RURAL DEVELOPMENT

PRINCIPLES, POLICIES AND MANAGEMENT

RURAL DEVELOPMENT

PRINCIPLES, POLICIES AND MANAGEMENT

4th Edition

KATAR SINGH

Former Director, Institute of Rural Management, Anand (IRMA), Gujarat

ANIL SHISHODIA

Information & Reference Services, Calgary Public Library, Canada

7/22, Ansari Road, Darya Ganj, New Delhi
Tel.: +91-11-4077 5252, 2327 3880
E-mail: orders@atlanticbooks.com
Web: www.atlanticbooks.com

Reprinted in 2026, 2025

This edition published in 2024 by Atlantic Publishers & Distributors (P) Ltd.

Previous edition published by Sage Publications in 2016

Printed & bound in India by Atlantic Print Services

Brief Contents

Contents

List of Tables

List of Figures

List of Boxes

List of Abbreviations

AAP	Annual Action Plan
ARTS	Advancement of Rural Technology Scheme
ACRP	Agro-climatic Regional Planning
ACS	Agricultural Capital Stock
ADB	Asian Development Bank
AI	Artificial Insemination
AIC	Agriculture Insurance Company of India
AIM	Asian Institute of Management
AMDP	Accelerated Maize Development Programme
AMIGS	Agricultural Marketing Infrastructure, Grading, and Standardization
ANM	Auxiliary Nurse Midwife
ANP	Applied Nutrition Programme
APDC	Anand-pattern Dairy Cooperatives
APMCs	Agricultural Produce Marketing Committees
APP	Agricultural Price Policy
APY	Atal Pension Yojana
ARWSP	Accelerated Rural Water Supply Programme
ATMA	Agricultural Technology Management Agency
AYUSH	Ayurveda, Yoga and Naturopathy, Unani, Siddha, and Homoeopathy
AWSs	Automatic Weather Stations
BAIF	Bhartiya Agro-industrial Foundation
BC	Business Correspondent
BDO	Block Development Officer
BIRD	Bankers Institute of Rural Development
BMS	Basic Minimum Services
BNP	Bharat Nirman Programme
BPL	Below the Poverty Line
BRO	Bureaucratic Re-orientation
CACP	Commission for Agricultural Costs and Prices
CAGR	Compound Annual Growth Rate
CAPART	Council for Advancement of People's Action and Rural Technology
CAPEX	Capital Expenditure
CAU	Central Agricultural University
CBs	Commercial Banks
CBDT	Central Board of Direct Taxes
CCAs	Cooperative Credit Agencies
CCI	Cotton Corporation of India
CDP	Community Development Program
CDS	Current Daily Status
CEO	Chief Executive Officer
CFCs	Chlorofluorocarbons
CFI	Consolidated Fund of India
CHC	Community Health Center
CII	Confederation of Indian Industry
CIMMYT	International Maize and Wheat Improvement Center
CIPHET	Central Institute of Post-harvest Engineering and Technology

CNG	Compressed Natural Gas
CPA	Community Projects Administration
CPIS	Coconut Palm Insurance Scheme
CPM	Critical Path Method
CPR	Common Pool Resource
CRAR	Capital to Risk Weighted Assets Ratio
CRAFICARD	Committee to Review Arrangements for Institutional Credit for Agricultural and Rural Development, 1981
CRDI	Composite Rural Development Index
CRSP	Central Rural Sanitation Programme
CSO	Central Statistical Office
CSR	Corporate Social Responsibility
CSS	Centrally-sponsored Schemes
CUs	Central Universities
CWC	Central Warehousing Corporation
DAPs	Development Action Plans
DDO	District Development Officer
DDP	Desert Development Programme
DLCC	District Level Coordination Committees
DPAP	Drought-prone Area Programme
DPR	Detailed Project Report
DRDA	District Rural Development Agency
DRI	Differential Rate of Interest
DRRPs	District Rural Roads Plans
DSFP	Deep Sea Fishing Policy
DUs	Deemed-to-be-universities
DWCRA	Development of Women and Children in Rural Areas
EAG	Empowered Action Group
ECAFE	Economic Commission for Asia and the Far East
ECLA	Economic Commission for Latin America
EEC	European Economic Community
EG	Expert Group
EIAs	End Implementing Agencies
EKC	Environmental Kuznets Curve
ENDP	Environmentally Adjusted Net Domestic Product
EOU	Export Oriented Units
EPC	Empowered Programme Committee
FAO	Food and Agriculture Organization
FCI	Food Corporation of India
FDAs	Forest Development Agencies
FDI	Foreign Direct Investment
FFDA	Fish Farmers Development Agency
FFW	Food-for-Work
FICCI	Federation of Indian Chambers of Commerce and Industry
FID	Financial Inclusion Department
FIF	Financial Inclusion Fund
FITF	Financial Inclusion Technology Fund
FPOs	Farmer Producer Organizations
FRA	Forest Resource Accounting
FSS	Farmers Service Society
FW	Family Welfare
HDI	Human Development Index

GCF	Gross Capital Formation
GCR	Gini Concentration Ratio
GDP	Gross Domestic Product
GKY	Ganga Kalyan Yojana
GMFC	Grow More Food Campaign
GNI	Gross National Income
GNP	Gross National Product
GWh	Gigawatt Hour
HC	Head Count
HSD	High Speed Diesel
HYV	High Yielding Variety
HYVP	High Yielding Variety Programme
IAAP	Intensive Agricultural Area Programme
IADB	Inter-American Development Bank
IADP	Intensive Agriculture District Programme
IAP	Integrated Action Plan
IAY	Indira Awas Yojana
IBPC	Inter-bank Participation Certificate
ICA	International Cooperative Alliance
ICAR	Indian Council of Agricultural Research
ICDP	Intensive Cattle Development Programme
IDC	Indian Dairy Corporation
IEA	Indian Economic Association
IHHL	Individual Household Latrines
ILO	International Labour Organisation
IMF	International Monetary Fund
INC	Indian National Congress
IPCC	Intergovernmental Panel on Climate Change
IPHS	Indian Public Health Standards
IPPE	Intensive and Participatory Planning Exercise
IPR	Intellectual Property Rights
IRC	Indian Roads Congress
IRD	Integrated Rural Development
IRDP	Integrated Rural Development Programme
IRRI	International Rice Research Institute
IT	Information Technology
ITC	Industrial Training Center
ITI	Industrial Training Institute
IUCN	International Union for the Conservation of Nature and Natural Resources
IWDP	Integrated Wasteland Development Programme
IWMP	Integrated Watershed Management Programme
JCI	Jute Corporation of India
JFM	Joint Forest Management
JFMCs	Joint Forest Management Committees
JRY	Jawahar Rozgar Yojana
KCC	Kisan Credit Cards
KVS	Key Village Scheme
KVIC	Khadi and Village Industries Commission
kWh	Kilowatt Hour
LAMPS	Large-sized Adivasi Multi-purpose Society
MFAL	Marginal Farmers and Agricultural Labourers
MFIs	Micro Finance Institutions

MFP	Marine Fishing Policy
MGNREGA	Mahatma Gandhi National Rural Employment Guarantee Act
MIDH	Mission for Integration Development of Horticulture
MIS	Management Information System
MIS	Market Intervention Scheme
MLAs	Members of Legislative Assemblies
MMA	Macro Management of Agriculture
MMP	Mid-day Meals Programme
MNAIS	Modified National Agricultural Insurance Scheme
MoU	Memorandum of Understanding
MP	Members of Parliament
MRP	Mixed Recall Period
MMRP	Modified Mixed Recall Period
MNP	Minimum Needs Programme
MoRD	Ministry of Rural Development
MoU	Memorandum of Understanding
MPCE	Monthly Per capita Consumption Expenditure
MRIN	Market Research Information Network
MRP	Mixed Recall Period
MSEs	Micro and Small Enterprises
MSG	Mission Steering Group
MSME	Micro, Small, and Medium Enterprise
MSP	Minimum Support Price
MWS	Million Wells Scheme
MYRADA	Mysore Resettlement and Development Agency
NABARD	National Bank for Agriculture and Rural Development
N-Ach	Need-for-achievement Motivation
NAEB	National Afforestation and Eco-development Board
NAFED	National Cooperative Agricultural Marketing Federation of India
NAIS	National Agricultural Insurance Scheme
NAP	National Afforestation Programme
NAPCC	National Action Plan on Climate Change
NAS	National Accounts Statistics
NCA	National Commission on Agriculture
NCDC	National Council for Development of Cooperatives
NCIP	National Crop Insurance Programme
NDA	National Democratic Alliance
NDC	National Development Council
NDDB	National Dairy Development Board
NDP	Net Domestic Product
NEP	New Economic Policy
NES	National Extension Service
NFA	"No-frills" Accounts
NFAD	National Fund for Agricultural Development
NFBS	National Family Benefit Scheme
NFFWP	National Food-for-Work Programme
NFP	National Forest Policy
NFS	Non-farm Sector
NFSIT	National Venture Fund for Software and Information Technology Industry
NFRD	National Fund for Rural Development
NIRD	National Institute of Rural Development
NKC	National Knowledge Management Commission

NLMs	National Level Monitors
NMBS	National Maternity Benefit Scheme
NMSA	National Mission for Sustainable Agriculture
NNI	Met National Income
NOAPP	National Old Age Pension Programme
NOAPS	National Old Age Pension Scheme
NPDP	National Pulses Development Project
NPK	Nitrogen, Phosphorus, and Potash
NRAA	National Rainfed Area Authority
NREP	National Rural Employment Programme
NRHM	National Rural Health Mission
NRLM	National Rural Livelihoods Mission
NRRDA	National Rural Roads Development Agency
NSDC	National Skill Development Corporation
NSS	National Sample Survey
NSSO	National Sample Survey Office
NSWP	National Social Welfare Programme
NWDB	National Wastelands Development Board
NWDPRA	National Watershed Development Programme for Rain-fed Areas
NWFP	Non-wood Forest Products
NWP	National Water Policy
OARs	Open Access Resources
ODS	Ozone-depleting Substance
OF	Operation Flood
OLP	Operational Linkage Programme
OMMAS	Online Monitoring, Management, and Accounting System
OOPP	Objective-oriented Project Planning
PAC	Public Accounts Committee
PACS	Primary Agricultural Credit Societies
PAI	Public Account of India
PEO	Programme Evaluation Organisation
PERT	Programme Evaluation and Review Technique
PIL	Public Interest Litigations
PFCE	Private Final Consumption Expenditure
PG	Poverty Gap
PHC	Primary Health Center
PIAs	Project Implementing Agencies
PIM	Programming and Implementation
PMCCC	Prime Minister's Council on Climate Change
PMGSY	Pradhan Mantri Gram Sadak Yojana
PMJDY	Pradhan Mantri Jan Dhan Yojana
POA	Programme of Action
PODF	Producer Organization Development Fund
PPP	Public Private Partnership
PPP	Purchasing Power Parity
PPT	Percentage Progress Technique
PRA	Participatory Rural Appraisal
PRADAN	Professional Assistance for Development Action
PRC	People's Republic of China
PRC	Performance Review Committee
PRIs	Panchayati Raj Institutions
PRODUCE	Producers' Organization Development and Upliftment Corpus'

PSS	Price Support Scheme
PURA	Provision of Urban Amenities in Rural Areas
PQLI	Physical Quality of Life Index
RBI	Reserve Bank of India
RCA	Royal Commission on Agriculture
RCCs	Regional Coordination Committees
RCD	Regional Cattle Development
RDMP	Rural Development Management Programme
RIDF	Rural Infrastructure Development Fund
RFCTLARR	Right to Fair Compensation and Transparency in Land Acquisition, Rehabilitation and Resettlement
RfP	Request for Proposal
RIDF	Rural Infrastructure Development Fund
RLEGP	Rural Landless Employment Guarantee Programme
RLP	Recursive Linear Programming
ROK	Republic of Korea
RRBs	Regional Rural Banks
RST	Remote Sensing Technology
RWP	Rural Works Programme
SAUs	State Agricultural Universities
SBD	Standard Bidding Document
SC	Scheduled Caste
SCARDBs	State Cooperative Agricultural and Rural Development Banks
SCBs	State Cooperative Banks
SDC	State Development Committee
SFDA	State Forest Development Agency
SFMFALP	Small Farmers, Marginal Farmers, and Agricultural Labourers Project
SHGs	Self Help Groups
SHG–BLP	SHG–Bank Linkage Programme
SGF	SME Growth Fund
SGSY	Swarnjayanti Gram Swarozgar Yojana
SIDBI	Small Industries Development Bank of India
SITRA	Supply of Improved Toolkits to Rural Artisans
SLCC	State Level Coordination Committee
SLDBs	State Land Development Banks
SLNA	State Level Nodal Agency
SLR	Statutory Liquidity Ratio
SLRCCDI	State Level Review and Coordination Committee on Credit Delivery Innovations
SPG	Squared Poverty Gap
SRDP	Special Rural Development Programme
SRRDA	State Rural Roads Development Agency
SSA	Sarva Shiksha Abhiyan
SSI	Small-scale Industry
ST	Scheduled Tribe
STA	State Technical Agency
STDs	Sexually Transmitted Diseases
SVCL	SIDBI Venture Capital Ltd.
SWCs	State Warehousing Corporations
SWDF	Sadguru Water and Development Foundation
SWOP	Social Welfare-oriented Programmes
TCA	Technical Cooperation Administration

TCM	Technical Cooperation Mission
TCPA	Technical Cooperation Programme Agreement
TMDD	Technology Mission on Dairy Development
TPDS	Targeted PDS
TPP	Twenty Point Programme
TRYSE	Training of Rural Youth for Self-employment
UGs	User Groups
UNCED	United Nations Conference on Environment and Development
UNDP	United Nations Development Programme
UPS	Usual Principal Status
URP	Uniform Recall Period
UTs	Union Territories
USAID	United States Agency for International Development
UV	Ultraviolet
VAs	Voluntary Agencies
VLWs	Village Level Workers
VMCs	Vigilance and Monitoring Committees
VVV	Vikas Volunteer Vahini
WB-NWMP	World Bank Assisted National Watershed Management Project
WBCIS	Weather-based Crop Insurance Scheme
WC	Watershed Committee
WCDC	Watershed Cell cum Data Centre
WCS	World Conservation Strategy
WCED	World Commission on Environment and Development
WDT	Watershed Development Team
WFP	World Food Programme
WPI	Wholesale Price Index
WRAs	Water Regulatory Authorities
WSHG	Women Self-help Group
WTO	World Trade Organization
WUAs	Water Users Associations

Preface to the Fourth Edition

The overwhelming success of the third edition of the book, which was published in 2009 as a text by SAGE, and the need for updating the redundant data presented in the tables in the third edition provided us the main rationale for revising the book. Also, many new rural development programs had been launched by the Government of India since the third edition came out and we realized the need to include those in this edition.

Like its earlier version, this edition of the book also comprises 15 chapters, which together deal with the basic concepts (Chapter 1), an overview of India's rural economy and its major problems (Chapter 2), measures of development (Chapter 3), theories/paradigms of development (Chapter 4), determinants of rural development (Chapter 5), policies, strategies, and programs of rural development (Chapters 6–11), and management of rural development (Chapters 12–15).

The major changes incorporated in this edition include: (a) the data and information presented in 26 tables in the third edition of the book was updated to the extent possible with the information available from various sources, including Internet resources; (b) 21 new tables were added containing the latest available data; (c) the section on poverty in Chapter 3 was thoroughly revised, expanded, and updated with the latest estimates of incidence of poverty in India and its states, presented in six new tables. Two new tables and a new section on an overview of various methodologies of estimating poverty, including the Rangarajan Expert Group methodology, were added; (d) one new box was added and three new sections in Chapter 6, namely, National Water Policy 2012, Land Acquisition Policy, and Agricultural Marketing Policy were added (e) a brief description of each of the National Mission for Sustainable Agriculture (NMSA) and the National Livestock Mission (NLM) was added in Chapter 9; (f) a minor restructuring of its contents was done in Chapter 10. The latest estimates of poverty presented in six tables were shifted to Chapter 3, a new section on National Rural Livelihood Mission (NRLM) or Aajeevika and two new boxes were added, and a brief description of each of the seven new programs, namely, Indira Gandhi National Old Age Pension Scheme (IGNOAPS), Indira Gandhi National Widow Pension Scheme (IGNWPS), Indira Gandhi National Disability Pension Scheme (IGNDPS), National Family Benefit Scheme (NFBS), Pradhan Mantri Jan Dhan Yojana (PMJDY), and Atal Pension Yojana (APY) was added; (g) a new section on "Planning Machinery in India" was added in Chapter 12, along with a short description of the NITI Aayog, which replaced the erstwhile Planning Commission; (h) all the original five tables in Chapter 14 were updated and two new tables, that is, "Sources and Uses of NABARD's Funds" as on March 31, 2015, and "Share of Non-institutional Sources in the Total Rural Credit Advanced in India—1951–2013" were added; and (i) details of the program of Monitoring and Evaluation of the Ministry of Rural Development in Chapter 15 were updated and a new section titled "Knowledge Management in Rural Development" was added.

Last but not least, Dr Anil Shishodia is associated as a co-author of this edition. He infused new energy and enthusiasm in the process of revision of the third edition of the book. He carefully read, edited, and reformatted all the 15 chapters and helped with the data and information used in updating the tables and identifying new sources of relevant data including websites.

Katar Singh
Anand, Gujarat

Anil Shishodia
Calgary, Canada

Preface to the First Edition

This book is the outcome of more than two decades of my professional experience in teaching, training, research, and extension activities in the field of agricultural and rural development. From July 1961, when I started my professional career as senior research assistant in charge of a research-cum-extension project in farm planning, I have had diverse experiences ranging from handling "nuts and bolts" type jobs to building conceptual and quantitative models of development. Most of the material presented in the book is based on my own ideas, observations, and research, and has been tested in some form or the other in my undergraduate and postgraduate classes, and in various short-term training programs at both G. B. Pant University of Agriculture and Technology, Pantnagar and the Institute of Rural Management (IRMA), Anand.

The book consists of 18 chapters which are grouped into three parts. Part I comprises five chapters which are devoted to an exposition of the meaning, objectives, measures, hypotheses, and determinants of rural development. Part II contains eight chapters, which deal with rural development policies, policy models, policy instruments, and selected rural development programs followed in India. Part III includes five chapters which together cover various organizational and managerial aspects of rural development, such as planning, organizing, financing, implementing, monitoring, and evaluation. Thus, the book is a comprehensive treatise on rural development covering all the three important aspects of the subject—principles, policies, and management.

This book is written for all those interested in contributing toward, and acquiring knowledge about, rural development. More specifically, this book is addressed to teachers, trainers, researchers, students, and agencies interested in rural development. In particular, it examines the meaning of rural development, its pace and level, the lessons learned from India's experience with various rural development program, and how these programs should be managed.

In writing this book and in the development of my thoughts and ideas about agricultural and rural development, I have benefited a great deal from my interaction with my teachers, colleagues, students, people in the rural areas, policy makers, planners, bankers, and from the writing of many development theorists. To name them all would be impossible and to mention a few individuals. I extend my sincere thanks to them all. My greatest debt is to my parents, Late Shrimati Anandi Singh and Late Shri Rajvir Singh, who taught me, through their work and attitude, the basics of farm and household development and management. My formal education has served only to corroborate and enrich what I learnt from them. I thank my wife, Vimala Singh, who kept me free from various household responsibilities and spent many lonely evenings and holiday ungrudgingly while I worked on this book.

I am extremely grateful to Shri R. N. Haldipur, Director, IRMA, who granted the permission and provided the necessary facilities and a congenial environment for writing this book, and whose advice and encouragement during the course of this work was invaluable. My sincere thanks are also due to Dr G. V. K. Rao, former member, Planning Commission and currently a member of IRMA's board of governors, for his valuable advice and suggestions to improve the book.

Finally, I want to thank my secretary, Mrs Lissy Varghese, who so willingly and carefully typed the final as well as earlier drafts of this book. Her cheerfulness, meticulous work, and patience made writing easier, quicker, and more of a pleasure.

February, 1986
Anand, Gujarat

Katar Singh

Acknowledgments

Several people have contributed to the development of this book and the revision of its first, second, and third editions. But we would like to place on record, in particular, our gratitude to Late Shri Tejeshwar Singh, former Managing Director, SAGE, who initially provided the first author the motivation and encouragement needed to write the book. Dr Sugata Ghosh, the then Vice-President, Commissioning and Ms Anjana Saproo, the then Commissioning Editor, facilitated the revision of the second edition of the book by providing the Microsoft Word version of the second edition of the book and rendering valuable advice from time to time. Mr Amit Kumar provided valuable inputs including suggestions gathered by him from several rural development teachers in India for adding some new topics in this edition. Ms Indrani Dutta suggested that we also provide some ancillary resources for instructors and students such as chapter-wise PowerPoint slides, instructor's manual/teaching notes, along with additional exercises/activities for students, and so on. With some initial reluctance to put in extra effort in producing those resources, we saw the merit of her suggestion and prepared some of the ancillary resources. Ms Priya Arora has carefully compiled the editorial queries and looked after the entire production process of the book. Ms Vimala Katar Singh provided, as in the case of first three editions of the book, the needed inspiration and moral support to finish up the work in time. Ms Deepali Anil Shishodia helped in the formatting of the texts and tables included in the book.

We are thankful to all of them.

Katar Singh
Anand, Gujarat

Anil Shishodia
Calgary, Canada

About the Authors

Katar Singh is currently Honorary (Founder) Chairman, India Natural Resource Economics and Management (INREM) Foundation, Anand, which is a nongovernmental academic organization committed to promoting teaching, training, and research in natural resource economics and environment management, and improving natural resource management policies and programs. He holds a PhD in agricultural economics from the University of Illinois, Urbana–Champaign, USA, and has done postdoctoral research and advanced coursework in natural resource economics in the Department of Agricultural and Resource Economics, Oregon State University, Corvallis, USA and in the Workshop in Political Theory and Policy Analysis, Indiana University Bloomington, USA.

He has over 50 years of teaching, training, research, and consulting experience in the areas of agricultural and rural development, and natural resource economics and management. He was the director and RBI Chair Professor in the Institute of Rural Management, Anand (IRMA), India, and also had a short stint as Director, Bankers Institute of Rural Development (BIRD), Lucknow. He has also taught at G. B. Pant University of Agriculture and Technology, Pantnagar, India.

He has coordinated and conducted several research and consultancy projects funded by national and international agencies. A prolific writer, he has published over 120 articles and papers in professional journals of repute and has authored/co-authored nine books, including a textbook, *Rural Development: Principles, Policies, and Management*, second ed. (SAGE, 1999), and another entitled *Environmental Economics: Theory and Applications* (SAGE, 2007), coauthored with Dr Anil Shishodia. He has also co-edited three books, namely, *Co-operative Management of Natural Resources* (SAGE, 1996), *Natural Resource Economics: Theory and Application in India* (1997), and *Designing and Managing Rural Development Organizations* (2000).

Professor Singh is a life member of numerous professional bodies, including the Indian Society of Agricultural Economics (ISAE), Indian Society for Ecological Economics, and International Society for Ecological Economics. He is a recipient of several awards and honors, including Rathindra Puraskar 2003, awarded by Visva Bharati University, Santiniketan, in recognition of his significant contribution to education in rural development and Sir Chhotu Ram National Award for the year 1996–97, awarded by CSS Haryana Agriculture University, Hisar, in recognition of his outstanding research work in the field of agriculture and rural development.

Anil Shishodia currently works in the Information/Reference Services Department of the Calgary Public Library in Calgary, Canada. He was formerly a Senior Lecturer in the Postgraduate Department of Economics, Sardar Patel University (SPU), Vallabh Vidyanagar, Gujarat. He was a World Bank Post-Doctoral Research Fellow in environmental economics at the Colorado State University, Fort Collins, USA, from August 1999 to May 2000, where he credited and audited a number of advanced courses in natural resources and environmental economics, including a course in environmental ethics. At SPU, he was instrumental in designing and offering a postgraduate level course in environmental economics. He has over 11 years of experience in teaching and research, and has published a number of articles on the subject.

Chapter 1

Introduction

LEARNING OUTCOMES

After having gone through this chapter, students should be able to:

- **Define and elaborate the basic concepts and elements of rural development;**
- **Distinguish between development and economic growth, and development and change;**
- **Elaborate the rationale for rural development in India;**
- **Explain the role of human beings as the pivot of development; and**
- **Illustrate the dogmas in rural development and how to resolve them.**

The term "rural development" is a subset of the broader term "development." Howsoever we define it, development is a universally cherished goal of individuals, families, communities, and nations all over the world. Development is also natural in the sense that all forms of life on planet Earth have an inherent urge to survive and develop. Given these two attributes, that is, its universal supremacy as a goal and its natural occurrence, development deserves a scientific study and analysis. Hence, it is not surprising that the subject of development has been studied by scholars of all faiths, ideologies, and disciplines. So much has been written and said about development that one finds it difficult to justify yet another book on this subject. However, it is my conviction that there is a need for a textbook on rural development; a book that extracts valuable insights and practicable lessons from the vast literature that is available on the subject and synthesizes them into meaningful forms. This book is intended to serve that purpose.

That such a book was needed was amply evident from the three editions of the book that have had a long innings of over three decades. Having said this, we now proceed to examine some of the commonly used connotations and definitions of development in general and rural development in particular. The objective is to arrive at a commonly acceptable definition that is easy to understand and use.

Concepts and Connotations of Rural Development

"Development" is a subjective and value-loaded concept and, hence, there cannot be a consensus about its meaning. The term is used differently in diverse contexts. It basically means "unfolding," "revealing," or "opening up" something which is latent. When applied to human beings it, therefore, means unfolding or opening up their potential powers. Generally speaking, the term development implies a change that is desirable. Since what is desirable at a particular time and place and in a particular culture may not be desirable at other places or at other times at the same place and in the same cultural milieu, it is impossible to think of a universally acceptable definition of development. But, generally speaking, development could be conceptualized as a set or vector of desirable societal objectives or a development index, which does not decrease over time (Pearce and Turner 1990, 2–3). Some of the objectives that are usually included in the set are as follows:

1. Increase in real income per capita (economic growth).
2. Improvement in distribution of income (equity).
3. Political and economic freedom.
4. Equitable access to resources, education, health care, employment opportunities and justice.
5. Security of life and property.
6. Hedge against natural calamities and man-made disasters.

Thus defined, the concept is applicable at all levels ranging from individuals to communities, nations, and the world as a whole. Development is cherished by all individuals, communities, and nations, irrespective of their culture, religion, and spatial location.

These days, the term "sustainable development" has become a buzzword. So we reproduce here a commonly accepted definition of the term. According to the World Commission on Environment and Development (WCED 1987, 43), "Sustainable development is development that meets the needs of the present without compromising the ability of future generations to meet their own needs." This definition underscores the need for society to ensure intergenerational equity in the sense that the present generation does not consume so much as to foreclose the option of the future generations to enjoy at least the present level of consumption and well-being. In simple words, sustainable development implies a process in which the set of desirable societal objectives or the development index does not decrease over time. Constancy of natural capital stock—including natural resources and the environment—is a necessary condition for sustainable development. The set of "sufficient conditions" includes an appropriate institutional framework and governance system for implementation of sustainable development policy at both the national and international levels.

The term "rural development" connotes the overall development of rural areas[1] with a view to improve the quality of life of the rural people. In this sense, it is a comprehensive and multidimensional concept, and encompasses the development of agriculture and allied activities, village and cottage industries, village art and crafts, socio-economic infrastructure, community services and facilities, and, above all, the natural and human resources in rural areas.

Rural development can be conceptualized as a process, a phenomenon, a strategy, and a discipline. As a *process*, it implies the engagement of individuals, communities, and nations in pursuit of their cherished goals over time. As a *phenomenon*, rural development is the end result of interactions between various physical, technological, economic, socio-cultural, and institutional factors and can be measured at any point in time. As a *strategy*, it is designed to improve the economic and social well-being of a specific group of people, that is, the rural poor. As a *discipline*, it is multidisciplinary in nature, representing an intersection of agricultural, social, behavioral, engineering, and management sciences.[2]

In the words of Chambers (1983, 147):

> Rural development is a strategy to enable a specific c group of people, poor rural women and men, to gain for themselves and their children more of what they want

and need. It involves helping the poorest among those who seek a livelihood in the rural areas to demand and control more of the benefits of rural development. The group includes small scale farmers, tenants and the landless.

Thus, the term "rural development" may be used to imply any one of the abovementioned connotations. To avoid ineffective floundering among the myriad definitions, we shall define rural development as "a process leading to sustainable improvement in the quality of life of rural people, especially the poor."

In addition to economic growth, this process typically involves changes in popular attitudes and, in many cases, even in customs and beliefs. In a nutshell, the process of rural development must represent the entire gamut of changes by which a social system moves away from a state of life perceived as "unsatisfactory" toward a materially and spiritually better condition of life. The process of rural development may be compared with a train in which each coach pushes the one ahead of it and is, in turn, pushed by the one behind, but it takes a powerful engine to make the whole train move. The secret of success in rural development lies in identifying and, if needed, developing a suitable engine to attach to the train. There are no universally acceptable blueprints to identify appropriate engines of rural development, if at all they exist. It is a choice that is influenced by time, space, and culture.

Basic Elements of Rural Development

Whatever the geographic location, culture and historical stage of development of a society, there are at least three basic elements, which are considered to constitute the "true" meaning of rural development. They are as follows (Box 1.1; Todaro 1995, 16–18).

The new economic view of development considers reduction or elimination of poverty, inequality, and unemployment as an important index of development. Seers (1969, 3) succinctly addressed the basic question of the meaning of development when he wrote: the questions to ask about a country's development are therefore:

1. What has been happening to poverty?
2. What has been happening to unemployment?
3. What has been happening to inequality?

If all three of these have declined from high levels, then, beyond doubt, this has been a period of development of the country concerned. If one or two of these central problems have been growing worse, especially if all three have, it would be strange to call the result "development" even if the per capita income doubled.

Some selected measures of development are presented in Chapter 3 of this book.

Growth Versus Development

While economic growth is an essential component of development, it is not the only one, as development is not a purely economic phenomenon. In the ultimate sense, it must encompass more than the material and financial aspects of people's lives. Development should, therefore, be perceived as a multidimensional process, involving the reorganization and reorientation of both economic and social systems. In addition to improvements in the level and distribution of incomes and output, it also involves radical changes in institutional, social, and administrative structures, and values and ethos of individuals and communities. To illustrate the difference between economic growth and development, let us consider the cases of states of Punjab and Kerala in India. The former ranks higher than the latter in terms of the level of economic growth as measured by the average per capita income alone, but the latter ranks superior to Punjab in terms of development as measured by—besides per capita income—literacy rate, infant mortality rate, sex ratio, and law and order situation. Finally, although development is usually defined in a national context, its widespread realization necessitates fundamental modifications of the international economic, social, and political systems as well.

The Vedic prayer *sarve bhavantu sukhinaha, sarve santu niramayaha*, that is, "May everybody (in this universe) be happy and free from diseases (healthy)," highlights the global and multidimensional nature of development.

Why Rural Development

Since time immemorial, India has been, still continues to be and will remain in the foreseeable future, a land of village communities. As a matter of fact, the village was the basic unit of administration as far back as the Vedic age. There is a reference to *gramini* (village leader) in the *Rig Veda*, the oldest of Indian scriptures. The predominantly rural character of India's national economy is reflected in the very high proportion of its population living in rural areas. It was 89% in 1901, 83% in 1951, 80% in 1971, 74% in 1991, 72% in 2001, and 69% in 2011. With more than 833 million of its people living in rural areas in 2011 and with agriculture—including forestry and fishing—contributing to about 18% of its gross domestic product (GDP) at current prices in 2013–14, no strategy of socio-economic development for India that neglects rural people and agriculture can be successful.

The rural character of the economy and the need for regeneration of rural life was stressed by Mahatma Gandhi. He wrote in *Harijan* on April 4, 1936 (cited in, Anonymous 1978: 2, 31):

> India is to be found not in its few cities but in its 7,00,000 villages. But we town dwellers have believed that India is to be found in its towns and the villages were created to minister to our needs. We have hardly paused to enquire if those poor folk get sufficient to eat and clothe themselves with and whether they have a roof to shelter themselves from sun and rain.

Box 1.1

BASIC ELEMENTS OF RURAL DEVELOPMENT

1. Basic Necessities of Life: *People have certain basic needs, without which it would be impossible (or very difficult) for them to survive. The basic necessities include food including water, clothes, and shelter. Besides, access to basic literacy, health care, productive job opportunities, and security of life and property is also necessary for a reasonably satisfactory level of living. When any one or all of them are absent or in critically short supply, we may state that a condition of "absolute underdevelopment" exists. Provision of basic necessities of life to everybody is the primary responsibility of all economies, whether they are capitalist, socialist, or mixed. In this sense, we may claim that economic growth (increased per capita availability of basic necessities) is a necessary condition for improvement of the "quality of life" of rural people, which is rural development.*
2. Self-respect: *Every person and every nation seeks some sort of self-respect, dignity, or honor. Absence or denial of self-respect indicates lack of development.*
3. Freedom: *In this context, freedom refers to political or ideological freedom, economic freedom, and freedom from social servitude. As long as a society is bound by the servitude of its people to nature,* ignorance, other men, institutions, and dogmatic beliefs, it*

> *cannot claim to have achieved the goal of "development." Servitude in any form reflects a state of underdevelopment.*
>
> *Servitude to nature implies excessive vulnerability of people to natural calamities such as floods, droughts, hail storms, tsunamis (A tsunami is a series of ocean waves generated by sudden displacements in the sea floor, landslides, or volcanic activity), forest fires, and so on.
>
> *Source:* Todaro (1995, 16–18).

He further wrote in *Harijan* on August 29, 1936 (cited in, Anonymous 1978), "I would say that if the village perishes, India would perish too. It will be no more India [*sic*]. Her own mission in the world will get lost. The revival of village life is possible only when it is no more exploited."

Rural development is, therefore, an absolute and urgent necessity in India now and will continue to be so in future. It is the sine qua non of development of India.

Rising Expectations and Development

The common man in India, as also in other developing countries, expects a higher standard of living for himself, his family, his community, and his nation. Particular expectations, of course, differ from person to person and from region to region, but the expectation of a marked improvement in material conditions of life is general throughout the world. People want and expect to have better diet, clothes, houses, education, a secured life, and freedom from servitude. This is the revolution of expectations that has swept over the third world countries.

There are many explanations for this phenomenon. First, the demonstration effect of the rural elite, urban rich, and foreign tourists engaging in ostentatious consumption of exotic and luxurious goods has distorted the consumption and utility functions of the poor. Second, films, radio, television, e-commerce websites such as Flipkart.com, Indiamart.com, and Amazon.in and aggressive advertising have exposed the masses to modern gadgets and lifestyles, and have thus aroused their expectations; they too want to have those things. Third, local and national politicians have assured the rural poor of the modern amenities of life, if they would vote for them. Fourth, the central governments have declared, time and again, that the eradication of poverty is their major policy goal. Under the influence of all these factors, the common man has first learned about the new products, gadgets and services; then, come to want them and, now, to demand them.

The economies of most developing countries (including India) cannot possibly fulfill these expectations in the immediate future and there is bound to be a collision between rising expectations and economic reality. The outcome will vary from country to country, but it will certainly involve disillusionment, demoralization, agitations, lockouts, and political upheavals, violence, and several other antisocial activities such as thefts, murders, smuggling, and trafficking in narcotics. It is this that makes rapid agricultural and economic development a national imperative in India to bridge the gap between rising expectations and economic reality.

Development and Change

Development is both a cause and a consequence of change. There is a two-way relationship between them, that is, development influences and is influenced by change. The change implies a physical, technological, economic, social, cultural, attitudinal, organizational, or political change. Whereas all manifestations of development can be traced to some change somewhere, sometimes not all changes lead to development. A change may be either for better (development) or for worse (retrogression). In the context of rural development, a "change" may be considered to be an instrument that can be used to promote rural development. In India, the introduction of technological changes in the mid-1960s (new high-yielding varieties of crops, fertilizers, improved farm machinery, and pesticides) led to the so-called Green Revolution in agriculture. Similarly, technological innovations such as modern milk processing and feed processing plants, artificial insemination of dairy animals, and organizational innovations such as the Anand-pattern dairy cooperatives introduced in India on a large scale in the early 1970s under the Operation Flood (OF) program, contributed significantly to the modernization and development of the dairy industry of the country. Elsewhere, such as in Taiwan and the People's Republic of China (PRC), agricultural development was largely a result of institutional reforms, especially land reforms and technological advances. Karl Marx was one of the great advocates of revolutionary (socio-economic) change as an instrument of development.

A change may occur naturally or autonomously, or may be induced. A development manager may accelerate the pace of development by both inducing a desirable change in a given system and by properly directing the autonomous change. It is important that the likely impacts of a contemplated change on various segments of the society be carefully evaluated *ex-ante* (before the change is introduced).

Human Beings as the Cause and Consequence of Development

Human beings are both the cause and consequence of development. It is the human factor that is the pivot of the process of development. Although the study of a human being is basic to the study of development, it cannot be of a human being in isolation but rather of human beings in relation to their fellows, or of humans in society and in their environment.

It is the creation of conditions, both material and spiritual, that enables the human being as an individual—and human beings as a species—to be at his best. Those who control a human being's livelihood, control the human being. A person's freedom is illusory when he depends upon others for the right to work and the right to eat. Equally, a nation is not independent if its economic resources are controlled by another nation. Political independence is meaningless if a nation does not control the means by which its citizens can earn their living. In other words, human development follows from economic development, only if the latter is achieved on the basis of equality and human dignity of all those involved. Human dignity cannot be given to a human being by the kindness of others. Indeed, it can be destroyed by kindness that emanates from an act of charity, for human dignity involves equality, freedom, and relations of mutual respect among humans; it depends on responsibility and on a conscious participation in the life of the society in which a human being lives and works. The whole structure of national societies and of international society is, therefore, relevant to the development of people. There are few societies in the world that can be said to serve this purpose. There are few, if any, that both accept and are organized to serve social justice, in what has been called the Revolution of Rising Expectations.

The greatest advances in technology and economic growth have been achieved under capitalism. However, the decisions pertaining to what goods shall be produced and how they shall be produced are made by a small number of people who have control over resources including land and capital. The determining factor in their decision-making is whether the activity will yield profit, power, or prestige to them as owners of land or capital. The needs of humankind are secondary, if they are considered at all.

There is no profit in producing cheap houses, so they are not produced; there is "no money" for schools and hospitals but enough for five star hotels, modern shopping complexes, and luxury apartments. The result is that a few people live in luxury, using the wealth produced by humans for their own grandeur and to ensure their own power. At the same time, masses of men, women, and children are reduced to beggary, squalor, and to the humiliation of that disease—the soul-destroying insecurity that arises out of their enforced poverty.

Let us be quite clear that if we are interested in a human being as an individual, then we must express this by our interest in the society of which those individuals are members, for humans are shaped by the circumstances in which they live. If they are treated like animals, they will *act* like animals. If they are denied dignity, they will act indignantly. If they are treated solely as a dispensable means of production, they will become soulless "hands," to whom life is a matter of doing as little work as possible and then escaping into the illusion of happiness and pride through vice.

Some Dilemmas in Development

The literature on development abounds in a variety of dilemmas and dogmas, such as rural versus urban development, agricultural versus industrial development, primacy of capital versus labor, and natural/autonomous versus induced/planned development. A brief critique of these dilemmas seems in order to clarify some of the issues.

Rural Versus Urban Development

Economic development in developed countries has been associated with growing urbanization, as reflected in the increasing proportion of the urban population. Hence, there is a tendency among economists to consider urbanization as an index of development. Growing urbanization is obviously the consequence of the growing concentration of infrastructural networks and capital-intensive industrial enterprises in urban centers. This type of concentration has resulted in the existence of what is known in the literature on the economics of development as "dualism" or coexistence of two separate economic subsystems in an economy, especially in many developing countries including India. On one hand, there exists in the economy a small but highly modern and developed urban subsector, which absorbs most of the material, financial, and educated and talented manpower resources. On the other hand, there is a very large but traditional and underdeveloped rural subsector, characterized by widespread poverty, unemployment and low productivity, which forms the majority of the population. In many developing countries, both the subsectors coexist, but without those linkages between them that were once the main factors that contributed to the development of today's developed countries.

At the other extreme, there is another dogma rapidly emerging in many developing countries that rural development is a prerequisite for overall development and, hence, it deserves the highest priority in terms of allocation of resources. In their enthusiasm to promote the cause of rural development, the proponents of this school of thought usually tend to either disregard or underplay the linkages between the rural and the urban subsectors of the economy. What is needed is a new approach to development, which explicitly recognizes the interlinkages and complementarity between the rural and the urban subsectors, and provides for integrating them completely.

Agricultural Versus Industrial Development

Closely analogous to the rural versus urban development dilemma is the dogma that industrialization alone can modernize agriculture and thereby raise agricultural productivity and wage rates and provide employment to the labor displaced by the mechanization of agriculture. This has led many development economists to associate development with industrialization. Following this dogma, many developing countries have established highly capital-intensive and sophisticated industrial enterprises, similar to those in developed countries. Such efforts, however, have often led to bitter disappointment when the desired results failed to materialize. Such projects are mere showcases whose contribution to development is negligible—and sometimes even negative—because they are built at the expense of enterprises that meet the basic needs of people. Nations with high agricultural potential spend enormous resources on agricultural imports and depend heavily on imported technology, capital, and management. At the same time, local agriculture stagnates and nutritional standards remain far lower than in the advanced countries. Distribution of income is tilted in favor of industrialists against farmers, workers, and consumers.

At the other extreme is agricultural fundamentalism, which holds that, in the initial stages of development when per capita incomes are low, agriculture alone can serve as an instrument of development and that increased agricultural productivity is a prerequisite to increased income and industrialization. The proponents of this dogma argue for allocation of more resources and attention to agriculture rather than to industry. They do not, however, realize that agriculture cannot develop alone and that the concomitant development of industry and supporting infrastructure is essential not only for the growth of the national economy but also for the advancement of agriculture itself. The non-agricultural sector must be developed to the extent that it is able to provide the agricultural sector with new farm inputs and services vital to its development, as also to absorb the manpower rendered surplus as a result of increased labor productivity in agriculture.

Agricultural fundamentalism has generally resulted in growth without development, mainly because of lack of linkages between the agricultural and non-agricultural sectors, and partly because of distribution of income being skewed in favor of big landlords. The establishment of small and less capital-intensive industrial enterprises in rural areas, along with introduction of new technology in agriculture is likely to establish linkages between agriculture and industry. The Israeli strategy of integrating agricultural and industrial sectors is worth emulating. In Israel, industrial enterprises were set up in rural areas along with the introduction of more efficient methods of agricultural production. Initially, the industrial enterprises included mostly services and industries connected with agriculture, such as feed mix plants, factories for processing agricultural produce and for producing tools and various accessories. Most of these enterprises were owned, either fully or in part, by the farmers themselves. In the course of time, the scope of industrial enterprises was widened to include activities completely unconnected with agriculture, such as jewelry manufacturing and ceramics (Weitz 1971, Chapter 9).

Capital Versus Labor Dogma

This is a legacy inherited by today's development economists from their predecessors in the developed countries, who considered capital to be the key instrument of development. The Harrod–Domar model represents a typical example of this dogma (Todaro 1995, 70–72). In this model, the rate of growth is expressed as the product of the savings rate and the output–capital ratio. Under the assumptions that capital and labor cannot be substituted for each other and that labor is in surplus supply, capital becomes the overriding constraint on economic growth. This dogma received a further fillip from those techno-economists who held that all new technology is embodied in capital.

Capital fundamentalism has been blindly accepted by development economists and planners in the developing countries. This has led to the promulgation of a number of policies in these countries, all aimed at increasing savings, redistributing income from the workers to the capitalists, granting monopoly rights to national and multinational corporations, transferring resources from the private to the public sector, increasing dependence on foreign aid and loans, and underpricing of capital, particularly foreign exchange for capital goods. This has resulted in a number of adverse effects on the economies of these nations. For example, underpricing of foreign exchange for capital goods has killed the incentive to develop labor-intensive technologies adapted to domestic needs and circumstances, and has led to premature and excessive mechanization in a number of sectors, resulting in the unemployment of labor and underutilization of other domestic resources.

Capital fundamentalism has extended to cover human capital formation as well. Higher education is highly subsidized in most developing countries, with the result that millions of college and university graduates are added annually to the pool of the unemployed, white-collar proletariat. In India, enormous investment has been made in the institutes of higher learning, particularly in the fields of engineering, technology, agriculture, medicine, and management. Many of the graduates of these institutes usually do not like the work environment and compensation rates prevailing in the country and seek jobs abroad. Thus, the scarce resources invested in their education and training are lost to the country. It seems that at this stage of India's economic and technological development, we need more institutes such as vocational schools to train barefoot agricultural and other technicians, engineers, doctors, and rural managers, rather than institutes for highly advanced training. Similarly, one wonders why we should produce more college and university graduates in disciplines such as arts, commerce, and agriculture and veterinary sciences than we need. The demand for higher education could be brought down to match the availability of jobs by pricing it at its real resources cost, which is markedly higher than the present cost.

In the US and other Western countries, most students terminate their studies at the high school level (10+2) and become self-employed as skilled workers such as electricians, plumbers, and motor garage mechanics. But their training is broad-based and highly practical and relevant to their context, with the result that high school graduates are able and confident to set up and manage their own small business or take up wage-paid jobs. We should learn from this experience and make our education less capital-intensive and more relevant to our requirements. We need to thoroughly overhaul our present education policy, which has become outdated and irrelevant in the context of our changed environment. More emphasis needs to be placed on the vocationalization of education.

Autonomous Versus Induced Development

In every country, some development takes place naturally or autonomously over time due to activities of individuals pursuing their own interests, but its level and pace may not be adequate to attain and maintain a reasonably satisfactory standard of living. In such situations, some sort of intervention is needed to speed up the pace of natural development. Development planning is one of the forms of intervention that has been adopted in many developing countries of the world and is considered a magic door to development. In fact, even the advanced countries have come to realize the need for some sort of planning or government intervention in the economic processes. It seems that there is a growing consensus around the statement that any planning is better than no planning at all and that decentralized planning is better than centralized planning.

However, we need to realize that planning can make a positive contribution only if it facilitates the achievement of development objectives more rapidly and more efficiently than if development followed the natural processes. It is now becoming increasingly apparent that the development effort cannot be left to the government alone. It must be shared by private, cooperative, corporate and other NGOs and agencies and, above all, by the people themselves. Planning by the government should complement and supplement the efforts of individuals and NGOs.

The main role of planning should be to provide a congenial economic and political environment for people to enable them to achieve their cherished goals and to set the rules of the game and enforce them strictly.

Key Points

1. The term "rural development" is a subset of the broader term "development." It implies an overall sustained improvement in the quality of life of rural people. Development is a universally cherished goal of individuals, families, communities and nations all over the world.
2. Nowadays, the term "sustainable development" has become a buzzword. According to the World Commission on Environment and Development (WCED), "sustainable development is development that meets the needs of the present without compromising the ability of future generations to meet their own needs." This definition underscores the need for maintaining intergenerational equity in terms of level of fulfillment of human needs. Constancy of natural capital stock including natural resources and environment is a necessary condition for sustainable development.
3. Rural development can be viewed as a process, as a phenomenon, as a strategy and as a discipline. As a *process*, it implies the engagement of individuals and communities in activities that lead to achievement of their cherished goals over time. As a *phenomenon*, it is a measure of quality of life at a particular point in time resulting from interactions between various physical, technological, economic, socio-cultural, and institutional factors. As a *strategy*, it is designed to improve the economic and social well-being of a specific group of people, that is, the rural poor. As a *discipline*, it is multidisciplinary in nature representing an intersection of agricultural, social, behavioral, engineering, and management sciences.
4. While economic growth is an essential component of development, it is not the only one, as development is not a purely economic phenomenon. In an ultimate sense, it must encompass more than the material and financial sides of people's lives. Development should, therefore, be perceived as a multidimensional process involving the reorganization and reorientation of both economic and social systems.
5. With more than 833 million of its people living in rural areas and with the agriculture and allied activities contributing about 18% of its GDP at current prices in 2013–14, no strategy of socio-economic development for India that neglects rural people and agriculture can be successful. Rural development is, in fact, the sine qua non of overall development.
6. The common man in India, as also in other developing countries, expects a higher standard of living for himself, his family, his community and his nation. These expectations cannot be fulfilled with the present low level of development and high level of inequality. This leads to frustration, disillusion and several antisocial activities, such as thefts, murders, violence and trafficking in drugs.
7. Development is both a cause and a consequence of changes. There is a two-way relationship between them, that is, development influences and is influenced by changes. The change implies a physical, technological, economic, social, cultural, attitudinal, organizational or political change. Whereas all manifestations of development can be traced to some change somewhere, sometimes not all changes lead to development. A change may be either for good (development) or for bad (retrogression).
8. Man is both the cause and consequence of development. It is the human factor that is the pivot of the process of development. But this basic truth is not taken into account in most of the countries of the world. For example, despite the greatest advances in technology and economic growth achieved under capitalism, the decisions pertaining to what goods shall be produced and how they shall be produced are made by a

small number of people who have control over resources including land and capital. The determining factor in their decision-making is whether the activity will yield profit, power or prestige to them as owners of land or capital. The needs of mankind are secondary, if they are considered at all.

9. Literature on development abounds in a variety of dilemmas and dogmas such as rural versus urban development, agricultural versus industrial development, primacy of capital versus labor and natural/autonomous versus induced/planned development. There is a need to recognize the futility of all such dogmas and take a practical and balanced view, recognizing the complementarity between rural and urban, agriculture and industry, capital and labor, and induced and autonomous dimensions of development.

Questions for Discussion

1. Is every change or everything new "development?" Yes/No. If yes, explain why and if no, why not? Illustrate your answer with examples.
2. Is economic growth as revealed in terms of increased production of food grains, milk, clothes, houses, roads, schools, motor cars, increased per capita income, increased purchasing power, and so on, "development?" Yes/No. If yes, explain why and if no, why not?
3. Illustrate with examples the concept of rural development as a process, as a phenomenon, as a strategy and as a discipline.
4. Can India become a truly developed nation while having such problems as growing disparities between urban and rural areas in terms of average per capita income, availability of basic infrastructure and security of life and property and rate of literacy? Yes/No. If yes, explain why and if no, why not?
5. Discuss why development of India's human resources, particularly the poor and disadvantaged sections of society, should be the major instrument and the ultimate goal of development planning and policy.
6. In the current Indian context, discuss the pros and cons of capital-intensive versus labor-intensive approaches to rural development.
7. Discuss how the rural sector and urban can develop in tandem and rural–urban disparities narrowed down.

Notes

1. Areas lying outside the administrative jurisdiction of municipal corporations and committees, and notified town area committees, cantonments and not classified as Census towns are considered rural areas.
2. In India and several other countries of the world, courses in rural development now are offered at both the undergraduate and postgraduate levels. As a matter of fact, Sage Publications India published in 2009 the 3rd edition of this book as a text book and it was very well received by both the teachers and students of rural development.

Chapter 2

Rural Economy of India

LEARNING OUTCOMES

After having gone through this chapter, students should be able to:

- **Identify the major segments and indicators of the size of the rural economy of India;**
- **List the major characteristics of the rural sector of India's economy;**
- **Illustrate the role of the agricultural sector in India's the recent past; and**
- **List the major initiatives taken by the government for its development at a faster pace and identify the major challenges and opportunities confronting the rural sector at present and in the foreseeable future, especially in the context of globalization and liberalization.**

Introduction

India is one of the oldest surviving civilizations and the biggest democracy in the world. It has a rich and diverse cultural heritage and it has two of the world's 18 hotspots of biodiversity. It ranks second after China in terms of population, first in terms of cattle and buffalo population, and sixth in terms of geographical area. It has the world's third largest reservoir of technically trained manpower and is now one of the seven nuclear weapons states. Its mainland covers an area of 3.29 million sq. km or 329 million hectares (mha), measures about 3,214 km from north to south between the extreme latitudes and about 2,933 km from east to west between the extreme longitudes. Over the last 68 years, since independence, India has achieved impressive progress in the fields of science and technology, and is now self-sufficient in food grains and milk production. On the negative side, India has not yet been able to fully develop and harness its human and natural resources for the benefit of its people, and it has yet to solve its problems of illiteracy, poverty, inequality, unemployment, and vulnerability to natural calamities.

India's economy is predominantly rural in character. This is evident from the fact that in 2011, nearly 69% of its population lived in its nearly 640 thousand villages and about 63% of the rural population was engaged in agriculture and allied activities as cultivators and agricultural laborers. Besides, agriculture and allied activities accounted for about 18% of India's gross domestic product (GDP) in 2013–14 at the current prices and about 14% at the 2004–05 prices (Planning Commission 2014a, 44). But despite its significance, rural economy of India is in doldrums. It is afflicted by several problems and the plight of most of the rural people is miserable. The increasing number of farmers committing suicides year after year is a testimony of their miserable financial condition.

In a predominantly agrarian country such as India, rural development is the sine qua non of overall development and agricultural development is a prerequisite for rural development. Therefore, in such a country, agricultural development should form the foundation of national development.

In this chapter, we first present an overview of the state of rural economy of India, with special reference to its agricultural sector and its role in India's overall development, then briefly discuss some of the major problems of agriculture, thereafter examine briefly the role of the non-agricultural subsector, and finally suggest a few feasible ways forward for the rural sector.

We begin with a description of the size and structure of India's rural economy, and its salient characteristics.

Size and Structure of the Rural Economy

An economy may be conceptualized as a collection of economic, social, institutional, legal, political, and technological arrangements through which individuals in society seek to increase their material and spiritual well-being. The two elementary functions of an economy are consumption and production. Consumption is considered as the prime pump of an economy. The classical dictum that "the consumer is sovereign" is based on the consumer power embodied in his demand, which is one of the crucial requirements for the existence of any business enterprise or, for that matter, any economic activity, including production.

India's economy can be thought of as comprising two main sectors, namely, the rural sector and the non-rural sector. The rural sector is, in turn, composed of two main subsectors, that is, the agricultural subsector and the non-agricultural subsector. The agricultural subsector comprises agriculture and allied economic activities, such as animal husbandry and dairying, fisheries, poultry, and forestry. The non-agricultural subsector consists of economic activities relating to small-scale village industries, rural craft, business, and services. Industry here refers to cottage and village industries, *khadi*, handloom, handicrafts, and so on. Business refers to microenterprises, trading of general goods, small shops, petty traders, and so on, whereas "services" refers to transport, communications, banking, input supply, marketing of farm and non-farm produce, and so on. The main stakeholders of the rural sector include farmers, agricultural and non-agricultural laborers, artisans, traders, moneylenders, and those engaged in providing such services as transport, communications, processing, banking, and education and extension.

The size of the rural sector could be measured in terms of the size of rural population, livestock population, and extent of land resources, water resources, forest resources, fisheries, quantum of production, inputs used, and the output produced.

Human Population

According to the 2011 population census, India's total population was 1210 million of which rural population was 833.1 million, which accounted for 68.84% of the country's total population. Of the total rural population, 118.7 million were cultivators and 144.3 million agricultural workers. The average annual exponential growth rate of rural population was 1.22% during the last decade, 2001–11, which was lower than 1.7% registered during the earlier decade, 1991–2001 decade. The decline in the growth rate was due partly to the

Table 2.1: *Some Salient Features of Rural and Urban Population of India, 1951–2011*

	Human Population (Million)			*Literacy Rate (%)*			*Life Expectancy at Birth (Years)*		
Year	*Rural*	*Urban*	*Total*	*Rural*	*Urban*	*Total*	*Male*	*Female*	*All*
1951	298.6 (82.70)*	62.5 (17.30)	361.1 (100)*	12.10	34.59	18.33	32.5	31.7	32.10
1961	360.3 (82.00)	78.9 (18.00)	439.2 (100)	22.50	54.40	28.30	41.9	40.6	41.30
1971	439.0 (80.10)	109.2 (19.90)	548.2 (100)	27.90	60.20	34.45	46.4	44.7	45.60
1981	525.6 (76.90)	157.7 (23.10)	683.3 (100)	36.00	67.20	43.57	50.9	50.0	50.90
1991	630.6 (74.50)	215.8 (25.50)	846.4 (100)	44.70	73.10	52.21	58.6	59.0	58.60
2001	742.6 (72.20)	286.4 (27.80)	1,029.0 (100)	59.40	80.30	65.38	61.6	63.3	61.60
2011	833.7 (68.90)	377.3 (31.10)	1,211.0 (100)	68.91	84.90	74.04	67.6	74.0	64.6

Sources: MoA (2014a, 10–11) and MoF (2015).
Note: *Figures in the parentheses are % of the total population.

decline in the birth rate and partly to the increase in rural–urban migration. The quality of human resources remains, by and large, poor in terms of literacy, life expectancy, technical knowledge, and skills. The average literacy rate in India in 2011 was 74% but for rural population it was only 69%. Similarly, the average life expectancy at birth in India, which is a catch-all variable for access to balanced nutrition and health care, was only 65 years in 2012 as compared to 83 years in Japan, 73 years in China, and the world average of 70 years (Planning Commission 2014a, 214). Consequently, according to the 2014 *Human Development Report*, out of 185 countries of the world, India ranked 135th with medium human development. This does not portend well about the status of human development in India. There is a need for concerted action to improve the quality of human resources through improving the access of people, particularly the rural poor, to appropriate education, health care, and skill-based vocational training. Some salient features of the quality of India's human resources are presented in Table 2.1.

Livestock Population

India is endowed with livestock resources of high genetic diversity and ranks first in the world in terms of the population of cattle and buffaloes. The livestock sector plays an important role in the socio-economic development of the country. The contribution of the sector to the national economy in terms of GDP was 4.1% at current prices in 2012–13. According to the 19th Livestock Census conducted in 2012, the country had 199.90 million cattle, 108.70 million buffaloes, 65.07 million sheep, 135.17 million goats, 10.29 million pigs and 729.21 million poultry birds in 2012 (MoA 2014b, 65). However, the livestock has relatively low productivity in terms of the average yield of milk, meat and wool per head. For example, the average milk yield of cows is only about 6.78 kg per day for exotic cows and 2.50 kg per day for non-descript (*desi*) cows as compared to about 13 kg per day in Ireland and about 11 kg per day in New Zealand (MoA 2014b, 146). Besides, livestock density is relatively high vis-à-vis the carrying capacity of grazing lands and fodder resources of the country. The livestock population exerts high pressure on the country's limited land and water resources, leading to their degradation in many ecologically fragile regions such as hilly, arid, and semiarid areas.

There is a need to increase the productivity of livestock through selective breeding, better feeding, culling, and effective disease control. It is feasible to replace the low yielding cattle and buffalo population by high yielding ones, thereby reducing the pressure of livestock on land and water resources of the country and increasing the livestock output with fewer heads of livestock.

Land Resources

Land is one of the natural resources that affects the level and pace of development in general and agricultural development in particular. India has the total geographical area of about 329 mha, of which about 120.40 mha was degraded in 2010–11, which is about 27% of the country's total geographical area. Of the degraded land, the land affected by wind and water erosion was 94.87 mha (79%); acidic soil was 17.93 mha (15%); alkaline soil was 3.7 mha (3%); saline soil 2.73 mha (1.8%); water-logged was 0.91 mha (1%) and mining and industrial waste 0.26 mha (0.20%) (MoA n.d.).

According to the *Wastelands Atlas of India 2011*, the extent of wastelands in India in 2006 was 47.22 mha, which was about 15% of the total area (MoRD 2013b, 11). It has been now well established through various land reclamation and watershed development projects that most of the country's degraded land could be put to productive use, especially for growing trees, fodder grasses, and medicinal herbs and shrubs (Singh and Shishodia 2007, 201–23).

In 2011–12, India had the total gross irrigated area of about 91.53 mha and net irrigated area of about 65.26 mha (MoA 2014a, 304–05) and it ranked first in the world in terms of irrigated area. The net irrigated area accounted for about 47% of the net area sown (140 mha) in the country and contributed about 55% to the country's total agricultural output. The cropping intensity was 138%. The average productivity of land in India in terms of crop yields is low when compared to that in some of the developed countries of the world. For example, in 2012, the average yield of paddy was 3,721 kg/ha in India as compared to 5,136 kg/ha in Indonesia and 6,775 kg/ha in China. Similar is the case for other major crops such as wheat, maize, and groundnuts (MoA 2014a, Table 7.1, p. 237). Thus, there is an urgent need to increase crop yield per ha of various crops. This is possible, as has been demonstrated in farmers' fields in many parts of the country, through the use of high yielding varieties of crops, balanced fertilizer application, and judicious use of water and integrated pest and disease control measures.

Water Resources

Water is a finite but renewable natural resource and, like other natural resources, it is an integral part of the environment. It is essential for the survival of all living beings on this planet and also for the socio-economic development of households, communities, and nations all over the world. It is also necessary to maintain and enhance biodiversity and quality of environment. India, as a whole, is reasonably well endowed with fresh water resources. The average annual rainfall in the country has been estimated to be about 1,170 millimeters (mm). It receives nearly 4,000 billion cubic meters (bcm) of fresh water annually through rainfall and snowfall. Most of the rainfall is concentrated in 100 to 120 days during the period of June through September. Besides, there are also wide variations in the annual rainfall from region to region: from as low as 100 mm in parts of western Rajasthan to as high as 11,000 mm in Cherrapunji in the eastern part of Meghalaya. Thus, the distribution and availability of water is not uniform over space. Similarly, there are wide year-to-year fluctuations in rainfall in the country.

It is estimated that out of the total quantity of rainwater received annually, 700 bcm seeps into the ground and 500 bcm is lost due to evaporation and transpiration. Of the total quantum of seepage, nearly 433 bcm is replenishable groundwater through recharging of underground aquifers, of which 396 bcm can be annually extracted economically. The surface run-off to the ocean is estimated at 1,869 bcm, which is approximately half of the total annual rainfall received. This leaves nearly 690 bcm as the fresh utilizable surface water, which together with the extractable groundwater of nearly 433 bcm makes the utilizable water resources of the order of 1,123 bcm. So far, of the total utilizable water resources, nearly 600 bcm has been put to use in the country (GoI 1999: 14–15).

It is estimated that India accounts for about 4% of the world's fresh water resources. This, when seen against India's share of 2.50% in the total land area of the world, seems more than adequate. However, when we consider the fact that India accounts for about 17.5% of the world's human population and 15% of the world's animal population the picture changes from optimistic to pessimistic. The picture is bleak when we consider the declining trend in per capita availability of fresh water.

The per capita renewable water resources availability in the country in 2014 was estimated to be only 1,526 cubic meters (cm) per annum as compared to 31,561 cm in the Russian Federation, 7,835 cm in Bangladesh, 2,005 cm in China, and 1,355 cm in Pakistan (FAO AQUASTAT 2015). It has been declining over time and will continue to do so in future also. While this is the picture at the aggregate national level, there are significant regional and temporal variations in water availability caused by spatial and year-to-year fluctuations in the annual rainfall that India receives. This causes the problems of regional and seasonal scarcity and surpluses.

Droughts and floods have been recurrent phenomena in many parts of the country for ages. They result in enormous economic loss to the nation and suffering to the millions of affected people. In view of all this, there is an urgent need for judicious development, use, and management of the country's water resources. We have the required technology, and financial and manpower resources available in our country but need a pragmatic national water policy, including a judicious water and power pricing policy.

Forest Resources

Forests are natural renewable resources and have always been an integral part of India's economy and culture since time immemorial. They are held in high esteem by people. The ancient religious, political, and literary writings are a testimony to the fact that people were considered as an integral part of nature and not superior to it.

Forests occupy an important place in India's economy in terms of their contribution to the GDP, employment, and livelihoods of poor people. In 2013–14, forests contributed ₹14,94,050 million at current prices to India's GDP at factor cost, which was 1.43% of India's total GDP (MoA 2014a, Tables 2.6b and 2.6c).

As per *India State of Forest Report*, 2013, the forest cover of India was 6,97,898 sq. km, of which 83,502 sq. km (about 12%) was very dense forest, 3,18,745 sq. km (about 46%) was moderately dense forest and 2,95,651 sq. km (about 42%) was classified as open forest. The forest area accounted for 21.23% of the total geographical area of the country (FSI 2013, Chapter 2). The National Forest Policy 1988 stipulates that the country as a whole should aim at keeping about one-third of the geographical area under forest cover. The forests are being degraded by the ever-increasing biotic pressure and, hence, they need to be rehabilitated by afforestation not only for environmental considerations but also for meeting the local demand for firewood, small timber, fodder, and for defense and industry.

In India, forests meet nearly 40% of the energy needs of the country of which more than 77% is utilized in the rural areas and they also meet about 30% of fodder needs of the cattle population. Forest products also play a very important role in rural and tribal economy as many of the non-wood forest products (NWFP) provide sustenance to the rural poor. For landless families and marginal farmers, forest-related activities often represent the primary source of income. Besides the direct tangible economic benefits mentioned previously, forests confer a number of benefits that are not directly visible to the human eye and, yet, they have a great influence in affecting the quality of life. Some of those benefits include the amelioration of climate, conservation of soil and soil moisture, and flood control.

Fishery Resources

India is now the third largest producer of fish and the second largest producer of inland fish in the world. India has a marine coastline of 12,700 km, maritime area of 452 thousand sq. km and an exclusive economic zone (EEZ) of 23.7 million sq. km. The fisheries subsector occupies an important place in the socio-economic development of India. In 2012, the total population of fisher folk in India was 4.056 million and the total number of fisherman families was 875 thousand (MoA 2014b, Table 75, p. 175).

In 2013–14, the fisheries subsector contributed 1.35% of India's total GDP at factor cost at current prices and 0.80% at the 2004–05 prices (MoA 2014a, Tables 2.6b and 2.6c). It is a source of cheap and nutritious food and is an important foreign exchange earner. In 2013–14, the value of fish and fish products exported from India was ₹30,627crore (US$5,062 million); MoA 2014a, Table 7.3(A), p. A 94. Besides, it is a major source of livelihood for over 4.056 million fishermen and women folk in the country, engaged fully or partially, or in subsidiary activities pertaining to the sector. Overfishing is a serious problem in many coastal areas of India and consequently fish yields have been declining over time. In view of this, there is a need to regulate and coordinate the fishing operations through appropriate policy measures including granting of sea tenure to local fishermen's organizations (Singh and Shishodia 2007, 302).

Use of Inputs and Outputs

The major inputs used in agriculture consist of seeds, organic manure, chemical fertilizers, pesticides, irrigation water, human labor, animal and mechanical power, electricity, livestock feed, and credit. Table 2.2 presents estimates of the quantities of seeds, chemical fertilizers, and pesticides used in India's agriculture. The total fertilizer consumption in the form of nitrogen, phosphorus, and potash (NPK) nutrients in India was merely 292 thousand tons in 1960–61. It increased to 16.70 million tons in 2000–01, and to 24.48 million tons in 2013–14. The average per ha consumption of NPK nutrients increased from a mere 1.90 kg in 1960–61 to 89.63 kg in 2000–01 and to 125.39 kg in 2013–14. The quantity of certified/quality seeds distributed increased from about 2.5 million quintals in 1980–81 to about 30 million quintals in 2013–14. The use of pesticides (technical grade) in India was only 8,620 tons in 1960–61. It increased to about 44,000 tons in 2000–01 and to about 56,000 tons in 2013–14 (MoA 2014a).

Judicious use of fertilizers is crucial in order to grow enough food to ensure food security. New Zealand is leading the Asia and Pacific region in fertilizer application rates with almost 1.4 tons per hectare, followed by China with 450 kg per hectare. Other top users are

Table 2.2: *Use of Major Agricultural Inputs in India: 2000–01 to 2013–14*

Input	*Unit*	*2000–01*	*2005–06*	*2010–11*	*2012–13*	*2013–14*
Production of breeder seeds	Thousand quintals	42.69	68.64	118.85	110.20	82.29
Production of foundation seeds	Thousand quintals	591	740	1,753	1,617	1,743
Distribution of certified seeds	Million quintals	8.627	12.675	27.734	31.344	30.139
Consumption of nitrogenous fertilizers (N)	Thousand tons	10,920	12,723	16,558	16,821	16,750
Consumption of phosphetic fertilizers (P)	Thousand tons	4,215	5,204	8,050	6,653	5,633
Consumption of potassic fertilizers (K)	Thousand tons	1,567	2,413	3,534	2,062	2,099
Total consumption of N+P+K	Thousand tons	16,702	20,340	28,122	25,536	24,482
Total consumption of N+K+P per ha	Kg	89.63	105.50	142.52	130.79	125.39
Consumption of pesticides	Thousand tons	43.58	39.77	55.54	45.62*	58.21*

Source: MoA (2014a, 321–22).
Note: *Updated on April 30, 2014.

Republic of Korea (ROK) with 293 kg, Malaysia, with 282 kg, Bangladesh with 227 kg, Japan with 243 kg, Pakistan with 194 kg and India with only 164 kg per hectare (FAO 2014, 16).

The level of use of energy is an important determinant of rural development. The rural households still have limited access to energy. About 45% of rural households lack access to electricity. Per capita consumption of electricity in rural areas is only 8 kilowatt hour (kWh) per month as compared to 24 kWh in urban areas (Planning Commission 2012, cited in IDFC 2013, 126). In 2011–12, consumption of electricity for agricultural purposes in India was only 1,40,960 gigawatt hours (GWh), which was 20.95% of the total energy consumption in India (MoA 2014a, 340). This was not adequate to meet even half the potential demand in the agricultural sector. It will be a challenging task to meet the growing demand for energy of households, industry, transport, agriculture, and business.

Farm mechanization is increasingly used in crop production, harvest and post-harvest operations. According to a study (Singh et al., cited in MoA 2013, 64), the share of agricultural workers and draught animals had come down from 63.50% in 1971–72 to 13.67% in 2009–10 whereas that of tractors, power tillers, and diesel engines and electric motors had gone up from 36.51% to 86.33% over the same period of time. India and Japan have by far the largest number of tractors in the Asia and Pacific region, over 2 million each (FAO 2014, 16).

The flow of institutional credit to agriculture in the country was ₹4,62,680 million in 1990–2000, which increased to ₹5,28,270 million in 2000–01 and to ₹71,16,210 million in 2013–14 (MoA 2014a, 343). Besides, farmers now have access to credit through 10,120 million Kisan Credit Cards (KCC) issued to them through a vast rural banking network in the country till March 31, 2014 (MoA 2014a, Table 14.10, p. 344). But still there is a huge unfulfilled demand for credit in the country.

Agricultural Production

Table 2.3 presents estimates of production of food grains, milk, and fish for selected years in India from 1950–51 to 2013–14. As shown in the Table, the total production of food grains increased from 51 million tons in 1950–51 to 265 million tons in 2013–14, milk production increased to 137 million tons and fish production increased to 9.58 million tons over the same period of time.

India now is self-sufficient in food grains and milk production. The average per capita availability of food grains in the country was about 469 gm/day in 2013 and that of milk 299 gm/day in 2012–13. However, the average per capita availability of food grains and milk does not reveal how the quantity available is distributed among different income groups. In fact, most of the poor people do not consume any quantity of milk as they cannot afford it. Similarly, not every poor person has access to enough food grains to meet his/her daily requirement. In view of this, we can say that not everyone in the country is food secure.

Fish production in the country has registered tremendous growth over the last decade, ranging from 2.91% to 6.87% per annum, which is much higher than that for the agricultural sector as a whole. The total fish production in India was only 0.75 million tons in 1950–51, which increased to about 9.58 million tons in 2013–14. Fish production can be increased significantly if judicious development, conservation, and harvesting of marine and inland fishery resources of the country by way of utilizing suitable scientific technologies and conservational measures were adopted.

The Role of the Agricultural Sector

The role of agriculture in economic development has been recognized and discussed since the time of the Physiocrats.[1] According to the Physiocrats, it was only the agricultural sector that produced an economic surplus over cost of production and, therefore, it played the most

Table 2.3: *Production of Food Grains, Milk, and Fish in India, 1950–51 to 2013–14*

Year	*Food Grains (Million Tons)*	*Milk (Million Tons)*	*Fish (Million Tons)*
1950–51	50.82	17.00	0.752
1960–61	82.02	20.00	1.16
1970–71	108.42	20.79	1.756
1980–81	129.59	31.60	2.442
1990–91	176.39	53.99	3.836
1999–2000	213.19	78.3	5.200
2004–05	198.36	92.50	6.30
2009–10	218.00	116.40	7.998
2010–11	259.30	127.90	8.70
2012–13	257.10	132.40	9.04
2013–14	264.80*	137.70	9.579(P)

Source: MoF (2015, Tables 1.12 and 1.20).
Note: *4th Advance estimate.
P: Provisional.

strategic role in economic development. They considered commerce and manufacturing as non-productive, in the sense that the value of raw materials handled by these sectors was enhanced only enough to pay for the labor and capital used in the process of production[2]. We now discuss in detail the role of the agricultural sector in the present Indian context.

Contribution to GDP

Table 2.4 presents data on the percentage contribution of agriculture and allied activities to India's GDP at factor cost at both the current prices and the constant 2004–05 prices. The GDP from agriculture, forestry, and fishing increased from ₹6,37,720 million in 2005–06 to ₹80,05,480 million in 2013–14 at constant 2004–05 prices. Agriculture and allied activities contributed 44.26% to the GDP at current prices and 47.65% at constant 2004–05 prices in 1960–61, but their share had declined to 18.20% in 2013–14 at current prices. As a matter of fact, the share of agriculture has been gradually declining ever since 1950–51, when it was 56.46%. The declining share of agriculture in the GDP does not, however, mean a retrogression of agriculture; it only means that the secondary and tertiary sectors of the economy are expanding at a higher rate. And this is what one would anticipate as the process of economic development moves forward. This has happened in developed countries all over the world (FAO 2014, Table 3, p. 24). In general, the more developed a country, the smaller is the share of agriculture in its national income.

Mainstay of Livelihood and Employment

As we stated earlier, a peculiar feature of India's economy is that a very high proportion (69% in 2011) of the country's population lives in its rural areas. Similarly, though the share of the agricultural sector in GDP has been declining over time, the proportion of the population

Table 2.4: *Contribution of Agriculture and Allied Activities to the Gross Domestic Product (GDP) of India: 1960–61 to 2013–14*

Year	*Total GDP at Factor Cost (₹ Millions)*		*Contribution of Agriculture & Allied Activities (%)*	
	At Current Prices	*At Constant 2004–05 Prices*	*At Current Prices*	*At Constant 2004–05 Prices*
1960–61	1,70,490	41,02,790	44.26	47.65
1970–71	4,43,820	58,97,870	41.95	41.66
1980–81	13,68,380	79,85,060	35.39	35.69
1990–91	53,18,130	1,34,78,890	29.02	29.53
1995–96	1,11,85,860	1,73,77,410	26.26	25.73
2000–01	1,99,19,820	2,34,27,740	23.00	22.42
2005–06	3,39,05,030	3,25,30,730	18.81	18.27
2010–11	7,24,88,600	4,91,85,330	18.21	14.59
2013–14 (RE)	10,47,28,070	5,74,17,910	18.20	13.94

Source: Planning Commission (2014a, 44).[2]
Note: RE: revised estimate as per data-book, December 2014.

dependent upon agriculture and allied activities has been more or less stagnant, or declining at a very slow rate. It is estimated that the agricultural sector is the main source of livelihood and employment for about half of India's population. In contrast, in the developed countries of the Asia and Pacific region, the proportion of population dependent on agriculture was only 4.1% in 2012. More specifically, it was 3.9% in Japan, 4.6% in Australia, and 8.8% in New Zealand as compared to 47.4% in India (FAO 2014, 22). The higher percentage of the population dependent upon agriculture in India indicates the inability of the industrial and services sectors to absorb the incremental rural population. The obvious remedy in such cases is to expand the industrial and services sectors at a faster rate.

Source of Raw Materials

Agriculture is the principal source of raw materials for India's leading industries such as sugar, cotton, jute, textiles, leather, tobacco, and edible oils. Many other industries such as fruit preservation and processing, *dal* mills, handloom weaving, *gur* making, and oil crushing also depend upon agriculture as a source of raw materials. The rate of growth in all these industries is, thus, dependent on the rate of growth in the agricultural sector, and agricultural development is prerequisite for their development.

Source of Foreign Exchange

Agriculture is an important source of earning foreign exchange, which is needed for importing capital goods for the rapidly expanding industrial sector. Agriculture makes its contribution to the net foreign exchange earnings through the displacement of current and potential imports, and through expanded exports. In the year 1990–91, the value of agricultural exports was ₹60,12,760 million, which accounted for about 18.49% of the total value of exports from India in that year. The value of agricultural imports in the same year was ₹12,05,860 million, which accounted for 2.79% of India's total imports (Table 2.5). The share of agricultural commodities in the total exports of India has been stagnant between 10–19% over time; in fact, it declined from 19.18% in 1995–96 to 14.17% in 2013–14. This is due to the fact that the exports of non-agricultural commodities have been increasing at a faster rate than the exports of agricultural commodities.

Table 2.5: *India's Imports and Exports of Agricultural Commodities*

(Value in ₹ Million)

Year	*Total Agricultural Imports*	*Total National Imports*	*% Share of Agricultural Imports*	*Total Agricultural Exports*	*Total National Exports*	*% Share of Agricultural Exports*
1990–91	12,059	4,31,704	2.79	60,128	3,25,273	18.49
1995–96	58,901	12,26,781	4.80	2,03,978	10,63,534	19.18
2000–01	1,20,862	22,83,066	5.29	2,86,574	20,13,565	14.23
2005–06	21,44,992	66,04,089	3.26	4,92,170	45,64,179	10.78
2010–11	5,73,343	1,68,34,670	3.41	11,74,836	1,14,29,219	10.28
2013–14 (P)	1,05,149	2,71,41,815	3.87	26,84,691	1,89,41,820	14.17

Source: MoA (2014a, Table 12.1, p. 283).

Market for Industrial Goods and Services

The agricultural sector provides a ready and big market for many goods manufactured and services provided by the secondary and tertiary sectors. Such goods include pesticides, insecticides, farm machinery, pumping sets, cattle and poultry feed, fish feed, pipelines, fencing material, veterinary medicines, and vehicles. Rural people also buy consumer goods manufactured by the industrial sector. In fact, now many big companies have their eyes on rural markets for their products and services.

Source of Cheap Food

Economic development is characterized by a substantial increase in the demand for food. Apart from autonomous changes in demand, the annual rate of increase in the demand (D) for food is given by $D = p + ng$, where p and g are the rates of growth of population and per capita income, respectively, and n is the income elasticity of demand for food. With the average annual exponential population growth rate of 1.64% per annum registered in India during the decade 2001–11, and with the annual growth in per capita net national income of nearly 10% at current prices, the annual rate of increase in demand for food in India is around 8% (assuming the income elasticity of demand for food to be 0.6). If food supplies fail to expand in pace with the growth of demand, the result is likely to be a substantial rise in food prices, leading to political discontent and pressure on wage rates, with consequent adverse effects on industrial profits, investment, and economic growth. The inflationary impact of a given percentage increase in food prices is much more severe in a developing country, such as India, than in a high-income economy. This is a simple consequence of the dominant position of food as a wage good in low-income countries, where 40% to 50% of the total consumption expenditure is devoted to food, compared with 20% to 25% in developed economies. There are, thus, severe penalties attached to the failure to produce adequate food in developing countries such as India.

Major Problems of the Agricultural Sector

The agricultural sector of India is afflicted by several problems. Some of the major problems are presented in Box 2.1 and briefly described in the following paragraphs.

Box 2.1

SOME OF THE MAJOR PROBLEMS OF INDIA'S AGRICULTURAL SECTOR

1. *High vulnerability to natural calamities and concomitant high risk and uncertainty*
2. *Preponderance of small uneconomic land and livestock holdings*
3. *Low capital–labor ratio*
4. *Low factor productivity*
5. *Long gestation and low rate of turnover*
6. *High incidence of poverty, inequality, and indebtedness*
7. *Preponderance of illiterate and unskilled workforce*
8. *Lack of remunerative prices of farm produce and post-harvest infrastructure*
9. *Lack of basic infrastructure and modern amenities*

Source: Authors.

High Vulnerability to Natural Calamities and Concomitant High Risk and Uncertainty

Agricultural production, being biological in nature, depends more on weather and other climatic factors than non-agricultural production. In India rain-fed agro-ecologies accounts for about 60% of the net sown area, where crop production wholly depends on the quantum and distribution of rainfall over the growing season. Given the wide fluctuations in rainfall in India from year to year and area to area, crop production—and, hence, farm incomes—vary widely. In a nutshell, Indian agriculture is vulnerable to several natural calamities such as droughts, floods, hailstorms, and cyclones and therefore has a high degree of risk and uncertainty. For example, nearly 60% of the Indian landmass is vulnerable to earthquakes, about 68% of the area is susceptible to droughts, over 40 mha of land is prone to floods and about 8% of the total area is prone to cyclones (Singh and Shishodia 2007, 345). This means that the degree of nature-induced risk and uncertainty in agriculture is higher than in the non-agricultural sector and so also the need for insurance against such risks.

Preponderance of Small Uneconomic Land and Livestock Holdings

In 1970–71, the number of operational landholdings in India was 71 million, which increased to 138.35 million by 2010–11 (MoA 2014b, 135). The average size of operational landholdings in India has been declining over time; it declined from 2.28 ha in 1970–71 to 1.84 ha in 1980–81, to 1.55 in 1990–91, and to 1.15 ha in 2010–11 (MoA 2014b, 135). Of the total landholdings in 2010–11, over 67% were operated by marginal farmers having less than 1 ha of land and 17.9% by small farmers having 1–2 ha of land (Table 2.6). Thus, marginal and small landholdings together accounted for about 85% of the total number of landholdings.

Similarly, it is estimated that most of about 70 million households in India owning milch animals are small holders having one or two animals. The land and livestock holdings are not only small in size but also widely scattered all over the countryside. Landholdings are also fragmented, particularly in those states where consolidation of landholdings has not yet been done. The small and fragmented landholdings are a great obstacle to economical use of farm labor and machinery.

Table 2.6: *Distribution of Operational Landholding in India*

	Total			*Distribution of Holdings (%)*				
Year	*No. of Holdings (Million)*	*Area (Million ha)*	*Average Size (ha)*	*<1 ha*	*1–2 ha*	*2–4 ha*	*4–10 ha*	*10 ha and Above*
1970–71	71.01	162.18	2.30	51.00	18.90	15.00	11.20	3.90
1980–81	88.88	163.80	1.80	56.40	18.10	14.00	9.10	2.40
1990–91	106.63	165.51	1.60	59.40	18.80	13.10	7.10	1.60
2000–01	119.93	159.44	1.30	62.90	18.90	11.70	5.50	1.00
2005–06	129.22	158.32	1.20	64.80	18.50	10.90	4.90	0.80
2010–11	137.76	159.18	1.20	67.00	17.90	10.00	4.30	0.70

Source: IDFC (2013, Table 2.3, p. 21).

A *Situation Assessment Survey* of farmers conducted by the National Sample Survey Office (NSSO) in 2003 showed that the monthly income of 94% of farm households owning less than 4 ha of land was less than their monthly consumption expenditure, making it difficult for them to continue in agriculture. It also revealed that 40% of the farmers reported that they would quit farming if given an option. But the lack of alternative opportunities compels them to continue in farming (NSSO 2005 quoted in IDFC 2013, 28).

Low Capital–Labor Ratio

Investment in agriculture in the form of capital formation is essential for sustaining the growth of agriculture. It is an important determinant of the pace and level of agricultural development. India's rural sector is starved of capital and overcrowded with human labor. Consequently, the amount of capital available per worker, that is, the capital–labor ratio is low and this is one of the main reasons of low productivity in the sector. For example, in 2007, the total agricultural capital stock (ACS) in Indian agriculture was $3,69,127 million and the number of cultivators and agricultural workers (agricultural population) in 2011 was 263 million. Thus, the total ACS per capita of agricultural population was $1,403.52 million as compared to $1,32,288.51 million in Australia, $1,72,800.00 million in New Zealand and $1,21,834.17 million in Japan. This means that capital per worker in Indian agriculture was very low and, hence, the agricultural productivity was low (FAO 2014, p. 22).

In 2011, the total public and private capital in agriculture and allied sectors was only ₹10,564 million at current prices per capita of agricultural population of 263 million comprising 118.7 million cultivators and 144.3 million agricultural workers.

To improve this ratio, it is necessary to step up capital formation in agriculture in both public and private sectors and to facilitate, through appropriate policies, the absorption of surplus workers in the non-agricultural sector. After a declining trend for a few years, now, both public and private investments in agriculture have been increasing. For example, public investment in agriculture and allied activities increased from ₹1,61,870 million at 2004–05 prices in 2004–05 to ₹2,38,860 million in 2012–13 and private investment from ₹5,99,090 million to ₹1,381,970 crore over the same period of time (for details, see Table 8.1). This buoyancy needs to be maintained to achieve the target growth rate of 4% per annum in the agricultural sector as envisaged in the Union Budget 2015–16.

Table 2.7 presents the estimates of gross capital formation (GCF) in agriculture and allied sectors at current prices along with their share in the total GCF of India. As shown in the Table, the GCF in agriculture and allied sectors had increased from ₹1,61,870 million in 2004–05 to ₹4,55,110 million in 2012–13 but its share in the total GCF was stagnant around 7–8% all through this period.

Low Factor Productivity

Low crop yields have been the bane of India's agriculture since long and continue to be so even now. For example, as shown in Table 2.8, in 2012, the average yield of paddy was 3,721 kg/ha in India as compared to 5,136 kg/ha in Indonesia and 6,775 kg/ha in China. Similar is the case for other major crops such as wheat, maize, and groundnuts (MoA 2014: Table 7.1, p. 237). As mentioned in the preceding section, the low factor productivity is mainly due to inadequate capital in the form of production inputs, raw materials, and improved machinery and equipment available per worker.

The low average crop yields in India as compared to those in other countries such as New Zealand, China, and Japan are due to low inputs of fertilizers and plant protection chemicals.

Table 2.7: *Gross Capital Formation (GCF) in Agriculture and Allied Sectors in India at Current Prices*

(₹ *Million*)

				Share of Agriculture & Allied Sectors in Total GCF in India (%)		
Year	*Public Sector*	*Private Sector*	*Total*	*Public Sector*	*Private Sector*	*Total*
2004–05	1,61,870	5,99,090	7,60,960	6.7	7.8	7.5
2005–06	2,07,390	6,92,040	8,99,430	7.1	7.4	7.3
2006–07	2,56,060	7,54,960	10,11,020	7.2	6.7	6.8
2007–08	2,76,380	9,56,790	12,33,170	6.3	6.8	6.7
2008–09	2,66,920	13,36,550	16,03,470	5.0	9.6	8.3
2009–10	3,32,010	15,13,250	18,45,260	5.6	9.2	8.3
2010–11	3,19,680	16,53,960	19,73,640	4.9	8.2	7.4
2011–12	3,68,870	21,48,180	25,17,050	5.3	9.2	8.3
2012–13	4,55,110	23,23,280	27,78,390	5.5	9.6	8.6

Source: MoA (2014a, Table 3.6(a), p. 54).

Table 2.8: *Average Yield Rates of Selected Major Crops in India and a Few Foreign Countries of the World in 2012*

(kg per hectare)

Country	*Paddy*	*Wheat*	*Maize*	*Sugarcane*	*Groundnuts (Shell)*
India	3,721	3,177	2,556	70,931	984
World	4,548	3,090	4,888	70,599	1,646
China	6,775	4,987	5,870	68,806	3,572
Indonesia	5,136	NA	4,899	70,000	2,236
Russian Federation	5,490	1,773	4,239	NA	NA
Philippines	3,845	NA	2,856	73,852	NA
Pakistan	4,068	2,709	4,268	55,829	NA
Bangladesh	4,421	NA	NA	42,770	NA
USA	8,349	3,115	7,744	80,057	4,699
Canada	NA	2,865	9,211	NA	NA

Source: MoA (2014a, Table 7.1, p. 237).
Note: NA: Not available.

For example, in 2011, in New Zealand, the average use of fertilizers was 1,400 kg/ha, in China 450 kg/ha and in Japan 243 kg/ha whereas in India it was only 164 kg//ha (FAO 2014, 16). Similarly, the low average milk yield per milch animal in India is due mainly to the low quantity of concentrated feed and the poor quality of fodder fed to the animals. What is required to improve the resource productivity in India's rural sector is to close the technology gap and reduce the redundant labor force.

High Incidence of Poverty, Indebtedness, and Suicides

The incidence of poverty in India is higher in the rural sector than in the urban sector. For example, in 2011–12, about 26% of the rural population was below the poverty line, as compared to about 14% in urban areas (Table 2.9). In absolute terms, of the total population of 269.7 million living below the poverty line in India in 2011–12, 216.6 million (80%) were in the rural areas.

Compared to the poverty lines based on the methodology of the Tendulkar Expert Group, the poverty lines estimated by the Rangarajan Expert Group are 19% and 41% higher in rural and urban areas, respectively. The Rangarajan Expert Group uses the Modified Mixed Recall Period (MMRP) consumption expenditure data of the NSSO as these are considered to be more precise compared to the Mixed Recall Period (MRP), which was used by the Tendulkar Expert Group and the Uniform Recall Period (URP), which was used for earlier estimations. About 67% of the increase in the rural poverty line and 28% of the increase in the urban poverty line is because of the shift from MRP to MMRP (Planning Commission 2014b, 4). As per the Rangarajan Expert Group report, in 2011–12, the poverty ratio was 39.9% in rural areas and 26.4% in urban areas, and the number of people below the poverty was 260.5 million in rural areas and 102.5 million in urban areas. This is in contrast to the corresponding estimates of 216.7 million and 53.1 million for rural and urban areas respectively, as per the Tendulkar Expert Group Report (Planning Commission 2014, Table 4.7, p. 69).

The rural–urban gap in poverty is further corroborated by the gap in the average monthly per capita consumption expenditure (MPCE). As per the household expenditure survey conducted by NSSO in 2011–12, the ratio of urban to rural per capita consumption increased from 1.76 in 1999–2000 to about 2.00 in 2011–12, which suggests that the urban–rural divide is widening. If the comparison is extended to gaps in the availability of other essential services, the chasm is much deeper.

However, in terms of Gini ratio, which is a measure of inequality in income distribution, rural areas fared better than urban areas in all the three reference periods, that is, 2004–05, 2009–10 and 2011–12 (Table 2.9). This shows that the average per capita income was more equally distributed in rural areas than in urban areas. This seems to be consistent with the common observation that it is the rural rich and the rural poor who migrate to urban areas; the former in search of greener pastures and the latter in search of jobs. This reduces income inequality in rural areas and increases it in urban areas.

Since ages, the high incidence of indebtedness among the rural poor has been the bane of India's rural economy. This situation has remained unchanged, if not deteriorated, till date. As per a recent *Situation Assessment Survey of Farmers* conducted by the NSSO, the total number

Table 2.9: *Poverty, Inequality, and Monthly Per-capita Consumption Expenditure in India, 2004–12*

Year	*Poverty* (%)*			*Inequality (Gini) Index*		*MPCE (₹) (2004–05 Prices)*	
	Rural	*Urban*	*Total*	*Rural*	*Urban*	*Rural*	*Urban*
2004–05	41.8	25.7	37.2	27.36	35.57	579.2	1,104.6
2009–10	33.8	20.9	29.8	27.58	37.06	632.7	1,249.7
2011–12	25.7	13.7	21.9	24.89	35.17	704.6	1,433.7

Source: IDFC (2013, 68).
Note: *Poverty estimates are as per the Tendulkar methodology.

of agricultural households in India was estimated to be 90.20 million in 2011–12. Of them 46.85 million households (51.9%) were in debt and the average outstanding debt was ₹47,000 per household. The highest incidence of indebtedness was in the landholding size class of 0.41–1.00 ha (34.90%). Uttar Pradesh had the highest number of farmers in debt, accounting for 16.90% of the total number of households in the state (MoA 2014a, Tables 16.2 and 16.3, pp. 373–76). It would not be an exaggeration to say that most of the small and marginal farmers are born in debt, live in debt, and die in debt.

Given the low coverage of crop insurance schemes, most of the farmers have to bear the losses due to crop failure themselves and resort to borrowing from money lenders and other sources to sustain themselves and their families. Due to the low and fluctuating farm incomes, they are not able to repay their debts and become broke in the process. Consequently, there have been numerous cases of farmers committing suicide in many ecologically vulnerable states such as Maharashtra, Andhra Pradesh, Karnataka, Madhya Pradesh, Chhattisgarh, Gujarat, and Odisha. It is estimated that 1,98,000 farmers in India committed suicide over the period 2001–12. Indebtedness and the confiscation of their land and other assets, such as tractors, by lenders were the main causes of suicides (IDFC 2013, 6).

Lack of Remunerative Price of Farm Produce and Post-harvest Infrastructure

Farmers—particularly small and marginal farmers—do not get a remunerative price for their produce. Most of them have small quantities of marketable surplus and low holding capacity due to poverty. As a result, they are forced to sell their produce in local markets at very low prices immediately after the harvest (distress sale), mostly to money lenders and traders from whom they had borrowed money. In most of the cases, the price that they receive does not cover even the cost of production. The government has intervened, both as regulator and buyer, to assure farmers of remunerative prices but with limited success. It is ironic that it is only the farmers who cannot fix the price of their produce the way all other producers and manufacturers do; they have to sell their produce at the price fixed by others.

Besides, there are inadequate decentralized storage facilities and other post-harvest infrastructure such as processing and grading. As a result, there is a lot of wastage of farm produce; in cases of vegetables and fruits, losses are as high as 18% (MoA 2013, 213–14). There are many instances when farmers had to virtually throw their produce on roads or burn in the fields. The way forward is the creation of adequate, post-harvest infrastructure including a chain of cold storage and processing facilities through public private participation. A study undertaken by the Central Institute of Post-harvest Engineering and Technology (CIPHET), Ludhiana, Punjab, has estimated the wastage in various types of farm produce (Table 2.10). Wastage occurs at all the stages in the food chain starting from production to marketing.

Table 2.10: *Wastage in Various Crops*

Crop	*Cumulative Extent of Wastage (%)**
Cereals	3.9–6
Pulses	4.3–6.1
Oilseeds	6.0
Fruits and vegetables	5.8–18

(Table 2.10 Continued)

(Table 2.10 Continued)

Crop	*Cumulative Extent of Wastage (%)**
Milk	0.8
Fisheries	2.9
Meat	2.3
Poultry	3.7

Source: MoA (2013–14).
Note: *Includes total wastage at all levels/stages from producer to wholesaler and retailer.

Lack of Basic Infrastructure

Indian villages miserably lack in such basic infrastructure as schools, health care centers (leave aside hospitals), all-weather roads, means of transport and communication, drinking water facilities, and electricity for domestic and agricultural purposes. It has been established through empirical studies that basic infrastructure is an important determinant of development. As matter of fact, the "growth center" theory of development is based on this premise. Although good progress has been made recently in many states under the Minimum Needs Programme (MNP), Bharat Nirman Programme (BNP), Sarva Shiksha Abhiyan (SSA), National Rural Health Mission (NRHM), Provision of Urban Amenities in Rural Areas (PURA) and other programs to provide the bare minimum infrastructure, there are millions of people living in remote tribal and hilly areas where not much has been done. An alarming 20% of rural households do not have three basic facilities, namely, drinking water within premises, sanitation, and electricity and only 18% have access to all three (IDFC 2013, 118). According to the 69th round of the NSSO survey of (covering the period of July–December, 2012) on drinking water, sanitation, hygiene and housing conditions, 11.5% of rural households had no access to improved sources of drinking during 2012; 62.3% did not have access to any bathroom facility; 59.4% had no latrine facilities; 20% had no electricity for domestic use; and 49.9% did not have any drainage system (NSSO 2014, Highlights, i–iii).

The Role of the Non-agricultural Subsector

In the following pages, we briefly discuss the role of the non-agricultural subsector in India's growth and development.

Importance of the Subsector

In most of the developing countries—including India—the rural labor force has been growing rapidly but employment opportunities have been dwindling. As the land available for expansion of agriculture becomes increasingly scarce, opportunities for non-farm employment must expand if deepening rural poverty is to be avoided. Given the expected growth and composition of large-scale urban industries, they are unlikely to be able to absorb the rising tide of workers migrating from the countryside to the cities. Looking toward the 21st century, we must slow the process of the urban spread, with its high social and environmental costs, such as congestion, pollution, skyrocketing land costs, growing violence, and increasing incidence of sexually transmitted diseases (STDs) such as AIDS. Expansion of the rural non-agricultural sector, with its emphasis on labor-intensive and small-scale enterprises, widens income opportunities for the poor, including small farmers, the landless, and women, enabling them to even out extreme fluctuations in their incomes.

In India, cottage and village industries have been an important occupation of the landless and other poor people in villages for ages. They are an important source of income and employment opportunities for them. As a matter of fact, agriculture and rural industries are complementary to each other. This sector has the second largest share of employment after agriculture. It touches the lives of the weaker and unorganized sections of the society, with more than half of those employed being women, minorities, and the marginalized. Fifty-seven percent of the micro and small enterprises (MSEs) units are owner-run enterprises with one person. They account for 32% of the workforce and 29% of the value added in non-agricultural private unincorporated enterprises.

The relative importance of the rural non-agricultural subsector and the composition of the various economic activities included in the sector differ widely from region to region in India. Broadly defined, this subsector includes economic activities outside agriculture, carried out in villages and varying in size from households to small factories. A few examples of these activities are cottage, tiny, village, and small-scale manufacturing and processing industries, and trade, transportation, construction, and services of various kinds. Household industries have declined over time, whereas small-scale, non-household industries have expanded. Cottage enterprises—based on part-time family labor—are relatively less efficient than small-scale, full-time, and specialized rural industries. As the cost of labor rises, enterprises with no scope for division of labor continue to lose their cost advantage. Subsequently, the rural towns that serve as trading and distribution centers for both urban and agricultural goods attract manufacturing activities.

The linkages between the rural non-agricultural and agricultural subsectors are critical for rural development. The growth in farm income provides an expanding market for consumption goods and agricultural inputs produced by the non-agricultural subsector, while agricultural raw materials are processed in the rural non-agricultural subsector. The relative strengths of the consumption and production linkages depend on the pace and pattern of growth in agricultural income, and the production technology used in agriculture. The higher the per capita income growth, the higher is the share of non-food consumption in rural expenditure and, hence, the greater is the stimulus to the growth of the rural non-agricultural subsector. The share of locally produced consumption goods (as against imports from urban areas or abroad) in consumption expenditure depends on the distribution of income in agriculture. It is higher among the medium or small farmers than among the rich.

More specifically, the subsector contributes to the growth and development of India's rural economy in the following ways.

Contribution to Employment Growth

Since agriculture cannot absorb all the growth in rural workforce, the non-agricultural sector has a crucial role as a source of employment for the unemployed rural workforce. In the last two decades or so, growth in the non-farm work has accelerated and now almost a third of rural workers and about 43% of rural households are engaged in non-farm work (IDFC 2013, Table 2.6, p. 33–34; NSSO 2011). Over the period from 1993–94 to 2009–10, rural employment increased by over 44 million and reached a total of 337 million adult workers (aged 15 years and above) and all new jobs were in the non-farm sector (Table 2.11). The share of non-farm employment in the total rural employment increased from 22% in 1993–94 to 32% in 2009–10. Almost two-thirds of the increase in the non-farm employment was in casual wage labor and one-fifth was in self-employment.

A striking feature of the non-farm employment is the casualization of labor. Now, almost two out of three new rural, non-farm jobs are casual labor, that is, unskilled daily wage jobs.

Table 2.11: *Rural Workers Employed in Farm and Non-farm Sectors in India*

(Million) Year	Agriculture			Non-agriculture			Total Employed		
	Male	Female	All	Male	Female	All	Male	Female	All
1993–94	139 (74)*	90 (86)	229 (78)	49 (26)	14 (14)	63 (22)	188 (100)	104 (100)	292 (100)
1999–2000	142 (71)	90 (85)	232 (76)	57 (29)	15 (14)	72 (24)	199 (100)	105 (100)	304 (100)
2004–05	146 (67)	103 (83)	249 (73)	73 (33)	21 (17)	94 (27)	219 (100)	124 (100)	343 (100)
2009–10	146 (63)	83 (79)	229 (68)	86 (37)	22 (21)	108 (32)	232 (100)	105 (100)	337 (100)

Source: IDFC (2013, Table 2.6, p.34).
Note: * Figures in parentheses are percentages of total employed.

But unlike regular salaried jobs, casual labor offers no job security or benefits but the wage rates are higher than those for agricultural labor. Besides, it offers an opportunity for social networking. For this reason, the move to casual labor is often not a distress move away from agriculture labor, but rather an intentioned one. Gradually, over time, this has bridged the gap between casual non-farm and farm wages as agricultural labor becomes scarce. Consequently, social hierarchies and traditional production systems in villages are disintegrating over time (IDFC 2013, 38–39).

Wages of casual workers in rural India increased at the fastest pace in seven years (2004–05 to 2011–12) across all categories of labor. As per NSSO, average rural casual wage rate increased by almost threefold during 2004–05 to 2011–12. On the whole, three factors, *that is,* rising construction activity, higher price support for farm products that trickled down to farm laborers, and Mahatma Gandhi National Rural Employment Guarantee Act (MGNREGA) seem to be pushing the rural casual wage rate upward (NABARD 2014, 4–5). This is a desirable change.

Contribution to Gross Domestic Product and Rural Net Domestic Product

There are now 36.1 million MSMEs in India that contribute 37.5% of the country's GDP. The increasing significance of non-farm subsector is evident from the fact that its contribution to the rural net domestic product (NDP) increased from 43% in 1993–94 to 61.1% in 2004–05, whereas that of agriculture, forestry and fishing declined from 57% to about 39% over the same period of time (IDFC 2013, Table 2.7, p. 35). The rapid growth of the non-farm subsector is driven by both the "push" and "pull" forces. The agrarian distress pushes the poor rural households to diversify into non-farm activities to increase their household income and/or to mitigate the risk from crop failure. The "pull" forces, and in particular urbanization, has been identified as a prime motivator for non-farm growth since the 1990s. Over the past decade or so, the trade, construction, and transportation activities have driven the non-farm job growth (IDFC 2013, 35).

The sector contributes over 40% of the gross turnover in the manufacturing sector, about 45% of manufacturing exports and about 35% of the total exports. They have a critical role in boosting industrial growth and ensuring the success of the "Make in India" program.

Policy Measures Taken by the Government

Given the increasing role of the non-agricultural subsector as a means of absorbing the additions to the rural workforce, the Government of India has taken several initiatives from time to time to promote the growth of this subsector. The first major initiative was the establishment of the Khadi and Village Industries Commission (KVIC) in 1956 under an act of Parliament, "Khadi and Village Industries Commission Act of 1956." KVIC is a statutory body formed by the Government of India. It is an apex organization under the Ministry of Micro, Small, and Medium Enterprises. It is mandated to "plan, promote, facilitate, organize, and assist in the establishment and development of khadi and village industries in the rural areas in coordination with other agencies engaged in rural development wherever necessary." The KVIC has identified 95 village industries for government support. These industries are divided into the following seven categories:

1. Mineral-based industries.
2. Forest-based industries.
3. Agro-based industries.
4. Polymer and chemicals based industries.
5. Engineering and non-conventional energy based industries.
6. Textile industry other than khadi.
7. Service industry.

In order to give a further boost to this sector, several policy initiatives have been taken by the Government of India, including a scheme of integrated infrastructural development, concessional rate of excise duty to non-registered units, quality certification scheme to acquire ISO 9000, raising project outlay from ₹3 million to ₹5 million in the single window scheme, and adequate and timely supply of credit as per the Nayak Committee (1992) recommendations. Besides, the investment limit for small-scale industry (SSI) units has been increased from ₹6 million to ₹30 million, for the tiny sector from ₹500 thousand to ₹2.5 million and the composite loan limit for SSI units from ₹50,000 to ₹2,00,000.

The Nayak Committee, set up by the Reserve Bank of India (RBI) in 1991 to examine the adequacy of institutional credit to the SSI sector and related aspects, observed that it would be safe to presume that the bulk of the financial needs of the rural segment of the SSI sector was met from private sources, including moneylenders. In regard to the overall SSI sector, it observed that:

1. There has been a dispersal of SSI units away from the metropolitan areas and large cities;
2. In spite of the increased flow of credit, the share of the tiny sector and village industries has been dismally low; and
3. Establishment of forward and backward linkages to ensure the success of enterprises has not kept pace with the increase in the flow of credit.

Credit is only one of the essential inputs for industrialization and only if other supporting facilities including adequate and timely availability of raw materials, skilled labor and marketing support are provided on an assured basis, will entrepreneurs be able to prepare viable proposals and obtain institutional finance. The Nayak Committee recommended, among other things, the creation of a separate fund for modernization, research and marketing, venture capital assistance for promoting viable projects by technocrat entrepreneurs, and detailed data collection for village and tiny industries.

Infusion of appropriate technology, design skills, modern marketing capacity building, and easier access to credit can make this segment an expanding base for self-sustaining employment and wealth generation and also foster a culture of creative and competitive industry. Agro-food processing, sericulture, and other village enterprises can check rural–urban migration by gainfully employing people in villages. This will also take the pressure off agriculture. The MSE sector can open up a window of opportunities in regions such as the North East where large industries cannot be set up due to infrastructure gap and environmental concerns. The income generated from various activities in this subsector is more evenly distributed than that generated in the large-scale manufacturing subsector. Besides, due to the low capital requirement per worker, the subsector can generate more jobs with a given amount of capital than the corresponding large-scale factory industries.

Lack of adequate infrastructure is a major impediment to the development of industries in the rural areas. Electricity, transport, communications, and availability of ancillary and allied services, such as suppliers of raw materials and other inputs, semi-skilled and skilled laborers to attend to the problems of machinery, marketing and credit support agencies, and so on, are essential for the growth of industries. In their absence, production activities of tiny units tend to concentrate around the peripheries of urban centers. The Sivaraman Committee (1981) has suggested that the responsibility for providing infrastructural and extension support to the development of industries in rural areas (including providing raw materials) be assigned to the state governments. In the absence of responsive and committed agencies for providing these essential services, banks find the task of supporting the development of rural industries frustrating.

Several ministries, departments and institutions deal with activities falling within the domain of the Micro, Small, and Medium Enterprise (MSME) sector, and have a variety of schemes to support the MSEs. Small Industries Development Bank of India (SIDBI), set up on April 2, 1990 under an act of the Indian Parliament, is the principal financial institution for the promotion, financing, and development of the MSME sector and for coordination of the functions of the institutions engaged in similar activities. However, the benefits accrue to only a small fraction of the MSMEs, as only 13% are registered. Now, we need to adopt a dual strategy to ensure that the unregistered MSMEs and units outside the cooperative fold are encouraged to get registered and are also able to benefit from government schemes, pending registration. In fact, the provision of voluntary filing of enterprise memoranda by the MSMEs in the new Micro, Small, and Medium Enterprises Development Act, 2006 is a step in that direction and should be implemented energetically.

There is a need to change the approach from emphasis on loosely targeted subsidies to creating an enabling environment. A cluster approach can help increase viability by providing these units with infrastructure, information, credit, and support services of better quality at lower costs, while also promoting their capacity for effective management of their own collectives. Further, in order to improve the competitiveness of the MSMEs, schemes for establishment of mini tool rooms, setting up design clinics, providing marketing support, sensitization to intellectual property rights (IPR) requirements and tools, adoption of lean manufacturing practices, wider use of information technology (IT) tools, and so on, should be evolved on a public private partnership (PPP) basis. Brand building can be used as an effective strategy to promote their products in national and international markets. Following an announcement made in the Union Budget 2008–09, a fund of ₹50,000 million was created in the National Bank for Agriculture and Rural Development (NABARD) in 2008–09 to enhance its refinance capacity for the MSME sector. Similarly, two funds of ₹20,000 million each were created in SIDBI; one for risk capital financing and the other for enhancing its refinance capacity for the MSME sector. SIDBI Venture Capital Ltd. (SVCL), a subsidiary of SIDBI set up in July 1999, is an asset management company, presently managing two venture capital funds, namely, the National Venture Fund for Software and Information Technology Industry (NFSIT) and the SME Growth Fund (SGF) for providing venture capital assistance to knowledge-based

MSMEs, especially in the areas of auto components, textiles, life sciences, clean technologies, retailing, light engineering, information technology, services, and so on.

A number of schemes are now being implemented for the establishment of new MSMEs and for promoting the growth and development of existing ones. These include: (a) the Prime Minister's Employment Generation Programme, (b) Micro and Small Enterprises Cluster Development Programme, (c) Credit Guarantee Fund Scheme for Micro and Small Enterprises, (d) Performance and Credit Rating Scheme, (e) Assistance to Training Institutions, and (f) Scheme of Fund for Regeneration of Traditional Industries (MoF, 95–96). All these measures would be more effective if targeted at identified clusters. It is also necessary to recognize the continuing need to facilitate graduation of these enterprises to higher levels, particularly from small to medium. There is a need to provide incentives for the graduation of MSMEs to medium and larger units through well-calibrated fiscal and non-fiscal measures.

Constraints and the Ways Forward

There are several constraints on the growth and development of MSMEs. We briefly discuss some of the major constraints and the ways forward to abate those constraints in the following pages.

Improving the Access to Capital

Micro and small enterprises are eligible for credit at reduced rates under priority sector lending schemes for non-farm activities along with agriculture. The RBI also introduced a General Credit Card Scheme in 2006 to provide access to credit to non-agricultural clients in rural and semi-urban areas along the lines of Kisan Credit Card scheme. However, a sizable section of the population, particularly the vulnerable groups such as weaker sections and low income groups, continue to remain excluded from even the most basic opportunities and services provided by the financial sector. In order to address the issues of financial inclusion, the Government of India constituted a "Committee on Financial Inclusion" under the Chairmanship of Dr C. Rangarajan. The Committee submitted its final report to the Union Finance Minister on January 4, 2008.

The Committee on Financial Inclusion has defined Financial Inclusion as "the process of ensuring access to financial services and timely and adequate credit where needed by vulnerable groups such as weaker sections and low income groups at an affordable cost." Among others, the Committee has recommended setting up of two funds—Financial Inclusion Fund (FIF) and Financial Inclusion Technology Fund (FITF).

Based on the recommendations of the Rangarajan Committee (2008), Government of India has constituted two funds, namely, Financial Inclusion Fund (FIF) for meeting the cost of developmental and promotional interventions of financial inclusion and Financial Inclusion Technology Fund (FITF) to meet the cost of technology adoption for financial inclusion. Each Fund consists of an overall corpus of ₹5,000 million, with initial funding to be contributed by the Government of India, RBI and NABARD in a ratio of 40:40:20. The funding was to be contributed in a phased manner over a maximum period of five years, depending upon the utilization of funds.[3]

Besides, to overcome this problem, banks also have taken several measures such as "no-frills" accounts (NFA) with zero or very low minimum balance, relaxed "know your customer" norms, electronic transfer of funds, and Business Correspondent (BC) model. As a result of these measures, there has been an almost four-fold increase in bank coverage from March 2010 to March 2012. To facilitate lending to the poor not having bank accounts, SHG-Bank linkage and Micro Finance Institutions (MFIs) are also playing an important role (IDFC 2013, 40–41).

Improving Marketing Infrastructure and Access to Markets

The government of India has intervened from time to time to improve the marketing infrastructure for rural producers engaged in MSMEs. The first policy intervention was the setting up of the All India Handicrafts Board as early as 1952. But as the focus shifted to industrialization, policies for artisans increasingly became welfare-oriented instead of growth-oriented. However, since 2000, this approach has changed and the government has now taken up several measures to create new marketing infrastructure and improve the existing one. Some of the measures include: (a) organization by the Ministry of Rural Development of SARAS *melas for* the sale of products produced by SHGs; (b) establishment of rural *haats* to provide permanent marketing centers at the village, district and state levels; (c) setting up of rural *bazaars* similar to ITC's e-choupals for facilitating ICT-based marketing; and (d) promoting demand-driven production by addressing market information asymmetries. This is done through provision of producers design and marketing inputs, coordination of production and quality control, and bringing together poor handloom craftsmen, fashion-conscious consumers, and organized retail sector and other supply chain partners such as Fabindia, Anokhi, and Contemporary Arts and Crafts; and (e) various forms of value chain interventions such as Professional Assistance for Development Action's (PRADAN's) sericulture initiative in Jharkhand and Bihar, which added new nodes to the tussar silk value chain to improve quality and productivity (IDFC 2013, 42).

Placement-based Skills

Failure to adequately develop the skills of the rural poor has been a major obstacle to improving their livelihoods. Many non-farm jobs require technical skills that are not imparted in schools. There are huge skill gaps in professions ranging from plumbing and electrical to nursing and teaching. India's vocationally skilled workforce is limited to only 10%—trained formally (2%) or informally (8%). Training capacity remains grossly inadequate. Taken together, all governmental and nongovernmental vocational training institutes can train only about 3.1 million people per year while 12.8 million people enter the workforce per year. To address these concerns, the government launched the National Skill Development Policy in 2009. The policy is aimed at catering to the emerging employment market needs by involving NGOs and private companies in imparting the required skills in their vocational training institutions. The policy is buttressed by the establishment in January 2010 of the National Skill Development Corporation (NSDC), which catalyzes the creation of private for-profit vocational institutions following the public private partnership (PPP) model. Rather than providing training by itself, NSDC subsidizes organizations that provide job-oriented skill development training through loans, equity and tax breaks. NSDC has a target of skilling/up-skilling 150 million persons by the year 2022 and, as of 2015, three proposals had been cleared to train 10,39,000 persons in next 10 years. The corporation is funded by a trust "National Skill Development Fund" to which the Government of India has contributed a sum of ₹9,951 million. The corporation is expected to mobilize about ₹1,50,000 million from other governments, public sector entities, private sector, and bilateral and multilateral sources. The corporation is expected to meet the skill training requirements of the labor market including that of unorganized sector.

Besides, the National Council for Vocational Training is also involved in improving the skill development training curricula of the Industrial Training Institutes (ITIs) and Industrial Training Centers (ITCs). But despite all these supply-side initiatives, the challenge of imparting necessary skills to the required number of persons remains unfulfilled and, ironically, the demand for vocational training remains low, due mainly to the poor quality of training and the high cost of financing vocational training (IDFC 2013, 43)

Challenges and the Ways Forward

There are many challenges that rural India has been facing for many years and continues to face even now. Similarly, many initiatives have been taken by the government and many more are needed to meet the emerging challenges and harness the opportunities that have opened up. We briefly describe some of the major challenges and the initiatives needed to meet them in the following pages.

Achieving and Maintaining Food Security

Thanks to the introduction and rapid spread of high yielding variety (HYV) seeds in the late 1960s and the early 1970s and increased public investment in infrastructure, research, and extension, India now produces enough food not only for its people but also for export. Foodgrain production, which was 820 million tons in 1960–61, has increased to over 265 million tons in 2013–14. However, despite this, a large number of India's poor still do not have access to enough food.

India has the potential to be a granary of the world, the country that the world should look up to for feeding its rising population. The present crop yields in India are, however, very low as compared to those in developed countries. For example, as stated earlier in this chapter, in 2012 the average yield of paddy was 3,721 kg/ha in India as compared to 5,136 kg/ha in Indonesia and 6,775 kg/ha in China and similar is the case for other major crops such as wheat, maize, and groundnuts (MoA 2014: Table 7.1, p. 237). The yield gap could be bridged through, inter alia, increased public and private investment in agriculture, widespread use of eco-friendly, appropriate new technologies, producer-oriented price policies, and professionally-managed programs. If the average cereal yield in India could be increased to the level of the world average, India can become the world's number one nation in terms of foodgrain production. Therefore, the biggest challenge before India is how to increase its crop yields to the world average level on a sustainable basis, despite such natural calamities as droughts, floods, and unseasonal rains and hailstorms to which India continues to be highly vulnerable even now.

To ensure food security to all, especially the poor, Parliament had passed, on September 12, 2013, a legislation called the National Food Security Act. This law aims to provide subsidized food grains to approximately two-thirds of India's 1.2 billion people. Under the provisions of the act, eligible beneficiaries are entitled to purchase 5 kg per eligible person per month of cereals at the following prices: rice at ₹3 per kg; wheat at ₹2 per kg; and coarse grains (millet) at ₹1 per kg. This act, if implemented faithfully by all state governments, could ensure food security to the poor people.

Preventing of Increasing Incidence of Indebtedness and Suicides by Farmers

Of late, there has been an increasing incidence of suicides by farmers due mainly to heavy losses suffered by them year after year in agriculture, and the consequent increasing indebtedness. There are no reliable estimates of the number of suicides committed by farmers in India. According to reports brought out by the National Crime Records Bureau,

Ministry of Home Affairs, Government of India,[4] some 1,98,000 farmers in India committed suicides over the period 2001–12. Most of suicides occurred in ecologically vulnerable states such as Maharashtra, Andhra Pradesh, Karnataka, Madhya Pradesh, Chhattisgarh, Kerala, and Odisha.

In view of this, the Government of India had approved a rehabilitation package of ₹1,69,787 million for suicide-prone districts in the four states of Andhra Pradesh, Maharashtra, Karnataka, and Kerala. The package was implemented over a period of three years, from 2007–08 to 2009–10. It included both immediate and medium term measures. The rehabilitation package aimed at establishing a sustainable and viable farming and livelihood support system through debt relief to farmers, improved supply of institutional credit, crop-centric approach to agriculture, assured irrigation facilities, watershed management, better extension and farming support services, and subsidiary income opportunities through horticulture, livestock, dairying, fisheries, and so on (GoI 2008). But despite all these measures, farmers still continue to commit suicides. We suggest the following measures for preventing farmers from committing suicides.

Compulsory subsidized crop and livestock insurance should be provided for all poor farmers with farmers paying a nominal amount of premium in normal crop years. The scope of agricultural insurance policies should become wider and should also cover health insurance, as envisaged under the Parivar Bima Policy.

Reasonably fair (remunerative) minimum support prices (MSP) of crop produce as per the recommendations made by the Swaminathan Committee (2006) in its report. The MSP should cover the total actual cost of production and provide a margin of 50% over and above the cost of production.

Poor farmers should be provided crop loans at subsidized rate of interest not exceeding 4% per annum with flexible terms and conditions of repayment over a period of five years.

As most of the poor marginal and small farmers grow high-value perishable crops, the MSP scheme should be extended to cover perishable crops also and necessary arrangements made to procure, store and process the produce when market prices fall below the MSP.

The rate of compensation for loss of crops should be reasonably high so as to cover at least 50% of the estimated loss/damage. For example, if the estimated loss is ₹20,000 per ha, the amount of compensation should be ₹10,000 per ha. The present rates are ridiculously low.

Helping Poor Marginal and Small Farmers Move out of Agriculture

Landholdings in India are not only small in size but also widely scattered all over the countryside. Landholdings are also fragmented in those states where consolidation of landholdings has not yet been done. The process of subdivision and fragmentation of landholdings continues unabated, generation after generation, under the existing land inheritance laws. Consequently, the average size of landholdings has been declining over time, that is, it declined from 2.3 ha in 1970–71 to 1.2 ha in 2010–11. Small and fragmented landholdings are a great obstacle to cost-effective use of farm labor and machinery. Besides, almost all of the landholdings less than one hectare in size are not economically viable and therefore sooner or later, the farmers owning such small landholdings will need to be moved out of farming. Further, the subdivision and fragmentation of landholdings needs to be stopped through appropriate legislative measures, such that landholdings below an economically viable level are not allowed to be subdivided further. Effecting such a reform in the structure of landholdings is a great challenge for policy makers and the ruling political parties. Besides, there is also an urgent need for tenancy reforms that protect the rights of tenants, without discouraging the practice of land leasing.

Bridging the Widening Gap Between Rural and Urban Areas

Bridging the widening gap between rural and urban areas in terms of real per capita incomes, basic infrastructure, and availability of civic amenities such as education, drinking water, sanitation, and health care, and thereby reversing the present trend of rural–urban migration is—and will continue to be so in near future—a great challenge for development policy makers, planners, and managers. Programs such as the MNP, BNP, SSA, and NRHM could be instrumental in narrowing down the rural–urban divide if they are implemented rigorously.

Enabling Farmers to Benefit from the Policy of Liberalization

Liberalization has opened up new opportunities for Indian farmers to benefit from higher global prices for their produce and lower prices for some of the inputs. Export orientation has brought in its wake the need for high-tech projects and for exploring international markets for exportable commodities. The assessment of credit demand, appraisal, and instruments of financing the high-tech projects are all difficult tasks. Meeting the credit needs of this emerging export-oriented, high-tech sector requires concomitant institutional innovations, for which a beginning has been made with the establishment of agricultural development finance companies. NABARD has to play—and, in fact, it is already playing—a crucial role in meeting this challenge.

Ensuring Forward and Backward Linkages of Agricultural Sector

Further, with uncertainties in global markets and hardening of the international prices of food, fuels and edible oils, domestic price stability, and food security critically depend on growth in this sector. This necessitates working out the forward and backward linkages that enhance productivity through balanced allocation and better utilization of available resources at all levels of implementation and quantifying output per unit of resource used. The issue of productivity and resource use assumes importance as agriculture continues to support more than half of our population.

Developing Human Resources Through Skill-based Training

Human resource development of the persons engaged in agriculture is necessary not only to have greater penetration of better technology, but also because new skill sets would be necessary to enable the underemployed labor in this sector to get absorbed in other fast growing sectors. This has acquired more importance in the context of "Make in India" policy of the government. Despite several measures taken by the government to impart skill-based training to unemployed rural youth, there still exists a huge gap between the requirement and availability of skilled labor force.

Promoting Eco-friendly Technologies

Of late, there has been a spectacular growth in public awareness about the adverse environmental impacts of economic growth and development. This has come from increasing air and water pollution, soil erosion, depletion of ground water aquifers, denudation and degradation of forests, and the increasing water-logging and soil salinity in canal command areas. In view of this, a new paradigm of sustainable development is emerging. This paradigm does not favor any blind pursuit of economic growth at the cost of environmental degradation. A serious challenge before the agricultural development policy makers today is how to achieve a faster rate of development, while keeping the natural resources and quality of the environment intact.

Facilitating the Expansion of the Non-farm Sector at a Higher Pace

The rural non-agricultural subsector will have to expand at a much faster rate to provide income and employment opportunities to the surplus rural people, particularly to the poor marginal and small farmers. This is possible if a well thought out long-term national policy for the rural non-farm sector development is formulated and implemented effectively. There is a need to improve the access of MSMEs to institutional credit and better marketing facilities.

Key Points

1. India's economy is comprised of two sectors, namely, rural sector and non-rural sector. The rural sector accounts for about 69% of India's total population. It is composed of two main subsectors, that is, the agricultural subsector and the non-agricultural subsector.
2. In the rural sector, agricultural subsector is the most prominent. This is evident from the fact that about one half of the country's population is dependent on agriculture and allied activities for its livelihood. Agriculture and allied activities contributed about 18% of India's GDP in 2013–14 at the current prices and about 14% at the 2004–05 prices and provided employment to 52% of the country's total labor force. It is also an important source of foreign exchange and raw materials for India's major agro-industries and provides a large market for industrial products. No program of India's development can ever succeed if it neglects the rural sector.
3. The non-agricultural subsector consists of several economic activities, such as cottage and village industries, khadi, handloom, handicrafts, trading of general goods, small shops, petty traders, and services such as transport, communication, banking, input supply, and marketing of farm and non-farm produce. The non-agricultural subsector has been growing at a faster rate than the agricultural sector, providing lots of new employment opportunities.
4. Despite the impressive progress that India has made since independence in the field of science and technology, the rural sector and rural people remain grossly underdeveloped with about 270 million (about 26% of India's rural population) of the rural people living below the poverty line in 2011–12 and 31% being illiterate in 2001.
5. The rural sector is characterized by, inter alia, the preponderance of small and scattered rural enterprises, lack of basic infrastructure, low productivity, high incidence of poverty and indebtedness, and excessive dependence on weather and climatic factors, and the consequent high degree of risk and uncertainty. In view of this, there is a need to reduce the weather induced risk in agriculture through appropriate crop insurance schemes. It is also necessary to consolidate the scattered and fragmented landholdings and prevent their further subdivision and fragmentation through appropriate legislative measures so that farm labor and machinery could be used more cost effectively.

6. Of late, there has been an increasing incidence of suicides by farmers due to heavy losses suffered by them year after year in agriculture and consequent increasing indebtedness, in the four states of Andhra Pradesh, Maharashtra, Karnataka, and Kerala. In view of this, there is an urgent need for the Government of India to take necessary measures including subsidized crop and livestock insurance and fair compensation for loss of crops.
7. Since agriculture cannot absorb all the growth in rural workforce, the non-agricultural sector has a crucial role as a source of employment for the unemployed rural workforce.
8. There are now 36.1 million MSMEs in India that contribute 37.5% of the country's GDP. The increasing significance of non-farm subsector is evident from the fact that its contribution to the rural net domestic product (NDP) increased from 43% in 1993–94 to 61.1% in 2004–05.
9. Over the period, 1993–94 to 2009–10, rural employment increased by over 44 million and reached a total of 337 million adult workers (aged 15 years and above) and all new jobs were in the non-farm sector.
10. Infusion of appropriate technology, design skills, modern marketing-capacity building, and easier access to credit can make this sector an expanding base for self-sustaining employment and wealth generation.
11. The income generated from various activities in the non-agricultural subsector is more evenly distributed than that generated in the large-scale manufacturing subsector. Besides, due to low capital requirement per worker, this subsector can generate more jobs with a given amount of capital than the corresponding large- scale factory industries.
12. The linkages between the rural non-agricultural and agricultural subsectors are critical for rural development. The growth in the agricultural subsector provides an expanding market for consumption goods and agricultural inputs produced by the non-agricultural subsector, whereas agricultural raw materials are processed in the rural non-agricultural subsector.
13. The Government of India has taken several measures from time to time to boost the growth of the non-agricultural subsector. They include, among other things, establishment of the KVIC in 1956 and NSDC in 2010 and measures to improve the access of MSMEs to credit, marketing facilities and skill development opportunities.
14. In the wake of increasing liberalization and globalization of its economy, India now faces several challenges to cope with and has many opportunities to benefit from. Some of the challenges include maintaining food security and environmental integrity, increasing resource productivity in agriculture and allied activities to at least match the corresponding world averages, bridging the gap between rural and urban areas in terms of basic infrastructure and civic amenities, and ensuring the financial viability of the agricultural sector through increasing farm incomes and reducing the weather induced risk and uncertainty.
15. The major opportunities opened up by globalization include increased access to the world markets and the consequent possibilities of securing higher prices for farm produce and lower prices for some of the inputs used by the rural producers. The export orientation has brought in its wake the need for high tech projects and for exploring international markets for exportable commodities. Meeting the credit needs of this emerging export oriented high tech sector requires concomitant institutional innovations, for which a beginning has been made with the establishment of agricultural development finance companies. NABARD is playing a crucial role in meeting this challenge.

Questions for Discussion

1. In India, the rich (nearly top 20% of the country's total population) live in a modernized and Westernized *India*, having easy access to everything that they desire and enjoying a comfortable life, whereas the poor four-fifths (80% or so) live in an underdeveloped and traditional *Bharat*, lacking access to even the bare necessities of life and highly vulnerable to manmade and natural calamities. Can India ever be a truly developed country so long as this kind of dualism exists and the yawning gap between the rich and the poor is not narrowed down? Yes/No. If yes, why; and if no, why not?
2. The share of the agricultural sector in India's GDP has been declining year after year. Is it a sign of retrogression of the sector? Yes/No. If yes, why; and if no, why not?
3. What are main characteristics of India's rural sector that are obstacles to rural development? How can those obstacles be removed?
4. How can India's rural non-agricultural sector grow at a faster rate so as to be able to solve the problems of rural poverty, inequality and unemployment?
5. What are the major challenges that India is facing now and will continue to face in near future, and how can India cope with those challenges?
6. Outline a strategy to enable India to harness the opportunities emerging in the new era characterized by globalization and liberalization.

Notes

1. The term, "*Physiocrats*" refers to a French school of economic thought of the 1760s, which believed that only agriculture produced an economic surplus or net product. This thought is, however, not accepted by any one now.
2. www.PlanningCommission.nic.in/data/datatable/data_2312/comp_data2312pdf. (Accessed on May 24, 2015).
3. https://www.nabard.org/english/FinancialInclusion2.aspx (Accessed on June 28, 2015).
4. http://ncrb.gov.in/adsi/main.htm (Accessed on July 24, 2015).

Chapter 3

Measures of Development

LEARNING OUTCOMES

After having gone through this chapter, students should be able to

- **Explain the necessity of rural development measurement for rural development policy makers and managers;**
- **Define various measures of level of rural development and use them;**
- **Define various measures of distribution of benefits from development and use them;**
- **Analyze through questions whether particular area, region or nation is on a path of development or retrogression; and**
- **Describe various concepts and measures of poverty and identify methodological problems in estimating rural poverty.**

Introduction

Statistical measurement of the level and pace of rural development is important for a number of reasons. Quantitative measures of rural development are needed to:

1. Indicate the extent of economic and social well-being of the rural people;
2. Serve as a benchmark for future planning;
3. Serve as instruments of monitoring, evaluation, and control of ongoing programs;
4. Facilitate spatial and temporal comparisons of development; and
5. Serve as criteria for advancing loans.

Needless to emphasize, if the measures are to be meaningful, they must be consistent with the objectives of rural development.

The main objectives of rural development in all societies, irrespective of their economic, political and socio-cultural systems are to:

1. Increase the availability and improve the distribution of life-sustaining goods and services, such as food, clothes, shelter, health, and security;

2. Raise the per capita purchasing power and improve its distribution by providing better education, productive and remunerative jobs, and cultural amenities; and
3. Expand the range of economic and social choices to individuals by freeing them from servitude and dependence.

Therefore, a measure of rural development should provide, at the minimum, an indication of the commonly accepted objectives of development, such as per capita availability of life-sustaining goods or per capita real income in rural areas, as well as some idea of the distribution of income, assets, and other means of socio-economic welfare.

There is, at present, no single indicator of rural development that adequately captures its multifaceted nature. A variety of indicators have been used by economists to reflect the multiplicity of goals that characterize rural development. For the sake of orderly presentation, we categorize the indicators into two classes, namely, measures of the level of rural development and measures of distribution of income. A critique of some of these indicators is presented in the following sections.

Measures of Level of Rural Development

The following measures are commonly used (or can be used) to measure the level of rural development at a particular time in a particular place, as well as over time and across space.

Per Capita Real Gross National Product (GNP)

The GNP or gross national income (GNI) is the market value of all final goods and services produced in a year, and attributable to the factors of production supplied by the normal residents of the country concerned. The GNP is computed at the prices prevailing during the reference year, that is, at current prices. When computed over a number of years, the changes in GNP would, therefore, include implicitly not only the effect of the changes in production but also the changes in prices. This estimate compared over time would not, therefore, give a true measure of the overall real increase in production of the country, or the economic welfare of the people, or growth of the economy. Therefore, it would be necessary to eliminate the effect of prices, or in other words to recompute the whole series at given prices of one particular (base) year. The GNP, thus, computed is termed as GNP at constant prices or in real terms. The Central Statistical Office (CSO) in the Ministry of Statistics and Plan Implementation, Government of India collects and publishes estimates of GNP, GNI, net national income (NNI)[1] and per capita NNI. Table 3.1 presents the CSO estimates of NNI, per capita NNI and index numbers of per capita NNI at both the current and constant prices for selected years since 1950–51 to 2014–15. As shown in the table, the real NNI had increased by about 17.27 times over the period, 1950–51 to 2014–15.

Per capita real NNI is the most widely used measure of the economic well-being of people. If computed for rural people separately, it could be used as a measure of the economic component of rural development. An increase in the average real NNI per capita means that, *ceteris paribus*, we are economically better off. But in reality, GNP has the following weaknesses as a measure of economic well-being:

1. It does not include the value of physical and mental satisfaction that people derive from leisure.
2. It does not include the value of non-paid housewives' services and home labor, such as gardening, painting, and care of pets and domestic animals. If a bachelor marries his maid, the GNP is reduced because he no longer pays for her services.

Table 3.1: *Net National Income (NNI) and Per Capita Net National Income Per Annum and Index Numbers of Per Capita NNI in India*

Year	*NNI at Market Prices (₹ Million)*		*Per Capita NNI at Market Prices (₹)*		*Index Numbers of Per Capita NNI*	
	Current Prices	*Constant Prices*	*Current Prices*	*Constant Prices*	*Current Prices*	*Constant Prices*
2004–05 series						
1950–51	98,290	26,97,240	274	7,513	100.00	100.00
1960–61	1,70,620	41,15,190	393	9,482	173.60	152.60
1970–71	4,45,500	59,64,700	823	11,025	453.30	221.10
1980–81	13,85,650	79,51,930	2,041	11,711	1,409.80	294.80
1990–91	52,60,170	1,34,20,310	6,270	15,996	5,351.90	497.60
2000–01	1,94,77,880	2,29,17,950	19,115	22,491	19,817.50	849.70
2010–11	6,94,20,890	4,65,74,380	58,534	39,270	70,631.20	1,726.70
2011–12 series						
2011–12	7,84,65,310	7,84,65,310	64,316	64,316	100.00	100.00
2013–14	10,05,65,230	8,75,18,340	80,388	69,959	128.20	111.50
2014–15	11,21,70,790	94,00,26,607	88,533	74,193	143.00	119.80

Source: MoF (2015, Statistical Appendix, Table 1.1: A1–A2).

3. It does not assign any negative values to those side effects of economic activities that reduce the total satisfaction from the output of those activities. The examples of such side effects are air pollution, water pollution, noise, and other disagreeable aspects that accompany industrialization.
4. It does not give any negative weight to the "disamenities" of living in dirty, noisy, and crowded cities and slums, compared to more clean, open, and pleasant surroundings. Nor does it assign any positive weight to such environmental amenities as clean air and water, and a pollution-free environment.
5. It is not only difficult but also time-consuming and expensive to determine per capita income of rural people, most of whom are self-employed and, being illiterate, do not keep any written records of their income and expenditure. It takes quite an experienced and well-trained rural researcher/investigator to find out the true per capita income of rural people.

Clearly, the GNP does not include everything that contributes to human happiness and does not exclude everything that diminishes it. But, despite all its weaknesses, per capita real GNP is the only quantitative indicator of the economic component of rural development available for intra-national and international comparisons over time and over space.

Per Capita Consumption Expenditure

Given the weaknesses of per capita income as a measure of rural development, per capita consumption expenditure of rural people is considered a better measure of rural development for several reasons, including relative ease of recall by the respondent of the expenditure incurred and the general tendency of rural people not to hide any expenditure, as compared

Table 3.2: *Per Capita Consumption Expenditure in Rural and Urban Areas at Current and Constant Prices in India*

(₹ per person per month)

Year	*Rural*		*Urban*	
	At Current Prices	*At Constant 1993–94 Prices*	*At Current Prices*	*At Constant 1993–94 Prices*
1973–74	53.01	219.86	70.77	350.80
1977–78	68.89	249.48	96.15	384.64
1983	112.45	258.62	164.03	399.05
1993–94	281.40	281.40	458.05	458.04
1999–2000	486.16	305.50	854.92	529.34
2004–05(URP)	558.80	322.83	1,052.40	549.75
2004–05(MRP)	579.20	334.61	1,104.60	577.01

Source: Planning Commission (2014a, 108–09).

to income. Per capita consumption expenditure is a reasonably good proxy variable for per capita income. The NSSO conducts sample surveys all over India at regular intervals to estimate the consumption expenditure for both urban and rural people. The latest round (68) was conducted in 2011–12. The NSSO estimates are considered reasonably reliable. Besides, other estimates of consumption expenditure are also available for selected areas from research reports of institutions and scholars. Like nominal income, nominal consumption expenditure also should be adjusted for changes in the prices over time and across space to make it useful for comparison purposes. This is done by estimating the per capita consumption expenditure at the constant price of a selected base year as is done in Table 3.2. As shown in the table, the per capita consumption has increased from ₹220 in 1973–74 to ₹335 in 2004–05 (MRP) at the constant 1993–94 prices.

Per Capita Public Expenditure on Community Facilities and Services

The level of rural development in a country is a function of the per capita quantity of various goods and services consumed by its rural population, in a particular reference period of time. It does not matter whether the goods and services consumed are purchased by a person with his personal income or he receives them without specific expenditure on his part. Certain services, facilities, and civic amenities such as schools, hospitals, roads, parks, police protection, and street lights are provided free by the government or at a nominal cost to its people. For example, the value of only two of these services, that is, education and health in 2011–12 was ₹157 and ₹58 per capita, per month respectively at the constant 2004–05 prices (Planning Commission 2014, 47). The availability of these facilities and services represents "real income" and, therefore, constitutes part of the level of living. Per capita public expenditure on such services and amenities is a good measure of socio-economic welfare. For comparisons over time and space, this measure should also be adjusted for changes/differences in the prices, that is, the estimates should be in real terms. This measure, used in conjunction with per capita income or expenditure, constitutes a reasonably satisfactory measure of rural development. However, estimates of this variable/measure are not made by any organization/agency in India. Therefore, one has to collect the requisite information from the office records of village panchayats and other village/block-level organizations to estimate this measure and use it.

Physical Quality of Life Index (PQLI)

This measure was developed by Morris and McAlpin (1982, 1–30) to determine the impact of development projects on their target groups. The measure is called the PQLI. It supplements the per capita real GNP, which is the most widely used measure of economic growth. It has three components, namely, infant mortality, life expectancy at age one, and basic literacy. These three component indicators lend themselves to intra-national and international comparisons, are simple to compute and understand, are fairly sensitive to changes in distribution of benefits of development, do not reflect the values of any specific cultures, and reflect results, not inputs.

In the calculation of GNP, various goods and services can be combined via a common element: market price. But the three component indicators of PQLI do not have any common element that values them all. Instead, a simple indexing system is used to combine them into a single index, PQLI. For each indicator, the performance of individual state/country is evaluated on a scale of 0 to 100, where 0 represents an absolutely defined "worst" performance, and 100 represents the "best" performance. Once the performance for each indicator is scaled to this common measure, a composite index is calculated by averaging the three indicators, giving equal weight to each of them. The resulting PQLI, thus, is also scaled 0 to 100.

Morris and McAlpin computed the PQLI for 150 countries. The range for each component index was based on the examination of the historical experience of the countries concerned. The literacy index ranged from 0 literacy to 100% literacy for the population aged 15 years and more, the infant mortality rate from 229 to 7 per thousand births, and life expectancy at age one from 38 to 77 years. Using these ranges and actual data for Nigeria, India, and the US, they computed a PQLI for each of them, as shown in Table 3.3. They argue that PQLI measures the combined effects of nutritional status, public health facilities, family income and social relations.

Table 3.3: *Life Expectancy at Age 1, Infant Mortality and Literacy: Actual Data and Index Numbers (Early 1970s)*

	Life Expectancy at Age 1[1]		*Infant Mortality*[2]		*Literacy*[3]		
Country	*Years*	*Index No.*	*Per 1,000 Live Births*	*Index No.*	*%*	*Index No.*	*PQLI*[4]
Nigeria	49	28	180	22	25	25	25
India	56	46	122	48	34	34	43
USA	72	87	16	96	99	99	94

Source: Morris and McAlpin (1982, 18).

Notes:
1. Years of life expectancy are converted to an index number according to the formula: (Life expectancy at age 1–38) 0.39.
2. The infant mortality rate is converted to an index number according to the formula: (229–Infant mortality rate per thousand) 2.22.
3. Literacy index numbers correspond to the actual data.
4. Average of life expectancy age 1, infant mortality, and literacy indices (equally weighted).

Composite Index of Rural Development

Duly recognizing the multidimensional nature of rural development, a composite index of rural development was developed by Mathur (2005, 159–90). Twenty-five indicators depicting all important dimensions of rural development were identified and grouped into nine key components as shown in Table 3.4.

Table 3.4: *Indicators of Rural Development by Group*

Group No.	*Group Name*	*Indicator Number and Description of Indicator*	
I	Agricultural productive efficiency	1.	Productivity per hectare
		2.	Productivity per worker
		3.	Percent of villages electrified
II	Workforce diversification	4.	Percent of non-agricultural workforce
III	Rural educational infrastructure	5.	Percent enrolment at primary and middle stage
		6.	Retention rate
		7.	Density of primary and middle schools in rural areas
		8.	Per capita number of primary and middle school teachers
IV	Rural health infrastructure	9.	Per capita number of primary health centers (PHCs)
		10.	Per capita number of rural doctors
		11.	Per capita number of nurses/*dais*/VLWs
		12.	Rural infant mortality rate
		13.	Rural female infant mortality rate
V	Rural amenities	14.	Percent of rural households with drinking water
		15.	Percent of rural households with electricity connection
		16.	Percent of rural households with toilets
		17.	Percent of rural *pucca* houses
VI	Transport infrastructure	18.	Percent of villages having surfaced roads
VII	Human capital content of workforce	19.	Percent of educated (primary and middle level) rural workforce
VIII	Rural financial infrastructure	20.	No. of commercial banks per capita
		21.	Rural credit of commercial banks per capita
		22.	Rural deposits of commercial banks per capita
		23.	Number of cooperative societies per capita
IX	Rural standard of living	24.	Per capita rural consumption expenditure
		25.	Per capita rural food consumption expenditure

Source: NIRD (2005, 160–61).

All the 25 indicators of state level rural development were converted into an index with the all-India values of these indicators equal to 100. For deriving an overall composite index of state level rural development based on the 25 indicators, a two-step procedure was followed. In the first step, nine separate group-level composite indices of rural development were computed. For this purpose, for all the six groups that had more than indicator, the group level indices were computed as a simple average of the indices of rural development belonging to each of the groups concerned. The nine composite indices, thus, computed portray different facets of state level rural development in India. In the second step, all the nine group level composite indices were aggregated into one to arrive at the composite index of state level rural development. For this purpose, two alternative methodologies were adopted. In the first alternative, a simple procedure of the type used for computing group-wise composite indices was followed. The Composite Rural Development Index (CRDI), thus, computed was called Simple Index. In this alternative, an equal weight was assigned to each of the nine group indices. In the second alternative, a weighted average was computed for combining the nine indices. The weights were derived from a variant of the First Principal Component.

Method (Kundu 1980). This index may be called the Weighted Index. Table 3.5 presents the simple and weighted indices of rural development for the years, 1981, 1991, and 2001, by state. As shown in the table, Kerala emerged as the most highly developed state in India in terms of both the Simple Index and the Weighted Index in all the three reference years and Punjab followed Kerala closely. At the other extreme, Madhya Pradesh was the least developed state in the years 1981 and 1991, and Bihar in 2001.

Table 3.5: *Simple and Weighted Composite Indices of Rural Development by State for the Years 1981, 1991, and 2001*

	1981		*1991*		*2001*		*Rank in 2001*	
State	*Simple Index*	*Weighted Index*	*Simple Index*	*Weighted Index*	*Simple Index*	*Weighted Index*	*Simple Index*	*Weighted Index*
Andhra Pradesh	91.2	233.7	83.7	231.9	99.3	209.8	11	11
Assam	106.1	272.5	93.6	259.9	81.5	174.0	16	16
Bihar	81.1	209.5	74.2	205.8	70.1	149.4	17	17
Gujarat	106.0	271.5	108.4	297.1	121.9	258.1	6	6
Haryana	136.0	347.5	129.0	351.5	118.3	251.6	7	7
Himachal Pradesh	177.5	443.8	131.3	359.3	156.1	325.7	3	3
Jammu & Kashmir	134.6	343.9	106.4	295.7	110.2	232.9	9	9
Karnataka	111.6	284.8	101.7	279.1	117.8	248.0	8	8
Kerala	190.8	487.7	194.8	536.3	185.6	391.3	1	1
Madhya Pradesh	70.8	183.3	71.5	201.0	86.8	183.2	14	14
Maharashtra	112.1	287.2	110.9	303.9	133.6	282.5	5	5
Orissa	82.1	212.2	75.3	210.6	93.3	196.2	12	12

(Table 3.5 Continued)

(Table 3.5 Continued)

State	1981		1991		2001		Rank in 2001	
	Simple Index	Weighted Index	Simple Index	Weighted Index	Simple Index	Weighted Index	Simple Index	Weighted Index
Punjab	190.0	479.3	172.7	467.5	165.8	349.8	2	2
Rajasthan	80.8	208.4	83.7	231.6	86.2	182.0	15	15
Tamil Nadu	135.9	342.5	124.8	341.2	151.0	321.0	4	4
Uttar Pradesh	85.0	219.2	86.5	237.9	87.2	186.0	13	13
West Bengal	104.2	267.9	103.7	286.5	103.2	219.7	10	10
India	100.0	100.0	100.0	100.0	100.0	100.0	100.0	–

Source: NIRD (2005, 160–61).

Human Development Index (HDI)

Rediscovering the truth that people must be at the center of all development, the United Nations Development Programme (UNDP) decided to bring out every year, beginning in 1990, a report on the human dimensions of development. The *Human Development Report 1990* was the first such report. The report addresses the question of how economic growth does or does not promote human development. It discusses the meaning and measurement of human development, proposes a new composite index of human development, summarizes the record of human development over the past three decades, and sets forth strategies for human development in the 1990s (UNDP 1990).

The *Human Development Report 1990* defined human development as the process of increasing people's options. It stressed that the most critical choices that people should have include the options to lead a long and healthy life, to be knowledgeable, and to find access to the assets, employment, and income needed for a decent standard of living.

Development, thus, defined, cannot be adequately measured by income alone. The report therefore proposed a new measure of development, the HDI, composed of three indicators: life expectancy, adult literacy, and income expressed in logs. The subsequent human development reports have made some refinements in the procedure of defining the component indicators and computing the HDI. The refinements include adjustment of income for differences in purchasing power and disparities in income distribution, combining adult literacy and mean years of schooling into an index of educational attainment, and computing disaggregated HDI for males and females and for different population groups. In addition, the HDI has also been supplemented by a Human Freedom Index, and indicators of human security for selected countries for which data are available.

The HDI for 1994 was calculated on a different basis from that in the previous years. Maximum and minimum values were fixed for the four basic variables: life expectancy (85 years and 25 years), adult literacy (100% and 0%), mean years of schooling (15 years and 0 years), and income adjusted for differences in purchasing power and expressed in terms of purchasing power parity (PPP) ($40,000 and $200). For income, the threshold value was taken to be the global average real GDP per capita of PPP $5,120. Multiples of income beyond the threshold were discounted using a progressively higher rate (UNDP 1994, 92).

The minimum and maximum values of component variables were fixed without reference to particular countries, that is, the values were norms. The minima were those observed

Table 3.6: *Basic Variables for Computing Human Development Index for Greece and India*

Country	*Life Expectancy*	*Adult Literacy (%)*	*Mean Years of Schooling*	*Income (PPP$)*
Greece	77.3	93.8	7.20	7,680
India	59.7	49.8	2.4	1,150

Source: UNDP (1994, 92–93).

historically, going back about 30 years, and the maxima were the limits of what could be envisioned in the next 30 years. This permitted more meaningful comparisons across countries and over time.

An index was prepared for each of the component variables of HDI, using the following formula:

$$\text{Component index} = \frac{\text{Actual value} - \text{Minimum value}}{\text{Maximum value} - \text{Minimum value}}$$

Illustration of the Procedure of Computing HDI

For illustration, we take pair of countries, one industrial (Greece) and one developing (India). Their basic variables are presented in Table 3.6.

Life expectancy index

$$\text{Greece} = \frac{77.3 - 25.0}{85.0 - 25.0} = \frac{52.3}{60.0} = 0.872$$

$$\text{India} = \frac{59.7 - 25.0}{85.0 - 25.0} = \frac{37.7}{60.0} = 0.578$$

Adult literacy index

$$\text{Greece} = \frac{93.8 - 0.0}{100.0 - 0.0} = \frac{93.8}{100} = 0.938$$

$$\text{India} = \frac{49.8 - 0.0}{100.0 - 0.0} = \frac{49.8}{100} = 0.498$$

Mean years of schooling index

$$\text{Greece} = \frac{7.0 - 0.0}{15.0 - 0.0} = \frac{7.0}{15.0} = 0.467$$

$$\text{India} = \frac{2.4 - 0.0}{15.0 - 0.0} = \frac{2.4}{15.0} = 0.160$$

Educational attainment index

$$\text{Greece} = 2(0.938) + 0.467 = 2.343/3 = 0.781$$

$$\text{India} = 2(0.498) + 0.160 = 1.156/3 = 0.385$$

Adjusted income

Greece's income is above the threshold, but less than twice the threshold. Thus, the adjusted income for Greece was computed as follows:

$$\begin{aligned}\text{Greece} &= 5{,}120 + 2(7{,}680 - 5{,}120)^{1/2}\\ &= 5{,}120 + 101\\ &= 5{,}221\end{aligned}$$

The indexed adjusted income for Greece was as follows:

$$\text{Greece} = \frac{5{,}221 - 200}{5{,}385 - 200} = \frac{5{,}021}{5{,}185} = 0.968$$

India's income is below the threshold, so it needs adjustment. To calculate the distance for income, we used the maximum adjusted income (5,385) and the minimum (200). The indexed adjusted income for India was as follows:

$$\text{India} = \frac{1{,}150 - 200}{5{,}385 - 200} = \frac{950}{5{,}185} = 0.183$$

The indices for the three component variables and the HDI, thus, computed for Greece and India, are presented in Table 3.7.

Countries having an HDI below 0.5 are considered to have a low level of human development, those between 0.5 and 0.8 a medium level, and those above 0.8 a high level (UNDP 1994, 92).

No change/modification in the method of computing HDI is contemplated in the near future. But greater emphasis will be placed on improving human development statistics. The HDI is by far the most widely accepted indicator of human development (and lack of development or poverty). In 2013, India's HDI was 0.586 and its rank was 135th among 187 nations of the world. There has been a marked increase in the India's HDI since 1990 when its value was 0.334. In 2013, Norway had the highest HDI (0.944) and Niger the lowest (0.337) (UNDP 2014).[2]

The HDI has been used to:

1. Stimulate national political debate;
2. Give priority to human development;
3. Highlight disparities within countries; and
4. Open new avenues for analysis.

Table 3.7: *Indices of Life Expectancy, Educational Attainment, Adjusted Income, and HDI for Greece and India*

Country	*Indexed Life Expectancy*	*Indexed Educational Attainment*	*Indexed Adjusted Income*	*All Three*	*HDI*
Greece	0.872	0.781	0.968	2.621	0.874
India	0.578	0.385	0.183	1.146	0.382

Source: UNDP (1994, 92).

The HDI is, however, not perfect measure of human development. It does not include important indicators such as gender or income inequality, respect for human rights, and freedom.

Measures of Income Distribution

The level of per capita real GNP and its distribution are both equally important from the point of view of aggregate economic welfare. In general, higher per capita real GNP and its more equitable distribution mean a higher level of economic well-being. A country with a high per capita real GNP but with a less equitable distribution of income would rank lower in terms of aggregate economic welfare than the one with the same level of per capita real GNP but with a more equitable distribution of income.

There are a wide variety of measures that are used by economists to measure income distribution. They include, among others, the Pareto index, the shares of the bottom 20% and the top 20% of households in the aggregate income, standard deviation of logarithms of incomes, the Lorenz curve and the Gini concentration ratio (GCR). A good measure of income distribution should possess two characteristics. First, it should be unaffected by equal proportional increases in all incomes, so that if the distribution of income for year X is simply a scaled-up version of that for year Y, then we should regard them as characterized by the same degree of inequality. Second, it should be sensitive to disproportionate changes at all levels of income, so that if from year X to year Y, the incomes of lower income households increase proportionately more than the incomes of the higher income households, this ought to lead to a strictly positive reduction in the index of inequality and not merely leave it unchanged (Atkinson 1970, 253–54).

The following is a brief description of the procedure for computing some of the commonly used measures of income inequality.

The Lorenz Curve

This is a graphical measure of income distribution and income inequality. The information required to draw a Lorenz curve consists of a frequency table showing the distribution of income by decile groups of households. In simpler words, the table should show for each of the decile groups, its share in the aggregate income, as is done in Table 3.8. To draw a Lorenz Curve, the cumulative percentage of income receiving households is represented on

Table 3.8: *Relative Shares of Aggregate Income Received by Various Decile Groups of Households in Aligarh District in 1963–64 and 1968–69*

	Percentage of Aggregate Income			
	1963–64		*1968–69*	
Decile Group	*Simple*	*Cumulative*	*Simple*	*Cumulative*
Bottom 10%	–0.42	–0.42	0.77	0.77
Second 10%	1.04	0.62	2.37	3.14
Third 10%	2.29	2.91	3.57	6.71
Fourth 10%	4.06	6.97	5.12	11.83
Fifth 10%	6.10	13.07	6.71	18.54

(Table 3.8 Continued)

(Table 3.8 Continued)

Decile Group	*Percentage of Aggregate Income*			
	1963–64		*1968–69*	
	Simple	*Cumulative*	*Simple*	*Cumulative*
Sixth 10%	8.00	21.07	8.89	27.43
Seventh 10%	10.31	31.38	11.55	38.98
Eighth 10%	13.94	45.32	13.86	52.84
Ninth 10%	18.39	63.71	17.56	70.40
Top 10%	36.29	100.00	29.60	100.00

Source: Singh (1973, 4).

the horizontal axis, the cumulative percentage of aggregate income on the vertical axis, and the curve represents the locus of all the combinations of the two cumulative percentages. The Lorenz Curves shown in Figure 3.1 are drawn on the basis of the figures presented in Table 3.8. The diagonal line represents a perfectly equal distribution of income and, hence, is known as the line of equality. In general, the farther the Lorenz Curve is from the line of equality, the higher the degree of income inequality is.

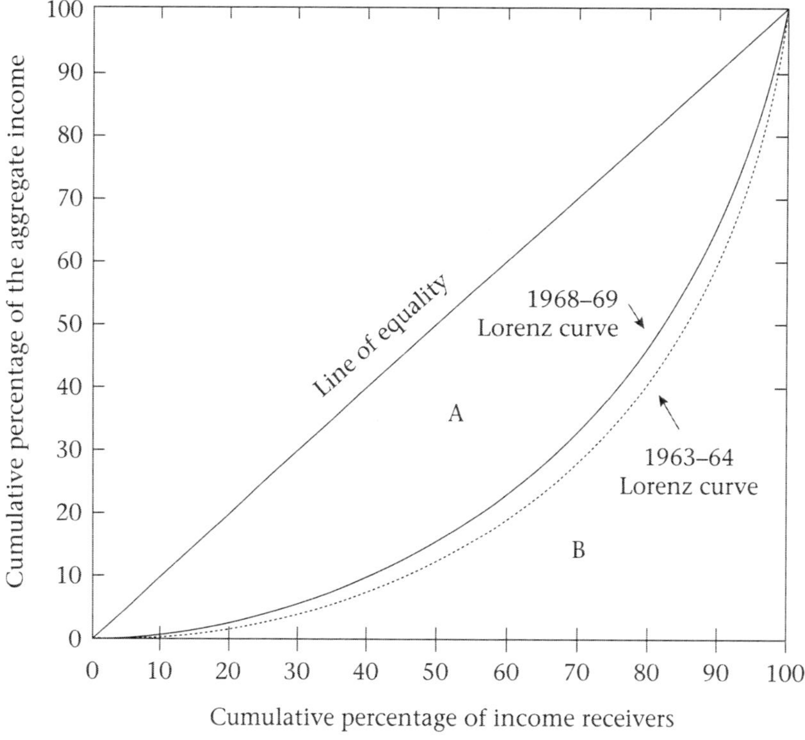

Figure 3.1 *Distribution of Farm Family Income in Aligarh District in 1963–64 and 1968–69*

Source: Singh (1973).

The Lorenz curve is a simple and commonly used measure of income inequality. It could be used to compare income distribution over time and across space. Its limitation is that, whereas it can show the difference in income inequality, it cannot quantify it. For instance, in Figure 3.1, since the Lorenz curve for the year 1963–64 lies above that for the year 1968–69, we could say that the income inequality was higher in 1963–64 than in 1968–69, but we cannot quantify the difference.

The Gini Concentration Ratio (GCR)

This ratio was invented by Corrado Gini in 1913. It is the most commonly used measure of income inequality these days. The ratio can be approximated either from the Lorenz curve or the mean difference.

When approximated from the Lorenz curve, it represents the proportion of the area lying between the diagonal and the Lorenz curve to the total area under the diagonal. If we denote the area inside the Lorenz curve as A and outside the Lorenz curve as B, the ratio would be $A/A + B$ (see Figure 3.1). Hence, the range of this ratio is from zero to one; zero being perfect equality and one being perfect inequality.

When computed from the mean difference, the GCR may be defined as:

$$\text{GCR} = \sum_{i=1}^{n}\sum_{j=1}^{n}\frac{f_i f_i / x_i - x_j}{2\bar{x}\text{N}}$$

where n is the number of income classes, f_i and f_j are the frequencies in the ith and jth classes, x_i and x_j are the mean incomes of the ith and jth classes, N is the total number of income receivers, and x the overall mean income. Hence, the ratio is one-half of the weighted average of all absolute differences between all possible pairs of incomes.

The GCR possesses both the properties of an ideal measure of income inequality described earlier.

The Standard Deviation of Logarithms of Incomes

This is another commonly used measure of income inequality. It is defined as:

$$\text{S.D.} = \left[\frac{1}{N}\sum_{i=1}^{n}(\log x_i - \log x)^2\right]^{1/2}$$

where N is the total number of individuals/households, x_i is the income of the ith individual/household and x is the mean income of all the individuals/households.

This measure is particularly useful when income is approximately log-normally distributed. A variable is log-normally distributed when its logarithm is normally distributed. Like the GCR, this measure also possesses both the properties of an ideal measure of income inequality, but it attaches more weight to income transfers at the lower end of the distribution.

Measures of Development Simplified

Realizing that reduction or elimination of rural poverty, inequality, and unemployment is an important index of rural development, we may specify a few simple measures by posing the following six questions:

1. Has the number of rural people below the absolute poverty line been declining over time?
2. Has the degree of income inequality in rural areas been declining over time?
3. Has the level of rural unemployment been declining over time?
4. Have the nature and quality of public educational, health and other social and cultural services in rural areas been improving over time?
5. Has economic progress enhanced individual and group esteem of rural people, both internally vis-à-vis one another, and externally vis-à-vis other nations and regions?
6. Finally, has economic progress expanded the range of choices available to rural people, and freed them from external dependence and internal servitude to other men and institutions?

If the answer to each of these questions is "yes," then clearly these phenomena constitute real rural development and a nation in which they are manifested can unquestionably be called "developed."

Concepts and Measures of Rural Poverty

The term "poverty" implies the lack of development, or underdevelopment, and, therefore, the knowledge of its measures also is as important for a student of rural development as that of measures of rural development. In this section, we present some commonly used connotations and measures of poverty.

Rural poverty is a worldwide problem; it exists in both developing and developed countries of the world. According to the 2014 *Human Development Report*, more than 15% of the world's people remain vulnerable to multidimensional poverty. The incidence of poverty is highly uneven among the regions of the world, among countries within those regions, and among localities within those countries. South Asia has the largest multidimensionally poor population, with more than 800 million poor and over 270 million near-poor—that is, more than 71% of its population. Nearly half of the world's poor live in South Asia, a region that accounts for roughly 30% of the world's population. India has the world's highest number of poor people numbering nearly 270 million in 2011–12, which is nearly 22% of India's total population. Alleviation of poverty has been an important objective of development policies and programs all over the world, including India.

Connotations and Definitions of Poverty

There is no universally acceptable definition of poverty, although there are several connotations and definitions of poverty in vogue. Poverty implies a condition of life characterized by deprivation of some sort or the other, and perceived as undesirable by the person(s) concerned or others. It is a multidimensional concept and phenomenon involving economic, social, cultural, and political elements. Generally, there is a consensus among scholars about poverty being conceived and defined as absolute or relative. Absolute poverty implies person's lack of access to objectively determined reasonably adequate quantities of goods and services to satisfy his material and non-material basic needs. Relative poverty, on the other hand, means that a person's access to the basic needs of life is relatively lower, as compared to some reference group of people. Between two households or two persons, one may be considered as poor while the other in comparison may not be so, even though both may be in a position to fulfill their basic material needs.

Criteria for Measuring Poverty

Measurement of poverty is beset with numerous conceptual, methodological, and empirical problems. Conceptually, it is difficult to define poverty in operational terms that are universally acceptable. Methodologically, there is no consensus among scholars about the best indicator or measure of poverty, and empirically, given the choice of a particular measure of poverty, it is very difficult to collect reliable data necessary for computing the value of the indicator/measure chosen. These problems notwithstanding, policy makers, planners, and scholars have attempted to measure poverty and have used poverty measures to monitor changes in the level/incidence of poverty and for other purposes.

The magnitude of poverty at any given point in time depends on the criteria or norms used to define poverty and determine the poverty line. The following two criteria or norms are usually employed to define the poverty line:

1. The norm based on the concept of a nutritionally adequate diet; and
2. The norm based on the concept of a minimum level of living.

A number of research scholars have attempted to estimate the cost of providing a nutritionally adequate diet. For example, Dandekar and Rath (1971, 8–9), on the basis of an average calorie intake of 2,250 per capita per day, estimated the poverty line to correspond to a consumer expenditure of ₹15 per capita, per month for rural households, and ₹22.50 for urban households at 1960–61 prices.

As far as the second norm based on the concept of a minimum level of living is concerned, a distinguished working group[2] constituted by the Planning Commission, Government of India, in July 1962, deliberated on the question of what should be regarded as the nationally desirable minimum level of consumer expenditure. The study group recommended that a per capita monthly consumer expenditure at 1960–61 prices of ₹20 for rural areas and ₹25 for urban areas should be deemed the national minimum. This does not include expenditure on health and education, which are expected to be provided by the state; the "minimum" for the urban areas assumed an element of subsidy in urban housing.

A "Task Force on Projection of Minimum Needs and Effective Consumption Demand" was constituted by the Planning Commission in 1979 under the chairmanship of Dr Y. K. Alagh. It defined the poverty line as that per capita expenditure level that the average per capita, per day calorie intake was 2,400 kcal for rural population and 2,100 kcal for urban population. The recommended poverty line was ₹49.09 per capita per month for rural population and ₹56.64 per capita per month for urban population at 1973–74 prices. The Task Force also recommended an adjustment in the consumption expenditure levels estimated by the NSSO by raising it by a "factor" to make it consistent with the total level of private consumption expenditure reported in the National Accounts Statistics (NAS), which was higher. This "factor" was small in the beginning but grew larger and larger over the years.

The expert group (EG) constituted by the Planning Commission in 1989 recommended the continuation of the task force poverty line (₹49.09 for rural areas and ₹56.64 for urban areas at 1973–74 prices) as the level separating the poor from the non-poor. The EG recommended specially constructed state-wise indices for updating the poverty line for price changes. It also recommended the abandoning of the adjustment of NSSO-based consumption expenditure with NAS consumption expenditure, since the reasons for the differences were diverse and the NSSO survey obtained direct information on consumption and, hence, was more reliable. Following the EG recommendation, the poverty series were revised by the Planning Commission from 1973–74 onward. Since then the official poverty estimates are based on the methodology recommended by the EG. The methodology suggested by the EG is summarized as follows (Radhakrishna and Ray 2005).

The poverty lines are anchored to a fixed commodity basket corresponding to the task force recommended poverty line (₹49.09 per person per month at 1973–74 prices for rural areas and ₹56.64 for urban areas, as specified in the previous paragraph). The rural commodity basket suggested by the EG contained 2,400 kcal per capita per day in rural areas and the urban food basket had 2,100 kcal per capita per day in 1973–74. The use of calorie norm was taken as an approximation to what may be considered as an acceptable "minimum needs." The consumption basket is common to all states. In order to take care of the changing tastes and preferences, the EG recommended that the consumption basket be revised once in five years. This was to take care of "minimum needs" as derived from the chosen nutrition attributes, as revealed by the behavior patterns of consumers.

The consumption basket, thus, identified separately for rural and urban areas, is evaluated at state-specific prices to arrive at state-specific poverty lines in the base year, 1973–74. The state-wise poverty lines computed for the base year 1973–74 are adjusted for prices for the subsequent years. For any year, poverty levels are estimated for each state using the state-level consumer expenditure distribution. Aggregating the state-wise poverty ratios, the all-India poverty ratio is estimated. Given the all-India poverty ratio, the poverty line is estimated using the consumer expenditure distribution for that year.

Some Common Measures and Indicators of Poverty

Though head count (HC) is the most popularly used measure, three other measures, that is, poverty gap (PG), squared poverty gap (SPG) and Sens's Index are also important for their properties. The first three measures belong to a class of additive measures. There are good surveys on the measurement of poverty (Atkinson 1987, Foster 1984). We briefly mention the main issues having a bearing on policy analysis. Let y denote per capita consumer expenditure and z denote the poverty line. Let $f(y)$ be the density function and $f(y)$ be the cumulative distribution function (CDF). A function $f(y, z)$, non-increasing in y and non-decreasing in z, is a measure of poverty. A desirable property for the function is homogeneity. In other words, the measure is scale neutral. Various ways of aggregating the $p(y, z)$'s have been proposed in the literature. However, additive measures satisfy sub-group consistency, which means that when poverty increases in any sub-group of the population (say agricultural laborers) without a decrease elsewhere, the aggregate poverty should also increase.

A sub-group inconsistent measure may mislead policy analysis, as the measure may not show decline in national poverty even when it declined in a particular area. The class of additive poverty measures is given by:

$$P(z) = \int p(y, z)\, f(y)\, dy \tag{3.1}$$

The limits of integration are 0 and q. All the three measures of poverty, that is, HC, PG and SPG are derived by taking $(1 - y/z)^{\alpha}$ for $p(y, z)$ and giving 0,1 and 2 to α:

$$P(z) = \int (1 - y/z)^{\alpha} f(y)\, dy \tag{3.2}$$

The limits of integration are 0 and q.

The Head Count (HC) Index

This measure is widely used now-a-days. It is simply the proportion of population whose consumption (y) is less than the poverty line (z). This is simply the value of $P(z)$ when $\alpha = 0$ in equation (3.2). The measure is easy to understand and communicate, but it has two serious drawbacks that affect policy analysis. First, it violates monotone axiom of welfare, which states that an improvement in the income of some people, given the incomes of others, should reduce poverty. The HC ratio is not sensitive to changes in income as long as these changes do not move a person from one side of poverty line to the other. Second, the measure also violates the transfer axiom of welfare, which states that transfers from a richer to a poorer person should reduce poverty. This violation has a serious implication that a given improvement of incomes through policy interventions will have high impact if those who are close to the poverty line are selected.

The Poverty Gap (PG) Index

This is obtained by setting $\alpha = 1$ in equation (3.2). It measures the depth of poverty as it depends on the distances from the poverty line as well as the number of the poor. The widely used income gap ratio is $I = 1 - \mu^P/z = PG/H$, where μ^P is the mean value of y for the poor. It measures the average proportionate shortfall below the poverty line. This is a deceptive measure because if a poor person with a standard of living above μ^P escapes poverty, the income gap ratio will rise though no one is worse off and one of the poor is, in fact, better off. Therefore, PG is a better measure than the income gap ratio. While it satisfies the monotone axiom, it is insensitive to transfers from a better off poor to another poor person, as the gap remains the same as long as both remain poor. While it gives depth of poverty, it does not indicate the severity of poverty, as it uses no weight for the gap from the poverty line.

The Squared Poverty Gap (SPG) Index

This measure, proposed by Foster, Greer and Thorbecke (1984), indicates the severity of poverty and it is obtained by taking $\alpha = 2$. This is strictly convex function, a desirable property of a welfare function.

Sen's Index

Sen (1976) proposed an index of poverty that combines the number of poor, the depth of poverty, and the distribution of the poor within the group. The formula is given by:

$$P_s = 2/(q + 1)\, n\, \Sigma\, (1 - yi/z)\, (q + i + 1) \tag{3.3}$$

where q is the number of poor and $q + i + 1$ is the weight accorded to the ith poor person from the poverty line. The formula can be expressed in terms of the average of the HC (P_0) and PG (P_1) measures weighted by the Gini coefficient of inequality among the poor (G^p).

$$P_s = P_0 Gp + P_1 (1 - G^P) \tag{3.4}$$

The Housing Index

Gibbons (1997) proposed this index as a cost effective measure/tool for identifying the poor. He asserts that this index has been found to be valid and useful in a number of countries, such as China, Vietnam, the Philippines, Indonesia, India, and Bangladesh, and that the index can help identify about 80% of the poor very quickly; it takes about five minutes for an experienced field assistant to use the index properly.

The Housing Index has three components, namely, (a) the size of the house; (b) the physical condition of the house, as reflected in the materials used in its construction; and (c) the type of materials used for making the roof of the house. All the three dimensions of the index can be looked at and assessed through going up and down the lanes/streets in a village. One does not have to conduct any interviews using questionnaires or schedules. According to Gibbons, the material of the roof is a simple but powerful indicator of poverty in most countries of Asia. The poor in those countries live in houses having thatched roofs, or roofs made out of woven bamboo or twigs, or plastic sheets that have holes, with the roofs leaking and creating health problems. Nobody wants to live in such houses unless one has to. So the people living in such houses are really very poor. If we combine this with the small size of the houses and the very simple building materials, such as mud, jute sticks, and such other things, then we are very close to identifying most of the very poor. Gibbons admits two limitations of this index. First, some poor people live in bigger and better houses because they inherited those houses, but now they no longer have any income. Second, in many countries (including India), the government provides reasonably good houses to the poor free of cost. So, in those areas, this index cannot identify the poor. To overcome these and other similar limitations, there is an appeal procedure. The poor people living in good houses could appeal to the field assistant and convince him/her that they are not rich. A senior officer could later interview such people and take final decision in the matter. In such cases, use of the Participatory Rural Appraisal (PRA) method of wealth ranking has been found to be useful. In the PRA method, all the villagers are brought together to find out who are the very poor, poor, not so poor, and not poor all. The two methods, Housing Index and PRA, were found to be comparable in terms of cost effectiveness and the time taken. They could both be used by governmental organizations and NGOs engaged in rural development, for identifying the poor for targeting their projects. The Housing Index has a serious limitation in the sense that it cannot be used for making international and even intra-national comparisons, when the type of houses varies widely from country to country, from state to state within the country. But the primary purpose of this index is to identify the poor in a particular area, for giving some benefits or services to them. For this purpose, the index seems alright. Another limitation is that there is no way to combine the three components into a single index. Hence, the name Housing Index is misleading.

Estimates of Poverty in India

In India, there is a long history of studies on measurement of poverty. There are, in fact, many approaches to measuring poverty used by various scholars. The first and foremost study of poverty in India was reported by Dandekar and Rath (1971). They used the criterion of a certain minimum level of consumption expenditure per person per month. Any household failing to meet that level of consumption expenditure was treated as a poor household. On the basis of an average calorie intake of 2,250 per capita per day, they estimated the poverty line to correspond to a consumer expenditure of ₹15 per capita per month for rural households, and ₹22.50 for urban households at 1960–61 prices (Dandekar and Rath 1971, 8–9). Thereafter, several approaches and methodologies were used by various scholars and expert committees constituted by the Government of India from time to time.

A chronology of various task forces/expert groups/expert committees constituted by the Planning Commission from time to time since 1962 until September 2012, is presented (Planning Commission 2014, 7):

1962: A working group on methodology of poverty estimation; report submitted in 1962 and accepted the same year.

1977: A task force under the chairmanship of Dr Y. K. Alagh; report submitted in 1979 and accepted the same year.

1989: An expert group under the chairmanship of Professor D. T. Lakdawala; report submitted in 1993 and accepted in 1997.

2005: An expert group under the chairmanship of Professor Suresh D. Tendulkar; report submitted in November 2009 and accepted in January 2011.

2012: An expert group under the chairmanship of Dr C. Rangarajan; report submitted in 2014.

The methodology adopted by the Tendulkar Expert Group generically belongs to its predecessors, namely the Working Group of 1962, the Task Force of 1977 and the Expert Group of 1989. Its methodology is based on an exogenously determined poverty line expressed in terms of per capita consumption expenditure in a month and the class distribution of NSS (National Sample Survey) consumer expenditure data of the National Sample Survey Office (NSSO). The poverty ratio (percentage of people living below the poverty line) was obtained by counting the persons lying below the poverty line from the class distribution of persons.

The methodology for estimation of poverty used by the Planning Commission has been based on the recommendations made by Working Group/Task Force/Expert Groups consisting of eminent experts in the field.[3] The Planning Commission has constituted these Groups from time to time to revisit the methodological issues related to the measurement of poverty so as to make the estimates more relevant to the contemporary economic situation. The methodology used by the Planning Commission at present (since January 2011) to estimate poverty is based on the recommendations of the Expert Group under the chairmanship of Professor Suresh D. Tendulkar.

In March 1997, the Government of India adopted the Lakdawala Expert Group methodology for poverty estimation as the basis for computing the official estimates of poverty and using this methodology the Planning Commission estimated the poverty ratios in rural and urban areas of different States/UTs for the year 1973–74 (NSS 28th Round consumer expenditure data, which was used to estimate the poverty line by the Task Force), and for the years 1977–78, 1983, 1987–88 and 1993–94 for which the large sample survey consumer expenditure data were then available from the 32nd, 38th, 43rd and 50th Rounds of the NSS. Subsequently, using the same methodology the Planning Commission estimated the poverty ratios at the national and states level for the years 1999–2000 and 2004–05, using the NSS large sample survey consumer expenditure data of 55th and 61st Rounds respectively.

The official estimate of poverty was derived by the Planning Commission using the Lakdawala Expert Group methodology and it was used until January 2011. The poverty ratio (i.e., the percentage of people living below the poverty line) and the number of poor for different years at the national level estimated by using the Lakdawala Expert Group methodology are given in Table 3.9. The Planning Commission released the estimates of poverty for 1993–94 and 2004–05 derived from the Tendulkar Expert Group methodology in January 2011. Subsequently, based on the same methodology, the poverty ratio for 2009–10 and 2011–12 were derived by the Planning Commission in March 2012 and July 2013 respectively. The estimate of poverty ratio and number of poor at the national level for the years 1993–94, 2004–05, 2009–10 and 2011–12 derived from the Tendulkar Expert Group methodology are presented in Table 3.10.

Table 3.9: *Poverty Ratio and Number of Poor: Lakdawala Expert Group Methodology*

	Poverty Ratio (%)			*Number of Poor (Million)*		
Year	*Rural*	*Urban*	*Total*	*Rural*	*Urban*	*Total*
1973–74	56.4	49.0	54.9	261.3	60.0	321.3
1977–78	53.1	45.2	51.3	264.3	64.6	328.9
1983	45.7	40.8	44.5	252.0	70.9	322.9
1987–88	39.1	38.2	38.9	231.9	75.2	307.1
1993–94	37.3	32.4	36.0	244.0	76.3	320.3
2004–05 (URP)	28.3	25.7	27.5	220.9	80.8	301.7

Source: Planning Commission (2014b, Table 2.1, p. 14).
Note: URP: Uniform Recall Period consumption in which the consumer expenditure data for all the items are collected from 30-day recall period.

Table 3.10: *Percentage and Number of Poor Estimated from Tendulkar Expert Group Methodology*

Year	*Poverty Ratio (%)*			*Number of Poor (Million)*		
	Rural	*Urban*	*Total*	*Rural*	*Urban*	*Total*
1993–94	50.1	31.8	45.3	328.6	74.5	403.7
2004–05	41.8	25.7	37.2	326.3	80.8	407.1
2009–10	33.8	20.9	29.8	278.2	76.5	354.7
2011–12	25.7	13.7	21.9	216.7	53.1	269.8

Source: Planning Commission (2014b: Table 2.2, p. 18).

As shown in the table, the poverty ratio had been consistently declining since 1993–94. The rate of decline in poverty ratio over the period, 1993–94 to 2004–05, was 0.75% per year for rural areas, 0.55% for urban areas, and 0.74% for the country as a whole. The corresponding figures for the period 2004–05 to 2011–12 were 2.32%, 1.69%, and 2.10% and for the period 1993–94 to 2011–12 were 1.36%, 1.01%, and 1.30% respectively for rural areas, urban areas, and India as a whole. Thus, the poverty ratio declined at a higher rate over the period 2004–05 to 2011–12 for the country as a whole as well as for the rural and urban areas. The state-specific poverty lines estimated using the Tendulkar methodology are presented in Table 3.11 and the number and percentage of population below poverty line by State in 2011–12 in Table 3.12.

Table 3.11: *State-specific Poverty Lines (Tendulkar Methodology)*

(₹ per capita per month)

Sl. No.	*State*	*Rural*			*Urban*		
		2004–05	*2009–10*	*2011–12*	*2004–05*	*2009–10*	*2011–12*
1.	Andhra Pradesh	433	694	860	563	926	1,009
2.	Arunachal Pradesh	547	774	930	618	925	1,060
3.	Assam	478	692	828	600	871	1,008
4.	Bihar	433	656	778	526	775	923
5.	Chhattisgarh	399	617	738	514	807	849
6.	Delhi	541	748	1,145	642	1,040	1,134
7.	Goa	609	931	1,090	671	1,025	1,134
8.	Gujarat	502	726	932	659	951	1,152
9.	Haryana	529	792	1,015	626	975	1,169
10.	Himachal Pradesh	520	708	913	606	888	1,064
11.	Jammu & Kashmir	522	723	891	603	845	988
12.	Jharkhand	405	616	748	531	831	974
13.	Karnataka	418	629	902	588	908	1,089
14.	Kerala	537	775	1,018	585	831	987
15.	Madhya Pradesh	408	632	771	532	772	897

(Table 3.11 Continued)

(Table 3.11 Continued)

Sl. No.	State	Rural			Urban		
		2004–05	2009–10	2011–12	2004–05	2009–10	2011–12
16.	Maharashtra	485	744	967	632	961	1,126
17.	Manipur	578	871	1,118	641	955	1,170
18.	Meghalaya	503	687	888	746	990	1,154
19.	Mizoram	639	850	1,066	700	939	1,155
20.	Nagaland	687	1,017	1,270	783	1,148	1,302
21.	Odisha	408	567	695	497	736	861
22.	Punjab	544	830	1,054	643	961	1,155
23.	Rajasthan	478	755	905	568	846	1,002
24.	Sikkim	532	729	930	742	1,035	1,226
25.	Tamil Nadu	442	639	880	560	801	937
26.	Tripura	450	663	798	556	783	920
27.	Uttar Pradesh	435	664	768	532	800	941
28.	Uttarakhand	486	720	880	602	899	1,082
29.	West Bengal	445	643	783	573	831	981
30.	Puducherry	385	641	1,301	506	778	1,309
	All India	447	673	816	579	860	1,000

Source: Planning Commission (2014b: Table B1, p. 28).

Table 3.12: *Number and Percentage of Population Below Poverty Line by States in 2011–12 (Tendulkar Methodology)*

Sl. No.	State	Rural		Urban		Total	
		% age of Persons	No. of Persons (million)	% age of Persons	No. of Persons (million)	% age of Persons	No. of Persons (million)
1.	Andhra Pradesh	11.0	6.18	5.8	1.70	9.2	7.88
2.	Arunachal Pradesh	38.9	0.42	20.3	0.07	34.7	0.49
3.	Assam	33.9	9.21	20.5	0.92	32.0	10.13
4.	Bihar	34.1	32.04	31.2	3.78	33.7	35.82
5.	Chhattisgarh	44.6	8.89	24.8	1.52	39.9	10.41
6.	Delhi	12.9	0.05	9.8	1.65	9.9	1.70
7.	Goa	6.8	0.04	4.1	0.04	5.1	0.08
8.	Gujarat	21.5	7.54	10.1	2.69	16.6	10.22
9.	Haryana	11.6	1.94	10.3	0.94	11.2	2.88
10.	Himachal Pradesh	8.5	0.53	4.3	0.03	8.1	0.56

(Table 3.12 Continued)

(Table 3.12 Continued)

Sl. No.	State	Rural		Urban		Total	
		% age of Persons	No. of Persons (million)	% age of Persons	No. of Persons (million)	% age of Persons	No. of Persons (million)
11.	Jammu & Kashmir	11.5	1.07	7.2	0.25	10.3	1.33
12.	Jharkhand	40.8	10.41	24.8	2.02	37.0	12.43
13.	Karnataka	24.5	9.28	15.3	3.70	20.9	12.98
14.	Kerala	9.1	1.55	5.0	0.85	7.1	2.39
15.	Madhya Pradesh	35.7	19.10	21.0	4.31	31.6	23.41
16.	Maharashtra	24.2	15.06	9.1	4.74	17.4	19.79
17.	Manipur	38.8	0.74	32.6	0.28	36.9	1.02
18.	Meghalaya	12.5	0.30	9.3	0.06	11.9	0.36
19.	Mizoram	35.4	0.19	6.4	0.04	20.4	0.23
20.	Nagaland	19.9	0.28	16.5	0.10	18.9	0.38
21.	Orissa	35.7	12.61	17.3	1.24	32.6	13.85
22.	Punjab	7.7	1.34	9.2	0.98	8.3	2.32
23.	Rajasthan	16.1	8.42	10.7	1.87	14.7	10.29
24.	Sikkim	9.9	0.04	3.7	0.01	8.2	0.05
25.	Tamil Nadu	15.8	5.92	6.5	2.34	11.3	8.26
26.	Tripura	16.5	0.45	7.4	0.08	14.0	0.52
27.	Uttar Pradesh	30.4	47.94	26.1	11.88	29.4	59.82
28.	Uttarakhand	11.6	0.82	10.5	0.34	11.3	1.16
29.	West Bengal	22.5	14.11	14.7	4.38	20.0	18.50
30.	Puducherry	17.1	0.07	6.3	0.06	9.7	0.12
31.	A & N Islands	1.6	0.004	0.0	0.0	1.0	0.004
32.	Chandigarh	1.6	0.0004	22.3	0.23	21.8	0.23
33.	Dadra & Nagar Haveli	62.6	0.12	15.4	0.03	39.3	0.14
34.	Daman & Diu	0.0	0.0	12.6	0.03	9.9	0.03
35.	Lakshadweep	0.0	0.0	3.4	0.002	2.8	0.002
	All India	25.7	216.66	13.7	53.12	21.9	269.78

Source: Planning Commission (2014b: Table B4, p. 31).

Duly realizing the urgency for sorting out various methodological issues involved in the measurement of poverty, the Planning Commission constituted an expert group in June 2012, under the chairmanship of C. Rangarajan to suggest a methodology for measurement of poverty. The report of the expert group was submitted in 2014 but it is not known as of December 2015 whether the report has been accepted by the NITI Aayog, the new *avtar* of Planning Commission. But in our opinion, the methodology adopted by the Rangarajan Expert Group is most appropriate for the purpose of estimating the extent of poverty. In view of this, we decided to present, in Tables 3.13 and 3.14, both state-specific poverty lines as well as the number and percentage of population below poverty line, by states, in 2011–12.

Table 3.13: *State-specific Poverty Lines for 2011–12 (Rangarajan Expert Group Methodology)*

(₹ Per capita per month)

Sl. No.	*State*	*Poverty Line*	
		Rural	*Urban*
1.	Andhra Pradesh	1,031.74	1,370.84
2.	Arunachal Pradesh	1,151.01	1,482.94
3.	Assam	1,006.66	1,420.12
4.	Bihar	971.28	1,229.30
5.	Chhattisgarh	911.80	1,229.72
6.	Delhi	1,492.46	1,538.09
7.	Goa	1,200.60	1,470.07
8.	Gujarat	1,102.83	1,507.06
9.	Haryana	1,127.82	1,528.31
10.	Himachal Pradesh	1,066.60	1,411.59
11.	Jammu & Kashmir	1,044.48	1,403.25
12.	Jharkhand	904.02	1,272.06
13.	Karnataka	975.43	1,373.28
14.	Kerala	1,054.03	1,353.68
15.	Madhya Pradesh	941.70	1,340.28
16.	Maharashtra	1,078.34	1,560.38
17.	Manipur	1,185.19	1,561.77
18.	Meghalaya	1,110.67	1,524.37
19.	Mizoram	1,231.03	1,703.93
20.	Nagaland	1,229.83	1,615.78
21.	Orissa	876.42	1,205.37
22.	Punjab	1,127.48	1,479.27
23.	Rajasthan	1,035.97	1,406.15
24.	Sikkim	1,126.25	1,542.67
25.	Tamil Nadu	1,081.94	1,380.36
26.	Tripura	935.52	1,376.55
27.	Uttar Pradesh	889.82	1,329.55
28.	Uttarakhand	1,014.95	1,408.12

(Table 3.13 Continued)

(Table 3.13 Continued)

Sl. No.	State	Poverty Line	
		Rural	Urban
29.	West Bengal	934.10	1,372.68
30.	Puducherry#	1,130.10	1,382.31
31.	Andaman & Nicobar Islands#	1,314.98	1,797.69
32.	Chandigarh#	1,303.17	1,481.21
33.	Dadra & Nagar Haveli#	1,008.39	1,540.81
34.	Daman & Diu#	1,200.60	1,434.93
35.	Lakshadweep#	1,327.77	1,458.69
	All India	972	1,407

Source: Planning Commission (2014b: Table 4.3, p. 64).
Note: #: union territory

Table 3.14: *Number and Percentage of Population below Poverty Line by States in 2011–12 (Rangarajan Expert Group Methodology)*

Sl. No.	State	Rural		Urban		Total	
		% age of Persons	No. of Persons (Million)	% age of Persons	No. of Persons (Million)	% age of Persons	No. of Persons (Million)
1.	Andhra Pradesh	12.7	7.15	15.6	4.57	13.7	11.73
2.	Arunachal Pradesh	39.3	0.43	30.9	0.10	37.4	0.53
3.	Assam	42.0	11.41	34.2	1.54	40.9	12.95
4.	Bihar	40.1	37.68	50.8	6.14	41.3	43.81
5.	Chhattisgarh	49.2	9.79	43.7	2.69	47.9	12.48
6.	Delhi	11.9	0.05	15.7	2.63	15.6	2.67
7.	Goa	1.4	0.01	9.1	0.08	6.3	0.09
8.	Gujarat	31.4	10.98	22.2	5.89	27.4	168.8
9.	Haryana	11.0	1.84	15.3	1.40	12.5	3.24
10.	Himachal Pradesh	11.1	0.69	8.8	0.06	10.9	0.75
11.	Jammu & Kashmir	12.6	1.17	21.6	0.76	15.1	1.93
12.	Jharkhand	45.9	11.70	31.3	2.55	42.4	14.25
13.	Karnataka	19.8	7.48	25.1	6.09	21.9	13.57
14.	Kerala	7.3	1.23	15.3	2.60	11.3	3.83
15.	Madhya Pradesh	45.2	24.14	42.1	8.63	44.3	327.8
16.	Maharashtra	22.5	13.99	17.0	8.84	20.0	22.83
17.	Manipur	34.9	0.67	73.4	0.63	46.7	1.29

(Table 3.14 Continued)

(Table 3.14 Continued)

Sl. No.	State	Rural		Urban		Total	
		% age of Persons	No. of Persons (Million)	% age of Persons	No. of Persons (Million)	% age of Persons	No. of Persons (Million)
18.	Meghalaya	26.3	0.64	16.7	0.10	24.4	7.4
19.	Mizoram	33.7	0.18	21.5	0.12	27.4	3.1
20.	Nagaland	6.1	0.08	32.1	0.19	14.0	2.8
21.	Orissa	47.8	16.90	36.3	2.60	45.9	19.50
22.	Punjab	7.4	1.29	17.6	18.7	11.3	3.16
23.	Rajasthan	21.4	11.20	22.5	3.95	21.7	15.15
24.	Sikkim	20.0	0.9	11.7	0.02	17.8	0.11
25.	Tamil Nadu	24.3	9.11	20.3	7.28	22.4	16.39
26.	Tripura	22.5	0.61	31.3	0.32	24.9	9.3
27.	Uttar Pradesh	38.1	60.09	45.7	20.82	39.8	80.91
28.	Uttarakhand	12.6	0.89	29.5	0.94	17.8	1.84
29.	West Bengal	30.1	18.86	29.0	8.68	29.7	27.54
30.	Puducherry	5.9	0.02	8.6	0.07	7.7	0.10
31.	Andaman & Nicobar Islands#	6.6	0.02	4.9	0.01	6.0	0.02
32.	Chandigarh#	12.0	0.0	21.5	0.23	21.3	0.23
33.	Dadra & Nagar Haveli#	55.2	0.10	15.3	0.03	35.6	0.13
34.	Daman & Diu#	0.0	0.0	17.6	0.04	13.7	0.04
35.	Lakshadweep#	0.6	0.0	7.9	0.0	6.5	0.0
	All India	2,605.2	2.64	1,024.7	2,095	3,629.9	2,60.52

Source: Planning Commission (2014b: Table 4.4, p. 66).
Note: #: union territory

The estimate of poverty ratio for the years 2009–10 and 2011–12 derived from the Rangarajan Expert Group methodology and Tendulkar methodology are summarized in Table 3.15.

As shown in Tables 3.10–3.15, the poverty lines estimated by the Rangarajan Expert Group are 19% and 41% higher for rural and urban areas, respectively. The expert group uses the MMRP consumption expenditure data of the NSSO as these are considered to be more precise compared to the MRP, which was used by the Tendulkar Expert Group, and the URP, which was used for earlier estimations. About 67% of the increase in the rural poverty line and 28% of the increase in the urban poverty line is because of the shift from MRP to MMRP (Planning Commission 2014b, 4). As per the Rangarajan Expert Group report, in 2011–12, the poverty ratio was 39.9% in rural areas and in 26.4% in urban areas, and the number of people below the poverty was 260.5 million in rural areas and 102.5 million in urban areas. This is in contrast to the corresponding estimates of 216.7 million and 53.1 million for rural and urban areas as per the Tendulkar Expert Group report (Planning Commission 2014b, Table 4.7, p. 69)

Table 3.15: *Poverty Estimates for 2009–10 and 2011–12 According to Rangarajan and Tendulkar Expert Groups*

Year	*Poverty Ratio (%)*			*Number of Poor (Million)*		
	Rural	*Urban*	*Total*	*Rural*	*Urban*	*Total*
			Rangarajan Expert Group			
2009–10	39.6	35.1	38.2	325.9	128.7	454.6
2011–12	30.9	26.4	29.5	260.5	102.5	363.0
Reduction (% age points)	8.7	8.7	8.7	65.4	26.2	91.6
			Tendulkar Expert Group			
2009–10	33.8	20.9	29.8	278.2	76.5	354.7
2011–12	25.7	13.7	21.9	216.7	53.1	269.8
Reduction (% age points)	8.1	7.2	7.9	61.5	23.4	84.9

Source: Planning Commission (2014b; Table 4.7, p. 69).

Some Methodological Issues in Estimation of Poverty

The major issues in estimating the poverty line are as follows: (Planning Commission 2014b, 30–47)

1. **Use of a Single Poverty Line of Poverty Line Basket (PLB) for India as a whole**
   This is questionable given the vast size of India that is marked by significant variability in living environment, in dietary patterns and preferences, and in prices of goods and services across states and between rural and urban areas even within the same state. But there is no other better alternative in terms of simplicity, in computability, and comparability over time and space.
2. **Use of Consumption Expenditure as a Proxy for Income**
   This practice is adopted in view of the significant difficulties of capturing household incomes through recall-based (typically with a 30-day reference period) surveys canvassed over a moving sample of households. These difficulties are particularly sizeable in the case of households with self-employment as the principal source of income. As per the NSS 68th Round (2011–12) survey, self-employed households form 49.8% of all households in rural India and 35.3% of all urban households. Another issue in using consumption expenditure is that there has been a considerable shift in consumption pattern over time with a sizeable reduction in the share of food in total expenditure, and, within food, a significant reduction in the share of calorie-rich cereals. The shifts in consumption patterns could be reflective of lower calorie requirements following the changes in occupational patterns toward a more sedentary life style, improvements in access to better sanitation and hygiene, and general improvements in health status leading to better retention of ingested calories and other nutrients. To obviate this problem, the Rangarajan Expert Group has re-computed the average requirements of calories, fats, and proteins on the basis of the 2010 ICMR norms; the age and gender distribution of the rural and urban populations as per the 2011 Population Census; and, the broad work status distribution

as per the 2011–12 Employment–Unemployment survey. The revised calorie norms are indeed lower—especially in rural India.

3. **Divergence Between Consumption Estimates Based on the NSSO Methodology and those Emerging from the National Accounts System (NAS) Aggregates**

The Indian statistical system generates two parallel estimates of private consumption. They are: (a) National Sample Survey (NSS) estimates, which are based on the household consumer expenditure survey and yield class distribution of consumption by sectors (rural and urban) and by regions (states, and sub-state level such as NSS regions, which are formed by grouping contiguous districts similar in density of population and cropping pattern); and (b) NAS estimates, originating from the CSO, that uses a scalar value of consumption for the nation as a whole, with no disaggregation by region or class (except by broad commodity groups). These two estimates of consumption (NSS and NAS) do not match in any country; India is no exception. What is alarming in India is that the difference between the NSS and the NAS consumption is widening over time. For example, the difference was less than 10% in the late 1970s; it rose to 50% in 2004–05. At the aggregate level, the NAS consumption has always been more than the NSS consumption. There are several intractable problems in reconciling the differences between the two sets of estimates.

In view of those problems, the Rangarajan Expert Group will continue with the current practice—initiated by the Lakdawala Expert Group and continued by the Tendulkar Expert Group—of estimating poverty in India solely by reference to the size-distribution of private consumer expenditure based on the NSSO methodology.

4. **Adjusting Poverty Lines for Spatial and Inter-temporal Variations in Prices**

While implementing the 1979 Task Force (Alagh) recommendations, the Planning Commission used a single common all-India poverty line for all the States—albeit separate ones for the rural and the urban populations. For adjusting the all-India poverty lines for price-inflation over time the Wholesale Price Index (WPI) was used to adjust both the rural and the urban poverty lines. This posed the obvious problem that the WPI had a substantial weightage for items that were not part of the consumption basket of the households. Subsequently, the Planning Commission used the implicit deflator underlying the current and the constant price values of Private Final Consumption Expenditure (PFCE) in the National Accounts. This, too, did not provide separate indicators for the rural and the urban populations. Subsequently, the Lakdawala Expert Group made a few key changes in that methodology but even then the problem posed by changing the consumption pattern over time and space remained unresolved. Thereafter, the Tendulkar Expert Group took cognizance of this problem and decided to work with Fisher price indices specifically estimated both for deriving state-specific poverty lines, given the all-India (urban) poverty line, and for updating the same over time.

The Rangarajan Expert Group (Planning Commission 2014b, 69–70) suggests that accounting for changing of consumption patterns requires the use of "Ideal index numbers" such as the Fisher Index to capture the "true" inflation faced by the population. In this context it may be noted that a rise in the share of food grains sourced by households from the public distribution system—which may gain pace as the National Food Security Act gets implemented—will be an important element of the changing composition of private consumption expenditure.

The use of Fisher index will require the weighting diagrams for both the base year and the terminal year, and, this can be drawn, as at present, from the large-sample NSS Consumer Expenditure surveys. The next requirement for the construction of Fisher indices is a set of price-relatives, at least for the major item- groups in the consumption basket. Recently, the CSO has started compiling the consumer price index at the state level for rural and urban areas. These state-wise price indices are available at a disaggregated level of commodity groups such as food, beverages and tobacco, fuel and light, housing (for urban areas only), clothing, bedding and footwear, and miscellaneous items from 2011. We could use the published price-indices for the listed item-groups for the construction of Fisher indices. Note, however, that with such highly aggregated item-groups, the impact of within-group changes in the composition of expenditures will not be captured. This is particularly problematic for the price indices for food as a single-item group since the weighting diagram underlying the currently available CSO consumer price indices relate to 2004–05. For the food–group, therefore, the Rangarajan Expert Group recommends that the current practice of relying on the unit values derivable from the NSSO Consumer Expenditure surveys should continue till such time a new CPI with a weighting diagram based on the 2011–12 pattern of consumption becomes available. In respect of non-food items, the price indices available in the exiting CSO Consumer Price Indices can be used in the construction of requisite Fisher indices.

Once the new series of Consumer Price Index numbers (with 2011–12 as the base year) become available, there will be a trade–off between the operational convenience of using these price indices as they are readily available and the desirability of using "ideal price indices" for capturing true inflation. A resolution of this trade–off will depend on an assessment of the extent of change in the structure of consumption at that point in time relative to the 2011–12 structure of consumption.

The procedure outlined above can be used to revise the state-wise poverty line for 2011–12 for subsequent years and, thereafter, compute state-level poverty ratios for later years.

5. Accounting for Public Expenditure on Social Services

In the seven-year period of 2004–05 to 2011–12, public expenditures on education and health per capita at constant 2004–05 prices have nearly doubled with an implied compound annual growth rate (CAGR) of close to 10% per annum. Given that these services are, typically, provided at heavily subsidized prices, the reported private expenditures as captured in the NSS Consumer Expenditure surveys on them would be lower than their true value. To that extent, this component of the PLB will carry a lower monetary value, relative to the true value of these services to the households, at that threshold. However, in the absence of data on the distribution of the public expenditures on these social services by size-class of private consumption expenditure, they can-not be factored into either the construction of the poverty line or in the assessment of their impact on measured poverty.

The monthly per-capita consumption expenditure (MPCE) of ₹972 in rural areas and ₹1,407 in urban areas constitute the new poverty lines at the all-India level as per the recommendation of the Rangarajan Expert Group They translate to a monthly per household expenditure of ₹4,860/ in rural India and of ₹7,035/ for urban India—assuming a family of five members in each case.

Now, the Government of India uses the estimates of poverty and state-specific poverty lines as recommended by the Tendulkar Expert Group. The methodology adopted by the Tendulkar Expert Group generically belongs to its predecessors, namely the Working Group of 1962, the Task Force of 1977 and the Expert Group of 1989. Its methodology is based on an exogenously determined poverty line expressed in terms of per capita consumption expenditure in a month and the class distribution of NSS consumer expenditure data of the NSSO. The poverty ratio (percentage of people living below the poverty line) was obtained by counting the persons lying below the poverty line from the class distribution of persons.

The Human Poverty Index (HPI)

The *Human Development Report 1997* (UNDP 1997) presents an HPI and ranks 78 poor countries using it. The report asserts that poverty is multidimensional, and poverty measures based on the income criterion do not capture deprivation of many kinds.

The HPI is based on the following three different types of deprivation (UNDP 1997, 17–23):

1. Survival deprivation, as measured by the percentage of people (in a given country) not expected to survive to age 40 years (P_1).
2. Deprivation in education and knowledge, as measured by the adult literacy rate (P_2).
3. Deprivation in economic provisioning (P_3), which is computed as the mean of three variables: population without access to safe water (P_{31}), population without access to health services (P_{32}), and underweight children under the age of five years (P_{33})—all three expressed in percentages.

The HPI is then obtained as the cube root of the average of the cubes of the three components of deprivation. This is a "power mean" of order three. The power mean of order one is the simple mean, the average of the values.

Out of the 78 developing countries, Trinidad and Tobago had the lowest HPI at 4.1 and Niger had the highest at 66.0. India's HPI was 36.7 and its rank was 47.

The report says that the HPI can be used in at least three ways: as a tool of advocacy, as a planning tool for identifying areas of concentrated poverty within a country, and as a research tool. For example, the HPI can help summarize the extent of poverty along several dimensions, the distance to go and the progress made.

This index has some drawbacks and, therefore, is not yet acceptable to scholars and policy makers (Krishnaji 1997, 2202–05). The HPI does not include certain critical dimensions of human poverty, such as low incomes, lack of political freedom, inability to participate in decision-making, lack of personal security, and threats to sustainability and intergenerational equity. In addition, the quality and reliability of data used for computing the HPI are also questionable in many cases.

Key Points

1. Measurement of the level and pace of rural development is useful for a number of purposes, such as the determination of the extent of economic and social well-being of the rural people, serving as a benchmark for future planning, facilitating the monitoring, evaluation and control of ongoing programs, and spatial and temporal comparisons of development.
2. To be meaningful, measures of rural development must be consistent with the objectives of rural development. A measure should provide, at the minimum, an indication of such commonly accepted objectives of development as per capita availability of life sustaining goods or per capita income in rural areas as well as some idea of the distribution of income, assets, and other means of socio-economic welfare.
3. There is no universally acceptable measure of rural development that captures its multifaceted nature. The choice of measure depends upon the purpose of measurement

and the availability of requisite data/information. Commonly used measures of rural development can be categorized into two classes, namely, measures of level of rural development and measures of distribution of rural development.

4. Some of measures of level of rural development include per capita real GNP, per capita consumption expenditure, per capita public expenditure on community facilities and services, the PQLI, composite index of rural development and the HDI.
5. Of all the measures of level, the composite index of rural development and the HDI, when computed separately for rural population, could be the most appropriate indicators of rural development.
6. The Lorenz curve and the GCR are two of the most popular measures of income distribution. They could also be used for measuring the distribution of benefits from rural development programs.
7. The HC ratio or index, the (PG index, the SPG index, Sen's index and the HPI are some of the commonly used indicators of rural poverty or lack of rural development. Estimation of poverty is beset with many conceptual, methodological and empirical problems including the lack of consensus about the definition of poverty, procedure of determination of poverty line and difficulty in gathering reliable data on income of rural households.
8. There are several estimates of poverty line and incidence of poverty in India as reported by various committees/expert groups constituted by the Planning Commission from time to time. The Planning Commission now uses the estimates of poverty derived from the Tendulkar Expert Group methodology, although the estimates made by the Rangarajan Expert Group are the latest ones but not yet accepted by the Planning Commission.
9. Some of the simple measures of rural development could be constructed in the form of questions such as these: (a) Has the number of rural people below the absolute poverty line been declining over time? (b) Has the degree of income inequality in rural areas been declining over time? (*c*) Has the level of rural unemployment been declining over time? Answers to these questions would indicate whether a particular area or country is developing or not.

Questions for Discussion

1. Why do we need to measure rural development?
2. What are the problems in measuring rural development?
3. Which is the most appropriate measure of development and why?
4. In India, the per capita income in Punjab is higher than that in Kerala. Does this imply that the level of overall development or quality of life in Punjab is better than in Kerala? Yes/No. If yes, why; and if no, why not?
5. Which one of the following three alternative states of an economy is better and why?
    (i) Increasing per capita income at a faster rate associated with increasing inequality in income distribution
    (ii) Increasing per capita income at a slower rate associated with decreasing inequality in income distribution
    (iii) No change in per capita income associated with decreasing inequality in income distribution

6. Write a critique of the Human Development Index (HDI) as a measure of development.
7. What are the main problems in estimating rural poverty and how they could be minimized?
8. What are the advantages and limitations of Wealth Ranking, done using the technique of Participatory Rural Appraisal (PRA) as compared to conventional sample survey methods?

Notes

1. NNI = GNI at market-price consumption of fixed capital.
2. http://hdr.undp.org/en/content/human-development-index-hdi-table (Accessed on October, 2015).
3. The Working Group comprised Professor D. R. Gadgil, Dr B. N. Ganguli, Dr P. S. Lokanathan, Mr M. R. Masani, Mr Ashok Mehta, Mr Shriman Narayan, Mr Pitamber Pant, Dr V. K. R. V. Rao, and Mr Anna Saheb Sahasrabudhe.

Chapter 4

Some Paradigms of Rural Development

LEARNING OUTCOMES

After having gone through this chapter, students should be able to:

- **List a few major characteristics of the modernization theory of development;**
- **Illustrate the genesis of the dependency theory of the Marxist school and its relevance in India's context;**
- **Compare and contrast the Rosenstein-Rodan's Theory of the "big push" and the Leibenstein's "Critical Minimum Effort Thesis" and determine which one is more relevant to India;**
- **critically examine the main assumptions of the Lewis' model of economic development and their validity under present Indian conditions;**
- **Appraise the Gunnar Myrdal's thesis of "spread and backwash" effects in the present context of India;**
- **Describe the salient features of the human capital model of development and its relevance to India vis-à-vis the Gandhian model of rural development, and**
- **Illustrate the basic concepts of "dualism" and "need for achievement," and their role in development.**

Introduction

There are several paradigms or models of development in vogue at present and so also many perspectives or viewpoints. A theory is expected to perform two major functions, namely, explanation and prediction, of a phenomenon. There is no universally acceptable model or theory of rural development, which can explain the existing phenomenon of rural development and predict its future course. What we have is a set of hypotheses and propositions that constitute higher level generalizations in the field of development. To the extent that rural development is a subset of development, the hypotheses of development apply to rural development as well. Many such hypotheses emphasize both economic and non-economic determinants of development, that is, they are quite comprehensive. Another characteristic of some of the hypotheses propounded by development theorists is that they are not fully operational, in the sense that it is very difficult to test them, that is, they are refractory. This chapter is devoted to a critical review of some of the contemporary paradigms of development and examines their relevance to rural development in the Indian context.

We begin with an examination of what the great thinkers of the past, particularly the classical economists, contributed to the subject. We can, then, in the light of subsequent experience, determine in what respects they were right or wrong. In this manner, we can free ourselves (at least partially) from the confines of our own times and can better equip ourselves for an objective analysis of the complex process of development.

The economists of the late 18th and early 19th centuries were primarily concerned with the conditions for economic growth. This was the period of the Industrial Revolution in Europe. The classical economists—including Adam Smith, David Ricardo, Thomas Robert Malthus, John Stuart Mill, and Karl Marx—lived through the period of take-off into sustained growth. The observations of these economists regarding the nature and causes of economic growth are, therefore, of considerable interest. We shall now present some basic ideas of the classical school of thought, which may still be relevant. An interesting element of the arguments of the classical economists was the concept of circularity that characterized the interrelationship between technology, investment, and profit. The circularity was inherent in their assertion that the level of technology depends on the level of investment, investment depends on profits, and profits depend partly on the level of technology. This circularity was no accident or oversight. It was precisely what the Classicists wished to stress, that is, in economic development, nothing succeeds like success and nothing fails like failure. In the circular argument, we already have a clue to the difference in the performance of developed and developing countries.

The classical economists did not focus their attention on development, or rural development per se. They perhaps assumed that economic growth would naturally lead to development. It was toward the end of World War II, around 1945, that development became an important field of study and attracted several scholars. Most of the initial writings on the subject dwelt on explaining the meaning of development, identifying factors affecting development, and exploring interrelationships among the factors. Two distinct schools of thought emerged in the 1950s, namely, the capitalist school and the Marxist school, and two distinct theories corresponding to them, namely, the "modernization theory" of the capitalist school and the "dependency theory" of the Marxist school.

The Modernization Theory

The dominant arguments of the capitalist school are embodied in what is known as the Modernization theory or the "Free World" model of development. The Modernization theory was the justification for the US hegemony in the context of the Cold War. Scholars who contributed to the growth and development of this theory comprised economists, sociologists, historians and anthropologists, and the determinants of development identified by them included both economic and non-economic factors. The essence of the theory was the transfer of Western technology and rationality, without changing class structure as a means of development, and removal of all social and ideological obstacles to such a process (Alavi and Shanin 1982, 2).

The Modernization theory was based on several assumptions, some of which are briefly stated here (Barnett 1988, 26; McKay 1990, 55):

1. Application of Western science and technology in order to increase production is essential for achieving development.
2. The process of development can be delineated into a series of stages, and all societies pass through those stages.

3. In the process of development, traditional social and political institutions are replaced by modern ones.
4. Traditional feudal forms of political power will be replaced by democratic forms of governance.

In a nutshell, the Modernization theory presented the "American way of life" as the epitome of modernity. It envisages that development can be achieved only through industrialization and urbanization, along with technological transformation of agriculture—an insight validated by the experience of the newly industrialized countries of East Asia and Southeast Asia.

In the context of rural development, the Modernization theory offers quite a few useful insights, such as the inevitability of the use of modern technology for increasing agricultural production and the need for replacing traditional feudal institutions by new democratic ones for a shift toward greater scientific temper, and secular values and norms. However, the theory has lost much of its appeal due to its failure to predict and explain many economic phenomena, such as the faltering of the post World War II boom in the 1960s, worldwide depression in the 1970s, and the shift in the terms of international trade in the favor of developed countries. The theory also did not foresee the adverse income inequality and environmental impacts of the capitalist/free market model of development and its unsustainability. In the face of these weaknesses and criticisms, the theory has taken a few new directions, such as International Keynesianism, with its emphasis on the establishment of a New International Economic Order and the Guarantee of Basic Needs and Structural Adjustments Programmes. However, these new initiatives do not directly address the problems of rural development and, to that extent, are not relevant.

The financial (currency and stock market) turmoil in the East Asian countries has proved that the free market economy model, or the capitalist path, cannot guarantee stable and sustainable economic development characterized by fast improving living standards. From Japan and South Korea to Malaysia and Indonesia, mounting bankruptcies, growing unemployment, and rising inflation had engendered not only the loss of economic self-confidence, but also threatened the region's political and military stability.

There is yet another reason for the failure of the Modernization Theory to be relevant in the context of developing countries such as India, and that is the non-existence or ineffective implementation of rules and controls aimed at preventing private companies or groups from dominating their domestic markets. In the free market-oriented Western democracies, such rules and controls are effectively implemented and, hence, they tend to even out the distribution of income and wealth. In the absence of strict control and regulation of the activities of private enterprises in developing countries, including India, not all the intended benefits from free markets accrue to society.

The Dependency Theory of the Marxist School

The growing disenchantment with the Modernization theory, owing to its failure to explain growing inequalities, poverty, violence, and military coups in the newly independent nations in Africa and Asia, forced development scholars to ask new questions and seek new answers, using an alternative paradigm. The intellectual foundation of the new paradigm was rooted in the ideas of Karl Marx, Friedrich Engels and other Marxist thinkers. Marx (1818–83) and Engels (1820–95) were the contemporaries of the proponents of the Modernization theory, notably Emile Durkheim (1858–1917) and Max Weber (1864–1924). Marx and Engels believed that the process of social change was not gradual and evolutionary, as assumed by the Modernization theory. Instead, it was characterized by conflict of interests between classes in society, or in other words, class struggle. The Marxists saw class struggle as the engine of social change and development.

The Marxists argued that imperialism, rather than being a benign political outgrowth of European civilization (as argued by the Modernization theorists), was an exploitative system of economic, social, and political relations. The system changed the colonized nations into sources of cheap inputs to production in the capitalist nations, as well as markets for their products. This arrangement always worked to the advantage of the imperial power. Such a view of the dynamics at work in the capitalist system meant a complete reversal of the logic of modernization from the promise of development to impoverishment. This was the fundamental argument of the Marxist school of thought, which came to be known as the Dependency theory.

The initial support for the Dependency theory came from Latin America, particularly from the work of Raul Prebisch and his associates at the Economic Commission for Latin America (ECLA). However, the chief spokesman for the theory was Andre Gunder Frank, who dismissed the Modernization theory as useless from a policy perspective. Frank asserted that the relation between rich and poor nations was not only non-beneficial to the latter, but also positively destructive, hindering, and distorting their development. In his view, development and underdevelopment were both results of interactions between societies. He drew up the detailed historical case studies of Chile and Brazil to support his assertions. The following are the main arguments of the dependency theory (McKay 1990, 55–56):

1. The developed countries (the First World) could not have achieved the level of development that they have, without the systematic exploitation of the developing countries (the Third World).
2. That the process of development passes through a series of stages is an illusion. Developing countries cannot attain development following the path adopted by developed countries, so long as the exploitative world system exists.
3. Countries that are now poor were not so to begin with; rather they have been *forced* into the stage of underdevelopment by a global system of capitalist exploitation.
4. Developing countries can develop only by snapping their links with the developed countries.

The Dependency theory was very popular in the 1970s as it provided a plausible explanation to the perpetuation of the problems of poverty and stagnation in developing countries, despite concerted efforts at solving them. Development scholars realized the need for critically examining the existing relations between rich and poor countries to find out whether they were benign and beneficial to the poor nations, or harmful. However, in the 1980s, the theory lost much of its initial popularity and was criticized as being "too deterministic" and "too simplistic." The basic argument of the theory, that "underdevelopment" in developing countries (the periphery) is the result of "development" in developed countries (the core/center), was falsified by the experience of the East Asian tigers. These tigers were initially dependent on the developed countries (that is, they were on the periphery), but in course of time they became highly developed and competitive, that is, they moved from the periphery to the core. Besides, the theory did not consider the role of several internal factors, such as excessive population growth, underdeveloped human resources, shortage of natural resources, and class struggle in explaining the existence of "underdevelopment."

In the context of rural development, we could say that the theory provides a useful caveat that, while identifying the determinants of rural development, we should critically examine various inter-sectoral linkages (both backward and forward) and interactions and determine whether they are beneficial to rural people or not. If not, necessary policy measures should be taken to make the linkages and interactions beneficial to the rural people. A similar exercise needs to be done at the national level to find out which international economic and political relationships are beneficial and which are harmful to economic development in general, and rural development in particular. Sadly, such an exercise is not done objectively anywhere in the world, including India, and, consequently, we drift either toward the capitalist model or the Marxist model.

Rosenstein-Rodan's Theory of the "Big Push"

According to this theory, there is a minimum level of resources that must be devoted to a development program, if it is to have any chance of success. Launching a country into self-sustaining growth is a little like getting an aeroplane off the ground. There is a critical ground speed, which must be passed before the craft can become airborne (MIT 1957, 70). The essence of this theory is: Proceeding "bit by bit" will not add up in its effects to the sum total of the single bits. A minimum quantum of investment is a necessary—though not sufficient—condition for success.

Rosenstein-Rodan (1970) identifies three different kinds of indivisibilities, which may be considered the main obstacles to the development of developing countries. These are, the indivisibility in the supply of social overhead capital (lumpiness of capital), the indivisibility of demand (complementarity of demand), and the indivisibility (kink) in the supply of savings. He argues that a big push in terms of a high quantum of investment is required to scale the economic obstacles to development created by these three kinds of indivisibilities and the external economies to which they give rise. This implies that the development process is a series of discontinuous "jumps," and each jump requires a "big push." Besides, there may finally be a phenomenon of indivisibility in the vigor and drive required for successful development policy. Isolated and small efforts may not add up to a sufficient impact on growth. An atmosphere of development may only arise after a critical minimum level of investment has been reached.

Rosenstein-Rodan does not offer any specific and practicable suggestions to overcome the adverse effects of the indivisibilities, but he suggests that international trade may reduce the size of the minimum push required to obviate the effect of indivisibility (complementarity) of demand. Mobilization of sufficient resources to provide the required "big push" continues to be the biggest hurdle, which developing countries cannot overcome on their own. Rosenstein-Rodan recommends that a trust—with capital from outside—be established to plan and finance investment for the entire area simultaneously. A major criticism of this theory is that the resources required to give the "big push" are of such a high order, that a developing country such as India cannot afford them. In fact, a country capable of mobilizing the requisite quantum of resources would not be a poor country. However, conceptually, this paradigm continues to be appealing to planners and scholars.

Leibenstein's "Critical Minimum Effort Thesis"

The central idea of Harvey Leibenstein's (1957) thesis is that in order to attain sustained secular growth, it is essential that the initial stimulant to development be of a certain critical minimum size. According to Leibenstein, economic backwardness is characterized by a set of interrelated factors, which have a certain degree of stability at their small equilibrium values. The actual values are different from the equilibrium values because the economy is always being subjected to stimulants or shocks. The stimulants have a tendency to raise per capita incomes above the equilibrium level. But in backward economies, long-term economic development does not take place because the magnitude of stimulants is too small. In other words, efforts to escape from economic backwardness, be they spontaneous or forced, are below the critical minimum that is needed for sustained growth.

For small values of the stimulant, the generated income-depressing factors are, in the long run, more significant than the induced income-raising forces, but the reverse is the case with high values of the stimulant. Population growth may be cited as an example of this phenomenon. A small increase in capital through raising incomes will stimulate more than an equivalent increase in population and a proportional decline in per capita income. There is, of course, a biologically determined maximum rate of population growth between 3% and 4%. As such, persistent capital accumulation above a certain minimum rate would eventually permit development. The need for a minimum effort arises to overcome internal and external diseconomies of scale, to overcome income-depressing obstacles, which may be generated by the stimulants to growth, and to generate sufficient momentum in the system so that the factors that stimulate growth continue to play their part.

Leibenstein's thesis is more realistic than Rosenstein-Rodan's "big push" theory. Giving a big push to the program of industrialization all at once is not practicable in underdeveloped countries, while the critical minimum effort can be properly timed and broken up into a series of smaller efforts to put the economy on the path of sustained development. This theory is also consistent with the concept of decentralized democratic planning, to which India, and most developing countries, are wedded. Therefore, this paradigm provides good clues as to the quantum of investment that is absolutely essential to make a program take-off.

Lewis' Model of Economic Development

W. Arthur Lewis' (1954, 139–92) model is based on the fact that in many developing countries there exist large reservoirs of labor whose marginal productivity is negligible, zero, or even negative. This labor is available in unlimited quantities at a wage equal to the subsistence level of living, plus a margin sufficient to overcome the friction of moving from the "subsistence sector" to the "capitalist sector," which may be called "subsistence-plus" wage. As the supply of labor is unlimited, new industries can be set up and the existing ones can be expanded without limit, at the ruling wage rate. The capitalist sector also needs skilled workers. But Lewis maintains that skilled labor is only a temporary bottleneck and can be removed by providing training facilities to unskilled workers.

Since the marginal productivity of labor in the capitalist sector is higher than the ruling wage rate, there results a capitalist surplus. This surplus is used for capital formation, which makes possible employment of more people from the subsistence sector. The increase in investment by the capitalists raises the marginal productivity of labor, which induces capitalist employers to increase their labor force till the marginal productivity of labor falls to a level equivalent to the ruling wage rate. This process goes on till the capital–labor ratio rises to the point where the supply of labor becomes inelastic. Some critics have pointed out that Lewis' optimism concerning development by absorption of disguised unemployment from agriculture is unfounded, because it is not possible to transfer a large number of workers permanently and on a full-time basis from agriculture to industry, without a drop in the agricultural output, that is, the marginal productivity of the labor in agriculture is not zero.

Technical progress in the capitalist sector may also increase the share of profits in the national income as long as there is surplus labor. The share of profits increases, both because the profit ratio within a capitalist sector of a given size may increase through innovation and because the capitalist sector itself grows. According to Lewis, this is the major way in which the rise in capital formation from 4% or 5% to about 12% to 15% of national income takes place.

Capital is created not only out of profits but also out of bank credit. In a developing country characterized by unemployed resources and scarcity of capital, credit creation will expand output and employment in the same way as profits do. Credit-financed capital formation, however, results in a temporary rise in prices. The inflationary process comes to an end when voluntary savings from increased profits are large enough to finance new investment, without resorting to bank credit.

According to Lewis, the process of growth cannot continue indefinitely and must come to an end on account of a number of factors. When this happens, the process of capital formation can still be kept going by stimulating immigration or by encouraging export of capital to countries that possess abundant supplies of labor at the subsistence wage rate. Since the former measure is strongly opposed by trade unions, the latter seems more practicable.

Lewis' model seems to provide a good framework to understand the process of economic development in labor-surplus developing countries such as India. Its basic premise is that labor productivity in agriculture must increase substantially in order to generate surplus in the form of food to be used for development of the non-farm sector, and to release the surplus labor from agriculture for meeting the growing needs of the non-farm sector. However, the relevance of the model is constrained by a number of factors. First, labor unions may push the wage rate up as labor productivity increases, and keep the rate of profit and rate of capital formation lower than expected. Second, the capitalist employers may use the surplus for speculative or non-productive purposes instead of ploughing it back for development purposes. This is, in fact, what has been happening these days in India and other developing countries. Third, to meet their rising expectations, rural people may consume more and save less than predicted by the model, and thereby dampen the pace of development.

The Lewis model does not present a satisfactory analysis of the agricultural sector, in the sense that it fails to consider the possibility of a change of productivity in agriculture. Building upon the Lewis model, Ranis and Fei (1970) propounded a theory of economic growth, by first analyzing the role of the "neglected" agricultural sector in a static sense and then generalizing the "static" analysis by introducing the possibility of an increase in agricultural productivity (Higgins 1966, Chapter 5). Cochrane (1969, Chapter 11) critically reviews the models of Lewis and of Ranis and Fei, and concludes that the creation of investment capital needed to employ the surplus workers released from agriculture is the critical missing element in these models. He then suggests that the resources to finance the expensive process of agricultural modernization can be obtained in any one or in a combination of three basic ways:

1. By squeezing more agricultural surplus.
2. By slowing down the rate of investment in the non-farm sector and in basic infrastructure.
3. By obtaining foreign loans and grants.

Of these three sources, foreign loans and grants are, he asserts, the most advantageous or least expensive. He further states that the growth rate of agricultural production in a developing country in the early stages must be raised high enough to meet its expanding food requirements. For this to happen, he argues, the pull exerted on agriculture through higher market prices will not be enough; agriculture must be pushed, and pushed hard, by a strategy emphasizing the use of modern technology and supporting infrastructure and services.

In our opinion, Cochrane's model is a good exposition of the process of agricultural development, and of the possibilities and limitations of agricultural development as a catalyst for overall national development. We would like to add two elements to Cochrane's model, and these are (a) population control measures; and (b) the international economic and political environment. No strategy of agricultural and national development would ever succeed in the absence of appropriate population control measures, and a congenial international economic and political environment. Whereas a developing country can always do something to control its exploding population, the creation of a suitable international environment is the responsibility of the world community and its organizations.

Gunnar Myrdal's Thesis of "Spread and Backwash" Effects

Gunnar Myrdal (1957) highlights low levels of income in most of the non-Soviet countries in the world, and international disparities in income, wealth, and investment. Myrdal finds the theoretical approach (automatic self-stabilization) inadequate to grapple with the problems of inequality. In his opinion, in a normal case, a change does not call forth countervailing changes, but, instead, supporting changes that move the system in the same direction as the first change, but much faster—the principle of circular and cumulative causation. As a result of such circular causation, a social process tends to move faster. A social process can be stopped by introducing new exogenous changes in the system. He elaborates this with an example of the African-American problem in the USA. Two factors, namely, white prejudices causing discrimination against the African-Americans and their "low plane of living," are interrelated. Their low standard of living is kept suppressed by discrimination by the whites. On the other hand, the African-Americans' poverty, ignorance, superstition, slum dwellings, health deficiencies, and their supposedly unclean appearance, bad odor, disorderly conduct, unstable family relations, and criminality stimulate and feed the antipathy of the whites for them. Both these factors mutually "cause" each other.

He also emphasizes the role of non-economic factors in development and highlights the backwash effects of growth brought out by the free play of market forces. The clustering of labor, capital, goods, and services in certain localities and regions leave the remaining areas, mostly rural, more or less in the backwaters and accentuate regional inequality. Concentration of firms, capital, and talented individuals in certain localities (growth points) at the expense of surrounding areas (the backwash) lowers the level of economic development below what it would have been, if growth points had never emerged.

Against the backwash effects there are, however, certain centrifugal "spread effects" of expansionary momentum from the centers of economic expansion to other regions. Empirical evidence shows that backwash effects are neutralized by spread effects only at a high level of development. This is one of the reasons why rapid sustained progress becomes an almost automatic process once a country has reached a high level of development. At low levels of development, the spread effects are either very weak, or are just strong enough to cancel the backwash effects, and the result in both cases is poverty and stagnation.

Similarly—at the international level—trade, capital movement, and migration have strong backwash effects on the developing countries. Examples can easily be cited of developing countries whose cultures have been impoverished as a result of the establishment of trading contacts with the outside world. But, generally speaking, the concepts of "back-wash effects" and "spread effects" are useful in the Indian context also and need to be considered while planning for rural development projects.

The Human Capital Model of Development

This model emphasizes the importance of human capital investment in the process of economic and social development. By human capital, we mean acquired mental and physical ability through education, training, health care, and pursuit of some spiritual methods such as yoga or meditation. The acquisition of human capital is largely through the investment of human effort and money. The simplest and most important of this type of model is a schooling model, which relates economic development to schooling. The classical and neoclassical economists did not explicitly include the quality of human resources in their theoretical frameworks; labor was taken to include both physical and mental effort (Alex 1983: 3–12). It was Theodore Schultz (1964) who elaborated the concept of human capital and explicitly considered the investment in human capital as an important determinant of economic development. Subsequently, quite a few other scholars got interested in the economics of human capital, especially the economics of education, and a large number of studies were conducted on the subject. The model considers the totality of human potential and emphasizes the need to harness it for the good of the people. It respects people's culture and religion, and social values and structures. It is more applicable to countries such as India than any other model. The human capital approach to rural development is based on the following three assumptions, which have been ignored in the classical theory of development:

1. Human physical and mental capabilities are partly inherited and partly acquired, and they vary from individual to individual, that is, the classical assumption of a homogeneous labor force does not hold.
2. Human capital directly contributes to development through its positive effect on productivity and through reduction in resistance to the diffusion of new technologies in the economy, especially in the rural sector.
3. Human resources are inexhaustible and are available in plenty in all developing countries of the world, including India. If properly developed and utilized, human resources can contribute significantly to development.

Thus, this model shifts the emphasis from physical capital formation to human capital formation and from industrial development to rural development as a basis for overall development. This model seems most appropriate for labor-surplus developing countries such as India, where a lot of underdeveloped human resources having high potential for development exist. Besides, human resources are renewable and, hence, inexhaustible. Therefore, human capital can be substituted for exhaustible, non-renewable physical capital in the process of development and, thus, relax the constraint on development imposed by the inadequacy of physical capital to a large extent. As a matter of fact, strategies for development of the tertiary (service) sector, which is now the fastest growing sector in India, requires skilled, and experienced and innovative human resources for their success. This is the path that India should choose to bring about overall sustainable development. Human resource development through nutrition, health care, appropriate education, training, and empowerment deserves the highest priority now in terms of allocation of resources for the purpose.

The Gandhian Model of Rural Development

Mohandas Karamchand Gandhi, popularly known as Mahatma Gandhi, played the leading role in securing for India political independence from the British Raj through organizing and mobilizing Indian people from all walks of life in a peaceful and nonviolent manner. He is, therefore, rightly called the "the Father of the Nation." Gandhiji's approach to India's rural development was holistic and people-centered. It was rooted in his conviction in the tenets of truth, nonviolence, and the goodness of human beings. Influenced as he was by Tolstoy, Ruskin, and the teachings of *The Gita*, he placed more emphasis on moral and spiritual values than on economic motives as a means of overall development. Some of the salient features of the Gandhian model are presented in the following pages.

Values and Premises Underlying the Model

The Gandhian model of rural development is based on certain values and premises (Box 4.1).

Box 4.1

BASIC VALUES AND PREMISES UNDERLYING THE GANDHIAN MODEL OF DEVELOPMENT

1. *Real India is found not in its cities, but in its villages.*
2. *The revival of villages is possible only when the villagers are no more exploited. In Gandhiji's opinion, exploitation of villagers by city dwellers was "violence."*
3. *Simple living and high thinking, implying voluntary reduction of materialistic wants, and pursuit of moral and spiritual principles of life.*
4. *Dignity of labor: everyone must earn his bread by physical labor and one who labors must necessarily get his subsistence.*
5. *Preference to the use of indigenous (swadeshi) products, services and institutions.*
6. *Balance between the ends and the means: Gandhiji believed that nonviolence and truth could not be sustained unless a balance between the ends and the means was maintained.*

Source: (Singh 1999: 86).

Principal Components of the Model

The principal components of the Gandhian model are as follows.

Self-sufficient Village Economy

Gandhiji's concept of self-sufficiency was not a narrow one, nor was it that of selfishness or arrogance. He realized the need for villagers to get those things from outside the village, which they could not produce in the village.

Decentralization

Gandhiji believed that human happiness with mental and moral development should be the supreme goal of society, and that this goal should be achieved through decentralization of political and economic powers.

Khadi and Village Industries

For Gandhiji, khadi was an instrument of decentralization of production and distribution of the basic necessities of life and of ensuring "work to all." He also favored the promotion of other village industries, such as hand grinding, hand pounding, soap making, paper making, metal making, oilseed crushing, tanning, and so on. He advocated the use of manual labor and opposed the introduction of machines, fearing that they would displace human labor. But he appreciated the role of new technologies if they were appropriate, indigenous, and did not affect the level of employment and standard of living.

Implementing Strategy

Gandhiji prescribed the following institutional structure and instruments for implementing his strategy, namely, panchayati raj, cooperatives, trusteeship, and *Nai Taleem* (new education). A brief description of each of these instruments follows.

Panchayati Raj

Gandhiji envisaged that each village in India would be a republic, where the village panchayat would have the full power of managing its affairs, including defense. He expected the panchayat to perform the legislative, executive, and judicial functions necessary for a smooth functioning of the village economy. Various developmental activities such as education, health, and sanitation would also be taken up by the village panchayat. It is good, and in conformity with Gandhiji's views, that India now has made panchayati raj institutions statutory bodies by passing the 73rd and 74th (Constitution) amendment acts. It is hoped that Gandhiji's dream of local self-governance through village panchayats would now be fulfilled.

Cooperatives

Gandhiji saw a great virtue in cooperation as an instrument of rural development. He assigned specific roles to cooperatives in the field of agriculture, commending the promotion of cooperative farming and thereby preventing further fragmentation of landholdings. He also advocated the establishment of other types of cooperatives, such as credit cooperatives, weavers and spinners cooperatives, and dairy cooperatives. In this matter also, we have perhaps lived up to the expectations of Gandhiji. India now has the world's largest network of cooperatives, which occupy an important place in India's rural economy. The OF program is a living example of what cooperatives can do to promote agricultural and rural development in India. There is, therefore, a need for us to adopt the cooperative path to rural development, as advocated by Gandhiji.

Trusteeship

Gandhiji considered trusteeship as an instrument of transforming the capitalist order of society into an egalitarian one. In his opinion, all the land belonged to God, that is, the community, and, therefore, he advocated that land and other natural resources should be collectively owned by—and operated for—the welfare of the community. Landlords should merely be trustees of land and other natural resources and capital assets. He saw in the principle of trusteeship a nonviolent method of persuading landowners to donate their land voluntarily for community welfare purposes, and of avoiding class conflicts.

Nai Taleem

Gandhiji had no faith in modern education, which emphasized only literacy and acquisition of information. In his opinion, modern education was "debauchery of the mind." Hence, he developed a new system of appropriate education and training that he called Nai Taleem. He believed that Nai Taleem would help develop the full potential of children and adults, through full development of their bodies, minds, and spirits. He wanted to see Nai Taleem to be self-supporting and practice oriented. It is unfortunate that India has not yet geared its education system to the needs of the country, and that is why its human resources remain underdeveloped and less productive as compared to other countries that have given the highest priority to education and training. However, of late, "universalization of elementary education" and "total literacy programs" have received higher priority than in the past, with a view to achieve the national objective of "Education for All." Similarly, vocational education at the post-high school (Class 10) level is now being considered as an alternative to the present traditional general education. This shows that we have now realized the relevance of Gandhiji's Nai Taleem and that we are gradually re-orienting our traditional education system.

The Gandhian model, like any other development model, has both its proponents and opponents. The proponents argue that under the prevailing socio-cultural and economic conditions in India the Gandhian model is still relevant, and is the only alternative available for bringing about equitable and sustainable rural development. They assert that panchayati raj institutions and cooperatives are still as relevant as when they were in Gandhiji's days and that the role of appropriate education cannot be overemphasized even in the present Indian context. The critics argue that Gandhiji's ideals of swadeshi, voluntary curtailment of one's wants, trusteeship, self-sufficient villages, and the use of manual labor in preference to machines sound obsolete these days, particularly in the wake of India's new economic policy characterized by privatization, liberalization, and globalization. As a matter of fact, they assert further that by adopting an economic growth oriented development path and by following the Western model of industrialization, both under the influence of Jawaharlal Nehru, India had abandoned the Gandhian model long ago. The main stream thinking in India now is in line with the critics' argument.

To conclude, we could say that Gandhiji wanted India to travel East but India decided to travel West, and we know that "the twain never meet." Now, we have gone probably too far in the wrong direction, and turning around and travelling eastward is perhaps not a feasible course of action. But, then, nothing is impossible and if there is a will, there is a way.

Development Theories from Other Social Sciences

Development is a complex process that is affected by both economic and non-economic factors. The importance of non-economic factors in development was duly recognized by the classical school. John Stuart Mill thought that non-economic factors, such as beliefs, habits of thought, customs and institutions, play an important role in economic development and he attributed the backwardness of underdeveloped countries to the despotic and anti-progressive character of their customs, institutions, and beliefs.

Boeke (1953) attempted to explain underdevelopment in terms of sociological dualism, which he defines as "the clashing of an imported social system with an indigenous social system of another style." On the basis of his analysis, largely based on the Indonesian experience, he concludes that the kindest thing the Western world can do for developing countries is to leave them alone; any effort to develop them along Western lines can only hasten their retrogression and decay. The acceptance of the dualism leads to two policy conclusions: (a) as a rule, one policy for the whole country is not possible; and (b) what is beneficial for one section of the society may be harmful for another. An appraisal of Boeke's theory would reveal that whereas there can be no question about the existence of dualism, its explanation lies not in the nature of society as Boeke perceives it, but in economic and technological terms. This is proved by the fact that not all efforts to promote development in the developing countries through technical and capital assistance from the West have been in vain.

For example, in India, a large part of the credit for bringing about the Green Revolution goes to the United States Agency for International Development (USAID) that helped India, both financially and technically, in setting up modern land-grant type state agricultural universities in the 1960s, and trained its agricultural scientists in American land-grant agricultural universities. Similarly, the OF program that is credited with modernizing India's dairy industry also benefited a lot from food aid in the form of skimmed milk powder and butter oil, first from the World Food Programme of the Food and Agriculture Organization (FAO), and then from the European Economic Community (EEC).

One may reject the theory of sociological dualism advanced by Boeke, and still consider sociological, cultural, and psychological factors important in economic development. Indeed, one may say that all economists who have specialized in economic development recognize the importance of the interplay of these factors with economic factors. In the words of Meier and Baldwin (1957, 355), "The psychological and sociological requirements for development are as important as the economic requirements. They deserve full consideration in their own right." Relatively few economists, however, have had the courage to attempt a systematic theory of development which would incorporate strategic sociological, cultural and psychological factors. Outstanding among these few are David McClelland and Everett Hagen (Higgins 1966, Chapter 13).

McClelland's "Need-for-Achievement Motivation" (N-Ach) theory seeks to establish a relationship between N-Ach and economic development. His theory rests on two propositions: (a) that group differences in the average level of certain motives, such as N-Ach, predict differences in the rate of economic growth and (b) that certain motive combinations predispose individuals to act like successful business entrepreneurs who have played key roles in all previous economic development. On the basis of his studies and analyses, he concludes that if we are to promote economic growth, it is necessary to first change the values and motives of individuals. This, in his opinion, can be done by: (a) persuasion or education; (b) introducing changes in the social system; and (c) early character training. Of the three, the third is by all odds the one most likely to succeed. For, in this way, values can be in-built from the very beginning. Early character training can he imparted by a corps of specially qualified nursery and primary school teachers carefully selected for the purpose.

Thus, McClelland's analysis leads to the conclusion that a take-off into economic development requires a large number of individuals with the entrepreneurial motivation complex and particularly with high N-Ach, and for this a long period of time is required to establish psychological preconditions.

Key Points

1. There is no universally acceptable theory of rural development that can explain the existing phenomenon of rural development and predict its future course. What we have is a set of hypotheses and propositions that constitute higher level generalizations in the field of development. To the extent that rural development is a subset of development, hypotheses of development apply to rural development as well.
2. The classical economists did not focus their attention on development or rural development per se; they perhaps assumed that economic growth would naturally lead to development. An interesting element of the arguments of the classical economists was the concept of circularity that characterized the interrelationship among technology, investment, and profit. The circularity was inherent in their assertion that the level of technology depends on the level of investment, investment depends on profits, and profits depend partly on the level of technology.
3. Two distinct schools of thought about development emerged in the 1950s, namely, the capitalist school and the Marxist school, and two distinct theories corresponding to them, namely, the "modernization theory" of the capitalist school and the "dependency theory" of the Marxist school.
4. The essence of the modernization theory was the transfer of Western technology and rationality to less developed countries without changing their class structure as a means of development and removal of all social and ideological obstacles to such a process.
5. In a nutshell, the modernization theory presented the "American way of life" as the epitome of modernity. It envisaged that development can be achieved only through industrialization and urbanization along with technological transformation of agriculture. It offers quite a few useful insights, such as the inevitability of the use of modern technology for increasing agricultural production and the need for replacing traditional feudal institutions by new democratic ones, for a shift toward greater scientific temper, and secular values and norms.

6. The intellectual foundation of the dependency theory of the Marxist school was rooted in the ideas of Karl Marx and Friedrich Engels, who believed that the process of social change was not gradual and evolutionary as assumed by the modernization theory. Instead, it was characterized by conflict of interests between classes in the society, or in other words, class struggle. The Marxists saw class struggle as the engine of social change and development.
7. The dependency theory was very popular in the 1970s, as it provided a plausible explanation to the perpetuation of the problems of poverty and stagnation in developing countries despite concerted efforts at solving them. The theory provides a useful caveat that while identifying the determinants of rural development, we should critically examine which international economic and political relationships are beneficial and which are harmful to economic development in general, and rural development in particular, and initiate policy measures to minimize the adverse ones.
8. Rosenstein-Rodan's theory of the "big push" maintained that there is a minimum level of resources that must be devoted to a development program if it is to have any chance of success. Launching a country into self-sustaining growth is a little like getting an aeroplane off the ground. There is a critical ground speed that must be passed before the craft can become airborne. A major criticism of this theory is that the resources required to give the "big push" are of such a high order, that a developing country such as India cannot afford them.
9. The central idea of Harvey Leibenstein's "critical minimum effort thesis" is that in order to attain sustained secular growth, it is essential that the initial stimulant to development is of a certain critical minimum size. Leibenstein's thesis is more realistic than Rosenstein-Rodan's "big push" theory in the sense that the critical minimum effort can be properly timed and broken up into a series of smaller efforts to put the economy on the path of sustained development. This theory is also consistent with the concept of decentralized democratic planning as practiced in India.
10. W. Arthur Lewis' model of economic development with unlimited supplies of labor is based on the fact that, in many developing countries, there exist large reservoirs of labor whose marginal productivity is negligible, zero, or even negative. Since the marginal productivity of labor in the capitalist sector is higher than the ruling wage rate, there results a capitalist surplus, which can be used for capital formation that makes possible employment of more people from the subsistence sector and initiates the process of development. The model provides a good framework to understand the process of economic development in labor-surplus developing countries such as India.
11. Gunnar Myrdal in his thesis of "Spread and Backwash Effects" asserts that the clustering of labor, capital, goods, and services in certain localities and regions leave the remaining areas, mostly rural, more or less in backwaters and accentuates regional inequality. Concentration of firms, capital, and talented individuals in certain localities (growth points) at the expense of surrounding areas (backwash) lowers the level of economic development below what it would have been if growth points had never emerged. Against the backwash effects, there are, however, certain centrifugal "spread effects" of expansionary momentum from the centers of economic expansion to other regions. Empirical evidence shows that backwash effects are neutralized by spread effects only at a high level of development.
12. The human capital model of development emphasizes the importance of human capital investment in the process of economic and social development. The human capital includes acquired mental and physical ability through education, training, health care and pursuit of some spiritual methods such as yoga or meditation. The

acquisition of human capital is largely through the investment of human effort and money. The simplest and most important of this type of model is a schooling model that relates economic development to schooling. This model is relevant to India and other developing countries.

13. The Gandhian model is holistic and people-centered. It is rooted in Gandhi's conviction in the tenets of truth, nonviolence, and goodness of human beings. It places more emphasis on moral and spiritual values than economic motives as a means of overall development. The proponents of the Gandhian model argue that under the prevailing socio-cultural and economic conditions in India, the model is still relevant and is the only alternative available for bringing about equitable and sustainable rural development. The critics argue that Gandhiji's ideals of *swadeshi*, voluntary curtailment of one's wants, trusteeship, self-sufficient villages, and use of manual labor in preference to machines are obsolete these days. The main stream thinking in India now is in line with the critics' argument.
14. There are a few other models of development propounded by other social scientists. They include Boeke's explanation of underdevelopment in terms of sociological dualism that he defines as "the clashing of an imported social system with an indigenous social system of another style" and McClelland's N-Ach theory. McClelland's analysis leads to the conclusion that a take-off into economic development requires a large number of individuals with the entrepreneurial motivational complex and particularly with a high N-Ach, and for this a long period is required to establish psychological preconditions. These Boeke's and McClelland's models are useful in providing insights into the role of non-economic factors in development.

Questions for Discussion

1. Why is it difficult, if not impossible, to have a universally acceptable theory of "development"?
2. Write a critique of the modernization theory of development in India's current context.
3. Is the dependency theory relevant to India? Yes/No. If yes, why; if no, why not?
4. Compare and contrast the Rosenstein-Rodan's theory of the "big push" and Harvey Leibenstein's "critical minimum effort thesis." Which one is more applicable to India and why?
5. What are the limitations of Arthur Lewis' model of economic development in India's context?
6. Illustrate with an example the "Spread and Backwash effects" of development as articulated by Gunnar Myrdal in his thesis.
7. What are the common features of the human capital model of development and Gandhian model of development? Examine critically the relevance of Gandhian model in the current context of India.
8. What do you understand by the term "sociological dualism"? How does its existence affect development?
9. Write a critique of the McClelland's "Need-for-Achievement Motivation" (N-Ach) theory in the India's context.
10. Is India's current approach to development as propounded by its Prime Minister Narendra Modi close to the capitalist model of development? If yes, why; if no, why not?

Chapter 5

Determinants of Rural Development

LEARNING OUTCOMES

After having gone through this chapter, students should be able to:

- **Explain why "changes in output" is considered as a proxy variable for "development" and its limitations;**
- **Illustrate the role of land and water resources in India's development in general, and agricultural development in particular;**
- **Identify the major attributes of human resources that significantly affect development;**
- **Define various forms of capital and their role in "development";**
- **Illustrate the role of new agricultural technologies in development in India; and**
- **Identify various forms of organizations and examine their role in India's rural development; describe various conceptual and methodological problems in measuring and quantifying the relation between rural development and its determinants, and the lessons of a few empirical studies of the relationship.**

Introduction

The factors affecting rural development favorably or adversely are so varied, and have combined over time in so many different ways, that it is very difficult to isolate a small number of crucial variables or determinants. There are many physical, technological, economic, socio-cultural, institutional, organizational, and political factors that affect the level and pace of rural development. These factors operate at all levels: household, village, district, state, nation, and the world as a whole. Depending upon how they are managed, these factors can have both favorable and adverse effects on development. For instance, if the human resources of a country are not properly developed by proper nutrition, health care, education, and training, and are not productively utilized, these resources become liabilities and obstacles to development. But if they are properly developed and utilized, then they become great assets and major factors contributing to development. Knowledge about the nature and magnitude of the impact of various determinants on rural development is necessary for rural development managers to be able to use these factors to achieve their goals efficiently and effectively. This chapter is devoted to identifying the major determinants of rural development and examining their role in promoting rural development.

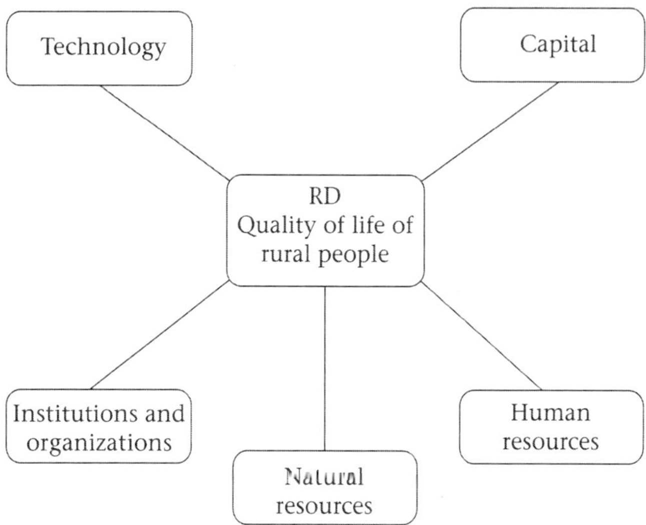

Figure 5.1: *Determinants of Rural Development*

Source: Author.

Rural development is characterized by multiple goals and, as stated in Chapter 3, there is no single index or indicator that can adequately capture the multifaceted nature of rural development. At the same time, unless we can measure the phenomenon of rural development, we are unlikely to know much about the quantitative impact of the factors that influence it.

In the absence of a single index of rural development, we shall use change in output as its proxy measure, and discuss the role of various factors that appear to us, on an a priori basis, as important determinants of this measure. Let us assume that change in output is a function of changes in natural resources, employment, capital, technology, and institutions and organizations. This can be expressed in notational form as follows:

$$\Delta Y = f(\Delta R, \Delta N, \Delta K, \Delta T, \Delta O)$$

where Y = output, R = natural resources, N = employment, K = capital, T = technology, O = organizational, and institutional framework, and delta (Δ) means "change in."

This equation states that changes in output is a function of changes in those variables appearing on the right hand side of the equation, that is, natural resources, employment, capital, technology, and organizational and institutional framework (Figure 5.1). The variables might be called the "instrument variables" of economic growth or change in output. Of course, it is not easy to determine the causal relationship between Y and the instrument variables. All of them change simultaneously, and the contribution of a single variable is difficult to isolate, but at least some statistical associations are often possible to determine, and have been established by a number of economists.

Changes in Output

Measuring changes in output over time is much more complex than often thought. For this, we need a system of accounts that provide indicators of output change. Many indicators may be used, but they are all subject to certain limitations. Before proceeding with a discussion of specific indicators of output change, a few observations will be made about economic growth as a means of promoting overall development.

A growing economy is one of the goals of economic policy in practically all countries, rich and poor. In recent years, however, particularly in developed countries, this preoccupation with growth has been challenged. It is now pointed out that growth should not be considered as an end in itself, but only as a *means* of promoting development. In fact, it is now widely believed that economic growth produces undesirable as well as desirable consequences. It has been alleged that our preoccupation with producing bigger, better and faster objects to satisfy our insatiable appetites and whims is a kind of "growth mania." The implication is that we have been so concerned about increases in some indicators of income or product that we have neglected some of the side effects of growth that deteriorate the quality of life of people.

Before growth can be considered an end of social policy, it must be demonstrable that economic activity will enhance the level of well-being of at least some human beings. The national income accounts have been designed to provide indicators of aggregate output or, alternatively, on the other side of the accounts, aggregate income to owners of the factors of production. Some of these indicators are GDP, NDP, GNP, net national product (NNP), GNI and net national income, personal income, and personal disposable income.

If we must have a single indicator that shows the growth that has occurred, that indicator must have a way of meaningfully aggregating physically unlike goods and services, such as wheat, milk, houses, clothes, steel, aeroplanes, banking, and insurance. The national income indicators accomplish this by converting these physical units of output into monetary values by multiplying the physical units by market prices. The monetary values of output are, thus, comparable and additive.

This valuation procedure is open to one basic question. Do market prices used as weights accurately reflect the contributions of the respective units of output to aggregate income? The answer seems to be that if product and factor markets are perfectly competitive, and no externalities are present in either consumption or production of the commodities being priced, they do. If the demand for a product is less than perfectly elastic, however, the additions to income due to increase in the output of the product will be reflected by marginal revenue rather than by price, because as output expands, the price of all units sold will decline. Furthermore, if externalities are present in consumption of the product, the market demand price will not reflect the "social" value of the product as it is consumed. By the same token, if externalities are present in production of the product, the product supply price will not reflect the complete "social" productivity of the factors of production. Externalities may be positive or negative, and when they can be shown to exist and can be meaningfully quantified, valuation adjustments may be made to reflect their significance.

An even more serious problem relates to the statistical coverage of the traditional national income indicators. What is needed, of course, is an indicator that captures all changes in the level of output. As a rule, the income accounts provide good coverage of those goods and services that pass through the market, but do not include many of those that do not. This means that the statistical coverage becomes more comprehensive as the economy becomes more complex and the market expands into more and more areas of the economy. If so, the consequence is that the real output of a less developed country is probably understated more by the income accounts than the real output of an advanced country.

Economists and others have recognized that a gross measure of output, such as the real GNP, is not the best indicator of the aggregate size of the growth-producing mechanism called the economy. The reason is that part of gross output is needed to maintain the stock of capital that is part of the productive base of the economy. Some of the category called "gross investment" constitutes net addition to the capital stock, and should, thus, be included in any measure of net productive capacity. But a substantial part of gross investment is simply replacement capital, called "capital depreciation allowance" in the income account. Gross product less capital depreciation allowance is net product. We would argue that change in real net national product is the best indicator of economic growth. But, as stated in Chapter 3, CRDI and HDI are more comprehensive measures of rural development than the real NNP. But, unlike real NNP, their estimation year after year is not yet institutionalized in India.

Although we cannot measure them in the income accounts, it is important to remember that other factors of production have precise parallels to the capital depreciation allowance. Labor sometimes depreciates as production occurs, and maintenance of the stock of human capital at a certain base requires investment in training, schooling, health, and nutrition. Resources taken from the natural environment are depleted and, to that extent, should be netted out of gross productivity figures in an exactly analogous fashion as with capital. The point is equally relevant with respect to the quality as well as well as the quantity of the factors. If the quality of the stock of human capital and of natural resources declines over time, latent productivity of the economy declines, and these deleterious changes should be subtracted from the net product of the system. Contrarily, if the quality of the factor stock improves due to technical advances and increases in knowledge, this latent capacity to produce should be added to the net product actually produced in a given time period.

Perhaps the most devastating limitation of our productivity accounts is the manner in which we deal with negative final products. These are those final outputs of production that cause disutility to human beings and that usually cause deterioration in the natural environment in the form of waste residues and environmental degradation. They also take the form of external diseconomies, such as crowding, pollution, congestion, and crime. Before a true estimate of the effects of growth on human well-being can be assessed, these negative influences on growth should be netted out from the positive ones.

Natural Resources

By a natural resource we mean any product, thing, or circumstance found by man in his natural environment that he may, in some way, utilize for his own benefit. In this sense, the resources provided by nature include air, climate, soil, water, plants, animals, mineral ores, mineral oil, coal, natural gas, solar radiation, and certain amenities that can be used for tourism. As time goes by, the world's resource pattern changes, not because nature's basic provision alters, but because of changes in what constitutes a resource. Natural resources can be classified into two categories: non-renewable or stock resources, such as metal ores, mineral oil, and coal deposits, and renewable or flow resources, such as solar radiation, animal and plant species, and winds, among others. This distinction is very important from the point of view of policies for resource development, conservation and utilization.

Natural resources play a very important role in the process of rural development. Mother Nature provides us natural resources free of cost and performs two important functions in the process of economic growth, namely, providing inputs to production processes and assimilating the wastes generated in the process of production (Figure 5.2). Since planet Earth is finite, closed, and non-growing, there is a natural limit to both these critical functions, that is, both inputs provisioning and waste assimilating capacities of our planet are limited. This means that one cannot go on increasing the production of goods and services using natural resources forever, that is, there are ecological/natural limits to economic growth, hence, it cannot be sustained forever. Sustainable development requires that, in the process of economic growth, we maintain our natural resources and environment intact and use/harvest only that quantity that is regenerated naturally, that is, we live on the "flows" and keep the "stock" of natural resources

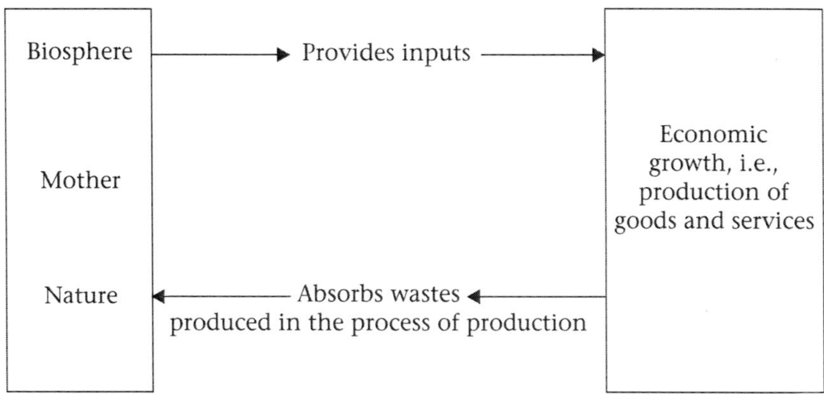

Figure 5.2: *Role of Mother Nature/Environment in Economic Growth*

Source: Author.

and the environment intact. However, we would like to add that it is now possible to augment—through appropriate technological and management interventions—the natural flows/harvest of the products of nature.

For example, fish catches can be increased sustainably through artificial feeding and breeding; crop yields can be increased through application of balanced organic and inorganic fertilizers, bio pesticides, and scientific soil and water management; and forests can be rejuvenated faster and their natural productivity increased through application of fertilizers and water. Thus, the carrying capacity of our biosphere in terms of the population of living beings is, to some extent, amenable to augmentation through technological and managerial interventions. Therefore, contrary to what growthmaniacs and technocrats believe, there are limits to economic growth and also, contrary to what ecologists assert, the limits are not absolutely rigid, that is, they can be relaxed. Proponents of sustainable development recognize this truth and advocate the middle path between the two extremes represented by technocrats and ecologists.

There are three major hypotheses that seek to propound the relation between the natural resources and development: (a) Neo-Malthusian hypothesis; (b) Cornucopian hypothesis; and (c) the Environmental Kuznets Curve (EKC) hypothesis. The proponents of the Neo-Malthusian hypothesis, mostly biologists and ecologists, believe that the carrying capacity of our planet Earth is limited, as the planet is finite, closed, and non-growing. In other words, there is a natural limit to both the critical functions of the environment, that is, the inputs provisioning and waste assimilating capacities of our planet Earth are both limited.[1] On the other extreme, the proponents of the Cornucopian hypothesis have an optimistic perspective. They are mostly technologists, agricultural scientists, and economists. They assert that there is no evidence or reason to fear the catastrophic collapse of societies postulated by the scholars subscribing to the Neo-Malthusian school. Thanks to the incentives provided by competitive markets, entrepreneurs are exploring and developing new sources of energy and minerals, and reserves of many commodities have increased due to new discoveries and/or recycling of wastes. Also, research in agricultural sciences has made it feasible now to augment through appropriate technological and management interventions the natural flows/harvest of products of nature. (Singh and Shishodia 2007, 42–44).

The EKC hypothesis proposes that there is an inverted U shaped relation between quality of environment as measured by some of the indicators of environmental degradation and per capita income, which is an important indicator of development (Figure 5.3). This means

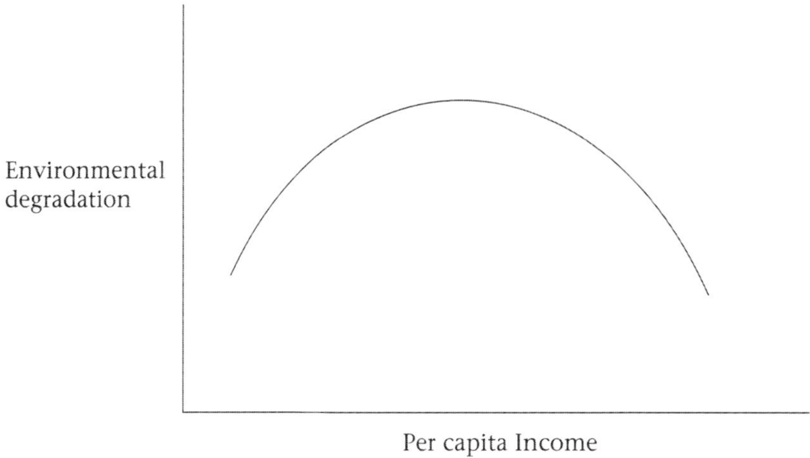

Figure 5.3: *A Typical Environmental Kuznets Curve*

Source: Author.

that environmental degradation is low initially when the per capita income is low, then it increases with increase in per capita income and, eventually, it declines with further increase in per capita income. The EKC is named after Simon Kuznets (1955) who proposed a hypothesis that the relationship between a measure of inequality in the distribution of income and the level of income is depicted by an inverted U-shaped curve. The EKC hypothesis has been interpreted by many scholars to imply that economic growth will eventually redress the adverse environmental impacts of the early stages of economic growth and that continued growth will lead to further improvements in the quality of environment. The hypothesis has been criticized by many scholars on both theoretical and empirical grounds (Stern 1998, 173–96). But overall, the general consensus is that it holds for some but not all environmental indicators and that economic growth alone cannot solve all environmental problems. The best fit is for air pollution and a few indicators of water pollution (Barbier 1997, 357–58).

Following the teachings of India's great philosophers, scholars and *gurus*, we believe in the middle path between the two extremes represented by biologists and ecologists, and technocrats and economists. This means that, contrary to what growthmaniacs and technocrats believe, there are limits to economic growth and, also, contrary to what ecologists assert, the limits are not absolutely rigid; they can be relaxed. We conclude with an optimistic view that, as argued by Simon and Kahn (1984), the 21st century will usher in an era characterized by higher living standards and reduced human impacts on the environment as a result of technological advancements and policy innovations. This view is consistent with the principles underlying sustainable development.

In India, common pool resources (CPRs), that is, resources used by people in common, play a very important role as sources of food, fuel wood, fodder, and many other basic needs of rural people, particularly the poor. India has nearly 100 mha of common pool land, about 30 mha of common pool forests, and the bulk of its water resources and fisheries are also CPRs. One of the major causes of rural poverty in India is the lack of access of the poor to privately owned natural resources and natural CPRs. With the growing commercial exploitation of natural CPRs, the rural poor people find it difficult to meet their basic requirements. Depletion of CPRs of land, forests and water has increased the misery and drudgery of the rural poor, particularly women, who now have to spend a lot of their energy and time in fetching water, fuel wood, and fodder from far-away places. Restoration and judicious management of natural CPRs is essential for improving the well-being of the rural poor, as also for improving the quality of the environment (Singh 1994, 16–20).

At any level of economic development, utilization of domestically available natural resources constitutes the bedrock of an economy. The quantity and quality of available natural resources along with the intensity and efficiency of their use determine, to a considerable extent, the level and pace of the economic development of a nation. Poverty of natural resources does not, however, exclude a high level of economic development, as is shown by the examples of Denmark, Switzerland, Israel, Hong Kong, and Japan. These countries have compensated for the lack of natural resources by appropriate technologies, institutions and organizations, and highly developed human resources. India is relatively well-endowed with natural resources but has not been able to develop and utilize them fully and judiciously for the benefit of its people. Hence, the low level of agricultural and rural development in India.

It is almost invariably true that the poorer a country is, the greater the percentage of its income that goes to the owners of natural resources, and, thus, the greater the importance of natural resources to its economic development. This can be easily demonstrated in the case of food production. In India, about 42% of the total private consumption expenditure (a proxy for income) is spent on food and beverages. Of the total cost of production, approximately 30% is paid out to the owners of land in the form of rent. Thus, approximately 13% of the community's total income is spent on land services alone. This means that so much of the capital wealth in India is held in the form of land. Who owns this land makes a tremendous difference, since economic, political, and social privileges also tend to be associated with land ownership. In a developed country such as the USA, on the other hand, about 10% of the total income is spent on food and approximately 20% of the cost of producing food goes toward land rent. Thus, only a little over 2% of the total community income goes to the owners of land. Land ownership, then, has far less economic and political significance in the US than in India.

The same point is relevant with respect to the production of other products that depend primarily on natural resources. If capital is scarce and labor tends to be unskilled, then the role of land and natural resources of other kinds tends to be very significant in production and their ownership becomes an important social issue.

Human Resources

The size, quality, and extent of utilization of human resources all play an important role in the process of development. The level of utilization in terms of employment is best considered from the viewpoint of the long run and the short run. Over the long run, employment is related primarily to population growth. The correspondence between employment and population growth is especially close in societies such as India where human beings enter the labor force at a young age, where much of the labor is utilized in agricultural pursuits and is, therefore, likely to be utilized even if underemployed. The higher the rate of population growth, the larger will be the amount of labor used relative to the other factors of production.

The important point in this connection, however, is that it takes time and investment to properly educate, and train human beings to make them fully productive. If the time is shortened by the necessity for children to work, the result tends to be less productive labor over the long run. On the other hand, if work is postponed and children go to school, the burden on public institutions, such as the educational establishments, becomes greater and the net consumption embodied in per capita incomes is reduced, as resources go into institutions for training and maintenance rather than for consumption. Thus, per capita incomes are temporarily reduced until people eventually get into the labor force, at which time the per capita incomes are increased if the labor is productive enough to compensate for the time that is spent on schooling and training.

In the short run, on the other hand, employment can be increased by providing more opportunities for people to work. This may be accomplished by offering remunerative wages, which attract previously unemployed workers into the labor force, and by providing a healthy economic environment where jobs are more plentiful.

Research undertaken in developed and developing countries of the world reveals that for an increase in output, the quality of labor is more important than the quantity. A clear picture emerges if one looks at the experience of different countries. No country with an educated, technically trained labor force is poor and no country with a predominantly illiterate, untrained labor force is rich. In general, the quality of the labor force is much more critical in economic development than is the availability of natural resources. Japan is a country that has almost no mineral or energy resources but has high economic productivity because of a highly literate, trained, and efficient working population.

It has also been seen that investment in education and training produces very high internal rates of return in economic output. The returns to basic literacy are especially high. The rate of returns to investment in schooling is in the neighborhood of 50% per year in many rich countries, and in developing countries such as India, the rate of return to primary schooling is even higher. Any poor country that wants to develop could do no better than use its scarce resources in schools, technical education, training, and management.

Another point to note about people and their importance in the development process is that their values and attitudes must be conducive to development. If development is to occur, an increase of income and wealth, held either privately or publicly, must be one of the dominant goals in life. That is, people must have a desire to acquire, accumulate, or consume at increasing levels. If not, development is practically impossible. There is no denying that it was this desire that produced Western technology, money and financial intermediaries, private property, and an economic structure based on free contract and exchange. Some would argue that even political liberty, which increased social mobility, which in turn contributed to development, resulted from the dominance of pecuniary considerations in the hierarchy of privately held goals.

India is a labor surplus country. According to the 2011 population census, India's rural population was 833.1 million, which accounted for 68.84% of the country's total population. Of the total rural population, 118.7 million were cultivators and 144.3 million agricultural workers. The average annual exponential growth rate of population was 1.22% during 2001–11, which was lower than 1.7% registered during the 1991–2001 decade. The quality of the rural labor force is poor in terms of skills, education, training, values and attitudes. Consequently, according to the 2014 Human Development Report, India ranks 135th among countries, with medium human development, out of 187 countries of the world (for which data was available). This does not speak well about the status of human development in India.

The literacy rate for the rural population in India in 2011 was 68.91% as compared to 84.90% for urban population. There is a positive correlation between the literacy rate and real per capita GDP. For a sample of 43 developing countries, the simple correlation between these two variables was 0.48. The poor quality of the rural labor force, in conjunction with very low per capita availability of capital, explains to a large extent the low productivity and, hence, the low per capita incomes in India's rural sector.

Capital

Most development economists from the developed Western countries consider capital to be the key instrument of economic development. The Harrod–Domar model represents a typical example of this school of thought. In this model, capital accumulation plays a crucial role in the process of economic growth, as the rate of economic growth is expressed as the product of the savings rate and output–capital ratio. Capital formation is, therefore, an important prerequisite of economic development. Much of new technology, such as high yielding seeds, chemical fertilizers and pesticides, tractors, combine harvesters, and food processing plants, is embodied in capital. Increases in the capital stock lead to increases in the marginal productivity of labor that, in turn, generally enhances wage rates.

Capital can be classified in various ways. Long-term capital is embodied in improvements in land, machinery, equipment, basic infrastructure, and other long-lived forms of capital, while operating capital exists in the form of seeds, fertilizers, fuel, and other raw materials that are used up annually in the production process.

Moreover, capital may also be classified according to whether it is owned publicly or privately. Private capital is managed by the individual entrepreneur and its examples are those listed previously in the examples of long-term and operating capital. Public capital, on the other hand, is the society's investment in infrastructure such as roads, schools, hospitals, national defense, and various government establishments. Private capital is, of course, acquired by individuals by their own decisions to consume less than they earn. Public capital, on the other hand, is produced by joint action through political processes, but can also come into being because the society earns more than it consumes. For promoting rural development, both private and public capital investments are necessary. At present, both types of investments in India fall short of the requirement and, hence, the level and pace of rural development have been affected adversely.

Looking at capital formation from the vantage point of the economy, capital resources can be acquired in one of the following two ways: First, by domestic saving, or second, by foreign aid. In most countries, domestic savings can be acquired from three sources. The first is from private citizens who consume less than their incomes and make the difference available in the form of investment to the economy. In rich countries, people save as a matter, of course, in their attempt to provide security against various contingencies and, thus, the saving takes the form of insurance premiums, retirement annuities, bank accounts, and so on. Since these choices are made voluntarily, people consider their well-being enhanced in the process of saving and, therefore, no deprivation is involved. In poor countries, on the other hand, saving is often painful, because most of the people live so close to the edge of hunger and disease and they need all their income for consumption alone. As a result, savings are usually meager. But, in India, of late, domestic saving has been increasing in all sectors. For example, as shown in Table 5.1, in 1950–51, the average rate of gross savings at current prices in all sectors was only 9.5% of India's GDP, which increased to 25.5% in 2000–01 and to 30.7% in 2013–14. Similarly, the average rate of gross saving in the household (private) sector increased from 6.5% in 1950–51 to 18.2% in 2013–14 and in the public sector, it marginally increased from 2.1% in 1950–51 to 2.6% in 2010–11 but declined to 1.6% in 2013–14, due perhaps to the launching of a new series (GoI 2014, Statistical Appendix Table 1.6) If the society needs more savings than are available by private decisions to save, then saving must be forced by inflation.

Second, savings can be acquired from corporations, which as a rule, in an effort to expand, take some of their earnings and plough them back into the firm for additional capital formation. In rich countries, where corporations are numerous, large, and powerful, this form of savings and the concomitant capital formation is extremely important. In India, the average rate of gross savings in both the private corporate sector and public sector has been increasing but is still very low. For example, as shown in Table 2.1, in 1950–51, it was 0.9% in the private corporate sector, which increased to 10.9% in 2013–14.

Third, governments can acquire resources for purposes of capital formation through taxes and inflation. Income tax, property tax, excise tax, value-added tax, and so on, all have their own

Table 5.1: *Gross Domestic Saving at Current Prices as % of Gross Domestic Product of India, 1950–51 to 2013–14*

Year	*Household Sector*	*Private Corporate Sector*	*Public Sector*	*Total*
1950–51	6.5	0.9	2.1	9.5
1960–61	6.5	0.9	2.1	9.5
1970–71	9.5	1.4	3.4	14.3
1980–81	12.1	1.6	4.1	17.8
1990–91	18.5	2.6	1.8	22.9
2000–01	21.7	4.3	0.5	25.5
2005–06	23.5	7.5	2.4	33.4
2010–11	23.1	8.0	2.6	33.7
2013–14*	18.2	10.9	1.6	30.7

Source: MoF (2014, Table 1.6, pp. A14–16, Statistical Appendix).
Note: *New series estimate.

advantages and disadvantages. However, space will not permit an evaluation of various forms of taxation.

Inflation is also a form of taxation. The government causes inflation by increasing the money supply, which creates excess demand for goods and services. This results in price rises and the average rise in a composite index of prices is known as inflation. With the money created by running printing presses or selling securities, the government buys goods and services. These may take the form of investment capital. Inflation is really a tax on cash balances, since those individuals and organizations in the economy who hold cash balances see their purchasing power getting eroded by inflation. There is, thus, a transfer of wealth from those who hold money in the form of cash balances to those (in this case the government) who obtain the resources through the creation of money. It is possible, of course, to analyze and evaluate the efficiency and equity effects of inflation vis-à-vis other forms of taxation to raise funds for government use. But this is not within the purview of this chapter.

Of course, saving is only one prong in the process of capital formation. Somehow the saving generated in the economy must be made available to the investors, that is, those who actually produce the capital formation. If the primary reliance is given to private savings, then an organizational base must be available to make the transfer of funds to investors. In most countries, these organizations are the commercial banks, savings and loan associations, insurance companies, and credit cooperatives. Likewise, if government funds are available for investment, whether they come from external aid, taxation, or money creation, there must be an institutional base to transfer the resources to investors. In many countries (including India), these take the form of central banks, and industrial and agricultural banks.

Foreign aid has been used extensively since World War II as a form of transfer of international capital from one country to another. It should be pointed out, however, that many of the advanced countries of today received much of their development capital from external sources. The US and Canada were aided tremendously in the take-off phase of their development by foreign capital shipments, particularly from the UK. There is one major difference, however, between that period and the present day. The bulk of the development capital that fueled the take-off in the US and Canada came from private foreign sources. Profit opportunities were unusually high and this attracted capital that was seeking these profits. It goes without saying that, since the capital transfer was made voluntarily, both borrowers and lenders were benefited by it.

There is also much private capital that goes abroad today. Large multinational corporations and international firms have established branches in many countries, including India. However, for development purposes, large quantities of financial resources are obtained from international organizations, such as the World Bank, the Asian Development Bank (ADB), the Inter-American Development Bank (IADB), and through foreign aid from government to government. Again, as long as the transfers are mutually beneficial and voluntary, there is a lot to be gained by both the grantor and the grantee. Since a large amount of international capital is available through grants or low-cost loans, the recipients do not worry too much about the economic feasibility of projects utilizing these funds. This is a needless waste of scarce resources. International grants and low-cost loans should be administered just as tightly and economically as high-cost loans. The real cost to the economy of using these funds, regardless of source or terms, are the foregone opportunities of using the resources in their most productive alternative. These capital funds should be allocated to uses where they generate the greatest productivity. Planning should be just as tight and rigorous with foreign aid resources, in terms of determining their use in the economy, as would be the case if the resources were generated through domestic saving.

India's rural sector is starved of capital, and this is perhaps one of the most serious constraints on rural development. The rate of capital formation in the rural sector has been low vis-à-vis the rate required for achieving a higher level of rural development. Furthermore, much of the surplus generated in the sector is siphoned off to the urban sector for a variety of reasons, including lack of institutional arrangements for mopping up small savings and providing incentives to small savers.

Technology

In all likelihood, technological advance is the most important factor that accounts for economic development. In many ways, it is the *sine qua non* of development, that is, it *is* development. Studies in the advanced countries have shown that increases in natural resources, employment, and capital have accounted for less than one-half of the increases in output over time. The bulk of growth must, therefore, be accounted for by qualitative rather than quantitative increases in the factors of production. In essence, this is what technological advance is—an improvement in the processes of production, which produces increases in output per unit of input. It is improvements in knowledge and knowhow; it is improved skills; it is utilizing better machinery and equipment, all of which combine to increase productivity.

Many students of development, notably Hayami and Ruttan (1970), Schultz (1964), and Rostow (1960) have constructed theories of development that have technological advance at the very center of concern. Schultz has argued that the transition from traditional to modern agriculture is essentially one of utilizing modern inputs, which are defined as those that are technologically advanced. In Rostow's scheme, once the static stage of traditional life has been disturbed, society passes through the later stages of: (a) establishment of the preconditions for growth; (b) take-off; (c) drive to maturity; and (d) mass consumption. During the period of the establishment of the preconditions for growth, the insights of modern science begin to be translated into new production functions. This is just another way of saying that technological advance is occurring.

Schumpeter (1949) distinguishes between the two classes of influences upon the dynamic evolution of an economy, such as: (a) the effects of changes in factor availability, which he calls the "growth" component; and (b) the effects of technological and social changes, which he refers to as "development" or "evolution." In his view, development covers five combinations, which are as follows:

1. The introduction of a new commodity.
2. The introduction of a new method of production.
3. The opening of a new market.
4. The conquest of a new source of supply of raw materials or half-manufactured goods.
5. The reorganization of an industry, such as the creation of a monopoly position or breaking down a monopoly situation.

In Schumpeter's model of economic development, the entrepreneur is the central figure. He revolutionizes the pattern of production by exploiting inventions, by exploiting untried technological possibilities for producing new commodities, by producing old commodities in new ways, and so on. For entrepreneurial activity to flourish, the capitalist rationality and bourgeois institutions are important prerequisites. Schumpeter also assigned an important role to credit as a means of enabling entrepreneurs to obtain productive resources and to carry out innovation. He emphasizes the importance of innovation in generating business cycles. In Schumpeter's opinion, there is no limit to the increase in the rate of output per head.

The critical question is, of course, how to promote a high rate of technical change. In the first place, the general economic climate must be conducive to innovation and knowledge building. As a rule, if incentives exist for individuals to innovate, they *will*. A country that has a sizeable, and educated and skilled middle class can rely largely on the profit motive to push inventors, scientists, and entrepreneurs to undertake technological advances. In conservative, traditional societies, however, public institutions must also play a very large role. Educational institutions are crucial at all levels. So are the experiment stations and the extension services. Empirical studies from both rich and poor countries clearly demonstrate that the rates of return from public investment in these knowledge building institutions and activities are very high. Over the long run, no country can afford to neglect these institutions that act as agents of change in producing and implementing technical change.

Prior to 1965, the outlook for agriculture in India was discouraging. But the post-1965 era was characterized by a marked spurt in the use of modern inputs, such as high yielding seeds, chemical fertilizers, plant protection chemicals, and improved farm machines, tools, and equipment.

In his 1970 presidential address to the Indian Economic Association (IEA), Dantwala (1970, 165–92) reviewed various economic, technological, institutional, and organizational factors that had been given credit for the so-called "technical breakthrough" or the Green Revolution in Indian agriculture. He concluded that land tenure, credit, marketing, extension services, education, relative prices, taxes, and subsidies were all of minor significance when compared with new technology. He arrived at his conclusion by a process of elimination: technology was the only causal factor that changed significantly between the pre-1965 stagnation and the post-1965 Green Revolution. What he did not appreciate was the fact that both the introduction and spread of new technology were facilitated by the efforts of various institutions and organizations, including agricultural universities, and provision of extension education services, credit, marketing, and subsidies. It is, however, true that new—and appropriate—technology is a necessary condition for economic growth. But new technology unsupported by appropriate institutions and organizations cannot bring about a transformation of traditional agriculture. Now India has access to the latest available new technology in the field of crop production, but still its average crop yields are very low when compared to developed countries (for details, see Table 2.8 in Chapter 2) What are the factors that can explain this vast yield differential? Certainly, natural resources and knowledge of new technology cannot. It is the level and intensity of the use of available new technology that explains these differentials, and which is a function of supporting institutions and organizations, including government policies and programs in the fields of input and output prices, credit, marketing, subsidies, and land reforms. One of the major factors responsible for low crop yields in Indian agriculture is the low level of use of fertilizers. Judicious use of fertilizers is crucial in order to grow enough food to ensure food security. New Zealand is leading the Asia and Pacific region in fertilizer application rates with almost 1.4 tons per hectare, followed by China with 450 kg per hectare. Other top users are Republic of Korea (ROK) with 293 kg, Malaysia, with 282 kg, Bangladesh with 227 kg, Japan with 243 kg, Pakistan with 194 kg, and India with only164 kg per hectare (FAO 2014, 16).

India has an impressive infrastructure for agricultural education and research comprising 53 state agricultural universities (SAUs), one Central agricultural university (CAU), five Institutes having deemed-to-be-universities (DUs) status (four of them are ICAR Institutes: IARI, New Delhi; IVRI, Izatnagar; NDRI, Karnal; and CIFE, Mumbai and, the fifth, Allahabad Agricultural Institute, Allahabad) and four Central universities (CUs) with agriculture faculty (BHU Varanasi; AMU Aligarh; Vishwa Bharti, Shantiniketan; and Nagaland University, Medziphema)

Besides, there are 45 national/Central research Institutes, all established by the Indian Council of Agricultural Research (ICAR), 17 national research centers, six national bureaux, eight regional agro-economic research centers, and numerous other public and private organizations engaged in research on issues of agricultural and rural development, and finding out solutions for them. Both ICAR institutions and SAUs have played a significant role in ushering in the Green Revolution in the country. What is needed now is a change in the orientation of researchers toward demand-driven, problem-solving and action-oriented research. There is also an urgent need to step up public and private investment in agriculture research.

While examining the role of new technology in rural development, I would like to caution that the adoption of technologies that are not appropriate may cause serious damage to the biosphere, albeit unintentionally. The general economic and political environments prevailing in the developing countries tend to favor and promote environmentally harmful technologies. For example, an indiscriminate use of chemical fertilizers, and the effluents discharged by firms producing such chemicals as napthol, and disulphonic acid and its derivatives, pollute the rivers, streams, land and air, and cause hazards to human health and reduce the longevity of the affected people. People in India, particularly the poor, suffer more from such hazards, as there are neither property rights nor liability rules to protect them. Therefore, it is necessary that the environmental impacts of new technologies are carefully evaluated before they are recommended for wider use.

Organizational and Institutional Framework

As already mentioned, rural development is influenced by a multitude of factors, such as natural resources, human resources (labor), capital, technology, and institutions and organizations. Although the classical and neoclassical economists emphasized the role of natural resources, labor, technology, and investment in economic development, they did not assign any significant role to institutions and organizations in the process of development. They assumed the institutional setup of the economy as a given (exogenous) and, hence, beyond scientific analysis. As a matter of fact, they even argued for minimizing the role of the government in the process of development and advocated a policy of laissez-faire. It was the institutional economists and Karl Marx who recognized the significant role that institutions and organizations play in the process of economic development.

The terms "organization" and "institution" are often used interchangeably. We consider organizations as a subset of the broader set of institutional structures or arrangements. An organization connotes coordinated acts or endeavors of two or more individuals. It is created to give effect to a certain institutional arrangement. The main function of an economic organization is to provide signals that will guide the self-interested economic agents/entities to act in the interest of the larger community. The main task of any nation-state is to create institutional arrangements that provide the needed signals to individual economic entities. Markets provide such signals efficiently, so long as they operate with low transaction costs. Non-market mechanisms, such as government agencies and NGOs, including cooperatives, can also provide such signals.

Institutions and organizations are important aids to development. They may affect agricultural and rural development in many different ways, including the provision of production inputs and services, reduction of transaction costs, enhancement of the bargaining power of rural producers vis-à-vis those to whom they sell their produce and from whom they buy production inputs and services, influencing investments and savings and bringing the two together, and so on. The economic life of any community takes place in a milieu of organizations and institutions. They largely determine the economic structure of the community, and set the rules in which the economic game is played. Changes in these organizations and institutions over time will probably have a pronounced effect on the economic output and development. Often these effects are difficult to isolate and measure because of the interdependence between changes in organizations and institutions, and between other instrument variables of agricultural development.

There are many forms of organizations, such as public (government), sole proprietorship, partnership, company, cooperative, and charitable trust, that can serve—and are, in fact, serving—the needs of the farmers in India. The form of organization suitable for promoting agricultural development should fully identify with the interests of the farmers and should be fully oriented to meeting their needs, both organizationally and operationally.

The government has been—still is and will continue in the near future to be—an important organization in the field of agricultural and rural development in India. Development is seen as the specific responsibility of the government. This has far reaching implications for the role of public bureaucracy, which is the arm of the state responsible for carrying out the wishes of the political leaders. Efforts to bring about improvement in the quality of life of the rural people depend heavily on government administration and bureaucrats.

At the institutional level, laws of property and contract have a profound impact on economic growth. The essential questions here are as follows:

1. What may a man do with his property?
2. What may others do to his property?
3. In what kinds of economic activity may he engage?

Some societies, such as Japan, are fairly liberal in permitting private firms and individuals to operate without restrictions, while others impose many restrictions that curtail private profits in the name of protecting the broad public interest. Other questions relate to what kinds of agreements private individuals may make; what kinds of claims and contracts can be enforced and to what extent, and so on.

All these questions relate to the influence of government regulation of business activity and its impact on economic growth. How tightly are specific kinds of business activities regulated by the government? How are the taxes, tariffs, subsidies, and other fees utilized to discourage certain activities and encourage others? How are the taxes and laws of inheritance used to control the distribution of income at the expense of economic growth? All these forces and factors determine the incentives for economic production and must not be neglected in the search for a favorable institutional and organizational climate for economic development.

The only organization that conceptually satisfies all the criteria of a good rural organization is a cooperative. The cooperative form of organization is solely designed for promoting the mutual interests of its user patrons on the basis of equality and equity. It is controlled by them on a democratic basis. It also resolves the conflict of interests between the lender and the borrower, or between the seller and the buyer, for, in it, the lender and the borrower, or the seller and buyer are the same person. The objective is not to do business for the sake of profits only, but for meeting the members' needs. It is a local organization, and provides for local participation. It is responsive to local needs, as its policy is decided democratically by the local members/users. It serves as a training ground for the rural people in business and in democracy.

In India, the Anand-pattern dairy cooperatives have demonstrated what appropriate institutions and organizations can do to initiate and foster agricultural and rural development. Similarly, sugar cooperatives also have contributed significantly to rural development.

Besides cooperatives, there are many other forms of formal and non-formal associations that could do a good job of promoting agricultural and rural development. For example, Sadguru Water and Development Foundation, a Dahod (Gujarat)-based NGO; SEWA, an Ahmedabad (Gujarat)-based NGO; and PRADAN, a Delhi-based NGO, promote people's organizations at the grassroots level to take up agricultural and rural development projects.

The role of the NGOs is to organize people and help them with technical information, training and, to some extent, with funds. Besides, they also help grassroots organizations to secure financial assistance from various governmental and nongovernmental sources. In most cases, the performance of the programs taken up under the auspices of the NGOs has been better than that of government programs. However, this statement cannot be generalized as there are many NGOs that do not have the necessary technical and managerial expertise, and financial discipline to initiate and support agricultural and rural development programs. Indian corporations and companies could play a pivotal role in promoting agricultural development. In fact, many blue chip companies such as the Tatas, Mafatlals, Larsen and Toubro, and Hindustan Unilever, and associations of industrialists such the Confederation of Indian Industry (CII) and the Federation of Indian Chambers of Commerce and Industry (FICCI), have already won laurels for their exemplary work in the field of agricultural and rural development, not only from Indian NGOs, and government organizations, but also from international donors and development agencies. Corporations can bring the benefits of modern science and technology, management, and world markets to the agricultural sector, and thereby promote agricultural development, particularly now, in the era of liberalization, deregulation, privatization, and globalization.

Relation Between Rural Development and Its Determinants

It is not easy to quantify the relationship between rural development and the various determinants discussed in the preceding section. For one thing, there are no time series data available on any acceptable measure of rural development, nor on these determinants, some of which cannot be quantified at all. Second, all these determinants keep changing simultaneously, and it is not possible to isolate and measure the contribution of any single determinant without resorting to some sophisticated econometric techniques.

A few attempts have been made in the past to measure the impact of some of these determinants on rural development. For instance, Hayami and Ruttan (1970, 895–911) attempted to explain the differences in agricultural output per worker (a proxy for agricultural development) between a representative group of developed and developing countries, and found that, (a) resource endowment (land and livestock); (b) technology (fertilizers and machinery); and (c) human capital (general and technical education) accounted for 95% of the differences. The implications of their analysis for an agricultural development strategy for developing countries are clear. An attempt must be made to close the gap in the use of modern industrial inputs, education, and research between the developed and developing countries. Agricultural surplus generated by closing the gap, over and above the amount necessary to maintain the growth of agricultural productivity, must be used to finance industrial development. In India as well, a number of studies have been conducted, mostly at the farm level, to determine the effect of land, water (irrigation), fertilizers, labor, and power on farm production and income. These studies furnish valuable information about the nature and magnitude of the impact of various determinants on farm income. However, there is a need for conducting macro-level studies aimed at determining the relationship between some acceptable measure of rural development and various factors affecting it.

Key Points

1. There are many physical, technological, economic, socio-cultural, institutional, organizational, and political factors that affect the level and pace of rural development. These factors operate at all levels: household, village, district, state, nation, and the world as a whole. Depending upon how they are managed, these factors can have both favorable and adverse effects on development. Knowledge about the nature and magnitude of the impact of various determinants on rural development is necessary for rural development managers to be able to use these factors to achieve their goals efficiently and effectively.
2. In the absence of a single index of rural development, we generally use change in output as its proxy measure and examine the role of various factors that appear to us, on an a priori basis, as important determinants of this measure. It is assumed that a change in output is a function of the changes in natural resources, employment, capital, technology, and institutions and organizations including governance.
3. Measuring changes in output over time is much more complex than often thought. For this, we need a system of accounts that provides the indicators of output change. The national income accounts provide the indicators of aggregate output. Some of these indicators are the GNP, NNP, national income, personal income, and personal disposable income.
4. Physically unlike goods and services, such as wheat, milk, houses, clothes, steel, aeroplanes, banking, insurance, and so on, are aggregated into a single measure by converting the physical units of output into monetary values by multiplying the physical units by market prices. The monetary values of output are, thus, comparable and additive.
5. A gross measure of output, such as the real GNP is not the best indicator of economic growth, as part of the gross output is needed to maintain the stock of capital in a productive form. In view of this, an increase in the real NNP is the best indicator of economic growth. The CRDI and the HDI are more comprehensive measures of rural development than the real NNP. But unlike the real NNP, their estimation year after year is not yet institutionalized in India.

6. Natural resources including the environment have a significant effect on output, or economic growth. The environment—or Mother Nature—performs two important functions in the process of economic growth, namely, provision of inputs to production processes and assimilation of the wastes generated in the process of production. Since our planet Earth is finite, closed and non-growing, there is a natural limit to both these critical functions. This means that economic growth cannot be sustained forever.
7. Sustainable development requires that in the process of economic growth, we maintain our natural resources and environment intact and use/harvest only that much quantity that is regenerated naturally. However, it is now possible to augment the natural flows/harvest of products of nature through appropriate technological and managerial interventions.
8. Poverty of natural resources does not exclude a high level of economic development, as is shown by the examples of Denmark, Switzerland, Israel, Hong Kong and Japan. These countries have compensated for the lack of natural resources by appropriate technologies, institutions and organizations, and highly developed and skilled human resources. India is relatively well endowed with natural resources, but has not been able to develop and utilize them fully and judiciously for the benefit of its people. Similarly, India's human resources are not properly developed and utilized. Hence, the low level of agricultural and rural development in India.
9. Human resources play an important role in the process of development. Research undertaken in the developed and developing countries of the world reveals that for an increase in output, the quality of labor is more important than the quantity. This is evident from the fact no country with an educated, technically trained and skilled labor force is poor, and no country with a predominantly illiterate, untrained and unskilled labor force is rich. Japan is a country that has almost no mineral or energy resources, but has high economic productivity because of a highly literate, trained and efficient working population.
10. The poor quality of the rural labor force in terms of education, training and skills, in conjunction with very low per capita availability of capital, explains to a large extent the low productivity and, hence, the low per capita incomes in India's rural sector.
11. Capital is considered by most development economists to be the key instrument of economic development. Capital formation is, therefore, an important prerequisite of economic development. Much of the new technology such as high yielding seeds, chemical fertilizers and pesticides, tractors, combine harvesters, and food processing plants, is embodied in capital. Increases in the capital stock lead to increases in the marginal productivity of labor that, in turn, generally enhances the wage rates.
12. Capital resources can be acquired by domestic saving and/or by foreign aid. Governments can also acquire resources for purposes of capital formation through taxes and inflation. India's rural sector is starved of capital and this is perhaps one of the most serious constraints on rural development.
13. The rate of capital formation in the rural sector has been low vis-à-vis the rate required for achieving a higher level of rural development. Furthermore, much of the surplus generated in the sector is siphoned off to the urban sector for a variety of reasons, including a lack of institutional arrangements for mopping up small savings and providing incentives to small savers.
14. Technological advance is the most important factor that accounts for economic development. In many ways it is the sine qua non of development, that is, it is development in and by itself. Studies in the advanced countries have shown that increases

in natural resources, employment, and capital have accounted for less than one-half of the increases in output over time. The bulk of growth must, therefore, be accounted for by technology. Many students of development, notably Schumpeter, Schultz, and Rostow, have constructed theories of development that have technological advance at the very center of concern.

15. The critical question is, of course, how to promote a high rate of technical change. This can be done by creating the general economic climate that is conducive to innovation and knowledge building. Educational and research institutions are crucial at all levels of development. In India, the extent of use of the available new technology in the rural sector is very low, which explains the low level of rural development to a large extent.
16. Institutions and organizations are important aids to development. They affect agricultural and rural development in many different ways, including the provision of production inputs and services, reduction of transaction costs, enhancement of bargaining power of rural producers, influencing investments and savings, and bringing the two together, and so on.
17. There are many forms of organizations, such as public (government), sole proprietorship, partnership, company, cooperative, and charitable trust, that can—and in fact, do—cater to the needs of the rural people in India. The form of organization suitable for promoting agricultural development should fully identify with the interests of the people, and should be fully oriented—both organizationally and operationally—to meet their needs. In India, the Anand-pattern dairy cooperatives have demonstrated what appropriate institutions and organizations can do to initiate and foster agricultural and rural development.
18. It is not easy to quantify the relationship between rural development and the various factors that affect it. This is mainly because there are no reliable time series data available on any acceptable measure of rural development or on its determinants. However, only a few attempts, including the one made by Hayami and Ruttan, have been made in the past to measure the impact of some of these determinants on rural development. There is need for conducting macro-level studies aimed at determining the relationship between some acceptable measure of rural development and the various factors affecting it.

Questions for Discussion

1. Discuss how human resources can have both favorable and adverse effects on development.
2. What are the limitations of real net national product (NNP) as a measure of rural development?
3. Most of India's natural resources and environment are degraded and polluted due to mismanagement. Suggest measures for their restoration and making them more productive so as to sustain, if not improve, the present rate of economic growth.
4. Outline a pragmatic strategy for development and proper utilization of India's human resources, particularly the rural poor.
5. India's rural sector is starved of capital and whatever surplus is generated in the sector is siphoned off to urban areas for various reasons. Suggest measures for reversing this trend.
6. India now has access to the latest agricultural technologies but its crop yields are still very low relative to those in such countries as China, Mexico, Israel, Japan, US, and Canada. Explain why.

7. Discuss the strengths and weaknesses of a cooperative as an organization for promoting rural development.
8. What are the problem in quantifying the relation between rural development and its determinants?

Assignment

Compare and contrast one relatively developed state, for example, Punjab, and one relatively under-developed state, for example, Chhattisgarh, in terms of the major determinants of development discussed in this chapter and identify the major factors that could explain the higher level of development in Punjab.

Note

1. The Club of Rome report, *The Limits to Growth* (Meadows, Meadows, Randers, and Behrens 1972), for example, predicted that if the current patterns of population growth and resource consumption continue, the world economic system would collapse by the mid-21st century. However, this has not happened and, hence, their prediction proved to be wrong.

Chapter 6

Rural Development Policies

LEARNING OUTCOMES

After having gone through this chapter, students should be able to

- **Define public policy and differentiate the concepts of "policy," "program" and "project";**
- **Illustrate how a public policy, say, rural credit policy, curbs as well increases the freedom of a farmer borrower;**
- **Identify the major reasons why we need a "Rural Development Policy" in India;**
- **Explain the major goals of "Rural Development Policy" and their rationale;**
- **Explain the concept of "Hierarchy of Policy Goals," and illustrate how and when a goal becomes a means of achieving a superior goal;**
- **Know the major Rural Development Policies of India and their salient features; and**
- **Critically examine the implications of globalization and liberalization for rural development.**

Introduction

Webster's dictionary defines "policy" as a definite course of action selected (as by the government, an institution, a group, or an individual) from among alternatives, and in the light of given conditions to guide and usually to determine present and future decisions. The most common social and political usage of the term "policy" refers to a course of action or intended course of action conceived of as deliberately adopted after a review of possible alternatives, and pursued or oriented to be pursued. The policy process is the formulation, promulgation, and application of these courses of action. Here, we will concern ourselves with public rural development policy, by which we mean the actions taken by the government in the pursuit of certain objectives of rural development. Rural development, as usual, includes agricultural development as well.

It is important to distinguish at the outset between: (a) policy, (b) program, and (c) project. Policy is a comprehensive term and connotes, as mentioned earlier, a set of intended actions. It subsumes programs that are narrower in scope than policy, but more specific with regard to what is to be done, how, by whom, and where. A policy has to be translated into a number of programs before it can be implemented. A project is highly specific and detailed in terms of its objectives, location, duration, funds, and executing agency and lends itself to planning, financing, and implementing as a unit. A program may consist of several projects. A rural development project may be defined as an investment activity, where resources are expended to create a producing asset from which we can expect to realize benefits over an extended period of time.

This chapter first presents a few basic elements of public policy, including a conceptual framework and rationale of public policy. This is followed by an overview of India's major public policies related to the rural sector. Finally, we briefly discuss the important implications of globalization for rural development. The main objective of the chapter is to familiarize the student with the basic elements of public theory and the salient features of India's rural development policies launched from time to time.

Freedom, Control, and Public Policy

Public policy is a form of social control. A farmer accepting a production loan from a nationalized bank and a subsidy from the government is restricted in the manner in which he can spend the borrowed money and subsidy, but his freedom to expand his output, improve his income and standard of living, and develop his individual talents is enhanced. The farmer is struggling with the dilemma of freedom and control. As an individual, he cherishes his dignity and independence; as a social being, he has to realize the necessity for discipline and control. However, like so many other dilemmas, this too is sophistry, based upon two alternatives that are made to appear exhaustive and mutually exclusive. Freedom and control are not mutually exclusive alternatives: they are two principles that can be compatible. In fact, the basic purpose of restraining certain actions through social controls is to safeguard the freedom for certain other actions.

A distinction between "license" and "freedom" is useful here. If license is defined as self-gratification harmful to others and freedom is defined as self-expression not harmful to others, then social controls can promote freedom by restricting license. Seen from this perspective, there is no necessary conflict between freedom and control. In fact, social controls can serve to expand individual freedom. So the real problem is not how we can avoid social control; it is rather, how we can make social controls so selective that they will restrain license and promote freedom in the larger interest of society.

Need for a Rural Development Policy

The farther away we move from simple, small-scale handicraft industry, and self-contained and subsistence agriculture, a greater need develops for public policy in the economic field. The individual, as a producer and as a consumer, depends more and more upon the general conditions of the market, of employment, output, and production efficiency of the nation as a whole, and upon the way income is distributed among the people; in short, upon the economic welfare of the country. Some specific reasons favoring government intervention in the rural sector are as follows.

India's Commitment to Set Up a "Socialist Pattern Society"

India has chosen to establish a "socialist pattern of society." This means that the basic criterion for determining the lines of development must not be private profit, but social gain, and that the pattern of development and the structure of socio-economic relations should be so planned that they result not only in appreciable increases in national income and employment, but also in greater equality in incomes and wealth (GoI 1961, 30). But the experience in India so far has been that the benefits of development have not been equitably shared by all. This has aggravated the problem of poverty, which has manifested itself in various forms, including rising unemployment and anti-social activities, malnutrition, growth of slums, fall in real wages, and impoverishment of marginal and small farmers. The problems of poverty and employment extant in India—even after 68 years of independence—undermine the principal objective of planned development, which is improvement in the standard of living of the masses. It has been acknowledged that a high rate of growth is not a substitute for deliberate policies that seek to ensure equitable distribution of the gains of development. Therefore, there is a need for a public policy to ensure growth with social equity or social justice.

Violent Fluctuations in Agricultural Production, Prices, and Incomes

Agricultural production, being biological in nature, is more vulnerable to the vagaries of nature than non-farm production and, hence, it fluctuates more violently than industrial production in response to such climatic aberrations as erratic rainfall, floods, hailstorms, and so on. Fluctuations in agricultural output lead to still higher fluctuations in agricultural prices and, hence, agricultural incomes. This is because the demand for most agricultural products is inelastic, having less than 1.00 value or, alternatively, because of higher price flexibility of agricultural produce with respect to changes in the supply. This means, in simple words, that a 1% increase in the price of a farm produce, say, wheat or rice, is associated with less than 1% decrease in its demand or, alternatively, a 1% decline in the price of a farm produce is associated with less than 1% increase in its demand. Most farmers, being small-scale operators and poor, cannot bear the consequences of fluctuations in farm output prices and incomes. They need some protection from the adverse effects of the free market and niggardly nature. Such protection can be provided only by the government in the form of price support, insurance, and credit policies.

High Incidence of Rural Poverty

As we stated earlier in Chapter 2 of this book, the incidence of poverty in rural areas in India is higher than in urban areas. As per the Rangarajan Expert Group Report, in 2011–12, the poverty ratio was 39.9% in rural areas and 26.4% in urban areas, and the number of people below the poverty was 260.5 million in rural areas and 102.5 million in urban areas. This is in contrast to the corresponding estimates of 216.7 million and 53.1 million for rural and urban areas as per the Tendulkar Expert Group Report (GoI 2014, Table 4.7, p. 69; see also Chapter 2). The rural–urban gap in poverty is further corroborated by the gap in the average MPCE. As per the household expenditure survey conducted by NSSO in 2011–12, the ratio of urban to rural per capita consumption increased from 1.76 in 1999–2000 to about 2.00 in 2011–12, which suggests that the urban–rural divide is widening. If the comparison is extended to gaps in the availability of other essential services, the chasm is much deeper.

Similarly, the average per capita income in rural areas is also lower than in urban areas. The average annual per worker income in the agricultural sector over the period 1998–99 to 2003–04 was ₹11,496 at 1993–94 prices, as against 59,961 in the non-agricultural sector (Radhakrishna 2008, 45). Thus, the material blessings of development in India have been more bountiful for urban people than for the rural masses. This is true for other countries as well. The injustice of the plight of the rural people is reason enough for government intervention to support rural income and improve its distribution through anti-poverty programs.

Small, Scattered, and Unorganized Rural Enterprises

Most rural enterprises are small, scattered, and unorganized. Due to these characteristics, their owners have very low or practically no bargaining power vis-à-vis those to whom they sell their produce and from whom they buy their supplies. This results in exploitation on both fronts—selling as well as buying. This heightens the need for government policies aimed at equalizing opportunities, strengthening the bargaining power of individuals and groups in rural areas, and restraining the powerful from exploiting the weak.

Inadequate and Poor Basic Infrastructure in Rural Areas

Rural areas are at a great disadvantage in relation to urban areas, as far as the provision of basic infrastructural facilities and services, such as roads, drinking water, electricity, schools, hospitals, police protection, transport, and communications, is concerned. Not only are these public facilities and amenities in rural areas inadequate, but they are also very poorly organized and undependable. As a result, poor villagers are damned, generation after generation, to poor education, poor health care facilities, poor sanitation, unemployment, and poverty. Improvement of their plight requires intensive government intervention. In fact, the government has intervened by launching programs such as the NRHM, MNP, TPP, and BNP and PURA (see Chapter 11 for details).

Predominant Place of Agriculture in India's Economy

Agriculture is the single largest sector of India's economy. In 2013–14, agriculture and allied activities contributed about 18% of India's GDP at current prices and 14% at the 2004–05 prices[1]. It is also the main source of livelihood for about two-thirds of India's population. Agricultural and rural development is, in fact, the sine qua non of national development. Therefore, a meaningful strategy of national development must have agricultural and rural development as one of its major planks.

Goals of Rural Development Policy

Rural development policies are designed to improve the conditions under which the rural people work and live. The goals of policies are governed by what people desire, and the measures of policies by what people think the government can and ought to do to bring about the desired change. This is the theory of public policy. Changes are desired only when people do not like the way things are going. Pressure for public action arises when people feel that they, individually, cannot bring about the desired adjustments. They have in mind some norm or some image of an ideal situation toward which they strive. These norms become the goals of policy toward which the objectives of specific programs are directed.

From the "Directive Principles of State Policy" enshrined in India's Constitution, it is possible to derive two dominant goals of economic policy: First, increasing the national income and second, improving the distribution of national income among the members of society. These goals are reflected in India's economic policies that are enunciated in its five year plans. The goals that seek to achieve "growth with equity" need to be seen in the context of the following four important dimensions of state policy:

1. The quality of life of the citizens;
2. The generation of productive employment;

3. Regional balance; and
4. Self-reliance.

All these objectives seem to be worthwhile and, therefore, deserve serious pursuit by the policy makers. However, to be of any use to society, these objectives should be translated into specific programs and projects that are manageable under the existing conditions. Many rural development policies are complex combinations of various goals, different sets of means or instruments, and are limited by various conditions. To understand such policies, we must break them down into several programs or projects. For each program, a clearly defined objective may be designated, which a particular government agency should pursue. The program measures can then be identified and appraised as to whether they are appropriate and efficient in serving the objective, and be adapted to the conditions outside the influence of that particular program. These conditions are often the decisive factors determining whether or not a certain program is "administratively" feasible.

Hierarchy of Policy Goals

Given the multiplicity of policy goals, it is necessary to study the relationships among them and see that they converge toward public interest, or, at least, do not militate against it. This can be done if various policy goals and program objectives are arranged in the form of a pyramid, as shown in Figure 6.1.

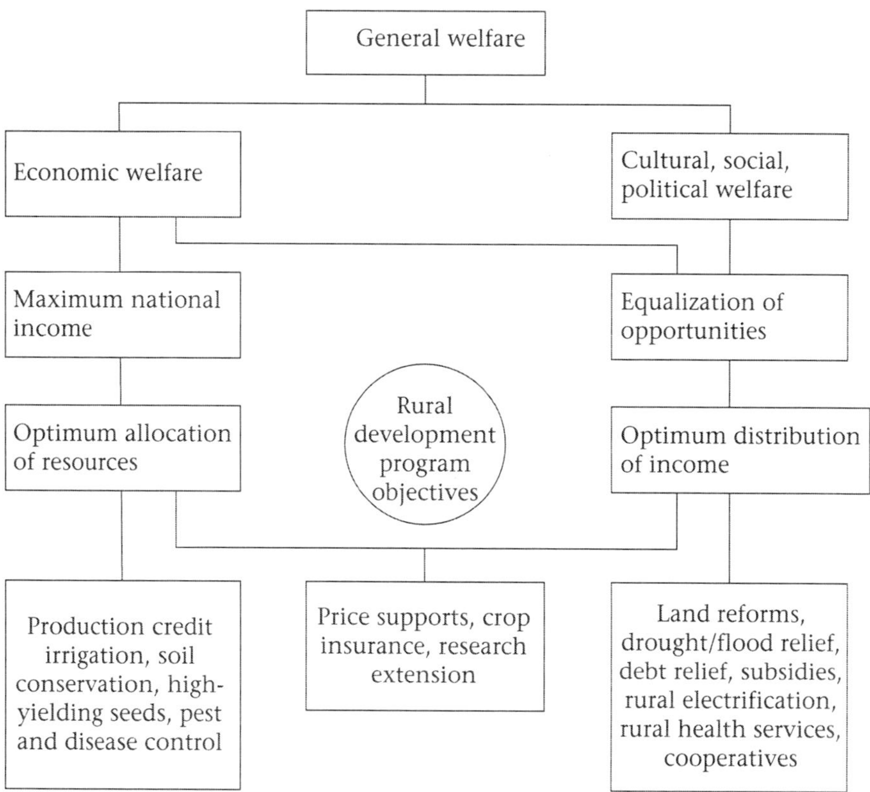

Figure 6.1: *Hierarchies of Rural Development Policy Goals*

Source: Author.

Descending the steps of the pyramid of policy goals from the lofty top of generality to the practical base of concrete issues would reveal the following hierarchy:

1. The master goal of economic policy is to promote general welfare, which comprises economic welfare and cultural, social, and political welfare. This master goal is served by two superior goals, namely, maximum national income and equal opportunities. The master goal and the superior goals together constitute the top level of the hierarchy.
2. Descending from the top level of the hierarchy, a series of goals is developed at a lower plane of generality. These goals deal with specific maladjustments in the various sectors of the economy and may be called the central goals of the major national policies. Each of these central goals is still quite general in scope and complex in nature. For practical application, these goals have to be broken down further into more specific program objectives, directed at a great variety of situations and concerning various groups of people, regions, and commodities.
3. At the next level, we find the objectives of specific government programs designed to correct maladjustments or remove the source of dissatisfaction suffered by certain groups of people. The central goal of agricultural policy, for instance, is broken down into various program objectives assigned to irrigation, soil conservation, agricultural credit, marketing, research, education, and extension.
4. We descend then to the lowest, most specific level of program units, the objectives of which are relatively simple and clear-cut. These are supporting specific farm commodities at specific prices, making loans to farmers for specific purposes, inducing farmers to follow certain soil conservation practices, and constructing dams and irrigation systems.

The method of formulating programs in which the objective and its means are clearly defined is indispensable for the study of policies. But the method is not simple to apply. Objectives become means and means become objectives, depending upon how one looks at them. Take, for example, the eradication of rural unemployment. From the viewpoint of the Union Ministry of Rural Development, it is an objective, and the means to accomplish it consist of budgetary allocation of funds to various employment-generating programs, grants to NGOs, institutional credit, and subsidies for the purchase of income-generating assets and rendering technical advice to the beneficiaries. From the viewpoint of the Planning Commission (now NITI Aayog), eradication of rural poverty is a means of improving income distribution and equalizing opportunities; those objectives again are means of improving social, cultural, and economic welfare, which, in turn, are means of attaining the master goal of general welfare. Thus, an objective in the context of a more specific program appears as a means in a more general action system. In evaluating the appropriateness of means, we take the objective for granted; in order to evaluate the appropriateness of an objective, we must place it in the position of a means serving a superior end.

Rural Development Policies in India

Tinbergen (1952, 2) distinguishes between a qualitative policy and a quantitative policy. A qualitative policy seeks to change the economic structure through the creation of new institutions, modification of existing institutions, and nationalization of private firms. A quantitative policy seeks to change the magnitude of certain parameters; for example, change in the tax rate. An example that represents both qualitative and quantitative policy is the introduction of an education system free of charge, if previously tuition fees were charged. It is qualitative because it represents a change in the economic structure, and is quantitative because it represents a change in the fee, from something to zero.

Heady (1965, 15) classifies agricultural policies into development policies and compensation policies. A development policy seeks to increase the supply of commodities and resources, and to improve the quality of products and inputs. A compensation policy is aimed at compensating its target group in various manners—through subsidies, price support, and so on.

India has a long history of government intervention in the rural sector of its economy. In the pre-independence era, the British government intervention was aimed at promoting the export of food and raw materials to Great Britain. There was no state policy for the development of resources of India for the welfare of its people. Introduction of a land tenure system, opening up of road and rail communications, and promotion of export trade in certain agricultural commodities were important measures taken by the British government. The other landmarks of that era were the creation of the Forest Department in 1864, and the Department of Agriculture in 1871, the appointment of the Royal Commission on Agriculture (RCA) in 1926, and the establishment of the Imperial (now Indian) Council of Agricultural Research in 1929. The report of the RCA was accepted as the basis for future development of agriculture in a conference convened by the Government of India in Shimla in October 1928. The report emphasized, inter alia, the importance of providing a minimum standard of life in villages and the modernization of agriculture through research, extension, and greater coordination of various departments dealing with agriculture and development of cooperative institutions. However, due to the lack of financial resources and the Great Economic Depression (1929–30), many of the recommendations of the RCA could not be implemented.

In January 1946, the Government of India issued a "Statement of Agriculture and Food Policy in India," which spelt out the objectives to be achieved, the measures to be taken, and the respective roles of the center and the provinces. According to the statement, the all-India policy was to promote the welfare of the people and to secure a progressive improvement of their standard of living (GoI 1976, 127–36).

Now we briefly discuss the salient features of major national level public policies in the field of agriculture and rural development.

National Forest Policy (NFP)

India is one of the few countries in the world that has had a forest policy since 1894. After independence, in recognition of the importance of forests in the national economy and to ensure the best possible use of land, a new forest policy was enunciated in May 1952. The new policy provided, inter alia, that the area under forests should be at least one-third of the total geographical area and that the forest areas should not be brought under cultivation of crops indiscriminately. The National Commission on Agriculture (NCA), 1976, recommended a further revision of the 1952 Forest Policy. The Forest Policy was revised in 1988. The main plank of the revised Forest Policy of 1988 is protection, conservation, and development of forests. The salient features of the revised policy are as follows:

1. A minimum of one-third of the total land area of the country has to be brought under forest or tree cover.
2. Total protection of tropical rain/moist forests.
3. The extent of forest use for grazing and extraction will be determined on the basis of the carrying capacity of the forests.
4. Involvement of tribals/forest dwellers in protection, regeneration, and development of forests to be encouraged.
5. Forest-based industries would have to raise their own plantations to meet their requirements and the practice of supplying forest produce to industries at concessional rates would cease.

These principles are necessary to ensure that the forest area can be increased from its present level of 75 mha to 110 mha (33% of the total land area). The revised forest policy has several implications for various sectors of the economy such as energy, industry, and agriculture. Development projects now are carefully examined to ensure that the ecological balance is not destroyed. This is done through an assessment of their impact on the ecosystem.

The Forests Rights Act 2006

Since times immemorial, the tribal communities of India have had an integral and close knit relationship with the forests and have been dependent on the forests for livelihoods and existence. The relationship was mutually beneficial and not one sided. However, rights were rarely recognized by the authorities and in the absence of real ownership of the land, the already marginalized local dwellers suffered. This was due mainly to the fact that the Indian Forest Act, 1927 empowers the government to declare any area to be a reserved forest, protected forest or village forest and the Wild Life (Protection) Act, 1972 allows any area to be constituted as a "protected area," namely a national park, wildlife sanctuary, tiger reserve, or community conservation area. Under these laws, the rights of people living in or depending on the area to be declared as a forest or protected area are to be "settled" by a "forest settlement officer." This basically requires that officer to enquire into the claims of people to land, minor forest produce, and so on, and, in the case of claims found to be valid, to allow them to continue or to extinguish them by paying compensation. To ameliorate this situation, Parliament passed the Scheduled Tribes and Other Traditional Forest Dwellers (Recognition of Forest Rights) Act, 2006 on December 18, 2006. The Forest Rights Act, 2006 represents a drastic shift from the earlier policies in the sense that it focuses on the rights of forest-dwelling communities to land and other resources, denied to them over decades as a result of the continuance of colonial forest laws in India. Supporters of the act claim that it will redress the "historical injustice" committed against forest dwellers, while including provisions for making conservation more effective and more transparent. The demand for the law has seen massive national demonstrations involving hundreds of thousands of people. However, the law has also been the subject of considerable controversy in the English press in India. Opponents of the law claim it will lead to massive forest destruction and should be repealed. A little over one year after it was passed, the act was notified into force on December 31, 2007. On January 1, 2008, this was followed by the notification of the rules framed by the Ministry of Tribal Affairs to supplement the procedural aspects of the act.

There have been numerous complaints regarding the manner in which the act has been implemented after its notification. For instance, in September 2010, the Council for Social Development, a New Delhi based think tank, released a "Summary Report on Implementation of the Forest Rights Act," which stated that all of the key features of this legislation have been undermined by a combination of apathy and sabotage during the process of implementation. In the current situation, the rights of the majority of tribals and other traditional forest dwellers are being denied and the purpose of the legislation is being defeated. Unless immediate remedial measures are taken, instead of undoing the historical injustice to tribal and other traditional forest dwellers, the act will have the opposite outcome of making them even more vulnerable to eviction and denial of their customary access to forests. Both the Central and the state governments have actively pursued policies that are in direct violation of the spirit and letter of the act.

However, in the past, India's forest policy has not been congenial to promoting a sustainable use and people-centric management of forest resources. The current policy also needs to be overhauled if the link between scarcity of forest resources and their prices is to be reestablished. Now that we are facing a growing scarcity of forest resources, forest product prices should be rising to slow down deforestation and accelerate reforestation. At present, not only are many of the forest products and services not priced at all, but even timber, which is an internationally tradable commodity, is priced below its true scarcity value due to implicit and explicit subsidies, and institutional failures. Forest concessions are typically inadequate to provide incentives for conservation and replanting. Failure to value non-timber goods and services results in excessive deforestation, conflicts with local communities, loss of economic value, and environmental damage. Promotion of local processing of timber often leads to inefficient plywood mills, excess capacity, wastage of valuable tropical timber, and loss of government revenues. Replanting subsidies often end up subsidizing the conversion of a valuable natural forest to inferior mono-species plantations, with the associated loss of the value of both tropical hardwoods and biological diversity.

There is also a need to adopt a better system of Forest Resource Accounting (FRA). The existing FRA system has several drawbacks. For example, there is no accounting of the free collection of fuel wood, grass, and other non-wood forest products; benefits from free grazing of animals in forest; and a whole set of intangible benefits, such as soil and water conservation, maintenance of productivity of adjoining lands, biodiversity conservation, moderation of micro climate, carbon sequestration, release of oxygen, recreation, and so on. This leads to gross underestimation of the forestry sector to India's GDP. In view of this, there is a need to adopt the new system of FRA.[2]

Further, in view of the rising demand for forest-based products, there is a need to pay far greater attention to increasing the productivity of forests and to their scientific management on modern lines. The NFP should rest on two pivotal points, namely, meeting the requirement of raw materials for the forest-based industries; small timber, fuel wood and fodder for the rural community; satisfying the present and future demands for protective and recreational functions of the forests and for environmental amenities. Social forestry and afforestation of wastelands should receive a very high priority.

In June 1990, the Union Ministry of Environment and Forests issued guidelines to the forest departments of all states and UTs, directing them to involve village communities and voluntary agencies for the regeneration of degraded forest lands on a usufruct sharing basis. Most of the state governments responded positively to the ministry's directive, and launched what have come to be known as Joint Forest Management (JFM) programs. The Ministry of Environment and Forests had issued fresh operational guidelines for the formulation of a new program called the NAP for the Tenth Five Year Plan (2002–07). These guidelines seek to encourage a participatory approach to the development of forests for the Government of India-sponsored afforestation schemes. Afforestation schemes operational during the Ninth Five Year Plan have been merged in the new NAP so as to avoid multiplicity of schemes with similar objectives and to ensure uniformity in the funding pattern and implementation mechanism (see Chapter 11: "Joint Forest Management [JFM] and National Afforestation Programme [NAP]" for details). The Tenth Five Year Plan provided for the universalization of the JFM in the country.

Land Reforms Policy

To lay the foundation for a progressive rural society, it is necessary to reorder the agrarian structure. A sound land reforms policy can contribute significantly to agricultural and rural development, and therefore, deserves a high priority. The land policy should be such that it ensures the scientific, sustainable and intensive use of land; creates productive employment; reduces disparities in the distribution of land; provides incentives to increase the productivity of land; and induces changes in property relations and social structure, with a view to enabling the wider participation of landowners and tenants in the process of rural development. The agrarian structure should be based on peasant proprietorship, strengthened and supplemented by cooperative and joint farming systems, and backed by necessary supplies and services for optimum utilization of land.

After independence, the Government of India formulated a comprehensive national land reforms policy for the first time in the First Five Year Plan. The main objectives of the policy were to remove such impediments to the modernization of agriculture as were innate in the agrarian structure inherited from the past, and the reduction of gross inequalities in the agrarian economy and the rural society. It accorded a high priority to programs that increased agricultural production, promoted diversification, reduced disparities in distribution of income and wealth, eliminated exploitation, and provided security to tenants and workers. This policy has been followed in all the subsequent five year plans with marginal reshuffling of the priorities of its components. Necessary land reform legislation has already been enacted by the state governments and is now in force. The policy and the programs framed thereunder have been periodically reviewed and evaluated. One of the common findings of the reviews is that the implementation of the programs has been lax. Many glaring gaps have occurred between the objectives of the policy and the legislation enacted to achieve them, and between the laws and their enforcement (Singh 1997, 152–55). The programs, therefore, need to be implemented more rigorously than in the past. For optimum results, the programs of land reforms, the consolidation of fragmented landholdings, land development, irrigation and drainage, and the acquisition of surplus land and its distribution should be integrated and executed properly. Special attention must be directed at the restoration of degraded common property land resources and their proper utilization for the larger benefit of the rural masses. With the establishment of the National Wastelands Development Board (NWDB), it is hoped that some 100 mha of India's wastelands would be properly developed and utilized.

The National Agriculture Policy 2000 stipulated the following approach to land reforms:

1. Consolidation of holdings all over the country on the pattern of north western states.
2. Redistribution of ceiling surplus lands and waste lands among the landless farmers and unemployed youth with initial startup capital.
3. Tenancy reforms to recognize the rights of the tenants and sharecroppers.
4. Development of lease markets for increasing the size of the holdings by making legal provisions for giving private lands on lease for cultivation and agro-business.
5. Update and improvement of land records, computerization and issue of land pass-books to the farmers.
6. Recognition of women's rights in land.
7. The rural poor will be increasingly involved in the implementation of land reforms with the help of panchayati raj institutions, voluntary groups, social activists, and community leaders.

The Land Acquisition Policy

Land acquisition in India refers to the process by which the union or a state government in India acquires private land for the purpose of industrialization, development of infrastructural facilities, or urbanization of the private land and provides compensation to the affected land owners and their rehabilitation and resettlement. The power to take property from the individual is rooted in the doctrine of "eminent domain," which states that the sovereign can do anything, if the act of sovereign involves public interest. The doctrine empowers the sovereign to acquire private land for a public use, provided the public nature of the usage can be demonstrated beyond doubt. The doctrine is based on the following two Latin maxims,

(a) *Salus populi suprema lex* (welfare of the people is the paramount law) and (b) *Necessitas publica major est quam* (public necessity is greater than private necessity). In the history of modern India, this doctrine was challenged twice (broadly speaking): Once when land reforms were initiated and another time when banks were nationalized. The Constitution of India originally provided the right to property (which includes land) under Articles 19 and 31. Article 19 guaranteed that all citizens have the right to acquire, hold, and dispose of property. Article 31 stated that "no person shall be deprived of his property save by authority of law." It also indicated that compensation would be paid to a person whose property has been taken for public purposes (often subject to wide range of meaning). The 44th Amendment of 1978 deleted the right to property from the list of fundamental rights with an introduction of a new provision, Article 300-A, which provided that "no person shall be deprived of his property save by authority of law." The Constitution's 44th Amendment came into effect on June 10, 1979. The amendment ensured that the right to property is no more a fundamental right but rather a constitutional/legal right/as a statutory right and in the event of breach, the remedy available to an aggrieved person is through the high court under Article 226 of the Indian Constitution and not the supreme court under Article 32 of the Constitution. State must pay compensation at the market value for such land, building, or structure acquired (inserted by Constitution, 17th Amendment Act, 1964); the same can be found in the earlier rulings when property right was a fundamental right. The legislature must "ensure that what is determined as payable must be compensation, that is, a just equivalent of what the owner has been deprived of.

Land acquisition in India is governed by the Right to Fair Compensation and Transparency in Land Acquisition, Rehabilitation and Resettlement (RFCTLARR) Act, 2013, which came into force from January 1, 2014. Till 2013, land acquisition in India was governed by the Land Acquisition Act of 1894. The National Democratic Alliance (NDA) government led by Narendra Modi introduced a land acquisition amendment bill in Lok Sabha on March 10, 2015. The bill amends the RFCTLARR Act, 2013. The land acquisition (amendment) bill seeks to ratify an ordinance or emergency executive order that was passed on December 29, 2014. The bill faced a tough resistance from the key opposition parties in India who have called the proposed amendments anti-farmer and anti-poor. The proposed amendments removed the requirements for approval from farmers to proceed with land acquisition under five broad categories of projects. While the bill was passed in Lok Sabha on March 10, 2015 by voice vote, it got stuck up in the Rajya Sabha (upper house), where the NDA government did not have a majority for the proposed amendments to become effective. Consequently, on May 30, 2015, the president of India promulgated the amendment ordinance for the third time. The Union Government of India has also made and notified the Right to Fair Compensation and Transparency in Land Acquisition, Rehabilitation and Resettlement (Social Impact Assessment and Consent) Rules, 2014 under the act to regulate the procedure. The bill was referred to a select committee of Rajya Sabha. But in the meantime, the NDA government decided not to proceed further with the bill, taking into account the continued agitation by a section of farmers with the support of the Congress and few other opposition parties.

The following were the main criticisms of the Bill:

- The RFCTLARR Act, 2013 defines "consent" clause as "land can only be acquired with approval of the 70% of the land owners for public private partnership (PPP) projects and 80% for the private entities. But the proposed amendments by the Narendra Modi government removed the consent clause for industrial corridors, PPP projects, rural infrastructure, affordable housing, and defense projects.
- The RFCTLARR Act, 2013 says the land unutilized for five years should be returned to the owner, but the amendment proposed by NDA government intends to change it to five years or any period specified at the time of setting up the project.

- The RFCTLARR Act, 2013 allows private companies to acquire land, but the proposed amendment allows any private entity to acquire land.
- According to the proposed amendment if any government official conducted any wrongdoing he or she could not be prosecuted without prior sanction from the government.
- The RFCTLARR Act, 2013 mandated the social assessment before land acquisition, but the NDA government's proposed bill did away with that requirement.

In India, more than 85% of farmers own land less than 2 hectares and all of them are not economically viable and are poor and in deep debt. Farming for them is losing proposition and keeps them perpetually in poverty. So they would like to quit farming as soon as a suitable opportunity arises for them to do so. Therefore, land acquisition for them affords a golden opportunity to get out of farming and poverty once and for ever. Even otherwise, they will be forced to sell their land sooner or later to pay back their accumulated debts to money lenders, banks, and others.

In our opinion, the land acquisition bill is in both farmers' and national interests. We do not understand why the opposition political parties call it "antifarmer."

National Water Policy (NWP)

Water is the most critical natural resource affecting the level and pace of agricultural and rural development. Optimum development and efficient utilization of water resources, therefore, assumes great significance. As we stated in Chapter 2 of this book, in 2011–12, India had the total gross irrigated area of about 91.53 mha and net irrigated area of about 65.26 mha (MoA 2014a, 304–05) and it ranked first in the world in terms of irrigated area. The net irrigated area accounted for about 47% of the net area sown (140 mha) in the country and contributed about 55% to the country's total agricultural output. The Union Ministry of Water Resources is responsible for laying down policies and programs for the development and regulation of the country's water resources. India's first national water policy (NWP) was announced by the Government of India in September 1987. It stressed that "water is a prime natural resource, a basic human need and a precious national asset. Planning and development of water resources need to be governed by national perspectives" (GoI 1987). It recommended an integrated and multidisciplinary approach to the planning, formulation, and implementation of projects in such a way as to be able to meet the demands of water from various sectors and to free the country, as far as possible, from the scourge of recurring floods and droughts. The NWP 1987 highlighted the following points:

- Need for efficient use of water.
- Need for a well-designed information system.
- Need for preservation of the quality of the environment and the ecological balance.
- Periodic reassessment on a scientific basis of the groundwater potential, taking into account the quality of water available and the economic viability of its exploitation.
- Integrated and coordinated development of surface water and groundwater, and their conjunctive use.
- Equity and social justice considerations in water allocation.
- Involvement of farmers in various aspects of water management, particularly water distribution and collection of water charges through water users' associations.

A new NWP was announced by the Government of India in April 2002 (GoI 2002c). It also highlights the similar concerns as the first NWP. The policy highlighted, inter alia, the need for the efficient use of water and for preservation of the quality of environment and ecological balance. This policy supersedes the 1987 policy but it also echoes similar concerns. The NWP 1987 and NWP 2002 neither clearly specify their goals, nor any operational guidelines as to how various provisions made in the policy documents would be actualized. In view of this, we could say that the policy framework is ineffective. In our opinion, its main goal should be to attain water security for all and forever through restoring, developing, conserving, utilizing, and managing the surface water and groundwater resources of the country in the socially optimum and ecologically sound and sustainable way. Besides, the policy should have a legal backup and operational guidelines to achieve its objectives. Also, the government must accept the access to water for survival as a basic human right and include it in the set of development goals and use it as an entry point for development work. A minimum of 40 liters of water per capita per day is required for meeting personal consumption, hygiene, and sanitation requirement (Water Supply and Sanitation Collaborative Council [WSSCC] 1999).

National Water Policy 2012[3]

The earlier two NWPs, NWP 1987 and NWP 2002, were reviewed and updated in 2012. Considering the fact that India accounts for about 18% of the world population and about 4% of the world's water resources, the policy advocated that one of the solutions to solve the country's water problems is to link its rivers taking into account the ecological needs of the rivers. The main emphasis of NWP 2012 is to treat water as an economic *good*, which requires its conservation and efficient use. This provision, which is intended to permit privatization of water-delivery services, has been criticized by various agencies. The policy also does away with the priorities for water allocation mentioned in NWP 1987 and NWP 2002. The policy was adopted, despite disapproval by many states.

The major provisions under the NWP 2012 are (MoWR 2012):

1. Establishing a standardized national information system with a network of data banks and data bases.
2. Resource planning and recycling for providing maximum availability.
3. Assessment of the impact of projects on human settlements and environment.
4. Prescription of guidelines for the safety of storage dams and other water-related structures.
5. Regulation of exploitation of groundwater.
6. Setting water allocation priorities in the following order: drinking water, irrigation, hydropower, navigation, and industrial and other uses.
7. Rationalization of water rates for surface water and groundwater with due regard to the interests of small and marginal farmers.
8. Evolving a national framework law as an umbrella statement of general principles governing the exercise of legislative and/or executive (or devolved) powers by the Centre, the states, and the local governing bodies.
9. Conferment of statutory powers upon Water Users Associations (WUAs) to collect and retain a portion of water charges, manage the volumetric quantum of water allotted to them and maintain the distribution system in their jurisdiction. WUAs should be given the freedom to fix rates subject to floor rates determined by Water Regulatory Authorities (WRAs).
10. Setting up of an independent statutory WRA by each state to fix prices of water for different uses.

11. Emphasis on the need for participation of farmers and voluntary agencies, improving water quality, water zoning, conservation of water, flood and drought management, control of erosion, and so on.

A national water board is intended to prepare a plan of action based on the NWP, as approved by the National Water Resources Council, and to regularly monitor its implementation. It is also expected state Water Policies would be drafted/revised in accordance with this policy keeping in mind the basic concerns and principles as also a unified national perspective.

In a nutshell, NWP 2012 is full of several other platitudes but we are afraid that like any other policies, it is also likely to suffer from lax implementation.

Agricultural Price Policy (APP)

Before independence, there was no semblance of an APP in India. After independence, the government introduced a price policy mainly to protect the interests of consumers, by making available to them food at reasonable prices, that is, the policy was consumer oriented. A broad framework for a price policy was specified for the first time in the terms of reference of the Agricultural Prices Commission (later renamed as the Commission for Agricultural Costs and Prices [CACP]), which was set up in 1965 for evolving a balanced and integrated price structure. The commission was required to keep in view the interests of both the producer and the consumer while formulating a price policy. The framework of the policy was reviewed and modified in 1980, and again in 1986. The latest review was done in 1991, after India became a signatory to the new world trade arrangement, which, for the first time, also included agriculture. The new price policy for the agricultural sector aims at setting the prices right and withdrawing the subsidies on inputs, targeting the public distribution system (PDS) to only the poor, abolishing the food management system, and liberalizing trade in agricultural commodities.

The main objectives of the price policy are:

1. To assure a remunerative and relatively stable price environment for farmers for inducing them to increase their production, and thereby augmenting the availability of food grains;
2. To improve the physical and economic access of the people to food; and
3. To evolve a production pattern that is in line with the overall needs of the economy.

Toward this end, MSPs for major agricultural products are announced each year, which are fixed after taking into account the recommendations of the CACP. MSPs have been a cornerstone of the agricultural price policy since 1965.The MSPs announced by the CACP in the last four years, 2010–11 to 2013–14 are presented in Table 6.1.

Cost of cultivation data for principal crops are collected under a plan scheme to generate state-wise and crop-wise estimates of cost of cultivation/production and made available to the CACP for use in making their recommendations of MSPs. The cost of cultivation/production takes into account all paid out costs such as those incurred on account of hired human labor, bullock energy, and machine energy (both hired and owned) and rent paid for leased-in land besides cash and kind expenses on use of material inputs such as seeds, fertilizers, manures, plant protection chemicals, irrigation charges including cost of diesel or electricity for operation of pump sets, and so on. Besides, cost of production includes imputed values of wages of family labor and rent for owned land. The cost also covers depreciation for farm machinery and building, transportation, and insurance charges. As such, the cost of production covers not only actual expenses in cash and kind but also imputed value of owned assets including land

Table 6.1: *Minimum Support Prices According to Crop Year*

(₹ *per quintal)*

Commodity	*2010–11*	*2011–12*	*2012–13*	*2013–14*
Kharif crops				
Paddy				
Common	1,000	1,080	1,250	1,310
Grade A	1,030	1,110	1,280	1,345
Jowar Hybrid	880	980	1,500	1,500
Jowar Maldandi	900	1,000	1,520	1,520
Bajra	880	980	1,175	1,250
Maize	880	950	1,175	1,310
Arhar/Tur*	3,000	3,200	3,850	4,300
Moong*	3,170	3,500	4,400	4,500
Urad*	2,900	3,300	4,300	4,300
Cotton				
Staple length-24.5–25.5 mm	2,500	2,800	3,600	3,700
Staple length-29.5–30.5 mm	3,000	3,300	3,900	4,000
Groundnut in shell	2,300	2,700	3,700	4,000
Sesamum	2,900	3,400	4,200	4,500
Rabi crops				
Wheat	1,120**	1,285	1,350	1,400
Gram	2,100	2,800	3,000	3,100
Rapeseed & Mustard	1,850	2,500	3,000	3,050
Other crops				
Copra	4,450	4,525	5,100	5,250
Sugarcane@	139	145	170	210

Source: MoA (2014, Table 8.1, p. 244–45).
Notes: *Additional incentive @ of ₹ 500/- per quintal of *tur, urad* and *moong* sold to procurement agencies payable during the harvest/arrival period of two months.
**An additional incentive bonus of ₹ 50/- per quintal is payable over the MSP.
@ Fair and Remunerative.

and family labor. The CACP, while recommending prices, takes into account all the important factors, such as:

- Cost of production;
- Changes in input prices;
- Input/output price parity;
- Trends in market prices;
- Inter-crop price parity;
- Demand and supply situation;

- Effect on industrial cost structure;
- Effect on general price level;
- Effect on cost of living;
- International market price situation; and
- Parity between prices paid and prices received by farmers (terms of trade).

Of all the factors, cost of production is the most tangible factor and it takes into account all operational and fixed costs. The government administers the Price Support Scheme (PSS) of the commodities through various public and cooperative agencies such as the Food Corporation of India (FCI), Cotton Corporation of India (CCI), Jute Corporation of India (JCI), National Cooperative Agricultural Marketing Federation of India (NAFED) and Tobacco Board, for which the MSPs are fixed. For commodities not covered under PSS, the government also arranges for market intervention on specific request from the states for specific quantity at a mutually agreed price. The losses, if any, are borne by the Center and the states on 50:50 basis. The price policy has paid rich dividends. The government has raised substantially the MSPs in recent years. Food and input subsidies have been used as complementary instruments of the Agricultural Price Policy (APP). Contrary to the general impression that the price support program, and input and food subsidies have benefited only a few crops and farmers in only some regions, it is now well established that these instruments have played an important role in achieving the objectives of food security and accelerated growth of the economy, and have benefited all the sections of society.

At present, 25 agricultural commodities are covered under the MSP program. Besides, some other commodities such as onions, potatoes and ginger are included under the Market Intervention Scheme (MIS). The FCI, which has been the nodal agency for implementing the price support policy for rice and wheat, was entrusted with the work of price support for coarse cereals also. As regards targeting the poorer sections, a revamped PDS was launched in 1992 with a view to extending the coverage of distribution of specially subsidized food grains to the population living in hilly and arid areas also. It is important for rural development that the overall relationship between input and output prices within agriculture, and the terms of trade between agriculture and other sectors of the economy are such that growth is stimulated in the rural areas. The major aim of an APP should be to correct market distortions, which are generally socially harmful. Being parts of the same policy, the interests of the producer should be safeguarded through price support (above the market price) operations when there is a sharp fall in market prices, and the interests of the consumers, particularly the vulnerable sections of the population, should be protected through distribution of food grains and other basic necessities at a fair price (below the market price) when there is a sharp rise in market prices. Since the MSP is expected to take into account changes in input prices, widespread use of input subsidy as an incentive to increase the production should, by and large, be avoided except in the case of small and marginal farmers and difficult areas.

The National Agriculture Policy 2000 stipulates that the Central government will continue to discharge its responsibility to ensure remunerative prices for agricultural produce through the announcement of MSPs for major agricultural commodities. The food, nutrition, and other domestic and exports requirements of the country are kept in view while determining the support prices of different commodities. The price structure and trade mechanism are continuously reviewed to ensure a favorable economic environment for the agricultural sector and to bring about an equitable balance between the rural and the urban incomes. The methodology used by the CACP in arriving at estimates of costs of production is periodically reviewed. The price structure of both inputs and outputs are monitored to ensure higher returns to the farmers and cost effectiveness throughout the economy. Domestic market prices are closely monitored to prevent distress sales by the farmers. The government intends to enlarge the coverage of future markets to minimize the wide fluctuations in commodity prices as also for hedging their risks. The endeavor will be to cover all important agricultural products under futures trading in course of time.

Price Supports Scheme (PSS)

The Department of Agriculture and Cooperation implements the PSS for procurement of oil seeds, pulses, and cotton, through NAFED that is the Central nodal agency, at the MSP declared by the government. NAFED undertakes procurement of oil seeds, pulses, and cotton under the PSS as and when prices fall below the MSP. Procurement under PSS is continued till prices stabilize at or above the MSP. Losses, if any incurred by NAFED in undertaking MSP operations are reimbursed by the Central government. Profit, if any, earned in undertaking MSP operations is credited to the Central government.

Under the PSS during 2010–11, procurement was made of Milling Copra in four states—Tamil Nadu (7,434 metric tons), Kerala (12,408 mertic tons), Andaman and Nicobar Islands (53, 35 metric tons), and Karnataka (30, 86 metric tons) for a total value of 1.35 billion.

Agricultural Marketing Policy (IDFC 2013, 29–30 & State of Indian Agriculture, 122–37)

Agricultural marketing plays an important role in promoting agricultural development. It adds value to farm produce through processing (form utility), storage (time utility), and transportation and distribution (place utility). As a matter of fact, value added through marketing is much more than the original value of the produce in case of perishable produce such as fruits, vegetables, milk, meat, and fishes. The increasing trend of agricultural production has brought in its wake, new challenges in terms of finding markets for the increased marketed surplus in the country. Challenges and opportunities that the global markets offer in the liberalized trade regime are also to be addressed. For the farming community to benefit from the new global market access opportunities, the internal agricultural marketing system in the country needs to be integrated and strengthened. Agricultural marketing reforms and the creation of marketing infrastructure has therefore been a prime concern of the government.

In India, rural producers, particularly marginal and small farmers, often face immense difficulties in marketing their produce. They have small quantities of marketable surplus and low holding power due to extreme poverty and indebtedness. As a result they have to sell off (distress sale) their produce in local markets at very low prices immediately after the harvest. Cases abound where perishable farm produce such as some of the seasonal fruits and vegetables selling at prices that do not cover even their cost of production and their producers suffer heavy losses and become broke. Duly taking cognizance of these problems, the Central and state governments have intervened from time to time to improve the markets and marketing though various policies and programs.

Unlike National Forest Policy and National Water Policy, there is no National Agricultural Marketing Policy as such. What we have is an assortment of government schemes aimed at improving the agricultural markets and marketing. The subject of agriculture and agricultural marketing is dealt with both by the state as well as the Central government in the country. Starting from 1951, various Five Year Plans laid stress on development of physical markets, on-farm and off-farm storage structures, facilities for standardization and grading, packaging, transportation, and so on. Most agricultural commodity markets generally operate under the normal forces of demand and supply. The role of government is normally limited to protecting the interests of producers and consumers, only in respect of wage goods, mass consumption goods and essential goods; and to promote the organized marketing of agricultural commodities in the country through a network of regulated markets.

Over the last several decades, the government has intervened in several ways, both as regulator and buyer, to assure farmers fair prices but with limited success. In the mid-1950s, state governments constituted Agricultural Produce Marketing Committees (APMCs) and set up regulated markets to sell certain notified agricultural products by a transparent open auction in the presence of an APMC official. The legal and administrative framework for regulation and management of agricultural produce markets has mainly been incorporated in the provisions of more than 27 regulated markets acts in vogue in different states and UTs of India.

To achieve an efficient system of buying and selling of agricultural commodities, most of the state governments and UTs have enacted several legislations to provide for regulation of the agricultural produce markets. The basic objective in the setting up of setting up of a network of physical markets has been to ensure reasonable gains to the farmers by creating a market environment where there is fair play of supply and demand forces, to regulate market practices and to attain transparency in transactions. With growing agricultural production, the number of regulated markets has also been increasing in the country. While, there were 286 regulated markets in the country at the end of 1950, their number had increased to 7,114 by 2014.

At a time when the private trade was underdeveloped and exploitative, this helped eliminate several malpractices in agricultural markets and ensured fairer deals to farmers. But as the regulated markets were not sufficiently spread out, most of the farmers could not access them and benefit from them. Besides, over time, facilities available in regulated markets became inadequate and auctions no longer remained transparent or fair. Consequently, informal private trade persisted and farmers continued to depend on *arhtiyas,* or middlemen to sell their produce at low prices. Besides, by preventing private investment in agricultural markets, regulated markets stifled competition and indirectly facilitated the states to exercise marketing monopoly power.

In view of this, the Central government moved to remove the monopoly power of state and to allow private sector participation in agricultural marketing. For this purpose, a new Model State Agricultural Produce Marketing (Development and Regulation) Act was passed by Parliament in 2003. The act provides for establishment of private markets/yards, direct purchase centers, consumer/farmers markets for direct sale and promotion of public private partnership in the management and development of agricultural markets in the country. It also provides for separate constitution for Special Markets for commodities such as onions, fruits, vegetables, flowers, and so on. A separate chapter has been included in the legislation to regulate and promote contract-farming arrangements in the country. It provides for prohibition of commission agency in any transaction of agricultural commodities with the producers. It redefines the role of present agricultural produce market committee to promote alternative marketing system, contract farming, and direct marketing and farmers/consumers markets. It also redefines the role of state agricultural marketing boards to promote standardization, grading, quality certification, market-led extension, and training of farmers and market functionaries in marketing-related areas. Provision has also been made in the act for constitution of the State Agricultural Produce Marketing Standards Bureau for promotion of grading, standardization, and quality certification of agricultural produce. This would facilitate the pledge financing, e-trading, direct purchasing, export, forward/future trading, and introduction of negotiable warehousing receipt system in respect of agricultural commodities.

Most states and UTs have either fully or partially adopted the Model Act. Consequently, a large number of private national corporates such as Ballarpur Industries, JK Papers, and Wimco; and multinational corporation such as Cadbury, PepsiCo, Unilever, Cargill, and ITC have entered into contract farming arrangements with farmers. But except for Karnataka, Tamil Nadu, and Andhra Pradesh where private firms work with small farmers for crops that require careful cultivation, most private firms work with large and medium farmers (Planning Commission 2011; Singh 2012). Contract farming has been criticized on several grounds including the procurement of only a portion of the farmers' produce without a firm commitment, lack of enforceable agreements and lack of provision for risk sharing (Singh 2012).

The Central and state governments are also substantial buyers (mainly wheat and rice) for the PDS and for strategic food security buffer stocks. The FCI is the largest buyer and traditionally concentrated in states such as Punjab, Haryana, western Uttar Pradesh for wheat, and Andhra Pradesh for rice. In 1997–98, the Central government encouraged decentralized procurement by state governments in order to extend the MSP to "non-traditional states" and increase efficiency in procurement.

Linking Farmers to Markets

Some of the initiatives taken for linking farmers to markets at the state and the national levels through infrastructure development and technological innovations are presented in Box 6.1.

Box 6.1

TYPES OF DIRECT MARKETING BY FARMERS

Rythu Bazar *is an initiative to create infrastructure facilities to enable farmers to sell their products directly to consumers thereby ensuring that farmers realize better prices and consumers receive fresh vegetables, fruits, and so on at reasonable prices and, thus, address constraints in the agricultural marketing infrastructure. Both producers and consumers are benefited from Rythu bazars as producer's share in consumer's rupee is more by 15 to 40% as compared to other markets and consumers get fresh vegetables, fruits and food items at 25–30% less prices than the prevailing prices in nearby markets. Typically, a Rythu Bazar covers 10 to 15 villages and at least 250 farmers including 10 groups (SHGs) who are selected by a team consisting of mandal revenue officers, horticulture officers and agriculture officers in the villages operate in the bazars. Adequate transport facilities are arranged for transport of goods to Rythu Bazars in consultation with the State Road Transport Corporation. In addition, online information of prices and commodities movements is provided on the internet. As of 2011, more than 100 Rythu Bazars were in existence benefiting 4,500 farmers and a large number of consumers. Rythu Bazars can play a key role in addressing marketing problems and there is, thus, a clear need to facilitate similar marketing infrastructure throughout the country.*

Shetkari Bazar *is a concept of direct marketing by producer (farmer) to consumers. By circumventing the intermediaries, the produce reaches in good shape with minimum handling. This results in better price realization for the farmer-producer and good quality produce to the consumer at reasonably lower price. This is expected to help small farmers with small quantity of perishable fruit and vegetables to get a fair price and escape commercial exploitation in the market place. In 2002, the Government of Maharashtra decided to set up Shetkari Bazars in the state and the Maharashtra State Agriculture Marketing Board was appointed as nodal agency for implementing this scheme. The Shetkari Bazars are located in all district and key taluka places and are managed by the Agriculture Produce Market Committees (APMC) of the area concerned. The produce brought by farmers is not levied cess. Local committees are set up to monitor the prices and take the commitment forward. A term loan up to one million is advanced to the APMCs for establishment of a Shetkari Bazar. As of 2011, an amount of 311 million has been sanctioned to 33 APMCs. There are 12 Shetkari Bazaars operating in the state and 33 additional markets have been sanctioned.*

Source: MoA (2011, Box 5.2, p. 133).

Impact of Farmers' Markets/Direct Marketing

Producers use different market outlets (commission agents, local traders, and farmers' markets) at different times of the year as a strategy to get the best price for their produce. Farmer's markets are especially beneficial for small producers, who have difficulties in selling small volumes during the dry season in the conventional market system. Farmers' markets have influenced producers' practices in two main ways namely: (a) diversification of production to include a wider variety of vegetables and (b) intensification to maximize the use of water and land resources throughout the year. Farmer's markets have also stimulated producers' adoption of marketing strategies through a better understanding of consumers' needs and preferences based on incomes, dietary habits, and local needs. Factors that affect the producers' capacity to adapt to changes include access to credit and financial assets, and institutional support across the system. These are key factors in ensuring that farmers fully benefit from the farmers' market initiatives, and deserve to be better addressed. Direct marketing enables farmers and processors and other bulk buyers to economize on transportation cost and to considerably improve price realization. This also provides incentive to large scale marketing companies to affect their purchases directly from producing areas.

Market Research Information Network (MRIN)

Market information is of vital importance to all in the marketing system whether farmers, traders, processors, or consumers who require market information for different purposes. For provision of information of prices of agricultural commodities prevailing in agricultural produce markets in the country, the Ministry of Agriculture launched in March 2000 the ICT-based Central sector scheme of Marketing Research and Information Network (MRIN). It provides electronic connectivity to important wholesale markets in the country for collection and dissemination of price and market-related information. The scheme was implemented in the year 2000–01 and now more than 3,000 markets from all over the country have been linked to a central portal.[4] These markets report the daily prices and arrivals for more than 300 commodities and 2,000 varieties from more than 1,900 markets covering nearly all the major agricultural and horticultural produce. The information on arrivals and prices is disseminated in 12 regional languages.

In addition to price, a lot of other market-related information is also provided on the portal, for example, the accepted standards of grade labeling; sanitary and phyto-sanitary requirement; physical infrastructure of storage and warehousing; marketing yards; fees payable; and so on. Efforts are underway to prepare a national atlas of agricultural markets on a GIS platform that would indicate the availability of the entire marketing infrastructure in the country including storage, cold storages, markets, and related infrastructure. Similarly, commodity profiles indicating the post-harvest requirements of important commodities are being loaded on to the portal.

Major stakeholders of the project are farmers, buyers, and commission agents of agricultural produce, media persons, government functionaries, academicians, market functionaries, agri-business consultants, and so on. The information available on the portal is in the public domain and can be instantly accessed from anywhere in the world. Farmers and stakeholders are accessing this information throughout the length and width of the country and many agencies are using the contents of the portal to generate market intelligence and making the same available to various stakeholders to support them in appropriate decision making. The project provides ready contents for the proposed 1,00,000 IT kiosks being installed in rural areas by the Department of Information Technology.

Construction of Rural Godowns Scheme (Grameen Bhandaran Yojana)

Modern, adequate, and affordable decentralize storage facilities and other post-harvest infrastructure play a crucial role in providing farmers, especially marginal and small farmers, holding power and linking them to organized markets. Presently, there is a limited warehousing capacity (108.75 mt) in the country as can be seen from Table 6.2.

To create additional storage capacity the government launched the Gramin Bhandaran Yojana on April 1, 2011, aimed at the creation of scientific storage capacity with allied facilities in rural areas. This will meet the requirement of farmers in manifold ways such as storing farm produce, processed farm produce, agricultural inputs, promotion of grading, standardization, and quality control of agricultural produce to improve their marketability, prevention of distress sales immediately after harvest by providing the facility of pledge financing and marketing credit. It will strengthen the agricultural marketing infrastructure in the country by paving way for the introduction of a national system of warehouse receipts in respect of agricultural commodities stored in such godowns and will help reverse the declining trend of investment in the agricultural sector by encouraging private and cooperative sector to invest in the creation of storage infrastructure in the country. The scheme was revised for implementation in the XI Plan period, with a provision of subsidy at 25% of the project cost to all categories of farmers, agriculture graduates, cooperatives and Central Warehousing Corporation (CWC) and State Warehousing Corporations (SWCs). All other categories of individuals companies and corporations are given subsidy at 15% of the project cost. In case of North Eastern states and other/hilly areas and SC/ST entrepreneurs and their cooperatives and women farmers, the subsidy is 33.33%. Since the inception of the scheme with effect from April 1, 2001 and up to July 31, 2012, 28,744 godowns having a capacity of 32.8.97 million tons with a subsidy release of 9.66.05 billion had been sanctioned by the NABARD and National Council for Development of Cooperatives (NCDC) for the country as a whole. The government has, from October 20, 2011 revised the cost norms under the scheme to encourage the creation of additional warehousing capacity, particularly in those areas where it is yet to fully pick up.

Table 6.2: *Storage Capacity Created by Agency in India as of 2011*

Name of Agency	*Storage Capacity (Million Tons)*
Food Corporation of India	32.05
Central Warehousing Corporation (CWC)	10.07
State Warehousing Corporations (SWCs)	21.29
State Civil Supplies Corporations/./Departments	11.30
Total Public Sector	**74.71**
Cooperative Sector	15.07
Private sector	18.97
Total	**108.75**

Source: State of Indian Agriculture (2011, Table 5.3, p. 134).

Development/Strengthening of Agricultural Marketing Infrastructure, Grading and Standardization (AMIGS) Scheme

The AMIGS is a reform-linked investment scheme to encourage rapid development of infrastructure projects in agriculture and allied sectors including dairy, meat, fisheries and minor forest produce. It is applicable in only such states/UTs that adopt reforms in the APMC act to allow direct marketing and contract farming and permit agricultural produce markets to exist in private and cooperative sectors. The scheme was launched in October, 2004. The assistance is provided for development of market infrastructure, linkages, and value addition by private entrepreneurs, cooperatives, and state agencies for projects such as cleaning, sorting, grading, drying and auction platform, pack-house, and so on. The scheme is credit linked and demand driven. The subsidy for the projects under the scheme is released through NABARD, NCDC and the directorate of marketing and inspection. The sanctioned projects include combined harvesters, milk chilling units, cotton ginning and processing units, paddy parboiling units, fruits packaging, grading and marketing units, fruit and vegetables market yards, and so on., which benefit the farmers during post-harvest management/marketing of agricultural produce. Under the scheme 6,214 projects with a subsidy release of 4.3954 billion had been sanctioned as of 2011.

The progress made in the construction of godowns has varied widely across states. Only five states, namely, Madhya Pradesh, Andhra Pradesh, Punjab, Maharashtra, and Haryana have more than 60% of the total capacity of godowns sanctioned in the country. Other states such as Karnataka, Uttar Pradesh, West Bengal, and Gujarat are picking up whereas there is little progress in the states such as Goa, Jharkhand, Kerala, Uttarakhand, Bihar and the North Eastern states. Long payback period and low levels of viability are attributed to be the main reasons for this imbalance. In the North Eastern region, there has been a lack of response also due to the reluctance of financial institutions to provide credit facilities to such back-ended credit linked projects due to a community landholding pattern, which does not facilitate land collateral in the name of individual borrowers.

There has been a lack of investment in the logistics of the retail chain, leading to a fragmented market chain. Across the states there is a wide variation in the availability of marketing infrastructure such as auction platforms, electronic weigh bridges, price dissemination terminals and display, storages and warehousing facilities, cleaning, grading and packaging facilities, processing and value addition, and so on. However, it is observed that despite some reform initiatives by the states, there has been a lukewarm response from the private sector for taking up projects for the development of marketing infrastructure. It is felt that this is mainly due to viability issues given the long gestation period of projects involving agricultural marketing infrastructure. It may not be possible to fund very large investment requirements of these projects fully from the limited budgetary resources of the Government of India alone. In order to remove this shortcoming and to bring in private sector investment and techno-managerial efficiencies, the government is promoting public private partnerships (PPP) in infrastructure development through a special facility envisaging support to PPP projects through "viability gap funding." Primarily, this facility is meant to reduce the capital cost of the projects by credit enhancement, and to make them viable and attractive for private investments through supplementary grant funding.

Rural Credit Policy

India has a long history of government intervention in the rural credit market. Duly recognizing the need for providing institutional credit to cultivators to protect them from the exploitation of private moneylenders and traders, the Government of India started granting loans to the cultivators under: (a) the Improvements Loans Act of 1883 and (b) the Agriculturists' Loans

Act of 1884. Such loans are called taccavi loans. The act of 1883 authorizes the grant of long-term loans for effecting permanent improvements on land. Under the act of 1884, short- and medium-term loans are granted to meet the current agricultural needs, such as purchase of seeds, fertilizers, and small tools and implements. The record of taccavi loans has been rather poor. Some of the drawbacks are inadequate amount, inordinate delays in sanctioning the loans, lack of supervision, poor recovery, and lack of coordination.

The RBI and the NABARD have both played a very important role in shaping the rural credit policies of India, and in building its rural economy through institutional credit. The rural credit policy has been reviewed by a number of committees from time to time. The following are the major landmarks in the history of the evolution of India's rural credit policy:

1. The Cooperative Credit Societies Act of 1904.
2. All-India Rural Credit Survey Committee (1954): Introduction of three-tier cooperative credit structure and state participation in the equity of cooperatives.
3. All-India Credit Review Committee (1969): Multi-agency approach with the entry of commercial banks in the field of rural credit.
4. Nationalization of 14 commercial banks in1969.
5. Nariman Committee 1971: Priority sector lending and Lead Bank Scheme.
6. Introduction of Differential Rate of Interest (DRI) Scheme 1972.
7. Narasimham Committee 1975: Regional Rural Banks (RRBs) were set up.
8. Committee to Review Arrangements for Institutional Credit for Agricultural and Rural Development, 1981 (CRAFICARD): NABARD was set up in 1982.
9. Agriculture Credit Review Committee 1989: A new credit policy was formulated.
10. Agricultural and Rural Debt Relief Scheme 1990.
11. Narasimham Committee 1991: Financial Sector reforms were introduced

Cooperative credit societies were the first of all types of cooperatives established in India, with the objective of liberating the poor cultivator from the clutches of the moneylender through providing adequate credit on easy terms. The credit cooperatives have played an important role in providing credit to the farmers and they occupy a significant place in India's rural credit system. In 1999–2000, they accounted for about 40% of the total institutional credit supply in the rural sector; their share has been declining since then and it had gone down to about 17% in 2013–14 (MoA 2014, Table 14.9, p. 343). Besides, their main objective also remains, by and large, unfulfilled even after more than 110 years of their existence in India. They suffer from many financial, organizational, managerial, and legal constraints. Their limited ability to mobilize resources, low levels of recovery, high transaction costs, frequent suspension of recovery, low administered interest rates, government controls, and political interference in their business and management affairs have all taken a heavy toll on their viability and sustainability. There is a need to liberate them from these constraints and revamp the cooperative credit structure to make it viable, vibrant, and robust enough to face the challenges posed by the new economic policy of liberalization and privatization. Otherwise, most of the credit cooperatives will have to die sooner or later.

The present credit policy needs to be reoriented, so that a package of all essential financial services is provided to the needy rural people to enable them to adopt new technologies and thereby enhance their income and socio-economic condition. Greater flexibility in timing the repayment of loans is also needed. In a nutshell, rural credit institutions should try to copy those practices of the private moneylenders that make them so popular even now, that is, after 68 years of independence.

The National Agriculture Policy 2000 asserts that progressive institutionalization of rural and farm credit will be continued for providing timely and adequate credit to farmers. The rural credit institutions will be geared to promote savings, investments, and risk management. Particular attention will be paid to the removal of distortions in the priority sector lending by commercial banks for agriculture and rural sectors. Special measures will be taken for the revamping of cooperatives to remove the institutional and financial weaknesses, and evolving simplified procedure for sanction and disbursement of agricultural credit. The endeavor will be to ensure distribution equity in the disbursement of credit. Microcredit will be promoted as an effective tool for alleviating poverty. SHGs and the SHG-Bank linkage system, suited to the Indian rural sector, will be developed as a supplementary mechanism for bringing the rural poor into the formal banking system, thereby improving banks outreach and the credit flows to the poor in an effective and sustainable manner.

National Agriculture Policy

The Government of India had announced a national policy on agriculture in July 2000. This could be considered as a formal pronouncement of the Government of India's latest national agricultural policy. The policy seeks to promote technically sound, economically viable, environmentally non-degrading, and socially acceptable use of country's natural resources—land, water, and genetic endowment—to promote sustainable development of agriculture. Measures are proposed to be taken to contain biotic pressures on land and to control indiscriminate diversion of agricultural lands for non-agricultural purposes. The unutilized wastelands are to be put to use for agriculture and afforestation.

The policy aims at attaining:

- Growth rate in excess of 4% per annum in the agricultural sector;
- Growth that is based on efficient use of resources and conserves our soil, water and biodiversity;
- Growth with equity, that is, growth that is widespread across regions and farmers;
- Growth that is demand-driven and caters to domestic markets, and maximizes benefits from exports of agricultural products in the face of the challenges arising from economic liberalization and globalization; and
- Growth that is sustainable technologically, environmentally and economically.

The highlights of National Agriculture Policy are presented in Box 6.2 and a brief description follows.

Box 6.2

HIGHLIGHTS OF NATIONAL AGRICULTURAL POLICY 2000

1. *Sustainable Agriculture*
2. *Food and Nutritional Security*
3. *Animal Husbandry and Fisheries Development*
4. *Generation and Transfer of Technology*
5. *Inputs Management*
6. *Incentives for Agriculture*
7. *Investments in Agriculture*
8. *Institutional Structure*
9. *Risk Management*
10. *Management Reforms*

Source: GoI (2002).

Food and Nutritional Security

Special efforts will be made to raise the productivity and production of crops to meet the increasing demand for food generated by unabated demographic pressures and raw materials for expanding agro-based industries. A regionally differentiated strategy will be pursued, taking into account the agronomic, climatic, and environmental conditions to realize the full growth potential of every region.

Animal Husbandry and Fisheries Development

Development of animal husbandry, poultry, dairying, and aqua-culture will receive a high priority in the efforts for diversifying agriculture, increasing animal protein availability in the food basket and for generating exportable surpluses. A national livestock breeding strategy will be evolved to meet the requirements of milk, meat, egg, and livestock products, and to enhance the role of draught animals as a source of energy for farming operations and transport.

Generation and Transfer of Technology

A very high priority will be accorded to evolving new location specific and economically viable improved varieties of agricultural and horticultural crops, livestock species and aqua-culture, as also conservation and judicious use of germplasm and other biodiversity resources. The regionalization of agricultural research, based on identified agro-climatic zones, will be accorded high priority. Application of frontier sciences such as biotechnology, remote sensing technologies, pre- and post-harvest technologies, energy saving technologies, and technology for environmental protection through national research system as well as proprietary research will be encouraged. The endeavor will be to build a well-organized, efficient, and result-oriented agricultural research and education system to introduce technological changes in Indian agricultural. Upgradation of agricultural education and its orientation toward uniformity in education standards, women empowerment, user-orientation, vocationalization, and promotion of excellence will be the hallmark of the new policy.

Inputs Management

Adequate and timely supply of quality inputs such as seeds, fertilizers, plant protection chemicals, bio-pesticides, agricultural machinery, and credit at reasonable rates to farmers will be the endeavor of the government. Soil testing and quality testing of fertilizers and seeds will be ensured and supply of spurious inputs will be checked. Balanced and optimum use of fertilizers will be promoted together with use of organic manures and bio-fertilizers to optimize the efficiency of nutrient use.

Incentives for Agriculture

The government will endeavor to create a favorable economic environment for increasing capital formation and a farmer's own investments by removal of distortions in the incentive regime for agriculture, improving the terms of trade with manufacturing sectors, and bringing about external and domestic market reforms, backed by the rationalization of domestic tax structure. It will seek to bestow on the agricultural sector, in as many respects as possible, benefits similar to those obtaining in the manufacturing sector, such as easy availability of credit and other inputs, and infrastructure facilities for development of agri-business industries, development of effective delivery systems, and freeing movement of the agro-produce.

Investments in Agriculture

The agricultural sector has been starved of capital. There has been a decline in the public sector investment in the agricultural sector. Public investment for narrowing regional imbalances, accelerating development of supportive infrastructure for agriculture and rural development, particularly rural connectivity, will be stepped up. Input subsidy reforms will be pursued as a combination of price and institutional reforms to cut down the costs of these inputs for agriculture. Resource allocation regime will be reviewed with a view to rechannelizing the available resources from support measures toward asset formation in rural sector. Private sector investments in agriculture will also be encouraged more particularly in areas such as agricultural research, human resource development, post- harvest management, and marketing.

Institutional Structure

Indian agriculture is characterized by the predominance of small and marginal farmers. Institutional reforms will be so pursued as to channelize their energies for achieving greater productivity and production. The reforms will include, inter alia, consolidation of holdings all over the country on the pattern of north-western states; private sector participation through contract farming and land leasing arrangements; progressive institutionalization of rural and farm credit for providing timely and adequate credit to farmers; active support for the promotion of cooperative form of enterprise and ensure greater autonomy and operational freedom to them to improve their functioning; and amendment and strengthening of the legislative and regulatory framework appropriately to achieve these objectives.

Risk Management

Despite technological and economic advancements, the condition of farmers continues to be unstable due to natural calamities and price fluctuations. National Agriculture Insurance Scheme (NAIS) covering all farmers and all crops throughout the country with built-in provisions for insulating farmers from financial distress caused by natural disasters and making agriculture financially viable will be made more farmer-specific and effective. An endeavor will be made to provide a package insurance policy for the farmers, right from the sowing of the crops to post-harvest operations, including market fluctuations in the prices of agricultural produce.

Management Reforms

Effective implementation of policy initiatives will call for comprehensive reforms in the management of agriculture by the Central and state governments. The Central government will supplement/complement the state governments' efforts through regionally differentiated work plans, comprising crop/area/target-group specific interventions, formulated in an interactive mode and implemented in a spirit of partnership with the states. The Central government will move away from a schematic approach to a macro-management mode and assume a role of advocacy, articulation, and facilitation to help the states in their efforts toward achieving accelerated agricultural development.

National Policy on Cooperatives

The cooperative movement in India traces its origin to the agriculture and allied sectors, and was originally evolved as a mechanism for pooling people's meagre resources with a view to providing them the advantages of the economies of scales. The first attempt to institutionalize the cooperatives began with the enactment of the Cooperative Credit Societies Act, 1904, the scope of which was subsequently enlarged by the more comprehensive Cooperative Societies Act of 1912. Under the Government of India Act, 1919, the subject of cooperation was transferred to the then provinces, which were authorized to enact their own cooperative laws. Under the Government of India Act, 1935, cooperatives remained a provincial subject. Presently, the item "cooperative societies" is a state subject under entry 32 of the state list of the Constitution of India. The Cooperative Societies Acts enacted by state governments are now in place in the states.

In order to administer the operations of cooperative societies where membership was from more than one province, the Government of India enacted the Multi-Unit Cooperative Societies Act, 1942, which was subsequently replaced by the Multi-state Cooperative Societies Act, 1984, under Entry 44 of the Union list of the Constitution of India.

In the pre-independence era, the government did not play an active role in the promotion and development of cooperatives. After independence, the advent of planned economic development ushered in a new era for the cooperatives. Cooperation came to be regarded as a preferred instrument of planned economic development and emerged as a distinct sector of the national economy. It was specifically stated in the First Five Year Plan document that the success of the plan should be judged, among other things, by the extent to which it was implemented through cooperative organizations. In the 1960s, special importance was attached to achieving an increased agricultural production as well as rural development through cooperatives. A significant development on the agricultural front, during 1966–71, was the implementation of a new agricultural strategy, the Green Revolution, which was aimed at achieving of self-sufficiency in food. The introduction of high-yielding and hybrid varieties of seeds and the allocation of large outlays for the provision of irrigation facilities and adequate application of farm inputs led to a manifold increase in the role of cooperatives. Thus, Green Revolution gave a big boost to the activities of the cooperative societies. The increased agricultural production and enhanced productivity in the aftermath of Green Revolution necessitated an emphasis on value-addition in the agricultural produce, and marketing and storage, and the development of allied sectors. As a result, specialized cooperative societies in the fields of milk, oil seeds, sugarcane, cotton, agro-processing, and so on, were set up. Many large cooperatives emerged in the fields of fertilizer manufacturing and marketing of agricultural produce. The role of cooperatives, thus, no longer remained confined to their traditional activities and expanded to new economic ventures as in the case of other such enterprises in the public or the private sector.

The role of cooperatives has acquired a new dimension in the changing scenario of globalization and liberalization of the nation's economy. Internal and structural weaknesses of these institutions combined with the lack of proper policy support have neutralized their positive impact. There are wide regional imbalances in the development of the cooperatives in the country. Notwithstanding their achievements and their phenomenal growth, cooperatives are beset with several financial, organizational, and management constraints and problems. In view of this, there is an urgent need for restructuring them. They are also in search of a new direction and a new strategy for their survival and growth in the changing national and international economic environment.

This has necessitated the need for a clear-cut national policy on cooperatives to enable sustained development and growth of healthy and self-reliant cooperatives for meeting the sectoral/regional aspirations of the people in consonance with the principles of cooperation. In this connection, it is also imperative to address the issues that require to be attended to by evolving a suitable legislative and policy support to these institutions.

In view of the state of cooperatives previously described, the Government of India announced a national policy on cooperatives in April 2002. The policy is an integral part of the concerted efforts of the Government of India to create a congenial environment for cooperatives through appropriate policy measures and legislative support with a view to revitalizing them. Some salient features of the policy are briefly described in this section. This augurs well for the millions of rural poor producers and consumers in the country. However, to impart credibility to them, the commitments of the Government of India need to be institutionalized through the passage of an appropriate (model) central cooperative law. It is hoped that the government will implement the new policy faithfully and honor its commitment to action. Then only will the good intentions of the government fructify.

The main objective of the national policy is to facilitate the all-round development of the cooperatives in the country. Under this policy, cooperatives would be provided necessary support, encouragement, and assistance, so as to ensure that they work as autonomous, self-reliant, and democratically managed institutions accountable to their members and make a significant contribution to the national economy, particularly in the areas that require people's participation and community efforts. This is all the more important in view of the fact that still a sizeable segment of the population in the country is below the poverty line and the cooperatives are the only appropriate mechanism to lend support to this section of the people.

The policy seeks to achieve its objectives mainly through several measures, including the following (GoI 2002d):

1. Ensuring the functioning of cooperatives based on the basic cooperative values and principles as enshrined in the declaration of the International Cooperative Alliance Congress, 1995.
2. Revitalization of the cooperative structure, particularly in the agricultural credit subsector.
3. Reduction of regional imbalances through provision of support measures by the Central/state governments, particularly in the underdeveloped states/regions, where cooperatives are weak.
4. Strengthening of the cooperative education and training.
5. Professionalization of management of cooperatives through human resource development.
6. Greater participation of members in the management of the cooperatives and promoting the concept of user members.
7. Amendment/removal of the provisions in cooperative laws, which seek to unnecessarily restrict and regulate the functioning of cooperatives as autonomous organizations.

The Government of India proposes to formulate a time-bound plan of action for implementation of the policy and back it up with adequate budgetary support in cooperation with the state governments and other concerned agencies including federal/national level cooperative organizations.

The policy commitments of the Government of India to do certain things and not to do certain other things are also laudable. But as the saying goes, the taste of pudding is in eating it. So it is the implementation of the policy and its impact on cooperatives and their stakeholders that will determine how good or bad the policy is. We would suggest the following steps to improve the chances of the policy being effective and successful in achieving its objectives: First, a time limit should be set for formulating "a time-bound plan of action for implementation." Second, a few reputed national-level organizations would have to be identified and designated as "Policy Implementing Agencies" (PIA). For example, the National Dairy Development Board (NDDB) could be designated as the PIA for dairy cooperatives, NABARD for credit cooperatives, and the National Cooperative Development Corporation (NCDC) for marketing and processing cooperatives.

Policies for Fishery Development

Until the first national policy for managing (marine) fisheries was announced in 2004, there was no national fisheries policy in India. However, the Government of India had sought to increase fish production in the country through several research and development programs. More specifically, the Government of India had established several fisheries research institutes under the aegis of the Indian Council of Agricultural Research (ICAR) to undertake research for development of composite fish culture and induced breeding technologies, and to promote their adoption. Besides, it also launched a national level program, Fish Farmer Development Agency (FFDA) in 1976 with initial assistance from the World Bank to promote aqua-culture in the country. The FFDA provided technical, financial and extension support to fish farmers for taking up culture fishery in common pool village ponds and tanks.

The Union Ministry of Agriculture has also paid due attention in the past decade to the development of deep-sea fisheries in the country. The declaration of an Exclusive Economic Zone (EEZ) in 1976 facilitated the exploration, exploitation and utilization of marine living resources in the sea around India extending to 200 nautical miles, thereby giving the nation immense opportunities and challenges to harvest the resources and manage them on a sound scientific basis. The past three decades have witnessed rapid initiatives by the government and private agencies in the marine fisheries sector of the country. Upon realizing that most of the deep-sea fishery resources beyond the conventional fishing limit and fishing capability of the indigenous craft can be gainfully exploited only if the upgraded and sophisticated vessels of adequate size and capabilities were inducted into the fishery, the Government of India facilitated the mobilization of capital and expertise indigenously to address this issue in the 1981 Charter Policy.

After the expiry of five years of operation of this policy, the government revised the policy to rectify the deficiencies noticed during its operation and to make it more beneficial to the country. Accordingly, a revised 1986 Charter Policy was pronounced. This Charter Policy envisaged acquisition of vessels by the Indian companies either through import/construction in India or through joint ventures. As a result of the Charter Policy, 97 companies were permitted to operate 311 foreign fishing vessels. Besides augmenting the marine fish production in the country, the policy also facilitated greater inflow of foreign exchange through export of fish caught by these vessels. All these vessels were operating on 100% Export Oriented Units (EOU) basis. The conditions for the acquisition of vessels of adequate type and number by the Indian companies who chartered vessels helped the growth of Indian deep-sea fishing fleet within a short span of time.

Having laid the foundation for the Indian deep-sea fishing industry, the government went ahead to broad base the initiatives through the Deep Sea Fishing Policy (DSFP) 1991. This policy envisaged to promote joint ventures, test fishing and leasing, besides allowing the vessels chartered under 1986 policy to operate till the validity of their permits lasted. From the beginning of 1994, the DSFP was criticized by various fishermen groups including Members of Parliament (MPs) and Members of Legislative Assemblies (MLAs), mechanized fishing vessel owners, fish processors and other stakeholders. The fishermen groups also resorted to agitation stating that their operational area is being encroached upon by the larger vessels operating under charter, joint ventures and lease arrangements. In response to those criticisms and agitations, the Government of India appointed a committee to review the Deep Sea Fishing Policy. The committee submitted its report in 1996. The government accepted all the 21 recommendations of this committee with minor modifications. Consequently, the government rescinded all the earlier policies on deep-sea fishing. It was also decided that the fishing policies of the government should be revised from time to time. Subsequently, the Government of India constituted a few other committees in order to gather inputs on the availability of the fishing craft, status of marine fishing resources, issues relating to the various stakeholder groups, and so on, and announced its first Marine Fishing Policy (MFP) in 2004 (GoI 2004c).

The 2004 policy seeks to address the concerns of the traditional and coastal fishermen together with those of the other stakeholders in the deep-sea sector so as to achieve harmonized development of marine fishery both in the territorial and extra-territorial waters of the country.

The rationale of the policy is enshrined in the National Agriculture Policy promulgated by the Government of India in 2000. The policy objectives are:

1. to augment marine fish production of the country up to the sustainable level in a responsible manner so as to boost the export of sea food from the country and also to increase per capita fish protein intake of the masses;
2. to ensure socio-economic security of the artisanal fishermen whose livelihood solely depends on this vocation; and
3. to ensure sustainable development of marine fisheries with due concern for ecological integrity and biodiversity.

Some of the salient features of the 2004 policy relevant to fishery resources management and environmental conservations are as follows:

Resource Management

In view of the overexploitation of living resources within 50-metre-deep zone, the policy stipulates the adoption of a stringent fishery management system. In particular, it provides for the following measures:

1. There would be a review of the Marine Fishing Regulation Acts (MFRAs) of coastal states and the Union Territories of India to ensure that they have adequate provisions for management of resources and fishing operations; if necessary, a fresh model bill on coastal fisheries development and management could also be proposed.
2. All existing boat-building yards shall be registered and construction of any new fishing units will be permitted only after obtaining a license. Standards for fishing vessel construction and registration, and for training, certifications and keeping watch over fishing vessel personnel would be fixed and enforced through a new legislation.
3. There will be a "closed season" mandate promulgated in both the coasts, the duration of which would be decided by a designated authority. Such closed seasons shall be uniform for neighboring states unless the geographic or climatic conditions warrant deviations. This would be supplemented by a strict ban on all types of destructive methods of fishing and regulation of mesh sizes in different parts of the fishing gear. The designated authority would be competent to declare any method as destructive after it is convinced so based on facts and data pertaining thereto. Penalties would be fixed for violations of mesh regulations;
4. The designated authority would, if necessary, decide the quota for different classes of fishing vessels in any region.
5. Catching of juveniles and non-targeted species and discarding less preferred species once they are caught would be strictly prohibited through legislation.
6. Posting of observers on commercial fishing vessels and enforcing monitoring control and surveillance (MCS) system would be ensured.
7. A resource enhancement program will be taken up on priority. This would capture of brood stock from these locations would be implemented. Besides, open sea cage culture would be promoted to rear or fatten commercially important species of fishes.

Environmental Concerns

Since they are the final destination for most of the wastes—solid, liquid, radioactive or otherwise—seas are getting more and more polluted over time. This adversely affects the health and productivity of living resources. Such adverse environmental effects of human activities on oceans need to be minimized. Besides, health hazards due to consumption of fish harvested from contaminated water is also becoming a matter of great concern in many parts of the world. The agencies responsible for legislation relating to environmental pollution will be urged to implement them more stringently, so that the impact of pollution on fisheries can be minimized.

The fishermen as the main stakeholder of the marine environment have to be sensitized about the growing land-based pollution. They also need to be educated about eco-friendly fishing practices, which would cause the least disturbance to the marine ecosystem including mangroves. Consumers also need to be protected from the deleterious effects of consuming fish contaminated with heavy metals and other hazardous chemicals discharged from industrial establishments. The 2004 policy, therefore, lays stress on the following aspects:

1. In order to minimize the impact on coastal waters of industrial effluents, the Central and state pollution control boards will need to work in harmony and consider enacting suitable legislation for all industrial establishments discharging effluents into the sea. Such regulations should provide for mandatory inclusion of the Hazard Analysis and Critical Control Points (HACCP) in effluent discharge systems.
2. Coastal area protection by planting mangroves with a view to producing nurseries for shrimp and fish would be introduced as a participatory program with the active involvement of coastal people, particularly in the fishing community.
3. The Coastal Regulation Zone (CRZ) notification would review the present zonation of areas keeping in view the topography of each region and ensure that any human activity in the high tide limit (HTL), which may cause degradation of the coastal environment is not permitted.
4. The policy provides, among other things, for India's participation in the Regional Fisheries Management Bodies (RFMB) to ensure greater cooperation amongst the neighboring countries in the region.

Infrastructure Development

Development of basin infrastructure for marine fisheries is of vital importance and requires an integrated approach. The policy provides for creation of such facilities as jetties, landing centers, provision for fuel, water, and ice, and repair of vessels and gear. For this purpose, a master plan for development of infrastructure for the next 10 years is proposed to be drawn up. Besides, alternatives to the present system of financing of the infrastructure projects by the Center and the state with cost sharing through "Build-Operate-Own" and "Build- Operate-Transfer" systems would be explored.

Areas such as use of information technology, strengthening of database in marine fisheries, human resource development and eco-labeling of marine products would also be paid needed attention.

The 2004 policy has, however, a few drawbacks. For example, it does not clearly state any long-term vision for the fisheries sector. Similarly, it does not specify any particular organizational structure or management system for implementing the policy and monitoring its progress, nor has it a coherent vision of genuine decentralized governance and grassroots empowerment. Also, no specific instruments have been identified for achieving the objectives of the policy. Last but not the least, there is no mention of gender in the entire policy document. This is despite the fact that fisherwomen play an active and important role in grading, processing and marketing of fish locally.

But notwithstanding these drawbacks, we could say that MFP 2004 is a good step in the direction of regulating over-fishing and marine fishery resources management. But the policy needs to be implemented faithfully using appropriate instruments and involving all major stakeholders, particularly fishermen and fisherwomen through their representatives and organizations

National Policy for Farmers (NPF)

The NPF as recommended by the National Commission on Farmers (NCF) has 10 major goals as summed up in Box 6.3 (GoI 2006d):

Box 6.3

OBJECTIVES OF NATIONAL POLICY FOR FARMERS

1. *Improve the economic viability of farming by ensuring that farmers earn a "minimum net income" and ensure that agricultural progress is measured by the advance made in improving that income.*
2. *Mainstream the human and gender dimension in all farm policies and programs, and give explicit attention to sustainable rural livelihoods.*
3. *Complete the unfinished agenda in land reforms.*
4. *Develop and introduce a social security system and support services for farmers.*
5. *Protect and improve the land, water, biodiversity, and climate resources essential for sustained advances in the productivity, profitability and stability of major farming systems by creating an economic stake in conservation.*
6. *Foster community-centered food, water, and energy security systems in rural India and to ensure nutrition security at the level of every child, woman and man.*
7. *Introduce measures which can help attract and retain youth in farming by making it both intellectually stimulating and economically rewarding, by conferring the power and economy of scale to small and marginal farmers both in the production and post-harvest phases of farming.*
8. *Strengthen the bio-security of crops, farm animals, fish, and forest trees for safeguarding both the work and income security of farmer families, and the health and trade security of the nation.*
9. *Restructure agricultural curriculum and pedagogic methodologies for enabling every farm and home-science graduate to become an entrepreneur and to make agricultural education gender sensitive.*
10. *Make India a global outsourcing hub in the production and supply of the inputs needed for sustainable agriculture, and products and processes developed through biotechnology, and information and communication technology.*

Many of the recommendation made by the NCF are similar to those incorporated in National Agriculture Policy 2004. What is needed most now is the faithful implementation of the recommendations made by the NCF and contained in the National Agriculture Policy. But in the absence of requisite administrative and management reforms in the existing system, there is little hope of any better implementations of these recommendations also.

Globalization and Rural Development

After the launching of the New Economic Policy (NEP) in India in August 1991, a process of privatization, deregulation and globalization has been set in motion. The statist model of rural development characterized by the predominant role of the state in initiating, fostering and directing rural development is likely to be abandoned, giving way to a market-driven and guided model. It has become fashionable once again these days to believe that a greater reliance on market forces and the integration of national economies within a global economy—that is, globalization—would reduce the problems of poverty and unemployment through speeding up the pace and level of economic growth. Furthermore, this new faith in market forces has also led to a reorientation of international development policies more in favor of liberal trade than aid as an instrument of development. But despite all this, there is a nagging doubt among the majority of development scholars and practitioners about the relevance of the new model for developing countries such as India, where a very large section of population is below the poverty line, and hence, outside the influence zone of market forces.

Indian agriculture has been protected from the influence of international market forces, mainly through a system of quantitative restrictions on the import of some 800 agricultural commodities. Now that India is a member of the World Trade Organisation (WTO) and a signatory to the Uruguay Round of General Agreement on Trade and Tariffs (GATT), we are under an obligation to replace non-tariff measures (quantitative restrictions/quotas) by reasonable levels of tariffs. Consequently, all quantitative controls on the import of merchandise have been done away with and import tariffs on non-agricultural goods have been reduced from 300% in 1991–92 to 125% in 2006–07. There are apprehensions that the liberalization of agricultural imports would hit our farmers and impair the growth prospects of the agricultural sector. According to a study conducted by Chand (1997, 1–6), liberalization of international trade in agricultural commodities may have the following major impacts on producers and consumers:

1. Removal of quantitative restrictions on international trade is expected to promote both imports and exports of agricultural commodities and production inputs. This would speed up the pace of commercialization and specialization on the basis of higher comparative advantage in the agricultural sector. Export orientation of agricultural production could necessitate the use of increased quantities of chemical fertilizers, pesticides and irrigation water, which would adversely affect the quality of the environment, unless adequate safeguards, such as the use of bio-fertilizers and bio-pesticides, provision of recharging of groundwater aquifers in water scarce areas, and of drainage in water-surplus waterlogged areas are taken.
2. Liberalization of international trade in agricultural commodities would pave the way for the entry of private companies and corporations in the import business, which at present is monopolized by government organizations, which are the sole canalizing agencies for imports of many commodities. Agricultural producers and consumers would be affected through changes in prices—producers from higher prices, and consumers from lower and/or better quality—due to increased competition and consequent increased efficiency.
3. Importers would have an advantage over domestic producers if the agricultural sector is not liberated from internal restrictions. Furthermore, government controls and intervention in the sector need to be reduced to encourage greater participation of the private sector in processing, marketing and distribution.

Like any other economic phenomenon, globalization is based on a set of values, such as competitiveness, efficiency, wealth accumulation and the free play of market forces. Globalization of business and trade without a global view of the society as a global family would lead to social tensions and economic strife, and this is what is happening today in many developing countries that have adopted the structural adjustment programs. In the paradigm of globalization, there is no place for such values as sympathy, kindness, compassion, world-brotherhood, cooperation, and so on. Because of the relatively easy flow of capital internationally as compared to labor, capitalists/portfolio investors would benefit the most from globalization. This would aggravate the problem of disparities in income and wealth between the rich and the poor. Further, globalization would also engender corruption, black money and other social evils, as portfolio investors would like to keep the bureaucrats and politicians on their side by bribing them. Besides, the powerful and rich countries define and redefine the rules of the game of globalization to suit their own national interests or the vested interest of their capitalist investors. This leads to clashes of interest and financial instability, as has been recently experienced in several East Asian countries.

It is clear that globalization is good for only a fraction of Indian society—may be the top 10% of people. The number of people who are likely to lose—or are already losing—from globalization, has been increasing, particularly in those poor countries that are outside North America, Europe and the Pacific Rim. But the issue is not whether globalization is good or bad, or whether it is inevitable. We should understand that globalization is here and that we are unavoidably part of the process of globalization, which demands a new focus and a restructuring and re-engineering of our polity and economy. The questions to be asked are: What can we do about it? How could we benefit from it?

The current opposition of farmers, workers, women and environmentalists to globalization in both developed and developing countries is increasing, as more and more people are questioning the drive for globalization and profit-seeking competition. In a nutshell, the current state of affairs suggests that we are in the process of redefining/remapping global economic and political relations to reflect a diversity of positions, as well as shared concerns and tensions. If the process is pursued to its logical conclusion, it could expose the hypocrisy of the old order and create a new political environment where the powerful hegemony of the transnational, commercial and financial institutions can be challenged through cooperative action by the losers. Acting individually, developing countries are unable to protect their people and natural resources from the havocs of globalization and transnational companies, which are taking over life-supporting industries. But acting collectively/cooperatively, they could face the challenges posed by globalization and benefit from the opportunities that it opens up. Similarly, within a country, rural producers' cooperatives could protect the small and marginal farmers from the adverse effects of globalization, and also enable them to benefit from it. What is needed most in the rural sector now is to liberate the rural producers and their organizations from the shackles of unnecessary government controls and archaic laws.

Consequent upon dismantling of Quantitative Restrictions (QRs) on imports as per the WTO Agreement on Agriculture (AoA), commodity-wise strategies and arrangements for protecting the grower from the adverse impact of undue price fluctuations in world markets and for promoting exports will need to be formulated. Apart from price competition, other aspects of marketing, such as quality, choice, health and bio-safety need to be promoted. Exports of horticultural produce and marine products deserve a high priority. A two-fold long-term strategy of diversification of agricultural produce and value addition, enabling the production system to respond to external environment, and creating export demand for the commodities produced in the country needs to be evolved with a view to providing the farmers incremental income from export earnings. A favorable economic environment and supportive public management system are also needed for promotion of agricultural exports. Quarantine, both of exports and imports need to be given particular attention so that Indian agriculture is protected from the ingress of exotic pests and diseases.

In order to protect the interest of farmers in aftermath of removal of QRs, continuous monitoring of international prices need to be undertaken and appropriate tariffs and other protection measures will need to be provided. Import duties on manufactured commodities used in agriculture need to be rationalized. The domestic agricultural market should be liberalized, and all controls and regulations hindering an increase in farmers' income should be reviewed and abolished to ensure that agriculturists receive prices commensurate with their efforts and investment. Restrictions on the movement of agricultural commodities throughout the country should be progressively dismantled.

Key Points

1. The term "policy" may be defined as a definite course of action selected (as by government, an institution, a group or an individual) from among alternatives and in light of given conditions to guide and usually to determine present and future decisions. The most common social and political usage of the term refers to a course of action or intended course of action conceived of as deliberately adopted after a review of possible alternatives and pursued or oriented to be pursued. Rural development policy implies the actions taken by the government in pursuit of certain objectives of rural development.
2. Public policy is a form of social control. A farmer accepting a production loan from a nationalized bank and a subsidy from the government is restricted in the manner in which he can spend the borrowed money and subsidy, but his freedom to expand his output, improve his income and standard of living and develop his individual talents is enhanced.
3. The farther we move away from simple, small-scale handicraft industry and self-contained and subsistence agriculture, a greater need develops for public policy in the economic field. The individual, as a producer and as a consumer, depends more and more upon the general conditions of the market, of employment, output and production efficiency of the nation as a whole, and upon the way income is distributed among the people; in short, upon the economic welfare of the country.
4. Some specific reasons favoring government intervention in the rural sector are: India's commitment to set up a "socialist pattern of society"; violent fluctuations in agricultural production, prices and incomes; rural poverty and income inequality; small, scattered and unorganized rural enterprises; and inadequate and poor basic infrastructure in rural areas.
5. Rural development policies are designed to improve the conditions under which rural people work and live. The goals of policies are governed by what people desire, and the measures of policies by what people think the government can and ought to do to bring about the desired change. This is the theory of public policy. Changes are desired only when people do not like the way things are going. Pressure for public action arises when people feel that they, individually, cannot bring about the desired adjustments. From the Directive Principles of State Policy enshrined in India's Constitution, one could derive two important goals of economic policy: first, increasing the national income; and second, improving the distribution of national income among the members of the society. These and other goals are reflected in India's economic policies that are enunciated by it from time to time.
6. Given the multiplicity of policy goals, it is necessary to study the relationships among them and see that they converge toward public interest, or at least do not militate against it. This can be done if various policy goals and program objectives are arranged in the form of a pyramid. At the top of the pyramid is the master goal of economic policy. At the next level, we have the objectives of specific government programs; and at the lowest level, relatively simple and clear-cut objectives of most specific level of program units are listed.
7. India has a long history of government intervention in the rural sector of its economy. In the pre-independence era, the British government intervention was aimed at promoting the export of food and raw materials to the Great Britain. There was no

state policy for the development of resources of India for the welfare of its people. Introduction of land tenure system, opening up of road and rail communications, and promotion of export trade in certain agricultural commodities were the important measures taken by the British government.

8. In January 1946, the then Government of India issued a "Statement of Agriculture and Food Policy in India," which spelt out the objectives to be achieved, the measures to be taken, and the respective roles of the Center and the provinces. According to the statement, the all-India policy was to promote the welfare of the people and to secure a progressive improvement of their standard of living.
9. India did not have a unified national policy for rural development until the year 2000, when the first National Agricultural Policy was announced. What existed until then was a National Forest Policy (NFP), an Agricultural Price Policy (APP), a Rural Credit Policy, a National Water Policy (NWP), some semblance of a land reforms policy and an assortment of agricultural and rural development programs not integrated with one another and coordinated properly. The main objectives of the National Agriculture Policy include, inter alia, the promotion of technically sound, economically viable, environmentally non-degrading, and socially acceptable use of country's natural resources—land, water and genetic endowment—to promote sustainable development of agriculture.
10. Besides the National Agriculture Policy, India now has a national policy on Cooperatives (2002), a National Policy for Farmers (2006) and a Marine Fishing Policy (2004). All these policies are designed to ultimately improve the well-being of rural people. But the intensions of the public policies in India are hardly realized, thanks to their lax and lackadaisical implementation.
11. In August 1991, the Government of India launched a New Economic Policy (NEP), which is characterized by privatization, deregulation and globalization. The statist model of rural development characterized by the predominant role of the state in initiating, fostering and directing rural development is likely to be abandoned giving way to a market-driven and guided model. It has become fashionable once again these days to believe that a greater reliance on market forces and integration of national economies within a global economy—that is, globalization—would reduce the problems of poverty and unemployment through speeding up the pace and level of economic growth.

Questions for Discussion

1. Does India need to have a separate national policy for rural development? Yes/No. If yes, why; if no, why not?
2. Illustrate with an example, the concept of hierarchy of policy goals.
3. In a democratic country such as India, who should determine the goals and measures of public policies and how?
4. Write a critique of the National Agriculture Policy 2000, with special reference to its objectives and the measures stipulated to achieve them.
5. Write an essay on why India's rural sector continues to be relatively backward and underdeveloped despite the fact the so many policies and programs for its development have been launched by the government from time to time over the last 68 years or so.

6. In what ways will the present economic policy of the Government of India characterized by privatization, deregulation and globalization affect the rural people, especially marginal and small farmers and rural artisans?

Notes

1. http:///dacnet.nic.in/agStat06-07.htm
2. See Singh and Shishodia (2007, Ch.10) for the details of a new system of FRA.
3. http://wrmin.nic.in/writereaddata/NationalWaterPolicy/NWP2012Eng6495132651.pdf (Accessed on September 9, 2015).
4. http://agmarknet.nic.in (Accessed on September 15, 2015).

Chapter 7

Strategies for Sustainable Development

LEARNING OUTCOMES

After having gone through this chapter, students should be able to:

- **Define and illustrate the term "strategy" in the context of development;**
- **Define the concept of sustainability and differentiate between "strong sustainability" and "weak sustainability";**
- **Define the term "sustainable development," and explain why it should be the supreme goal of public policy;**
- **Identify the major indicators of non-sustainable development;**
- **Describe India's major strategies of rural development followed in the past and their merits and demerits and**
- **Illustrate the basic elements of an ideal strategy of sustainable development.**

Introduction

According to Wikipedia, the free encyclopedia, a strategy is a long-term plan of action designed to achieve a particular "goal," most often "winning." Strategy is differentiated from "tactics" or immediate actions with resources at hand by its nature of being extensively premeditated, and often practically rehearsed. The word derives from the Greek word *strategos*, which derives from two words: *stratos* (army) and *ago* (ancient Greek for "leading"). *Strategos* referred to a "military commander" during the age of Athenian democracy. This chapter deals with strategies for sustainable development.

Sustainable development has recently risen to the top of international economic and political agenda. The report of the WCED (1987), "Our Common Future," was the first major international initiative that enhanced the awareness of policy makers about sustainable development and the complexity of relationship between environmental problems, economic growth, and needs of people, rich and poor. One of the follow-up actions initiated by the UN to implement the recommendations of WCED culminated into the UNCED held in Rio in June 1992. The UNCED has further heightened the global concern over deteriorating environment and the interest in the search for practicable strategies for sustainable development.

This chapter first presents the basic concepts and connotations of sustainability and sustainable development, and then a few indicators of non-sustainable development. This is followed by a critical review of India's strategies of rural development and, finally, the presentation of basic elements of a new strategy of sustainable development.

The Concepts of Sustainability and Sustainable Development

The concept of sustainability basically implies a characteristic of a system, a program, or a resource to last intact forever. The concept first came into prominence in 1980 in the context of the WCS of the International Union for the Conservation of Nature and Natural Resources (IUCN). Thereafter, the WCWD, or the Brundtland Commission, in its 1987 report, "Our Common Future," emphasized the key role of agricultural sustainability as the basis of sustainable development (WCED 1987). Currently, there are two distinct concepts of sustainability in vogue. First, the economist's worldview of sustainability is concerned about the long-term constancy of economic output, income, or consumption. Second, the ecologist's and biologist's concept of sustainability relates to long-term preservation of biosphere, that is, the sustenance of human populations and biodiversity conservation in a given geographical area/region, endowed with limited natural resources (Bartelmus 1997, 326–27; FAO 1989, 65). The former, that is, the economic sustainability, is production- and consumption-oriented, and the latter, that is, the ecological sustainability, has sustenance of people and biodiversity conservation as its focal points.

Economic sustainability implies the maintenance/constancy of produced capital and natural capital (natural resources and environment) used in the production of goods and services. Ecological sustainability can be defined in terms of compliance with the number of people (limit) a natural system/area/watershed can sustain indefinitely, or for a specified time period, at a particular standard of living. Obviously, carrying capacity depends on the level of desirable standard of living, type of production technologies in use, time horizon of analysis, and external trade with other regions/countries. Variations in all these parameters/factors render the concept inapplicable except at the global level, which is a utopia.

As stated earlier in Chapter 1, the WCED (1987, 43) defined sustainable development as "development that meets the needs of the present without compromising the ability of future generations to meet their own needs." This definition emphasizes the need for the present generation to ensure intergenerational equity by safeguarding the interests of future generations through maintaining the natural resources capital of this planet intact. In these respects, it is very similar to the concept of sustainable livelihood by which we mean secure access of both present and future generations to basic necessities of life such as food, clothes, shelter, security, freedom, basic literacy, and health care on a long term basis. This concept of sustainable livelihood is almost synonymous with that of human survival with freedom and dignity, or human development, which should be, in our opinion, the supreme goal of mankind. Few would dispute that sustainable livelihood (survival) as a goal is more environment-friendly and more globally acceptable than the goal of economic growth.

Sustainable development requires that, in the process of economic growth, we maintain our natural resources and environment intact and use/harvest only that much quantity that is regenerated naturally, that is, we live on the "flows" and keep the "stock" of natural resources and environment intact. However, we would like to add that it is now possible to augment the natural flows/harvest of products of nature through appropriate technological and management interventions.

In the context of sustainability, two questions are important:

1. How long will our natural resources last, given current consumption patterns?
2. How should we manage our natural resources and environment so that the future generations have access to the same quality of life as the present generation?

The first question of resource longevity is really one of prediction and accounting: How do technology, taste, population, and natural regeneration influence the stock of environmental goods that will be available from one year to the next? Thus, the ethical motives behind sustainability are derived from a concern for the future, and the fear that the current trends in production and consumption are threatening the well-being of future generations.

Questions about how long resources will last have long concerned planners and economists who have worried that the world is running out of agricultural land, fish, and other important environmental goods. A variety of indices have been developed to measure the degree to which resources are being consumed sustainably. In their most basic form, these indices simply divide stocks by consumption rates. More elaborate indices take into account the fact that changes in taste or technology may reduce future demand while natural regeneration, especially of biological resources, may increase stocks to keep pace with the increasing demand. Generally, most predictions about resource sustainability lack accuracy. Clearly, a better understanding of the trends in demand and technology are necessary before we can say with confidence how environmental quality and goods will fare in a consumption-oriented world.

The second question of sustainability, "how should we manage our resources," requires that we have some management target for the way in which resources are distributed across generations. The concept of Pareto optimality, useful in the analysis of welfare within a generation, is not applicable when we do not know the tastes, preferences, or technologies of the future generations. Consumers, particularly the poor, tend to attach a higher preference to consumption today than tomorrow. Should we ignore this tendency when thinking of sustainability, or should we include the society's time preference by discounting the value of future consumption when we decide how to manage for sustainability? What about expected improvements in technology? Could saving too much of our natural and environmental resources make the future generations better off at the expense of the present generations?

The "we" in the second question of sustainability, "how should *we* manage...," implies that there is some sort of shared vision about the goals of sustainability. However, there is no universal consensus about a single indicator of sustainability. But the most commonly used indicator of sustainability of any proposed resource-use over time is the maximization of net present value, as proposed by the neoclassical economists (Grafton, Pendelton and Nelson 2001, xxvi–ix).

However, the question whether sustainability and sustainable development ought to refer to the maintenance of the status quo, economic growth, redistribution of wealth, the protection of capital stocks, or the preservation of natural capital, is still debatable. The answer would vary from society to society and with the stage of economic development within a society. Related to this question are the notions of "weak sustainability" and "strong sustainability." The former is defined as the maintenance of the value of the aggregate stock of capital. It implies that we can substitute human-made capital for natural capital in production and consumption, such that economic growth can be associated with improvements in environmental quality. More rigorously, "weak sustainability" can be defined as follows:

$$K + H + SC + N \geq X^*,$$

where K is man-made capital, H is human capital, SC is social capital, N is natural capital, and X^* is some predetermined threshold level of all the forms of capital expressed in monetary terms. This implies that under a policy of weak sustainable development, depletion of the stock of natural capital could be made good by investment in man-made capital. But it is important to note that the substitution of one form of capital for another form is possible only to a certain extent. This means that a certain minimum quantum of each form of capital is essential for development.

By contrast, "strong sustainability" posits that natural and human-made capital are complements and cannot be substituted for each other in either production or consumption. Consequently, economic growth that uses natural resources and generates wastes must increase environmental degradation. A rigorous definition of "strong sustainability" is as follows:

$$K \geq K^*;\ H \geq H^*;\ SC \geq SC^*; \text{ and } N \geq N^*.$$

This definition implies that each type of capital stock be maintained in its own right above some minimum level. Daly (1990) has specified the following three principles for attaining and maintaining strong sustainable development:

1. Renewable resources must be harvested at or below the growth rate for some predetermined stock of the resource.
2. As non-renewable resources are depleted, renewable substitutes must be developed so as to maintain the flow of goods and services over time.
3. Pollution emissions should be limited to the assimilative capacity of the environment.

The scale of sustainability is also an important factor affecting the success of a policy of sustainability. The scale ranges from local to global and, accordingly, we could think of local sustainability and global sustainability. The scale determines the type of problems that can be addressed locally, nationally, or globally. For example, the problem of global warming or depletion of ozone layer can be addressed effectively only at the global level and not at the local level. The distinction between local sustainability and global sustainability can be related to "weak sustainability" and "strong sustainability." In most discussions of sustainability, "weak sustainability" and "strong sustainability" are thought of as competing paradigms. However, it is more useful to recognize that both these measures could be valid in different contexts concurrently. For global sustainability, it is essential to maintain stocks of some critical resource, say biodiversity, above a "safe minimum standard" level for sustainable development, a condition for strong sustainability. But the local economy, while dependent on strong global sustainability, may seek weak local sustainability by depleting its renewable resources, say fisheries or forest, to maintain its material well-being, without adversely affecting global sustainability.

Some Indicators of Non-Sustainable Development

The following indicators and data support the non-sustainability of current patterns of production, consumption, and economic growth (WRI 1992, xi; Bartelmus 1997, 325).

Land Degradation

Over the past 50 years or so, 1.2 billion hectare (bha) of land—an area larger that of China and India taken together—has been degraded and its productivity reduced (WRI 1992, xi). It is also estimated that 500 billion tons of topsoil has been lost since 1972 (Brown et al. 1993)

Table 7.1: *Extent of Land Degradation in India: 2010–11*

Sl. No.	*Type of Degradation*	*Area in Million Hectare*	*% of Total Degraded Land*
1.	Wind and water erosion	94.87	79.00
2.	Acidic soil	17.93	15.00
3.	Alkaline soil	3.72	3.00
4.	Saline soil	2.73	1.80
5.	Water-logged	0.91	1.00
6.	Mining and industrial waste	0.26	0.20
7.	All	120.40	100.00

Source: Land Degradation and Its Management in India, Ministry of Agriculture, Government of India, New Delhi, Mimeo.

and 5 mha are lost annually due to desertification. If such human-caused losses continue, feeding the world population, which is projected to nearly double by the middle of the 21st century, will be a very difficult task. In India, it is estimated that the total land degraded in 2010–11 was 120.40 mha. Of this, the land affected by wind and water erosion was 94.87 mha (79%); acidic soil was 17.93 mha (15%); alkaline soil was 3.7 mha(3%); saline soil 2.73 mha (1.8%); water-logged was 0.91 mha (1%); and mining and industrial waste 0.26 mha. (0.20%); see Table 7.1.

Thus, about 27% of the total geographical area of India is undergoing various forms of degradation. Besides, about 25 of the total area is affected by desertification (GoI, 2014, i).

Land degradation can result from both intrinsic attributes, such as location, environment, and chemical and physical properties of the soil, as well as from manmade circumstances. Whatever its underlying causes, land degradation has significant adverse impacts on crop productivity and the environment. Joshi and Jha (1991), in a study of four villages in Uttar Pradesh, found that a 50% decline in crop yields over a period of eight years was due to salinization and waterlogging caused by the irrigation system.

A characteristic feature of land resources in India is the preponderance of common pool lands, that is, the lands that are used in common by identifiable groups of people. These lands, irrespective of their legal ownership, are accessible to local people without any restrictions and are used without any rules and regulations. In this sense, they may be called open access resources (OARs). All OAR suffer from what Hardin (1968) called "the tragedy of the commons." Most OARs are degraded, eroded, denuded of vegetation, encroached, and polluted. Thus, with more than half of its land being degraded, India has very bleak prospects of sustaining even the existing (low) rate of food production in the coming decades.

Degradation and Depletion of Water Resources

Water is essential for the survival of all forms of life on this planet. Adequate and timely availability of water for irrigation is an important factor affecting agricultural production and, thereby, food security. The global renewable water resources are estimated at 41,022 cubic kilometer (ckm) and, in 1998, the per capita availability of water was 6,918 cubic meter (cm) with wide variations from nation to nation ranging from merely 11 cm in Kuwait to 6,06,498 cm in Iceland (WRI 1998, 305).The per capita renewable fresh water availability in India in 2011 was estimated to be only 1,184 cubic metres (cm) per annum as compared to 31,534 cm in Russian Federation. 8,252 cm in Bangladesh, 74,863 cm and 22,094 cm in Australia (FAO 2014, Table 5, p. 26). It has been declining over time and will continue to do so in future also. While this is the picture at the aggregate national level, there are significant regional and temporal variations in water availability caused by spatial and year-to-year fluctuations in the annual rainfall that India receives. This causes the problems of regional and seasonal scarcity and surpluses.

Due to the increasing area being brought under irrigation, growing industrialization and urbanization, and increasing human and animal populations, the pressure on water resources has increased tremendously and, consequently, both surface water and groundwater resources are being depleted and degraded at a fast rate in most of the countries of the world. Some people believe that in the 21st century, there will be more water wars—both internationally and intra-nationally—than any other kind of war. This trend poses a real threat not only to sustainable development but also to human survival.

Both surface water and groundwater resources in India are in a serious state of degradation and pollution. The extent of degradation of water resources has reached a stage when immediate intervention by governmental and nongovernmental agencies through appropriate measures has become absolutely essential. Surface water is hardly fit for drinking. The river Ganga, which is worshiped by devout Hindus as "Mother Ganga" and taking a dip into its waters is supposed to cleanse the "sins," is no exception. It is highly polluted at several places and several projects including Ganga Action Plans aimed at reducing the pollution have failed.[1] After getting elected, the NDA led by India's prime minister, Narendra Modi, affirmed to work for cleaning the river and controlling pollution.[2] Subsequently, the Namami Ganga project was announced by the government in July 2014 budget for this purpose.

Similarly, groundwater in many arid and semi-arid areas has been depleted due to over-extraction, and degraded due to leaching of fertilizers and pesticides' residues from cultivated fields. Consequently, the incidence of waterborne diseases has increased significantly in recent years.

Furthermore, mismanagement of both surface water and groundwater resources in conjunction with the growing demand of water for agricultural, industrial, and domestic uses has engendered many problems, such as depletion and degradation of groundwater aquifers, pollution of surface water bodies, and acute shortage of freshwater in arid, semi-arid and hard rock areas in the country. Groundwater table has gone down drastically in many areas of the country, such as Mehsana district in north Gujarat, western Uttar Pradesh, and Coimbatore district in west Tamil Nadu. It is estimated that in Mehsana district, water table has been falling at the rate of 5–8 m annually and that some 2,000 wells dry up every year (Moench and Kumar 1997, 305). In the coastal areas of Gujarat, excessive extraction has depleted the groundwater aquifers and the vacuum so created has been filled in by intrusion of seawater, a phenomenon called salinity ingress. It is estimated that salinity ingress is increasing at an alarming rate of half-a-kilometer to one kilometer a year along 60% of the 1,100 km-long Saurashtra coast in Gujarat (*TOI* 1998). The salinity ingress has rendered groundwater in those areas unfit for both domestic and agricultural uses, and has adversely affected crop yields. Most of the problems in the use and management of water resources could be traced to the lack of well-defined property rights and absence of appropriate institutions for regulating the use of water. Restoring the loss of sustainability of renewable water resources requires governmental intervention in such forms as creation and enforcement of appropriate property rights, rational pricing of water, regulation of water use, taxes, and cooperative management by users' groups or associations (Singh 1998).

Degradation and Depletion of Forest Resources

Forests are a valuable renewable resource providing the vital life support system and are essential for sustainable development. With the fast growing population, the demand for forest resources has progressively increased. Consequently, forest resources are being depleted at a rate that is higher than the natural regeneration rate. The world's total forest area is just over 4 bha, which constitutes about 31% of the world's total geographical area. This corresponds to an average of 0.6 ha of forest area per capita. The present rate of deforestation in the world shows signs of decreasing, but is still alarmingly high. Around 13 mha of forest were converted to other uses or lost through natural causes each year in the last decade (2000–10) compared with 16 mha per year in the decade of 1900–2000 (FAO 2010, xiii).

Although, there is no consensus about the extent of deforestation of tropical forests in the world, environmentalists point with alarm to the eroding hillsides, barren dry lands studded with trunks of once-thriving trees, and burned out tropical forests. At a regional level, South America suffered the largest net loss of forests between 2000 and 2010—about 4.0 mha per year—followed by Africa, which lost 3.4 mha annually. Asia, which had a net loss of forest of some 6,00,000 ha annually in the 1990s, reported a net gain of forest of more than 2.2 mha per year in the period 2000–10, primarily due to the large-scale afforestation reported by China and despite continued high rates of net loss in many countries in South and Southeast Asia (FAO 2010, xvi)

In India, millions of rural people depend on forests for their livelihood. In view of this, the sustainability of the flow of forest products is essential for sustaining their livelihoods. But, over the last three decades or so, forest resources have been under great biotic and abiotic pressures. They have been subject to overexploitation, degradation, and encroachment (Singh 1994, 226). It is estimated that about 36 mha of the total forestland is deforested and degraded (SPWD 1984). Being OAR, "open forest" areas, which account for about 42% of the total forest area are all highly degraded and denuded. Besides, substantial chunks of forest land are being diverted to non-forestry uses. Consequently, the forests' area, productivity and production have declined, and their sustainability is threatened. The low productivity of forests in India in terms of the volume of growing stock is evident from the fact that the volume of growing stock in India in the year 2000 was 43 cm/ha, as compared to 119 cm in Malaysia and 100 cm in Nepal (FAO 2001). All this poses a threat to the survival of millions of poor people, especially tribals, who mainly depend on forests for their livelihood.

Depletion of Conventional Sources of Energy

The world's consumption of commercial energy from conventional sources is increasing at a rapid rate, depleting the world's reserve of fossil fuels. In the central scenario of the World Energy Outlook 2014 (WEO-2014), world primary energy demand will be 37% higher in 2040, putting more pressure on the global energy system. But this pressure would be even greater if not for efficiency measures that play a vital role in holding back global demand growth. The scenario shows that world demand for two out of the three fossil fuels—coal and oil—will essentially reach a plateau by 2040, although, for both fuels, this global outcome will be a result of very different trends across countries. At the same time, renewable energy technologies will gain ground rapidly, helped by falling costs and subsidies (estimated at $120 billion in 2013). While coal is abundant and its supply relatively secure, its future use is constrained by measures to improve efficiency, tackle local pollution, and reduce CO_2 emissions. Coal demand will be 15% higher in 2040, but growth will slow to a near halt in the 2020s. Regional trends will vary, with demand reaching a peak in China, dropping by one-third in the US but continuing to grow in India.

In an in-depth focus on nuclear power, WEO-2014 sees installed capacity growing by 60% to 2040 in the central scenario, with the increase concentrated heavily in just four countries (China, India, Korea, and Russia). Nuclear power plays an important strategic role in enhancing energy security for some countries. It also avoids almost four years' worth of global energy-related carbon-dioxide (CO_2) emissions by 2040. However, nuclear power faces major challenges in competitive markets where there are significant market and regulatory risks, and public acceptance remains a critical issue worldwide. Many countries must also make important decisions regarding the almost 200 nuclear reactors due to be retired by 2040, and how to manage the growing volumes of spent nuclear fuel in the absence of permanent disposal facilities.

A critical "sign of stress" is the failure to transform the energy system quickly enough to stem the rise in energy-related CO_2 emissions (which grow by one-fifth to 2040) and put the world on a path consistent with a long-term global temperature increase of 2°C. In the central scenario, the entire carbon budget allowed under a 2°C climate trajectory is consumed by 2040, highlighting the need for a comprehensive and ambitious agreement at the COP21 meeting in Paris in 2015.

In India, the per capita consumption of commercial energy is very low when compared with that in developed countries. For example, in 2012, it was merely 18 giga joules per annum as compared to 248 giga joules in Canada and 192 in the US (UN 2012, 47–64). But given the very large size of its population, even this level of energy consumption is not sustainable unless non-conventional sources of energy are fully developed and harnessed.

Loss of Biodiversity

The diversity of species is necessary for the normal functioning of ecosystems and the biosphere as a whole. The genetic material in the wild species contributes billions of rupees to the world economy in the form of improved crop species, new drugs and medicines, and raw materials for industry. But utility aside, there are also moral, ethical, cultural, aesthetic, and purely scientific reasons for conserving wild beings.

There are no reliable estimates of the extent of biodiversity available worldwide. Estimates vary from two million to 100 million species with the best estimate being somewhere near 10 million, of which only 1.4 million have actually been named so far. The biological heritage of the planet Earth is increasingly at risk. It is estimated that one-quarter of all species are in danger of extinction, and 5,000 to 1,50,000 species are lost annually due to the destruction of biomass and habitat by destructive agriculture, deforestation, pollution, and destructive fishing and grazing practices (Bartelmus 1997, 325). Much of the world's biodiversity is found in developing countries and it is estimated to be disappearing at 50 to 100 times the natural regeneration rates (World Bank 1988, 26). Nearly half the world's vascular plant species and one-third of terrestrial vertebrates are endemic to 25 "hotspots" of biodiversity, each of which has at least 1,500 endemic plant species. None of these hotspots have more than one-third of their pristine habitat remaining. Historically, they covered 12% of the land's surface, but today their intact habitat covers only 1.4% of the land. As a result of this habitat loss, we expect many of the hotspot endemics to have either become extinct or—because much of the habitat loss is recent—to be threatened with extinction.

India is endowed with an immensely rich biodiversity. It is rated as one of the 12 mega diversity countries in the world, accounting for 60% to 70% of the world's biodiversity. India has 6% of the world's flowering plant species, 14% of the world's birds, one-third of the world's identified plant species numbering over 45,000, and about 81,000 identified species of animals (World Bank 1996, 1). India's natural resources and biodiversity are economically important, both nationally and globally. As one of the world's oldest and largest agricultural countries, India has an impressive diversity of crop species and varieties. At least 166 species of crop plants and 320 species of wild relatives of cultivated crops originate in the subcontinent. About 90% of all medicines in India come from plant species, many of which are harvested in the wild. Medicinal plants and other non-timber forest products are particularly important as a source of income and sustenance for the tribal population. Natural ecosystems strongly influence natural resources development and management, which is important not only for agriculture but also for industrial and municipal development.

In India, there has been a tremendous loss of biodiversity due to deforestation. Many plant and animal species are on the brink of extinction. Although the extinction of 23 species has been confirmed, it is suspected that many more have died unnoticed. Although, loss of habitat, over-harvesting, and pollution are immediate causes of loss of biodiversity in most of the cases, the underlying causes of these actions are several socio-economic factors, such as population pressure, poverty, unemployment, ignorance, and lack of incentives for using natural resources and biodiversity on sustainable basis in the best interest of society. So long as the human and animal population was within the carrying capacity of locally available natural resources and the local environment, there was no environmental degradation and no loss of biodiversity due to human actions. But as the population increased and local economies got integrated with external economies through trade, the process of degradation of natural resources and loss of biodiversity started. Further, many communities depend directly on natural resources for their livelihood. They are very poor and ignorant, and have no alternative employment opportunities. This compels them to overexploit and degrade the natural resources accessible to them, which, in turn, poses a great threat not only to their own survival, but also to ecological security and integrity. It is high time that India adopted a responsible national policy of natural resources and biodiversity conservation, which is in tandem with its economic and social development policies.

Climate Change

Climate change is a change in the statistical distribution of weather patterns when that change lasts for an extended period of time (i.e., decades to millions of years). Climate change may refer to a change in average weather conditions, or in the time variation of weather around longer term average conditions (i.e., more or fewer extreme weather events). Climate change is caused by factors such as biotic processes, variations in solar radiation received by Earth, plate tectonics, and volcanic eruptions. Certain human activities have also been identified as significant causes of recent climate change, often referred to as "global warming."

There have been perceptible changes in climate all over the world, particularly in the last two decades or so. The major changes include global warming, depletion of ozone layer, acid rains, and increased incidence of droughts, floods, cyclones, and hailstorms. According to the Intergovernmental Panel on Climate Change (IPCC) (1995), atmospheric accumulations of greenhouse gas emissions have led to global warming to the extent of 1°C to 3.5°C. (Bartelmus 1997, 325). This is further substantiated by the Fourth Assessment Report (2007) of the IPCC. Of particular concern is the emission of carbon dioxide (CO_2) from the combustion of fossil fuels, which now supply around 95% of the world's commercial energy. Scientific understanding of global warming is increasing. The IPCC reported in 2014 that scientists were more than 95% certain that most of global warming is caused by increasing concentrations of greenhouse gases and other human (anthropogenic) activities.[3] Current concentrations of CO_2, methane, nitrous oxide, and other greenhouse gases have reached levels well above those of the preindustrial era.

If the growth in global emissions continues unabated, the atmospheric concentration of CO_2 is likely to double, relative to its preindustrial level, mid-way through the next century. The accumulation of the greenhouse gases poses significant risks to the world's climate and to human well-beings. Potential impacts include a rise in sea levels, greater frequency of floods and droughts, shifts in agricultural production, threats to human health from increased range and incidences of diseases, changes in availability of freshwater supplies, and damage to ecosystems and biodiversity. Another disturbing aspect of this problem is the disproportionately high share of the industrialized and oil-producing countries in the world's total emissions. To stabilize atmospheric concentrations of CO_2, the emissions must be cut by 60% from the present levels. The Kyoto Agreement, signed in December 1997 by the US and 159 other countries, provides for placing binding limits on industrial countries' emissions of greenhouse gases. The agreement also provides opportunities for the industrial nations to trade rights to emit greenhouse gases with each other.

The climate change performance index is an instrument intended to enhance transparency in international climate politics. Its aim is to encourage political and social pressure on those countries that have, up to now, failed to take ambitious actions on climate protection as well as to highlight countries with best-practice climate policies. On the basis of standardized criteria, the index evaluates and compares the climate protection performance of 58 countries that are, together, responsible for more than 90% of global energy-related CO_2 emissions. Eighty percent of the evaluation is based on objective indicators of emissions trend and emissions level (50% for emissions trend and 30% for emissions level). Twenty percent of the index results are built upon national and international climate policy assessments by more than 200 experts from the respective countries. The emissions trend is the most important indicator set within the CCPI, as it constitutes 50% of the ranking's weight. Therefore, if countries wish to improve their ranking, it is vital for them to lower their emissions trend.[4] Table 7.2 presents for the top 10 countries of the world the emissions emitted and their CCPI rank. The poor performance of the majority of the 10 largest CO_2 emitters is particularly alarming. These countries account for more than 60% of global CO_2 emissions. In the case of India also, the trend is alarming and requires urgent attention of policy makers.

Table 7.2: *World's Top Ten Carbon Emitters and Their CCP Rank*

Country	*Share of Global CO_2 Emissions (%)*	*CCPI Rank*	
		2011	*2012*
United Kingdom	1.61	8	5
Germany	2.59	7	6
India	5.47	10	23
Korea, Republic	1.78	34	41
Japan	3.77	38	43
USA	17.91	54.52	52
Canada	1.80	57	54
Russia	5.28	48	55
China	23.71	56	57
Iran	1.84	52	60

Source: Climate Change Performance Index 2012: Results.[5]

Ozone Layer Depletion

Increasing industrialization and deforestation are changing the chemical composition of the earth's composition in ways that threaten agriculture, ecological balance and human health. The atmospheric changes pose two major threats: First, ozone layer depletion by the production and use of chlorofluorocarbons (CFCs) and other related compounds, and second, greenhouse effect resulting from the concentration of CO_2 and other greenhouse gases. The ozone layer or ozone shield refers to a region of Earth's stratosphere that absorbs most of the Sun's ultraviolet (UV) radiation. It contains high concentrations of ozone (O_3) relative to other parts of the atmosphere, although still very small relative to other gases in the stratosphere. The ozone layer contains less than 10 parts per million of ozone, while the average ozone concentration in Earth's atmosphere as a whole is only about 0.3 parts per million. The ozone layer is mainly found in the lower portion of the stratosphere, from approximately 20 to 30 km (12 to 19 miles) above Earth, though the thickness varies seasonally and geographically. The UN General Assembly has designated September 16 as the International Day for the Preservation of the Ozone Layer. The ozone layer can be depleted by free radical catalysts, including nitric oxide (NO), nitrous oxide (N_2O), hydroxyl (OH), atomic chlorine (Cl), and atomic bromine (Br). While there are natural sources for all of these elements, the concentrations of chlorine and bromine increased markedly in recent decades due to the release of large quantities of man-made organohalogen compounds, especially CFCs and bromofluorocarbons. By 2009, nitrous oxide was the largest ozone-depleting substance (ODS) emitted through human activities.

Ozone is a powerful oxidant, and it absorbs much of the sun's damaging ultraviolet rays. An increase in the ultraviolet radiation can cause skins cancer and cataract, may disrupt the marine food chain and damage crops. Recent measurements indicate that peak ozone destruction has reached 60% over Antarctica and there are indications of an Arctic ozone hole over the North Pole. Only equatorial regions so far show no significant ozone losses (WRI 1992, 9). Ozone levels have dropped by a worldwide average of about 4% since the late 1970s. For approximately 5% of the Earth's surface, around the north and south poles, much larger seasonal declines have been seen, and are described as "ozone holes."

The ozone layer in 1993 was at an all-time low of 90 Dobson units, with the ozone hole 15% larger than in previous years (Brown et al. 1993). The 2005 ozone hole was one of the biggest ever, spanning 24 million sq. km in area, nearly the size of North America. While the ozone hole over Antarctica continues to open wide, the ozone layer around the rest of the planet seems to be on the mend.[6] This is caused by the use of CFCs and halons in refrigeration, insulation, and packing. For countries such as India, no reliable information is available about the extent of the loss of ozone.

All the indicators of the loss of sustainability necessitate radical changes in the conventional economic planning and policy making. Generally speaking, in response to such threats to sustainability, two new paradigms are emerging: "eco-nomics" (coined by Postel 1990) and "sustainable development." The former focuses on the internalization of environmental costs into conventional micro- and macro-economics, and the latter advocates compliance with the social and environmental norms in the processes and activities necessary for economic growth. Economics can be seen as an attempt to accommodate externalities in the conventional economic analysis, while, at the same time, incorporating in it the criteria of intergenerational equity defined as long-term maintenance of per capita consumption. This implies a shift from GDP maximization toward more sustainable growth, which can be defined as environmentally adjusted net domestic product (ENDP). Several UN conferences held recently have adopted a number of goals for the 21st century. One of the goals is: "implementing national strategies for sustainable development by 2005 to ensure that the current loss of environmental resources is reversed globally and nationally by 2015" (World Bank 1998, 10).

Now, we shall first present an overview of the major strategies of development followed in India in the past, and then some salient elements of a new strategy for sustainable development.

A Critical Review of India's Strategies of Rural Development

A review of various rural development programs and policies followed in India after independence revealed the following four major strategies of development.[7]

Holistic-cum-equity-oriented Strategy

Agricultural and rural development has been accorded a high priority in India's Five Year plans. The First Five Year Plan was dominated by the Community Development Programme (CDP), which reflected India's overriding concern with nation building and equity. The major strategy underlying the CDP was holistically designed to simultaneously achieve the goals of growth, welfare, equity, and community participation. This paradigm takes a very comprehensive but integrated view of the basic problems of poverty, unemployment, and inequality and seeks to address the physical, economic, technological, social, motivational, organizational, and political bases of these problems. The multiple goals of this strategy are sought to be achieved by building the capacity of the community to involve itself in development in partnership with the government. The critical assumption underlying this approach is that the government can restructure the societal power relationships and centralized bureaucracies can learn to share power with community groups. Successful implementation of this strategy requires complex decentralized matrix structures, with permanent mechanisms for vertical and lateral integration, a combination of specialist and generalist skills, institutional leadership, social intervention capability, and systems management (Ickis 1983, Chapter 1). Some other programs launched after the CDP, such as the Integrated Rural Development Programme (IRDP), National Rural Employment Programme (NREP), and Training of Rural Youth for Self-Employment (TRYSE), were intended to follow this paradigm. But given the existing organizational structure and governance system in India, which does not have many of the prerequisites discussed earlier for the successful implementation of this strategy, this strategy did not yield the desired results.

Growth-oriented Strategy

By the middle of the Second Five Year Plan, it became increasingly evident that whatever the success of the CDP, a new approach would be required if agricultural production was to stay ahead of the demands of India's mounting population. In 1957–58, India faced its first post-independence food crisis. In response to this crisis, and on the basis of the recommendations of the Ford Foundation-sponsored team of American agricultural production specialists, a new program called the Intensive Agriculture District Programme (IADP), (popularly known as package program) was formulated and launched in seven selected districts in the country in 1960–61, and was later extended to eight more districts.

The IADP represented a significant departure from the CDP, in that it employed the concentration principle in deploying resources, as opposed to the equity criterion of the CDP. Its main objective was to achieve rapid increases in agricultural production through the use of all complementary inputs and services (package approach) at the farm level. Farm planning formed the core of IADP. By 1966, the basic concept of concentration and the effective use and better management of resources had gained national acceptance, and a number of new agricultural development programs, such as the Intensive Agricultural Area Programme (IAAP), the HYVP and the Intensive Cattle Development Programme (ICDP) had been patterned like the IADP. All these programs were growth oriented; they did not address themselves to equity issues. They demonstrated, on one hand, the effectiveness of the concentration principle in achieving rapid increases in food production, and on the other hand, the failure of the growth-oriented strategy to solve the basic problems of rural poverty and income inequality. The most important lesson learned from the experience with these programs was that a rising economic growth rate was no guarantee against worsening poverty and that a direct frontal attack on the basic problems of poverty and unemployment was called for.

Welfare-oriented Strategy

This seeks to promote the well-being of the rural population in general, and the rural poor in particular, through large-scale social development programs such as the MNP, Applied Nutrition Programme (ANP), Mid-day Meals Programme (MMP), National Old Age Pension Programme (NOAPP), and so on. The primary means used in this strategy are free provision/distribution of goods, services, and civic amenities in rural areas. The critical assumptions of this strategy are that people are not competent to identify and resolve their problems, and that government specialists can identify their needs and meet them with the financial and administrative resources available with the government. The role of villagers is that of passive receptors of services. This strategy has a paternalistic orientation. The performance of the programs is judged by the quantity of goods, services, and civic amenities delivered. The welfare-oriented programs present a mixed picture; the rural poor have benefited significantly through some programs in a few areas but not in others. There are three major criticisms of this strategy as follows:

1. It has created dependence.
2. It requires resources that are beyond the means of governments.
3. It has opened the doors for large-scale corruption among those responsible for delivering welfare benefits.

Facilitating and Participatory Strategy

This strategy is aimed at helping rural people help themselves through their own organizations, active participation, and other support systems. Its concern is with responding to the felt needs of the rural people as defined by *them*. The role of the government is to facilitate the self-help efforts of the villagers by providing technologies and resources that are not locally available. The critical assumption of this strategy is that the rural poor will identify and resolve their problems if provided with minimal support, and otherwise left to their own devices and initiatives. Community participation in—and control of—project activities is the primary performance indicator of this strategy. India's OF, which was launched in 1970 in 18 milksheds in 10 selected states, is a good example of this strategy. OF aimed at modernizing and developing India's dairy industry through a three-tier structure of Anand-pattern dairy cooperatives. Many voluntary agencies are also following this paradigm of development.

To conclude we could say that what is needed now is an integrated or holistic strategy that combines all the positive features of the earlier four strategies, and which is implemented faithfully through the creation of an appropriate organizational and institutional framework.

Some Elements of a New Strategy of Rural Development

Given the failure of the rural development strategies followed so far in India to solve the problems of rural poverty and unemployment, there is a need for us to design strategies that will allow us to move from the present, often unsustainable processes of growth and development, on to sustainable development paths. This will require policy changes in all countries, with respect to their own development and to their impacts on other nations' development possibilities. Generally speaking, in our opinion, some of the important elements of a pragmatic strategy for sustainable development are as follows (Singh 1999).

Sustainable Agriculture, Food Security, and Ecological Security

Food security, which depends on sustainable agriculture, is a prerequisite for sustainable livelihoods, which, in turn, constitutes an integral element of sustainable development. Food security at the national level may be defined as the secured access of all individuals and households in a country to adequate quantity of food for an active and healthy life on a long-term basis. Now the concept of food security has been broadened and is used to connote livelihood security, that is, secured physical and economic access to balanced diet, safe drinking water, environmental sanitation, primary education, and basic health care (Swaminathan 1996, 66). The three components of food security, namely, physical availability, economic access, and sustainability, are essential for maintaining peace and social harmony, both nationally and internationally. Therefore, it would be logically correct to say that food security is a sine qua non of peaceful sustainable development.

To attain food security, top priority must be given to promoting sustainable agricultural production systems. Increasing agricultural production at the cost of degraded soil and depleted and polluted water bodies is an antithesis of sustainable agriculture. Land use in agriculture should be based on a scientific assessment of the land capability. Furthermore, annual depletion of top soil, fish stock, or forest resources must not exceed the rate of their natural regeneration. Future increase in productivity, in both developed and developing countries, should be based on a better controlled application of water and agro chemicals, as well as on more extensive use of organic manures and non-chemical means of pest control. As we stated in Chapter 2 of this book, the biggest challenge before India is how to increase its relatively low crop yields to the world average level on sustainable basis, despite such natural calamities as droughts, floods, and unseasonal rains and hailstorms to which India continues to be highly vulnerable even now.

To ensure food security to all, especially the poor, Parliament had passed on September 12, 2013, a legislation called the National Food Security Act. This law aims to provide subsidized food grains to approximately two-thirds of India's 1.2 billion people. Under the provisions of the Act, eligible beneficiaries are entitled to purchase 5 kg per eligible person per month of cereals at the following prices: rice at ₹3 per kg; wheat at ₹2 per kg; and coarse grains (millet) at ₹1 per kg. This Act, if implemented faithfully by all state governments, could ensure food security to the poor people.

Judicious Management of Natural Resources and Natural Disasters

The natural resources of land, water, plants, animals, forests, fisheries, and environment constitute the basic support systems of life on Earth. Sustainable development depends on how wisely such natural resources are used. In India, most of the natural resources, especially those held and/or used in common, that is, common pool resources (CPRs) and OARs are highly degraded and their productivity is very low. Most of the CPRs and all OARs suffer from what Hardin (1968) calls "the tragedy of the commons." It is estimated that nearly 100 mha of land in India is common pool land, and about 30 mha of forests, and the bulk of water and fisheries resources also belong to the category of CPRs and OARs (Singh 1994, vii).

The restoration and wise management of CPRs and OAR is crucial to the well-being and livelihoods of millions of the rural poor who depend on them. If the process of degradation of natural resources including environment is not reversed, it will not be possible to attain the goal of sustainable development. Fortunately, being biological systems, the CPRs of land, water, forests, and fisheries are dynamic and amenable to management interventions that can provide sustainable benefit flows in the form of food, fodder, fuel wood, fiber, timber, and various environmental amenities.

The management of CPRs on a sustained yield basis depends upon a careful orchestration of policies and management practices. Agricultural economists, especially those specializing in natural resource economics, have special advantage over other technical and social scientists in developing socially optimum strategies for using and managing CPRs. There are several alternative property regimes or management systems under which natural resources are—and could be—managed. They include private, cooperative/collective, corporate, and public property regimes (Singh 1994, 49–70). Creating and enforcing appropriate property rights in OAR could be an instrument of averting their "tragedy" and improve their productivity (Singh 1997, 136–50). In many cases, cooperative management has been found to be a promising alternative for sustaining CPRs (Singh and Ballabh 1996, 16–18). India's experience with various watershed development projects shows that the watershed approach could ensure the sustainable use of renewable CPRs (Singh 1995). There is a need for us to determine which resource is likely to be judiciously used and managed under what property regime and under what conditions, and how the watershed approach could be more widely adopted in India, especially in the rain-fed areas.

Natural disasters have been a bane of India's economy since time immemorial. In ancient Indian literature, there are references to natural disasters, such as prolonged droughts, flash floods, hail storms, landslides, cyclones, and forest fires. About 60% of the landmass in India is vulnerable to earthquakes, over 40 mha is prone to floods,[8] about 8% of the total area is prone to cyclones and about 68% of the total area is susceptible to droughts. An 8,000 km long coastline is prone to severe cyclonic formations. About 55% of the total area lies in seismic zones III and V and is vulnerable to earthquakes. Sub-Himalayan regions and Western Ghats are vulnerable to landslides (Kanwar 2001, 7; GoI 2004a, 32).

Economic development is unsustainable if it increases the vulnerability of people to natural and manmade crises. A drought may force the farmers to sell their animals or other productive assets needed for sustaining production in future years. A pestilence may damage a crop wholly and leave the crop-growers bankrupt. Similarly, a drop in prices of farm produce may reduce farm incomes and, thereby, cause the farmers to overexploit the natural resources. According to Pursell and Gulati (1993), liberalization of domestic and external trade in agricultural commodities may aggravate the food insecurity problem of the India's poor through higher cereal prices. To guard against the adverse effects, the PDS will need to be better targeted and made more effective as a safety net for the poor.

To conclude, we could say that a development path that combines growth with reduced vulnerability is more sustainable than one that does not.

Optimal Development and Utilization of Human Resources

Human development is both a means and an end of overall societal development. The focus of the development policies and programs should be people and their well-being. People should be provided freedom and opportunities to develop their capabilities and should be educated, empowered, and motivated to contribute to achieving sustainable and equitable development. Human resource development is a crucial requirement not only to build up technical knowledge and capabilities, but also to create new values to help individuals and nations cope with the rapidly changing social, environmental, and developmental realities. Knowledge, shared globally, would assure greater mutual understanding and greater willingness to share global resources equitably. Providing more and better education, health care, and other related social services is an essential element of any strategy of sustainable development. Current priorities need to be changed to commit more public funds for providing basic services and amenities to all, particularly the poor. According to a recent study, developing countries could usefully redirect much of their current spending—over 2% of their GDP—toward human development. Efforts to reduce military expenditure, halt capital flight, combat corruption, and privatize loss-making public enterprises could make large amounts of money available to support human development (UNDP 1991, 5).

The sustainability of development is also intimately linked to the dynamics of population growth. Projections of India's population to the year 2150 have been made based on several alternative scenarios. Of all the scenarios, the medium fertility scenario seems most probable. Under this scenario, fertility is assumed to stabilize at replacement levels of slightly above two children per woman. Under this scenario, India's population is projected to grow from 929 million in 1995 to 1,533 million in 2050, 1,617 million in 2100 and 1,669 million in 2150 (UN 1998, 187).

Urgent steps are needed to limit the present (high) rate of India's population growth. Choices made now will influence the level at which the population stabilizes around 1.25 billion people. But this is not just a demographic issue; providing people with education, incentives, and facilities that allow them to choose the size of their families is a way of assuring, especially for women, the basic human right of self-determination. Inculcating values and habits that are congenial to sustainable development among the people from the very childhood days is the key requirement for sustaining livelihoods in perpetuity. India's Vedic system of livelihood was sustainable in the sense that it emphasized, among other things, frugality and harmony with—and conservation of—natural resources and environment. There are hymns in the *Rig Veda*, in praise of *Prithvi devata* (the Earth), *Indra devata* (the rain), *Surya devata* (the sun; the source of inexhaustible solar energy), *Vayu devata* (the air), and so on. Gandhiji also commended those values and lifestyle. There are also Vedic prayers seeking bounties from the *devatas* in the form of food, livestock, health, and wealth. This means that the attitude of people in Vedic era was to respect nature and accept with gratitude whatever it gives to them. But, sadly, the attitude today of most of the people is to exploit nature for self-aggrandizement, degrading its productivity. Most of the Indians, particularly the urban elite, now ape Western values and lifestyles and indulge in ostentatious consumption, which is not sustainable. Perhaps they would accept the Vedic way of living if someone from the West commends it to them.

Removing Market Imperfections and Getting the Prices Right

In a well-functioning market, the price of a good or service reflects both its marginal value to the consumer and its marginal cost to the producer. So long as there is no divergence between the private and the social values and costs of these goods and services, the market system is likely to bring about the most efficient allocation of economic resources. However, it is true that in many situations prices are distorted and that a market economy may fail to allocate resource efficiently. Potential sources of market failure are (a) externalities, (b) incomplete or asymmetric information, (c) public or collective goods, and (d) imperfect competition. When market failures occur, appropriate government interventions are needed to improve upon the market performance and enhance the overall economic well-being. Economists can provide important insights into the circumstances in which government can intervene to improve upon the market performance, how it can do so in a cost-effective manner, and how the costs and benefits of such interventions are likely to be distributed.

Given the wide year-to-year and place-to-place fluctuations in agricultural production and given the inelastic demand for staple food grains, free market forces cannot be depended upon to safeguard the interests of farmers, and to attain and sustain food security in India. Therefore, government intervention in agricultural markets and marketing has been accepted as fully legitimate all over the world.

To enable Indian farmers to derive full benefits from the new liberalized world trade regime, it is necessary to remove various constraints and deficiencies in the existing domestic markets and marketing practices. The policy instruments that were developed and used to regulate markets and marketing in a food scarcity era need to be carefully reviewed and then scrapped if they are no longer necessary, or if they create unnecessary obstacles in the way of efficient marketing. Such instruments include administered prices, procurement of rice and sugar from millers/processors as levy, restrictions on inter-state trade/movement of food grains, purchase/sales taxes, rural development cess, monopoly procurement by the government, and so on.

Farmers' organizations, especially the Anand-pattern producers' cooperatives, could play an important role in protecting the farmers from adverse effects of the new world trade regime and in enabling them to derive full benefits from it. With appropriate farmers' (cooperative) organizations at the secondary level for processing and marketing of agricultural produce, including high value export-oriented commodities, preponderance of small size of landholdings in India would not be a handicap (Vyas 1998: 14). The role of the state agricultural marketing boards, commodity boards, FCI and state and national agricultural cooperative marketing federations also need to be re-examined in the light of new policy of privatization, deregulation, and globalization.

In developing countries such as India, most of the natural resources and their products are highly undervalued, and that has led to the overexploitation of those resources and ecological degradation. Realistic pricing of natural resources and their products, and the recognition of the value of environmental amenities would promote more sustainable development.

Mainstreaming Gender in Development Strategy

Despite the fact that development cannot be sustained unless it is a joint responsibility shared by women and men, there has been a glaring lack of gender perspective in development strategies in both developed and developing countries of the world, including India. A gender perspective emphasizes the relations between men and women, and the relationships that both men and women have with their social and natural environment. It recognizes that the success of projects to foster sustainable development largely depends on the extent to which both women and men participate in project design, planning, implementation and monitoring. In India, where women constitute about 65% of total employment in agriculture, need for mainstreaming them in decision making is all the more important. Women farmers generally have less access to productive resources compared to men and fewer opportunities. Narrowing this gender gap would deliver significant gains in terms of food security. According to FAO's 2010–11 *State of Food and Agriculture* report, "If women had the same access to productive resources as men, they could increase yields on their farms by 20–30 percent." When developing policies to promote rural and agricultural development, policy-makers will need to keep this in mind (FAO 2014, 14).

There are many ways of institutionalizing a gender-sensitive approach to sustainable development. The first and foremost requirement is the policy of equal development of both men and women in development projects. Next, women should be assigned specific roles, responsibilities and rights in making various decisions, rather than simply attending project meetings. Besides, the development project team, as a whole, has to be sensitized to gender issues if gender awareness is to be encouraged. The team also has to be trained and made responsible for the implementation of the gender sensitive approach. Finally, it is also important to clearly define the objectives to be achieved and the measures to be employed to achieve each of the objectives and develop quality and process-oriented indicators in order to monitor the progress of the projects in achieving the intended objectives.

Creating a Congenial International Economic and Political Environment

Economic, political, and ecological links between nations have grown rapidly. This has increased the vulnerability of the developing countries to the adverse consequences of widening international inequalities in economic growth. The asymmetry in international economic relations compounds the inequalities, as developing nations are generally influenced by but are unable to influence international conditions.

International economic relationships pose a particular problem for developing countries such as India trying to manage their environments, since the export of natural resources remains a large factor in their economies. The processing of certain raw materials, for example, pulp and paper, oil, and alumina, can have a substantial environmental side-effects. Industrial countries have generally been more successful than developing ones in seeing to it that export product prices reflect the cost of environmental damage and of controlling that damage. Thus, in the case of exports from industrial countries, these costs are paid by the consumers in importing nations, including those in the developing countries. But in the case of exports from developing countries such as India, such costs continue to be borne entirely domestically, largely in the form of damage costs to human health, property, and ecosystems.

The inability and adverse price trends faced by most of these countries make it impossible for them to manage their natural resource bases for sustained production. The rising burden of debt servicing and the decline in new capital flows intensify the forces that lead to environmental deterioration and resource depletion, occurring at the expense of long-term development.

International trade in fish, for example, is a major factor underlying the depletion of marine fisheries in India. Foreign exchange earnings from exports encourage many entrepreneurs and private companies to use large mechanized trawlers to harvest fish at a rate faster than that at which fish can be regenerated. This over-fishing not only accelerates the loss of species and genetic resources, but also causes the loss of livelihoods of those poor people who exclusively depend on fishing, and pollutes the sea (Singh 1997, 61). The increase in protectionism in industrial countries stifles export growth and prevents diversification from traditional exports. A recent study of the International Monetary Fund (IMF) and the World Bank indicated that protectionism in the industrialized countries costs developing countries twice as much in lost export earnings as they receive in development assistance (Stoltenberg 1989, 22). According to Ekins (1991, 66–68), global trade, aid, and debt are all inimical to the interests of the poor in the developing countries. It is only the rich in developed and developing countries who benefit from all these three power instruments of the North.

Growth in many developing countries also requires external capital inflows. Without reasonable flows, the prospect for any improvements in living standards is bleak. But as goods and capital flow freely within an integrated global economic system seeking highest short-term profits, national governments lose their ability to regulate and manage their own economies in the public interest and become puppets in the hands of the World Bank, IMF and other financiers, and sub-serve their interests. To attract investment funds, they offer cheap labor, weak environmental health and safety standards, low taxes, well-developed infrastructure, and least restricted access to natural resources. All this results in the depletion of their natural resources and degradation of their environment at a faster rate.

A larger portion of total development assistance should go to investments needed to enhance the environment and the productivity of the resource sectors. Such efforts include reforestation and fuel wood development, watershed protection, soil conservation, agro forestry, rehabilitation of irrigation projects, small-scale agriculture, low cost sanitation measures, and harnessing of solar energy. Experience has shown that most effective efforts of this type are small projects with maximum grassroots participation. The programs most directly related to the objective of sustainable development may, therefore, involve higher local costs, a higher ratio of recurrent to capital costs, and a greater use of local technology and expertise.

In the short run, for most developing countries including India, the new era of economic growth hinges on effective and coordinated economic management among major industrial countries designed to facilitate expansion, to reduce real interest rates, and to halt the slide to protectionism. In the longer term, major changes are also required to make consumption and production patterns sustainable in a context of higher global growth.

Key Points

1. Sustainable development has recently risen to the top of international economic and political agenda. The report of the WCED, "Our Common Future," was the first major international initiative that enhanced the awareness of policy makers about sustainable development. The UNCED held in Rio in June 1992 had heightened the global concern over deteriorating environment and the interest in the search for practicable strategies for sustainable development.
2. The concept of sustainability basically implies a characteristic of a system, a program or a resource to last intact forever. Currently, there are two distinct concepts of sustainability in vogue. First, the economist's worldview of sustainability is concerned about the long-term constancy of economic output, income or consumption. Second, the ecologist's and biologist's concept of sustainability relates to long-term preservation of biosphere.
3. The WCED defined sustainable development as "development that meets the needs of the present generation without compromising the ability of future generations to meet their own needs." This definition emphasizes the need for the present generation to ensure intergenerational equity by safeguarding the interest of future generations (intergenerational equity) through maintaining the natural resources capital of this planet intact.
4. Related to the term sustainability, there are two notions of "weak sustainability" and "strong sustainability." The former is defined as the maintenance of the value of the aggregate stock of capital. It implies that we can substitute human-made capital for natural capital in production and consumption, such that economic growth can be associated with improvements in environmental quality. By contrast, "strong sustainability" posits that natural and human-made capital items are complements and cannot be substituted for each other in either production or consumption. Consequently, economic growth that uses natural resources and generates wastes must increase environmental degradation.
5. There are several indicators of non-sustainability of current patterns of production, consumption, and economic growth. They include land degradation, degradation and depletion of water resources, degradation and depletion of forest resources, depletion of conventional sources of energy, loss of biodiversity, climate change, and, ozone layer depletion.

6. A review of various rural development programs and policies followed in India after independence reveal four strategies of development, namely, holistic and equity-oriented strategy, growth-oriented strategy, welfare-oriented strategy, and facilitating and participatory strategy. The major strategy underlying the CDP was holistic, designed to simultaneously achieve the goals of growth, welfare, equity, and community participation. The growth-oriented strategy was adopted in the IADP, HYVP, the welfare-oriented strategy in social programs such as the MNP, ANP), MMP and OAPP, and the facilitating and participatory strategy in the OF program.
7. Generally speaking, the following are some of the important elements of a pragmatic strategy for sustainable development: sustainable agriculture, food security and ecological security; judicious management of natural resources and natural disasters; optimal development and utilization of human resources; alleviation of poverty and inequality through higher economic growth; reorienting technology and reducing risk; optimal use and management energy resources; removing market imperfections and getting the prices right; mainstreaming gender in development strategy, and creating a congenial international economic and political environment.

Questions for Discussion

1. Are the current patterns of production, consumption and economic growth in India sustainable? Yes/No. If yes, why; if no, why not?
2. What is the most important prerequisite of sustainable development and why?
3. Which of the two notions of "weak sustainability" and "strong sustainability" is more realistic under Indian conditions and why?
4. Write a critique of the growth-oriented strategy of development.
5. Compare and contrast the holistic strategy and facilitating strategy of development.
6. In this chapter, we have identified several indicators of non-sustainable development. List a few indicators of sustainable development and illustrate their applications.
7. Write a critique of the new strategy of sustainable development proposed in this chapter.

Notes

1. According to a Green Media report dated January 25, 2006, over three lakh sadhus, who had assembled in Allahabad for Magh Mela that started on January 1, 2006, had launched an agitation complaining against the high level of pollution in the river Ganga in Allahabad, and demanding government intervention to prevent the pollution and keep the Ganga waters clean.
2. https://en.wikipedia.org/wiki/Pollution_of_the_Ganges - cite_note-6 (Accessed on October 6, 2015).
3. https://en.wikipedia.org/wiki/Global_warming (Accessed on April 18, 2016).
4. http://germanwatch.org/klima/ccpi.pdf, pp. 5–8 (Accessed on September 1, 2015).
5. http://germanwatch.org/klima/ccpi12tm.pdf, Table (Accessed on September 2, 2015).
6. http://www.sciencedaily.com/releases/2006/05/060527093645.htm (Accessed on March, 2008).
7. On the basis of a general survey of recent strategies of rural development followed in five Central American governments, John C. Ickis has identified three basic approaches, namely, growth, welfare, and responsive strategies. For details, see John C. Ickis (1983).
8. India is one of the most flood prone countries in the world and accounts for one-fifth of the global death count due to floods. Over 30 million people are displaced annually due to the floods.

Chapter 8

Policy Instruments of Rural Development

LEARNING OUTCOMES

After having gone through this chapter, students should be able to:

- **Define and illustrate the concepts of "policy instrument" and "policy measure";**
- **Know the meaning and components of the conceptual framework for public policy as propounded by Nobel Laureate Jan Tinbergen;**
- **Identify the relationship between various components of the conceptual framework, that is, social welfare function, policy goals, and policy instruments;**
- **Define the term "action system" in the context of development management and identify its components and utility; and**
- **Describe various types of policy instruments, that is, "public finance," "money and credit," "direct controls," "exchange rate," and "changes in institutional framework" and the purposes for which they are used, when, how, and by whom.**

Introduction

An instrument is defined as something that a manager or an actor can change or manipulate in order to produce a desired effect. It may be an economic quantity such as interest rate, or it may be part of the institutional framework such as nationalization of banks. An instrument, therefore is the means by which an objective is pursued. A measure is the use of a particular instrument at a particular time in order to promote one or more objectives. For instance, the decision to raise the bank rate on a certain day, or to reduce income tax in a particular budget year, is an instrument. The removal of a measure, for instance, the removal of price control, is also a measure. Knowledge about what instruments can be used to achieve the objectives of various rural development programs is essential for rural development policy makers and managers in order for these programs to be effective and successful. This chapter is devoted to a discussion of some instruments that can be used by rural development policy makers, administrators, and managers to achieve their objectives.

A Conceptual Framework

Perhaps the most useful framework to illustrate the relationship among policy instruments, target variables and social welfare, and for policy analysis, has been provided by Nobel Laureate Jan Tinbergen (1952, Chapter 2). This is illustrated in Figure 8.1.

The important elements of the framework for policy analysis are W, the Y_i, the Z_j, and the structural relationships that link the Z_j to the Y_i. Each of these elements needs elaboration.

Social Welfare Function (W)

Economists call W the social welfare function. It reflects the level of well-being achieved by a society. As such, it represents the aggregate of the satisfaction reached by the individuals comprising the society. "Utility" is "consumed" ultimately only by individuals, and no social or community welfare function exists independent of the well-being achieved by individuals. Because no method has yet been found to measure utility or well-being, W is entirely psychological and subjective. It is nevertheless a useful concept, since it suggests that the end of all policy and planning is the well-being of people. It is well to emphasize that W consists of much more than purely economic factors. In fact, even the size and distribution of incomes extant in the society are really only the means to superior human ends. W is composed of such final ends as freedom, equality, justice, opportunity, and security. Thus, social, political, and cultural factors as well as economic ones must be included in any conceptualization of welfare

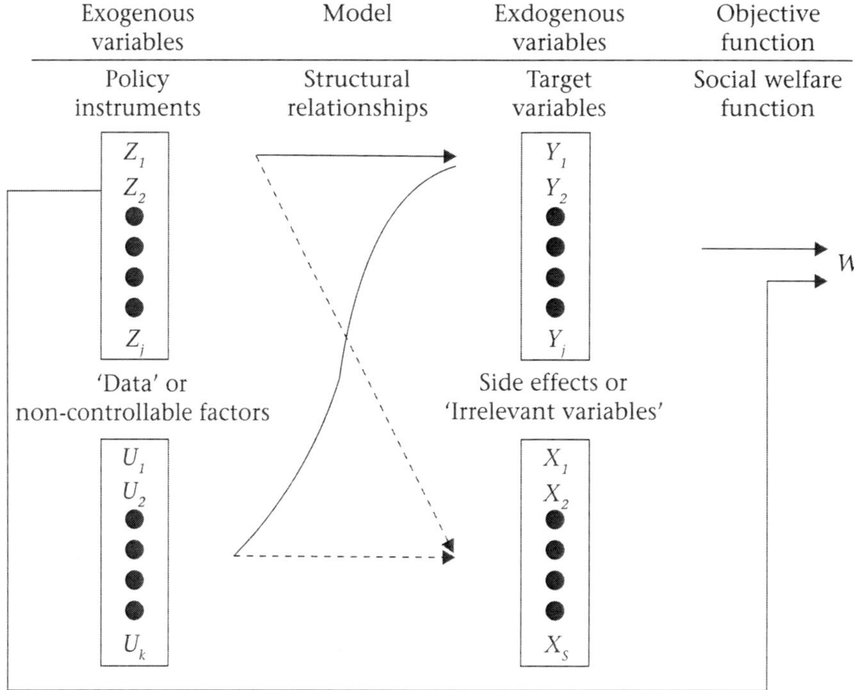

Figure 8.1: *A Conceptual Framework for Policy Analysis*

Source: Tinbergen (1952, Chapter 2).

and must be evaluated in any policy analysis. In democratic society, W is best regarded as given to the policy makers, that is, W is the welfare function of the society and not that of the policy maker. He must look outside himself for the society's ultimate values: to statutes enacted by the representatives of the people, to the constitution under which the people are governed, to rulings of the judicial system, and so on. Of course, determining precisely what the society's values are is often a difficult problem, the solution of which the policy maker may participate in or give articulation to. But he should not assume the responsibility of deciding what social values should be.

Policy Goals (Y_i)

The Y_i are the articulated goals of policy. They are deduced from the values of W. An example will illustrate this. An element of W may be an improvement in the range of opportunities for the members of the society—the target goal may be a rise in per capita incomes by 5% per annum, a rise in the average literacy level to 70%, or the complete eradication of poliomyelitis. It should be obvious that W and the Y_i are related, and the precise nature of the relationship between the two should be as clear as possible.

The policy maker may well decide the Y_i. In a democratic system, the people at the ballot box will judge the reasonableness of the Y_i chosen by the policy maker, as well as whether or not the targets are achieved. A great deal of thought and care should be given to the matter of selecting appropriate target variables.

It is especially important that the Y_i be framed in such a way that they are capable of being evaluated. It is hard to evaluate vaguely stated goals. Contrast the following goals: (a) incomes should be increased and (b) average annual per capita real incomes should be increased by 5%. The first statement is general and vague and cannot be easily appraised. The second is specific and quantitative, and can be readily evaluated.[1]

Policy Instruments (Z_j)

The policy instruments available to achieve the target goals are the Z_j. For example, to reduce unemployment to 5% of the workforce (a target to be sought), various policies (Z_j) may be utilized. The government may increase the quantity of money in the economic system, believing that more demand for goods will ultimately reduce unemployment; or, a tax reduction may be given to businesses that invest in new capital equipment, under the theory that capital growth will produce more jobs. A great number of policies may be stated to contribute to the accomplishment of the target. Policy analysis is largely composed of looking for—and evaluating—alternative ways to achieve the target goals. The great bulk of science, and most of economics, is concerned with these tasks.

Like any other scientific study, policy analysis should utilize scientific methods. Hypotheses that postulate how a given policy is expected to theoretically influence a given target should be formulated. Experimentation is the process of determining whether or not, in fact, the policy works in the way expected. Scientists call the set of theoretical hypotheses a model, and this is the analytical bridge between policy instruments and target variables. Models must be tested, however, both for logical consistency and empirical validity. A set of statistical relationships must be established that reveal the processes of getting from the Z_j to the Y_i, and how efficient the processes are.

It should be remembered that just as the Y_i *are* prescribed by the ultimate values of society, so are the Z_j, that is, the Z_j *must* be evaluated in terms of political and moral acceptability as well as efficiency in reaching the target. Certain kinds of policies, accepted and even encouraged in one class of society, are anathema to another class. Most democratic or non-totalitarian societies would never permit policies that seriously compromise the rights of individuals.

Non-controllable Factors and Irrelevant Variables (U_k and X_s)

There are some factors that affect the targets and that cannot be manipulated or affected by policy. In the framework previously stated, these are the U_k. An example might be the weather. Any target of agricultural production would be affected by rainfall or by frost, but, till now, man has been largely ineffective in controlling these factors. They must be treated simply as "non-controllable" in any policy analysis, but nonetheless must always be recognized and accounted for.

Finally, some effects of policy do not apply to the targets, or do not directly enter the community's welfare function, but should nevertheless be monitored because they are potentially significant. These are the X_s in the above framework and are called the "side effects" of policy. A policy to shift the production of energy from steam engines to internal combustion engines will have side effects that will not be significant for most situations. Internal combustion engines produce a variety of invisible pollutants in the air that are not a problem, until they reach certain dangerous threshold levels. These types of side effects must be watched, but may not affect the evaluation of policy until they reach problem proportions, in which case they may be shifted into the category of Y_i.

The policy framework is primarily a taxonomic device and should be of value in elucidating what is being sought, the available means of reaching what is being sought, and at what cost. It helps the policy maker to keep things straight. In most of the policy documents, this simple framework is not made operational or is not properly elaborated.

The model can also be expressed in the form of an econometric model or a mathematical programming model.

An Action System

In the context of development management, an action system may be conceived of as consisting of four elements: the manager/actor, the objectives, the conditions (physical, technological, economic, social, and political), and the means or instruments. Their relationships can be indicated by a simple diagram, as shown in Figure 8.2 (Schickele 1954, 60)

The manager or actor may be an employee of a public, private, cooperative, corporate or any other entity. The manager in any given system makes the decisions as to what means should be employed toward a given objective or set of objectives. The objectives are what the manager wants to accomplish. They need to be clearly defined in operational terms.

The conditions of an action system are all those technical, financial, political, and institutional circumstances beyond the control of the manager, at least with respect to the particular program under consideration. The instruments chosen must be adapted to—or compatible with—the conditions under which the program must operate.

The instruments are the policy measures or program provisions employed to achieve the objectives. There are often many different instruments that could possibly serve a certain objective. Knowledge of economics is especially useful in making a wise choice in the selection of instruments.

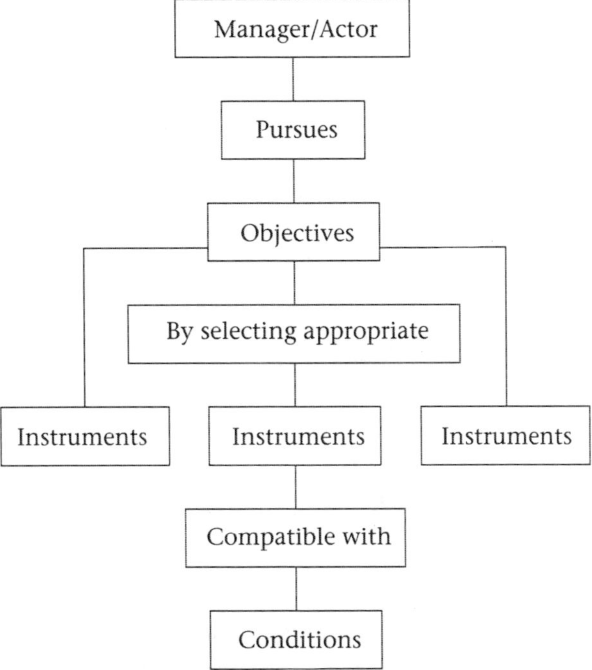

Figure 8.2: *Diagram of an Action System*

Source: Schickele (1954, 60).

Policy Instruments

The policy instruments can be grouped in the following five categories (Kirschen et al. 1964, Chapter 13):

1. Public finance,
2. Money and credit,
3. Exchange rate,
4. Direct controls, and
5. Changes in the institutional framework.

A brief description of some of the major instruments follows.

Public Finance

This set of instruments covers most income and expenditure items of the Central, state and local governments. Government expenditure is largely devoted to the objective of the satisfaction of collective needs of people.

The main occasion for the use of the instruments of public finance is the annual budget. Consequently, many (but not all) of these instruments can be employed at annual intervals only. Because these instruments involve sums of money paid in or out of government accounts, the statistical documentation is required. Not all items of government expenditure and income can be regarded as instruments of economic policy. There are some flows that enter the public accounts, but that the government cannot, or does not, seek to change in order to achieve economic objectives. This is true, for instance, of the interest paid on public debt, the imputed rent of government buildings, sales of government goods and services, its income from property, and its depreciation allowance.

The financial transactions of public enterprises are excluded from public finance because, in general, public enterprises behave in the same way as private ones.

Classification

There are 17 instruments in this category, and they can be further classified as follows.

Two Balances

1. The current balance, or government net saving, and
2. The overall balance, or the change in the government's net claims on other sectors.

Governments use both the current and overall balances as instruments of economic policy. They frequently decide to first increase or reduce the size of the current or overall deficit or surplus, and subsequently decide which items of income or expenditure to adjust. In this sense, the use of the current and overall balances is a separate instrument from the use of items of income and expenditure.

The extent to which governments can use the current and overall balances is limited by the fact that it is not easy to cut back government expenditure. People have opposed the idea both of a budget current surplus and a budget current deficit.

Eight Expenditure Instruments

1. *Government (Public) Investment*: This is the most powerful of the expenditure instruments. But, in the short run, it is not always easy to change government investment. In the short run, the main form of government intervention is to advance or postpone the starting dates for public investment. Government investment is good for serving long-term objectives, and it is a major instrument of rural development in India.

Investment in agriculture in the form of capital formation is essential for sustaining the growth of agriculture. It is an important determinant of the pace and level of agricultural development. Investment is needed for creating basic infrastructural facilities, such as roads, markets, transport, communication, power generation, cold storage, and other post-harvest facilities, irrigation, and so on. During the late-1980s and early 1990s, concern over the falling share of public sector capital formation in agriculture was articulated. With the presumption that there exists high complementarity between public and private capital formation, it is contended by various studies that a declining trend in the former is likely to have an adverse impact on overall capital formation.

After a declining trend for a few years, now, both public and private investments in agriculture have been increasing. For example, public investment in agriculture and allied activities increased from ₹1,61,870 million at 2004–05 prices in 2004–05 to ₹2,38,860 million in 2012–13 and private investment from ₹5,99,090 million to ₹13,81,970 million over the same period of time (Table 8.1). However, the share of total investment in the GDP in 2004–05

Table 8.1: *Public and Private Investment in Agriculture and Allied Activities at 2004–05 Prices in India*

(₹ Million)

Year	*Public Investment*	*Private Investment*	*Total Investment*	*Total Investment as % of GDP*
2004–05	1,61,870 (0.5)*	59,909 (1.8)	76,096 (2.3)	2.3
2005–06	1,99,400 (0.6)	66,664 (1.9)	86,604 (2.4)	2.4
2006–07	2,29,870 (0.6)	6,90,700 (1.8)	9,20,570 (2.4)	2.4
2007–08	2,32,570 (0.5)	8,24,840 (1.9)	10,57,410 (2.5)	2.5
2008–09	2,05,720 (0.5)	10,65,550 (2.4)	12,71,270 (2.9)	2.9
2009–10	2,26,930 (0.5)	11,04,690 (2.3)	13,31,620 (2.8)	2.8
2010–11	1,98,540 (0.4)	11,28,800 (2.1)	13,27,340 (2.5)	2.5
2011–12	2,11,840 (0.4)	13,59,880 (2.4)	15,71,720 (2.8)	2.8
2012–13	2,38,860 (0.4)	13,81,970 (2.3)	16,20,830 (2.7)	2.7

Source: MoA (2014a, Table 3.6 C, p. 56).[2]
Note: *Figures in the parentheses are percent of total GDP at the 2004–05 prices.

has been more or less stagnant around 2.5% throughout this period of time. This needs to be increased or at least maintained to achieve the target growth rate of 4% per annum in the agricultural sector as envisaged in the Union Budget 2015–16.

The establishment by the Government of India of a Rural Infrastructure Development Fund (RIDF) under the NABARD in 1995–96 was a welcome step in the right direction. The fund is utilized for creating necessary infrastructure under the technical guidance and supervision of NABARD. The initial corpus of the fund was ₹20,000 million under RIDF I in 1995–96. The funds lends to the state governments every year in tranches at the interest rate that is 0.50% higher than the prevailing bank rate. Rural roads and irrigation projects have claimed the highest share in the fund, accounting for about 40% and 39% of the corpus, respectively. The RIDF is a major source of funds for the states for the development of rural infrastructure. The cumulative resources routed through the RIDF stood at ₹21,75,000 million as on March 31, 2015. The Union Budget 2015–16 has announced an allocation of ₹2,50,000 million under RIDF XXI (NABARD 2015, 31).

2. *Subsidies and Capital Transfers to Enterprises*: A subsidy, often viewed as the converse of a tax, is an instrument of fiscal policy. Derived from the Latin word *"subsidium,"* a subsidy literally implies coming to assistance from behind. A subsidy is a form of financial aid or support extended to an economic sector (or institution, business, or individual), generally with the aim of promoting economic and social development. Support for agriculture in the form of subsidies dates back to the 19th century. It was developed extensively in the EU and USA across the two World Wars and The Great Depression to protect domestic food production, but remains important across the world today. Today, agricultural subsidies are defended on the grounds of helping farmers to maintain their livelihoods and in that sense they are used as an instrument of rural development. They seek to change the behavior of the users of production inputs and services by motivating them to use them in socially desirable quantities and ways. There are several types of subsidy that are used in India and other countries of the world. The major types of subsidies include production subsidy, consumption (food) subsidy, export subsidy, employment subsidy, and tax subsidy.

The subsidies could be used in two situations. First, when the private marginal benefit to the user at the socially optimum level of resource use is less than the social benefit, that is, when a positive externality exists. Second, when the marginal social cost of using an input at the level of private optimum is higher than the marginal private cost, that is, when a negative externality exists. In both the cases, subsidies abate the externalities involved—in the former, by equalizing the marginal private benefits and marginal social benefits, and in the latter, by equalizing the marginal private costs and marginal social costs. As in the case of taxes, aggregate welfare effects of subsidies also could be counter-intentional (Singh 1994, 80–81).

Subsidies are, in principle, fairly flexible and they can be used selectively and given to any particular inputs, or type of activity, or a particular region. The main objective that this instrument can serve is protection and priorities, either to particular regions or to particular inputs or activities. The instrument can take several forms, such as the promotion of use of new inputs by subsidizing their prices, promotion of investment (by subsidizing interest rates) or exports, keeping down the prices of the products of rural industries and, thus, helping to keep up their sales. When subsidies on investments or exports are given for long periods of time, they serve the objective of expansion.

Agricultural subsidies in India were originally introduced on fertilizer, irrigation water, and rural electricity—that drove many of the irrigation pumps—in the 1960s to support the successful drive for the Green Revolution. Now, subsidies are provided on food, canal irrigation water, electricity for agricultural uses, fertilizers, institutional credit to certain categories of borrowers, and purchase of certain income-generating assets by the poor under poverty alleviation and employment programs, such as the Million Wells Scheme (MWS) and the Ganga Kalyan Yojana (GKY). Table 8.2 presents the Central government expenditure on major types of subsidies—food, fertilizers, petroleum and all types of subsidies used in India. As shown in the table, there has been a substantial increase in the quantum of expenditure on all subsidies over the period of time, 2002–03 to 2013–14, the expenditure on total subsidies increased from ₹435.33 billion to ₹2,606.58 billion over this period of time. We have not included the quantum of expenditure on subsidies on irrigation water, and power for agricultural uses in the Table, as we could not have access to the required information.

Table 8.2: *Total Central Government Expenditure on Major Subsidies in India as in July 2014*

(₹ billion)

Year	*Food*	*Fertilizers*	*Petroleum*	*Interest Subsidies*	*Total Subsidies*	*Subsidies as % of GDP at Current Prices*
2002–03	241.36	110.15	52.250	7.50	435.33	1.72
2005–06	230.77	184.60	26.83	21.77	475.22	1.29
2010–11	638.44	184.60	383.71	46.80	1,734.20	2.22
2011–12	728.22	700.13	684.84	50.49	2,179.41	2.43
2012–13	850.00	656.13	968.80	72.70	2,570.79	2.54
2013–14 RE	920.00	679,710	854.80	81.75	2,555.16	2.25
2014–15 Budget	1,150.00	729.70	634.27	83.13	2,606.58	2.02

Sources: Planning Commission (2014). Data-book compiled for use of Planning Commission.
Note: RE: Revised estimate.

Subsidies may have several adverse spill-over effects. Directly, they are expensive to governments by directing resources away from other legitimate priorities (such as environmental conservation, education, health, or infrastructure. Indirectly, they could cause environmental degradation, for example, pollution, loss of landscape, misuse, and overuse of supplies. They tend to benefit the few at the expense of the many, and the rich at the expense of the poor.

In India, agricultural subsidies have been criticized by those who do not understand their rationale as well their magnitude vis-à-vis other sectors in India as well as other countries. For example, agricultural subsidies in EEC are $82 per ha, Japan $35 per ha, USA $32 per ha and China $30 per ha as compared to only $14 per ha in India (Salunkhe and Deshmukh 2012, 45).

In the wake of the new economic policy, there is a strong pressure on the government from the World Bank and the IMF, as also from certain sections of the Indian society, to phase out all kinds of subsidies. However, the government has so far withstood all the pressures, as it is a politically hazardous decision for any government to withdraw subsidies given to the rural sector, which constitutes the biggest vote bank and, hence, determines the fate of political parties. Besides, there is also a strong economic rationale for subsidies to the rural sector. First, the rural sector produces and supplies the basic necessities of life to people and, thus, provides food security, for which no amount of cost (subsidies) is high enough. In economics terminology, the social benefits from agricultural subsidies far exceed the private benefits to farmers receiving them. Second, it has been established through empirical studies that Indian agriculture is net-taxed, that is, considering the producer prices of agricultural produce and the input prices paid by the farmer vis-à-vis the corresponding world prices, the agricultural sector gives more to our society than it receives from it in terms of subsidies and grants (Gulati 1989, A57–A65; Gulati and Sharma 1992, A106–A116). Third, the extent of the subsidies in Indian agriculture is much less than in many developed countries, such as the EEC, USA, Canada, Japan, China, and so on. A simple rule of thumb in determining whether to provide a subsidy or not is to compare the estimated loss of revenue due to the subsidy and estimated gains to the beneficiaries of the subsidy (consider both gains in the producer surplus and the consumer surplus). If the gains exceed the loss, then the subsidy is economically justified. A serious weakness of this instrument is that it is very difficult to withdraw a subsidy once it is granted. Politically, it is highly undesirable for popular governments to withdraw subsidies even when they are no longer justified on economic grounds.

3. *Transfers to Households*: Governments in many developed countries pay pensions to old people, sickness allowances to invalids, unemployment benefits, and so on. Such expenditure is financed partly by contributions paid to the social security agencies and partly by transfers from the Central government. Although this expenditure is large, it is not of great value as an instrument of economic policy, certainly not for a short-term policy. Its influence is mainly limited to its effects on income distribution–transfer from taxpayers to lower income groups. In India, this instrument so far has been of relatively minor importance. However, a significant step in this direction was taken by the Central government by launching, on August 15, 1995, a National Social Welfare Programme (NSWP). The program comprises three components, namely, the National Old Age Pension Scheme (NOAPS), the National Family Benefit Scheme (NFBS) and the National Maternity Benefit Scheme (NMBS; GoI 1997a, 53–54).

Another significant initiative in this direction was the Pradhan Mantri Jan Dhan Yojana (PMJDY) that was launched on August 28, 2014 with a revised target of 100 million bank accounts by January 26, 2015. The scheme had yielded deposits of ₹83,690.55 million with 106.39 million new bank accounts as on January 3, 2015. Payment solutions are an important part of financial inclusion for which a new card payment scheme known as RuPay Card has been in operation since May 8, 2014. Banks have further been asked to provide universal coverage across all the six hundred thousand villages of the country by providing at least one basic banking account per household, with indigenous RuPay Debit Card having inbuilt accident insurance of ₹1,00,000 and life insurance cover of ₹30,000. The RuPay Card is on par with other debit cards. These two schemes are complementary and will enable achievement of multiple objectives such as financial inclusion, insurance penetration, and digitalization.

4. *Pradhan Mantri Atal Pension Yojana (APY)* named after the ex-prime minister of India, Atal Bihari Vajpayee, acronymed as APY scheme, was launched in continuation to the Jan Dhan Yojana scheme to bring those employed in rural and unorganized sector under the ambit of pension schemes. The idea of the scheme is to provide a definite pension to all Indians. However, in order to get pension in old age, one needs to contribute accordingly. The more one can contribute the more pensions one would get during old age. The scheme is backed by Ministry of Finance, Government of India. The scheme would mostly touch those working under unorganized sector. Any Indian national within the age group of 18 to 40 years is eligible to contribute under the APY. However, any member of a statutory social security scheme is not eligible to get the government's contribution for this pension scheme. But he will get all normal benefits of the Yojana.
5. *Government Stock Changes*: Governments sometimes build up stocks themselves by direct controls or subsidies for the satisfaction of collective needs and security of supply; for example, stockpiling of food grains, minerals, metals, coal, and so on. Stockpiling of wheat, rice, and sugar represents the use of this measure in India. Stocks of food grains consist of buffer stocks and of operational stocks. Buffer stocks include the base level stocks that cannot be pulled out of the system, and operational stocks are those that are used to reduce fluctuations in availability and prices of food grains, and to reach the food grains to the poor at reasonable prices through fair price shops under the revamped PDS.
6. *Current Purchases of Goods and Services*: This instrument can be selective; for example, purchases in a particular region or from a particular subsector. Purchases can be delayed or advanced, with the objective of price stability or full employment. Some governments try to concentrate their orders, particularly their military orders, in periods of slackening economic activity. There are many examples of current purchases of goods by the Central and state governments in India.
7. *Wages and Salaries*: Governments do not often attempt to manipulate their wage and salary bill for purposes of economic policy. Some expenditure on in-service education or training can serve to increase the mobility of labor or to improve income distribution. In India, wages and salaries in the public and organized sectors are linked to the cost of living index and, hence, are revised from time to time, usually every five years, to neutralize the effect of inflation on incomes.
8. *Transfers to the Rest of the World*: This is not a very important instrument in India. Transfers are usually made to poor countries such as Nepal and international institutions like the UNDP and the International Labour Organization (ILO)

Eight Revenue Instruments

1. *Direct Taxes on Incomes of Households*: There are fairly strict limits on the extent to which governments, in times of peace, can increase their revenue from personal income tax. First, this tax is very unpopular with the middle and upper income groups. Second, it is a tax that is often avoided or evaded, and the higher it is, the greater is the temptation to evade it. However, direct taxes are very important in an economic

policy because they are progressive, they redistribute income, and they act as built-in stabilizers; their yield varies more than incomes and, therefore, stimulates demand in periods of depression and reduces it in boom periods, thus, serving the objectives of full employment and price stability. With a "pay as you earn" system, there is not much time-lag before the stabilizing action comes into play. In India, income from agriculture is exempt from tax mainly because: (a) most of the 90% of farms having landholdings of four hectares or less are not financially viable, and their income is well below the level of income exempted from income tax under the Income Tax Act 1961; (b) it is very difficult and costly to assess farm incomes correctly; and (c) the cost of collection of the tax is very high vis-à-vis the revenue collected.

2. *Direct Taxes on Enterprises' Incomes*: Company profits are taxed as a whole, that is, with no distinction between distributed and undistributed profits. They also have an automatic anticyclical effect, as in economic fluctuations, profits tend to vary more than national income as a whole. Investment can be encouraged by special depreciation allowances and tax breaks for specified periods of time.
3. *Indirect Taxes on Internal Transactions*: They are the largest of the income instruments and have two great advantages. First, they are politically convenient because their incidence is less obviously painful than those of income taxes. Second, they can be made highly selective. One minor disadvantage of these taxes is that there may be awkward economic effects if people expect a change; there may be a rush of anticipatory buying if they think the tax will go up, or demand may fall sharply, if they think the tax will fall.
4. *Customs Duties*: Export duties are rarely used, but import duties are used universally. They can be both flexible and selective, but their use is limited by international agreements and the fear of reprisals by foreign governments. The main purpose of the imposition of these duties is protection, usually of particular industries and particular commodities. In India, until the end of the 1980s, both imports and exports of agricultural commodities, excepting tea, coffee, tobacco, and spices, were restricted through tariff (customs duties) and non-tariff barriers. But now, under the new trade policy, import duties on most of the agricultural commodities have been drastically reduced or completely waived.
5. *Social Security Contributions*: They have been rarely used in India as instruments of economic policy. They have a regressive effect on income distribution, that is, the rich benefit more than the poor.
6. *Taxes on Property:* They include both taxes on wealth, and separate taxes on land and buildings, and serve as instruments for the distribution of incomes.
7. *Succession Duties and Inheritance Tax*: They have some effect on income distribution.
8. *Transfers from the Rest of the World*: Donations from the rich to the poor countries are important aids to development.

Constraints on the Use of the Instruments of Public Finance

The main purpose of public expenditure is to satisfy collective needs, and this limits the extent to which it can be manipulated for other objectives. Political pressures and pressure groups can have a very strong influence on policies in the field of public finance.

Taxation is the most widely used policy instrument. It was Pigou (1962) who had argued that taxes and subsidies could be used to encourage economic agents to internalize externalities, that is, the unintended side effects of economic activities. The logic of taxation schemes is to raise the private costs of entry and/or use (or equivalently to lower the benefits) to the point where individual action will result in the socially optimum level of production of a good, whose production involves a negative externality, for example, pollution.

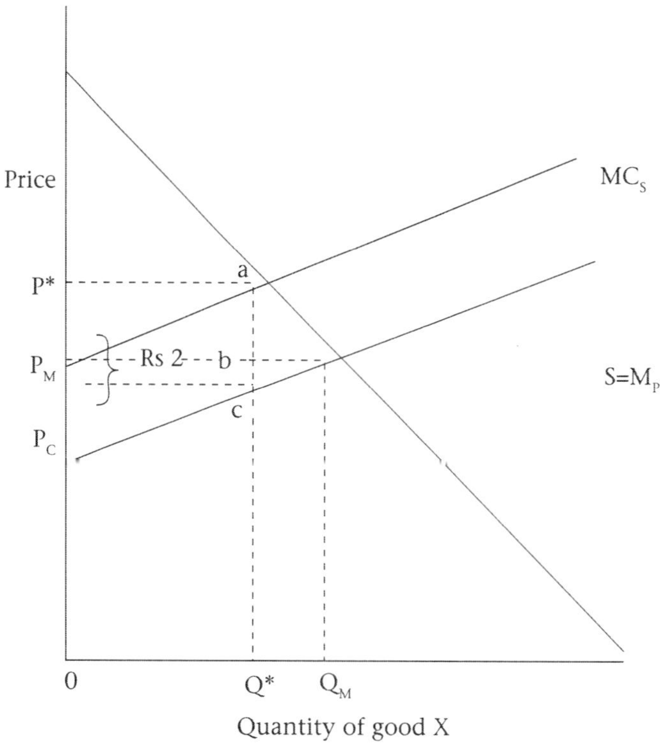

Figure 8.3: *Effect of a Pollution Tax*

Source: Author.

Figure 8.3 depicts the typical supply and demand curves for a good X. However, in this case, we have labeled the supply curve $S = MC_P$ because it represents the marginal private costs associated with producing the good. The free market equilibrium output and price are Q_M and $P_{M,}$ respectively. Now suppose that there is a negative externality (pollution) associated with the production of each unit of the good X, then the MC_P curve would not represent the real costs to society of the good. If each unit of the good produced imposes an externality costing ₹2 on a third party, then the true marginal social cost will be MC_s. The pollution tax shifts the private marginal cost curve, $MC_{P,}$ upward by ₹2 at every point to MC_s in the figure. Q^* is the socially optimum level of production of good X and P^* is the socially optimum price at the new intersection between the demand curve and MC_s. Thus, by internalizing the social costs of pollution, the actual output of the polluting good X is reduced from Q_M to Q^* while the price charged to the consumer rises from P_M to P^*, and the price received by the producer is reduced from P_M to P_C. Depending upon the relative elasticities of the demand and supply curves, the burden of the pollution tax is shared by both consumers and producers. In our example, the consumer pays *ab* and the producer *bc* of the total tax *ac*. Thus, the pollution tax affects both producers' and consumers' behavior.

It is important in this context to realize that the aggregate effect of a tax could be counter-intentional, if there were no restrictions on the number and the size of firms in an industry causing a negative externality, say, water pollution. This is so because, although the contribution of each individual firm to pollution after taxation would be smaller than before taxation, all the firms together are likely to generate more pollution than what can be assimilated by the water body into which the effluents are discharged (Bromley 1991, 62–63).

There are two important issues in using taxation as an instrument of equalizing social and private costs, and social and private benefits. First, how should the tax be administered: on yield or produce or inputs? Second, how should the tax revenues be used? A method commonly suggested in the literature for levying tax has been first to consider alternative specifications of technology and resource growths, and then to study the adjustment of prices and yield rates until (if ever) a steady rate emerges. While the details vary slightly the principal conclusions on this issue are that optimal taxes exist and can be levied on either inputs or outputs, and that when harvesting requires more than one input and when at least one input is fixed, the optimal tax policy needs to differentiate between the inputs or must tax outputs. Price uncertainty is shown by Anderson (1982) to favor a tax on revenue (an income tax). Another important determinant of tax policy is whether the stock of the resource and of harvesting capital is above or below the optimal level.

Ciriacy-Wantrup (1968, Chapter 13) discusses in detail the various aspects of taxation as a tool of conservation policy. His major conclusions are:

1. Progression in taxation tends toward conservation and regression toward depletion;
2. A high tax on income (from a resource) in conjunction with a lower capital-gains tax may result in conservation;
3. Yield taxes are superior to most other taxes in terms of economy and accuracy of assessment and administration, but are inferior to net revenue taxes from the standpoint of ability to pay and social justice; and
4. Lump sum taxes are inflexible and generally regressive, and may, therefore, lead to depletion.

A simple rule of thumb in determining whether to levy a tax or not is to compare the estimated loss of revenue/utility to the taxpayer and others who use the resource/resource commodity (consider both the loss of the producer surplus and the loss of the consumer surplus) and the estimated gain of revenue to the tax authority. If the gains exceed the loss, then the tax is economically justified. A serious weakness of this instrument is that it is politically very inconvenient to levy a new tax, particularly a direct tax (Singh 1994, 77–80).

Instruments of Money and Credit

This set of instruments includes those that serve to make it either more difficult or easier for persons, companies, or governments to borrow money. In contrast to budgetary measures, which can be described as open decisions openly arrived at, a great deal of mystery and mystique surrounds monetary and credit policy. It is not always possible to find out exactly what is being done.

The government and the RBI are responsible for promulgating these instruments. The list of instruments may be classified as follows:

Government's New Borrowing and Lending

1. Lending abroad,
2. Lending to households and enterprises,
3. Borrowing from abroad, and
4. Borrowing from households and enterprises.

Government Operation in Existing Debt

1. Open-market operations in short-term securities, and
2. Other open-market operations.

Interest Rate Instruments

1. Bank rate,
2. Legal imposition of maximum rates, and
3. Government guarantees of loans.

Instruments Acting on Credit Creation by Banks

1. Reserve ratios (statutory liquidity ratio and cash reserve ratio),
2. Quantitative stops on advances,
3. Approval of individual loans, and
4. Other directives, recommendations and persuasion.

Instruments Acting on Lending or Borrowing by other Agents

1. Control of borrowings of local authorities and nationalized enterprises,
2. Control of borrowings of private companies by new issues,
3. Control of hire purchase transactions, and
4. Control of other financial institutions.

Instrument of Exchange Rate

This instrument has the following three main features:

1. It is extremely powerful, and can have considerable effects on the economy of the country concerned, and also on the countries from which it imports and exports,
2. It has a strong emotional content. The exchange rate of a country's currency gives its price in terms of gold and foreign currencies. Any reduction in this price is considered a kind of national defeat, and
3. Further, any reduction brings with it the risk that it will lead to a loss of confidence in the national currency. Moreover, it leads to price rises and changes in the distribution of incomes, which seem particularly perilous.

The exchange rate is a single instrument and not a set of instruments. But there are different types of exchange rates and, consequently, different types of changes in them. The exchange rate can be single or multiple, or fixed or floating.

Decisions to alter the exchange rate are, of course, national decisions. But foreign and international influences can often be very important. In most countries, it is the decision of the Cabinet, and it is the prime minister and minister of finance who together take the responsibility of changing the exchange rate. Parliament is virtually never concerned with the decision to devalue or revalue. The rules of the IMF require that all member countries should consult the fund and obtain its prior approval to all changes of 10% or more.

Changes in exchange rate must either be revaluations or devaluations. The objectives of revaluation are price stability and, to a lesser extent, the international division of labor. Devaluations are always meant to improve the balance of payments, sometimes to expand production and also for the international division of labor.

If there is some unutilized capacity in the country that devalues (whereas the countries that buy its exports are fully employed), then its elasticity of supply will be high enough for it to be able to meet the increased demand for its exports. If the country that devalues is fully employed, devaluation might worsen the balance of payments. Devaluation can be used as a method of increasing employment in an underemployed country, since it stimulates exports and holds back imports.

As most of the resource-based commodities produced in India are internationally traded or tradable (e/g., tea, coffee, spices, jute, cotton, fish, rice, and rubber), or are substitutes for tradable commodities (e.g., natural gas, lignite, and hydropower), an overvalued exchange rate would reduce their depletion by reducing their price relative to non-tradable goods (e.g., transport, services, and construction). An overvalued exchange rate and export taxes have similar effects in that they discourage exports (and encourage imports) of resource-based commodities, thereby reducing the pressure on the domestic resource base. Increased exports of primary commodities may have an adverse effect on the environment, unless the prices of inputs and outputs involved fully reflect the true scarcity of the resources being used and the environmental costs incurred.

Reduction of export duties on certain crops, such as horticultural and plantation crops, helps diversify the economy away from soil-eroding crops, such as rice and sugarcane, and toward high value perennial export crops, such as fruits, tea, coffee, and rubber with positive environmental side-effects. Increased incentives for perennial crops vis-à-vis annual field crops, such as cotton and rice, can help protect the soil on gentle slopes but are not a substitute for natural forest cover on steep or fragile slopes. India could use tariff reform as an opportunity to favor import or manufacture of environmentally benign technologies and machinery, and discriminate against highly polluting technologies.

There is a tendency for exchange rate to be used as an instrument of last resort, when all other weapons that serve the same objectives have failed. There is a strong hostility to the use of this instrument among politicians, certain pressure groups and the public in general.

The Instruments of Direct Controls

Direct controls are powerful instruments of economic policy. They can take effect very quickly and they can be selective. Because of their quick effect, these instruments are particularly used in crises, emergency and periods of war, and to deal with short-term economic problems. The results are graduated and fairly precisely calculable. In general, direct controls are less effective in dealing with long-term problems than with short-term ones. Three main categories of this set of instruments can be identified.

Control of Foreign Trade, Foreign Exchange and Immigration

1. Control of private imports,
2. State import trading,
3. Control of private exports,
4. Exchange control, and
5. Control of immigration.

Control of Prices

1. Price control of goods and services,
2. Rent control,
3. Dividend control, and
4. Control of wages.

Other Controls on the Internal Economy

1. Control of investment,
2. Raw material allocation,
3. Control of operations,
4. Regulation of conditions of work,
5. Control of exploitation of natural resources,
6. Rationing of consumer goods, and
7. Quality controls and standards.

Direct controls are normally administered by the ordinary civil service departments. Sometimes special institutions are set up for this purpose. In the field of international trade, decisions are taken in the framework of international institutions and agreements.

Direct controls are very effective in the short-term in holding back economic activity, but they are much less effective in stimulating it. Businessmen and consumers can be prevented by controls from doing certain things, but it is often virtually impossible to compel them to take positive action.

Direct controls have also been used much more to deal with short-term than with long-term or structural problems. Controls do not, as a general rule, modify the underlying market forces that brought about the situation that needed control. Consequently, two things may happen in the long run. First, the market forces that are held back by controls in one sector may break out in another. Second, if it is in the interests of both consumers and producers to evade the controls, then, as time goes on, evasion is likely to become more widespread; black markets will spring up, and administration will become more expensive. Third, there is a cultural dimension. In societies like India, where there is a little respect for the law and where the reflex is to violate the law rather than to obey it, this form of intervention is likely to be less effective and more expensive than in societies where there is respect for the law. For all these reasons, the use of regulatory instruments in isolation from other measures is unlikely to be the least cost method of achieving rural development objectives in many cases. Control and regulation compare unfavorably with the use of market-based approaches, such as taxes and emission charges.

With this instrument, as with others, there are psychological complications to be taken into account. Any prior warning that controls may be imposed will cause consumers to stock up.

Changes in the Institutional Framework

The instruments described so far have all been instruments that are used within the existing institutional framework and the changes made in these instruments can be quantified. Changes in the institutional framework do not lend themselves easily to quantification and usually require a change in the laws. Since it takes time to change the institutional framework, these changes are usually made with long-term rather than short-term objectives in mind. But there are occasions on which the institutional frameworks are changed in order to facilitate the use of the instruments for short-term policy. The nationalization of 14 major commercial banks in India in 1969 is a good example of the use of this instrument.

There are the following three categories in this set of instruments:

Institutional Changes Involving Other Instruments

1. Changes in the system of transfers to households (public finance),
2. Changes in the system of subsidies to enterprises (public finance),

3. Changes in the tax system (public finance),
4. Changes in the credit system (money and credit), and
5. Changes in the system of direct controls (direct control).

Institutional Changes Directly Affecting Production

1. Agricultural land reforms,
2. Changing the conditions of competition (restriction on monopolies),
3. Changes aimed at increasing labor's influence in management,
4. Changes in the extent of public ownership in industry, and
5. Creation of national institutions.

Institutional Changes in the International Framework

This includes the creation of international institutions, such as the World Bank, IMF, UNDP, the World Trade Organisation (WTO), and so on.

There are the following constraints on the use of changes in the institutional framework:

1. The establishment of a new institution or a major change in the institutional framework is usually a fairly major policy step that often meets with more opposition than does the use of an existing instrument, and
2. Since changes of this kind usually involve new laws, they have to go through a lengthy procedure of parliamentary approval.

In a developing country such as India, institutional changes constitute the most important instrument of promoting rural development. Institutional changes, particularly land reforms, contributed significantly to agricultural development in China and Taiwan. In India, although the process of institutional reforms including land reforms was initiated in the early 1950s, it is not yet complete, and rural development still continues to be stifled by the lack of appropriate institutions and organizations.

Creation of new markets, creation of property rights and Public Interest Litigations (PIL) are some of the of policy instruments that can help in internalizing environmental damages on the production side because the government creates a market to use the environment as a waste sink or issues pollution permits. These rights can be traded, that is, bought and sold like any other commodities. Tradable pollution permits are good examples for market creation, as they allow a company to buy or sell the rights to pollute the environment with an allowable level of pollution. This ensures that a specific level of pollution or emission will be attained at the lowest cost to society.

The creation and assignment of property rights can be used to internalize an externality and it does not matter, in terms of economic efficiency, as to which party (the party causing the externality or the party suffering from the externality) is assigned the right. Economic efficiency will be achieved as long as property rights are fully allocated and that completely free trade of all property rights is possible. The importance of this instrument is in demonstrating that it does not matter who owns what initially but only that everything should be owned by someone. Trade will place resources in their highest value occupation eventually. In India, this instrument has been used for averting the degradation of common pool[3] wastelands by creating private property rights and conferring them on the poor landless households.[4]

Thanks to the growing judicial activism in India, the instrument of PIL is now being used quite frequently for resolving environmental problems. We have numerous examples of cases in which high courts and the Supreme Court in India, *suo moto*, or in response to PILs, have pronounced orders for relocating polluting industries out of cities, using compressed natural gas (CNG) in place of diesel for operating buses and auto-rickshaws in several cities, including Delhi, and keeping the cities clean by institutionalized collection and disposal of garbage by the municipalities/municipal corporations concerned. For illustration, we would like to present a gist of a few of the significant environmental decisions taken by the Supreme Court in 1996 (Box 8.1).

Box 8.1

A FEW EXAMPLES OF COURT ORDERS FOR PREVENTION OF POLLUTION

8 July 1996: *The Supreme Court orders closure of 168 Delhi-based industries by November 30, 1996 and directs the chief secretary, Delhi government, to fix responsibility on government officials who had been negligent in their duty.*

6 August 1996: *The Supreme Court orders closure of 69 foundries in Howrah, West Bengal, following their failure to install pollution control devices.*

28 August 1996: *On the basis of a petition from the Vellore Citizens Welfare Forum, the Supreme Court imposes fines of ₹10,000 on each of the 700-odd tanneries in Tamil Nadu, and asks them to pay compensation for polluting the environment; the tanneries are also asked to install pollution treatment plants before December.*

9 October 1996: *The Supreme Court orders closure of 39,000 illegal industrial units operating in residential areas in Delhi.*

11 December 1996: *The Supreme Court orders closure of aqua-culture farms within 500 meters of the coast along India's 6,000 km coastline by 31 March 1997; it also passes the directive that employees of the farms be paid six years' compensation in lieu of loss of employment.*

19 December 1996: *The Supreme Court directs shifting of 550 tanneries located in east Calcutta by September 30, 1997, and the setting up of an environment pollution fund, with each unit depositing ₹10,000 as fine. This money is to be used for restoring the pollutant-ridden Hooghly river.*

Source: CSE (2001, 161).

Key Points

1. An instrument is defined as something that a manager or an actor can change, or manipulate in order to produce a desired effect. It may be an economic quantity, such as interest rate, or it may be a part of the institutional framework, such as nationalization of banks. An instrument, therefore, is the means by which an objective is pursued. A measure is the use of a particular instrument at a particular time in order to promote one or more objectives; for instance, the decision to raise the bank rate on a certain day, or to reduce income tax in a particular budget year.
2. The most useful framework to illustrate the relationship among policy instruments, target variables and social welfare, and for policy analysis has been provided by Nobel Laureate Jan Tinbergen. The model relates the main goal of a policy to various targets, and instrument variables and helps the policy makers in making rational choice of instruments for achieving the specified targets/objectives of the policy. In

India, in most of the policy documents this simple framework is not made operational, or is not properly elaborated and this is one of the reasons of lax implementation of policies.

3. In the context of development management, an action system may be conceived of as consisting of four elements: the manager/actor, the objectives, the conditions (physical, technological, economic, social, and political), and the means or instruments.
4. To achieve the objectives of a rural development policy efficiently, it is necessary that a set of appropriate instruments be identified for each of the objectives of the policy and that the chosen instruments are set at their optimal levels. Identification of appropriate instruments and determination of their optimal levels are both better done by public policy analysts than anyone else.
5. Choice of appropriate instruments needs to be made carefully, keeping in view the prevailing socio-economic and political environment. In many cases, instruments are not properly selected and their levels are not consistent with the objectives they seek to achieve. This results in the wastage of valuable public resources and unnecessary delays in achieving the objectives.
6. The policy instruments can be grouped in the following five categories: (a) public finance; (b) money and credit; (c) exchange rate; (d) direct controls; and (e) changes in the institutional framework.
7. Of all these types of instruments, subsidies, public investment and taxes that belong to the "public finance" category are most commonly used in India for achieving the objectives of agricultural and rural development programs.
8. Direct controls are powerful instruments of economic policy. They can take effect very quickly and they can be selective. Because of their quick effect, these instruments are particularly used in crises, emergency and periods of war, and to deal with short-term economic problems. Controls do not, as a general rule, modify the underlying market forces which brought about the situation that needed control and, in most cases, they lead to emergence of black markets and corruption.
9. In a developing country like India, institutional changes constitute the most important instrument of promoting rural development. Institutional changes, particularly land reforms, contributed significantly to agricultural development in China and Taiwan. In India, although the process of institutional reforms including bland reforms was initiated in the early 1950s, it is not yet complete and rural development still continues to be stifled by the lack of appropriate institutions and organizations.
10. The instrument of PIL is now being used quite frequently for resolving environmental problems. We have numerous examples of cases in which High Courts and the Supreme Court of India, either suo moto or in response to PILs, have pronounced orders for relocating polluting industries out of cities, using CNG in place of diesel for operating buses and auto-rickshaws in several, cities including Delhi, and keeping the cities clean by institutionalized collection and disposal of garbage by the municipalities/ municipal corporations concerned.

Questions for Discussion

1. Citing an example, differentiate between an instrument and a measure.
2. Write a critique of Tinbergen's policy framework. Can it be expressed in the form of an econometric model, or mathematical programming model? Yes/No and how?
3. In the context of development management, what is the relevance of an action system?

4. In what circumstances, the use of 'changes in the institutional framework' as a policy measure is desirable and why? What are its limitations?
5. Examine the pros and cons of using "direct controls" as a policy measure in India.
6. Cite a few examples when the instrument of "public finance" has been used in India to achieve certain objectives of a rural development program.
7. For what purposes can we use the instrument of "exchange rate"? What are the limitations of this instrument?

Assignment

Prepare a list of all the major policy instruments currently in use in India and examine their effectiveness.

Notes

1. http://dacnet.nic.in/eands/agStat06-07htm (Accessed on March 2008).
2. http://agricoop.nic.in/Agristatisticsnew.html (Accessed on May 24, 2015)
3. In common pool resources (CPRs), property rights are not clearly defined and, hence, they are vulnerable to degradation, encroachment and misuse.
4. See for details, Singh and Shishodia (2007): Chapter 8, Section 8.4.3.

Chapter 9

Equity-oriented and Growth-oriented Programs

LEARNING OUTCOMES

After having gone through this chapter, students should be able to:

- **Describe the contexts of various equity- and growth-oriented rural development programs and their main objectives;**
- **Describe the salient features of various equity-oriented rural development programs, such as the CDP, TRYSE) scheme, and Small Farmers, Marginal Farmers and Agricultural Laborers Project, and the major lessons of experience with them and;**
- **Illustrate the salient features of various growth-oriented programs such as the IADP, ICDP, HYVP and OF program, and the lessons of experience with them.**

Introduction

India has a very long history of experimenting with various approaches to rural development. Even in the pre-independence era, a number of rural reconstruction experiments were initiated by nationalist thinkers, social reformers, and missionaries. Well known among them were the Gurgaon Experiment of F. L. Brayne (1920), the Marthandam Experiment of Spencer Hatch (1921), the Sriniketan Experiment of Rabindra Nath Tagore (1920s), the Sewagram Experiment of Mahatma Gandhi (1933), the Firka Development Scheme (1946) and the Etawah Pilot Project of Albert Mayer (1948). Besides these experiments in rural development, various departments of the government, such as agriculture, cooperation, irrigation, health, and education also had tried in their own way to address rural problems falling within their respective jurisdictions.

Since the launch of the First Five Year Plan in 1951–52, the government has initiated numerous agricultural and rural development programs from time to time. For orderly presentation, we have classified those programs into the following three broad categories:

1. Equity- and growth-oriented programs.
2. Poverty and unemployment alleviation programs.
3. Natural resources and infrastructure development programs.

Given the limited space available here, it is not possible to present a detailed account of each of the rural development programs launched in India so far, nor is it of great relevance and interest to the contemporary rural development student to get bogged down with the details of those programs that now are part of historical archives. In our opinion, it would suffice to present briefly some of the salient features of the major programs and the lessons learnt from their experience. The main objectives of this overview are to acquaint the student with the historical perspective of the process of proliferation of rural development programs over time. Accordingly, we have chosen to devote a chapter to each of the three categories of the programs. In this chapter, we present an abridged account of a few major rural development programs that were aimed at promoting equity in terms of distribution of benefits of development, and growth in terms of increased production using new technologies. The main objective of the chapter is to familiarize the student with the nature, strategy, objectives, and contents of those programs, and the lessons thereof.

Equity-oriented Programs

A brief presentation of the salient features of the major programs that fall in this category follows.

Community Development Programme (CDP)

The CDP was India's first large-scale, well-planned and organized initiative for promoting agricultural and rural development with the main focus on equity. It was launched in October 1952. We now briefly describe its genesis and some of its salient features.

The Genesis

Launched in 1943, in the wake of the Bengal famine, the Grow More Food Campaign (GMFC) was India's first organized effort to increase food production. The campaign had a two-pronged approach. First, to bring idle but potentially productive land under the plough and, second, to stimulate cultivator interest in increasing crop yield per hectare. In 1948, the GMFC was reviewed by the Thakurdass Committee and, following its recommendations, the campaign was reoriented in 1950–51. In the following year, the GMFC became part of India's First Five Year Plan. In 1952, the Government of India appointed the Grow More Food Inquiry Committee under the chairmanship of Sir V. T. Krishnamachari to evaluate the campaign. The committee found, inter alia, that (a) all aspects of village life are interrelated and no lasting results can be achieved if individual aspects of it were dealt with in isolation and (b) the movement touched only a fringe of the population and did not arouse widespread enthusiasm and, hence, did not become in any sense a national program. The committee also made a number of recommendations regarding the future policy of the GMFC. One of the recommendations was that an extension agency should be set up for rural work, which would reach every farmer in the country and assist in the coordinated development of rural life. It was out of this background and experience that the CDP was designed and launched.

The Basic Premises

The basic premises underlying the India's decision to create the national CDP 1952 are presented in Box 9.1 (Ensminger 1968, 3).

One of the major initial moving forces in community development was Prime Minister Jawaharlal Nehru's interest in the program. Nehru felt that one of India's most important undeveloped resources was the people living in its some 6,00,000 villages. Nehru saw in community development the way to involve the village people in building a new India. He visualized that,

Box 9.1

BASIC PREMISES OF COMMUNITY DEVELOPMENT PROGRAM

1. *The overall development of the rural community can be brought about only with effective participation of the people, backed by the coordination of technical and other services necessary for securing the best from such initiative and self-help. It was to provide the necessary institutional structure and services that early attention was given to the development of basic democratic village institutions, especially panchayati raj, cooperatives, and village schools.*
2. *The problems of rural development have to be viewed from a holistic perspective and the efforts to solve them have to be multifaceted.*

Source: Ensminger (1968, 3).

through their involvement in self-help-oriented programs, would come the development of the people and people's institutions, both of which are essential ingredients in moving India towards one of its most clearly stated objectives, that is, developing India into a viable democracy.

The Objective

The main objective of the CDP was to secure the total development of the material and human resources of rural areas, and to develop local leadership and self-governing institutions, so as to raise the levels of living of rural people. This objective was to be attained by bringing about a rapid increase in food and agricultural production by strengthening programs of natural resource development, such as minor irrigation and soil conservation, by improving the effectiveness of farm-inputs supply systems and by providing agricultural extension service to farmers. The First Five Year Plan was dominated by the CDP, which reflected India's overriding concern with nation building and equity. Thus, the strategy underlying the CDP was holistic and equity-oriented.

The Coverage

The CDP was formally inaugurated on October 2, 1952. Initially it was launched in 55 project areas located in different parts of the country. Another 110 areas had to be added to the original 55 in the course of six months in response to popular demands from the members of state legislatures and the Members of Parliament (MPs). A new, somewhat less ambitious, scheme called the National Extension Service (NES) was evolved and launched in 1953. Whereas in the CDP, intensive development was taken up in all fields, the NES scheme was designed to provide the essential basic staff and a small amount of funds with which the people could start the development work essentially on the basis of self-help. The NES blocks were subsequently converted into CDP blocks. From April 1, 1969, the CDP was transferred from the central sector to the state sector.

The CDP had to be expanded phenomenally under political pressure and soon it became a national program encompassing 400 million rural people across the four corners of the country. Consequently, both the program as well as the inputs had to be diluted under this abnormal rate of expansion. The CDP now covers all the rural areas in the country.

The Activities

A large number of rural community development activities were undertaken in such varying degrees (within the limits of the available funds) as were advisable under the circumstances peculiar to each block. The number of activities taken up under the CDP was 46, categorized in the following eight broad heads (Ensminger 1972):

1. Agricultural and related matters (18)
2. Communication (3)
3. Education (3)
4. Health (6)
5. Training (5)
6. Social welfare (5)
7. Supplementary employment (4)
8. Housing (2)

Thus, the CDP was perhaps the most comprehensive program ever launched in India.

The Organization Structure

The CDP was undertaken and implemented by the Government of India and the state governments in cooperation with one another. For this purpose, an innovative multi-tier organizational structure was designed under the Technical Cooperation Programme Agreement (TCPA) on January 5, 1952 between the Government of India and the government of the US. At the national level, the Government of India formed a Central committee with the prime minister as the chairperson, the members of the Planning Commission, and the minister of food and agriculture as members, to lay down the broad policies and provide the general supervision for the agreed projects. All nation building ministries were directed to collaborate with the program through the Community Projects Administration (CPA), which was specially created for the purpose. The CDP organization at the national level has undergone a number of changes over time. Now, the Ministry of Rural Development is the administrative ministry in charge of all the centrally-sponsored rural development programs, including the CDP, in the country.

At the state level, a State Development Committee (SDC) headed by the chief minister was responsible for directing and coordinating the program within the state. Many state governments had constituted state planning commissions or state planning boards for this purpose. The program falls within the administrative purview of the state departments of rural development.

At the district level, a District Development Officer (DDO) is responsible for the CDP in his district. Now, after the 73rd Constitution amendment, statutory zila parishads are responsible for implementation of the program in the districts. The zila parishad is chaired by an elected non-official and the DDO is the Chief Executive Officer (CEO) of the zila parishad. However, there are state to state variations in the organizational structure of the CDP at the district level. At the block level, the statutory block parishad or samiti, or block panchayat samiti, which is chaired by an elected non-official, oversees the implementation of the CDP. The Block Development Officer (BDO) is the secretary to the block samiti and is responsible for implementation of the program.

At the village level, Village Level Workers (VLWs), or gram sevaks and gram sevikas, are responsible for implementing the program within a cluster of villages. VLWs work under the advice and control of the BDO. With the establishment of panchayati raj in all states now, the village or gram panchayat, which is headed by an elected non-official, is responsible for implementing the program within its jurisdiction. The VLW assigned to the panchayat acts as its secretary.

Financing

The CDP was conceived, planned, and initiated as a people's self-help program. The Parliament appropriated funds annually on the condition that the funds had to be committed within the year appropriated or reverted to the treasury. Initially, financial and technical assistance to the CDP was made available by the US government, under the TCPA signed on January 5, 1952. To meet the local expenditure on the implementation of the CDP, funds were drawn from the Government of India and the state governments, as well as the people. The Technical Cooperation Administration (TCA) provided technical assistance to the CDP at both the central and the state levels. At the central level, the services of the director of the TCA were made available to the central committee.

Evaluation and Lessons Learnt

There have been a number of surveys and studies that have highlighted the tangible achievements of the CDP in terms of distribution of improved seeds, use of chemical fertilizers, plant protection chemicals, improved farm tools and equipment, construction of roads, wells, and irrigation canals, establishment of primary health centers, rural dispensaries, *balwadi*s (nurseries), and so on. On the basis of these studies, it would be fair to say that the CDP contributed significantly towards the creation of basic rural development machinery and infrastructure in the country for the first time, and helped expand and improve the production base of the rural economy of India. The CDP has also fulfilled, to a large extent, the equity norm of rural development.

However, the CDP failed to achieve the expected increase in agricultural production. This failure could be attributed to its diffused character, as it did not put sufficient and direct emphasis on agricultural production. The financial, material, and administrative resources of the CDP were spread too thinly, albeit uniformly, all over the countryside to produce any tangible impact on agricultural production and rural poverty. In other words, the resources devoted to agricultural production fell short of the "critical minimum" required to escape from the perpetual problem of low productivity in Indian agriculture.

The Small Farmer Development Agency (SFDA)

The report of the All India Rural Credit Review Committee (1969) recommended the establishment of an agency to assist the small farmers who had not benefited from the gains of the Green Revolution. Accordingly, the Fourth Five Year Plan laid special emphasis on enabling the small farmers to participate in the process of development and share in its benefits. To achieve this objective, the plan provided for the initiation of a project, namely, the SFDA scheme, which was sanctioned during 1970–71, but the actual implementation started only during 1971–72. The objective of the SFDA was to ensure the viability of the small farmers. An autonomous agency registered under the Societies Registration Act 1860 was established at the district level to implement the SFDA projects.

The SFDA acted as a catalyst in identifying small farmers and their problems and helping them to obtain inputs from various developmental organizations.

The SFDA was a Central sector scheme until 1978–79 with 100% assistance from the Central funds. From the year 1979–80, it became a joint venture of the central government and the state governments, each sharing the cost of the scheme in the 50:50 ratio.

The Marginal Farmers and Agricultural Laborers (MFAL) Scheme

Like the SFDA, the MFAL scheme was also launched in 1970–71 following the recommendations of the All India Rural Credit Review Committee (1969). Its objective was to assist the marginal farmers (with landholdings below 2.50 acres) and agricultural laborers to improve their productivity and income through a variety of activities like crop husbandry, including multiple cropping, increased use of new inputs, water harvesting techniques, minor irrigation, livestock, poultry, and fishery, among others. During the Fifth Five Year Plan, based on the recommendations of the National Commission on Agriculture, the SFDA and MFAL schemes were merged into one composite scheme called the Small Farmers, Marginal Farmers, and Agricultural Labourers Project (SFMFALP). The District Rural Development Agency (DRDA) is responsible for implementation of both the schemes, as also all other rural development program in the district.

In a study conducted by the Planning Commission, it was found that proper care was not exercised in the selection of some of the project areas, that very little attention had been paid to the identification of agricultural laborers, and that the progress of identification of the participants was, on the whole, slow in most of the project areas. As a result of improper identification and verification of beneficiaries, the benefits of the schemes accrued to undeserving persons to the extent of about 9% in both the SFDA and MFAL projects (GoI 1975).

Growth-oriented Programs

By the middle of the Second Five Year Plan, it became increasingly evident that whatever the success of the CDP, a new approach would be required if agricultural production was to stay ahead of the demands of India's mounting population. In 1957–58, India faced its first post-independence food crisis. In response to this crisis, and on the basis of the recommendations of the Ford Foundation-sponsored team of American agricultural production specialists, a new program called the Intensive Agriculture District Programme (IADP), popularly known as package program, was formulated and launched in the country in 1960–61. Based on the principle of concentration underlying the IADP, the following programs had been designed and launched. All these programs were growth oriented; they did not address themselves to equity issues.

1. The ICDP
2. Green Revolution or HYVP
3. All India Coordinated Projects and Technology Missions
4. OF Program
5. Fish Farmers Development Agency (FFDA)

A brief description of each of the growth-oriented programs follows.

The Intensive Agriculture District Programme (IADP)

The IADP represented a significant departure from the CDP, in that it employed the concentration principle in deploying resources, as opposed to the equity criterion of the CDP. Its main objective was to achieve rapid increases in agricultural production through the use of all complementary inputs and services (package approach) at the farm level. Farm planning formed the core of IADP.

The Objectives

As its immediate goal, the IADP sought to achieve rapid increases in agricultural production through concentration of financial, technical, extension, and administrative resources. Its aim in the long run was to achieve a self-generating "breakthrough" in productivity and raise the production potential by stimulating the human and physical processes of change. The program was also intended to provide lessons for extending such intensified agricultural production programs to other areas.

The Coverage

The IADP was initially implemented in seven selected states of India. The state governments selected the following seven districts for implementation of the IADP: Thanjavur (Tamil Nadu), West Godavari (Andhra Pradesh), Shahabad (Bihar), Raipur (Madhya Pradesh), Aligarh (Uttar Pradesh), Ludhiana (Punjab), and Pali (Rajasthan). The Government of India approved the implementation of the program in these seven districts in June 1960. The seven districts were delimited into 140 community development blocks with 14,038 villages and the total gross cropped area of about 4.5 mha. At the behest of the Government of India, the IADP was later extended to eight more districts, one each in eight other states.

The Activities

In the districts selected for implementation of the IADP, all the inputs and services required to increase production were provided simultaneously. The activities taken up under the IADP are presented in Box 9.2.

Box 9.2

ACTIVITIES OF THE INTENSIVE AGRICULTURE DISTRICT PROGRAMME IN INDIA

1. *Adequate and prompt supply of credit based on production plans and made available through strengthened cooperative societies.*
2. *Adequate and timely supply of production requisites, such as fertilizers, pesticides, and implements, channeled mainly through cooperatives.*
3. *Arrangements for marketing and other services through cooperatives, so as to enable the cultivators to obtain a remunerative price for their marketable surplus.*
4. *Adequate storage facilities for supplies, such as seeds, fertilizers, implements, and pesticides, and for farm produce, so that the cultivators do not have to travel long distances to procure supplies and market their produce.*
5. *Intensive educational efforts, particularly through crop demonstrations, to disseminate knowledge of improved agricultural practices.*
6. *Strengthening of transport arrangements to ensure mobility of supplies and staff.*
7. *Village planning for increased production and strengthening of village organizations like cooperatives and panchayats.*
8. *Analysis and evaluation of the program from its initiation to its completion.*
9. *Establishment of agricultural implements workshops, seed and soil testing laboratories, and implementation of local works programs having a direct bearing on production.*

Source: Singh (1999, 171–72).

The Organization and Administration

A machinery specifically responsible for supervising the IADP was created at the center; the existing machinery at the state level was strengthened for guiding the program, and a district functionary was designated as project officer and made responsible for program administration at the district level. At the block level, the normal complement of the CDP staff was strengthened by providing additional staff. Appropriate machinery was provided for at various levels to coordinate the activities of different departments and agencies. To ensure quick and speedy action, adequate financial and administrative powers were delegated to the district collectors and project officers. These powers were reviewed from time to time and additional powers, wherever necessary, were given to the officers to meet the needs of the program.

The Implementation Strategy

The implementation of the IADP involved two broad stages. The first may be termed a "preparatory stage" during which the following activities were undertaken:

1. Selection of areas within the district for implementing the program
2. Creating general awareness among the farmers and non-official agencies such as panchayats and cooperatives and securing their participation
3. Strengthening of the cooperative institutions in the areas selected for coverage
4. Selection, appointment, and posting of additional staff
5. Training of staff
6. Organization of a resource and production benchmark survey
7. Assessment of the supplies needed
8. Constructing and/or hiring storage godowns to bring the supplies within easy reach of the farmers
9. Strengthening of the transport arrangements

It was only after these preparatory measures were completed that the program entered the second stage, that of operation and execution. The activities at this stage included

1. Preparation and follow-up of farm and village production plans;
2. Adequate and prompt supply of credit based on production plans;
3. Adequate and timely supply of production requisites, such as seeds, fertilizers, pesticides, and implements to be channeled primarily through cooperatives;
4. Intensification of information and extension education activities, such as demonstrations and use of other creative information media;
5. Arrangements for marketing and other services through cooperatives; and
6. Analysis and evaluation of the program.

Farm planning was the core of the IADP. Planned utilization of production resources, use of scientific knowledge and improvement of management skills formed the modus operandi to increase agricultural production and productivity. The farm plan proforma, which was developed to suit the farming needs of each geographically homogeneous area emphasized the following basic elements:

1. An inventory of the resources
2. The present land use and cropping system
3. Improved production practices to be adopted
4. Production supplies that have to be purchased for cash
5. Production credit to be tied to the additional production due to improved practices and not to tangible security
6. Expected net returns from all enterprises
7. A repayment plan
8. A credit application that links production needs to credit requirements

Farm planning under the IADP had been effective on the whole in getting a substantial number of cultivators to use simple improved practices, such as improved seeds, fertilizers, and plant protection measures. It made considerable progress in the first seven districts during the period the program has been in operation.

Training

National, regional, and district level training conferences were organized under the IADP for the district and state level program staff. Block level training camps for the village-level staff and the cultivators were also organized. Special training programs were conducted for the office bearers of the cooperative and marketing institutions. The staff of the central and state governments, and of the Ford Foundation invariably assisted in these programs. The training conferences were aimed at enhancing the competence of the participants in certain areas.

Financing

In the first seven districts, the IADP was implemented with financial assistance from the Ford Foundation. A memorandum of agreement (MoA) between the Government of India and the Ford Foundation was signed on June 18, 1960 setting forth the financial obligations of the different parties involved in the program, namely, the Government of India, the participating state governments, and the Ford Foundation.

The program also envisaged provision of funds in the form of short- and medium-term credit to enable the cultivators to purchase various wherewithal of production and also to meet such requirements as purchase of bullocks, construction and repair of minor irrigation works, purchase of implements and equipments, land development measures, and so on. The short-term loans were provided mainly by the cooperatives with the assistance of the RBI, and the medium-term loans partly by the government and partly by the cooperative institutions. Apart from financial assistance, the Ford Foundation also rendered technical assistance through a team of subject matter specialists and consultants. These consultants were located in New Delhi, and they assisted the central and state governments in the planning, implementation and evaluation of the program. Besides the Ford Foundation, the Technical Cooperation Mission (TCM) of the USAID also provided technical experts. These experts were assigned to the IADP districts and they assisted the district staff in the study of field problems, and in analyzing and resolving those problems.

Evaluation

A large number of problem-oriented analytical studies covering various aspects of the IADP have been conducted mostly by scholars working in agricultural universities and agro-economic research centers. Besides, the performance of the IADP has been analyzed from time to time by an expert committee on assessment and evaluation, which was set up by the Ministry of Food and Agriculture in June 1961 for this purpose.

In its fourth assessment of the IADP covering the period from its inception in 1960 through 1967–68, the Expert Committee on Assessment and Evaluation sought to identify useful lessons from eight years of experience with the IADP. The committee concludes that (GoI 1968, v):

> [T]he programme in general has lived up to its promise in the setting in which it operated. It has shown that where effectively organized and where improved technology was available, it has been able to move agricultural production forward more rapidly than did earlier approaches and to reach a wider range of farmers—large, medium and small.

One of the major drawbacks of the IADP was its neglect of the equity aspect of development. It has been criticized for having aggravated the inter-district and intra-district inequalities in income distribution. However, a study conducted by Singh (1973) in IADP, Aligarh, showed that the degree of inequality in farm income distribution had decreased from 1963–64 to

1968–69, due to the easy access of marginal and small farmers to improved seed, fertilizers, institutional credit, and irrigation ensured under the IADP.

Lessons

By 1966, the basic concept of concentration, and effective use and better management of resources had gained national acceptance, and a number of new agricultural development programs were designed and launched on their pattern. The growth-oriented programs demonstrated, on the one hand, the effectiveness of the concentration principle in achieving rapid increases in food production, and on the other hand, the failure of the growth-oriented strategy to solve the basic problems of rural poverty and income inequality. The most important lesson learned from the experience with these programs was that a rising economic growth rate was no guarantee against worsening poverty, and that a direct frontal attack on the basic problems of poverty and unemployment was called for.

Intensive Cattle Development Projects (ICDPs)

The first systematic attempt in India to improve the quality of cattle was the Key Village Scheme (KVS) initiated during the First Five Year Plan. The program was invigorated with the introduction of the ICDPs in 1965. The ICDPs were designed to provide cattle owners a package of improved practices, and envisaged intensive coverage of 1,00,000 cows and buffaloes of breedable age for achieving marked impact on milk production. The ICDPs were located in selected areas that had good potential and conditions to respond to cattle development programs. The ICDPs had a three-tier structure in which projects—regional cattle development (RCD) blocks (four per project), and Stockmen centers (25 per RCD block) each looking after 1,000 cattle—were placed in the descending order of the pyramid.

The ICDPs were not expected to yield spectacular results within a short span of time. However, after five years of operation of the program, an evaluation study was taken up by the Programme Evaluation Organisation (PEO) at the instance of the agriculture division of the Planning Commission in 1970–71, with a view to suggest the required correctives. Some of the major findings of the study were as follows:

1. A good number of cattle owners in various states pointed out that the male progeny of the exotic breed was comparatively less suitable for various farm operations.
2. In majority of the selected areas, it was found that artificial insemination (AI) had received increasing appreciation, but the follow-up action in this respect was not satisfactory.
3. Despite the several limitations like small holdings and inadequate irrigation facilities, the program of feeding and fodder development yielded satisfactory results.
4. Regular vaccination attenuated the incidence of contagious diseases and epidemics.
5. For marketing, milk cooperative societies were formed in many projects but some of them were ineffective.

Lessons

The following lessons could be teased out of the experience with the ICDPs:

1. To encourage breeding, cattle owners should be educated about the breed and quality of the cattle.
2. Regular pregnancy and sterility camps should be organized in all the ICDP areas, which should be attended by functionaries at all levels. Good quality of draught cattle needs to be ensured in abundance to meet the requirements of farm operations.

Green Revolution/High Yielding Varieties Programme (HYVP)

The term "Green Revolution" is commonly used to imply the rapid transformation of agriculture worldwide, including India, that led to significant increases in agricultural production between the 1940s and the 1960s.[1] As the Green Revolution was made possible mainly because of the widespread use of HYV seeds of a few crops, it is also known in India as the HYVP.

The Rockefeller Foundation was instrumental in initiating the process of Green Revolution in Mexico in an informal international research institution set up in 1959, which in 1963 was formally named as the International Maize and Wheat Improvement Center (CIMMYT). The second nation to which the Green Revolution spread was India. The Ford Foundation was instrumental in introducing the Green Revolution to India. The foundation and the Indian government collaborated to import a huge amount of wheat seed from the CIMMYT. The seeds of dwarf variety of wheat (red in color originally) were first multiplied in the mid-sixties in the experiment station of the GB Pant University of Agriculture and Technology, Pant Nagar, which was the first and foremost agricultural university in India set up on the land grant pattern agricultural universities of USA[2]. Later the seeds were multiplied at the Punjab Agricultural University, Ludhiana and then at the Indian Agricultural Research Institute, Pusa, New Delhi. India then began its own research and development programs involving plant breeding, irrigation development, and financing of agrochemicals. The Rockefeller Foundation and the Ford Foundation jointly established the International Rice Research Institute (IRRI) in the Philippines in 1960. The HYV of rice spread throughout that country, as well as Indonesia, Pakistan, Sri Lanka, other non-Soviet bloc countries, Latin American, Asia, and North Africa.

In India, the Green Revolution was brought about by the introduction of HYV seeds of wheat, paddy, and maize after 1965, and the increased use of fertilizers and irrigation. This led to rapid and significant increase in the foodgrain production needed to make India self-sufficient in foodgrains. The HYV of wheat, rice, and maize introduced in India had been developed in Mexico and in the Philippines. Of the high-yielding seeds, wheat produced the best results. Production of coarse grains, the staple diet of the poor, and pulses, the main source of protein, lagged behind, resulting in reduced per capita availability.

The total area under the HYVP was negligible at 1.9 mha in 1960. Since then, growth has been spectacular, increasing to nearly 15.4 mha by 1970, 43.1 mha by 1980 and 63.9 mha by 1990. The rate of growth decreased significantly in the late 1980s, however, as additional suitable land was not available.

The major benefits of the Green Revolution in India were experienced mainly in northern and northwestern India between 1965 and the early 1980s. The program resulted in a substantial increase in the production of food grains, mainly wheat and rice. Food grain yields continued to increase throughout the 1980s, but the dramatic changes in the years between 1965 and 1980 were not duplicated. By 1980, almost 75% of the total cropped area under wheat was sown with HYV. For rice, the comparable figure was 45%. In the 1980s, the area under HYV continued to increase, but the rate of growth overall was slower. The Eighth Five Year Plan aimed at making HYV available to the whole country and developing more productive strains of other crops.

The Indian Green Revolution created wide inter-regional and inter-state disparities. The program was implemented only in areas with assured supplies of water and the means to control it, large inputs of fertilizers and adequate farm credit. These inputs were easily available in parts of the states of Punjab, Haryana, and western Uttar Pradesh. Thus, yields increased most in these states. In other states, such as Andhra Pradesh and Tamil Nadu, in areas where these inputs were not assured, the results were limited or negligible, leading to considerable variation in crop yields within these states. The Green Revolution in India also increased income disparities: higher income growth and reduced incidence of poverty were found in the states where yields increased the most, and lower income growth and little change in the incidence of poverty in other states.

A revolution of this magnitude was bound to create some problems of its own. Critics charged that the Green Revolution resulted in environmental degradation and increased income inequality, inequitable asset distribution, and increase in absolute poverty. Some of these criticisms are valid and have been or still need to be addressed. But there is a tendency today to overstate the problems and to ignore the appropriate counter-factual situation: what would have been the magnitude of hunger and poverty without the yield increases of the Green Revolution and with the same population growth?[3]

Operation Flood (OF)

The OF was the world's biggest dairy development program. It heralded the so-called White Revolution in India. It was designed and launched in 1970 by the National Dairy Development Board (NDDB), then an NGO but now a statutory corporate body. Dr Verghese Kurien, who is regarded as "the Father of White Revolution" and Dr Michael Halse, then FAO advisor at NDDB, were instrumental in conceptualizing, designing, and launching of the OF. It was aimed at creating a virtual "flood" of rurally produced milk in India, by helping rural milk producers in 18 milksheds in 10 selected states of India to organize Anand-pattern dairy cooperatives (APDC). The basic philosophy behind OF was that milk production in the rural milksheds could be encouraged only by providing an efficient channel and a ready market for the rurally produced milk at remunerative prices. The milk production, procurement, processing, and marketing operations were to be organized on Anand model cooperatives, which had already proved their worth as an organization structure suitable for small-scale and scattered milk producers. The OF was implemented in three phases: OF-I, OF-II and OF-III. OF-I was formally launched on July 1, 1970 by the newly formed Indian Dairy Corporation (IDC). The IDC was a wholly Government of India-owned corporation, specifically set up to serve as a "finance and promotion" house for the OF. Originally, OF-I was to conclude in five years, but it had to be extended until March 31, 1981. Concurrently, OF-II was launched on October 2, 1979. It concluded on March 31, 1985. OF-III was launched on April 1, 1985 and concluded on March 31, 1996. Since April 1, 1996, OF-IV has been underway in some selected unions that are currently financially viable, but vulnerable to threats from competition of the private trade, or those that are currently sick, but can be turned around.

As stated earlier, the OF program sought to replicate the APDC structure in selected milksheds in India. The APDCs have a three-tier organizational structure consisting of a milk producers' cooperative society at the village level, a cooperative milk producers' union at the district level, and a cooperative milk producers' federation at the state level. This structure permits the horizontal and vertical integration of all the dairy development activities in a state, and makes it possible to realize the economies of scale in procurement, processing, and marketing of milk through the use of modern technology. The APDCs formulate and implement their own policies and programs for dairy development in their area, and hire professional managers and technicians for their implementation. The role of the government is limited to assisting the cooperatives financially in implementing their own programs. The government funds for dairy development are placed at the disposal of the cooperatives.

The OF is a living example of a nongovernmental initiative that has been successful in promoting people-centered development more efficiently and effectively than the government-sponsored programs. The OF is also a unique example of the use of foreign aid in the form of dairy commodities, namely, skimmed milk powder and butter oil, to create, expand, and modernize the production, processing, and distribution facilities in the country, such that the dependence on foreign aid was eventually eliminated. It also demonstrated that the food aid need not necessarily depress the domestic prices below the levels, which are low enough to kill the domestic producers' initiative to produce more. The OF has enabled India to increase its milk production from about 21 million tons in 1968–69 to about 138 million tons in 2013–14. The number of dairy cooperatives established under the OF in India had increased to 1,62,186 by the end of the year 2013–14 and the number of member milk producers to 15.46 million (NDDB 2014, 62–63). In 2013–14, the dairy cooperatives procured about 12.5 million tons of milk, as compared to 12.2 million tons in the previous year, and liquid milk marketing by the cooperatives stood at 11 million tons, as compared to 10.4 million tons in the previous year. Now, another ambitious dairy development, the National Dairy Plan Phase I (NDP-I) is being implemented by NDDB through end implementing agencies (EIAs). NDP I is a Central Sector Scheme to be implemented over a seven-year period, 2011–12 to 2018–19. It will be implemented with a total investment of about ₹22.42 billion. Its main objectives are: (a) to help increase productivity of milch animals and thereby increase milk production to meet the rapidly growing demand for milk and (b) to help provide rural milk producers with greater access to the organized milk processing sector. The project is a scientifically planned multi-state initiative with focus on 14 major milk producing states. The NDP-I will put in place scientific and systematic processes that in the long run would put India firmly on the path of improving the genetics of milk producing animals in a consistent manner. It will enable prudent use of the country's scarce natural resources; help reduce methane emissions; improve the quality of milk; help strengthen regulatory and policy measures to provide an enabling environment for the growth of dairying; and ultimately, benefit small holder milk producers who are the bedrock of India's milk production system (NDDB 2014, 46–47).

Thanks to the OF program, India continues to be the world's highest milk producing country. Evaluation studies of the OF show that the program has significantly improved the income of rural milk producers, especially marginal and small farmers, and landless laborers (Singh 1999a, 218–22).

Technology Missions

Technology Missions on oilseeds, pulses, maize, and cotton were launched in the Seventh Five Year Plan to further intensify research and provide a fillip to technology adoption by removing some bottlenecks and constraints. The technology mission on oilseeds has achieved a major breakthrough in the production of oilseeds. During 1998–99, a record production of 25.2 million tons of oilseeds was achieved for the first time in India. As oilseeds crops are predominantly grown in rain-fed areas in the country, their production fluctuates widely depending upon the fluctuations in the rainfall. In the year, 2013–14, the production of all oilseeds in the country was 32.88 million tons, and cotton increased from 9.84 million bales in 1990–91 to 32.59 million bales in 2013–14 (MoA 2014, 103–104, 118–119).

In view of the success achieved in the oilseeds production, pulses were also brought under the ambit of the technology mission in 1990. There has been an increase in the production of pulses after their inclusion in the mission. In 2005–06, the production of pulses in India was estimated to be about 13.40 million tons, which increased to 19.27 million tons in 2013–14 ((MoA 2014, 91–92). Besides the mission, a centrally sponsored National Pulses Development Project (NPDP) is also underway in the country. Maize had also been included in the technology mission in 1995 in view of the versatility of the crop and its importance as a food grain, animal feed, and an industrial raw material. For increasing the production of maize, the Accelerated Maize Development Programme (AMDP) was formulated during the Eighth Five Year Plan. Consequently, the production of maize in the country increased from merely 8.96 million tons in 1990–91 to 24.35 million tons in 2013–14 (MoA 2014, 88–89).

A Technology Mission on Dairy Development (TMDD) was constituted by the Government of India in August 1988 to complement and supplement the efforts made under the OF program for dairy development. The main objective of TMDD was to optimize the use of available inputs, resources and infrastructural facilities established under the OF. Under the Operational Linkage Programme (OLP), which was implemented under the auspices of TMDD in 171 districts in 14 states, integrated district annual plans were prepared by the District Level Coordination Committees (DLCCs). These plans were prepared taking into account the resources available for dairy development with the state governments, the dairy cooperatives and the concerned NGOs (NDDB 1997, 34).

A national horticulture mission was launched in 2005–06 as a Centrally-sponsored scheme to promote holistic growth of the horticulture sector through an area based regionally differentiated strategies. The scheme has been subsumed as a part of Mission for Integration Development of Horticulture (MIDH) during 2014–15. Presently, India is the second largest producer of fruits & vegetables in the world. The mission covers fruits, vegetables, root and tuber crops, mushrooms, spices, flowers, aromatic plants, coconut, cashew, cocoa, and bamboo. While the Government of India contributes 85% of total outlay for developmental programs in all the states except the states in North East and Himalayas, a 15% share is contributed by state governments. In the case of the North Eastern and Himalayan states, the Government of India's contribution is 100%. The mission adopted the following strategies:[4]

1. Ensure an end-to-end holistic approach covering production, post-harvest management, processing, and marketing to assure appropriate returns to growers/ producers.
2. Promote R&D technologies for production, post-harvest management, and processing.
3. Enhance acreage, coverage and productivity through (a) diversification from traditional crops and (b) extension of appropriate technology to the farmers for high-tech horticulture cultivation and precision farming.
4. To establish convergence and synergy among multiple on-going and planned programs for horticulture development.
5. To promote, develop and disseminate technologies, through a seamless blend of traditional wisdom and modern scientific knowledge.
6. To create opportunities for employment generation for skilled and unskilled persons, especially unemployed youth.

Yet another mission, the National Mission for Sustainable Agriculture (NMSA) is one of the eight missions under the National Action Plan on Climate Change (NAPCC).[5] The mission document was accorded, in principle, approval by the Prime Minister's Council on Climate Change (PMCCC) on September 23, 2010. The mission seeks to address issues regarding *sustainable agriculture* in the context of risks associated with climate change by devising appropriate adaptation and mitigation strategies for ensuring food security, equitable access to food resources, enhancing livelihood opportunities, and contributing to economic stability at the national level.

The mission, therefore, seeks to transform Indian agriculture into a climate-resilient production system through suitable adaptation and mitigation measures in the domain of crops and animal husbandry. These interventions would be embedded in research and development activities, absorption of improved technology and best practices, creation of physical and financial infrastructure, and institutional framework, and facilitating access to information and promoting capacity building. While promotion of dryland agriculture would receive prime importance by way of developing suitable drought and pest resistant crop varieties and ensuring adequacy of institutional support, the mission would also expand its coverage to rainfed areas for integrating farming systems with management of livestock and fisheries, so that agricultural production continues to grow in a sustainable manner.

The mission identifies 10 key dimensions for promoting the sustainable agricultural practices by implementing a program of action (POA) covering both adaptation and mitigation measures through four functional areas, namely, *research and development, technologies, products and practices*, and *infrastructure* and *capacity building*. While modern technologies and research would continue to play an important role in promoting the sustainability of agricultural production, the mission also recognizes the need to harness traditional knowledge and agricultural heritage for in-situ conservation of genetic resources.

Detailed operational guidelines for the mission were issued by the Ministry of Agriculture, Government of India in 2014 (MoA 2014c). The State Department of Agriculture will have the overall responsibility for implementing NMSA in a mission mode at state level.

The National Livestock Mission (NLM) is the latest in the series of missions. It was launched by the Department of Animal Husbandry, Dairying and Fisheries, Government of India in the Financial Year 2014–15 with the main objective of ensuring quantitative and qualitative improvement in livestock production systems and capacity building of all stakeholders. The mission has the following four sub-missions:[6]

Sub-mission on Livestock Development

The sub-mission includes activities that address the concerns for overall development of livestock species including poultry, other than cattle and buffalo, with a holistic approach. The risk management component of the sub–mission will, however, also cover cattle and buffalo along with other major and minor livestock.

Sub-mission on Pig Development in North Eastern Region

The sub-mission will strive to forge synergies of research and development organizations through appropriate interventions, as may be required for holistic development of pigs in the North Eastern region, including genetic improvement, health cover, and post-harvest operations.

Sub-mission on Feed and Fodder Development

The sub–mission is designed to address the problems of scarcity of animal feed and fodder resources, to give a push to the livestock sector making it a competitive enterprise for India, and also to harness its export potential. It will especially focus on increasing both production and productivity of fodder and feed through adoption of improved and appropriate technologies best suited to specific agro–climatic region in both arable and non–arable areas.

Sub-mission on Skill Development, Technology Transfer and Extension

At present, the extension machinery at field level for livestock activities is not adequately strengthened. As a result, farmers are not able to adopt the technologies developed by research institutions. The adoption of new technologies and practices requires linkages between stakeholders. The sub-mission will provide a platform to develop, adopt, or adapt the technologies including frontline field demonstrations in collaboration with farmers, researchers and extension workers, and so on, wherever it is not possible to achieve this through existing arrangements.

Fisheries Development Programs

As stated in Chapter 2, the fisheries sector occupies an important place in the socio-economic development of India. In 2013–14, the fisheries contributed 1.35% of India's total GDP at factor cost at current prices and 0.80% at the 2004–05 prices (MoA 2014 a, Tables 2.6b and 2.6c).

It is a source of cheap and nutritious food, and is an important foreign exchange earner. In 2013–14, the value of fish and fish products exported from India was (₹)306.27 billion (US$ 5,062 million) (MoA 2014a, Table 7.3(A), p. A 94). Besides, it is a major source of livelihood for over 4.056 million fishermen and women folk in the country, engaged fully or partially, or in subsidiary activities pertaining to the sector. Besides, it is considered as a major source of livelihood for nearly 11 million people in the country, engaged fully or partially, or in subsidiary activities pertaining to the sector. It is estimated that fisheries sector alone can provide one million jobs in next five years.

India is now the third largest producer of fish and the second largest producer of inland fish in the world. Its coast line measures 8,118 km and continental shelf is 530,000 km^2. The fish production in the country has registered tremendous growth over the last two decades or so, ranging from 5.5% to 5.8% per annum, which is much higher than that for the agricultural sector as a whole. Fish production can be increased significantly if judicious development, conservation, and harvesting of marine and inland fishery resources of the country, by way of adopting suitable scientific technologies and conservational measures, were adopted.

Like other CPRs, the fisheries in India also suffer from what Hardin (1968) called "the tragedy of the commons." In 2014, India had a huge fleet of 1,99,141 fishing crafts comprising 52,982 traditional (non-motorized) crafts, 73,410 motorized crafts and 72,749 mechanized boats (MoA 2014, 128). Consequently, marine fisheries are overexploited and the fish catch has been declining over time.

Being part of the environment, they affect it and are affected by it. Until the first national policy for managing (marine) fisheries was announced in 2004, there was no national fisheries policy in India. However, the Government of India had sought to increase fish production in the country through several research and development programs. More specifically, the Government of India had established several fisheries research institutes under the aegis of the Indian Council of Agricultural Research (ICAR) to undertake research for the development of composite fish culture and induced breeding technologies, and to promote their adoption. Besides, it also launched a national level program, the FFDA in 1976 with the initial assistance from the World Bank to promote aquaculture in the country. The FFDA provided technical, financial, and extension support to fish farmers for taking up culture fishery in common pool village ponds and tanks. Consequently, the national average fish yield in the FFDA-supported ponds increased from 50 kg/ha per year in 1974–75 to about 2,135 kg/ha in 1994–95, and this increasing trend in the yield continues to date (Katiha 2006, 19). In addition to the Government of India, the state fisheries departments also promote inland fishery culture through granting leases to poor fishermen to take up culture fishery in public/common pool village water bodies and provision of subsidies.

The Ministry of Agriculture (Government of India) has also paid due attention to the development of deep-sea fisheries in the country. The declaration of an EEZ in 1976 facilitated the exploration, exploitation, and utilization of marine living resources in the sea around India extending to 200 nautical miles, thereby giving the nation immense opportunities and challenges to harvest the resources and to manage them on sound scientific basis. Besides, many other initiatives have been taken by the government and private agencies in the marine fisheries sector of the country. On realizing that most of the deep-sea fishery resources beyond the conventional fishing limit and fishing capability of the indigenous craft can be gainfully exploited, only if the upgraded and sophisticated vessels of adequate size and capabilities were inducted into the fishery, the Government of India facilitated the mobilization of capital and expertise indigenously to address this issue in the 1981 Charter Policy.

After the expiry of five years of operation of this policy, the government revised the policy to rectify the deficiencies noticed during its operation and to make it more beneficial to the country.

Accordingly a revised 1986 Charter Policy was pronounced. This charter policy envisaged the acquisition of vessels by the Indian companies either through import/construction in India or through joint ventures. As a result of the charter policy, 97 companies were permitted to operate 311 foreign fishing vessels. Besides augmenting the marine fish production in the country, the policy also facilitated greater inflow of foreign exchange through the export of fish caught by these vessels. All these vessels were operating on 100% export oriented units (EOU) basis. The conditions for acquisition of vessels of adequate type and number by the Indian companies who chartered vessels helped the growth of Indian deep-sea fishing fleet within a short span of time. Having laid the foundation for the Indian deep-sea fishing industry, the government went ahead to broad base the initiatives through the Deep Sea Fishing Policy (DSFP) 1991. This policy envisaged to promote joint ventures, test fishing, and leasing, besides allowing the vessels chartered under the 1986 policy to operate till the validity of their permits lasted. The Government of India had announced its first Marine Fishing Policy (MFP) in 2004 (GoI 2004c).[7]

The 2004 policy seeks to address the concerns of the traditional and coastal fishermen together with those of the other stakeholders in the deep-sea sector, so as to achieve the harmonized development of marine fishery, both in the territorial and extra-territorial waters of the country. The rationale of the policy is enshrined in the National Agriculture Policy promulgated by the Government of India in 2000.

Key Points

1. India has a very long history of experimenting with various approaches to rural development going back to the pre-independence era. Since the beginning of the First Five Year Plan in 1951–52, a large number of agricultural and rural development programs have been launched in the country from time to time. These programs could be classified into the following three broad categories: Equity- and growth-oriented programs, poverty and unemployment alleviation programs, and natural resources and infrastructure development programs.
2. The CDP was India's first large scale, well-planned and organized initiative to promote agricultural and rural development, with the main focus on equity. It was launched in October 1952. Its main objective was to secure total development of the material and human resources of rural areas, and to develop local leadership and self-governing institutions, so as to raise the levels of living of the rural people. It laid the foundation for agricultural and rural development programs.
3. The financial, material and administrative resources of the CDP were spread too thinly, albeit uniformly, all over the countryside to produce any tangible impact on agricultural production and rural poverty. In other words, the resources devoted to agricultural production fell short of the "critical minimum" required to escape from the perpetual problem of low productivity in Indian agriculture. However, the CDP was successful in achieving the objective of equity.
4. The SFDA scheme and the MFAL scheme were the two other major equity-oriented programs. They were both launched in 1970–71, following the recommendations of the All India Rural Credit Review Committee (1969). During the Fifth Five Year Plan, both the schemes had been merged into one composite scheme called the SFMFALP. These programs did not succeed in achieving their objectives, mainly due to improper identification of their beneficiaries.

5. The first growth-oriented program launched in India in the wake of the food crisis of 1957–58 resulting mainly from the failure of the CDP to increase agricultural production rapidly and significantly, was the IADP. It was initiated in 1960–61 in seven selected districts in the country and was later extended to eight more districts. The IADP employed the concentration principle as opposed to the equity principle of the CDP. It aimed at attaining rapid increases in agricultural production in selected areas through intensification of the use of the full set of production inputs and services. It was successful in achieving this objective to a great extent.
6. Based on the success of the IADP, several other programs, such as the ICDP, Green Revolution or HYVP; the OF program; technology missions; and the FFDA were designed based on the concentration principle. All these programs led to rapid increases in agricultural production but aggravated the inter-regional and intra-regional disparities in the distribution of benefits of development.

Questions for Discussion

1. Compare and contrast the equity-oriented approach with the growth/efficiency-oriented approach to rural development. Which one of these is more appropriate under the current situation in India and why?
2. What was the main reason for the failure of the Community Development Programme (CDP) to achieve significant increases in agricultural production?
3. What were the major lessons of the experience with the Integrated Agriculture District Programme (IADP), and to what extent they were replicated in other programs?
4. The High Yielding Varieties Programme (HYVP) made India self-sufficient in foodgrains, but it was criticized by social scientists on several grounds. What were the major criticisms of the HYVP?
5. In India, we have dozens of rural development programs currently underway. Some of them have contradictory objectives. This creates a lot of confusion among the villagers. Why cannot we have a comprehensive program of rural development encompassing all aspects of rural life as the CDP did?

Assignment

Write a critique of various 'Technology Missions' underway now in India focusing on how they are different from earlier agricultural development programs or they are simply "old wines in new bottles".

Notes

1. The term "Green Revolution" was first used in 1968 by the former USAID Director, William Gaud, who noted the spread of the new technologies and said, "These and other developments in the field of agriculture contain the makings of a new revolution. It is not a violent Red Revolution like that of the Soviets, nor is it a White Revolution like that of the shah of Iran. I call it the Green Revolution." (http://en.wikipedia. org/wiki/Green_Revolution).
2. The Government of Uttar Pradesh had granted about 6,500 hectares of its Terai farm in Nainital district (then in Uttar Pradesh but now in Uttarakhand) to set up the new university at Pant Nagar, named after the first Chief Minister of Uttar Pradesh, Govind Ballabh Pant. The senior author of this

book, Katar Singh, was then an Assistant Professor in the Department of Agricultural Economics in the Pant Nagar University and saw the dwarf wheat growing in Pant Nagar.

3. http://www.ifpri.org/pubs/ib/ib11.pdf (Accessed on March 2008).
4. http://nhm.nic.in/Archive/midh(English).pdf (Accessed on April 18, 2016).
5. The Eight national missions on climate change are: National Solar Mission; National Mission for Enhanced Energy Efficiency; National Mission on Sustainable Habitat; National Water Mission; National Mission for Sustaining the Himalayan Ecosystem; National Mission for Green India; National Mission for Sustainable Agriculture; and National Mission on Strategic Knowledge on Climate Change.
6. http://dahd.nic.in/dahd/division/national-livestock-mission.aspx (Accessed on October 3, 2015).
7. Some of the salient features of the Policy are presented in Chapter 6 of this book.

Chapter 10

Poverty and Unemployment Eradication Programs

LEARNING OUTCOMES

After having gone through this chapter, students should be able to:

- **Explain the genesis of various rural poverty and unemployment eradication programs**
- **launched in India from time to time;**
- **Describe the present poverty scenario in India and the trends in it;**
- **Describe the present unemployment scenario in India and the trends in it;**
- **Describe the genesis and salient features of the National Rural Livelihood Mission (Aajeevika);**
- **Describe the genesis and salient features of MGNREGA and the scheme formulated thereunder for alleviation of unemployment; and**
- **Explain the salient features of major social welfare-oriented programs (SWOP) of India, including their objectives and target groups.**

Introduction

Poverty and unemployment have been the bane of India since long. Their reduction has been one of the major goals of India's development planning since the beginning of the planning era in 1951–52 and the planning process has been sensitive to the needs of the poor. Accordingly, the Government of India has launched various programs from time to time aimed at alleviation of poverty and unemployment, and creating adequate livelihood opportunities for the poor through provision of employment and public services. Poverty and unemployment are interrelated problems and have a two-way relation, that is, one is both the cause and effect of the other. Poverty in India is not merely an economic phenomenon but a social one as well. While poverty is an outcome of multiple deprivations, its measurement has largely dealt with economic deprivation (income/consumption expenditure). The recent body of literature highlights the multidimensionality of poverty and also the heterogeneity of the poor. It also highlights the need to go beyond income poverty by using indices of human development and overall welfare. Since the determinants of poverty and unemployment are interrelated, a comprehensive approach is needed to address these two problems.

Poverty alleviation schemes and programs have been in place in India for a long time now. The programs and schemes have been modified, consolidated, expanded, and improved over time. The Ministry of Rural Development now categorizes various targeted programs into four broad categories: (a) rural poverty alleviation programs; (b) rural wage-employment program; (c) rural connectivity programs; and (d) social welfare-oriented programs.

There are numerous Centrally-sponsored schemes (CSS) belonging to all the four categories. The CSS are designed by the Center, administered by the Ministry of Rural Development (MoRD), but implemented by the state governments, which generally contribute 25% of their costs. In addition, some state governments have their own schemes. The multiplicity of the programs is advocated on the grounds of multidimensionality of poverty and regional variations in the efficacy of the delivery systems. There is also recognition that it is problematic to close a scheme even if it is cost ineffective because of adverse publicity and political fallout associated with the closure. Hence, there is a plethora of schemes now underway in the country, all purporting to address the problems of poverty and unemployment.

In Chapter 3, we presented the various methodologies followed in India for estimating the incidence of poverty as also the latest estimates of poverty in the country. In this chapter, we first present the current poverty scenario and trends, then unemployment situation and trends thereof in the recent past, and, finally, examine the salient features of the two major poverty and unemployment alleviation programs currently under way in India, namely, National Rural Livelihood Mission (NRLM/Aajeevika), and the MGNREGA and the scheme formulated thereunder. The main objective of the chapter is to enhance the awareness of the student about poverty and unemployment situation, and the measures taken by the government from time to time to resolve them and lessons thereof.

Current Poverty Scenario and Trends

Several attempts have been made in India to estimate the incidence of poverty and trends thereof. The estimates are, however, not comparable because of differences in the methodologies used to define the poverty lines and size of samples taken. However, by and large, we could say that the proportion of India's population living below the poverty line has fluctuated widely over time and across states in the past, but the overall trend has been downward. We could broadly examine the incidence of poverty and trends therein under the following three phases (Muthalagu 2007, 4).

Phase I: 1950 to the Mid-1970s

Incidence of poverty shows no discernible trend. In 1951, 47% of India's rural population was below the poverty line. The proportion went up to 64% in 1954–55; it came down to 45% in 1960–61 but in 1977–78, it went up again to 51%.

Phase II: Mid-1970s to 1990

Poverty declined significantly between the mid-1970s and the end of the 1980s. The decline was more pronounced between 1971–78 and 1986–87, with rural poverty declining from 51% to 39%. It went down further to 34% by 1989–90. Urban poverty went down from 41% in 1977–78 to 34% in 1986–87 and further to 33% in 1989–90.

Phase III: Post-1991 Era

The post-economic reform period evidenced both progress and setbacks. Rural poverty increased from 34% in 1989–90 to 43% in 1992, and then fell to 37% in 1993–94. Urban poverty went up from 33.4% in 1989–90 to 33.7% in 1992 and declined to 31% in 1993–94.

Due to methodological changes in the collection of NSS data in the 55th round (1999–2000), comparison of the pre- and post-reform period trend in poverty is beset with problems. The trend in the incidence of poverty depends on whether we include or exclude the 55th and 56th rounds of the NSS. The exclusion of both the rounds shows substantial slowdown in the rate of decline in the percentage of rural population living in poverty during 1990–98, but inclusion tends to suggest some improvement in the rate of decline during 1990–2001.

The existing official Planning Commission poverty lines for 2011–12, based on the Tendulkar Expert Group methodology and derived from the Mixed Recall Period (MRP) consumption distribution of the NSSO, are ₹816 and ₹1,000 per capita per month respectively for the all-India rural and urban populations. The Rangarajan Expert Group poverty lines, based on consumption estimates on MMRP are 19% higher for rural India and 41% higher for urban India. Because of the differences in the underlying recall periods, only a part of the total difference (₹156 for rural India and ₹407 in urban India) between the current official poverty lines and those proposed by the Rangarajan Expert Group is real.

As per the Rangarajan Expert Group report, in 2011–12, the poverty ratio was 39.9% in rural areas and in 26.4% in urban areas and the number of people below the poverty was 260.5 million in rural areas and 102.5 million in urban areas. This is in contrast to the corresponding estimates of 216.7 million and 53.1 million for rural and urban areas as per the Tendulkar Expert Group Report (Planning Commission 2014, Table 4.7, p. 69).

Undoubtedly, India has made some progress in the reduction of income poverty. Yet, in 2011–12, as many as 363 million persons (29.5%) were living below the poverty line in India (for details, see Table 3.15). A large number of the hardcore poor are located in remote and inaccessible areas. The problem of poverty alleviation is going to be far more difficult than in the past, since those who were near the poverty line might have crossed it temporarily for some time but may have slipped again below the poverty line and now living as the hardcore poor.

Current Employment Scenario and Trends

In development economics, the link between employment and poverty is one of the most debatable issues, particularly in the light of their relationship with the general growth rate of the economy. A higher rate of growth of (GDP does not necessarily reduce poverty, if the distribution of benefits of the growth is highly unequal. Employment is a source of income and livelihood, and also a reflection of the overall living condition of people. The approach paper to the Tenth Five Year Plan prescribed that in order to ameliorate poverty, it is essential to create "gainful high quality" employment for the existing as well as prospective additions to the labor force. Growth in employment is usually linked with growth in earnings of the households and, hence, has a direct bearing on the poverty levels. As most of the poor rural households are primarily engaged in occupations that, since the initiation of the economic reforms in the 1990s, have not experienced a significant increase in productivity, amelioration of poverty for this group, in the immediate future, has to come mainly through additional employment generation. Hence, it is widely acknowledged that creating adequate employment opportunities should constitute one of the important objectives of the development strategy of the country.

The all-India Employment and Unemployment surveys of NSSO are the primary sources of labor market data at the national and state levels. The labor force indicators at national and state/UT levels, generated from these surveys, provide the critical inputs required for planning and policy formulation exercises of various government organizations and also are useful to other users/researchers. NSS surveys on employment and unemployment, with large sample of households are conducted quinquennially. As of 2015, nine such comprehensive surveys on the employment and unemployment have been conducted by NSSO, beginning from 27th round (October 1972–September 1973) until the 68th round survey (July 2011–June 2012).

NSSO rounds are quinquennial and therefore information on the employment/unemployment situation in the country is available only after a gap of five years. To make the data available in the interregnum, the labor bureau conducts household employment–unemployment surveys on annual basis and has also been bringing out quarterly survey reports on the effects of the economic growth/slowdown on employment in select sectors in India since 2009. The results of the latest quarterly survey on employment conducted in July 2014 indicated an increase in employment by 3.5 million since the first survey.

Estimates of Employment

As per the NSSO data, during 1999–2000 to 2004–05, employment on usual status (US) basis increased by 59.9 million persons from 398.0 million to 457.9 million as against the increase in labor force by 62.0 million persons from 407.0 million to 469.0 million. After a period of slow progress during 2004–05 to 2009–10, employment generation picked up during 2009–10 to 2011–12, adding 13.9 million persons to the workforce, but not keeping pace with the increase in labor force (14.9 million persons; Table 10.1). Based on current daily status (CDS), CAGR in employment was 1.2% and 2.6% against 2.8% and 0.8% in the labor force respectively for the same periods. A cause for concern is the deceleration in the CAGR of employment during 2004–05 to 2011–12 to 0.5% from 2.8% during 1999–2000 to 2004–05 as against CAGRs of 2.9% and 0.4% respectively in the labor force for the same periods of time.

Tables 10.2 and 10.3 show the unemployment rates as per the 55th round and 61st round of the NSSO for rural areas and urban areas of India, respectively. As one could see from the

Table 10.1: *Employment and Unemployment Scenario in India*

Method	*1999–2000*	*2004–05*	*2009–10*	*2011–12*
Persons in labor force (million)				
US*	407.0	469.0	468.8	483.7
CDS**	363.3	217.2	428.9	440.4
Persons and person days employed (million)				
US*	398.0	457.9	459.0	472.9
CDS**	336.9	382.8	400.8	415.7

Source: MoF (2015, Table 9.1, p. 135).
Notes: US* (Usual Status) (principal + subsidiary) measures employment in terms of number of persons. CDS** measures employment in term of person days employed.

Table 10.2: *Unemployment Rates for 55th Round and 61st Round of NSSO in Rural India (in %)*

	Rural					
	Male			*Female*		
NSSO Round	*UPS*	*CWS*	*CDS*	*UPS*	*CWS*	*CDS*
55th (1999–2000)	2.1	3.9	7.2	1.5	3.7	7.0
61st (2004–05)	4.4	3.8	8.0	3.1	4.2	8.7

Source: GoI (2007b).
Note: UPS: Usual Principal Status; CWS: Current Weekly Status; CDS: Current Daily Status.

Table 10.3: *Unemployment Rates for 55th Round and 61st Round of NSSO in Urban India (in %)*

	Urban					
	Male			*Female*		
NSSO Round	*UPS*	*CWS*	*CDS*	*UPS*	*CWS*	*CDS*
55th (1999–2000)	4.8	5.6	7.3	7.1	7.3	9.4
61st (2004–05)	4.4	5.2	7.5	9.1	9.0	11.6

Source: GoI (2007b).
Note: UPS: Usual Principal Status; CWS: Current Weekly Status; CDS: Current Daily Status.

tables, unemployment rates were lower in rural areas than in urban areas for both males and females. Within the rural areas, unemployment rates for males were higher than those for women, except for the CDS in the 61st round. But in the urban areas, the opposite was true.

Of late, there have also been structural changes in the pattern of employment. For the first time, the share of the primary sector in total employment has dipped below the halfway mark (declined from 58.5% in 2004–05 to 48.9% in 2011–12), while employment in the secondary and tertiary sectors increased to 24.3% and 26.8% respectively in 2011–12 from 18.1% and 23.4% respectively in 2004–05. Self-employment continues to dominate, with a 52.2% share in total employment. What is critical is the significant share of workers engaged in low income-generating activities. The contribution of the agricultural sector in the employment of rural workforce has declined from 83% in 1977–78 to 63% in 1999–2000. The annual growth rate of workforce in agriculture was 1% during 1977–99, while the same in non-agricultural occupations was 4.3% during 1977–88 and 2% during 1987–2000. In agriculturally developed states, non-agricultural households in rural areas are gradually withdrawing completely from cultivation to concentrate fully on non-agricultural occupations. Employment diversification occurred even in some semi-arid regions wherein toddy tappers and shepherds reverted to their traditional occupations from casual labor in agriculture. Expansion of the rural non-farm sector has been influenced by the growing commercialization in the rural economy. This is the normal pattern of development and in fact, the process has been very slow in India.

There are other issues of concern such as poor employment growth in rural areas, particularly among females. Though employment of rural males is slightly better than that of females, long-term trends indicate a low and stagnant growth. Such trends call for diversification of livelihood in rural areas from agriculture to non-agriculture activities. In order to improve generation of productive employment under the MGNREGA, the Intensive and Participatory Planning Exercise (IPPE), has been initiated to prepare the labor budget for financial year 2015–16 in selected 2,500 backward blocks using participatory rural appraisal technique. Emphasis has been laid on agriculture and allied activities to ensure that at least 60% of the works in a district in terms of cost is for creation of productive assets linked to agriculture and allied activities through development of land, water, and trees.

A major impediment to the pace of quality employment generation in India is the small share of manufacturing in total employment. However data from the 68th NSSO round (2011–12) indicates a revival in employment growth in manufacturing from 11% in 2009–10 to 12.6% in 2011–12. This is significant given that the National Manufacturing Policy 2011 has set a target of creating 100 million jobs by 2022. Promoting growth of MSME is critical from the perspective of job creation which has been recognized as a prime mover of the development agenda in India. Although total informal employment increased by 9.5 million to 435.7 million between 2004–05 and 2011–12, it is significant that informal unorganized sector employment

Table 10.4: *Share of Formal–Informal Employment across Organized–Unorganized Sectors in 2011–12 and 2004–05 (in %)*

Sector	*Organized*	*Unorganized*	*Total*
Formal	45.4 (52)	0.4 (03)	8.1 (7.3)
Informal	54.6 (48)	99.6 (99.7)	91.9 (92.7)
Total	17.3 (13)	82.7 (87)	100.00

Source: MoF (2015, Table 9.12, p. 136).

declined by 5.8 million to 390.9 million, leading to an increase in informal organized sector employment by 15.2 million. Consequently the share of unorganized labor has declined from 87% to 82.7% (Table 10.4).

The composition of employment (self-employment, regular salaried employment, and casual employment) has also been changing. While self-employment is on the decline, casual employment is on the rise. The share of self-employed in the rural workforce declined from 63% in 1977–78 to 56% in 1999–2000, while the proportion of casual labor has increased from 30% to 37%. During the same period, regular employment has declined marginally from 7.7% to 6.7%.

Some of the highlights of the 68th round of NSS survey are presented below (NSSO 2015, Highlights: i–iii):

- In 2011–12, in rural India, proportion of households with self-employment as the major source of income was the highest among "others" category (58.4%) followed by OBC (52.9%), ST (49.5%) and SC (33.7%).
- In rural India, proportion of households with casual labor as the major source of income was much higher among SC (52.6%) and ST (about 38.3%) than among the OBC (32.1%) and "others" (21%).
- In urban India, proportion of households with income from casual labor as major source, was higher among the SC and ST (20.5% and 18%, respectively) than among OBC (14.3%) and others (5.9%).
- In rural India, proportion of households with regular wage/salary earning as the major source was the highest among "others" category (13.3%) followed by OBC (9%), SC (8.5%) and ST (6.3%).
- In urban India, proportion of households with regular wage/salary earning as the major source was the highest for ST (46.5%) followed by others (44.5%), SC (44%) and OBC (37.6%).
- About 38.4% of the households in rural areas had MGNREG job cards.
- A higher proportion of households belonging to ST or SC category had MGNREG job cards than OBC or others category of households: 57.2 % of ST households and 50% of SC households had MGNREG job cards compared to 34.2% of OBC households and 27.1% of "others" category of households.

Poverty and Unemployment Alleviation Programs

The failure of the growth-oriented strategy of the 1960s to make any significant dent on the problems of rural poverty and unemployment led to its re-examination in the late 1960s. Inequitable distribution of benefits of the growth-oriented programs between rich and poor households within an area was officially acknowledged in the early 1970s, and a number of corrective measures in the form of programs were taken to ameliorate the problems. Here, we discuss the major programs taken up by the government with the main objective of alleviation of poverty and unemployment.

Public Distribution System (PDS)

The PDS is perhaps the oldest of all the programs that were designed to ensure food security in India, particularly of the poor. It is perhaps the world's largest food distribution network having within its fold over 4,35,000 fair price shops, distributing commodities worth more than ₹1,50,000 million annually. The basic objective of the PDS is to ensure that essential commodities are made available to the people at reasonable price, so as to provide them a safety net against inflation.

The PDS has been an integral part of India's food policy since World War II, when statutory rationing was introduced in big cities, such as Mumbai and Kolkata. After independence also, the Government of India has continued to follow the system, although the nature and the extent of government intervention has varied over time, depending on fluctuations in food grains production and price rise. The First Five Year Plan emphasized the distribution of food grains through the statutory rationing system in cities and towns having a population of more than 5,000 persons and in chronically food-deficit areas of the country. In the Second Five Year Plan, the PDS was extended to cover, besides food grains, other essential commodities as well. In the Third Five Year Plan, a procurement and distribution system was created for ensuring price stabilization. In the Fourth Five Year Plan, the scope of the PDS was further widened by covering all rural areas in the country and distribution of other goods of mass consumption with the help of cooperative stores. In the Fifth Five Year Plan, the PDS was focused on the poor. The Sixth Five Year Plan emphasized the distribution of food grains to the disadvantaged groups. In the Seventh Five Year Plan, the PDS was included in the MNP. The Eighth Five Year Plan laid emphasis of the intensification of the PDS in the rural and disadvantaged areas, and the strengthened the infrastructure by establishing new fair price shops. The Ninth Five Year Plan took a broader view of the food security system and included nutritional security in it. The system was continued in the Tenth Five Year Plan and is continuing as of date.

In order to remove some of its drawbacks, the PDS was revamped in 1992 and the revamped system was launched in tribal, arid, hilly, drought-prone, and other remotely located areas of the country. The objective of revamping the PDS was to increase its reach on the basis of area approach, and to eliminate the leakages and malpractices that had crept in the system. In June 1997, a new policy of targeted PDS (TPDS) was introduced as an important constituent of the strategy of poverty alleviation. One of the important features of the implementing strategy of the Tenth Five Year Plan was the crucial role given to the panchayati raj institutions (PRIs) in the delivery of TPDS. To ensure food security to all, especially the poor, Parliament had passed a legislation called the National Food Security Act on September 12, 2013. This law aims to provide subsidized food grains to approximately two-thirds of India's 1.2 billion people, especially through the PDS. Under the provisions of the act, eligible beneficiaries are entitled to purchase 5 kg per eligible person, per month of cereals at the following prices: rice at ₹3 per kg; wheat at ₹2 per kg; and coarse grains (millet) at ₹1 per kg. This act, if implemented faithfully by all state governments, could ensure food security to the poor people.

Several attempts have been made to study the impact of the PDS. Gulati (1989) found that the PDS had a positive impact on the nutritional status of the malnourished and the poor. An evaluation study conducted by the Planning Commission in 1995 identified several deficiencies in the implementation of the revamped PDS including (a) proliferation of bogus ration cards; (b) inadequate storage arrangements; (c) ineffective functioning of vigilance committees and (d) failure to issue ration cards to all eligible households (Jena 1998: 915).

The PDS has also been criticized on the ground that there has been large scale diversion of food grains from fair price shops to black markets. *The Economic Times* (September 17, 2007) reported that wheat and rice worth ₹3,10,000 million had been siphoned off the PDS in the three years, 2004–05 to 2006–07 (Box 10.1).

Box 10.1

LARGE-SCALE DIVERSION OF PDS FOOD GRAINS IN INDIA

Every year, India's poor are cheated of 53.3% of the wheat and 39% of the rice meant for them. With the exception of 11 states and the Union Territories, large-scale diversion of PDS food grains takes place everywhere in India. In three years, 2004–05, 2005–06, and 2006–07, wheat and rice worth ₹3,10,000 million had been diverted from the PDS, thanks to the widespread corruption and inefficiency in the system. The North East (NE) states fared the worst in terms of the extent of leakage. For example, in six of the eight NE states, namely, Sikkim, Meghalaya, Manipur, Mizoram, Nagaland and Assam, 100% of the PDS wheat was diverted. If the political and policing problems in the NE states could be blamed for such large scale leakages, other states have no alibi. In terms of the extent of loss to the exchequer, Uttar Pradesh fared the worst, followed by West Bengal, Madhya Pradesh, Assam, Rajasthan and Maharashtra. Such large-scale leakages in the PDS have been known for decades now but no correctives are taken to fix the problem. Good governance is the only answer to the problem.

Source: Economic Times (2007).

Rural Poverty Alleviation Programs

There were several Centrally-sponsored rural poverty alleviation programs in vogue in India until 2006 when a comprehensive program called National Rural Livelihood Mission (NRLM) subsuming all earlier programs was launched. The salient features of major rural poverty alleviation that have been subsumed in NRLM are presented in Appendix 10.1. We now present the salient features of NRLM.

Aajeevika—National Rural Livelihoods Mission (NRLM)

The Genesis of Aajeevika

At the national level, the (MoRD, Government of India, is responsible for planning, designing, and overseeing the implementation of rural poverty alleviation programs directly targeted at the rural poor households. The major programs of the MORD that directly targeted poor families for creation of assets, skill development and self-employment started with Integrated Rural Development Programme (IRDP) in the year 1980 and included several other programs such as the TRYSEM, Development of Women and Children in Rural Areas (DWCRA), Supply of Improved Toolkits to Rural Artisans (SITRA), GKY, and the MWS. On account of multiplicity of programs, which were viewed as separate programs in themselves, the desired linkages among these programs were not established effectively. These were more concerned with achieving individual program targets rather than focusing on the substantive issue of sustainable income generation.

The Planning Commission set up a committee under the chairmanship of Professor S. R. Hashim in 1997, to review and rationalize various Centrally-sponsored schemes for poverty alleviation and employment generation. The committee recommended the integration of all programs allied with IRDP for better linkages. The report formed the base for shifting from an individual beneficiary approach to a group approach for poverty alleviation. Based on the recommendations of the Planning Commission, the schemes of TRYSEM, SITRA, GKY, DWCRA and MWS were merged into a single self-employment program, namely, Swarnjayanti Gram Swarozgar Yojana (SGSY), to be implemented by the states, with effect from April, 1999. SGSY had the objective of improving the family incomes of the rural poor while, at the same time, providing for a flexibility of building institutions of the poor at the grassroots level to suit local needs and resources. The objective of the restructuring was to provide sustainable income generation through microenterprise development, both land-based and otherwise. SGSY moved from the individual-oriented approach of the earlier programs such as the IRDP, TRYSEM and so on to a group based approach with SHGs of rural Below Poverty Line (BPL) families as the unit of assistance. The cornerstone of the SGSY strategy was that the poor need to be organized and their capacities built up systematically so that they can access self-employment opportunities. This restructuring also helped in establishing effective linkages between the various components of the program, such as capacity building of the poor, credit availability, technology transfer/upgradation, marketing, and infrastructure development.

Performance of SGSY was assessed through concurrent evaluation, studies, and reports including those conducted by the National Institute of Rural Development (NIRD), Hyderabad, the Bankers Institute of Rural Development (BIRD), Lucknow, Centre for Management Development, Thiruvananthapuram, reports of the Steering Committee constituted by the Planning Commission for the Eleventh Plan and the Professor Radhakrishna Committee on Credit Related Issues related to SGSY, set up by the MoRD in April 2008. Accordingly, based largely on the recommendations of the Professor Radhakrishna Committee, SGSY has been restructured as NRLM, subsequently renamed as "Aajeevika," to implement it in a mission mode across the country. The program was formally launched on June 3, 2011.

Lessons from Earlier Poverty Alleviation Programs

The key lessons for NRLM from the two-decade-long work of state-wide livelihoods projects in Andhra Pradesh, Kerala, and Tamil Nadu and the work of outstanding NGOs in the country are as follows:

1. There is a need for a sensitive support structure right from state level to district and sub-district levels. The sensitive support structure has the responsibility for inducing social mobilization and building strong grassroots institutions of the poor, particularly women.
2. The key role of the sensitive support structure is to build and nurture strong institutions of poor women at SHG level, village level, and block (sub-block) level. These institutions provide the continuous nurturing support which a poor household require during this journey out of poverty.
3. For a poor family to come out abject poverty, a nurturing and handholding support of its own organizations for a period of six–eight years is extremely critical.
4. Rural women poor households, organized into developing synergies through institutions of the poor SHGs require repeated doses of finance at affordable rates such that over a period of 6-8 years they have accessed at least ₹1,00,000.
5. The strength of individual SHG in providing support to their members is multiplied when all the poor in a village are organized into SHGs and all the SHGs come together at the village level and form a federation.

6. A second tier of federation of the village federations at the block or sub-block level is required to provide necessary linkages with ongoing government programs and to link with the subdivisional level structure of the State Livelihoods Missions.
7. The poor need to overcome livelihoods risks by developing a variety of livelihoods. This enables them to survive shocks to any particular livelihoods streams.
8. Poor are highly vulnerable to shocks and they need safety nets and they need their organizations to access safety needs entitlements under various government programs such as MGNREGA, social assistance programs, PDS, and so on.

It was also seen that the various states are at different stages of progress in terms of institution building and hence require state-specific strategies. Common centralized guidelines/strategies would not meet the needs of all the states. Hence differentiated or state-specific strategies need to be developed to cater to the specific requirements of each individual state. Aajeevika has incorporated learning from the implementation of earlier programs, primarily from the successes and failures of SGSY and from the various states' initiatives in the rural livelihoods sector, and accordingly adapted the approach and strategies in implementing the program.

NRLM Approach

NRLM has set out with an agenda to cover 70 million rural poor households, across 600 districts, 6,000 blocks, 2,50,000 gram panchayats and 6,00,000 villages in the country through self-managed SHGs and federated institutions and support them for livelihoods collectives in a period of 8–10 years.[1] Being conscious of the wide variations in livelihoods activities, NRLM works on three pillars- enhancing and expanding existing livelihoods options of the poor; building skills for the job market outside; and nurturing self-employed and entrepreneurs. Toward building, supporting and sustaining livelihoods of the poor, NRLM harnesses the innate capabilities of the poor, complements them with capacities (information, knowledge, skills, tools, finance and collectivization) to deal with the rapidly changing external world. Dedicated support structures build and strengthen the institutional platforms of the poor. These platforms, with the support of their human and social capital, offer a variety of livelihoods services to their members. These services include financial and capital services, production and productivity enhancement services that include technology, knowledge, skills and inputs, market linkages etc. The interested rural BPL youth would be offered skill development after counseling and matching the aptitude with the job requirements, and placed in jobs that are remunerative. Self-employed and entrepreneurially-oriented poor would be provided skills and financial linkages and nurtured to establish and grow with microenterprises for products and services in demand.

Strategy of NRLM:

NRLM implementation is in a Mission Mode. This enables:

a) Shift from the present allocation based strategy to a demand driven strategy, enabling the states to formulate their own livelihoods-based poverty reduction action plans;
b) Focus on targets, outcomes, and time bound delivery;
c) Continuous capacity building, imparting requisite skills, and creating linkages with livelihoods opportunities for the poor, including those emerging in the organized sector; and
d) Monitoring targets of poverty outcomes. As NRLM follows a demand driven strategy, the states have the flexibility to develop their livelihoods-based perspective plans and annual action plans for poverty reduction. The overall plans would be within the allocation for the state based on inter-se poverty ratios.

The second dimension of demand-driven strategy implies that the ultimate objective is that the poor will drive the agenda, through participatory planning at grassroots level, implementation of their own plans, reviewing and generating further plans based on their experiences. The plans will not only be demand-driven, they will also be dynamic. NRLM recognizes and values the iterative nature of the processes. Aajeevika supports a phased implementation approach and an Intensive Block Strategy: Intensive Block is a block (sub-district unit) identified by State Rural Livelihoods Mission (SRLM) in the first phase of Aajeevika implementation to demonstrate the best practices and processes in Participatory Identification of Poor (PIP), targeting the poorest of poor, financial and economic inclusion, enhancement of livelihoods by creating strong institutional platforms of the poor in three years. Once the intensive work is completed in these selected blocks, it provides social capital of the poor for scaling up and replicating Aajeevika mandate to other blocks in a systematic manner. This approach serves as a large sized proof of concept. In addition, the intensive blocks also serve as immersion and training sites for the project staff and also the SHG members.

Monitoring, Evaluation, and Lessons

Aajeevika is process-intensive and therefore at various levels, it would constantly review, assess and learn from the qualitative and quantitative progress achieved. A robust IT-based Monitoring, Evaluation and Learning (MEL) system would be in place to facilitate learning and continuous improvement and support informed decision making at all levels.

Mechanisms of Monitoring

Aajeevika would put in place the following mechanisms for monitoring:

(i) Accountability in institutions of the poor including institutional self-monitoring, peer internal audit of processes and local social audit;
(ii) Management Information System (MIS) based input-output monitoring including results framework-based MIS; milestones linked to investments/inputs; web-based MIS; real time input-output monitoring at various levels; and MIS with partners' data;
(iii) ICT-framework for dedicated digital grid includes national databases of poor, their institutions, and skill development (jobs/self-employment), national livelihoods portal, communication/knowledge dissemination channels, thematic e-groups etc.;
(iv) Internal review mechanisms at various levels;
(v) External social audit, public expenditure tracking and community score cards;
(vi) Impact Assessment: State level baseline assessments and external interim impact evaluation studies of progress on key result indicators; independent national assessment of household level well-being through panel studies at periodic intervals (sample would be large enough to enable quantitative assessments up to district levels); and periodic thematic national assessments Benefitting the poor through partnerships with dairy federations; and
(vii) SRLM Annual Reports and Aajeevika Annual Report.

Fund Tracking System

Aajeevika would put in place a comprehensive financial management system at the SRLMs to ensure transparency, efficiency and accountability. Aajeevika would position an IT-based fund tracking system and promote e-book keeping in institutions of the poor and in support structures.

Aajeevika Website

Aajeevika's bilingual website[2] and a logo were launched in 2012. The website serves as a knowledge hub for NRLM stakeholders, where guidelines and policy documents, AAP, SPIP, sanctions and communication are posted on a regular basis.

Funding Pattern
Aajeevika is a Centrally-sponsored scheme and the financing of the program is shared between the Centre and the states in the ratio of 75:25 (90:10 in case of North Eastern states including Sikkim; and completely from the Centre in case of UTs). The Central allocation earmarked for the states are distributed in keeping in view the incidence of poverty in the states.

Project Components of NRLP

The Government of India has availed of a credit of $500 million from the International Development Association (IDA) for implementing NRLP under NRLM. The NRLP is being implemented in 107 districts, 422 blocks in 13 high-poverty states, covering 90% of rural poor of the country (MoRD, 2014, Annual Report 2014–15, pp. 25–26). The activities detailed in the components are intended to create an enabling environment for the effective utilization of all the resources allocated by the Government of India to the NRLM. With the exception of Component B that will be implemented in the 12 targeted states, the remaining components will provide support at the national level to enable the smooth rollout of the NRLM throughout the country.

Component A: Institutional and Human Capacity Development
The objective of this component is to transform the role of MoRD into a provider of high quality technical assistance in the field of rural livelihoods promotion. This component will finance primarily staff, technical assistance consultancies, and training and related course material. Support under this component will be for all states.

Component B: State Livelihood Support
The objective of this component is to support state governments in the establishment of the necessary institutional structures and mechanisms for the implementation of NRLM activities from the state to the block level, including support to the formation of institutions of the rural poor.

Component C: Innovation and Partnership Support
The objective of this component is to create an institutional mechanism to identify, nurture and support innovative ideas from across the country to address the livelihood needs of the rural poor. Support under this component will be for all states.

Component D: Project Implementation Support
The objective of this component is to strengthen the National Mission Management Unit for effective project management at the national level that develops key systems and processes for coordination and management of the proposed project and the NRLM.

NRLM Progress During 2014–15

As of December 2014, all states except Goa have transited to NRLM, that is, all states have set up a State Rural Livelihood Mission (SRLM) as society/company, appointed Chief Executive Officer (CEO) and core team, and prepared action plan. Among the Union Territories, Puducherry has transited to NRLM. Goa and the remaining union territories (except Chandigarh and Delhi) are expected to transit in FY 2014–15 (MoRD, 2014, Annual Report 2013–14, p. 29).

By the end of December 2014, NRLM implementation had brought under its fold 28 states (except Goa) and Union Territory of Puducherry. As of January 2015, 2.09 million SHGs in 2125 intensive blocks in 316 districts have been promoted. It had newly formed or strengthened and provided revolving and community investment funds amounting to ₹43,089.9 million to the SHGs/Federations (MoRD, 2015, Annual Report 2014–15, Annexure X, p. 254).

Wage-employment Generating Schemes (WEGS)

Wage-employment programs have become important instruments for alleviating poverty and smoothening consumption during critical periods including, drought and flood situations. They have been perceived to be both protective (via income transfer) and promotional (via infrastructure development) forms of safety nets.

The Rural Works Programme (RWP) was the first major government intervention aimed at providing employment to the unemployed, particularly in the lean season. It was introduced in 1971. However, due to its limited scope, and its various organizational and administrative deficiencies, it did not make any significant dent in the problem of unemployment. A series of special employment programs followed the RWP. The major programs of the series were as follows:

1. The Crash Scheme of Rural Employment (CSRE), introduced in April 1971,
2. The Food-for-Work (FFW) Programme, introduced in April 1977,
3. The Jawahar Rozgar Yojana (JRY), launched in April 1989,
4. The Sampoorna Grameen Rozgar Yojana (SGRY), launched in 2001,
5. The Employment Assurance Scheme (EAS), launched on October 2, 1993, and
6. The National Food-for-Work (NFFW) Programme, launched in 2005–06.

After the launching of the Mahatma Gandhi National Rural Employment Guarantee Act (MNREGA) in 2006, earlier rural employment programs were subsumed in it.

Mahatma Gandhi National Rural Employment Guarantee Act (MNREGA) and Rationale of Rural Wage Employment Programs

A majority of the poor in rural areas of the country depend mainly on the wages they earn through unskilled labor. They are often on threshold levels of subsistence and are vulnerable to the possibility of sinking from transient to chronic poverty, in the event of inadequate labor demand or in the face of unpredictable crises that may be general in nature such as natural disaster or personal like ill-health, all of which adversely impact their employment opportunities.

In the context of poverty and unemployment, wage employment programs provide unskilled manual workers with short-term employment on public works such as irrigation infrastructure, reforestation soil conservation, road construction etc. These programs provide income transfers to poor households during critical times and so also enable consumption smoothing specially during slack agricultural seasons or years. Durable assets created under these programs have the potential to generate sustainable livelihood.

History of Rural Wage Employment Programs

The need to evolve a mechanism to supplement existing livelihood sources in rural areas was recognized early in development planning in India. The government has implemented wage employment programs that offered wage-employment on public works on minimum wages. The wage employment programs started as pilot projects in the form of Rural Manpower Programme (RMP, 1960–61), Crash Scheme for Rural employment (CRSE, 1971–72), Drought

Prone Area Programme was started as Rural Work Programme (RWP, 1972), Small Farmers Development Agency (SFDA), Marginal Farmers & Agricultural Labour Scheme (MF&AL) to the poorest of the poor. These experiments were translated into a full-fledged wage-employment program in 1977 in the form of Food for Work Programme (FWP). In 1980's this program was further streamlined into the National Rural Employment Programme (NREP) and Rural Landless Employment Guarantee Programme (RLEGP), Jawahar Rozgar Yojana (JRY 1993–94) and Employment Assurance Scheme (EAS). The Jawahar Rozgar Yojana (JRY) was merged with Jawahar Gram Samridhi Yojana (JGSY) from 1999–2000 and was made a rural infrastructure program. The program was merged with Sampoorna Grameen Rozgar Yojana during the year 2001–02 and NFFWP (2005).

These wage-employment programs implemented by state governments with Central assistance were self-targeting and the objective was to provide enhance livelihood security, specially of those dependent on casual manual labor. At the state level, the Government of Maharashtra formulated the Maharashtra Employment Guarantee Scheme and Maharashtra Employment Guarantee Act, 1977 to provide wage employment to those who demanded it.

Based on the experience of these programs, the Mahatma Gandhi National Rural Employment Guarantee Act (MGNREGA) was enacted in 2005 to reinforce the commitment toward livelihood security in rural areas. This Employment Guarantee Act is the most significant legislation in many ways. For the first time, rural communities have been given not just a development program, but a regime of rights. The MGNREGA is a legal guarantee that people can use to secure their entitlement of wage employment. It holds the government responsible for making this employment available to the people. It is a legal instrument in the hands of the poor based on the demand of the workers.

Main Features of MGNREGA

Mahatma Gandhi National Rural Employment Guarantee Act (MGNREGA) with its legal framework and rights-based approach was notified on September 5, 2005. It aims at enhancing livelihood security by providing at least one hundred days of guaranteed wage employment in a financial year to every rural household whose adult members volunteer to do unskilled manual work. The act covered 200 districts in its first phase, on February 2, 2006, and was extended to all the rural districts of the country in phases. During the FY 2013–14, the scheme had provided employment to around 47.91 million households with more than 22.02 million person days of employment being generated at a total expenditure about of ₹38,672 million (MoRD, 2015, Annual Report 2014–15, 250–251). The average wage rate per day has increased from ₹65 in 2006–07 to about ₹115 in 2011–12.

The women workforce participation under the Scheme has surpassed the statutory minimum requirement of 33% and the trends indicate an increase in the participation rate at the national level. Since inception, every year, women's participation has been around 48%. MGNREGA is the first ever law, internationally, that guarantees wage employment at an unprecedented scale. The primary objective of the act is meeting demand for wage employment in rural areas. The works permitted under the act address causes of chronic poverty such as drought, deforestation and soil erosion, so that the employment generation is sustainable. The act is also a significant vehicle for strengthening decentralization and deepening processes of democracy by giving a pivotal role to local governance bodies, that is, the panchayati raj institutions.

Key Achievements of MGNREGA

The key achievements of the program in the last six year of its implementation are presented in Box 10.2.

Box 10.2

KEY ACHIEVEMENTS OF MGNREGA SINCE 2006 UNTIL DECEMBER 2013

1. *Since its inception in 2006, around ₹1,290 billion had been disbursed directly as wage payments to rural households.*
2. *13,480 million person-days of employment has been generated*
3. *On an average; 50 million households had been provided with employment every year since 2008.*
4. *Scheduled Castes and Scheduled Tribes have accounted for 51% of the total person-days generated.*
5. *Women have accounted for 47% of the total person-days generated. This is well above the mandatory 33% as required by the act.*
6. *Since the beginning of the program, 14.6 million works have been taken up under the act.*
7. *Average wage per person-day has gone up by 81% since the Scheme's inception, with state-level variation. The notified wage now varies from ₹122 in Bihar and Jharkhand to ₹191 in Haryana.*

Source: MoRD (2013) Annual Report 2012–13, Ch. 2, p. 14.

The salient features of the act are as follows:

1. Rights based framework: For adult members of a rural household willing to do unskilled manual work,
2. Time bound guarantee: 15 days for provision of employment, else unemployment allowance to be paid,
3. Up to 100 days in a financial year per household, depending on the actual demand,
4. Labor-intensive works: 60:40 wage and material ratio for permissible works at the Gram Panchayat; no contractors/machinery,
5. Decentralized planning,
6. Gram abhas to recommend works,
7. At least 50% of works to be done by Gram Panchayats for execution,
8. Principal role of PRIs in planning, implementation, and monitoring,
9. Work site facilities: Crèche, drinking water, first aid and shade provided at worksites,
10. Women empowerment: At least one-third of beneficiaries should be women Protection wall built under MGNREGA in Manipur,
11. Transparency and accountability: Proactive disclosure through wall writings, citizen information boards and MIS and Social Audits,
12. Funding: 100% cost toward unskilled wages and 75% toward skilled, semi-skilled, and material is borne by Central government and 25% of skilled, semi-skilled and material costs is contributed by states. In addition 6% administrative expenses are borne by the Centre for effective implementation of the act, and
13. Financial Inclusion of the poor: With a view to universalize the system of wage payments through institutional accounts, it has been recommended to all states to disburse wages through Post Offices and Bank Accounts.

Concurrent Monitoring and Evaluation of MGNREGA

The Ministry of Rural Development has set up a Concurrent Evaluation Office (CEO), a system by which the schemes of the Ministry including MGNREGA will be evaluated in real time during implementation to identify weaknesses in structure and execution, and enable the government to effect mid-course corrections. Concurrent evaluation would mark a change from the present method of annual studies undertaken to evaluate schemes. Besides, the Vigilance and Monitoring Committees (V&MCs) are constituted at state and district levels to function as important instrument for effective monitoring of implementation of the programs of the ministry. The ministry strongly supports the use of Information Communication Technology (ICT) to improve program efficiency, streamline processes as well as place information in public domain.

It provides an objective summary of both, the positive impacts of the Scheme as well as its constraints. Main findings from the Sameeksha are presented in Box 10.3.

Box 10.3

MAIN FINDINGS ABOUT THE IMPACT OF MGNREGA

1. *MGNREGA is important as a supplementary source of income and its income is being used by rural households for starting their own ventures.*
2. *MGNREGA has caused a significant increase in monthly per capita consumption expenditure of rural households.*
3. *MGNREGA is succeeding as a self-targeting program with high participation from marginalized groups including the SCs and STs. In the case of both SCs and STs, the participation rate exceeds their share in the total population.*
4. *MGNREGA has reduced the traditional gender wage discrimination, particularly, in the public works sector and has had a positive impact on the socio-economic status of the women.*
5. *MGNREGA with its intersectoral approach opens an opportunity for convergence with different programs with an aim to optimize public investment.*
6. *MGNREGA works have been described as "Green" and "Decent," that is, the scheme creates decent working conditions by ensuring workers' rights and legal entitlements, providing social protection and employment and environmentally sustainable works that re-generate the eco-system and protect bio-diversity.*
7. *MGNREGA has had a more direct and positive impact on reducing distress migration as compared to migration taken-up for economic growth and other reasons.*

Source: MoRD (2013, Ch. 2, pp. 11–18).

Social Welfare-oriented Programs

The Directive Principles of State Policy enunciated in the Constitution of India enjoin upon the state to undertake within its means a number of welfare measures. In particular, Article 41 of the Constitution of India directs the state to provide public assistance to its citizens in case of unemployment, old age, sickness and disablement and in other cases of undeserved want within the limit of its economic capacity and development. It is in accordance with these noble principles that the Government of India on August 15, 1995 included the National Social Assistance Programme in the Central Budget for 1995–96.

The National Social Assistance Programme (NSAP) then comprised National Old Age Pension Scheme (NOAPS), National Family Benefit Scheme (NFBS) and National Maternity Benefit Scheme (NMBS). The programs were meant for providing social assistance benefit to the aged, the BPL households in the case of death of the primary bread winner and for maternity. The programs were aimed at ensuring minimum national standards in addition to the benefits that the states were then providing or would provide in future. NMBS was transferred to Ministry of Health and Family Welfare with effect from 2001–02 and subsumed in Janani Suraksha Yojana. On April 1, 2000, a new scheme known as Annapurna Scheme was launched. This scheme aimed at providing food security to meet the requirement of those senior citizens who, though eligible had remained uncovered under the NOAPS. Under Annapurna Scheme, 10 kg of food grains per month is provided free of cost to the beneficiary. In February 2009 two new Schemes, namely, Indira Gandhi National Widow Pension Scheme (IGNWPS) and Indira Gandhi National Disability Pension Scheme (IGNDPS) were introduced under NSAP.

Implementation of NSAP Schemes

In 2002–03, NSAP and the Annapurna scheme were both transferred from Centrally-sponsored scheme to state plan. The funds for NSAP and Annapurna are allocated by Planning Commission and are released as Additional Central Assistance (ACA) by the Ministry of Finance in a combined manner for all the schemes under NSAP on the recommendation of the Ministry of Rural Development. NSAP is being implemented mainly by Social Welfare Departments in the states. In some states it is being implemented by Rural Development Departments and in a few others by Women and Child Development Departments.

Indira Gandhi National Old Age Pension Scheme (IGNOAPS)

Government of India on September 13, 2007 modified the eligibility criteria for grant of old age pension to persons aged 65 years or higher and belonging to a household below the poverty line according to the criteria prescribed by the Government of India. With this modification, National Old Age Pension Scheme (NOAPS) was renamed as Indira Gandhi National Old Age Pension Scheme (IGNOAPS). With the modification of eligibility criteria to cover all persons living below the poverty line as of December 2012, the number of beneficiaries covered under Indira Gandhi National Old Age Pension Scheme (IGNOAPS) was 22.3 million. With effect from April 1, 2011 under IGNOAPS, the eligibility for old age pension has been reduced from 65 years to 60 years and the amount of pension has been raised from ₹200 to ₹500 per month for those who are 80 years or above.

Indira Gandhi National Widow Pension Scheme (IGNWPS)

In February 2009, Government of India had approved this scheme for BPL widows in the age group of 40–64 years. The amount of pension is fixed at ₹200 p.m. per beneficiary. Consequent upon the lowering of age under IGNOAPS the upper age limit under IGNWPS has been lowered from 64 years to 59 years. With effect from Oct 1, 2012, the amount of pension under IGNWPS has been increased to ₹300 p.m. and upper age limit increased to 79 years. Hence, IGNWPS is applicable to widows in the age group of 40–79 years and belonging to households living below the poverty line (BPL) as per criteria prescribed by the GoI. Until December 1, 2012, 4.2 million beneficiaries had been covered under the scheme.

Indira Gandhi National Disability Pension Scheme (IGNDPS)

In February 2009, Government of India had also approved this pension scheme under Indira Gandhi National Disability Pension Scheme (IGNDPS) for BPL persons with severe or multiple disabilities between the age group of 18–64 years. The amount of pension is fixed ₹200 p.m. per beneficiary.

Consequent upon the lowering of age under IGNOAPS the upper age limit under IGNDPS has been lowered from 64 years to 59 years.

With effect from October 1, 2012 the amount of pension under IGNDPS has been increased to ₹300 p.m. and upper age limit has been increased to 79 years. Hence, IGNDPS is applicable to persons with severe or multiple 78 disabilities between the age group of 18–79 years and belonging to household living below poverty line (BPL) as per criteria prescribed by GoI. Till December 2012, 800,000 beneficiaries had been covered under the scheme.

National Family Benefit Scheme (NFBS)

At inception, grant of ₹5,000 in case of death due to natural causes and ₹10,000 in case of accidental death of the "primary breadwinner" was provided to the bereaved household under this scheme. The primary breadwinner specified in the scheme, whether male or female, had to be a member of the household whose earning contributed substantially to the total household income. The death of such a primary breadwinner occurring whilst he or she was in the age group of 18 to 64 years, that is, more than 18 years of age and less than 65 years of age, made the family eligible to receive grants under the scheme. In 1998, the amount of benefit under NFBS was raised to ₹10,000 in case of death due to natural causes as well as accidental causes. W.e.f., October 18, 2012, amount of assistance under NFBS has been increased to ₹20,000 and upper age limit of death of primary breadwinner has been reduced to 59 years. Hence, NFBS is applicable in case of death of primary breadwinner in the age group of 18–59 years. Till December 2012, 291,000 BPL families had benefited under the Scheme.

Aam Admi Bima Yojana (AABY)

The AABY was launched on October 2, 2007. Under this scheme, insurance to the head of the family of rural landless households in the country is provided against natural death as well as accidental death and partial/permanent disability. It extends life and disability cover to persons between the age of 18 years to 59 years, living below and marginally above the poverty line in 47 identified vocational/occupational groups, including rural landless households. The Scheme is also available to all Rashtriya Swasthya Bima Yojana (RSBY) beneficiaries. This cover is ₹75,000 on death due to accident and permanent disability due to accident, ₹37,500 in case of partial permanent disability due to accident and ₹30,000 in case of death of a member, prior to terminal date. The premium to be charged under the scheme is ₹200 per annum per member, 50% of which is to be contributed by the Central government and remaining by state governments. It also provides an add-on-benefit of scholarship of ₹100 per month per child subject to the maximum of two children.

Rashtriya Swasthya Bima Yojana (RSBY)

The RSBY was formally launched on October 1, 2007. All workers in the unorganized sector who come in the category of BPL and their families are covered under the scheme. The scheme also has a provision of smart cards to be issued to the beneficiaries to enable cashless transaction for health care. The total sum insured is ₹30,000 per family per annum, with the Government of India contributing 75% of the annual estimated premium amount of ₹750, subject to a maximum of ₹565 per family per annum, while the state governments are expected to contribute 25% of the annual premium as well as any additional premium. The cost of the smart card would also be borne by Central government.

Pradhan Mantri Jan Dhan Yojana[3]

Pradhān Mantrī Jana Dhan Yōjanā (PMJDY) was launched by Prime Minister Narendra Modi on August 28, 2014. He had announced this scheme on his first Independence Day speech on August 15, 2014. Prior to that Finance Minister Arun Jaitley had made an announcement about the scheme in his Union Budget 2015–16 Speech. PMJDY's main objective is to ensure universal access of all citizens of India, especially the financially excluded sections of society, that is, weaker sections and low income groups, to financial services, namely bank savings/deposit accounts, remittance services, credit, insurance, pension in an affordable manner. The scheme is administered by the Department of Financial Services, Ministry of Finance, Government of India.

As of October 2015, 196.0 million accounts had been opened with the total balance of ₹280.124 billion (US$4.2 billion). On the inauguration day, 15 million bank accounts were opened under this scheme which is a Guinness World Record. Of the total number of accounts opened, 195.5 million accounts were 'rural accounts'. The scheme has been started with a target to provide 'universal access to banking facilities' starting with "Basic Banking Accounts" with overdraft facility of ₹5,000 after six months and *RuPay* Debit card with inbuilt accident insurance cover of ₹1,00,000 and *RuPay* Kisan Card. In the next phase, micro insurance and pension will also be added.

Under the scheme:

1. Account holders will be provided zero-balance bank account with *RuPay* debit card, in addition to accidental insurance cover of ₹1,00,000.
2. Those who open accounts by January 26, 2015 over and above the 1,00,000 rupee accident claim will also be given life insurance cover of ₹30,000 (to be given by LIC).
3. After six months of opening of the bank account, holders can avail an overdraft of up to ₹5,000 from the bank.
4. With the new technology introduced by National Payments Corporation of India (NPCI), a person can transfer funds, check balance through a normal phone which was earlier limited only to smart phones so far.
5. Mobile banking for the poor would be available through National Unified USSD Platform (NUUP) for which all banks and mobile companies have come together.

The scheme has been criticized by many experts from the banking sector as an effort to please voters and that it has created unnecessary work-burden on the public-sector banks. The opposition party Congress alleged that PM Narendra Modi was trying to take credit of the financial inclusion scheme started by the UPA government and that the new Yojana had got nothing new. According to the experts, temptations presented by the Prime Minister such as zero balance, free insurance and overdraft facility would result in duplication. Many individuals who already have bank accounts may have had accounts created for themselves, lured by the insurance cover and overdraft facilities. As per the scheme, very few people are eligible to get the life insurance worth ₹30,000 with a validity of just five years. However, these 'secret' conditions were not shown in the TV advertisements of the scheme. The claimed overdraft facility has been completely left to the discretion of the banks. As per the government notice, only those people would get the overdraft facility whose transaction record is satisfactory. It is quite unlikely that many people would get this facility as the banks would avoid potential Non Productive Assets (NPAs). The claimed accidental insurance has also proved to be a non-existing scheme as the card holders have got no legal paper for any such accidental insurance.

Atal Pension Yojana

The Government of India has been concerned about the old age income security of the working poor and is focused on encouraging and enabling them to join the National Pension System (NPS). To address the longevity risks among the workers in unorganized sector and to encourage the workers in unorganized sector to voluntarily save for their retirement, who constitute 88% of the total labor force of 472.9 million as per the 66th round of NSSO Survey of 2011–12, but do not have any formal pension provision, the government had started the Swavalamban Scheme in 2010–11. However, the coverage under the Swavalamban Scheme is inadequate mainly due to lack of clarity of pension benefits at the age after 60.

The Finance Minister has, therefore, announced a new initiative called Atal Pension Yojana (APY)[4] in his Budget Speech for 2015–16. The APY will be focused on all citizens in the unorganized sector, who join the National Pension System (NPS) administered by the Pension Fund Regulatory and Development Authority (PFRDA) and who are not members of any statutory social security scheme. Under the APY, the subscribers would receive the fixed pension of ₹1,000 per month, ₹2,000 per month, ₹3,000 per month, ₹4,000 per month, ₹5,000 per month, at the age of 60 years, depending on their contributions, which itself would vary on the age of joining the APY. The minimum age of joining APY is 18 years and maximum age is 40 years. Therefore, minimum period of contribution by the subscriber under APY would be 20 years or more. The benefit of fixed pension would be guaranteed by the government. The Central government would also co-contribute 50% of the subscriber's contribution or ₹1,000 per annum, whichever is lower, to each eligible subscriber account, for a period of 5 years, that is, from 2015–16 to 2019–20, who join the NPS before December 31, 2015 and who are not income tax payers. The APY has become functional with effect from June 1, 2015. The existing subscribers of Swavalamban Scheme would be automatically migrated to APY, unless they opt out.

Benefit of APY: Fixed pension for the subscribers ranging between 1,000 to ₹5,000, if he joins and contributes between the age of 18 years and 40 years. The contribution levels would vary and would be low if subscriber joins early and increase if he joins late.

Eligibility for APY: Atal Pension Yojana (APY) is open to all bank account holders who are not members of any statutory social security scheme.

Age of joining and contribution period The minimum age of joining APY is 18 years and maximum age is 40 years. Therefore, minimum period of contribution by the subscriber under APY would be 20 years or more.

Focus of APY: Mainly targeted at unorganized sector workers.

Enrolment and Subscriber Payment: All bank account holders under the eligible category may join APY with auto-debit facility to accounts, leading to reduction in contribution collection charges.

Enrolment agencies: All Points of Presence (Service Providers) and Aggregators under Swavalamban Scheme would enroll subscribers through architecture of National Pension System.

Operational Framework of APY: It is Government of India Scheme, which is administered by the Pension Fund Regulatory and Development Authority. The institutional structure of NPS would be utilized to enroll subscribers under APY.

Funding of APY: Government would provide (a) fixed pension guarantee for the subscribers; (b) would co-contribute 50% of the subscriber contribution or ₹1,000 per annum, whichever is lower, to eligible subscribers; and (c) would also reimburse the promotional and development activities including incentive to the bank.

The effectiveness of the poverty alleviation programs in targeting the poor and alleviating poverty has been a mixed bag of success in some of the states and failure in other states. Variations in effectiveness are largely due to efficiency or otherwise of the implementing machinery, that is, the delivery system, strengths of the PRIs, existence or non-existence of community-based organizations of people, and initiative and innovativeness of the states in evolving approaches and institutional arrangements in harmony with the ground conditions. In the block of Northern states where the concentration of poverty is high, and which have also generally not done well in terms of economic growth, the implementation of poverty alleviation programs has been weak. Andhra Pradesh and Kerala, on the other hand, have evolved very effective institutional models for poverty alleviation efforts (GoI 2006b).

Key Points

1. Poverty and unemployment have been the bane of India since long. Their reduction has been one of the major goals of India's development planning since the beginning of the planning era. Accordingly, the Government of India has launched various programs from time to time aimed at alleviation of poverty and unemployment.
2. Poverty alleviation schemes and programs have been in place for a long time now. The programs and schemes have been modified, consolidated, expanded and improved over time. The targeted programs fall into four broad categories: (a) poverty alleviation programs, now subsumed in Aajeevika; (b) wage-employment programs, now subsumed in MGNREG Scheme; (c) public distribution system (PDS); and (d) other social welfare oriented programs (SWOP), such as National Social Assistance Programme (NSAP) and the Aam Admi Bima Yojana (AABY).
3. Several attempts have been made in India to estimate the incidence of poverty and trends thereof. The estimates are, however, not comparable because of differences in the methodologies used to define the poverty lines and size of samples taken.
4. The existing Official Planning Commission poverty lines for 2011–12, based on the Expert Group (Tendulkar) methodology and derived from the Mixed Recall Period (MRP) consumption distribution of the NSSO, are ₹816 and ₹1,000 per capita per month respectively for the all-India rural and urban populations. The Rangarajan Expert Group poverty lines, based on consumption estimates on MMRP are 19% higher for rural India and 41% higher for Urban India.
5. As per the Rangarajan Expert Group report, in 2011–12, the poverty ratio was 39.9% in rural areas and in 26.4% in urban areas and the number of people below the poverty was 260.5 million in rural areas and 102.5 million in urban areas. This is in contrast to the corresponding estimates of 216.7 million and 53.1 million for rural and urban areas as per the Tendulkar Expert Group Report.
6. The all-India Employment and Unemployment Surveys of National Sample Survey Office (NSSO) are the primary sources of labor market data at the national and state levels. NSS surveys on Employment and Unemployment, with large sample of households are conducted quinquennially. As of 2015, nine such comprehensive surveys on the employment and unemployment have been conducted by NSSO.
7. As per the NSSO data during 1999–2000 to 2004–05, employment on usual status (US) basis increased by 59.9 million persons from 398.0 million to 457.9 million as against the increase in labor force by 62.0 million persons from 407.0 million to 469.0 million. After a period of slow progress during 2004–05 to 2009–10, employment generation picked up during 2009–10 to 2011–12, adding 13.9 million persons to the workforce, but not keeping pace with the increase in labor force (14.9 million persons).
8. As per the 55th and 61st rounds of the NSSO surveys for rural areas and urban areas of India, respectively, the unemployment rates were lower in rural areas than in urban areas for both males and females. Within the rural areas, unemployment rates for males were higher than those for women.
9. Of late, there have also been structural changes in the pattern of employment. For the first time, the share of the primary sector in total employment has dipped below the halfway mark (declined from 58.5% in 2004–05 to 48.9% in 2011–12), while employment in the secondary and tertiary sectors increased to 24.3% and

26.8% respectively in 2011–12 from 18.1% and 23.4% respectively in 2004–05. Self-employment continues to dominate, with a 52.2% share in total employment.

10. A major impediment to the pace of quality employment generation in India is the small share of manufacturing in total employment. However data from the 68th NSSO Round (2011–12) indicates a revival in employment growth in manufacturing from 11% in 2009–10 to 12.6% in 2011–12. This is significant given that the National Manufacturing Policy 2011 has set a target of creating 100 million jobs by 2022. Promoting growth of Micro, Small, and Medium enterprises (MSME) is critical from the perspective of job creation.
11. The poverty alleviation programs were aimed at tackling the problems of poverty and backwardness directly by helping the weaker sections to increase their incomes through self-employment and wage-employment.
12. The public distribution system (PDS) is perhaps the oldest of all programs that were designed to ensure food security in India, particularly of the poor. It is perhaps the world's largest food distribution network. The basic objective of the PDS is to ensure that essential commodities are made available to the people at reasonable price, so as to provide them a safety net against inflation. To ensure food security to all, especially the poor, Parliament had passed on September 12, 2013, a legislation called the National Food Security Act. This law aims to provide subsidized food grains to approximately two-thirds of India's 1.2 billion people, especially through the PDS.
13. Several attempts have been to study the impact of the PDS. Gulati (1989) found that the PDS had a positive impact on the nutritional status of the malnourished and the poor. An evaluation study conducted by the Planning Commission in 1995 identified several deficiencies in the implementation of the revamped PDS. Large-scale diversion of food grains, particularly rice and wheat, to unauthorized uses has been a major criticism of the PDS.
14. Now all of the self-employment programs including the IRDP and SGSY are subsumed in the National Rural Livelihood Mission (NRLM) or Aajeevika, which was launched in June 2011. NRLM has incorporated learning from the implementation of earlier programs, primarily from the successes and failures of SGSY and from the various states' initiatives in the rural livelihoods sector.
15. NRLM works on three pillars: enhancing and expanding existing livelihoods options of the poor; building skills for the job market outside; and nurturing self-employed and entrepreneurs. It is implemented in a Mission Mode. This facilitates a shift from the present allocation based strategy to a demand-driven strategy, enabling the states to formulate their own livelihoods-based poverty reduction action plans. It focuses on targets, outcomes and time bound delivery.
16. A majority of the poor in rural areas of the country depend mainly on the wages they earn through unskilled labor. They are often on threshold levels of subsistence and are vulnerable to the possibility of sinking from transient to chronic poverty. In the context of poverty and unemployment, wage employment programs provide unskilled manual workers with short-term employment on public works such as irrigation infrastructure, reforestation, soil conservation, and road construction etc. The Central and state governments have launched several wage-earning programs from time to time.
17. Now all of the Centrally-sponsored wage-earning programs have been subsumed in the MGNREGA, which with its legal framework and rights-based approach was notified on September 5, 2005. It aims at enhancing livelihood security by providing at least one hundred days of guaranteed wage employment in a financial year to every

rural household whose adult members volunteer to do unskilled manual work. The act covered 200 districts in its first phase, on February 2, 2006, and was extended to all the rural districts of the country in phases.

18. Since its inception in 2006 until December 2013, around ₹1,290 billion had been disbursed directly as wage payments to rural households under the scheme, 13,480 million person-days of employment had been generated, on an average, 50 million households had been provided with employment every year since 2008. Scheduled Castes and Scheduled Tribes have accounted for 51% of the total person-days generated and women have accounted for 47% of the total person-days employed.
19. An anthology of over 130 evaluation studies of MGNREG scheme revealed, inter alia, that MGNREGA was important as a supplementary source of income and its income was used by rural households for starting their own ventures, that it had caused a significant increase in monthly per capita consumption expenditure of rural households, that with its inter-sectoral approach, it opens an opportunity for convergence with different programs with an aim to optimize public investment, and that it has had a more direct and positive impact on reducing distress migration as compared to migration taken-up for economic growth and other reasons.
20. Besides the self-employment and wage-employment schemes, there are a few other social welfare-oriented programs also underway in the country. They include the National Social Assistance Programme (NSAP), the Aam Admi Bima Yojana (AABY), the Rashtriya Swasthya Bima Yojana (RSBY), the Pradhan Mantri Jan Dhan Yojana (PMJDY) and the Atal Pension Yojana.

Questions for Discussion

1. Illustrate with an example that poverty and unemployment are inter-related problems and have two-way relation, that is, one is both the cause and effect of the other.
2. Write a critique of the current poverty and unemployment situation in India.
3. Despite the plethora of poverty and unemployment eradication programs that have been launched in India from time to time since the beginning of the planning era, why do these two problems still remain unresolved?
4. Write a critique of the public distribution system (PDS) as it is implemented at present, and suggest better ways of its implementation to achieve its objectives.
5. Write a critique of Aajeevika as a means of resolving the problem of poverty in India.
6. What are the problems and prospects of the Mahatma Gandhi National Rural Employment Guarantee (MNREG) scheme as an instrument of eradicating the problems of poverty and unemployment?

Appendix 10.1

Poverty Alleviation Programs Prior to NRLM

The Integrated Rural Development Programme (IRDP)

The IRDP was the most important program that belonged in the category of self-employment programs. It was the single largest anti-poverty program that was underway in all the community development blocks in the country. It was launched in 1978–79 in 2,300 selected blocks in the country and was extended to all the blocks in the country with effect from October 2, 1980. It aimed at providing income generating assets and self-employment opportunities to the rural poor to enable them to rise above the poverty line once and for ever. The IRDP in effect sought to redistribute assets and employment opportunities in favor of the rural poor and thereby reduce income inequality. It was a Centrally-sponsored scheme and was funded on 50:50 bases by the Centre and the states. The IRDP beneficiaries were assisted through viable bankable projects which were financed partly by subsidy and partly by bank loans. The subsidies were provided at differential rates ranging from 25% to 50% of the capital cost of the scheme, subject to a maximum of ₹5,000 in DPAP areas and ₹4,000 in non-DPAP areas; for a SC/ST or disabled beneficiary the limit was ₹6,000.

The IRDP was implemented by an autonomous agency called the DRDA. At the national level, the Ministry of Rural Development was responsible for the release of the Central share of the funds, policy formulation, overall guidance, direction, coordination, monitoring, and evaluation of the IRDP.

The Ministry of Rural Development had also provided for concurrent evaluation and impact studies of the IRDP as an aid to administer the program effectively. The state governments had been advised to undertake evaluation studies from time to time to ascertain the impact of the program and to measure the extent to which the beneficiaries had directly derived additional income and employment from the investments made under the program. The state governments were free to make use of their own evaluation machinery, wherever practicable, to undertake concurrent evaluation and impact studies, or entrust that work to selected academic/research institutions of standing and repute in this field.

Several all-India evaluation studies of the IRDP have been carried out by the NABARD, the RBI, the PEO of the Planning Commission and academic institutions. The Public Accounts Committee (PAC) of the Indian Parliament made some recommendations in its report about reshaping the IRDP. Some of the major inadequacies of the IRDP pointed out by the PAC report are as follows (Hirway 1988):

1. The per capita investment (loans plus subsidy) was too low to generate enough income to bring the beneficiary family above the poverty line,
2. Inadequate infrastructural support for various income generating activities,
3. Inadequate representation of the concerned agencies on the governing body of the DRDA, and
4. Absence of people's participation in the program.

The subsidies provided under the IRDP had attracted the interest of politicians wishing to divert the subsidies to their current or potential supporters. This had contributed to the low repayment rates on the loan component, since defaulters (and bank staff) were aware of the political support enjoyed by this category of beneficiaries. It had also meant that a high proportion of beneficiaries were not 'BPL'.

Malpractices by lower level officials had been pervasive. Surveys in some areas indicated that a 10% deduction was made by bank officials as informal 'charges'. In other localities, over 20% of the subsidy component was charged in various ways as 'speed money'. Another common form of corruption prevalent in some areas was the collusion between officials and local middlemen, who provided the asset, specified by the beneficiaries and got some money from the beneficiaries for allowing the over-invoicing of the cost of the asset and shared the booty with the local officials. This practice was contrary to the regulations, which required that the specified asset be provided by approved suppliers and not by middlemen.

Training of Rural Youth for Self Employment (TRYSEM)

A special scheme called TRYSEM was initiated in 1979 with the principal objective of removing unemployment among the rural youth. The TRYSEM was an integral part of the IRDP and was concerned with equipping rural youth in the age group of 18–35 years with the necessary skills that would enable them to be self-employed. Any rural youth below the poverty line was eligible for selection but preference in selection was given to SC), ST, and women candidates. The TRYSEM training was sharply focused on trades whose products have high potential demand and can lead to sustainable IRDP projects.

A TRYSEM evaluation study covering a sample of 6,686 beneficiaries arrived at the following conclusions: Of the total beneficiaries covered, around 54% were women, which is more than the prescribed norm that 40% of the TRYSEM beneficiaries should be women. Caste-wise distribution showed that 32% of the total beneficiaries belonged to SC and 21% to ST, which was as per the norms of the program (that 50% beneficiaries should be SC or ST). There had been a 20% increase in the employment levels of the beneficiaries after training under the TRYSEM. About 15% of them had started their own employment ventures. Only 26% of them received any subsidy/rebate/concession. More than 80% of the TRYSEM beneficiaries were satisfied with the quality of training imparted and stipend offered to them during training.

Development of Women and Children in Rural Areas (DWCRA)

The DWRCA program was launched in 1982 as part of the IRDP. Its aim was to empower rural women living BPL by way of organizing them to create sustainable income generating activities through self-employment. It was the first program of its kind that specifically focused on improving the quality of life of rural women. A unique feature of the DWCRA, unlike the other IRDP components, was that along with the improvement in income, it also focused on access to health, education, safe drinking water, sanitation, nutrition, and so on. Thus, it not only aimed at promoting economic development, but also facilitated social development. Another unique feature of the program was that it emphasized group activity. It was thought that in the long run, women's empowerment depends on creation of a movement that promotes awareness and self-reliance

An evaluation study of the DWCRA brought out that it had a direct and significant impact on employment and group activities. As high a proportion as 93% of the beneficiaries reported that the DWCRA had created a desire for self-employment, whereas about 89% of the beneficiaries felt that the DWCRA had raised their incomes. The DWCRA had a visible impact on savings, economic conditions, and social prestige, but it had less impact on health, sanitation, drinking water, and children's education, which are more of community services.

Swarnjayanti Gram Swarozgar Yojana (SGSY)

The SGSY was operationalized in April 1999 after restructuring and combining the IRDP with allied programs into a single self-employment program. The basic objective of the SGSY is to bring the assisted poor families above the poverty line by providing them income-generating assets through bank credit and government subsidy. Formation of organizations of the poor at the grassroots level through a process of social mobilization for poverty reduction is central to the program. The approach of the SGSY is based on women's SHGs that have to act as a financial intermediary and a vehicle for women's empowerment. The NGOs are expected to facilitate the formation of such groups. Community involvement is emphasized in the programs, in contrast to IRDP.

The program has been conceived as a holistic self-government program, covering all aspects of self-employment of the rural poor, such as organization of the poor in SHGs, their capacity building, selection of key activities, planning of activity clusters, infrastructure build-up, and technology and market support. The program aims at establishing a large number of microenterprises in rural areas based on the ability of the poor and the potential of each area. Assistance under the SGSY is given in the form of subsidy by government and credit by the banks. Credit is a critical component of the SGSY, and subsidy is back-ended, a minor and enabling element. Therefore, SGSY, in contrast to IRDP, envisages greater involvement of the banks in the planning and preparation of project reports, identification of activity clusters, choice of activities of SHGs, selection of individual beneficiaries, and post-credit monitoring including loan recovery. The interface among the DRDAs, the line departments of state governments, banks, NGOs and PRIs is necessary for the effective implementation of this program. The program has in-built safeguards for the weaker sections. Thus, the main tenets of the SGSY are (a) key activities, (b) cluster approach, and (c) group method. The first reduces the number of activities; the second shrinks the geographical spread to fewer contiguous or selected villages; and the third reduces the number of clients from a large number of individuals to a small number of groups. All these are expected to reduce the burden of follow-up and the training and education inputs for providing backward and forward linkages.

The scheme is being implemented on a cost sharing basis of 75:25 between the Centre and states. The number of SHGs has been growing rapidly; as on December 2007, about 2.74 million groups had been formed since April 1999, and 9.32 million *swarozgaris* had been assisted with a total outlay of ₹1,93,403.2 million.

The total investment (credit plus subsidy) during 2006–07 is expected to be about ₹38,500 million. The investment per assisted family is about ₹25,000. Evaluation studies show that only about one-fourth of assisted families could cross the poverty line. The Central and state governments had allocated ₹14,660 million (66% for subsidies, 12% revolving fund, 12% infrastructure, and so) for the SGSY during 2006–07.

SHGs had a positive and significant impact in Andhra Pradesh, Kerala, and Tamil Nadu, but have not yet made their presence felt in the poorer states such as Bihar, Orissa, and Uttar Pradesh. Most of the factors responsible for their poor performance relate to the delivery systems. They include ad-hocism in planning and implementation processes, inadequate reach of delivery systems, negative attitude of bankers toward credit disbursal to the poor, and lack of understanding and appreciation of complexity of livelihood issues. Cluster approach has also been a non-starter in many of the states. The DRDAs and the line departments of the state governments have failed in providing non-credit inputs to the beneficiaries. Above all, the building up of a gender perspective in the program has been conspicuously absent.

Appendix 10.2

Wage-employment Programs Prior to MGNREGA

The Food-for-Work (FFW) Programme

This program provided temporary employment with food grains as wages. Its objective was to ensure employment and food security to the rural people affected by natural disasters such as droughts and floods. A new program called the NFFWP was launched in 150 most backward districts in November 2004. It was a 100% Centrally-sponsored scheme. It aimed at generating supplementary wage-employment and providing food security through creation of need-based economic, social and community assets.

Jawahar Rozgar Yojana (JRY)

The JRY was the single largest wage-employment program implemented in all the villages of the country through the PRIs. The JRY was launched in April 1989, after merging the then ongoing two wage- employment programs, that is, NREP and RLEGP. The main objective of the

JRY was to provide additional gainful wage-employment to unemployed and underemployed persons in the rural areas during the lean agricultural seasons. The JRY was targeted at people living below the poverty line. The expenditure under the program was shared between the Centre and the states in the ratio of 80:20.

The JRY contributed to the creation of durable assets in the form of school buildings, roads and other infrastructure. It was, however, felt that a stage had come when the development of village infrastructure had to be taken up in a planned manner. Keeping this in view, the JRY was restructured in 1999 and renamed as the JGSY. The main features of the JGSY were

1. Creation of rural infrastructure;
2. Implementation of JGSY entirely by village panchayats;
3. Direct channelization of funds to the village panchayats through the DRDAs/zila panchayats;
4. Vesting in the village panchayats the sole authority for preparation of Annual Action Plan (AAP) and its implementation with the approval of the Gram Sabha;
5. Empowerment of the gram sabha to approve the schemes;
6. Wage employment restricted to below poverty line (BPL) families;
7. 30% of the employment opportunities reserved for women;
8. Delegation of administrative power to panchayats to suitably adjust the 60:40 wage material ratio for building demand-driven rural infrastructure;
9. Authorization of the gram sabhas to undertake social audit; and
10. Assignment of responsibility to DRDAs/zila parishads for overall guidance, supervision and monitoring and periodical reporting.

Sampoorna Grameen Rozgar Yojana (SGRY)

A new scheme called the SGRY was launched in 2001. It combined the various features of EAS, FFW and JGSY, and replaced those schemes. The main aim of the SGRY remains the same as of previous employment programs, which is, providing wage employment in rural areas and creation of economic assets. Under the scheme, wages are paid in both cash and food grains. The scheme is being implemented through the PRIs. Studies have shown that it provided only 29 days of employment per beneficiary per annum. Indiscriminate use of machines, underpayment of wages and leakage of food grains were the major lacunae of the SGSY (GoI 2006b).

Employment Assurance Scheme (EAS)

The EAS was launched on October 2, 1993. It guaranteed 100 days of employment per annum to rural poor, particularly during lean seasons. It also provided for materials for the creation of durable assets and was, to a large degree, self-targeting, assuming that only the poorest will opt to work for the basic minimum wage. The use of food grains for payment in kind is minimal in the EAS, and its regulations prohibit the engagement of contractors or middlemen. But this provision is widely flouted, and has been accompanied by falsification of attendance lists and other irregularities. Some estimates suggest that, given the widespread malpractices among administrators and contractors, only 25% of the wage funds, to which beneficiaries are entitled, actually reaches them, with the remaining 75% disappearing through leakages of various kinds.

National Food-for-Work Programme (NFFWP)

Duly taking cognizance of the need for alleviating the chronic problems of rural poverty and unemployment, and reducing the interregional disparities in economic growth and development in India, the Planning Commission designed and launched in 2004–05 a new program, called the NFFWP. It identified the 150 most backward districts in India on the basis of incidence of poverty as indicated by the proportion of SC/ST population, agricultural productivity per worker and agricultural wage rate. Most of the districts identified are tribal dominated districts. The main objective of the NFFWP is to generate supplementary wage employment and provide food security through the creation of need-based economic, social and community assets. This is to be done through the provision of additional resources, over and above the resources available under the SGRY, to the identified districts of the country. The NFFWP is a 100% Centrally-sponsored scheme. A five year Perspective Plan was prepared for each of the 150 districts.

The Crash Scheme of Rural Employment (CSRE)

In the early 1970s, when the planning strategy emphasized a direct attack on poverty, the CSRE was introduced in April 1971 as a crash scheme to alleviate the prevailing conditions of unemployment and underemployment in rural areas by generating additional employment through additional rural works. Apart from employment generation, the other objective of the CSRE was to generate assets of a durable nature in the areas of minor irrigation, land development, roads, afforestation, school buildings and other durable assets.[5]

Notes

1. http://aajeevika.gov.in/content/welcome-national-rural-livelihoods-mission-nrlm. (Accessed on October 5, 2015).
2. http://www.aajeevika.gov.in/ (Accessed on October 5, 2015).
3. For further details of the Scheme see, brochure, Pradhan Mantri Jan Dhan Yojana, Department of Financial Service, Ministry of Finance, Government of India (www.financialservices.gov.in).
4. For further details of the Scheme see, brochure, Pradhan Mantri Jan Dhan Yojana, Department of Financial Service, Ministry of Finance, GoI (www.financialservices.gov.in).
5. https://data.gov.in/catalog/physical-and-financial-progress-under-pardhan-mantri-gram-sadak-yojna-pmgsy-swarnajayanti (Accessed on October 8, 2015); http://rural.nic.in/netrural/rural/sites/downloads/annual-report/Annual_Report_2014_15_English.pdf MoRD Annual Report 2014-15 (Accessed on October 8, 2015).

Chapter 11

Natural Resources and Infrastructure Development Programs

LEARNING OUTCOMES

After having gone through this chapter, students should be able to:

- **Illustrate the genesis of various natural resource-based and infrastructure development programs launched in India from time to time;**
- **Identify the role of natural resources and infrastructure in rural development;**
- **Describe the salient features of major natural resource-based programs such as the Drought-prone Area Programme (DPAP), the Desert Development Programme (DDP), the Integrated Wasteland Development Programme (IWDP), the National Watershed Development Programme for Rain-fed Areas (NWDPRA) and so on;**
- **Explain the rationale for National Crop Insurance Programme (NCIP) and the pilot Weather-based Crop Insurance Scheme (WBCIS) and their main features; and**
- **Describe the salient features of major infrastructure development programs currently underway in India, Indira Awas Yojana (IAY), Pradhan Mantri Gram Sadak Yojana (PMGSY), PURA and the RIDF and National Rural Health Mission.**

Introduction

As stated in Chapter 5, natural resources of land, water, forests, minerals, air, and solar radiation play a very important role in the process of rural development. Mother Nature provides us natural resources free of cost and performs two important functions in the process of economic growth, namely, providing inputs to production processes and assimilating the wastes generated in the process of production. Similarly, basic infrastructure[1] such as roads, schools, health care centers, markets, electricity, water supply structures, and means of transport and communication play a critical role in the process of development through rapid spread of technologies and increased access of rural people to markets and institutional credit. Several research studies have shown that the average rate of return to investment in basic infrastructure, particularly rural roads and irrigation facilities, are very high. Improved infrastructure also helps reduce the incidence of poverty; there is an inverse relationship between poverty and Infrastructure Development Index (Fan, Hazell, and Haque 1998; Satish 2007, 32–50). Together with natural resources, infrastructure constitutes the production base of India's economy. The rural areas of India are at a great disadvantage vis-à-vis the urban areas in terms of provision of basic infrastructure. Provision of adequate, dependable, and good quality infrastructure in rural areas of India is, therefore, a prerequisite for rural development. The Government of India seems to have recognized the need for provision of basic infrastructure in the rural areas of the country and have launched from time to time several programs for the purpose.

Inequitable distribution of the benefits of the growth-oriented programs such the IADP and the High Yielding Variety Programme (HYVP) between prosperous and backward areas was officially acknowledged in the early 1970s. As the backward areas in India are very poor in natural resources endowment as well the basic infrastructure, corrective measures in the form of several area-specific/natural resources-based and infrastructure development programs were launched in those areas.

This chapter first presents an overview of some of the major natural resource-based development programs and then some salient features of some of the major infrastructure development programs launched in India from time to time. The main objective of the chapter is to familiarize the student with the salient features of the programs, their effectiveness, and the lessons that could be derived from their experience.

Natural Resources-based Programs

A brief description of major programs in this category follows.

Drought-prone Area Programme (DPAP)

A Rural Works Programme (RWP) was initiated in 1970–71 with the focus on the execution of rural works and employment generation in an attempt to mitigate the conditions of scarcity in drought-prone areas. Subsequently, it was realized that a mere RWP would not help in attaining these goals. The program was sought to be reoriented on the basis of an area development approach and was redesignated as the DPAP at the time of mid-term appraisal of the Fourth Five Year Plan. The program was confined to those areas that were originally taken up under the RWP. The basic objectives of the program are:

1. To reduce the severity of the impact of drought;
2. To stabilize the income of the people, particularly weaker sections of the society;
3. To restore the ecological balance.

Some of the important elements of the DPAP are:

1. Development and management of water resources;
2. Soil and moisture conservation;
3. Afforestation;
4. Restructuring of cropping pattern and pasture development;
5. Changes in agronomic practices;
6. Livestock and dairy development; and
7. Development of small farmers, marginal farmers, and agricultural laborers.

During the Fourth Five Year Plan, the DPAP was a central sector scheme with 100% financial assistance from the Center. From the Fifth Five Year Plan onward, this scheme has been operating with funds being shared between the Center and the states in a 50:50 ratio. Under the new strategy of rural development adopted in the Sixth Five Year Plan, the DPAP was merged with the IRDP. There are 183 districts spread over 16 states in India that are classified as drought-prone districts. They are all covered under the DPAP. The program is now under the administrative jurisdiction of the Department of Land Resources in the Ministry of Rural Development (MoRD). A technical committee constituted by the Government of India under the chairmanship of C. H. Hanumantha Rao studied, inter alia, the implementation and impact of DPAP and made some recommendations for improving its effectiveness.

DPAP has been under implementation in 972 blocks of 195 districts in 16 states. Till March 1999, the funds were shared on the 50:50 basis between the Central government and the state governments. However, with effect from April 1, 1999, the funding is shared on the 75:25 basis between the Center and the state government. The projects with size of about 500 ha were sanctioned under the program. With effect from April 1, 2001, uniform treatment cost norms at ₹6,000 per ha have been introduced. These norms are applicable to projects sanctioned during and after 2000–2001.

Between 1995–96 and 2006–07, 27,439 projects covering an area of 13.72 mha had been sanctioned. From 11th Plan onward, no new DPAP projects were sanctioned. A total number of 27,344 projects covering an area of 13.67 mha were completed/closed until March 31, 2014 and ₹42,768.4 million had been released. During 2013–14, 380 projects had been completed as of March 31, 2014 and an amount of ₹175.7 million had been released to the states concerned (MoRD 2014, 167)

Desert Development Programme (DDP)

The DDP was launched in 1977–78 in the hot desert areas of Rajasthan, Gujarat, and Haryana, and cold desert areas of Jammu and Kashmir and Himachal Pradesh as a central sector scheme with 100% financing by the Center. Subsequently, with effect from April 1, 1999, the program is being funded on the basis of 75:25 (Central share: state share) for the watershed projects sanctioned on or after April 1, 1999. The funds are released directly to the district rural development agencies/zila parishads for implementation of the program.

The DDP aims at mitigating the adverse effects of drought on crops, and human and livestock populations through controlling further desertification of the desert areas and enhancing productivity of local resources to raise the income and employment levels of the local inhabitants. The strategy adopted to achieve the objectives of the program involves the development of the selected areas on a watershed basis.

The activities taken up under the DDP include afforestation, water harvesting, rural electrification, and animal husbandry. In hot sandy desert areas, sand dune stabilization and shelter belt protection were given a higher weightage than other activities. With a view to identifying the weaknesses of the program and to consider the requests of some state governments for including more areas under the program, the Ministry of Rural Areas and Employment, Government of India, constituted in 1993 a technical committee on DPAP and DDP under the chairmanship of C. H. Hanumantha Rao. The committee submitted its report in April 1994. Based on the recommendations of the committee, new districts/blocks were brought under the fold of the program and fresh guidelines for watershed development applicable to DPAP and DDP were issued in October 1994 and made applicable from 1995–96. The committee found the performance of the program poor. The main reasons identified by the committee for the poor performance included the failure of the implementing agencies to adopt the watershed approach, lack of people's participation in planning and implementation of the program, inadequacy of funds, and non-availability of trained personnel (GoI 1997a, 42–43). The program is now under the administrative jurisdiction of the Department of Land Resources in the MoRD.

It is under implementation in 235 blocks of 40 districts in seven states, namely, Andhra Pradesh, Gujarat, Haryana, Himachal Pradesh, Jammu & Kashmir, Karnataka, and Rajasthan. As of March 31, 2014, a total number of 13,421 projects covering an area of 6.711 mha had been completed and 2026 projects closed. An amount of ₹31,557.6 million had been released until March 31, 2014. (MoRD 2014,168).

Integrated Wasteland Development Programme (IWDP)[2]

The Genesis of IWDP

India has vast tracts of wastelands that are normally defined as degraded lands, which, at reasonable cost and effort, can be brought under vegetative cover. Casual estimates of the extent of wastelands in India vary from 75 mha to 200 mha (Balooni and Singh 2003, 1). As stated in Chapter 2, India has a total geographical area of about 329 mha, of which about 120.40 mha was degraded in 2010–11, which is about 27% of the country's total geographical area. India needs to reclaim its degraded land and make it productive, so as to meet the increasing demands of its rapidly growing population and increasing affluence.

There are several wastelands development projects currently underway in India including the IWDP. This program has been under implementation since 1989–90 under the auspices of the NWDB, which was established in 1985, under the Ministry of Environment and Forests. With effect from July 1992, both the NWDB and the programs sponsored by it have been operating under the administrative control of the Department of Wastelands (now Department of Land Resources), Ministry of Rural Development. From April 1, 1995, the IWDP is being implemented on watershed basis. The projects under IWDP follow the guidelines that were in operation in the year of sanction of the particular project, namely, Guidelines for Watershed Development (April 1, 1995 to March 31, 2000), Revised Guidelines for Watershed Development (April 1, 2000 to March 31, 2003), and Hariyali Guidelines (April 1, 2003 to March 31, 2008). The department has integrated this program along with other watershed programs of the department, namely, DDP and DPAP, into a single modified program called Integrated Watershed Management Programme (IWMP) with effect from February 26, 2009.

Objectives of IWDP

The program is aimed at integrated development of wastelands/degraded lands based on village micro-watershed plans. More specifically, the main objectives of the program are as follows:

- Developing wastelands/degraded lands on watershed basis, keeping in view the capability of land, site conditions and local needs.
- Promoting overall economic development and improving socio-economic condition of the poor and disadvantaged sections inhabiting the program areas.
- Restoring ecological balance by harnessing, conserving and developing natural resources, that is, land, water & vegetative cover.
- Encouraging village community for sustainable community action for the operation and maintenance of assets created and further development of potential of the natural resources in the watershed.
- Employment generation, poverty alleviation, community empowerment, and development of human and other economic resources of the village.

Coverage

The projects under the program are sanctioned in the blocks not covered by DDP and DPAP. So far, the projects under the program have been implemented in 470 districts of the country.

Funding Pattern

Prior to March 31, 2000, watershed development projects under the program were sanctioned at a cost norm of ₹4,000 per hectare. These were funded entirely by the Central Government. The cost norms were revised to ₹6,000 per hectare for the projects sanctioned since January 4, 2000. Funding of the projects is shared between the Center and states in the ratio of ₹5,500 per ha and ₹500 per ha respectively. However, the old projects sanctioned until March 31, 2000 continue to be funded entirely by the Central Government.

Physical and Financial Progress

Since 1995–96 to 2006–07, 1,877 IWDP projects covering an area of 10.722 mha have been sanctioned and ₹45,493.5 million had been released as of March 31, 2014. To focus on completion of ongoing projects, no new projects were sanctioned under IWDP since 2007–08. As the department has integrated IWDP, DDP, and DPAP into a single modified program called IWMP with effect from February 26, 2009, new watershed projects are being sanctioned under IWMP from 2009–10. A total number of 1,227 projects covering an area of 7.22 mha had been completed until March 31, 2014, out of which 63 projects were completed during 2013–14. Under IWDP, during 2013–14, a sum of ₹363.8 million had been released to the states.

Integrated Watershed Management Programme (IWMP)[3]

The main features of the IWMP are as follows:

1. The activities to be taken up under IWMP are distributed over three phases. The preparatory phase (1 to 2 years) involves preparation of DPR, entry point activities, and institution and capacity building. The watershed works phase (2 to 3 years) involves the watershed development works, livelihood activities for the assetless persons, and production system and microenterprises. Withdrawal phase (1 to 2 years) involves the consolidation and completion of various works.
2. The cost norm for IWMP is ₹15,000 per ha for hilly and difficult area, ₹12,000 per ha for other areas and up to ₹15,000 per ha for IWMP projects in Integrated Action Plan (IAP) districts.
   The funding pattern under the scheme is in the ratio of 90:10 between the Center and states. The projects under IWMP undertake a cluster of micro-watersheds of area about 5,000 ha in rainfed/degraded areas having no assured irrigation. Dedicated institutions are also provided at Centre, state and district levels. The program lays emphasis on meticulous planning and capacity building, by providing a special provision of 1% for preparation of detailed project report (DPR) and 5% for institution and capacity building. A watershed development fund was established in 1999–2000 with an initial corpus of ₹2,000 million, contributed equally by the Government of India and NABARD. The corpus was augmented over the years by the interest differential earned under the RIDF and interest accrued on the unutilized portion of the Fund. As of March 31, 2015, the total corpus stood at ₹10,849.4 million.
3. Institutional set up for implementation of IWMP
   - **Ministry Level:** A steering committee has been constituted at national level in the Department of Land Resources under the chairmanship of the secretary

(land resources) with members from the Planning Commission, NRAA, related ministries/departments/institutes, and organizations including NGOs to administer the IWMP.

- **State Level:** State Level Nodal Agency (SLNA) constituted with professional support is the dedicated institution for implementation of IWMP in the state.
- **District Level:** Watershed Cell cum Data Centre (WCDC) is the district level institution to supervise and coordinate IWMP projects in the district. WCDC is set up in DRDA/zila parishad/district level implementing agency/department in all program districts as per the convenience of the state governments.
- **Project Level:** Projects under IWMP are supervised by Project Implementing Agencies (PIAs). Government and NGOs may act as PIAs, as per the provisions in the *Common Guidelines for Watershed Development Projects*, 2008 (revised in 2011), for providing technical back up for IWMP projects. Each PIA has a Watershed Development Team (WDT) comprising at least 4 members.
- **Village Level:** A Watershed Committee (WC) is constituted by the gram sabha for implementation of the project at field level. It comprises of at least 10 members, half of which are representatives of SHGs and User Groups (UGs), SC/ST community, women, and landless. One member from WDT is also represented in the WC.

4. Criteria for allocation of target area to states under IWMP. Keeping in view the mandate of the Department of Land Resources and its watershed schemes, the following criteria are adopted for the allocation of target area among the states.
    - Identified DPAP/DDP areas in the state as percentage of total DPAP and DDP area in the country.
    - Total treatable wastelands in the state as percentage of total treatable wastelands in the country.
    - Total SC/ST population of the state as percentage of total SC/ST population of the country.
    - Percentage of rainfed area in the state to total cultivated area in the country.
    - 10% mandatory allocation to North Eastern states.

Progress Under IWMP

The SLNA for overseeing the implementation of IWMP has been notified in all the 28 states. A total assistance of ₹1,480.2 million has been released under professional support to 27 states for the establishment/engagement of personnel at state and district levels institutions from 2009–10 to 2013–14. During 2013–14, Central funds to the tune of ₹396.7 million had been released.

Under IWMP, a target for covering 22.65 mha was set for the Eleventh Five Year Plan. Against this, a total area of 24.213 mha (5,087 projects) had been sanctioned by the SLNAs of 27 states. The target for sanction of new projects under IWMP for the year 2013–14 is 5.0 mha. A total of 1,051 projects covering an area of 5.051 mha had been appraised/sanctioned by SLNAs and a total amount of ₹21,628 million had been released during 2013–14. As of 2013–14, a total amount of ₹87,475.5 million had been released toward the Central share for the projects sanctioned under IWMP.

Initiatives Under Watershed Program

The Department of Land Resources proposes to implement the World Bank Assisted National Watershed Management Project (WB-NWMP) "Neeranchal" in support of IWMP. The objective of the program is to support IWMP through technical assistance to improve incremental conservation outcomes and agricultural yields for communities in selected sites and adoption of more effective processes and technologies into the broader IWMP in participating project states.

Neeranchal is primarily designed to address the following concerns:

- Bring about institutional changes in watershed management practices in India,
- Build systems that ensure watershed programs are better focused and have quantifiable results,
- Devise strategies for the sustainability of improved watershed management practices in program areas, even after the withdrawal of "Neeranchal."

The project would be implemented through the following four components:

Component 1: Central Institutional and Capacity Building,
Component 2: National Innovation Support,
Component 3: IWMP Implementation Support in Participating States, and
Component 4: Project Management and Coordination.

The project will be implemented in eight states, namely, Andhra Pradesh, Chhattisgarh, Gujarat, Jharkhand, Madhya Pradesh, Maharashtra, Odisha, and Rajasthan, which together cover approximately 60% of the total IWMP area. The total outlay of the project is ₹21,420 million (USD 357 million at the exchange rate of ₹60 for every $1) and the cost share between the Government of India and WB is 50:50. The duration of the project is six years, from 2014–15 to 2019–20.

Concurrent Monitoring and Evaluation

The Department of Land Resources has taken a new initiative for concurrent monitoring and evaluation of the IWMP projects. In this regard many of the states have already selected the independent evaluation agencies. States were also advised to involve the voluntary organizations in social mobilization and capacity building.

Joint Forest Management (JFM) and National Afforestation Programme (NAP)

It was the NCA 1976, which recommended for the first time in India the plantation of trees on degraded forest and non-forest lands to enhance the forest cover in the country. Subsequently, the Government of India launched a social forestry programs including farm forestry on a large scale during the 1970s and 1980s to rope in people in the afforestation programs on private as well as community lands. The National Forest Policy (NFP) of 1988 emphasized the role of people's participation in forest protection and management. The Ararbari experiment in West Bengal in involving local people in the protection and management of degraded forests gave rise to a new concept called the Joint Forest Management (JFM), which means co-management of forests by the local people and the forest department, mediated in most cases by a local NGO.[5] As a follow-up to the NFP of 1988 and based on the experience with the Ararbari experiment, the Government of India has issued orders and guidelines on the JFM from time to time. The first policy directive was a JFM circular issued on June 1, 1990 by the Ministry of Environment and Forests, Government of India, for the involvement of village communities and voluntary agencies in regeneration of degraded forests. Subsequently, the state governments also passed their own resolutions on JFM.

The Ministry of Environment and Forests had issued fresh operational guidelines for the formulation of a new program called the National Afforestation Programme (NAP) for the

Tenth Five Year Plan (2002–07). These guidelines seek to encourage a participatory approach to development of forests for the government-sponsored afforestation schemes. Afforestation schemes operational during the Ninth Five Year Plan have been merged in the new NAP, so as to "avoid the multiplicity of schemes with similar objectives" and to ensure "uniformity in funding pattern and implementation mechanism."

These guidelines stipulate that all the new Centrally-sponsored afforestation schemes will be implemented by a two-tier setup consisting of Forest Development Agencies (FDAs) at the forest division level and Joint Forest Management Committees (JFMCs) at the village level, to allow for greater participation of the community in planning and implementation. The FDA is a new institutional setup, which is a registered society under the Societies Registration Act 1860, constituted at the territorial wildlife forest division level. Other than JFM committees, already existing village institutions with different nomenclatures are the implementing agencies at the grassroots level. The FDAs work in tandem with JFM Committees by signing a memorandum of understanding (MoU). On one hand, the FDAs will strengthen the existing JFM committees and on the other they will create new JFM committees. To be concise, the purpose of the NAP is to make JFM a "central integral part" of all the afforestation projects in the country. We now present the salient features of the NAP (MoEF 2015, 138–144).

NAP is a major Afforestation scheme of the National Afforestation and Eco-Development Board (NAEB) in the Ministry of Environment, Forests and Climate Change, Government of India. Launched in 2000–02, the scheme has acquired a pan-India ambit over the last eight years of the its implementation and was being implemented by 28 states of the country through a twin institutional set up of FDAs at the forest division level and JFMCs at the village level. From the year 2010–11, SFDA has been constituted at the state level to smoothen the fund flow to the FDAs. The program is now implemented through a three tier system of SFDAs at the state level, FDAs at the district/forest division level, and JFMCs at the village level. Under entry point activities, community assets are created with a "care and share" concept.

The objectives of the scheme are as follows:

1. Protection and conservation of natural resources through active involvement of the people,
2. Checking land degradation, deforestation, and loss of biodiversity,
3. Ecological restoration and environmental conservation and eco-development,
4. Evolving village level people's organization that can manage the natural resources in and around villages in a sustainable manner,
5. Fulfillment of the broader objectives of productivity, equity, and sustainability for the general good of the people,
6. Improve quality of life and self-sustenance aspect of people living in and around forest areas, and
7. Capability endowment and skill enhancement for improving employability of the rural people.

Achievements

- Twenty eight SFDA projects have been operationalized in the country at an expenditure of ₹35,138.1 million to treat an area of 2.09 mha since the inception of the NAP scheme.
- During the year, till December 31, 2014, ₹2,124.7 million had been released under the NAP scheme sanctioning an advance area of 73,435 ha for afforestation in 2015 monsoon.

New Initiatives Under the Scheme

A number of initiatives have been taken by the Ministry to expedite the implementation of the scheme as well as to improve the qualitative aspects of implementation. These include:

- Comprehensive amendment in guidelines of the NAP scheme has been made to promote further decentralization by delegating more responsibilities to state forest departments with respect to processing of the FDA project proposals, greater organic linkage of JFMCs with gram panchayats, increased security of the elected members of JFMCs through longer tenure of JFMC presidency, capacity building in particular of frontline staff of forest department, and JFMC members especially with regard to local management and administrative responsibilities.
- In general, women are the largest beneficiary group of all interventions by the NAEB. In addition to being users of the resource, and their participation in the labor force, the empowerment of women is being also ensured by requesting the states to increase their representation to 50% in FDA. Similarly, the revised guidelines of NAP scheme also require 50% women in the JFMCs. It is proposed to monitor the benefit of the NAP scheme to women members in quantifiable terms. Accordingly, the formats for progress reports of FDA projects under NAP scheme have been modified.
- While formulating proposals under NAP, states have been advised to give adequate representation to SC/ST in FDA and JFMC at village level. Information received from FDAs reveal a larger participation of SCs/STs, in afforestation program, and there has been corresponding increase in generation of employment in the project areas.
- Adequate emphasis has been given to the development of North Eastern states including Sikkim. *Jhum* areas in the North East have been given special priority. The Board is also supporting new initiatives and new technologies to support states efforts in tackling the problem of jhum land degradations. An Alder-tree based jhum rehabilitation project is also being implemented and, if found suitable, would be scaled up in the coming years. In view of the fact that a majority of forest lands in the North East is owned by clans and communities, adequate emphasis will be given on supporting projects proposed on these lands under NAP.
- A website of NAEB[4] has been launched and the relevant information on the approvals is being provided on the website. SFDA/FDA is required to discuss the approved works in the general body of the JFMCs.

National Watershed Development Project for Rainfed Areas (NWDPRA)[5]

Introduction

Rainfed areas constitute about 57% of the total 140.30 mha cultivated the country. Rainfed agriculture is characterized by low levels of productivity and low input usage. Variability in rainfall results in wide variation and instability in yields. The bulk of the rural poor live in the rainfed regions. Therefore, the Government of India accords highest priority to the holistic and sustainable development of rainfed areas through watershed development approach. The scheme of NWDPRA was launched in 1990–91 in 25 states and two UTs based on twin concepts of integrated watershed management and sustainable farming systems.

The NWDPRA combines the features of the DPAP, DDP, and IWDP, with the additional dimension of improving arable lands through better crop management technologies. During the Ninth Five Year Plan, the scheme was extended to three newly formed states of Uttaranchal, Jharkahand, and Chhattisgarh. The scheme of NWDPRA has been subsumed under the scheme for Macro Management of Agriculture (MMA) from 2000–2001. At present, this scheme is being implemented as a program of centrally sponsored scheme of MMAe in 28 states and two UTs. Funds are released to the states based on an approved annual work plan. The scheme is presently being implemented on the basis of *Common Guidelines for Watershed Development Projects* issued by National Rainfed Area Authority (NRAA).

Objectives

The main objectives of the scheme are as follows:

- Conservation, development, and sustainable management of natural resources,
- Enhancement of agricultural production and productivity in a sustainable manner,
- Restoration of ecological balance in the degraded and fragile rainfed ecosystems by greening these areas through appropriate mix of trees, shrubs and grasses,
- Reduction in regional disparity between irrigated and rainfed areas, and
- Creation of sustained employment opportunities for the rural community including the landless.

Financing Pattern

Financing pattern of NWDPRA program is applicable as per the financing pattern of MMA, that is, 90:10 of Central and state government. For North Eastern states, it is a 100% grant.

Main Components of the NWDPRA

The main components include:

Preparatory phase:
- Entry point activities
- Institution and capacity building
- Detailed Project Report (DPR)

Watershed Works Phase:
- Watershed development works
- Livelihood activities for the assetless persons
- Production system and microenterprises

Consolidation Phase

Progress of NWDPRA

Major Achievements

Impact evaluation studies both on the ground and through remote sensing techniques have shown that watershed based interventions have led to:

- Increase in groundwater recharge,
- Increase in number of wells and water bodies,
- Enhancement of cropping intensity,
- Changes in cropping pattern, and
- Higher yields of crops and reduction in soil losses.

National Crop Insurance Programme (NCIP)[6]

Introduction and Genesis

Keeping in view the risks involved in agriculture and to insure the farming community against various risks, the Ministry of Agriculture introduced a crop insurance scheme in 1985 and thereafter brought improvements in the erstwhile scheme(s) from time to time, based on the experience gained and views of the stakeholders, states, farming community, and so on. To enlarge the coverage in terms of farmers, crops, and risks, NAIS was started in 1999. To make the crop insurance schemes more farmers friendly, a re-structured Central sector scheme, namely "NCIP," has been approved by merging the erstwhile pilot schemes of Modified National Agricultural Insurance Scheme (MNAIS), WBCIS, and Coconut Palm Insurance Scheme (CPIS) with some improvements for full-fledged implementation from *rabi* 2013–14 season throughout the country. NAIS was to be discontinued after implementation of NICP from rabi 2013–14 season. However, on the representations from states, it has been continued during 2013–14 and 2014–15. The scheme is optional for the state governments and they can notify crops and areas according to provisions of the schemes. The components under the scheme are being implemented on "area approach method" where yield of notified areas under MNAIS and weather data of notified reference automatic weather stations (AWSs) under WBCIS are taken as one unit for assessment/payment of claims for widespread calamities. However, claims are also being paid on the basis of losses at individual farms due to localized calamities like hailstorm and landslides under MNAIS and WBCIS (as add on/index-plus coverage).The penetration/coverage of these schemes in terms of number of farmers has reached about 30% of the total number of landholdings in the country.

The coverage of farmers under NCIP by the terminal year of the Twelfth Five Year Plan (i.e. 2016–17) has been projected to be at 50% due to the improvements/changes made in NCIP component schemes of MNAIS, WBCIS, and CPIS. Salient features of NCIP are listed below:

- Implementation is made compulsory for loanee farmers,
- Two indemnity levels of 80% and 90% would be available instead of three, that is, 70%, 80%, and 90% under MNAIS,
- Under WBCIS, provision for add-on/index plus products for horticultural crops for compensating losses due to perils of hailstorm, cloudburst, and so on,
- For successful implementation of WBCIS, 5,000 AWS will be set-up in the country through the model of private public participation,
- Pilots for use of modern technology like Remote Sensing Technology (RST)/Satellite imageries to supplement the yield assessment through CCEs,
- Insurance eligibility condition of having at least 10 healthy palms by farmer has been reduced to five palms under CPIS.

The total funds released by the Government of India under various schemes for crop insurance till December 31, 2014, were ₹1,72,049.8 million (MoA 2015, 81).

Weather-based Crop Insurance Scheme (WBCIS)

With the objective to bring more farmers under crop insurance fold and to overcome the shortcoming regarding delays in settlement of claims, etc. under NAIS, a pilot WBCIS was announced in the Union Budget for 2007–08 and was approved for implementation in 20 states on pilot basis. WBCIS is implemented as a full-fledged component scheme of NCIP from rabi 2013–14 season. WBCIS intends to provide insurance protection to the farmers against adverse weather incidence, such as deficient and excess rainfall, high or low temperature, humidity, and so on, which are deemed to impact adversely the crop production. Under WBCIS, actuarial rates of premium are being charged. However, to make the scheme affordable to the farmers, subsidy up to 50% of the premium is provided by the government that is shared by the Center and the concerned state on a 50:50 basis. Actuarial rates of premium are capped at 10% during *kharif* and 8% during rabi for food crops and oilseeds. For annual commercial/horticultural crops, a cap of 12% on actuarial rates of premium is applicable. Both loanee and non-loanee farmers are covered under WBCIS irrespective of their size of holding.

Table 11.1: *Progress of Weather-based Crop Insurance Scheme (WBCIS) in India (From Kharif 2007 to Rabi 2013–14)*

No. of Farmers Insured (Million)	*Area Insured Million (ha)*	*Sum Insured Million (₹)*	*Gross Premium Million (₹)*	*Claims Million (₹)*	*No. of Farmers Benefited (Million)*
52.10	687.37	9,24,629.23	84,652.10	57,147.91	31.36

Source: MoRD (2015, 85).

Like NAIS, the loanee farmers are covered on compulsory basis in a notified area for notified crops whereas for non-loanee farmers the scheme is voluntary. Further, to provide competitive service to the farmers, private insurance companies have been involved in implementation, besides the Agriculture Insurance Company of India (AIC) Ltd.

Achievements of the WBCIS as on December 31, 2014 are presented in Table 11.1. As shown in the Table, as of rabi 2013–14, 52.10 million farmers had been covered under the scheme and 31.36 million farmer had benefited in 18 selected states where the scheme was underway. The area insured was 687.37 mha and the sum insured was over ₹925 billion.

Infrastructure Development Programs

The presence of appropriate physical and social infrastructure is a core need to support agriculture and rural development and to facilitate effective forward and backward linkages to farm produce. In this context, the Government of India has launched a number of infrastructure development programs from time to time and taken numerous forward-looking initiatives to fund and support the creation of rural infrastructure. A brief description of the major programs now underway in India follows.

Indira Awaas Yojana (IAY)

Introduction and Genesis

Housing is universally recognized as one of the basic human rights. It is the responsibility of the government to ensure that every citizen has a safe, secure, and healthy place to live and work and lead a life of dignity. In other words, by ensuring the right to adequate housing in rural areas, the need to enhance quality of life and opportunity of growth is addressed. A large number of rural households, specially those belonging to the vulnerable sections, are unable to access good housing and civic amenities due to low income. Besides absolute shortage, congestion, and obsolescence, damage due to vagaries of nature such as floods, cyclones, and earthquakes, as well as incidence of violence, has added to the problem of housing shortage.

Fulfilling the need for rural housing and tackling housing shortage particularly for the poorest is an important task to be undertaken as part of the poverty alleviation efforts of the government. The Indira Awaas Yojana (IAY) is a flagship scheme of the Ministry of Rural Development to provide houses to BPL families in the rural areas. Under IAY, since inception until the end of 2013–14, over 32 million houses had been constructed, incurring an expenditure of ₹1,055.18 billion.

Evolution of the Scheme

The IAY was launched during 1985–86 as a sub-scheme of the Rural Landless Employment Guarantee Programme (RLEGP). IAY, thereafter, continued as a sub-scheme of Jawahar Rozgar

Yojana (JRY) since its launch in April, 1989. Six percent of the total JRY funds were allocated for implementation of IAY. In the initial years the housing scheme addressed the needs of SC and ST families and families of bonded laborers in BPL category.

From the year 1993–94, the scope of IAY was extended to cover non-SC/ST families in the rural areas. IAY was de-linked from JRY and made an independent scheme with effect from January 1, 1996. It is now a flagship program of the Ministry of Rural Development, as part of the larger strategy of rural poverty eradication, to provide dignity of an address to the poor households and to enable them to access benefits of other rural development schemes.

Salient Features IAY (MoRD 2014, 66–70)

The IAY has the following components: (a) assistance for construction of new houses; (b) upgradation of *kutcha* or dilapidated houses; and (c) provision of house sites.

The criteria for allocation of IAY funds to states/UTs and from states/UTs to districts, blocks, and wherever the states desire to the village panchayats would be on the basis of selection of houseless people from among the BPL population for each category of target beneficiaries, that is, SC, ST, minorities, and others. The ministry does the annual allocation of funds for the states/UTs on the basis of 75% weightage to housing shortage in rural areas as per the latest census data and 25% weightage to the number of people who are BPL.

At the national level, 60% of the funds are earmarked for SCs and STs with the proportion between SCs and STs being fixed by the Ministry of Rural Development and reflected in the targets. From the year 2011–12 onward, 60% of total allocation under IAY is being earmarked for SCs/STs under a separate budget head. Further, 15% of the funds are set apart for beneficiaries from among the minorities. The states should ensure that at least 3% beneficiaries of IAY are from among persons with disabilities. The earmarking is only the minimum limit that should be achieved by the state and states, if they so desire, may add to the target under these categories.

Under IAY, with effect from April 1, 2013, a BPL family is given grant of ₹70,000 for new construction in plain areas and ₹75,000 in hilly/difficult areas including LWE districts. Further, IAY funds can also be utilized for upgradation of a kutcha house for which a subsidy of ₹15,000 per unit is provided. For purchase of house sites, an assistance of ₹20,000 is provided to the landless poor. With effect from March 1, 2013, a provision has been made for utilization of 4% of funds allocated for administrative expenses.

The funding of IAY is shared between the Center and states, (except in North Eastern states and Sikkim) in the ratio of 75:25 respectively. In the case of North Eastern states and Sikkim, funding is shared in the ratio of 90:10. In the case of UTs, entire funds of IAY are provided by the Center. The cost of providing house sites is shared in the ratio of 50:50 between the Government of India and state governments. Government of India provides for the full cost in respect of UTs. Up to 95% of the total budget can be utilized for the components relating to new houses, upgradation of houses, and provision of house sites and administrative expenses. The remaining 5% is to be retained in the Center and is reserved for special projects that can be proposed for:

- Rehabilitation of BPL families affected by natural calamities, and law and order problems,
- Settlement of families of vulnerable tribal groups, FRA beneficiaries, families of bonded laborers, and manual scavengers,
- Rehabilitation of persons affected by occupational diseases, and
- House construction for demonstration of eco-friendly, appropriate, and locally relevant technology.

Up to 4% of the funds released can be utilized for administrative expenses of which up to 0.5% can be retained at the state level and the balance is to be distributed to the districts. The administrative expenses may be used for:

- IEC activities, MIS evaluation studies
- Social audit
- Capacity building initiatives
- Technology demonstration

The administrative expenses shall be shared by the Center and states in the same ratio as applicable to the program expenditure.

The construction of a house should be carried out by the beneficiary himself/herself. No contractor should be involved in the construction of houses under IAY. But construction may be facilitated by government agencies in the case of very old beneficiaries above 60 years of age and persons with disabilities who may not be able to stand the strain of supervising construction and who request for such support in writing. Government departments or agencies can provide technical assistance and may arrange coordinated supply of material for the convenience of beneficiaries.

States can also accredit reputed CSOs, institutions, and agencies for providing support services for adoption of suitable design, technology, and material.

Achievements

Bharat Nirman

IAY has been implemented with the objective of providing adequate, affordable, and durable homes to BPL families, addressing on priority the urgent needs of the poorest and the marginalized, particularly STs, SCs, and minorities' families in rural areas, including such families who have been rendered houseless due to man-made or natural calamities. Rural housing is one of the components of Bharat Nirman, which was launched in 2005 as a time bound action plan for rural infrastructure. In phase I of Bharat Nirman, 6 million houses were to be constructed under IAY (in the period 2005–2009). Against this, 7.18 million houses were constructed with an expenditure of ₹2,17,204.9 million.

In phase II of Bharat Nirman (2009–14) the target was fixed at 12 million houses under IAY. Against this target, 12.131 million houses have been constructed with an expenditure of ₹6,20,422.5 million.

New Initiatives

IAY Guidelines have been revised with effect from April 1, 2013 with the objective of making the scheme flexible. States and experts in the sector were consulted before finalizing the guidelines. The major new initiatives are as follows:

a) Priority to vulnerable categories:
   Among the eligible BPL families, to ensure coverage of the most vulnerable categories, priority should be given to:
   - Families of manual scavengers and bonded laborers
   - Households with single girl child
   - Physically and mentally challenged persons
   - Transgenders

- Widows/next of kin of defense/paramilitary/police personal killed in action in (even if not BPL)
- Households where a member is suffering from leprosy or cancer
- People living with HIV (PL HIV)

b) Social audit

To ensure public accountability in implementation, states have been directed to conduct at least one social audit every year in a gram panchayat. Social audit teams and resource persons should be identified and trained to verify the processes and procedures regarding selection, construction, completion, timelines, and quantum of payment, support services provided, grievance redressal, and so on. Detailed instructions have been issued in this regard.

c) Special projects

To address special needs of the eligible families the provisions for special projects has been expanded by including by including following categories:

- Families forced to relocate along international borders
- Households benefited under FRA
- Houses built for technology demonstration
- Families affected by natural calamities and law and order problem
- Families belonging to particularly vulnerable tribal groups
- Persons/Families affected by occupational diseases or epidemic

An empowered committee has been set up at the ministry level, which among other functions will sanction special projects submitted by state governments every year. Five percent of the IAY allocation will be retained every year at the Center for funding these projects.

d) Flexibility in identification of Difficult Areas

Presently the North East states, states of Himachal Pradesh, Jammu & Kashmir, and Uttarakhand and all 82 LWE districts are identified as difficult and hilly areas. These states/districts are eligible for sanction of IAY house at ₹75,000 per house. In the new guidelines, provision has been made for states to identify difficult areas, where due to reasons like low availability of material, poor connectivity, and adverse geo-climatic conditions, the cost of construction is very high. For this, the gram panchayat may be treated as a unit, and the states can submit the proposals, with adequate justification for a one-time approval of the empowered committee in the ministry.

e) Appropriate building technologies

States should proactively identify appropriate building technologies focusing on use of local materials. Geo-climatic factors and socio-cultural issues should be addressed while developing design options. Options like prefabricated structures, reuse and recycling of construction material, and facilitation of supply of building material at reasonable rates should be explored and adopted for the convenience of beneficiaries. In congested localities, where cost of land is high, construction of multi-storied house should be allowed, but it should not exceed three floors.

f) Convergence

A house is not just a dwelling place, but a socioeconomic asset for the rural family. The larger strategy of rural housing is to support development of an environmentally sound habitat with adequate provision for safe drinking water, sanitation, electricity, infrastructure like road, schools, and so on. A state-level mechanism to supervise and oversee the convergence initiatives with an action plan has been suggested. IAY beneficiaries should be provided services through schemes such as MGNREGS, RGGVY, RSBY, Aam Admi Bima Yojana, NSAP, and so on. Convergence with NBA for construction of Individual House hold Latrines (IHHL) has been made mandatory and joint instructions for implementation have been issued along with Ministry of DWS.

g) Capacity Building

To strengthen the quality of implementation the states should have a comprehensive capacity building plan, with the following elements:

- Training of district level officials and functionaries
- Training of cutting edge level functionaries
- Training of masons, extension workers
- Training of SHGs, CRPs, panchayat functionaries
- Training of Quality Monitors
- Smooth fund flow

The revised guidelines enable smooth fund flow, in two installments. The first installment will be automatically released to all states/UTs, except to those districts who have not availed of a second instalment in the previous year. The second installment will be to those districts that have utilized at least 60% of total available funds and fulfillment of conditions imposed in previous release. A checklist and format has been provided for submission of proposals. It has been envisaged that the state share should be released as soon as the Central share is received so that disbursement is regular. States may decide the number of instalments for release to the IAY beneficiaries, although a suggestive pattern has been given in the guidelines.

h) IT Enabled Monitoring & Implementation through AwaasSoft

AwaasSoft is a workflow-based management information system (MIS) designed to capture the implementation process through its target setting and fund management modules. The beneficiary management module captures details of the beneficiary and status of his/her sanction. Real-time reports generated by the system are useful tools for monitoring of progress and reporting. This was launched in July 2010. Reports are available in the public domain for all citizens to know the progress of the scheme in their area. The system also provides for an online grievance redressal platform to register grievances and track the status of action taken on them. The software captures all relevant data of beneficiary including the category he/she belongs to, the Aadhaar number, and so on. There is a provision for uploading of photographs of houses under different stages of construction.

Prime Minister's Gram Sadak Yojana (PMGSY)[7]

History and Evolution of Scheme

Rural connectivity is a critical component in the socio-economic development of rural people as it provides amenities like education, health, marketing, and so on. Historically, there has been skewed development of the rural road network in country. Some states provided cent percent connectivity while some others did not have enough financial resources at their disposal and consequently rural connectivity remained at low levels. There were also problems of inadequate funds for maintenance, upgradation and renewal of existing rural roads. In this context, a network approach and provision of sustainable accessibility with assured maintenance was surely desirable.

In 1951, India had around 4,00,000 km of serviceable road network. Accessibility to villages was poor as only about 20% had all-weather road links. Over the years for development of roads, several long-term 20-year plans were formulated under the aegis of the Indian Roads Congress (IRC). They have served as sound reference framework for the Central and state governments to formulate their successive Five Year Plans. A major thrust to the development of rural roads was accorded at the beginning of the Fifth Five Year Plan in 1974, when it was made a part of the Minimum Needs Programme. In 1996, this was merged with the Basic Minimum Services (BMS) programs. The works of village roads were also taken up under several employment generation and poverty alleviation programs of the Central and state governments. Notwithstanding the efforts made, over the years, at the state and Central levels, through different programs, around 40% villages were still not connected by all-weather roads at the turn of century. A major initiative in this direction taken by the Government of India as the part of poverty reduction strategy is PMGSY that was launched on December 25, 2000 as a Centrally-sponsored scheme to assist the states, though rural roads is in the state list under the Constitution. The primary objective of PMGSY is to provide connectivity by way of an all-weather road (with necessary culverts and cross-drainage structures, which is operable throughout the year), to the eligible unconnected habitations as per Core Network with a population of 500 persons (as per 2001 Census) and above in plain areas. In respect of "special category states" (North East, Sikkim, Himachal Pradesh, Jammu & Kashmir, and Uttarakhand), the desert areas, the tribal (schedule V) areas, and 88 selected tribal and backward districts as identified by the Ministry of Home Affairs/Planning Commission, the objective is to connect eligible unconnected habitations as per Core Network with a population of 250 persons and above (Census 2001). The program envisages single all-weather connectivity to all eligible habitations. In critical LWE affected blocks (as identified by MHA), additional relaxation has been given to connect habitations with population 100 to 249 persons.

Key Features of PMGSY

1. **Decentralized Planning:** The program draws upon the model of decentralized network planning for rural roads. The District Rural Roads Plans (DRRPs) have been developed for all the districts of the country and Core Network has been drawn out of the DRRP to provide for at least a single connectivity to each target habitation under PMGSY. This planning exercise has been carried out with full involvement of the three-tier panchayati raj institutions.
2. **Standards and Specifications:** A manual on geometric standards, design, construction and maintenance of rural roads has been published by the IRC. Subsequently, IRC has prepared and published several codes, which are used in designing of low volume rural roads.
3. **Detailed Project Reports and Scrutiny:** As an important step to achieve quality output for each road under the program, proper survey and adequate investigations are stipulated. A DPR is a pre-requisite for project clearance. Independent scrutiny of the project proposals to ensure the adequacy of design and project preparation is carried out by over 60 prominent institutions of engineering and technology in the country, identified as State Technical Agencies (STAs).
4. **Institutional Arrangements:** Ministry of Rural Development is the nodal ministry for implementation of the program at Central level. National Rural Roads Development Agency (NRRDA) has been constituted to provide technical and managerial support for implementation of the program at the Central level. The state governments have identified state nodal departments and State Rural Roads Development Agencies (SRRDAs) have been constituted for the program implementation at the state level.
5. **Procurement Process:** Based on best national and international practices, a Standard Bidding Document (SBD) has been developed for procurement of works under the PMGSY. All the works under the program are being procured and managed on the basis of provisions of the SBD. To ensure transparency and harness various advantages of electronic tendering, the entire bidding for procurement of works under the program is being carried out only through e-procurement.
6. **Quality Assurance:** Quality is the essence of this program. As such, a three-tier quality management mechanism has been institutionalized under PMGSY.

7. **Maintenance:** With a view to ensure sustainability of road assets created under the program, each contract under the program provides for defect liability of five years along with paid routine maintenance after completion of the work by the same contractor.
8. **Online Monitoring, Management, and Accounting System:** In view of full transparency in various aspects of program implementation, a web based online monitoring, management, and accounting system (OMMAS) has been developed for the program.
9. **Operations Manual and Program Monitoring:** All the operations under the PMGSY program have been systematically laid down in the "operations manual" that was published in 2005. This manual provides for details of all the processes encompassing institutional structures, planning, design, project preparation, procurement, targets, and achievements.

Funds Requirement

Total cost of sanctioned projects, including the projects for upgradation of roads under PMGSY, is ₹1,851.190 billion. Net funds required during Twelfth Fifth Year Plan (at 2010–11 prices) for completing the works sanctioned and yet to be sanctioned has been projected to Planning Commission. Accordingly, an allocation of ₹1,050.000 billion has been made for the Twelfth Five Year Plan (2012–17) period. Details about the current sources of funds for the Program are as under:

- Cess on High Speed Diesel (HSD) at 0.75/liter)
- Budgetary Support
- Asian Development Bank (ADB)
- World Bank Loan
- NABARD Loan

Progress of MGSY as a Component of Bharat Nirman

The Government of India has identified "Rural Roads" as one of the six components of "Bharat Nirman" with a goal to provide connectivity to all eligible unconnected habitations with a population of 1,000 persons and above (as per 2001 census) in plain areas and 500 persons and above in the case of hilly or tribal (schedule V) areas with an all-weather road.

As of March, 2014 a total of 51,253 habitations had been connected out of 63,940 habitations to be connected and works for connecting 62,876 habitations had been sanctioned.

Provision of Urban Amenities in Rural Areas (PURA)[8]

Lack of livelihood opportunities, modern amenities, and services for decent living in rural areas force people to migrate to urban areas. There are wide gaps in the availability of basic infrastructure and social amenities between rural and urban areas. To address these issues, the former president of India Dr A. P. J. Abdul Kalam articulated a vision of transformation of rural India through launching a mega mission for PURA. Seven pilot projects were implemented from 2004–05 during the Tenth Five Year Plan in Basmath (Maharashtra), Bharthana (Uttar Pradesh), Gohpur (Assam), Kujanga (Odisha), Motipur (Bihar), Rayadurg (Andhra Pradesh), and Shahpura (Rajasthan), with a total budget of ₹300 million. There were seven clusters selected in the seven states, with budgets of ₹40—50 million per cluster. The implementation of the pilot phase did not yield the desired results as it faced the following issues (Planning Commission 2013, 311–13).

- The pilot projects lacked a detailed business plan and there was limited participation by the private sector.
- The pilot projects were predominantly infrastructure-oriented, with limited attention being given to the implementation of economic activities.
- The criteria for selection of the clusters did not consider the growth potential for that area.
- There was no ownership at the state government level and the entire implementation lacked an appropriate institutional structure with dedicated professional support.
- There was no convergence with other schemes of rural development or other departments.

Given the experience of the pilot projects, and based on the feedback/comments received during consultations with officials of state governments, a restructured PURA was launched in the Eleventh Five Year Plan as a demand-driven program through public private partnership (PPP) between gram panchayats and private sector partners.

The restructured scheme proposes holistic and accelerated development of compact areas around potential growth center in a gram panchayat (or a group of gram panchayats) through public private partnership (PPP) framework for providing livelihood opportunities and urban amenities to improve the quality of life in rural areas. The scheme is being implemented on pilot basis.

An illustrative list of amenities and economic activities proposed to be provided under PURA are presented in Table 11.2.

The PURA schemes administered by the Ministry of Rural Development/other Ministries are converged in Capital Expenditure (CAPEX) provision of PURA projects. The implementation is done following the guidelines stipulated for each of the identified schemes. It is expected that the developer shall invest some capital on his own to fund the essential infrastructure. In addition, a capital grant limited to a maximum of 35% of the project cost or ₹420 million whichever is less is provided to private developers. Under the scheme the private developer shall be responsible for creating and managing the designated infrastructure and amenities in the panchayat area over a period of ten years.

A concession agreement is signed between the gram panchayat as the grantor and the private developer as the concessionaire. It includes details of minimum service level standards,

Table 11.2: *An Illustrative List of Proposed Amenities and Economic Activities under PURA*

Amenities to be Provided under MoRD Schemes (Compulsory Activities)	*Amenities to be Provided under Non-MoRD Schemes*	*Add-on Projects*
• Water and sewerage • Construction and maintenance of village streets • Drainage • Solid waste management • Skill development • Development of economic activities	• Village street lighting • Telecom • Electricity, etc.	• Village-linked tourism • Integrated rural hub, rural market • Agri-common Services Centre, • Warehousing, etc. • Any other rural-economy based project

Source: MoRD (2014), Annual Report 2013–14, p. 76.

performance guarantees, and so on. A state support agreement is also signed between the Ministry of Rural Development, state government and private developer.

As at the end of the Financial Year 2014, the first batch of PURA pilot projects (PURA 1.0) was underway in five states, namely, Kerala, Andhra Pradesh, Uttarakhand, Rajasthan, and Maharashtra. For the second batch of PURA pilot projects (PURA 2.0), 47 private sector entities had been qualified and the request for proposal (RfP) had been issued to the qualified entities.

Rural Infrastructure Development Fund[9]

NABARD has created a special fund, called the RIDF in 1995–96. The fund is augmented by channelizing the shortfall in the mandatory share of priority sector lending by commercial banks. Though the fund initially focused on incomplete irrigation, flood protection and watershed management projects, funding for rural infrastructure became more broad-based through the years. The RIDF now covers 34 activities related to rural infrastructure development. With allocations in every Union Budget since its inception, RIDF has evolved as a major and popular source of finance to state governments. This long-term partnership between NABARD and the state governments has strengthened over the last two decades.

With its experience of managing the RIDF for nearly 20 years, NABARD has gathered significant insights in matters related to rural infrastructure. As an indirect outcome, NABARD has developed internal capabilities in financing and facilitating the creation of rural infrastructure and has expanded its contribution to this domain through various other initiatives as well.

An amount of ₹2,50,000 million was allocated to the Tranche XX of the RIDF in the Union Budget 2014–15. This is a 25% growth over the past two financial years. From an initial allocation of ₹20 billion under RIDF I, the cumulative resources routed through the RIDF reached ₹2,175 billion including the Tranche XX.

National Rural Health Mission (NRHM)[10]

Rural health care infrastructure is an important determinant of rural development. The rural areas in India are at a disadvantage vis-a-vis urban areas in terms of adequacy and reliability of health care system. The health care infrastructure in rural areas has been developed as a three-tier system and is based on the population norms as presented in Table 11.3.

Sub centers are the most peripheral and first contact point between the primary health care system and the community. Sub centers are assigned tasks relating to interpersonal communication in order to bring about behavioral change and provide services in relation to maternal and child health, family welfare, nutrition, immunization, diarrhoea control, and control of communicable diseases programs. Each sub center is required to be manned by at least one auxiliary nurse midwife (ANM)/female health worker and one male health worker. As on March 31, 2015, there were 1,53,655 subcenters functioning in the country.

Table 11.3: *Population Norms for Creation of Health Care Facilities in Rural Areas of India*

Type of Health Care Facility	*Population Norm*	
	Plains Areas	*Tribal/Hill/Other Remote Areas*
Sub-center	5,000	3,000
Primary Health Center (PHC)	30,000	20,000
Community Health Center (CHC)	1,20,000	80,000

PHC is the first contact point between village community and the medical officer. The PHCs were envisaged to provide an integrated curative and preventive health care to the rural population with emphasis on preventive and promotive aspects of health care. The PHCs are established and maintained by the state governments under the MNP/BMS program. As per minimum requirement, a PHC is to be manned by a medical officer supported by 14 paramedical and other staff. Under NRHM, there is a provision for two additional staff nurses at PHCs on contract basis. It acts as a referral unit for six sub centers and has four–six beds for patients. The activities of PHC involve curative, preventive, promotive, and family welfare services. As on March 31, 2015, there were 25,308 PHCs functioning in the country.

Community health centers (CHCs) are established and maintained by the state government under MNP/BMS program. As per minimum norms, a CHC is required to be manned by four medical specialists, that is, surgeon, physician, gynecologist, and pediatrician supported by 21 paramedical and other staff (See Annexure-I for IPHS norms). It has 30 in-door beds with one OT, X-ray, labor room and laboratory facilities. It serves as a referral center for four PHCs and also provides facilities for obstetric care and specialist consultations. As on March 31, 2015, there were 5,396 CHCs functioning in the country.

The NRHM was launched on April 12, 2005, to provide accessible, equitable, affordable, and quality health care to the rural population, especially the vulnerable groups. Under the NRHM, the Empowered Action Group (EAG) states as well as North Eastern states, Jammu & Kashmir, and Himachal Pradesh have been given special focus. The thrust of the mission is on establishing a fully functional, community owned, decentralized health delivery system with inter-sectoral convergence at all levels, to ensure simultaneous action on a wide range of determinants of health such as water, sanitation, education, nutrition, and social and gender equality. Institutional integration within the fragmented health sector was expected to provide a focus on outcomes, measured against IPHS for all health facilities. The NRHM was initially focused on addressing the health needs of 18 states that had been identified as having weak public health indicators.

Key Features of NRHM

In order to achieve its goals, the mission lays special emphasis on making the public health delivery system fully functional and accountable to the community, human resources management, community involvement, decentralization, rigorous monitoring and evaluation against standards, convergence of health and related programs from village level upward, innovations and flexible financing, and also interventions for improving the health indictors.

Institutional Set Up

At the national level, there is a mission steering group (MSG) headed by the union minister for Health and Family Welfare (FW) and an Empowered Programme Committee (EPC) headed by the union secretary for Health and FW. The EPC will implement the mission under the overall guidance of the MSG.

At the state level, the mission would function under the overall guidance of the State Health Mission headed by the chief minister of the state. The functions under the mission would be carried out through the state Health and Family Welfare Society.

NRHM aims to undertake architectural correction of the health system to enable it to effectively handle increased allocations and promote policies that strengthen public health management and service delivery in the country. It has the following key components:

- Provision of a female health activist in each village;
- A village health plan prepared through a local team headed by the Village Health, Sanitation and Nutrition Committee (VHS&NC) of the panchayat;

- Strengthening of the rural hospital for effective curative care and made measurable and accountable to the community through Indian public health standards (IPHS); and
- Integration of vertical health and family welfare programs, optimal utilization of funds and infrastructure, and strengthening delivery of primary healthcare.

NRHM seeks to revitalize local health traditions and mainstream ayurveda, yoga and naturopathy, unani, siddha, and homoeopathy (AYUSH) into the public health system. It further aims at effective integration of health concerns with determinants of health like sanitation and hygiene, nutrition, and safe drinking water through a district plan for health. It seeks decentralization of programs for district management of health and to address the inter-state and inter-district disparities, especially among the 18 high focus states, including unmet needs for public health infrastructure. It also seeks to improve access of rural people, especially poor women and children, to equitable, affordable, accountable, and effective primary healthcare.

Key Points

1. Natural resources and infrastructure constitute the production base of India's economy and play an important role in the process of development. The rural areas of India are at a great disadvantage vis-à-vis the urban areas in terms of provision of basic infrastructure.
2. As the backward areas in India are very poor in natural resources endowment as well the basic infrastructure, corrective measures in the form of several area-specific, natural resources-based, and infrastructure development programs were launched in those areas from time to time.
3. The major natural resources development programs launched in economically backward and environmentally fragile areas include the DPAP, the Desert DDP, the IWDP, NAP, and the NWDPRA.
4. To protect the farmers against the adverse effects of climatic aberrations, such as drought and floods, two schemes, namely, NAIS and the pilot scheme for WBCIS were launched. Now both these schemes as also other agricultural insurance schemes are subsumed in the NCIP, which is now underway throughout the country. The WBCIS was initially implemented on a pilot basis in the state of Karnataka and now is being implemented as an independent scheme of NCIP in 18 selected states beginning rabi 2013–14 season.
5. The major infrastructure development programs now underway in India are the IAY and the PMGSY, the PURA, and the NRHM. The creation of the RIDF under the NABARD was a major landmark in the government's effort to improve the rural infrastructure.
6. There are no rigorous evaluation studies of the impact and effectiveness of most of natural resources and infrastructure development programs available. However, a Technical Committee on DPAP and DDP under the chairmanship of C. H. Hanumantha Rao reviewed those programs. The committee found the performance of the programs poor. The main reasons identified by the committee for the poor performance included the failure of the implementing agencies to adopt the watershed approach, lack of people's participation in planning and implementation of the program, inadequacy of funds, and non-availability of trained personnel.

Questions for Discussion

1. Illustrate with an example the role of natural resources, especially, land, water and forests, in the process of rural development.
2. Illustrate with an example the role of electricity and rural roads in the process of rural development.
3. Discuss how good rural infrastructure can reduce the incidence of poverty (Hint: see the paper by P. Satish, referred to in this chapter.)
4. Write a critique of the Drought-prone Area Programme (DPAP) and Desert Development Programme (DDP).
5. Write a critique of the public private partnership (PPP) approach to infrastructure development.

Notes

1. Infrastructure is an umbrella term that subsumes many activities referred to as Social Overhead Capital (SOC) by development economists.
2. This section is largely based on MoRD 2014: 168–69.
3. This section is largely based on MoRD 2014: 170–72.
4. http://naeb.nic.in/ (Accessed on April 18, 2016)
5. www.agricoop.nic.in/dacdivision/NWDPRA8410.pdf (Accessed on December 3, 2015).
6. This section is largely based on MoRD 2015: 80–86.
7. This section is largely based on (MoRD 2014, Ch. 5: pp. 27–48) www.rural.nic.in
8. This section is largely based on (MoRD 2014, Annual Report 2013–14: 76–77).
9. This section is reproduced from NABARD 2015, Annual Report 2014–15, 141–42.
10. This is largely based on the Rural Health Care System in India, Ministry of Health and Family Welfare, GoI, New Delhi (http://nrhm.gov.in)

Chapter 12

Planning for Rural Development

LEARNING OUTCOMES

After having gone through this chapter, students should be able to:

- **Define the terms 'plan' and 'planning', and explain their rationale;**
- **Enumerate the functions of planning at the micro, meso, and macro levels;**
- **Explain why decentralization of planning in countries such as India is necessary;**
- **List the major steps in micro-level planning with special reference to agriculture;**
- **Describe the methodology for block- and district-level planning followed in India, and**
- **List the major components of an ideal development project.**

Introduction

A plan is a blueprint for action. It points out a precise way to reach a predetermined goal, or a set of goals, within a predetermined period of time with the means that are available with the planner and under the prevailing circumstances. Planning is the process of formulating a plan. Development planning as a process involves the application of a rational system of choices among the feasible courses of investment and other development possibilities, based on a consideration of economic and social costs and benefits. In the context of a quantitative planning model, planning may be defined as a process of determining an optimal mix of alternative investment activities, so as to maximize the objective function under the given constraints. Howsoever we define planning, it implies an organized, conscious, and continued effort to achieve specific goals in the future.

In every country, some development always occurs naturally (autonomous development), but it may not be sufficient to maintain a socially desirable level of living in the country. Therefore, some sort of government intervention in the economic system is needed in almost every country to initiate and foster a higher rate of development (induced development). These days, governments in virtually all the countries are engaged in one way or another, and to a small or large extent, in planning and regulating their economic activities. However, planning makes a positive contribution only if, through it, the objectives are achieved more rapidly and more efficiently than if development followed natural forces. Planning can contribute to development mainly through direct provision and allocation of scarce resources by the government, regulation and direction of resource allocation decisions in the private sector, coordination of public and private actions, and guiding the use of private resources through the manipulation of market forces.

Levels and Functions of Planning

Problems in planning can be identified and, consequently, planning can be carried out at the national and state levels (macro level), at the level of the individual unit of production (micro level), and at the intermediate level (meso level). The planning function at the national and state levels consists mainly of defining the goals of development effort; projecting population growth, and demand and supply of important goods and services; estimating and mobilizing the necessary domestic and foreign resources of money and skills; and allocating them to those specific uses among different sectors of the economy that seem likely to make the greatest contribution to achieving the national goals. Macro-planning is, of necessity, based on highly aggregated data and on considerations that are usually of broad significance. Planning at the district and block levels may be considered as meso-level (intermediate) planning. The main function of meso-level planning is to translate the macro-level plan into concrete and operational programs and projects, taking into consideration the peculiar characteristics and requirements of the district/block concerned.

Micro-level planning refers to planning at the level of the basic unit of production, which may be a farm, a factory, a household enterprise, or any other production/service unit. Micro-planning is concerned with the what, how much, how, when, and where questions relating to production, consumption, credit, and marketing. In a nutshell, micro-level planning is concerned with the allocation of the resources of the planning entity concerned, to maximize whatever goals the entity may have.

In the context of rural development planning, micro-level planning has the following major roles to play:

1. Reveal the prospective needs of farmers (or any other rural producers) for production inputs and credit, so that a suitable supply scheme could be designed.
2. Determine the best alternatives for reorganization of the rural business units, so as to utilize the public services and facilities completely.
3. Furnish basic information for the formulation and evaluation of rural development projects.
4. Aid in projecting the effects of changes in technology, prices, and public programs and policies on rural production, income, and employment.
5. Serve as an aid to the rural development extension worker in establishing an effective working relationship with rural producers, and in educating them in scientific methods of farming.

If micro-level planning is to play an effective role in the modernization of India's rural economy, it must be treated as an integral part of development planning. Micro-planning, in and of itself, is not of much use in the formulation and implementation of national development plans and policies. Micro-plans should be vertically integrated with national plans via the regional/area planner. He/she is at an intermediate level between the micro- and macro-planning systems, and his/her job should be to blend them together, relying on his/her knowledge of the overall plan and familiarity with the micro details of the region. It is his/her task to bring about a synthesis of macro- and micro-planning in such a way that what is desirable at the national/state level will be made worthwhile and feasible for the individual producer and consumer.

Horizontal integration embraces inter-sectoral coordination between different sectors—agriculture, industry, and services—within a specific spatial framework. Micro-plans should be horizontally integrated with the plans for supply of production inputs and credit, marketing, infrastructure development, and industrial development for the area.

India's approach to development planning has been predominantly macro-oriented, emphasizing national goals and priorities. The national planners really do not know whether their targets can, in effect, be achieved and what it takes to achieve them. And the planners at the sub-national levels do not know what the effect of their plans would be on the aggregate input requirements and aggregate output of the country as a whole. Thus, for successful and effective planning, it is necessary that the macro- and micro-plans are harmonized at some intermediate (region/area) level. In a nutshell, to make development planning effective, we must follow a two-pronged approach, working simultaneously and in a coordinated way from the grassroots level up, and the national level down.

The term "area planning" is highly fashionable nowadays, and is widely acclaimed in both advanced and developing countries. The term is used in many different ways and in vastly divergent contexts. We shall use the term to refer to planning for the overall development of a single area, usually an economically backward and ecologically fragile area, within the broad framework set by the national development planning. In essence, we imply, by this term, a multi-level and decentralized planning approach to the overall development of an economy.

Rural development is the end result of interactions between various technological, economic, social, and institutional factors. For example, to increase total output from an individual farm, it is necessary to introduce new technology adapted to local ecological and socio-economic conditions, to educate and train the farmer in its use, to provide him/her with sufficient resources at the proper time and place, and to create the necessary infrastructure of service facilities for supply and marketing. Ultimately, however, it is the response of the individual producer to these measures that determines the success or failure of the development plan. The area approach to development planning, therefore, emphasizes the role of the people, their potentialities, and their motivations. Besides, this approach is integrative, in the sense that it assesses the significance of all the factors affecting the development process.

The area approach to development planning can contribute to the achievement of the following main objectives of national planning in India:

1. Accelerate the development of lagging areas.
2. Reduce interregional disparities in development and growth.
3. Provide the basic disaggregation of national planning with respect to agriculture and other sectors of the economy.
4. Facilitate coordination and integration of planning and implementation at various levels.
5. Coordinate agricultural and rural development with the overall area development plans.
6. Facilitate the wider involvement of people in the process of preparation and implementation of development projects.

Decentralization of Planning

In view of different agro-climatic, techno-economic and socio-cultural factors occurring in different regions of India, national planning, to be realistic and effective, has to be decentralized to sub-national/sub-state levels. Decentralization or regionalization of planning and development is a logical step for a democracy. This is a movement that permits the wider involvement of people in the process of planning and implementation, and reduces the discrepancies between national and sub-national plans that arise from regional or area characteristics that differ from national assumptions.

The need for decentralization was recognized in the Fourth Five Year Plan and a modest beginning was made in the direction of extending planning to the state, regional and district levels. In September 1969, the Planning Commission issued detailed instructions to the state governments on how to formulate district plans. In the Fifth Five Year Plan, special emphasis was laid on the area/regional approach to development planning, particularly in the backward areas. In November 1977, the Planning Commission appointed a working group under the chairmanship of M. L. Dantwala to draw up guidelines for block level planning. The group submitted its report in 1978, which emphasized the need for strengthening the planning team at the district level and for the integration of the block plan with the district plan. In 1979, the Union Department of Rural Development prepared a brochure on the methodology for planning and implementation of the IRDP.

There have also been quite a few attempts by state governments and other organizations to frame block level plans. Having taken cognizance of all these efforts, the Planning Commission, in December 1979, issued "Guidelines for Block Level Planning." These guidelines covered only some broad and essential aspects of block level planning, and it was understood that the Union Ministry of Rural Development and the state governments would supplement and elaborate these guidelines further from time to time, as considered necessary.

In 1980, the then Union Ministry of Rural Reconstruction (now Ministry of Rural Development) prepared a "Manual on Integrated Rural Development Programme," which included, inter alia, procedures and formats for preparing household, village, and block plans (GoI 1980). The block and district level plans for the IRDP were to be formulated as per the Planning Commission's "guidelines for block level planning." In April 1982, the Union Ministry of Rural Development issued "operational guidelines for block level plans for Integrated Rural Development Programme" in consultation with the Planning Commission, the state governments and other organizations involved in rural development. These guidelines were in the nature of a broad frame of reference to enable those who were engaged in the implementation of IRDP, to draw up sound and locally appropriate programs and action plans. The guidelines envisaged preparation of a five-year development profile or a perspective plan, as well as an annual action plan for each block.

The block level perspective plans were to be aggregated at the district level, based on the practical possibilities of development in the primary, secondary, and tertiary sectors. The Integrated Rural Development (IRD) block plan was to be integrated with the development programs of other departments, and it was eventually to be a component of the comprehensive block development plan. A five-year credit plan and an annual credit plan were also to be prepared for each block, and were to be a part of the IRD block plan. The procedures and formats for the preparation of the five-year perspective plan, block credit plan, cluster plan, and household plan were specified in the guidelines. But sadly, no comprehensive integrated plans were developed at the block and the district levels, following the manual, due to the lack of requisite manpower and expertise. However, five-year credit plans at the block and the district levels were prepared in most of the states. Later, at the instance of Planning Commission, comprehensive five year plans were prepared by selected NGOs for 150 most backward districts in the country under the new Food-for-Work (FFW) Programme. However, to sum up, we could say that so far there has not been any meaningful decentralization of planning in India below the state level.

Methodology of Micro-level Planning

Micro-planning is essentially a two-stage process of diagnosis and prescription. The first stage consists of a preliminary survey of local conditions for an appraisal of natural and human resources, institutions, and infrastructural facilities and services available in the area to obtain a proximate view of the organization and management of individual rural enterprises, including farms and their major handicaps and shortcomings, and to identify the major constraints on—and opportunities for increasing—income and employment. The second stage is to work out improved micro plans for representative types and size groups of rural enterprises.

To be successful and effective, micro-planning requires an interdisciplinary approach. The technical agricultural scientists—the agronomist, the horticulturist, and the agricultural engineer—and the social scientists should work together to identify the major possibilities of—and key constraints on—increasing production and income in the area, to design appropriate research and action programs to remove or minimize the constraints, and to exploit the potentialities and to test, on a limited scale, these programs under real world conditions.

The important components of a sound micro-planning program can be elaborated as follows, with special reference to the farm subsector.

Farm Planning and Programming

The first step necessary to implement this component of the program is to identify and delineate the major farming areas of the country. Two types of areas may be identified to meet different agricultural planning needs. First, crop regions that would be appropriate for central production planning of major crops. Second, agro-climatic regions/areas that could be used for overall agricultural planning by the district, state, and central governments.

In India, several attempts have been made in the past to delineate areas based on several criteria. The most comprehensive work on agro-climatic classification of the country was the one done by the Agro-climatic Regional Planning (ACRP) unit of the Planning Commission. The unit has recommended the adoption of the ACRP approach for bringing about balanced, sustainable agricultural and rural development. The ACRP approach was based on the optimum utilization of land and water resources through decentralized and participatory planning, which has been facilitated by the 73rd and 74th Constitution amendments. The ACRP project was launched by the Planning Commission in 1988. The project had generated a large volume of high quality research-based information, useful for agricultural planning (Basu and Guha 1996; Basu and Kashyap 1996). However, like so many other good initiatives, the ACRP approach also was not institutionalized and it did not become an integral part of overall national and regional development planning.

Ideally, for each major agro-climatic region or area, a sample of 50–100 typical farms should be selected on the basis of their representativeness of the most important farm types (with respect to soils, farm size, and so on) of the area. In cooperation with the selected farmers, a farm business survey should be conducted, and information about input–output coefficients, resource availability, and the kind and level of predetermined activities collected. Cooperation with agronomists is necessary to acquire information on improved crop varieties and their yield response to fertilizers, with animal scientists for information on high-yielding breeds of milch animals and appropriate feeding practices, and with agricultural engineers on the technical feasibility of using tractors and machinery for various field operations and transportation. This information may be generated by conducting sample trials and demonstrations on farmers' fields. On the basis of these technical data and the data obtained from the sample farmers, a set of alternative farm plans are worked out, indicating the range of different crops and livestock combinations that are technically feasible.

Linear programming is by far the most commonly used tool for micro-level planning. This technique can be used to determine:

1. The most profitable combination of crop and livestock activities under varying assumptions about the level of technology, resource availability, and input and output prices;
2. The optimal amount of outside financing needed to maximize the returns to the farmers' fixed resources;
3. The least-cost methods and techniques of production to employ in those cases where alternative techniques are available;
4. The sensitivity of the farm plans to variations in the values assumed for various economic factors included in the model; and
5. The shadow prices of scarce resources/inputs, which would serve to direct the type of investment that should be made.

The inputs and outputs from the farm plans are aggregated for the major farming areas and the nation, and are evaluated with respect to national production needs and the possibilities of meeting the supply requirements for various inputs and services. Not many details are required, and only a few selected major products and input items are handled.

Harmonizing Local Farm Plans and National Production Targets

The farm management specialist works out a set of farm plans for a certain area, without reference to what would be the effect of the farm plans so prepared on aggregate output and aggregate supply requirements of the various farming areas and the country as a whole. On the other hand, the macro-economist works out a set of production targets on the basis of past production records, prospective demand, nutritional needs, foreign exchange requirement, and so on, none of which are based on the particular agricultural resources and the potential production capacity of various agricultural areas of the country. Hence, the national planners really do not know whether their production targets can, in effect, be achieved, or what it takes to achieve them. The farm management researchers really do not know what effect the adoption of a series of specific improvements in farming methods and enterprise combinations would have on the aggregate output of various products, on the aggregate requirements of inputs, on the total supply and demand, and on the import and export situation of the country.

Harmonizing local farm plans and national production targets requires a tentative breakdown of the national production targets into the major farming areas, and comparison with the aggregated farm plans for the farming areas and the nation as a whole. Major discrepancies between the national plan targets and the national production (aggregated from farm plans for important individual agricultural products) are harmonized by working out alternatives acceptable from the point of view of both the national needs and local production feasibility. Similarly, the aggregate input requirements derived from the farm plans are evaluated in the context of national supply prospects, financial feasibility, and foreign exchange considerations. Infrastructural investments needed for the facilities of transporting, marketing, storing, and processing are stressed, as this makes the required supplies of inputs available to the farms in various areas, and moves the increased output efficiently through the market channels.

Improving External Environmental Conditions

Changes in the external socio-economic and institutional conditions affecting the farmers' incentive to adopt a desirable farm plan and their ability to implement it, are explored in each farming area. We must identify those external factors that impede the implementation of the farm production plans, and indicate the specific incentives required for farmers to improve their production efficiency. Among these factors, the prevailing tenure arrangements, cost–price relationships, marketing facilities, availability of inputs at the farm level, nature and effectiveness of extension and other government services, cooperatives, and so on are of crucial importance.

The methodology of micro-level planning specified previously is an ideal one. In practice, this methodology was never followed in India except in cases where some reputed research institute specializing in agricultural planning, or an agricultural economist trained in farm planning and management, was involved in formulating the micro plans. The main reason for not following the ideal methodology is the lack of requisite manpower and expertise at the block and district levels.

Methodology for Block- and District-level Planning

Almost all past efforts at development planning are characterized by the lack of an appropriate methodology for both planning and implementation at the sub-national levels. Conscious of this fact, as stated earlier in the section "Decentralization of Planning" of this chapter, the Planning Commission constituted a working group in 1977 under the chairmanship of M. L. Dantwala in order to draw up detailed guidelines for block level planning. The Dantwala Working Group asserted in its report that no serious attempt had been made so far to induct technical skills in planning at the district level, even in states that have set up some sort of district planning machinery. The working group recommended the following guidelines for planning at the block and district levels (GoI 1978b, 4):

1. Prepare and analyze resource inventories to assess the prevailing level of development, potential for further development, and to identify constraints on further development.
2. Determine priorities of various programs proposed for the area and identify a catalytic program.
3. Formulate programs and projects for development, and establish their spatial and temporal linkages within an integrated frame work.
4. Devise a plan for fuller utilization of manpower resources.
5. Assess the availability of financial resources from various sources, such as the district budget, banking system, and private sector, and mobilize the same.
6. Provide for monitoring and concurrent evaluation, or parallel audit of development plans and their modification from time to time in the light of experience.

These guidelines define the scope of the functions of the planning team alright, but they are of little help to the planner as far as the actual mechanics of formulating, evaluating, and integrating various projects is concerned. The planner needs a framework that could guide him in collecting and processing data, and in formulating, ranking, and combining various projects in optimal proportions, given a set of technical, economic, and institutional constraints, and a choice criterion.

We now make a modest attempt to outline such a framework. The planning framework consists of a number of components, which are described as follows.

Delineation of Viable Areas for Planning

This is the first logical step in the process of rural development planning. Several factors, such as cohesiveness, locus of economic activities, an adequate resource base for self- sustained growth, and the nature of the development programs, need to be considered in identifying and delineating the areas for planning.

The question of an appropriate basic planning unit still continues to be controversial. But it seems that the community development block has been accepted as the primary unit for local planning. But block level planning will have to be built within the framework of district level planning, which has to be adjusted to the state plan, which forms part of the national plan. On the other hand, the use of the district as the basic planning unit is advocated on the grounds that time series area and production data are not available in published form for any units smaller than the district.

In the present situation in India, the block may be a convenient administrative unit for planning and implementing area development programs, with clusters of villages delineated on the basis of micro-watersheds/command areas within the block serving as the ultimate units for micro-level planning. The framework for integrated planning outlined in this chapter is based on the concept of multi-level planning, with clusters of villages (sub-areas) serving as the ultimate units of micro-level planning.

Determination and Quantification of Plan Objectives

This is the second step in the process of area planning. The objectives set for the area plan should represent the collective needs of the people living in the area, and should be realistic and operational. From the past experience with planned development, it has become abundantly clear that it is no longer appropriate to formulate the principal objectives of a plan in terms of a specific target of growth only. The rate of growth in income and production that is achieved during the plan period is of little importance, if it does not result in the reduction of the worst forms of poverty and unemployment. The essential point is that a high rate of growth has not been, and is not, any guarantee against worsening poverty and unemployment. "How much is produced, how fast, and what is produced and how" are all equally important. Keeping this in view, we can specify the following as the main objectives of planning at the block and district levels:

1. Maximizing production in agriculture and allied activities in the rural areas using most cost-effective techniques and methods.
2. Eradication of unemployment and significant underemployment.
3. An appreciable improvement in the level of living of the poorest sections of the population.
4. Provision by the state of certain basic amenities such as drinking water, elementary education, adult literacy, health care, rural roads and rural housing for the landless.

Identification of Target Groups

To achieve the plan objectives, a comprehensive and integrated area plan covering the entire rural population is called for. For the purposes of planning, the target population can be broadly classified into four categories, as follows:

1. Farm households possessing landholdings of economic size
2. Farm households possessing landholdings of uneconomic size
3. Landless agricultural laborers
4. Rural artisans

The population falling in the first category would require technical assistance and guidance, as well as supply of inputs and institutional finance in order to be able to adopt the new farm technology appropriate for the area. If farmers in this category adopt new farm technology, it will substantially increase farm production, and will also generate considerable employment opportunities to absorb a significant proportion of the rural unemployed.

For the households in the second category, high-value and labor-intensive crops will need to be identified, and their production and marketing facilitated. Besides crop production, some complementary and supplementary enterprises, such as dairying, poultry, bee-keeping, pisciculture, and sericulture will also need to be introduced on these farms to supplement their income.

For landless agricultural laborers and rural artisans, a set of cottage and small-scale industries, and rural crafts will need to be identified and evaluated in terms of their technical and economic feasibility, and social acceptability. A massive program of appropriate rural crafts and industries would require upgrading of traditional skills, setting up a chain of training-cum-production centers, supply of raw materials and credit, and institutional arrangements for marketing of the output.

In the first two years of the plan, the first category of target population may be left out of the plan fold, and the resources available for development may be devoted to the betterment of the quality of life of the lowest three strata of the population.

Resource Appraisal and Identification of Constraints on Development

After identifying the target groups, the next step in the process of area planning is to appraise the quantity and quality of natural, human, and artificially created resources available in the area, and those likely to be available from outside the area for the implementation of the plan. The process of resource appraisal would also facilitate the identification of constraints on any further development of the area. Resource appraisal is a multidisciplinary endeavor, requiring the collaboration of meteorologists, hydrologists, plant scientists, animal scientists, soil scientists, agricultural engineers, and social scientists.

Technical scientists appraise the environmental attributes (land, water, plants, fish, livestock, and mineral resources) and the available technologies to exploit them, whereas social scientists appraise the attributes of human resources, institutions, and organizations. The end product of the appraisal is a comprehensive resource inventory of the biophysical and socio-economic phenomena. The use of a proforma facilitates the resource appraisal exercise and the preparation of resource inventories.

Most of the information required for preparing a resource inventory is usually available with various government departments, and other public and private agencies and organizations. Some of the information, such as input use, yield rates, income and expenditure patterns, and sources and structure of employment will need to be collected afresh from a representative sample of the target population. Preparation of a preliminary plan format would help in gathering the right kind of information and should, therefore, precede data collection.

The resource inventory should be analyzed to identify the major constraints on the achievement of the objectives of area planning. Some of the constraints may be technological, others economic and institutional, and still others social and cultural in nature. The constraints may be identified by direct contact with the people, area leaders, extension workers, and program administrators. Some of the constraints could be removed or relaxed within the plan period with the resource, technology, and institutional framework already available in the area.

On the other hand, there could be some other constraints that may require a longer time to be removed than the proposed plan period. Their alleviation may require further basic and/ or applied research and/or a new institutional structure, which may not be feasible during the proposed plan period. After their identification, the constraints should be listed according to (a) their significance, as measured in terms of economic losses suffered by the people when they are present and (b) the relative ease with which they can be removed within the plan period.

Identification and Selection of Development Projects

The next step in the process of area planning is to prepare a list of all technically feasible activities/enterprises, which could be taken up in the area. This is again a multi-disciplinary endeavor. Insights gained from resource appraisal would prove helpful in the identification of (agro-technically) appropriate activities for the area. The activities would include those that are already prevalent in the area, as well as those found successful under similar conditions elsewhere. The following four criteria seem to be appropriate in identifying such projects:

1. The activities should be technically and organizationally feasible.
2. The activities should directly or indirectly contribute to the objectives of the plan.
3. The activities should be legally permissible.
4. The activities should be, by and large, socially acceptable.

The criteria for selection of projects for an area are largely furnished by the values and preferences of the people living in the area. Generally speaking, four criteria—efficiency, equity, employment, and sustainability—can be used to make a choice from amongst a shelf of projects initially identified as appropriate.

Formulation of Development Projects

After having identified and selected various projects for inclusion in the plan, the next step is to formulate detailed projects for the activities so selected. Each of the projects should specify the following:

1. Title of the project
2. Rationale for the project
3. Duration of the project
4. Objectives of the project
5. Location of the project
6. Target groups to be covered
7. Details of the technology to be adopted
8. Cost-benefit calculations
9. Indicators of success
    - Increase in production of major produce
    - Increase in income

- Incremental employment
- Distribution of project benefits among the target groups
- Impact on environment and ecology
- Social acceptability
- Sustainability

10. Financing strategy
    - Total financial outlay needed
    - Amount likely to be available from the target groups
    - Amount likely to be available from other ongoing government projects
    - Amount likely to be available from various institutional sources
    - Balance to be met from fresh allocations
11. Linkages with other projects
12. Implementation: organizational structure, staffing, flow of funds, and work schedules
13. Arrangements for supplying inputs and disposing output
14. Arrangements for monitoring, feedback, control, and evaluation
15. Anticipated externalities and conflicts, and procedures for their resolution

It is important that a separate project be formulated for each distinct process or activity. For example, if wheat can be produced by three different methods—that is, (a) with the adoption of a complete package of improved inputs and practices, (b) with 50% of the recommended dosage of NPK, and all other improved practices, and (c) with no fertilizers and no other improved practices,—then three separate projects would need to be formulated for it. Similarly, if two different scales of a cottage industry are to be considered, two different projects should be formulated.

The task of project formulation is highly technical in nature and, therefore, can be handled satisfactorily only by a multidisciplinary team of experts. Expertise in project formulation is not usually available at sub-state levels and, therefore, this very crucial phase of planning remains, by and large, neglected. The competence of the planning staff at all levels in the areas of project formulation and appraisal needs to be upgraded. This should be done through special in-service training programs.

Determining Optimal Mix of Development Projects

After having formulated detailed projects, the next step in the process of area planning is to determine the optimal mix or combination of various projects, so as to attain the objectives of the area plan under the given conditions of resource availability, and the technical, economic, institutional, and social constraints. A number of quantitative techniques are now available for planning at both the micro and the macro level. But of all the planning techniques, linear programming is by far the most powerful and flexible tool that can be used for planning. This technique can facilitate:

1. Annual re-planning exercises within the framework of a five-year rolling plan;
2. Testing the effects of changes in projected resource availability, prices and government policies on plan objectives through sensitivity analysis;
3. Estimation of the amount of outside financing needed to meet the objectives of the plan;
4. Estimation of the amount of labor employment that would be generated as a result of the plan; and
5. Investment planning on the basis of shadow prices generated in the linear programming solutions.

A multi-period linear programming model can be used to determine the optimal mix of various activities/projects for an area, a block, a district or a watershed. The model is constructed essentially in a linear programming framework, adding to it the appropriate dynamic equations characterized by flexibility coefficients on the lines of so-called recursive linear programming (RLP). These dynamic equations reflect the dynamic structure of agricultural production, and the psychological and cautious responses of producers to innovations. The formal structure of the model can be presented in its mathematical form as follows (Ramakrishnaiah 1980):

1. Maximize $Z(t) = \sum_{j=1}^{n} C_j(t)X_j(t)$ ($j = 1, \ldots, n$ and $t = 1, \ldots, 5$

   Subject to the constraints

   (i) $\sum_{j=1}^{n} a_{ij}(t)X_j(t) < b_i(t), \; (i = 1, \ldots, m)$

   (ii) $\sum_{j=1}^{n} a_{ij}(t)X_j(t) = b_i(t), \; (i = m + 1, \ldots, p)$

   (iii) $\sum_{j=1}^{n} a_{ij}(t)X_j(t) \geq b_i(t), \; (i = p + 1, \ldots, r)$

   (iv) $X_j(t) \leq (1 + \bar{\beta}_j)X_j\,(t - 1)$

   (v) $X_j(t) \geq (1 - \underline{\beta}_j)X_j\,(t - 1)$

   (vi) $\sum_{j=1}^{n} X_j(t) \leq (1 + \bar{\alpha}) \sum_{j=1}^{n} X_j(t - 1)$

   (vii) $\sum_{j=1}^{n} X_j(t) \geq (1 + \underline{\alpha}) \sum_{j=1}^{n} X_j(t - 1)$

   (viii) $X_j(t) \geq 0$

In the given equations,

$Z(t)$ = returns over variable costs in rupees in year (t);
$C_j(t)$ = returns over variable costs per unit of the jth activity in rupees in year (t);
$X_j(t)$ = units of the jth activity in year (t);
$a_{ij}(t)$ = requirement ($a > 0$) or contribution ($a < 0$) of the jth activity for the ith constraint;
$b_i(t)$ = the ith constraint level of supply—a resource capacity in equation (2), an accounting balance in equation (3), and a requirement to be met in equation (4);
$\bar{\beta}$ = upper flexibility coefficient with respect to the *jth* activity;
$\underline{\beta}_j$ = lower flexibility coefficient with respect to the *jth* activity;
$\bar{\alpha}$ = upper flexibility coefficient with respect to a group of related activities; and
$\underline{\alpha}$ = lower flexibility coefficient with respect to a group of related activities.

This model was used for the formulation of a set of five-year agricultural development plans for a small watershed in the hills of the erstwhile state of Uttar Pradesh (now Uttarakhand) under the guidance of the senior author of this book. The objective function of the model was to maximize the aggregate returns over the variable costs for the watershed, subject to various constraints. The model included 72 activities and 47 constraints. To sum up, we could say that the model is a very powerful and highly flexible tool for formulating multi-period integrated development plans at both micro and macro levels.

It is hoped that with the introduction of computers at the district level, preparation of household, cluster, block and district plans would be facilitated. However, a computer cannot be a substitute for trained and experienced rural development planners, who are a scarce resource at present in India.

Institutional Structure for Planning

At the national level, until January 1, 2015 when the Government of India led by Prime Minister Narendra Modi announced the creation of a new institution called NITI Aayog, the Planning Commission[1] was responsible, among other things, for the formulation of India's Five Year Plans, their mid-term appraisal and allocation of resources to various Centrally sponsored schemes and state governments. The Planning Commission had formulated 12 Five Year Plans during its existence. Now its avatar, NITI Aayog, is supposed to foster the involvement and participation of state governments in the economic policy-making, a "bottom-up" approach to planning in contrast to the Planning Commission's tradition of "top-down" decision-making. NITI Aayog will provide opportunities to represent the economic interests of the state governments and UTs of India. NITI Aayog will act more like a think tank or forum and execute programs by taking the states along with them. This is in sharp contrast with the defunct Planning Commission that imposed five-year-plans and allocated resources while running roughshod over the requests of the various states.

The NITI Aayog comprises the following:

1. Prime minister of India as chairperson
2. Governing council comprising the chief ministers of all the states and UTs with legislatures and lieutenant governors of other UTs.
3. Regional councils will be formed each for a specified tenure to address specific issues and contingencies impacting more than one state or a region. The regional councils will be convened by the prime minister and will be composed of the chief ministers of states and lieutenant governors of UTs in the region. These will be chaired by the chairperson of the NITI Aayog or his/her nominee
4. Experts, specialists, and practitioners with relevant domain knowledge as special invitees nominated by the prime minister
5. Full-time organizational framework (in addition to prime minister as the chairperson) comprising:
   - Vice-chairperson—Arvind Panagariya.
   - Members—Three full-time: Economist Bibek Debroy, former DRDO chief V. K. Saraswat, and agriculture expert Ramesh Chand.
   - Part-time members—Maximum of two from leading universities research organizations and other relevant institutions in an ex-officio capacity. Part-time members will be on a rotational basis.
   - Ex officio members—Maximum of four members of the union council of ministers to be nominated by the prime minister.
   - Chief executive officer—To be appointed by the prime minister for a fixed tenure, in the rank of secretary to the Government of India. Ms Sindhushree Khullar has been appointed as the CEO.
   - Secretariat as deemed necessary.

At the state level, many state governments have constituted state planning commissions or state planning boards for formulating state Five Year Plans. An SDC headed by the chief minister is responsible for directing and coordinating the development programs within the state.

At the district level, after the 73rd Constitution amendment, statutory Zila Parishads are responsible for planning and implementing development programs in the districts. The Zila Parishad is chaired by an elected non-official and the DDO is the CEO of the Zila Parishad. However, there are state to state variations in the organizational structure at the district level.

At the block level, the statutory block parishad or samiti, or block panchayat samiti, which is chaired by an elected non-official, oversees the implementation of development programs in the block. The block development officer (BDO) is the secretary to the block samiti and is responsible for implementation of various development programs.

At the village level, VLWs, or gram sevaks and gram *sevikas*, are responsible for implementing the development programs within a cluster of villages. VLWs work under the advice and control of the BDO. With the establishment of panchayati raj in all states now, the village or gram panchayat, which is headed by an elected non- official, is responsible for implementing the program within its jurisdiction. The VLW assigned to the panchayat acts as its secretary.

The organizational structure described in the preceding paragraphs was developed and came into existence under the CDP, which was launched in the country in October 1952.

Key Points

1. A plan is a blueprint for action. It points out a precise way to reach a predetermined goal or a set of goals within a predetermined period of time with the means that are available with the planner and under the prevailing circumstances. Development planning as a process involves the application of a rational system of choices among feasible courses of investment and other development possibilities, based on a consideration of economic and social costs and benefits.
2. These days, governments in virtually all countries are engaged in one way or another, and to a small or large extent, in planning and regulating their economic activities. However, planning makes a positive contribution only if, through it, the objectives are achieved more rapidly and more efficiently than if development followed natural forces.
3. Planning can contribute to development, mainly through direct provision and allocation of scarce resources by the government, regulation and direction of resource allocation decisions in the private sector, coordination of public and private actions, and guiding the use of private resources through the manipulation of market force.
4. Problems in planning can be identified and, consequently, planning can be carried out at the national and state levels (macro level), at the level of the individual unit of production/enterprise (micro level), and at an intermediate level (meso level).
5. If micro-level planning is to play an effective role in the modernization of India's rural economy, it must be treated as an integral part of development planning. India's approach to development planning has been predominantly macro-oriented, emphasizing national goals and priorities. For successful and effective planning, it is necessary that the macro and micro plans are harmonized at some intermediate (region/area) level.
6. In view of the different agro-climatic, techno-economic, and socio-cultural factors occurring in different regions of India, national planning, to be realistic and effective, has

to be decentralized to sub-national/sub-state levels. Decentralization or regionalization of planning and development is a logical step for a democracy. Despite several attempts at it, there has not been any meaningful decentralization of planning in India below the state level.

7. Planning is essentially a two-stage process of diagnosis and prescription. The first stage consists of an appraisal of natural and human resources, institutions, and infrastructural facilities and services available in an area, and to identify major constraints on—and opportunities for—increasing income and employment. The second stage is to work out improved micro plans for representative types and size groups of rural enterprises.
8. The important components of a sound micro-planning program in the farm subsector are: (a) farm planning and programming; (b) harmonizing local farm plans with national production targets and (c) improving the external environment by removing various constraint.
9. A sound planning framework consists of a number of components such as: (a) delineation of viable areas for planning; (b) determination and quantification of plan objectives; (c) identification of target groups; (d) resource appraisal and identification of constraints on development; (e) identification and selection of development projects/activities; (f) formulation of development projects and (g) determining optimal mix of selected projects.
10. A number of quantitative techniques are now available for planning at both micro and macro levels. But of all the planning techniques, linear programming is by far the most powerful and flexible tool that can be used for planning.
11. At the national level, up until January 1, 2015 when the Government of India led by Prime Minister Narendra Modi announced the creation of a new institution called NITI Aayog, the Planning Commission[1] was responsible, among other things, for formulation of India's Five Year Plans, their mid-term appraisal and allocation of resources to various centrally sponsored schemes and state governments. The Planning Commission had formulated 12 Five Year Plans during its existence. Now its avatar, NITI Aayog, is supposed to is to foster the involvement and participation of state governments in the economic policy-making, a "bottom-up" approach to planning in contrast to the Planning Commission's tradition of "top-down" decision-making.

Questions for Discussion

1. Discuss the problems and prospects of rural development planning in India.
2. Most of the developed countries of the world, including the US and Japan, do not prepare five year plans of development like India does, but despite that they are developed. Why?
3. Why is the integration of micro plans and macro plans necessary? What are the problems in integration?
4. Why is decentralization of planning in India necessary and why there has not been any meaningful decentralization of planning so far?
5. What are the main components of an ideal development project? Select any development project you can have access to and appraise it vis-à-vis an ideal project.

6. Select a district level plan available in your library, or elsewhere, and appraise it with reference to an ideal planning framework.
7. Examine the pros and cons of creation of NITI Aayog in place of the Planning Commission.

Note

1. India's first Prime Minister Jawaharlal Nehru, a socialist who admired Joseph Stalin's drive to industrialize the Soviet Union, set up and chaired the Commission to map out a development path for India's agrarian economy.

Chapter 13

Organizing for Rural Development

LEARNING OUTCOMES

After having gone through this chapter, students should be able to:

- **Define the term "organization" and examine the role of organizations in rural development;**
- **Explain various organizational models and their relevance in India's context;**
- **List some important criteria for designing an appropriate organization; and**
- **Critically examine the suitability of government organizations, panchayati raj institutions (PRIs), cooperatives and voluntary agencies (VAs)/NGOs, and corporations for promoting rural development.**

Introduction

By "organizing for rural development," we mean (a) designing appropriate organizational structures, (b) facilitating desirable human behavior within the organization, and (*c*) organizing the clientele of a program, such that the stated goals of the organization and/or the program under consideration are achieved as efficiently as possible.

The term "organization" is derived from the Greek word, *organon*, which means a tool or an instrument. An organization may be thought of as the coordinated actions of two or more people for the purpose of meeting an objective. In the context of management, we may conceptualize an organization as a concrete and tangible entity, comprising men, machines, and material resources that are organized and interrelated in a particular manner. The main purpose of an organization is to transform something—materials, people, information—in a manner that adds value to what is transformed and allows the organization to survive and prosper.

The term "organization" is also used to refer to any government, or governmental subdivision or agency, corporation, trust, estate, partnership, cooperative, or association. In this sense, it connotes various forms of organization. An organization becomes an institution when nobody is indispensable for its survival and growth, that is, when it becomes self-sustaining, irrespective of its employees who leave it or who join it.

An organizational structure may be thought of as made of goals, tasks, resources, relationships, reward-and-punishment systems, communication systems, authority systems, and so on. The net effect of "structure" is a specific set of behavioral patterns. Therefore, any structural change basically involves a behavioral change. In a human being, however, behavior must be consistent with his attitudes. When there is inconsistency or dissonance, unpleasant tensions arise, which the individual seeks to resolve. When he cannot alter his behavior (because he cannot leave the structure), he changes his attitudes to attain consistency.

The rationale of organizing the program clientele is based on the participative model of organizations. According to the proponents of this model, "the overall objective of the organization is to achieve satisfactory integration between the needs and desires of the members of the organization and the persons functionally related to it, such as shareholders, suppliers, consumers [programme beneficiaries]" (Lorsch and Lawrence 1972, 12).

An organization performs a variety of functions. Some of the important organizational functions are presented in Box 13.1.

Box 13.1

FUNCTIONS OF AN ORGANIZATION

1. *Formalizing rules and procedures for facilitating the repetition of desired actions.*
2. *Ensuring that desired actions will fit together in a systematic way, and that these will be co-ordinated.*
3. *Making the behavior of organization members predictable.*
4. *Storing information and "learning" in the course of their existence.*
5. *Establishing an identity independent of the people within it, thereby ensuring its existence in spite of members who leave it.*
6. *Allocating rewards to contributors and claimants.*

Source: Singh 1999: 263.

To understand and interpret information about an organization, a manager should adopt the following three elemental strategies:

1. *Measures of events*: a case study of an organization
2. *Measures of association*: determining the correlation between two measures
3. *Measures of causation*: identification of causal variables by using experimental procedures.

This chapter first briefly presents a few organizational models, then lists a few criteria of designing an appropriate organization for rural development, and, finally, it critically evaluates the suitability of various forms of organizations for rural development.

A Detour to Organizational Models

Like the person who solves problems in other fields, the rural development manager concerned with organizational issues needs analytical tools and models that can help him analyze the problems he faces and evolve solutions to the problems. When a manager wants to build an organization, or when he sets out to change an existing organization, he has in mind a theoretical model of what the reorganized structure should resemble. A manager can be more effective if he is explicit about the organizational models he chooses to use.

Now we discuss the salient features of a few major organizational models of possible relevance to rural development.

Gouldner (1959, 404–06) defines the following two types of organizational models.

The Rational Model

In the rational model, the organization is regarded as a rationally conceived instrument or means to the realization of group goals. It assumes that decisions are made on the basis of a rational survey of the situation and well-received knowledge with an orientation to a legal framework. Basically, the model is "mechanical," with explicit focus on legal structures or "blueprinted" patterns, which can be inspected and rationally manipulated with a view to realize the group goals. Individual organizational elements can be subjected to planned modifications and the organization as a whole can be brought into conformity with explicitly held plans and goals. This model is widely used by managers in analyzing issues of organizational design.

The Natural-system Model

This model regards the organization as a natural whole or system that is oriented to the realization of group goals. Its elements are seen as interdependent and emergent institutions, which can be understood only in relation to the diverse needs of the total system. The organization continues to strive to survive and to maintain its equilibrium even after its goals have been attained and, thus, it becomes an end in itself with its distinct needs that have to be satisfied. Changes in organizational patterns are considered the results of cumulative, unplanned. and adaptive responses to threats to the equilibrium of the system as a whole. The organization is seen as growing organically, with a natural history of its own, which is modifiable only at a great cost, if at all.

Buckley (1967, 36–41) has criticized the mechanical rational model and the biological natural-system model and has offered an alternative modern system theory, which he feels is more consistent with the observed functioning of organizational systems. He points out that organizations are more like "socio-cultural systems" than either mechanical or biological systems. To many managers, both the rational and the natural-system models may seem inappropriate. Yet many, if not most, managers implicitly or explicitly rely on one, particularly the rational model, and sometimes on an eclectic mixture of both, when they think about issues of organizational design.

To understand why these two models are so widely used, it would be helpful if we develop a general understanding of the "classical" and "participative" models, which have a clear connection to Gouldner's "rational and natural-system" dichotomy, and the "socio-technical" and "cognitive models that have captured more of the complexity of organizational phenomena.

The Classical Model

This model focuses primarily on the relationship between management and workers. Workers are viewed as instruments, solely motivated by economic incentives and existing to carry out organizational objectives. Managers, on the other hand, are characterized as rational, omniscient, and possessing outstanding personal qualities, such as kindness and fairness. However, despite these qualities, the manager's role defines that he be firm with workers.

Because of the model's view of the worker as an "economic man," rewards and punishments to the workers should be economic in nature. An astute classical manager would give detailed instructions to his subordinates. Then, according to the model, he must measure or assess exactly what has been done by the workers and whether the employee should be rewarded or punished for his/her performance in executing the task. The essence of this model is: fitting the "right" man into the "right" job. This fit is to be defined by personal characteristics, such as physical strength, manual dexterity, or specific craft skills.

The classical organization pattern resembles a pyramid. Within this structure, both the chain of command and the channels of communication are vertical. The vertical chain of command stipulates that each person in the organization is to have only one superior or boss. Similarly, each member is to have some authority delegated to him, which is equal to his responsibility.

The Participative Model

While the classical model is derived from an analysis of the experience of practitioners, the participative model is derived from the work of behavioral scientists. According to the proponents of this model, the individual in the organization is engaged in a multidimensional process of development. Within this dynamic developmental process, the individual is seen as moving through the process of maturity. As he/she matures, this individual's needs, goals, and desires tend to move in a specific direction. The individual seeks to be in a position of relative independence in which he/she has some level of self-determination about his/her future. He/she begins to seek deeper, more consistent, and increasingly complex interests with which to be challenged. He/she also seeks a greater depth to his behavioral interactions within the organization.

According to participative theorists, the overall objective of the organization is to achieve a satisfactory integration between the needs and desires of the members of the organization and the persons functionally related to it, such as consumers, shareholders, and suppliers. It is assumed that the management can make full use of the potential capacities of its human resources only when each person in the organization is a member of one or more effectively functioning work groups, thus, participating in the overall organizational effort. Further, it is required that these groups have a high degree of group loyalty, effective skills, and goals of high performance.

The organizations that perform best, according to this model, are those that motivate the individual to "cooperate," not compete. In achieving this cooperation, the group leader is accountable and must accept final responsibility for the performance of the group. However, in spite of the leader's responsibility for group performance, he/she must consider accepting those group decisions with which he/she does not concur, if he/she feels he/she could adversely affect group loyalty by neglecting to take the group's decisions into account.

The Socio-technical Model

This model views the organization as a system interacting with its environment—a system in which behavior is influenced by human, technological, social, and organizational inputs. All these variables are interdependent, so that a change in one influences the others.

In this model, the organization is seen as an open system, exchanging resources with its environment in the form of an input–conversion–output process. The enterprise takes in raw materials, energy, and manpower and converts them into output of goods and services. The ability of an organization to satisfy and adapt to its environment determines its success or failure, in terms of accomplishment of the "primary task" for which it is built.

In this model, the organization is viewed as consisting of a "formal organization" and an "informal organization," and both these components are expected to be as congruent as possible. The major strength of this model is in its systematic treatment of the complex realities of the organization life, thereby allowing us to identify the diverse causes of behavior in organizations. The model is very useful for planning of division of work and allocating primary tasks with a view to enhance organizational efficiency. Its limitation is that it is difficult to use as a design tool without practice and formal training (Lorsch and Lawrence 1972, 22).

The Cognitive Model

This model is also known as the "behavioral theory of decision making." This approach to the analysis of complex organizations was developed by Herbert Simon, James March, and their colleagues at the Carnegie Institute of Technology, mainly to aid them in building quantitative models of the decision process (March and Simon 1958). Their model assumes that price and output decisions are made by a group of managers whose goals are often in conflict with each other and who possess imperfect information, rather than by an individual entrepreneur who has perfect information, as presumed under the economic theory of the firm. In their opinion, organizations tend to "satisfice" rather than optimize profit by the very nature of their decision processes. They view the organizational decision process as built around the development of alternative courses of action and execution of a choice from amongst these alternatives, on the basis of available information and under constraints imposed by the environment, as well as the structural aspects of the situation.

Although the cognitive model may seem overly complex, it provides a number of useful insights into the functioning of complex organizations. As an analytical approach, it leads us to view an organization as a "process" that evolves from the interaction of structure, human cognitive mechanisms and the nature of the decisions that must be made. In this sense, it is a dynamic model, which emphasizes the development and adaptation of organizational systems under varying conditions.

The Search for a New Paradigm

The organizational models reviewed in the preceding section are not very helpful in designing appropriate organizational structures for rural development in India, as also in other developing countries. This is mainly because these models were all built out of the Western experience, which, to begin with, was confined to relatively simple and well-defined organizational activities, since the state functions were essentially of regulation and maintenance. Under those conditions, it was relatively easy to develop an administrative theory capable of analyzing—through both inductive and deductive systems—the various organizational issues. Having done that, it was also possible to design an operating system capable of performing various tasks.

In a developing country such as India, with a mixed economy, it is difficult to observe any uniform pattern either in the activities or in the behavior of a development organization. In the fields of agriculture, community development, health, family planning, and in many other areas of social welfare, it is virtually impossible to establish clear-cut roles for social, economic, political, and administrative organizations. Under these circumstances, it has not been possible to identify the behavioral patterns that have to be changed or the methods by which they can be changed, nor has it been possible to design an administrative structure that can bring both the change agent and the clientele system in any kind of effective working relationship. As a result, the various organizations engaged in rural development crisscross each other, causing a great deal of confusion in the operations and wastage of resources in the process.

Even so, the organizational models serve considerable purposes in their applications to discrete projects, such as those relating to fertilizer production, power generation and irrigation. In these projects, the functions, activities and tasks to be performed can be fairly accurately measured and identified, making it easy to prescribe what is to be done organizationally to achieve them. However, when it comes to diffused programs such as agricultural and rural development programs, where the goals are intertwined with different sets of forces and are not so easy to describe, it has not been possible to develop appropriate organizational structures for effective implementation and management. Therefore, the search for appropriate organizational designs and structures for rural development still continues.

Numerous individuals and institutions are engaged in the search for new paradigms of development, based on structures that meet the criteria of efficiency, sustainability, equity, well-being, and participation. Toffler (1980, 368), among others, argues that sustainable social development should be based on exploitation of the one resource that is inexhaustible—information and the human capacity for creative imagination. The structures of social institutions must be designed with the intention of gaining complete advantage of the potentials of this resource. This is basic not only to sustainable and equitable material well-being, but to the non-material advancement of human beings as well.

Berger and Neuhaus (1977, 2–3) suggest policy actions to strengthen the role of intermediate human institutions, such as the family, the neighborhood, the self-managing work group, the voluntary agencies, and so on, which perform a mediating role between the individual and the mega-structure (government bureaucracies, big corporations, and so on), providing a source of personal support and recognition, and facilitating solutions to problems at the local level and creative innovation.

Korten (1981, 610) asserts that

> [T]he answer rests not in abolishing society's mega-structures since they are basic to the functioning of any modern society. Rather it rests in substantially reforming them, in loosening central control and strengthening the feedback systems that increase potential for self-direction and direct participation at local levels consistent with the well-being of the larger society. It will be necessary to move beyond more primitive forms of bureaucratic organization, able only to control or to substitute for local action, to substantially more sophisticated forms which can work to strengthen capacities for creative local self-help action and self-control. Though most calls for greater reliance on local level solutions to global problems look to such an action as a substitute for bureaucratic action, it is neither so easy to dismiss their stifling regulatory power or to achieve effective problem solving on the scale required without access to their massive resources.

In the Introduction to a series of studies on bureaucracy, Littrell (1980, 263) concludes:

> Although many critically important problems face us today, most of the problems as well as proposals for their solutions are defined and shaped in bureaucratic organizations. Our capacity to understand and modify bureaucracy in the present decade will greatly determine our capacity to solve our problems and thus shape the decades to come.

Criteria for Designing an Appropriate Organization

While the organizational structure for rural development may differ from state to state, depending upon the variations in the role assigned by the states to NGOs and the PRIs for agricultural and rural development, an ideal rural development organization should satisfy certain criteria, as presented in Box 13.2.

Box 13.2

CRITERIA FOR DESIGNING AN APPROPRIATE ORGANIZATION

1. *It should provide for effective coordination of macro-planning and micro-planning, that is, vertical integration of planning.*
2. *It should provide for the formulation of inter-sectoral plans, programs, and projects, and for their horizontal integration.*
3. *There should be a mechanism for maintaining a dynamic relationship between planning and implementation.*
4. *The delivery system should be in a position to channelize the benefits of development programs to the target groups and should be strong enough to resist vested interests that have in the past stood in the way of these benefits reaching the poor.*
5. *It should have a high degree of technical and professional competence.*
6. *It should provide for the maintenance of a direct and continuing relationship between the planners and people, and for the meaningful participation of the people in the process of development planning and implementation.*
7. *It should provide for checks, balances, and correctives, so that target groups belonging to the weaker sections are not deprived of the benefits meant for them.*
8. *It should be sensitive to the needs of its clientele and responsive to changes in its external environment.*
9. *It should provide for participation of its target group(s)/clientele in making its policies that affect them.*
10. *It should be financially viable and sustainable.*

Source: Singh (1999, 270).

We now briefly describe the salient features of various forms of organizations engaged in rural development in India, and critically appraise their suitability for the purpose.

Government Organizations

The government has been, still is, and will continue in the near future to be an important organization in the field of agricultural and rural development in developing countries, including India. Development is seen as the specific responsibility of the government in all such countries. This has far-reaching implications for the role of public bureaucracy, which is an arm of the state responsible for carrying out the wishes of political leaders. In most of these countries, efforts to bring about improvement in the quality of life of rural people depend heavily on government administration and bureaucrats. According to Bauer (1991, 190–91), economic development is not the result of forced mobilization of people's resources, forced modernization of attitudes and behavior of people, large-scale state-sponsored industrialization, or of achievement of political independence. It is the result of individual voluntary responses of millions of people to emerging or expanding opportunities, brought to their notice primarily through the operation of the market. The government has a limited role to play in this process and does not have to incur huge expenditure of public funds. The primary role of the government should be to create and nurture an institutional setup that provides the needed incentives and facilities to economic agents to do what they want to do, and which is flexible and adaptable to changing social and economic conditions. Besides, the government should also establish mechanisms for coordinating the activities of atomistic economic agents and for removing uncertainty about human behavior or solving the assurance problem that characterizes the classic prisoner's dilemma.[1] More specifically, the main functions of governmental organizations/institutions can be seen at the following six levels:

1. Facilitating policy formulation;
2. Harmonizing the actions of various economic agents and coordinating program implementation;
3. Providing incentives for collective action and self-regulation;
4. Enforcing regulations and policing;
5. Resolving conflicts and providing arbitration;
6. Providing technical assistance.

After independence, certain changes were effected in the administrative system with a view to reorient it to meet the needs of development. The nation-building departments of agriculture, rural development, education, and health have expanded considerably. New development agencies and corporations have been set up. The district is the focal unit of rural development administration, and developmental activity is one of the numerous responsibilities of the district collector. His/her prime responsibility is and will, in the foreseeable future, continue to be the maintenance of law and order. He/she is so preoccupied with this that it is impossible for him/her to do justice to the developmental responsibility. The district collector leans heavily on the DDO for the purpose, but as all the authority is vested in the district collector, the DDO only plays the second fiddle and is not able to achieve what is desired. Further, hierarchically, the DDO, being lower than the district collector, is unable to provide the requisite leadership and obtain the cooperation of—and adequate input from—the officers of other departments/disciplines, which is so vital for coordinated development.

Due to the unethical value system and highly inflammable socio-cultural environment in which we are operating, the law and order situation has deteriorated over the years, requiring greater attention from the district magistrates, which in turn means less attention, both quantitatively and qualitatively, for developmental activity. The result is that the goals of development have become mirages. There is yet another aspect of this matter. The machinery charged with the responsibility of law and order cannot handle the development portfolio adequately. The qualities required for the efficient discharge of the responsibility of law and order are just the ones which hinder developmental responsibility. For example, the efficient discharge of the law and order responsibility requires qualities of evasiveness, toughness, circumspectness, and the capacity to dispense expedients. For developmental work, however, one needs to be receptive, open-minded, communicative, and empathetic, and should have the capacity to go deep and find real and lasting solutions. In these days of specialization, how can one be expected to become adept at simultaneously handling varied responsibilities requiring contrasting skills?

It is, therefore, not surprising that even after more than six decades of development planning, rural administration still displays serious faults. It generally fails to deliver services and supplies promptly, efficiently, and equitably. The failure is due partly to inadequate resources, partly to an elitist bias, and partly to the lack of coordination. Rural administration generally fails to secure popular participation. Traditional attitudes have prevented any synthesis with local institutions or a real partnership with the people.

From a management perspective, the central challenge of our times is to understand and modify bureaucratic organizations by building into them a capacity for innovative learning, leading to a fundamental orientation in their purposes and modes of operation. This is what is called Bureaucratic Re-orientation (BRO). What we need most urgently now are operational prescriptions for rural development organizations, which may want to implement the new strategy of BRO. Sadly, very little is known at present to advise a development agency about what it should do to achieve BRO and how.

Korten (1981, 610) suggests that BRO should give priority to the management of systems over the management of projects, to innovation over compliance, and to methodologies for continuous self-monitoring and rapid self-correction over formalized planning and evaluation methodologies. To achieve these, he suggests the formation of social learning clusters and networks within the system, linking together those individuals who have commitment to appropriate action, and providing them mutual support and the operational methodologies needed to translate their good intentions into effective action.

Jesus (1984), on the basis of action-research activities of the Asian Institute of Management (AIM) through its Rural Development Management Programme (RDMP) team working with three agencies undertaking BRO, has attempted to construct a conceptual framework to capture the process of BRO. The salient features of his framework are presented in Box 13.3.

Box 13.3

A CONCEPTUAL FRAMEWORK FOR BUREAUCRATIC REORIENTATION

1. *BRO assumes a decision by the agency to initiate a fundamental change in its objectives, or a radical shift in its strategy. Only the strongest—present or imminent—pressures from the external environment are likely to budge bureaucracies from their settled ways.*
2. *Once the new strategy is identified and accepted, the BRO process can begin.*
   Access to the top management of the agency is a precondition for any attempt at BRO to get started and prosper.
3. *BRO takes a long time, possibly longer than the tenure of the executive who starts the process. His/her departure from the scene inevitably results in some disruption of the BRO process.*
4. *For the purposes of triggering and sustaining the BRO process, it is vitally important that some source of external funds, such as a foundation or an international development agency be associated with the agency undertaking BRO. As with the stimulus for changes, resources for bringing about BRO have to come from outside the agency.*
5. *Training of agency personnel seems to be a tactically sound first step in the process of BRO. A training program can serve not only to develop skills, but also to initiate or sustain the process of change.*
6. *A manager aiming to elicit certain behavior patterns from his staff ought to focus on changing the structures within the organization, rather than the attitudes of the people. But this assertion holds more strongly for private enterprise than for a government or public sector organization. Public sector managers place a high premium on convincing people to change their views about their work. Not everyone will respond to the appeal for an attitude change, but not everyone will need to. A few "champions" can have pervasive effects.*

Source: Korten (1981, 610).

Panchayati Raj Institutions (PRIs)

It was Gandhiji who realized the importance of the village panchayat as an important instrument of rural development, and of promoting and nurturing democracy at the grassroots. He asserted that unless panchayats were invested with adequate powers, villagers cannot have real *swaraj*. In fact, Para iv in Article 40 of the Constitution of India was introduced at his insistence.

The article states: "The State shall take steps to organize village panchayats and endow them with such powers and authority as may be necessary to enable them to function as units of self-government." In January 1957, the Government of India appointed a committee under the chairmanship of Balwantray Mehta to study the working of the CDP and suggest how best it could be maintained and implemented. The committee recommended a three-tier system of local government, christened "panchayati raj" by Jawaharlal Nehru.

Village panchayats were to be formed at the grassroots or village level, panchayat samitis at the middle or block level, and zila parishads at the apex or district level. The new bodies were to have a wide range of powers and adequate finance. The committee offered two broad directional thrusts: (a) it argued that there should be administrative decentralization for effective implementation of development programs and (b) the decentralized administrative system should be under the control of elected bodies. The three-tier structure of the PRIs was brought into existence after the Mehta Committee scheme was approved by the National Development Council (NDC) in January 1958. The NDC affirmed the objectives behind the introduction of democratic institutions at the district and block levels, and suggested that each state should work out the structure that suited its conditions best.

The new system of PRIs was first adopted in Rajasthan and Andhra Pradesh in 1959, and, thus, PRIs have been in existence in India since then. However, there were inter-state variations in the structural pattern, tenure, and responsibilities entrusted to them. With a view to grant a constitutional status to PRIs in the country and to bring about uniformity, the Indian Parliament passed the 73rd Constitution Amendment Act 1992, in December 1992. This act came into force with effect from April 24, 1993. It envisages the establishment of panchayats as units of local self-government in all states and UTs, except the tribal areas in the states of Nagaland, Meghalaya, and Mizoram and certain other scheduled areas. Subsequently, in December 1996, the provisions of the 73rd Amendment were extended to the tribal and other scheduled areas also, through an act of Parliament. Adequate powers and responsibilities were to be devolved upon the PRIs at the appropriate levels, to enable them to prepare and implement schemes for economic development and social justice, as entrusted to them under the items listed in the Eleventh Schedule to the Constitution. Significantly, the 73rd Amendment does not have a provision for the constitution of gram sabhas, but their powers and functions have to be specified by the state legislatures. However, in the extended act, the constitution of gram sabhas is mandatory.

The salient features of the 73rd Constitution Amendment Act, 1992 are as follows:

1. The gram sabha has been envisaged as the foundation of the panchayati raj system. It shall perform such functions and exercise such powers as may be entrusted to it by the state legislatures.
2. There shall be three tiers of panchayats, at the village, intermediate, and district levels. Only states having population not exceeding two million will have the discretion to not constitute panchayats at the intermediate level.
3. Seats in a panchayat at every level are to be filled by direct election from territorial constituencies demarcated for this purpose. In addition, there would be ex-officio members also, as provided in the state legislation.
4. Seats shall be reserved at every level of panchayat for SCs and STs in proportion to their population in a given panchayat area, and for women to the extent of not less than one-third of the total number of seats. Reservation for offices of chairpersons of panchayats at every level shall also be made in the same proportion as the population of the SC and ST in the state bears to the total population of the state, and for women to the extent of not less than one-third of the total number of offices of chairpersons in the panchayats at each level.

5. The term of office of panchayats shall be five years, and elections must be completed before the expiry of its duration; if dissolved earlier, elections must be completed within six months from the date of dissolution.
6. A State Finance Commission shall be constituted in every state, to go into the principles governing the distribution and devolution of financial resources between the panchayats and states.
7. The superintendence, direction and control of the preparation of electoral rolls and conduct of all elections to panchayats shall be vested in a State Election Commission.
8. The Eleventh Schedule has been added to the Constitution, which denotes 29 subjects/functions that could be entrusted to the PRIs.

A national committee of state panchayat ministers has been constituted by the Central government to review the progress of implementation of the constitutional provisions and guide and advise the states in this regard.

While PRIs have on one hand been criticized as having generated tensions, factions, and party politics in village communities, on the other hand they have been considered as the only hope for achieving people's participation, which is the soul of the democratic system. Whereas the introduction of panchayati raj in the year 1959 was in itself a major landmark in the history of administrative reforms, the system was not implemented faithfully in most of the states, largely due to the indifferent attitude of bureaucrats toward it. Consequently, there have been more failures than successes. After the operationalization of the 73rd Amendment Constitution Act, 1992, it is hoped that PRIs will emerge stronger and more dynamic to face various challenges and problems that still lie ahead of them. Their success in the future will depend on the extent of transfer of rural development functions and devolution of financial and administrative powers to them by the state governments. If the deliberations of the conference of chief ministers and panchayat raj ministers held in New Delhi on August 3, 1997 are any guide, the new panchayati raj structure will take a long time to be fully functional. A major concern expressed at the conference was the slow pace of devolution of powers, functions and responsibilities to the PRIs. The conference recommended that the process of devolution of powers be completed latest by the end of December 1997, but it seems that this has not been done by most of the states yet. Similarly, the district rural development agencies have not been restructured to permit the PRIs to perform their intended functions effectively and efficiently.

While it is too early to assess the impact of the constitutional status given to PRIs, the report of the first concurrent evaluation survey of the JRY, which covered 448 districts in the country, throws some light on certain aspects of elected village panchayats, and the people who head them. The evaluation covered a one-year period from January 1992 to December 1992. The survey was conducted before the introduction of the 73rd Amendment to the Constitution. Some of the major findings of the evaluation are as follows:

In West Bengal, as many as 89% of the elected panchayat heads were landless and marginal farmers, whereas in states such as Maharashtra, Punjab, and Andhra Pradesh, over 25% of the *pradhans* were big farmers, owning at least 10 ha of land. As expected, a majority of the panchayat pradhans (77%) were from the upper classes. Only 7% of them were from the SC and another 15% from the ST. About 3% of the sample panchayats were headed by women, of whom 41% belonged to the SC. Of the panchayat pradhans, 13% were graduates, about 24% had education up to primary level, and 7% were illiterate. The level of deliberations in the panchayat level meetings was extremely poor. During the 12-month period preceding the survey, 39% of the sample panchayats did not meet even once (Gangrade 1997, 755–56). In a study conducted in Orissa, it was found that women entered panchayat politics due to persuasion of their family members, or pressure from the village community or political parties. However, the women who reluctantly entered politics showed greater maturity in outlook, enthusiasm, political consciousness, and consciousness about their role and responsibilities (Panda 1997, 663). Given these features of panchayats and their elected heads, there is a need for building the capacity of elected leaders through education and training. This is all the more necessary, given a variety of administrative and financial functions expected to be performed by the elected leaders, as also the ambivalent attitude of the bureaucracy and the reluctance of the state leaders to part with power.

Cooperatives

If the goals of agricultural and rural development are to be achieved, it will be necessary that the people are organized within an institutional structure that gives them access to the national economic and social systems. Organizing people is a political act because it alters the distribution of power within the community by increasing the number of people who are making decisions. Cooperatives are one of the institutional forms of organizing villagers. A cooperative is generally viewed as a socio-economic organization that can fulfill both social and economic objectives of its members, and that has its members' interests truly at heart. Cooperation has three dimensions, that is, economic, social, and moral, which are equally crucial for its success. The very motto of cooperation, "each for all and all for each," signifies loyalty, trust, faith, and fellowship. A cooperative is a perfect democratic institution of the members, for the members, and by the members, and is based on the "one member, one vote" system of decision-making.

A cooperative is based on certain values and principles of its own, which distinguish it from other forms of organizations. The International Cooperative Alliance (ICA) congress, held in Manchester on September 23, 1995, adopted the following seven principles:

1. Voluntary and open membership;
2. Democratic member control;
3. Members' economic participation and limited interest on share capital;
4. Autonomy and independence;
5. Provision of cooperative education, training, and information;
6. Cooperation among cooperatives; and
7. Concern for the community.

The cooperative as a business organization is similar in many ways, and different in many other ways, from other forms of organizations. The similarities are in the domain of roles and functions, and the differences in the manner in which the roles and functions are performed. Cooperatives are expected to reflect in their day-to-day practices the principles and values of cooperation, which emphasize, inter alia, equality, equity, and mutual self-help.

Like any other business organization, cooperatives are expected to ensure efficiency and profitability in their operations. But, unlike other business organizations in the private and public sectors, the cooperative is both a social organization and a business enterprise and, therefore, has a dual purpose: it serves both a social as well as an economic function. A cooperative manager must be concerned not only with the economic aspects, but also with the social obligations of his organization.

Cooperatives have a higher comparative advantage over other forms of organizations in involving people in their activities, in mobilizing people's resources and political power for achieving their goals, in identifying and developing local leaders through democratic processes, in securing vertical and horizontal integration of production, procurement, processing, and marketing functions, and in facilitating equitable distribution of benefits of development. All these advantages can help cooperatives in improving their competitive position as a business organization vis-à-vis their competitors.

The economic rationale for a cooperative organization lies in its endeavor to secure for its members advantages of modern technology and economies of scale. A cooperative organization that does not want or cannot secure these two advantages is doomed to fail sooner or later. Theoretically speaking, there is hardly a better organizational structure than the cooperative for achieving the dual goal of social and economic development, but the final success depends on the level of operational efficiency achieved (Dulfer 1974).

The major difference between cooperative management and management in other organizations is the greater need for cooperatives to involve their directors, members, and staff in key positions in problem solving and decision-making. This is no small task. Managers trained in traditional management schools, when confronted with a difficult situation, feel they must think it through for themselves and find a solution. That is what they have learnt in management courses. Cooperative theory requires a different response. Cooperative managers are expected to take the problem out to the members and staff, and involve various interest groups in the development of solutions.

Cooperatives occupy an important place in India's rural economy in terms of their coverage of population and their share in the total supply of agricultural inputs, including credit. India can rightly claim to have the largest network of cooperatives in the world. In India, as of 2009–10, there were 610 thousand cooperatives of all types, having a total membership of some 249.367 million and working capital of ₹7,295.766 billion. They covered 98% of India's villages and 67% of all rural households in the country and accounted for 19% of the total credit supplied in rural areas, 36% of the total quantity of fertilizers distributed, 26.3% of the total quantity of fertilizers produced, 39.7% of total sugar produced, and 49% of branded edible oil produced in the country (NCUI 2012, 32–34).[2]

Of all the types of cooperatives, the Anand-pattern dairy cooperatives are considered to have been most successful in serving their members, as well as society at large. Growth and development of milk producers' cooperatives in Kheda (Kaira) district of Gujarat, under the umbrella of the Kaira District Cooperative Milk Producers' Union Ltd, popularly known as AMUL, during the 1950s and the 1960s demonstrated the potential of cooperatives as an instrument of dairy development. The then Prime Minister Lal Bahadur Shastri was convinced about the suitability of the Anand model, and advised the Government of India to set up an organization under the chairmanship of V. Kurien to replicate the Anand-pattern dairy cooperatives in India. Consequently, the NDDB was established in 1965 with its headquarters in Anand. The NDDB designed a program called OF to replicate Anand-pattern cooperatives in the country. The OF is perhaps the world's largest dairy development program in terms of its scope, coverage. and longevity. It enabled India to emerge as the highest milk producer in the world and become an exporter of some of the dairy products.

Despite their overwhelming importance in India's rural economy, most of the rural cooperatives are not financially viable due to mismanagement. Cooperatives need to be managed by professional managers, if they are to survive and grow in the wake of India's new economic policy characterized by deregulation, delicensing, privatization, and globalization. Several obstacles hinder the professionalization of management of agribusiness cooperatives, such as the lack of professional managers having values and ethos congenial to cooperative management; excessive government control and interference; lack of enlightened leadership; small size of business and, hence, the inability to hire professional managers; lack of performance-based reward systems; and internal work culture and environment not being congenial to professionalization of management.

Voluntary Agencies/Nongovernmental Organizations

Voluntary action in India is as old as the emergence of organized society itself. It originated as pure philanthropy or charity, and this motivation sustained the effort all through history. Even the establishment of the Indian National Congress (INC) in 1885 was a voluntary effort initiated by Allan Octavian Hume, acclaimed as its "father and founder." Addressing the graduates of Calcutta University in 1883 in an open letter, Hume gave a clarion call to the educated youth (Maheshwari 1987, 560–61):

> You are the salt of the land. And if amongst you the elite, 50 men cannot be found with sufficient power of self-sacrifice, sufficient love for and pride in their country, sufficient genuine and unselfish heartfelt patriotism to take the initiative, and if needs be, devote the rest of their lives to the cause, then there is no hope for India. Her sons must and will remain mere humble and helpless instruments in the hands of foreign rulers, for they who would be free themselves must strike the blow.

Emphasizing the role of voluntary agencies in rural development, the working group on block level planning, 1978 (Vaishnav and Sundaram 1978; GoI 1978b, 45), shares the view that

> [T]he country's social and economic problems are so vast and multifarious that the government's administrative machinery alone cannot tackle them. The establishment of a self-reliant society implies progressive curtailment of people's dependence on the government. From times immemorial, voluntary agencies in our country have played a significant part in promoting people's welfare.... The planning team at the district level should consult and actively seek the assistance of the voluntary agencies in their area while preparing the plan and selectively entrust to them the implementation of some sectoral plans in which they may have requisite expertise and experience.

VAs or NGOs can—and, in fact, some of them do—play a very important role in rural development. They can enthuse the rural population to prepare meaningful plans for rural development and also to take part in their implementation. There are now quite a few VAs in the country that have the requisite technical and managerial resources available with them to undertake rural development projects, and to manage them successfully. For example, the Bhartiya Agro-industrial Foundation (BAIF) of Urlikanchan (Maharashtra) has acquired a high level of technical competence in the field of animal husbandry, and is implementing a number of projects in this field now in many areas in the country. Similarly, Sadguru Water and Development Foundation (SWDF) based in Dahod, Gujarat, is known nationally and internationally for its expertise in the field of natural resource management, particularly water resources development in poor tribal regions of the country. The Mysore Resettlement and Development Agency (MYRADA) of Bangalore has developed expertise in the fields of irrigation, wastelands development, watershed development and resettlement of released bonded laborers, and it has a number of projects in these fields in operation in the southern states of the country. Besides, there are many other NGOs doing good rural development work. There is a definite need for the government to support genuine voluntary effort in rural development.

At the national level, the Council for Advancement of People's Action and Rural Technology (CAPART) is the nodal agency responsible for promoting voluntary action in rural development. CAPART was registered under the Societies Registration Act, 1860, on September 1, 1986, with its headquarters in New Delhi. It is now under the administrative control of the Ministry of Rural Development. It aims at encouraging, promoting, and assisting voluntary action for rural development. In pursuance of these objectives, CAPART makes available financial assistance to VAs/NGOs under the following schemes:

1. Promotion of voluntary action in rural development
2. Development of Women and Children in Rural Areas
3. Accelerated Rural Water Supply Programme (ARWSP)
4. Central Rural Sanitation Programme (CRSP)
5. Organization of beneficiaries of anti-poverty programs
6. MGNREGA and NRLM
7. Advancement of Rural Technology Scheme (ARTS)
8. Panchayati Raj (PR)
9. Rehabilitation of disabled people

Its funds mainly consist of grants from the Union Ministry of Rural Development. The council can also obtain grants from various other Central and state government departments, and accept donations and contributions from other sources. CAPART has set up six Regional Coordination Committees (RCCs) at Jaipur, Ahmedabad, Hyderabad, Bhubaneswar, Guwahati, and Lucknow to decentralize its functioning. These committees have been given the mandate to sanction and monitor projects involving an outlay of ₹0.5 million or less.

The 1990s have witnessed a proliferation of development initiatives taken by NGOs. It is no longer an issue of concern for the elite. Now, development action is perceived as an alternative career option even by the common person. The idea of undertaking socially meaningful activities as a full-time occupation is not an alien concept for a large majority of those working with NGOs. However, the ideological fervor, or a sense of nationalism in society as a whole, has been waning gradually over time.

Large-scale support from the government has also necessitated the routinization of development interventions. This has also been encouraged by the fact that many common people, who are not innovators, are involved in delivery of goods and services, which are not adequately catered to by the state or market institutions.

Most new organizations that are coming up now are those promoted by the common people. They do not attract highly trained or highly competent personnel. Most old, large organizations, which attracted some of the best brains during the phase of innovation, are either saturated at the top (with a small group, if not one, of development innovators at the helm of affairs) or have routinized functions to such an extent that they have ceased to remain attractive for the competent youth. However, the liberalized market economy now offers much more attractive opportunities to the talented youth, as compared to the development initiatives that they had even a few years ago.

The present generation of NGO workers has a very different set of aspirations and motivation from those of the leaders of the NGO sector a decade or so ago. Many of the norms of personal need (gratification, accountability, and transparency) evolved around people of high social motivation. These norms need changes in the present context, with people having different sets of motivations and aspirations.

With development funding agencies refocusing their attention on supporting small organizations, small NGOs have received a boost. This has also made it necessary for funding agencies to take a more proactive role than they did earlier. Many of them now play the role of a resource center, contributing to the planning and implementation of programs, and competence building of the NGO teams.

The known processes of development interventions have become more complex with enhanced understanding of the development process itself. Though in the 1950s, service delivery was the focus of development initiatives, by the 1960s, development activists were talking about transfer of technology. In the 1970s, it was recognized that technology transfer remained inadequate, unless backed with competence building. In the 1980s, the initiatives concentrated on multiple or comprehensive sets of services, backing up technology transfer with training, credit, and market linkages. But in the 1990s, it was recognized that the development inputs, to be sustainable in an eco-friendly manner, have to have much more than this. The ability of the NGOs to deliver high quality development services had also been recognized by the state machinery. This had also led to fairly high expectations from these organizations.

But now most of the NGOs are left with poor quality manpower to address this even more complex task. This may have serious implications for the quality of services being delivered by those organizations. Though substantial weightage is being given to building the competence of development teams by various support agencies, developing human resources is also being seen as one more task by a large majority of these organizations. Further, most of NGOs are dominated by one person, often their founders, and there is lack of professionalism in their functioning and management, leading to the misuse of public money.

Corporations and Rural Development

Corporations could make a significant contribution to rural development in India through establishing and/or supporting institutions that bring corporate resources, new technologies, modern management, and expertise to bear on the problems of rural development. There are, at least, the following four reasons why involvement of corporations in rural development is desirable (Raymond 1996):

1. *Win–Win Outcome*: Promoting the involvement of corporations in rural development is a classic "win–win" strategy. Corporations gain by demonstrating their commitment to rural communities, thereby building their credentials as good corporate citizens. This improves their image in the marketplace and contributes to their commercial success. The rural people benefit from new expertise and resources used by the corporations to solve their problems and fulfill their felt needs. The government wins because the corporations supplement the limited public resources available for rural development.
2. *Stable Democracy*: The involvement of business houses in rural development and the emergence of non-profit institutions, such as charitable trusts and societies boost institutional pluralism and people's participation in the policy-making process. Indeed, independent private institutions are vital to ensuring the stability of democratic processes in times of political change and economic crisis.
3. *Sustainability*: Government-funded rural development programs are vulnerable to changes in policy and budgetary allocations. Involvement of private corporations and their executives, who are not affected by political changes, in rural development projects could help make those projects sustainable. Sustainability depends on both the availability of funds as well as the commitment of institutions and their employees over the long term. Commitment of government employees to rural development is often short-lived, as compared to that of their counterparts in the private sector development organizations. How many Kuriens of Anand and the Jagawats of Water and Development Foundation, Dahod, Gujarat can you find in government organizations?
4. *Locking-in Economic Reforms*: When economic reforms fail to bring any real benefits to rural people, rural voters may throw the political party which introduced the reform out of power. Cuts in subsidies on fertilizer, irrigation water, electricity, and withdrawal of social welfare programs can erode the electoral support for reforms. If policy makers respond by slowing down the process of reforms, the result may be a decline in investment and the rate of economic growth. In contrast, successful economic reforms make

private corporations and enterprises more robust, and then corporate voluntarism delivers the benefits of growth and prosperity to the underprivileged and poor people.

In India, the government provides many incentives to the corporate sector for making contributions to the cause of rural development. Through the Finance Act 1978, two new Sections, 35 CC and 35 CCA, were added to the Income Tax Act 1961. These sections provide fiscal incentives to corporations and cooperatives to undertake rural development activities, directly as well as indirectly to promote such activities through rural development agencies approved by a prescribed authority notified by the Central Board of Direct Taxes (CBDT). These sections stipulate that the expenditure incurred by a corporation or a cooperative on rural development activities would be considered as normal expenditure, and would be deductible from the income of the tax payer (donor) to compute the taxable profit. The Finance Act of 1983 has amended Section 35 CCA to provide for the setting up of a National Fund for Agricultural Development (NFAD) for providing financial support to VAs to undertake rural development work. However, Section 35 CC has been retained, and private companies and business houses can avail the tax concession by undertaking rural development activities directly.

Fortunately, India's corporate sector, with its powerful economic status, is able to influence the policy makers in the country. However, most business houses in the past have confined their roles to their business and in maximizing profits. Nevertheless, some business houses do make attempts to address the problems of the community. This is, however, in no way adequate. When the majority of India's population is struggling for survival, how can corporations turn a blind eye and plan for their progress and prosperity? The corporate sector cannot continue to prosper unless the economy and quality of life of our common people is improved.

In all the programs implemented by both the governmental organizations and the NGOs, good management is the critical input for success. It is here that the corporate sector can play a major role. Transfer of management skills from business houses to the agencies in charge of rural development can easily enhance the productivity of natural resources.

Business houses with experience in management can assist the rural people directly, or through local voluntary organizations, to generate employment and to improve the quality of life. Some of the important areas where corporate can support the development of the rural areas are as follows:

1. Arranging financial assistance in the form of grants and loans to invest in various income and employment generating activities.
2. Direct procurement of produce as industrial raw material, or for the consumption of their employees; eliminating in this process the middlemen at various levels.
3. Imparting management skills to field workers and village leaders involved in rural development to improve their project management skills.

To begin with, a corporate house can start work in villages where its plants are located. By constructing roads, installing hand pumps, starting primary schools and a health center, corporates can not only earn goodwill, but also establish good relationships with the people.

Subsequently, corporates can spread their work to nearby areas. A good example to emulate is of the Tata Steel, which started rural development work in rural areas in Jamshedpur in erstwhile parts of Bihar (now Jharkhand). As a result, the company earned a lot of goodwill of the beneficiaries as well as of the government.

The private sector can also join hands with government agencies such as the KVIC and CAPART to develop rural areas. These agencies not only provide cheap funds, but their wide network can also prove useful to new entrants.

After having said this, we would like to highlight some points. First, corporations do not come forward spontaneously to take up rural development activities; public policy must create a congenial legal and policy environment for them to get into this arena. Tax relief and other incentives for rural development endeavors are pivotal. Second, both the corporations and the community must be partners in identifying the felt needs, and formulating programs that are beneficial to both the parties involved. Third, socially oriented corporations having good credentials and hands-on experience will need to provide leadership and advice to other interested companies and enterprises. Fourth, leaders in the public and private sectors must support the establishment of well-managed, non-profit rural development organizations. The Government of India now encourages the private corporations to participate in many areas of rural development including creating basic infrastructure through public private partnership (PPP) arrangements. Consequently, many corporations and big industrial houses now have set up corporate social responsibility (CSR) cells, which provide financial and technical support to reputed NGOs for undertaking rural development work.

Key Points

1. By "organizing for rural development," we mean: (a) designing appropriate organizational structures; (b) facilitating desirable human behavior within the organization, and (c) organizing the clientele of a program, such that the stated goals of the organization and/or the program under consideration are achieved as efficiently as possible.
2. The term "organization" is also used to refer to any government or governmental subdivision or agency, corporation, trust, estate, partnership, cooperative, or any other association of people. In this sense, it connotes various forms of organization. An organization becomes an institution when nobody is indispensable for its survival and growth, that is, when it becomes self-sustaining, irrespective of its employees who leave it or who join it.
3. An organization performs a variety of functions. The failure to organize properly can result in wasted energy and resources, the inability to accumulate knowledge, a dependency on the presence of certain people for existence and a failure to provide incentives for contribution by its members.
4. There are several organizational models developed in Western countries to help guide managers in designing and managing organizations. The important models include the rational model, the natural-system model, the classical model, the participative model, the socio-technical model and the cognitive model. These models have limited relevance in India's context because of its mixed economy and highly heterogeneous socio-economic conditions. In view of this, no single model is appropriate in India's context.
5. In India, there coexist many different forms of organizations in the rural sector. Of all the organizations, the government has been, still is, and will continue in the future to be the most important actor in the field of rural development. However, it alone cannot effectively tackle all the problems of rural development. PRIs, cooperatives, VAs, and private companies and corporations can—and, in fact, most of them do—play important roles in the process of development by complementing and supplementing the functions and activities of the government.
6. The role of the government should be to define the roles of other agencies, coordinate and, if necessary, regulate their activities, and provide such infrastructural facilities

and services as cannot be provided by other agencies. Above all, the government should help organize the rural poor within an institutional framework that can give them access to the nation's economic and political systems.

7. PRIs can help achieve the goal of local self-governance, thereby realizing Gandhiji's dream of swaraj. Cooperatives that are owned and controlled by their members and managed professionally can ensure to the producer a fair share in the consumer's price, and supply of good quality products at reasonable prices to the consumer. NGOs have a special advantage over other forms of organizations in educating and training rural people, in enlisting their participation in rural development programs, and in working closely with them.
8. Corporations could make a significant contribution to rural development through establishing and/or supporting institutions that bring corporate resources, new technologies, modern management, and expertise to bear on the problems of rural development.

Questions for Discussion

1. Differentiate between an organization and an institution, citing an example. Which one is better in India's context and why?
2. Drawing upon the theoretical organizational models presented in this chapter and using an eclectic approach, outline the salient features of an ideal organizational model for rural development in India.
3. Write a short critique of the following organizations vis-à-vis an ideal organization of rural development:
   (*i*) Government as an organization
   (*ii*) Panchayat raj institutions (PRIs)
   (*iii*) Cooperatives
   (*iv*) Nongovernmental organizations (NGOs)/Voluntary Agencies (VAs)
   (*v*) Private companies/corporations

Notes

1. For details of the classic prisoner's dilemma, see Singh and Shishodia (2007, 100–02).
2. http://ncui.coop/profile.html (Accessed on April 11, 2016).

Chapter 14

Financing Rural Development

LEARNING OUTCOMES

After having gone through this chapter, students should be able to:

- **List the purposes for which capital is required and the major sources of funds for rural development;**
- **List the various domestic institutional sources of financing rural development projects and critically examine their role;**
- **Illustrate the role of non-institutional agencies in financing rural development projects;**
- **Describe how deficit financing can help mobilize funds for rural development projects; and**
- **Critically examine the role of foreign sources of funds for rural development, especially, loans, grants and foreign direct investment.**

Introduction

The capital requirements of agricultural and rural development are enormous. Capital is required not only for on-farm investment to improve the production apparatus and to provide various farm inputs and services, but also for a vast array of supportive infrastructural facilities, such as power, roads, transportation, communication, markets, storage, warehouses, education, training, research, and extension. Capital is also required for the creation of non-farm jobs through the provision of factories and their complementary machinery and equipment. There are no precise estimates available about the capital requirements of agricultural and rural development in India. But the amount required is in thousands of billions of rupees. Funds for investment in rural development projects come from two main sources: domestic and foreign. Further, in each category, there are institutional and non-institutional sources (Figure 14.1). Domestic institutional sources include the government, government undertakings including public enterprises, the RBI, NABARD, cooperative banks, commercial banks and RRBs, charitable

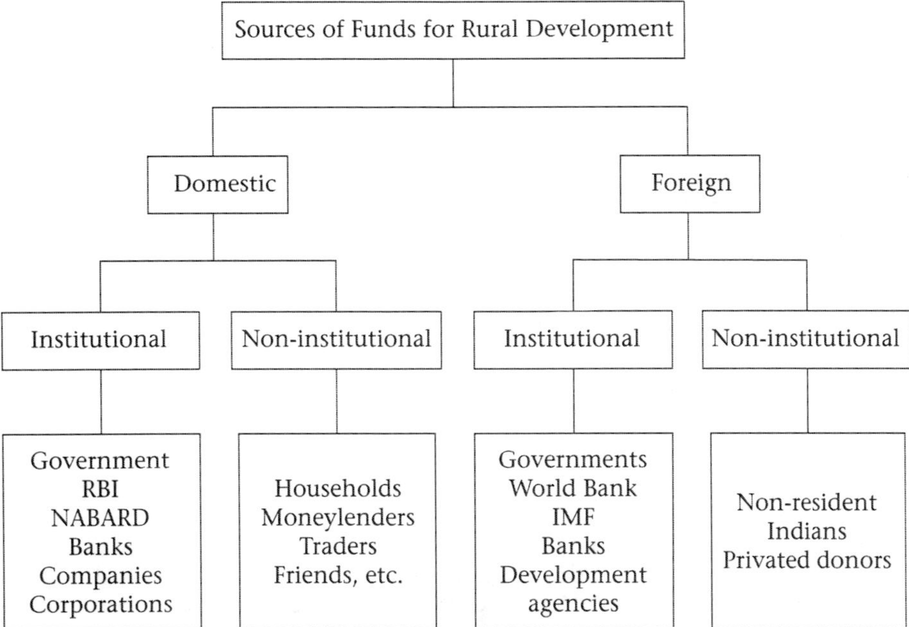

Figure 14.1: *Sources of Funds for Rural Development*

public trusts, foundations, and private companies and corporations. Non-institutional sources include households, moneylenders, traders, and friends and relatives. Foreign institutional sources include foreign governments, development agencies, the World Bank, the ADB, the IMF, foreign banks, multinational corporations, and so on. Foreign non-institutional sources include NRIs and foreign nationals.

In countries such as India, which are both poor and nationalistic, neither sacrifices from current consumption nor heavy reliance on foreign aid and investment is popular with the political leaders and electorate as means of financing development. However, there are no other alternatives for the government but to follow these painful paths to development. Without a certain amount of national sacrifice, economic development will not occur. The sacrifice may take one, more, or all of the following forms:

1. Working harder and more efficiently.
2. Saving voluntarily to finance development investment, public or private.
3. Paying higher taxes to finance development investment.
4. Controlling inflation, with whatever hardships it may cause to the people (deficit financing).
5. Encouraging foreign investment, no matter what temporary sacrifices of opportunities for national businessmen may be involved.
6. Accepting foreign aid, with whatever commitment is required as a condition for receipt of such aid.
7. Changes in sectoral terms of trade.

Working harder and better is not "finance" in the ordinary sense, and it will not raise standards of living very much unless accompanied by capital formation. Therefore, the government depends on the other six sources of financing development.

In this chapter, we briefly discuss the role of domestic and foreign sources of funds for rural development, and examine their suitability in the Indian context.

Domestic Institutional Sources

Domestic institutional sources of rural credit include the government, the RBI, NABARD, cooperative banks, commercial banks (CBs), RRBs and Self Help Groups (SHGs). We now briefly discuss the role of each of these agencies.

Central and State Governments

The government in the past has been, still is, and will continue in future to be the most important source of funds for rural development in India. At the national level, the Union Ministry of Finance is responsible for the mobilization, allocation and administration of financial resources for various purposes, including rural development. It also regulates the expenditure of the government, including transfer of resources to the states. Power to raise and disburse public funds has been divided under the Constitution of India between the Union and state governments. The Finance Commission of India, which was established in 1951 under Article 280 of the Indian Constitution, makes recommendations to the president of India about the distribution of the net proceeds of taxes between the Union and states and also the allocation of the same amongst the states themselves. It is also under the ambit of the Finance Commission to define the financial relations between the Union and the states. They also deal with devolution of non-plan revenue resources. Now the Fourteenth Finance Commission (2015–20) has been constituted under the chairmanship of Y.V. Reddy, former RBI governor.

The sources of revenue for the Union and states are, by and large, mutually exclusive, if shareable taxes and duties between the two are excluded. The Constitution provides that: (a) no tax can be levied or collected except by the authority of law; (b) no expenditure can be incurred from public funds except in the manner provided in the Constitution; and (c) executive authorities must spend public money only in the manner sanctioned by the Parliament in the case of the Union and by the state legislatures in the case of states.

All receipts and disbursements of the Union are kept under two separate heads, namely, the Consolidated Fund of India (CFI) and the Public Account of India (PAI). All revenue received, loans raised and money received as the repayment of loans by the Union form the consolidated fund. No money can be withdrawn from this fund except under the authority of an act of Parliament. All other receipts, such as deposits, service funds, and remittances go into the PAI, and disbursements therefrom are not subject to the vote of the Parliament. To meet unforeseen needs not provided in the Annual Appropriation Act, a contingency fund of India has been established under Article 267(1) of the Constitution. The Indian Constitution provides for the establishment of a consolidated fund, a public account and a contingency fund for each state.

The main sources of the Union tax revenue are customs duties, Union excise duties, and corporate and income taxes. Non-tax revenues largely comprise interest receipts, including the interest paid by the railways and telecommunications ministries, dividends, and profits. The main heads of revenue in the states are taxes and duties levied by the respective state government, a share of taxes levied by the Union and the grants received from the Union. Property taxes, octroi, and terminal taxes are the mainstay of local finance. Devolution of the resources from the Union to the states is a salient feature of the system of federal finance of India. Apart from their share of taxes and duties, state governments receive statutory and other grants, as well as loans for various development and non-development purposes. An estimate of all anticipated receipts and expenditure of the Union for the ensuing year is laid before the Parliament. This is known as the Union Budget, and it covers the central government's transactions of all kinds in and outside India occurring during the preceding year, the year in which the statement is prepared, as well as the ensuing year, or the "budget year," as it is known. Government funds are made available in the form of investment, grants, subsidies, and loans. Allocations are made through the annual budgetary process. The total public (government) sector plan outlay and expenditure on agriculture and allied activities, including rural development and special area programs under the Five Year Plans are presented in Table 14.1. As shown in the table, the total expenditure on agriculture and rural development in the public sector since the beginning of the planning era (1951–52) until the Eleventh Five Year Plan (2007–12) aggregated ₹3,58,276.700 billion at current prices As a percentage of the total plan expenditure in the public sector, the share of agriculture and rural development varied from around 11% to 17%, with an overall average of around 15% for the entire period. In the Eleventh Five Year Plan, the total expenditure on agriculture and rural development was ₹3,58,276.700 billion at current prices, which accounted for 13.7% of the total public sector expenditure.

Table 14.1: *Public Sector Outlay and Expenditure on Agriculture and Allied Activities in India's Five Year Plans*

	Agriculture and Rural Development (₹ Billion)*		*Total (₹ Billion)*		*Share of Agriculture and Rural Development (%)*	
Five Year Plan	*Plan Outlay*	*Actual Expenditure*	*Plan Outlay*	*Actual Expenditure*	*Plan Outlay*	*Actual Expenditure*
First Plan (1951–56)	3.540	2.900	23.780	19.600	14.9	14.8
Second Plan (1956–61)	5.100	5.490	45.000	46.720	11.3	11.7
Third Plan (1961–66	10.860	10.890	75.000	85.770	14.5	12.7
Annual Plans (1966–69)	10.370	11.070	66.650	66.250	15.6	16.7
Fourth Plan (1969–74)	27.280	23.200	159.020	157.790	17.1	14.7
Fifth Plan (1974–79)	47.660	48.650	393.220	394.260	12.1	12.3
Annual Plan (1979–80)	18.150	19.960	126.010	121.760	14.4	16.1
Sixth Plan (1980–85)	125.390	152.010	975.000	1,092.920	12.9	13.9
Seventh Plan (1985–90)	222.330	315.090	1,800.000	2,187.300	12.3	14.4
Annual Plan (1990–91)	91.420	85.420	647.170	583.690	14.1	14.6
Annual Plan (1991–92)	100.580	90.600	723.170	64.750	13.9	14.0

(Table 14.1 Continued)

(Table 14.1 Continued)

Five Year Plan	Agriculture and Rural Development* (₹ Billion)		Total (₹ Billion)		Share of Agriculture and Rural Development (%)	
	Plan Outlay	Actual Expenditure	Plan Outlay	Actual Expenditure	Plan Outlay	Actual Expenditure
Eighth Plan (1992–97)	636.420	232.510	4,341.000	1,609.330	14.7	14.4
Ninth Plan (1997–2002)	1,209.970	1,187.610	8,592.000	79,274.000	14.1	15.0
Tenth Plan (2002 07)	2,017.400	1,376.650	15,256.390	NA	13.2	NA
Eleventh Plan (2007–12)	4,637.790 (at 2006–07 prices)	4,919.950 (at current prices)	3,644.718 (at 2006–07 prices)	3,58,276.700 (at current prices)	12.7	13.7
Twelfth Plan (2012–17)	9,011.070 (at current prices)	NA	7,669.807 (at current prices)	NA	11.7	NA

Sources: (GoI 2007a, 2008b),[1,2] MoF (2015, A46–A47 for 11th and 12th Plans).
Note: *Includes agriculture, animal husbandry and dairying, research and education, forestry and wildlife, plantation, agricultural marketing and rural godowns, food storage and warehousing, rural development, cooperation and special area programs.

In India, the government is probably the oldest institutional source of rural credit. The government provides financial assistance by granting loans to the cultivator under: (a) the Improvements Loans Act of 1883 and (b) the Agriculturists' Loans Act of 1884. Such loans are known as *taccavi* loans. The act of 1883 authorizes the grant of long-term loans by the taluka/tehsil-level officers of the government for effecting permanent improvements on land, such as construction of wells, land leveling, protection of lands from floods or erosion, and so on. Such loans are generally granted for periods extending over 25 years, on the security of landed property at a relatively low rate of interest.

Under the Act of 1884, short- and medium-term loans are granted by the government to meet the current agricultural needs, such as the purchase of seeds, fertilizers, and small tools and implement. Such loans are repayable over a period of six months to one year, mostly after the harvest of crops. The rate of interest charged on these loans is lower than the rate charged by CBs and cooperatives.

The record of taccavi loans has been rather poor. Some of the drawbacks are the inadequate amount, inordinate delays in sanctioning the loan, lack of supervision, poor recovery, and lack of coordination. In view of the rapidly expanding role of cooperative credit institutions, CBs, and RRBs in the sphere of rural credit, the relative importance of taccavi loans has been declining over the years.

With a view to encouraging individuals, corporate and non-corporate bodies to participate in the national effort of rural development, a National Fund for Rural Development (NFRD) was established by the Union Ministry of Rural Development in February, 1984. The fund is managed by a committee under the chairmanship of the Prime Minister. Donations made by all categories of taxpayers to the NFRD are deductible while computing taxable income, under

Sections 35 CCA and 80 CCA of the Income Tax Act, 1961. The NFRD projects can be executed through an implementing agency, having the legal status of

1. An irrevocable public charitable trust registered under the Income Tax Act, 1961;
2. A society registered under the Societies Registration Act, 1860, or under any other law corresponding to that act in force in any part of India;
3. A company incorporated under Section 25 of the Companies Act, 1956; and
4. A corporation established by or under a central/state act concerned with the development of rural areas. Donors, while making donations, may recommend their preference for the area or locality and the rural development programs for which the donations may be utilized, as also the implementing agency through which the program may be undertaken and implemented. The recommendations, if any, of the donors, are given due consideration to the extent deemed appropriate by the government/management committee of the fund.

The Reserve Bank of India (RBI)

The RBI was established under the Reserve Bank of India Act, 1934, on April 1, 1935, and nationalized on January 1, 1949. The RBI is the sole authority for issue of currency in India, other than one rupee coins and subsidiary coins and notes. As the agent of the Central government, the RBI undertakes distribution of one rupee notes and coins as well as small coins issued by the government. The RBI acts as the banker to the Central government, state governments, CBs, state cooperative banks (SCBs), and some of the financial institutions. It formulates and administers monetary policy, with a view to ensuring stability in prices, while promoting higher production in the real sector through proper deployment of credit. The RBI plays an important role in maintaining the stability of the exchange value of the rupee and acts as an agent of the government in respect of India's membership of the IMF. The RBI also performs a variety of developmental and promotional functions.

The RBI was a pioneer central bank in the sphere of rural credit. Its founding act of legislation and subsequent amendments entrusted to it the responsibility for enlarging the availability of rural credit. The bank shouldered this responsibility rather reluctantly until 1947, when, after independence, this responsibility was reinforced and became a major responsibility of the bank. The activities of the RBI in the sphere of rural credit can be broadly divided into three categories: (a) financing functions; (b) promotional, advisory, and coordinating functions; and (c) regulatory functions. The first category covers the provision of long-term loans to state governments from the National Agricultural Credit (long-term operations) Fund to enable them to contribute to the share capital of the cooperative credit institutions, provision of medium-term loans to the SCBs to refinance the seasonal crop (short-term) loans of credit cooperatives, granting medium-term loans to the SCBs from the National Agricultural (stabilization) Fund to enable them to repay their short-term loans to the RBI under conditions of drought or famine, and short-, medium-, and long-term loans to NABARD. Its promotional and coordinating functions include formulation of programs for cooperative credit under the five year plans, annual reviews of the progress of various credit schemes, and assistance to the Central and state governments, and cooperative credit institutions in tackling their problems in implementing various credit schemes. The regulatory functions include establishing credit limits and credit norms for various purposes, and control of advances by commercial and cooperative banks.

Though the flow of credit to the agricultural sector has improved from ₹1,12,020 million 1991–92 to ₹4,68,291 million in 2010–11, and to ₹8,40,643 million in 2014–15, the RBI perceives that investment in agriculture, particularly non-farm investments in agriculture, has not kept pace with demand to encourage credit flow to the agricultural sector.

National Bank for Agricultural and Rural Development (NABARD)

A major landmark in the history of development of rural credit in India was the establishment of NABARD in July 1982, by merging the Agricultural Refinance and Development Corporation, the Agricultural Credit Department of the RBI, and the Rural Credit and Planning Cell of the RBI. The RBI owns 50% of the share capital of NABARD and the rest is held by the Government of India. As on March 31, 2015, the total amount of NABARD' fund stood at ₹2,858,090 billion, which is a huge amount by any standards (NABARD 2015, xiii). The sources and uses of funds of NABARD are presented in Table 14.2. The main sources of NABARD's funds consist of the National Rural Credit (long-term operations) Fund and the National Rural Credit (stabilization) Fund transferred to it by the RBI at the time of its establishment, Bonds and Debentures, Reserves and Surpluses, RIDF Deposits, STCRC Fund, and borrowings from the RBI, the Government of India and the market. The Government of India also provides to NABARD funds received from the World Bank and other external agencies under various credit projects. Most of the amount of funds shown under "loans and advances" constitute the most important use of the funds.

Table 14.2: *Sources and Uses of NABARD's Funds as on March 31, 2015*

Sources	*Amount (₹ Million)*	*Uses*	*Amount (₹ Million)*
Capital	50,000	Cash and Bank Balances	1,29,610
Reserves & Surplus	1,96,010	Collateralized Borrowing and Lending Obligation	1,650
		Investments	
National Rural Credit (LTO) Fund	1,44,850	a) GOI Securities	30,990
National Rural Credit (stabilization) Fund	15,850	b) ADFC Equity	1,310
Deposits	3,010	c) AFC Equity	10
Bonds and Debentures	3,40,070	d) SIDBI Equity	480
Borrowings from GoI	200	e) AICI Ltd.	600
Borrowings JNN Solar Mission*	360	f) NCDEX Ltd, UCX & MCX Ltd.	340
Foreign Currency Loan	7,270	g) Nabcons	50
Commercial Paper	28,980	h) Biotech Venture Fund	960
CBLO**	52,810	i) Treasury Bills	53,460
Term Money Borrowings	5,150	j) Commercial Paper	9,750
RIDF deposits	8,96,030	k) Non-Convertible Bonds	1,500

(Table 14.2 Continued)

(Table 14.2 Continued)

Sources	*Amount (₹ Million)*	*Uses*	*Amount (₹ Million)*
STCRC Fund@	6,00,000	l) Equity Shares of Other Institution	620
Short Term RRB Credit Refinance Fund	3,00,000	m) Debentures in Nature of Advance	64,690
Warehouse Infrastructure Fund	15,500	n) Certificate of Deposits	41,610
Long Term Rural Credit Fund	50,000	o) Mutual funds	6,000
		Loans and Advances	
Other Liabilities	94,090	a) Production & Marketing Credit	8,87,110
Other Funds	57,100	b) Conversion of Production Credit into MT Loans	0
		c) MT & LT Project Loans	6,19,170
		d) Loans under Warehouse Infrastructure Fund	11,540
		e) LT Non Project Loans	590
		f) Other Loans	1,05,050
		g) RIDF Loans	8,35,450
		h) Co-finance (net of provision)	100
		Fixed Assets	3,250
		Other Assets	5,220
Total	**28,58,090**	**Total**	**28,58,090**

Source: NABARD (2015, xiii).
Notes: *JNN Solar Mission: Jawaharlal Nehru National Solar Mission.
**CBLO: Collateralized Borrowing and Lending Obligation.
@STCRC: Short Term Cooperative Rural Credit (STCRC) Refinance Fund.

The main functions of NABARD include refinance (short-, medium-, and long-term) to the cooperative banks and RRBs, refinance to CBs against term lending (medium- and long-term), short-term accommodation for special cases, and overall policy, planning, coordination, and monitoring of all agricultural and rural lending activities in the country. Besides, it also undertakes training, research, and consultancy relating to rural credit.

The main objective of the establishment of NABARD was to provide institutional credit through banks for promotion of agriculture, small-scale industries, cottage and village industries, handicrafts and other types of rural craft and allied activities in rural areas. NABARD provides refinance facilities to CBs, SCBs, State Land Development Banks (SLDBs), now known as State Cooperative Agricultural and Rural Development Banks (SCARDBs) and RRBs, to enable them to advance short-, medium-, and long- term loans for specified bankable projects. CBs and SLDBs are supported only for term (medium and long) loans. Financial assistance is also provided by NABARD to state governments to enable them to contribute to the share capital of cooperative credit institutions. From the financial year 1995–96, NABARD has also entered into the area of direct financing. Initially, it directly financed big high-tech projects only. The development of agriculture (farm sector) on a sustainable basis has always been the main agenda of NABARD. In pursuance of this goal, it has taken a number of initiatives such as watershed-based programs, livelihood-based programs, natural resource management programs, transfer of agricultural technology, the development of tribal farmers, enhancing the resilience of agriculture against climate change, and the promotion and financing of producers' organizations.

Hitherto, the farm sector had been the major focus of rural development. The non-farm sector (NFS) has of late assumed importance in view of its potential for employment generation in rural areas. Several refinements in policies relating to credit for the farm sector, as well as new initiatives relating to the NFS have been introduced by NABARD. Even after considerable expansion of the network of the formal credit institutions, certain sections of the population have not been reached. The bank has actively supported innovations in credit delivery, to extend the outreach of credit to these sections.

NABARD works in close cooperation with various Central government agencies to refinance various priority schemes, such as watershed development and management, dry land farming, warehouses and godowns, wastelands development, forestry, aquaculture, and poverty alleviation programs. Besides, it has made quite a few innovations in both the structures and methods of delivering rural credit. A few of its innovative schemes include Vikas Volunteer Vahini (VVV) program, promotional grants to VAs and NGOs, establishment of a cooperative development fund, establishment of a rural infrastructure development fund (RIDF), establishment of a watershed development fund and a warehouse infrastructure fund and promotional schemes for NFS, and financing of rural health services.

Indian economy in general and banking services in particular have made rapid strides in the recent past. However, a sizeable section of the population, particularly the vulnerable groups, such as weaker sections and low income groups, continue to remain excluded from even the most basic opportunities and services provided by the financial sector. In order to address the issues of financial inclusion, the Government of India constituted a committee on financial inclusion[3] under the Chairmanship of C. Rangarajan. The committee submitted its final report to the Union finance minister on January 4, 2008. The committee had recommended, among other things, setting up of two funds—FIF and FITF.

Based on the recommendations of the Rangarajan Committee, the Government of India has constituted two funds, namely, FIF for meeting the cost of developmental and promotional interventions of financial inclusion and FITF to meet the cost of technology adoption for financial inclusion. The two funds have been established in NABARD, which is the coordinating agency of financial inclusion initiatives with Financial Inclusion Department (FID) as the nodal department Each fund consists of an overall corpus of ₹5,000 million, with initial funding contributed by the Government of India, RBI, and NABARD in the ratio of 40:40:20. The funding was to be contributed in a phased manner over a maximum period of five years, depending upon the utilization of funds. However, the RBI has now decided that the relative margin available to NABARD in excess of 0.5% in respect of deposits placed by banks under RIDF and STCRC will be credited to FIF with effect from April 1, 2012 and funds for FITF will be, by way of transfer from FIF, RBI and the Government of India. It was also decided that FIF and FITF may be managed with such margin and there will be no more contribution by them.[4] The RBI on October 15, 2015 announced the merger of the two funds to create a new FIF with a corpus of ₹20,000 million to support "developmental and promotional activities" for expanding the reach of banking services. While presenting the Union Budget for 2014–15, the Union Finance Minister announced that a "Producers' Organization Development and Upliftment Corpus" Fund of ₹2,000 million to be utilized for building of 2,000 Farmer Producer Organizations (FPOs) in the next two years to supplement NABARD's Producer Organization Development Fund (PODF). Pursuant to this announcement, the Government of India has created a Producers' Organization Development and Upliftment Corpus'(PRODUCE) fund of ₹2,000 million in NABARD. The fund is intended to meet the initial requirements of the emerging FPOs, which would subsequently be able to avail of new business opportunities with the support of credit from financing institutions. The fund has become operational and 835 FPOs had been approved during the financial year 2014–15.

Cooperative Credit Agencies (CCAs)

Cooperative credit societies entered the field of rural finance with the adoption of the Cooperative Societies Act of 1904. Since then, the government has been making deliberate attempts to nurture the cooperative movement in the country in the larger interests of the rural people. Credit cooperatives have been recognized as the best institutions to provide rural credit to the farmer because they satisfy all the important criteria of sound agricultural credit.

Credit cooperatives have many advantages over other sources of credit. First, being located right in the rural areas where their borrowers reside, they are in close proximity to their clients. Second, they have more intimate knowledge of the character and abilities of their members than any other financial institution. Third, they can easily supervise the use of credit, so that it is used for productive purposes. Fourth, the credit provided by the cooperative societies is bound to be cheap, due to their lower administrative costs and lower cost of their funds. Fifth, the credit provided by the credit cooperatives is neither too rigid nor too elastic; it is also safe, as it assists, and does not hamper, the borrowers' stability and productive capacity.

Despite these positive aspects, cooperative credit suffers from the following weaknesses:

1. The tendency of cooperative credit has been to flow mainly toward big cultivators. The small and marginal farmers have been handicapped in their access to cooperative credit, both for current inputs and viable investment.
2. The experience of cooperative credit in India shows that, despite improvements over the years, the proportion of cooperative credit to total borrowings of cultivators has been declining over time.
3. The orientation of cooperative credit to production needs has, by and large, been inadequate.
4. The cooperative credit system has been vulnerable to political interferences and rigid bureaucratic controls.
5. A large number (over 65%) of primary agricultural credit societies are neither viable, nor even potentially viable, and must be regarded as inadequate and unsatisfactory agencies for dispensing production-oriented credit.
6. Cooperative credit has frequently fallen short of standards of promptness, adequacy, and dependability. This has been due to various reasons, including the paucity of resources, lack of eligibility, time consuming and cumbersome procedures, poor management, and efficiency in working methods.
7. Coordination between the authorities and agencies in charge of cooperative credit, and those in charge of supplies and extension education under agricultural programs, has generally been inadequate.

The cooperative credit system in the country comprises short-term and long-term credit structures. In 2010–11, the short-term cooperative credit structure comprised 31 SCBs, 371 District Central Cooperative Banks (DCCBs) and over 93,413 Primary Agricultural Credit Societies (PACS) including Large-sized Adivasi Multi-purpose Society (LAMPS) and Farmers Service Society (FSS), operating at the apex, middle, and ground levels, respectively (NCUI 2012, pp. 36–43).

In 2010–11, the long-term cooperative credit structure in the country consisted of 19 SCARDBs, originally known as land mortgage banks/land development banks, having a unitary structure in eight states and a federal/mixed structure in 11 states, operating through 2,610 operational units (including 701 Primary Cooperative Agricultural and Rural Development Banks (PCARDBs) (NCUI 2012, 46). In Andhra Pradesh, there is an integrated structure wherein the units of the short-term structure provide all types of agricultural credit under a "single window" credit delivery system. In the North Eastern region, only three states are served by the long-term structure.

As far as the flow of ground level agricultural credit is concerned, the share of the cooperative banks has been declining over time. In 2002–03, it was about 34%, which had declined to 17% by the year 2010–11 and has been stagnant around that level since then, whereas the share of commercial banks had increased from 57% in 2002–03 to 74% in 2010–11 but had decline marginally to 71% by 2014–15. During 2014–15, all of the banks in India disbursed ₹8,406.43 billion (provisional) credit to the agricultural sector, against the target of ₹8,000.00 million. Commercial banks, cooperative banks, and RRBs disbursed ₹5,996.91 billion (provisional), ₹1,384.69 billion, and ₹1,024.83 billion, respectively (Table 14.3). Cooperative credit societies and cooperative banks suffer from several internal and external problems. Quite a significant proportion of cooperative banks are not financially viable, in 2010–11, 41% of the PACS were in loss, and the proportions of SCB branches, DCB branches, and SCARDBs in loss were about 17%, 36% and 74% respectively (NCUI 2012, 37–43). As on March 31, 2014, the aggregate accumulated losses of SCBs, DCBs, SCARDBs, and PCARDBs stood at ₹7,039.2 million, ₹38,680 million, ₹24,112 million, and ₹51,120.7 million respectively (NABARD 2015, 81). There is no formal system of corporate governance extant in the cooperative banks. As a result, a number of cooperative banks have come to be the hot bed of political patronage, unscrupulous financial practices, and gross mismanagement. In certain cases, these have become private fiefdoms of individual political and other functionaries sustaining themselves on public money. In the past 15 years or so, over a dozen cooperative banks have been defrauded. On the financial landscape, cooperative banks, politicians, and scamsters have come to form a destructive antisocial nexus, thanks to the bad governance (Law 2002, 46). Consequently, most of the cooperative credit societies and banks are not financially viable.

In view of all this, there is need for putting effective corporate governance in place in cooperative banks. The RBI has recently taken some steps to improve the governance in the cooperative sector (RBI 2000). In January 2006, the Government of India announced a package

Table 14.3: *Flow of Institutional Credit to Agriculture and Allied Activities in India by Agency*

(₹ Billion)

Agency	*2010–11*	*2011–12*	*2012–13*	*2013–14*	*2014–15 P*
Commercial banks	3,458.77 (74)	3,686.16 (72)	4,324.91 (71)	5,090.05 (71)	5,996.91 (71)
Regional Rural banks	442.93 (9)	544.50 (11)	636.81 (11)	826.52 (12)	1,024.83 (12)
Cooperative banks	781.21 (17)	879.63 (17)	1,112.03 (18)	1,199.64 (17)	1,38.69 (17)
Total	4,682.91 (100)	5,110.29 (100)	6,073.75 (100)	7,116.21 (100)	8,406.43 (100)

Source: NABARD (2015, Table 1.8, p. 18).

for the revival of short-term rural cooperative credit structure involving financial assistance of ₹1,35,960 million. NABARD has been designated as the implementing agency for the purpose. A department for cooperative revival and reforms has been set up in NABARD for facilitating the implementation process. States are required to sign a Memorandum of Understanding (MoU) with NABARD, committing to implement the legal, institutional, and other reforms as envisaged in the revival package.

Commercial Banks (CBs)

The commercial banking system in India in 2012–13 consisted of 89 comprising 26 public sector banks, 13 old private sector banks, seven new private sector banks and 43 foreign banks (RBI 2013, 1–8). In all, all the 89 commercial banks in India had 92,114 branches. 14 major CBs were nationalized in July 1969 and another six in 1980. Now there are 26 public sector banks having a mandate to provide credit to rural people. In addition, 246 private CBs are also operating in the country. These CBs provide short-, medium-, and long-term credit for various agricultural and rural development activities. Until the nationalization of major CBs in 1969, the official policy was to give a fillip to the cooperative banking system as the channel best suited for institutional credit for agriculture. Before their nationalization, CBs supplied only a negligible share of rural credit: 0.9% in 1951–52 and 0.6% in 1961–62. Even after the nationalization, they were a bit hesitant in going full steam ahead in financing agriculture; four years after the nationalization, in 1973–74, their share in total rural credit was only 5%. However, since the mid-1990s, there has been a substantial increase in their involvement in agricultural lending. The total number of branches of all CBs in India in 2006 was 69,616, which increased to 92,114 in 2012–13 and their share in direct agricultural advances went up from 1.3% of bank credit in July 1969 to 69% in 2014–15. In the years to come, the Indian banking system has a strategic role to play in increasing the national savings rate, in canalizing the available savings to finance high priority investments, in better utilization of available capacities both in agriculture and in industry through adequate supply of credit as working capital, and in promoting the cause of social justice by increased emphasis on the credit needs of the hitherto neglected sectors and sections of population, as also by providing finance for such anti-poverty programs.

Regional Rural Banks (RRBs)

The RRBs were established consequent to the acceptance by the Government of India of the recommendations of a working group on rural banks appointed by the Union finance ministry in July 1975, under the chairmanship of M. Narasimham. The first five RRBs were established on October 2, 1975, following the promulgation of the RRBs ordinance by the Government of India on September 26, 1975. The ordinance was subsequently replaced by the Regional Rural Bank Act, 1976. The issued and paid up share capital of RRBs as in 2015 was ₹1,970 million, share capital deposit 61,730 million reserves 1,84,620 million and deposits 27,13,290 million (NABARD 2015, 91). The share capital is held by the Government of India, the sponsor bank, and the concerned state government in the proportion of 50:35:15. The management of each RRB is vested in a board of directors headed by a chairman (usually an officer of the sponsor bank and appointed by the Government of India).

Initially, RRBs were mandated to cater to the credit needs of the weaker sections of the rural community comprising small and marginal farmers, agricultural laborers, artisans, and small entrepreneurs. With effect from December 1993, their mandate has been expanded to include non-target group borrowers also. These RRBs were intended to be low-cost "small man's banks," combining the advantages of cooperatives (close rapport with villagers) and CBs (business acumen). To enable RRBs to keep their costs down, the salary and perks of their staff were fixed at par with those of the comparable district level staff of the state government concerned. The statutory liquidity ratio (SLR) was fixed at a lower level as compared to commercial banks, and low cost refinance from NABARD and sponsor banks up to prescribed levels was permitted.

The RRBs advance short-, medium-, and long-term loans for various rural development activities, including crop production, purchase of tractors, setting up of small village industries, village crafts, various artisans' activities, retail trade, consumer durables, house construction, purchase of mini buses, and so on. Their share in the total quantum of credit disbursed to the agricultural and rural development activities in 2010–11 was 9%, which increased to 12% in 2014–15.

The RRBs were established as a new set of state-sponsored, rurally-oriented, region-based, low cost banks, having the ethos of cooperatives and business acumen of CBs for providing credit in the rural areas, particularly to the relatively weaker sections of society. It would be fair to say that the RRBs have succeeded in spreading banking services to far flung rural areas, mobilizing rural savings, opening up more avenues for rural poor through institutional credit, and generating employment opportunities. However, their mandate of financing only the target group borrowers, coupled with an administered interest rate structure, poor recovery performance, increasing establishment costs, and low level of operational efficiency have resulted in the RRBs incurring losses and losing their financial viability right from their inception (Deshpande, Mudgal, and Gupta 1996, 22–23).

With a view to enabling the RRBs to achieve current and sustainable financial viability, several policy measures were initiated, including revamping of the RRBs by infusion of capital. The concept of development action plans (DAPs) was initiated by NABARD, and the RRBs and sponsor banks signed a MoU for ensuring performance obligations/commitments. Initially, 49 RRBs and, subsequently, another 53 were selected for restructuring during 1994–95 and 1995–96, respectively. Financial support aggregating ₹7,471.4 million was provided for the purpose. During 1996–97, an additional 36 RRBs were selected, and the central government provided ₹1497.7 million for strengthening their financial position. Further, a second dose of assistance was also provided to 16 RRBs during 1996–97, aggregating ₹502.3 million. An equal amount was contributed by the sponsor banks and state governments. The Central government made a further provision of ₹2,700 million in the 1997–98 budget and ₹2,650 million in the 1998–99 budget to carry forward the process of rehabilitation and recapitalization of the RRBs. As a result of all these measures taken under the direction of NABARD, a perceptible improvement in the performance of the RRBs in all spheres has been observed (NABARD 1997, 47).

As per the review undertaken by the K. C. Chakraborty Committee on "Recapitalization of RRBs for improving the Capital to Risk Weighted Assets Ratio (CRAR)" in 2010, of the 82 RRBs, 42 were deemed capable of bringing the CRAR to the desired level of 9% on their own. The Government of India, along with other shareholders, decided to recapitalize the remaining 40 RRBs, infusing ₹22,000 million in the proportion of 50:35:15 (Government of India: sponsor banks: state governments), as per the recommendations of the committee. As on March 31, 2015, a cumulative amount of ₹20,765 million had been released to 38 RRBs from 20 states. Of the released amount, ₹10,382.4 million was the Government of India's contribution, ₹7,267.8 million, the sponsor banks' contribution and ₹3,114.9 million being the contribution of various state governments (NABARD 2015, 91–92).

The RBI in 2001 constituted a committee under the chairmanship of V. S. Vyas on "Flow of Credit to Agriculture and Related Activities from the Banking System," which examined the relevance of RRBs in the rural credit system and the alternatives for making it viable. The consolidation process, thus, was initiated in the year 2005 as an off-shoot of V. S. Vyas Committee recommendations. The first phase of amalgamation was initiated in 2005 sponsor bank-wise within a State and the second phase was started in 2012 across the sponsor banks within a State. The process was initiated with a view to provide better customer service by having better infrastructure, computerization, experienced work force, common publicity and marketing efforts, and so on. The amalgamated RRBs also benefit from larger area of operation, enhanced credit exposure limits for high value, and diverse banking activities.

After their amalgamation, as in March 2015, there were 56 RRBs in the country with a network of 20,059 branches covering 644 notified districts in 26 states and the UT of Puducherry. As a result, the deposits of RRBs increased to ₹27,13,290 million crore by the end of 2014–15, registering a growth of 13.29% over the previous year. The aggregate loans and advances outstanding with RRBs improved to ₹18,48,430 million as on 31 March 2015—excluding the Inter-bank Participation Certificate (IBPC)—registering a growth of 15.9% over the previous year. During 2014–15, out of the 56 RRBs for which data is available, 51 had earned aggregate profits to the tune of ₹29,580 million, compared to 57 RRBs earning an aggregate profit of ₹26,940 million in 2013–14. While no RRB incurred losses during 2013–14, as many as five reported losses amounting to ₹1,770 million in 2014–15. Thus, the net profit of RRBs marginally increased to ₹27,810 million by the end of March 2015. The proportion of RRBs that are sustainably viable, that is, earning profits and carrying no accumulated losses, has decreased from 86% (49 out of 57) as on March 31, 2014 to 84% (47 out of 56) as on March 31, 2015 (NABARD 2015, 90).

Self Help Groups (SHGs)

An SHG is a small group of individual members who voluntarily come together and form an association for achieving a common objective. In most cases, SHGs are constituted by persons known to one another and coming from the same village, community, or neighborhood, that is, SHGs are small in size with membership ranging from 10 to 25, are homogeneous, and have certain pre-group social binding factors. The purpose for which SHGs are formed varies from managing a CPR, such as an irrigation facility and tree plantation on common lands, to providing such basic amenities as a school, a health center, and so on. In the context of micro-finance, SHGs are formed around the theme of savings and credit. In February 1992, NABARD launched a pilot project on "Linking SHGs with Banks" after consultations with the RBI, selected banks, and NGOs. The main objective of the project was to develop innovative participatory and self-sustaining credit delivery systems for improving the access of the rural poor to institutional credit. The systems are intended to complement and supplement the role of the formal rural credit system. Under the project, credit is provided to SHGs by banks using a simplified procedure that requires minimum documentation.

Under the SHG-Bank Linkage Programme, three linkage models have broadly emerged: (a) SHGs formed and financed by banks; (b) SHGs formed by other agencies, including NGOs, but directly financed by banks; and (c) SHGs financed by banks using financial intermediaries. The SHG–Bank Linkage Programme (SHG–BLP) has expanded substantially since it was first launched on a pilot scale in 1992. As of March 31, 2014, there were more than 7.43 million savings-linked SHGs, covering over 97 million poor households. The total savings of these SHGs with banks amounted to ₹98,974.2 million. The number of credit-linked SHGs under the program was 4.20 million.

The program is being expanded with a view to covering all eligible poor rural households, with a focus on resource-poor states, providing livelihood opportunities to SHG members and covering the areas that have not been reached. Efforts are being made to revive dormant SHGs and prevent the functional ones from disintegrating, through measures such as capacity-building and hand-holding support. In close coordination with the NRLM, an attempt is being made to form and nurture groups by involving NGOs and a community-support system for promoting and nurturing SHGs is being suitably incentivized.

During 2014–15, NABARD had spent a sum of ₹.410 million from the FIF and the Women Self-Help Group (WSHG) Development Fund on various microfinance-related activities. These included the formation and linkage of SHGs, training and capacity-building of stakeholders, promotion of livelihoods, documentation, generation of awareness, and introduction of innovations (NABARD 2015, 123–25).

NABARD has been networking with a large number of NGOs. These NGOs act either as facilitators, or both as facilitators and financial intermediaries, in effecting the linkage of SHGs with banks. With a view to increase the involvement of NGOs/SHGs in improving the outreach of credit to the rural poor, the RBI constituted a working group in November 1994, under the chairmanship of the managing director of NABARD. Based on the recommendations of the working Group, banks were advised to consider lending to SHGs as a normal business activity under the priority sector, and internalize the training of their officers. As a follow-up measure, NABARD constituted, in each state, a State Level Review and Coordination Committee on Credit Delivery Innovations (SLRCCDI) comprising senior officials of the RBI, banks, prominent NGOs, and a few state government departments, with the officer-in-charge of the bank's regional office acting as the chairman-cum-convener. These committees review the progress periodically in various credit delivery innovations to improve the access of the rural poor to credit.

The Role of Non-institutional Agencies

Non-institutional agencies that supply credit to farmers and other rural people include professional moneylenders, agricultural moneylenders, landlords, traders, commission agents, and friends and relatives. Traditionally, these agencies have played an important role in meeting the credit requirements of villagers. Most of the money advanced by them used to be—and still is—spent on household consumption, and social and religious ceremonies, and very little, if any, on production activities. The interest rates were very high, usually ranging from 24% to 60% per annum. The incidence of indebtedness was very high, and most of the rural poor were "born in debt, lived in debt and died in debt." Table 14.4 presents the estimates of the share of non-institutional sources in the total rural credit advance in India over the period, 1951 to 2013. As shown in the table, the share of non-institutional sources as a proportion of the total quantum rural credit advanced in India declined rapidly over the period 1951–81, it was about 93% in 1951 but declined rapidly to about 36% in 2001 However, the trend seems to have reversed during the period 1991 to 2013; their share increased from 36% in 1991 to 43.9% in 2013.

Table 14.4: *Share of Non-institutional Sources in the Total Rural Credit Advanced in India: 1951–2013*

Source	*1951*	*1961*	*1971*	*1981*	*1991*	*2002*	*2013*
Money lenders	69.7	68.8	36.9	16.9	15.7	29.6	33.2
Relatives, friends etc.	14.2	6.9	13.8	9.0	6.7	7.1	8.5
Traders, & commission agents	5.5	7.7	8.7	3.0	7.1	2.6	0.1
Land lords	1.5	0.9	8.6	4.0	4.0	1.0	0.7
Others	1.9	8.9	2.8	4.9	2.5	2.6	1.4
All	**92.8**	**85.2**	**70.8**	**38.8**	**36.0**	**42.9**	**43.9**

Source: Hoda and Terway (2015, Table 1(a), p. 6).

Although there has been a marked decline in the share of non-institutional sources in the total rural credit advanced over the period 1951 to 2001, due partly to growing competition from institutional sources and partly to various agrarian reforms implemented since independence, they still continue to be in business. Notwithstanding the criticism that has been leveled against them, these sources do provide valuable service, which is not available from any other alternative sources and for which they are amply rewarded.

Deficit Financing or Controlled Inflation

Some economists have suggested that the simplest way to finance development in developing countries is to print money or borrow from the banking system; in short, by deficit financing or controlled inflation. In this fashion, it is maintained that the population will be "forced" to save, since the rise in prices will necessitate a reduction in the volume of consumption of goods and services.

As we have already mentioned in Chapter 5, inflation is also a form of taxation. It is really a tax on cash balances, since those individuals and organizations in the economy who hold cash balances see their purchasing power eroded by inflation. There is, thus, a transfer of wealth from those who hold money in the form of cash balances to those who obtain the resources (in this case the government) through money creation. The government borrows heavily to finance spending, including that for rural development programs. The Government of India's rupee debt as well as the payment of interest on the debt decrease due to inflation. Suppose inflation increases by three percentage points then, in real terms, the value of debt and interest decreases by 3%, which is a whopping sum. Thus, inflation is an invisible tax on those the government borrows from, in the sense that it erodes the value of their capital and their interest payment. So, inflation tax affects hundreds of millions of people, yet very few of them realize it. Most people value their investment and income without adjusting it for inflation. This is what is called money illusion in economics. Hence, inflation is a politically easier way of taxing people than direct taxes. According to Bronfenbrenner (1966, 465–66), there are two ways in which inflation may prove beneficial. First, it may permit the authorities to raise the relative prices of the types of labor and capital goods required for development projects without imposing on other sectors of the economy the reductions in money wages and prices which would otherwise be required. This device (which was deliberately used by the Canadian government in the first two years of World War II) permits re-allocation of resources, in a manner conducive to development, in relatively painless fashion. Second, and more important to Professor Bronfenbrenner's argument, is the money illusion.

A slow inflation, or even a rapid one, in its early stages, induces laborers to work more intensively for real incomes which are no higher and which may be lower than their previous level. To a lesser extent, owners of land and capital may be induced to put their property to work more intensively in the same way when money incomes rise. Thus, judicious inflation may result in increased output, which, if properly allocated, could significantly accelerate the development process. The accompanying forced saving helps to re-allocate demand from consumer goods to capital goods. Beyond a certain point, however, further inflation will reduce the output, partly because investment shifts to speculative hoarding of inventories, and partly because supply curves of various factors of production turn backwards as higher incomes are reached (workers prefer more leisure to more income, investors prefer more safety and liquidity to more income).

But we would like to mention that even controlled inflation can have grave consequences for a developing country such as India, which still suffers from a tendency on the part of investors to go in for speculative holding of inventories, rather than for the establishment or expansion of productive enterprises. A constantly rising price level tends to aggravate this tendency by making speculation all the more profitable. Moreover, export industries, whose prices are determined in the world market, are confronted with constantly rising costs and, thus, become increasingly unprofitable, leading to aggravation of balance of payments difficulties on one hand, and increasing demand for export subsidies on the other. In view of these probable adverse effects of inflation, the Government of India and the RBI keep a close watch on the rate of inflation and take appropriate corrective measures if and when the inflation crosses a given limit.

Inflationary (deficit) financing of the regular budget in the hope that a rising price level will in itself provide incentive for private investment in development projects is unlikely to be successful. However, if the government undertakes a large-scale development program, recognizing that the level of deficit financing is in itself inflationary and mops up increases in income through tax policy, monetary policy, and direct controls, then mild inflation can have a positive impact on economic development. The extent of current account fiscal deficit in India for 2013–14 was estimated at $45 billion, which is lower than the last fiscal year's deficit of $88 billion. As per the Union Budget 2015–16, the fiscal deficit target of 3% of GDP is to be achieved over next three years, instead of two years. The 4.1% target was met in 2014–15, despite tax buoyancy being lower.

Foreign Sources of Funds

As we mentioned earlier in this chapter, foreign sources of funds for rural development include a variety of institutional and non-institutional agencies. The funds are given in the form of grants, loans, and investments. Table 14.5 lists the major foreign development agencies/donors who provide assistance for rural development and other purposes. Besides, there are four major international NGOs, namely, the Aga Khan Foundation, CARE India, the Ford Foundation, New Delhi, and the Save the Children Fund, UK, that provide substantial assistance to India for various rural development projects.

We now briefly discuss the role of foreign investment and foreign aid in rural development.

Table 14.5: *External Sources of Development Assistance to India*

	Bilateral Partners		*Multilateral Partners*
1.	Canada/Canadian International Development Agency (CIDA)	1.	Asian Development Bank (ADB)
2.	Canada/International Development Research Centre (IDRC)	2.	European Union (EU)
3.	Denmark	3.	Food and Agriculture Organization (FAO)
4.	France	4.	International Fund for Agricultural Development (IFAD)
5.	Germany	5.	International Labour Organization (ILO)
6.	Japan/Japan International Cooperation Agency (JICA)	6.	United Nations International Children's Emergency Fund (UNICEF)
7.	Japan/Overseas Economic Cooperation Fund (OECF)	7.	United Nations Development Fund for Women (UNDFW)

(Table 14.5 Continued)

(Table 14.5 Continued)

	Bilateral Partners		*Multilateral Partners*
8.	Netherlands	8.	United Nations Development Programme (UNDP)
9.	New Zealand	9.	United Nations Industrial Development Organization (UNIDO)
10.	Norway	10.	United Nations Population Fund (UNDF)
11.	Sweden	11.	World Food Programme (WFP)
12.	Switzerland	12.	World Health Organization (WHO)
13.	The United Kingdom (UK)	13.	World Bank/International Bank for Reconstruction and Development (IBRD)

Source: UNDP (1996a).

The Role of Foreign Investment

Foreign investment is almost indispensable for promoting vigorous economic growth in developing countries. This is because many of them cannot raise the additional capital resources they need for the purpose. If a developing country wants to bring about economic development depending only on its own resources, it will have to wait for decades to be able to do so. Even if a country is fortunate enough to be able to meet its total capital requirements from domestic savings and taxes, it may nevertheless face a foreign exchange problem. As total outlays for development increase, foreign exchange requirements also go up.

In India, foreign exchange is mainly required to import modern technologies, heavy machinery and equipment, fertilizers, fighter planes, fossil fuels, pulses, vegetable oils, and so on. The foreign exchange needed for development must be obtained by (a) restricting imports of other goods and services; (b) increasing exports; and (c) obtaining loans and grants from foreigners. Reducing imports, in and of itself, is inflationary; it reduces the availability of goods and releases cash to be spent in other ways. Therefore, whereas it is good for a poor developing country to have an austere import policy, it offers no panacea for financing its development.

There can be no argument against a policy to increase exports. However, four observations need to be made about the role of expanding exports in financing development. First, the volume of exports depends very much on the world market conditions, on which individual developing countries have little control. Second, measures to increase exports are for the most part likely to operate rather slowly. Third, an export surplus, no less than a cut in imports, involves sacrifices; an export surplus means sending more goods abroad than one gets in return. Fourth, an export surplus is in itself inflationary; it reduces the supply of goods and services and increases the supply of money. It is not, therefore, a substitute for increased savings/taxes at home.

The third alternative for a developing country to secure the needed foreign exchange is obtaining loans or grants from foreigners—foreign private investors, foreign governments, or international agencies. It is better for a developing country to obtain part of its additional requirements from each of the three sources, rather than from only any one of them. Certain development projects can be more easily organized and more efficiently managed if carried out on a private enterprise basis, with assistance from a foreign private investor. Other development projects that are highly beneficial to the country, but which do not attract any private investors, may be better handled through government channels, either on a bilateral basis or on a multilateral basis through an international agency such as the World Bank.

Many people in developing countries still believe that a huge flood of foreign capital is waiting to inundate their lands if only the gates were opened. This is very far from the truth. There is a lot of competition for capital amongst both the developed as well as developing countries. Furthermore, the prospective investor wants to be sure about the climate for foreign investments in the receiving countries. In Box 14.1, we list the elements that constitute just such a favorable climate from the investor's point of view (ECAFE 1950: 4–5).

Box 14.1

CERTAIN ELEMENTS OF A FAVORABLE ENVIRONMENT FOR FOREIGN INVESTMENT

1. *Political stability and freedom from external aggression.*
2. *Security of life and property.*
3. *Availability of opportunities for earning profits.*
4. *Prompt payment of fair compensation and its remittance to the country of origin in the event of compulsory acquisition of a foreign enterprise.*
5. *Facilities for the remittance of profits, dividends, interest, and so on.*
6. *Facilities for the immigration and employment of foreign technical and administrative personnel.*
7. *A system of taxation that does not impose a crushing burden on private enterprise.*
8. *Freedom from double taxation.*
9. *Absence of vexatious controls.*
10. *Non-discriminatory treatment of foreigners in the administration of controls.*
11. *Absence of competition of state-owned enterprises with private capital.*
12. *A general spirit of friendliness for foreign investors.*

Source: ECAFE (1950, 4–5).

It is unlikely that even highly favorable laws governing foreign investment will encourage sufficient inflow of private capital to meet a large share of the requirements of developing countries, including India. Therefore, foreign investment has a substantial role to play in financing economic development in India. FDI has been increasing over time, thanks largely to the opening up of India's economy in the wake of its new economic policy.

The Role of Foreign Aid

The so-called aid for development is provided by the so-called donors to the so-called recipients. Perhaps it would be appropriate to refer to "aid" as "involvement" of the more developed countries in the economic, political, military, and social sectors of developing countries, either directly or through international agencies.

Donors may be foreign governments, corporations, individuals, international organizations, or private foundations. "Aid" may be people serving as actual workers, or just advisors endeavoring to impart knowledge, techniques, and institutions in the form of commodities, tools, and machines. These items may be provided as gifts, loans, or investments. Loans and investments comprise the great bulk of "aid."

What are the objectives of the aid policies of donors? They are a mixed bag, mainly economic and political, with a dash of humanitarianism. One of the most general facts of human nature and conduct is a "tendency to assume that things which are associated in the society we know must necessarily be associated in all other societies."

The United Nations Panel on Foreign Investments in Developing Countries, in its meeting in Amsterdam in February 1969, called for a massive increase in the flow of foreign capital to developing countries in order to provide a reasonable rate of per capita growth (SID 1969). These conclusions, though they may be false, have been accepted—more or less voluntarily—by many of the developing countries, resulting in heavy obligations not only to foreign governments and international lending agencies, but also to private investors who have acquired the privilege of exploiting mineral, forest, and land resources to produce commodities for export and the privilege of building electric power, communication and transportation facilities, and industrial plants. In this way, the "donors" promote their own exports, obtain raw materials, and make very substantial profits. These operations are assumed to be in the national interest of both the "donors" and the "recipients." What is good for the donors must be good for the recipients! This concept of the national interest rests on the further assumption that the way to better living for the people of all nations is in the direction of integrating their economies with those of other countries so that they can maximize their access to the markets and resources of the world.

The governments of developed countries, in order to protect their foreign loans and the investments of their citizens, help recipient governments stay in power by strengthening their military and police forces. This arrangement leaves the large landowners, the military, the industrial and mining interests, the traders, and the government bureaucracy in firm control of a country. Any change—social, economic, or political—which threatens this power structure is deemed "subversive" and dealt with accordingly. Should a government that attempts significant reforms come into power, there is always a military coup at hand to remove it from the scene.

As a consequence of a mutuality of interests between the dominant power groups in the donor and recipient countries, substantial "aid" and indigenous resources have been used for the construction of luxury hotels, apartments, and office buildings, and for the manufacture of luxury consumer goods and services, as well as for obtaining resources for the establishment of capital-intensive industries. In agriculture, the more affluent landowners have been the first to obtain the benefits accruing from the introduction of HYV of rice and wheat. However, foreign aid has undeniably contributed substantially to present and potential progress in some sectors of the India's economy, including the agricultural sector (Box 14.2). Most of the infrastructural projects, such as roads, dams, electric power generation and transmission facilities, and some of the education programs, such as the strengthening of medical, engineering and technology, agricultural, business management, and public administration schools, have furnished a foundation for further economic and social progress.

Nevertheless, certain major aspects of foreign aid have helped create conditions that give little promise of dealing effectively with the need to advance a technology that will be suited to small farms, and the need to create non-farm employment opportunities for a rapidly growing rural labor force. In so far as aid is responsible for maintaining governments in power, which are unwilling to carry through meaningful land tenure reforms, or devise a tax system that provides sufficient revenue to support appropriate education and health programs, or accept responsibility for the creation of sufficient employment opportunities in rural areas is concerned, then aid has been inimical to rural development.

In so far as aid has contributed to an emphasis on the expansion of capital-intensive industries in urban areas, and has given priority to the larger landowners in programs to increase the

Box 14.2

FINANCING OF THE OPERATION FLOOD (OF) PROGRAM

India's OF was the world's biggest dairy development program. An ingenious method was designed and used for financing phase I of the program, by way of using the funds generated from the sale of 1,26,000 tons of skimmed milk powder and 42,000 tons of butter oil donated to India by the World Food Programme (WFP), an agency of the FAO of the UN. The original 1970 allocation for OF-I was ₹954 million crore for a period of five years, 1970–71 to 1974–75. This was subsequently revised to ₹1,164 million. The funds generated from the sale of donated dairy commodities since the inception of the program till March 31, 1981 amounted to ₹1,146.80 million and the actual disbursements over the same period of time were ₹1,165.5 million. The donated commodities were received, and sold, on behalf of the Government of India, by the IDC, which was the financing agency for the program. The funds were disbursed by the IDC as 30% grant and 70% loan to the implementing agencies nominated by the participating state governments. This method of financing through aid was innovative in the sense that the sale proceeds of the donated dairy commodities were used as investments to create the basic infrastructure needed for modernizing India's dairy industry and the donated dairy commodities were used in such a way as to stabilize the domestic price of milk at a level that was fair to the consumer and remunerative enough for the producer to provide him the needed incentive to increase his milk production. OF enabled India not only to be self-sufficient in milk production, but also to be able to export some dairy products.

Source: Singh (1999, 209–10).

output of food and export products, it has served to create islands of affluence, while still leaving the bulk of the people with a traditional technology and at a subsistence level of well-being. A country with a dual society of this nature can never build a domestic consumption base to ensure the full realization of its technological potential, either in agriculture or in industry. It leaves a major portion of its human resources untapped.

Rising pressures to produce for export distorts the allocation of resources in agriculture, causing production to increase regardless of export prices. The terms of trade worsen for the recipient, making still greater production for export imperative. More and more resources, which might have been used to produce for domestic consumption, must be allocated to produce for export, as debt and profit service requirements grow. Food production may have to be sacrificed to produce exportable products. Existing land tenure systems will remain entrenched because they will most effectively produce surplus for export. Unless there are drastic changes in the concept and direction of foreign aid and in the strategy for achieving goals in the developing nations, the standard of living of cultivator families will not be improved much.

It is intriguing to contemplate what might have happened if these poor countries with colonial and feudal backgrounds had been permitted to exercise a greater measure of responsibility for the development of their respective societies without external intervention or, indeed, what could happen even now if they relied more on themselves.

A very minimal amount of loan and investment and a very minimal number of "technicians" from external sources would best serve the national interest of these countries. In discussing the contribution of "aid" to development, Mikesell (1968) concludes that

> [A]s a general proposition, external capital or aid is neither a necessary nor a sufficient condition for development.... By and large, countries that are not making satisfactory progress, regardless of their per capita income, have failed to realize the potential

returns from their own resources. What is required are policies and programs for mobilizing, adapting and re-allocating those resources, including the training of human resources for the operations of modern economy.

The foreign aid that a developing nation needed, and still needs, is the kind that would enable its citizens to utilize their own natural resources, accumulate their own capital, and operate their own economy by themselves and exclusively for themselves, even though the process would be gradual, over a considerable period of time.

Table 14.6 presents the estimates of the inflow of foreign aid in the form of loans and grants to India for selected years from 1980–81 to 2014–15. As shown in the Table, the amount of both loans and grants has been increasing over time; the amount of foreign loans increased from about ₹37,712 million in 1980–81 to about ₹20,488 million in 2014–15, but the amount of foreign grants decreased from about ₹758 million to about ₹421 million over the same period of time. However, it is noteworthy that most of the foreign aid has been in the form of loans, which accounted for about 96% of the total foreign aid in 2010–11 and almost 100% in 2014–15 (provisional).

Besides, foreign loans and grants, FDI is also an important source of financing development projects. Foreign companies invest in India to avail themselves of the benefits of cheaper wages and a favorable business environment. Economic liberalization started in India in wake of the 1991 economic crisis and since then FDI has steadily increased in India. In first half of the 2015, India attracted investment of $31 billion compared to $28 billion and $27 billion of China and the US respectively. The Government of India has amended the FDI policy to increase FDI inflow. In 2014, the government increased the foreign investment upper limit from 26% to 49% in insurance sector. It also launched the "Make in India" initiative in September 2014 under which FDI policy for 25 sectors was further liberalized. As of April 2015, FDI inflow in India increased by 48% since the launching of "Make in India" initiative on September 25, 2014. India was ranked 15th in the world in 2013 in terms of FDI inflow, it rose up to 9th position in 2014 and in 2015 India became the top destination for foreign direct investment. During 2014–15, India received most of its FDI from Mauritius, Singapore, Netherlands, Japan, and the US. About 10% of India's GDP is based on construction activity. Indian government has plans to invest $1 trillion on infrastructure from 2012–2017. About 40% of this $1 trillion is to be funded by the private sector. Now, 100% FDI under automatic route is permitted in construction sector for cities and towns.[5]

Table 14.6: *Inflow of Foreign Aid in the Form of Loans and Grants in India (in ₹ Million)*

Year	*Loans*	*Grants*	*Total*
1980–81	37,712.0	758.0	38,470.0
1990–91	76,013.0	5,221. 0	81,234.0
1995–96	1,08,332.0	13,300.0	1,21,632.0
2000–01	1,71,841.0	9,406.0	1,81,247.0
2005–06	1,73,091.0	16,288.0	1,89,379.0
2010–11	3,58,951.0	15,365.0	3,74,316.0
2014–15 P	2,07,488.0	421.0	2,07,909.0

Source: MoF (2015, A113).
Note: P: Provisional.

Table 14.7: *External Debt of India Outstanding as at the End of March of Selected Years (in ₹ Billion)*

	Source of Debt	*1991*	*2000*	*2005*	*2010*	*2012*	*2014QE*
1.	Multilateral	403.86	1,371.32	138.92	1,934.36	2,570.89	3,286.92
2.	Bilateral	223.78	79.28	74.17	101.98	137.09	143.85
3.	IMF	51.32	1.43	0	272.64	315.28	363.40
4.	Export credit	83.74	29.56	21.80	760.11	971.17	949.05
5.	Commercial Borrowing	19.727	869.63	1,182.43	3,192.21	6,146.23	9,941.75
6.	NRI deposit (Longer than one year)	NA	NA	1,432.67	2,170.62	2,998.40	6,694.33
7.	Rupee debt	NA	NA	100.71	74.80	69.22	89.44
8.	Total long term debt	NA	NA	5,087.87	9,424.50	14,442.05	22,763.41
9.	Total short term debt	NA	NA	775.28	2,361.88	3,999.620	5,322.27
10.	Total debt	959.97	333.08	3,531.30	5,863.05	11,786.38	28,085.68

Sources: GoI (2007a),[6] MoF (2015, Table A125–26).

Table 14.7 presents the estimates of India's total outstanding foreign debt from all sources. As shown in the table, it, has been increasing over time.

In 1991, it was estimated to be around ₹959.97 billion, which increased to ₹3,531.30 billion in 2005, and to ₹28,085.68 billion in 2014. This trend indicates that we have yet to go a long way before we reach our proclaimed goal of self-reliance. Another important observation that we would like to make in this connection is that the bulk of the foreign debt is on account of multilateral sources and commercial borrowings.

Key Points

1. The capital requirements of agricultural and rural development are enormous. Capital is required not only for on-farm investment to improve the production apparatus and to provide various farm inputs and services, but also for a vast array of supportive infrastructural facilities.
2. Funds for investment in rural development projects come from two main sources: domestic and foreign. Further, in each category, there are institutional and non-institutional sources. Domestic institutional sources include the government, the RBI, NABARD, cooperative banks, CBs and RRBs, and private companies and corporations. Non-institutional sources include households, moneylenders and traders, and friends and relatives.

3. Foreign institutional sources include foreign governments, development agencies, the World Bank, the ADB, the IMF, foreign banks, multinational corporations, and so on. Foreign non-institutional sources include NRIs and foreign nationals.
4. The government in the past has been, still is, and will remain, in future also, the most important source of funds for rural development in India. Government funds are made available in the form of investment, grants, subsidies, and loans—called taccavi. Allocations of funds are made through the annual budgetary process. the total expenditure on agriculture and rural development in the public sector since the beginning of the planning era (1951–52) until the Eleventh Five Year Plan (2007–12) aggregated ₹3,58,276.70 billion at current prices As a percentage of the total plan expenditure in the public sector, the share of agriculture and rural development varied from around 11% to 17%, with an overall average of around 15% for the entire period. In the Eleventh Five Year Plan, the total expenditure on agriculture and rural development was ₹3,58,276.700 billion at current prices), which accounted for 13.7% of the total public sector expenditure.
5. The RBI was a pioneer central bank in the sphere of rural credit. Its founding act of legislation and subsequent amendments entrusted to it the responsibility for enlarging the availability of rural credit. The bank shouldered this responsibility rather reluctantly until 1947, when, after independence, this responsibility was reinforced and became a major responsibility of the bank.
6. A major landmark in the history of development of rural credit in India was the establishment of the NABARD in July 1982, by merging the Agricultural Refinance and Development Corporation, the Agricultural Credit Department of the RBI, and the Rural Credit and Planning Cell of the RBI. The main functions of NABARD include the provision of refinance facility to the cooperative banks and RRBs, CBs against term lending, and overall policy, planning, coordination, and monitoring of all agricultural and rural lending activities in the country. Besides, it also undertakes training, research and consultancy relating to rural credit.
7. Although both the RBI and NABARD have played important roles in making cheap credit available to rural people through cooperative banks, CBs and RRBs, the needs of the rural poor still continue to be unfulfilled.
8. Cooperative credit societies entered the field of rural finance with the adoption of the Cooperative Societies Act of 1904. Since then, the government has been making deliberate attempts to nurture the cooperative movement in the country in the larger interests of the rural people. Credit cooperatives have been recognized as the best institutions to provide rural credit to the farmer because they satisfy all the important criteria of sound agricultural credit. They have many advantages over other sources of credit.
9. The share of the cooperative banks has been declining over time; in 2002–03, it was about 34%, which had declined to 17% by the year 2010–11 and has been stagnant around that level since then.
10. Cooperative credit societies and cooperative banks suffer from several internal and external problems. There is no formal system of corporate governance extant in cooperative banks. As a result, a number of cooperative banks have come to be the hot bed of political patronage, unscrupulous financial practices, and gross mismanagement. Most of the cooperative credit societies and banks are not financially viable.
11. CBs are now playing a strategic role in increasing the national savings rate, in canalizing the available savings to finance high priority investments, and in better utilizing

the available capacity both in agriculture and in industry through adequate supply of credit as working capital. They also provide finance for antipoverty programs. Fourteen major CBs were nationalized in July 1969 and another six in 1980. Before their nationalization, CBs supplied only a negligible share of rural credit: 0.9% in 1951–52 and 0.6% in 1961–62.

12. Since the mid-1990s, there has been a substantial increase in the involvement of CBs in agricultural lending. The total number of branches of all CBs in India in 2006 was 69,616, which increased to 92,114 in 2012–13 and their share in direct agricultural advances went up from 1.3% of bank credit in July 1969 to 69% in 2014–15.
13. The RRBs were established consequent to the acceptance by the Government of India of the recommendations of a working group on rural banks. Initially, they were mandated to cater to the credit needs of the weaker sections of the rural community comprising small and marginal farmers, agricultural laborers, artisans, and small entrepreneurs. With effect from December 1993, their mandate has been expanded to include non-target group borrowers also. They were intended to be low-cost "small man's banks," combining the advantages of cooperatives (close rapport with villagers) and CBs (business acumen).
14. Most of the RRBs have been incurring losses and losing their financial viability right from their inception. This is due to several reasons including their mandate of financing only the target group borrowers, coupled with an administered interest rate structure, poor recovery performance, increasing establishment costs, and low level of operational efficiency. After their amalgamation, as of March 2015, there were 56 RRBs in the country with a network of 20,059 branches covering 644 notified districts in 26 states and the UT of Puducherry. Their performance has improved slightly after certain corrective measures had been taken by NABARD, including their amalgamation.
15. SHGs have emerged as an important source of micro finance. They are formed around the theme of savings and credit. In February 1992, NABARD launched a pilot project for "linking SHGs with banks" after consultations with the RBI, selected banks, and NGOs. The main objective of the project was to develop innovative, participatory and self-sustaining credit delivery systems for improving the access of the rural poor to institutional credit.
16. The SHG–BLP has expanded substantially since it was first launched on a pilot scale in 1992. As of March 31, 2014, there were more than 7.43 million savings-linked SHGs, covering over 97 million poor households. The total savings of these SHGs with banks amounted to ₹98,974.2 million. The number of credit-linked SHGs under the program was 4.20 million.
17. Non-institutional agencies that supply credit to farmers and other rural people include professional moneylenders, agricultural moneylenders, landlords, traders and commission agents, and friends and relatives. Traditionally, these agencies have played an important role in meeting the credit requirements of villagers. However, the share of non-institutional sources as a proportion of the total quantum rural credit advanced in India declined rapidly over the period 1951–81, it was about 93% in 1951 but declined rapidly to about 36% in 2001. The trend seems to have reversed during the period 1991 to 2013; their share increased from 36% in 1991 to 43.9% in 2013.
18. Deficit financing or controlled inflation is one of the ways to finance development in developing countries. It is argued that, due to inflation, the population will be "forced" to save since the rise in prices will necessitate a reduction in the volume of consumption of goods and services. Inflationary (deficit) financing of the regular

budget in the hope that a rising price level will in itself provide incentive for private investment in development projects is unlikely to be successful. However, if the government undertakes a large-scale development program, recognizing that the level of deficit financing is in itself inflationary and mops up increases in income through tax policy, monetary policy and direct controls, then mild inflation can have a positive impact on economic development.

19. Many people in developing countries still believe that a huge flood of foreign capital is waiting to inundate their lands if only the gates were opened. This is very far from the truth. There is a lot of competition for capital amongst both the developed as well as developing countries. Furthermore, the prospective investor wants to be sure about the climate for foreign investments in the recipient countries.
20. The amount of foreign aid in the form of both loans and grants has been increasing over time; the amount of foreign loans increased from about ₹37,712 million in 1980–81 to about ₹20,488 million in 2014–15, but the amount of foreign grants decreased from about ₹758 million to about ₹421 million over the same period of time. The foreign aid that a developing nation needed, and still needs, is the kind that would enable its citizens to utilize their own natural resources, accumulate their own capital and operate their own economy by themselves, and exclusively for themselves, even though the process would be gradual, over a considerable period of time. An exemplary way of using this mode of foreign aid was demonstrated by the OF program.
21. Besides, foreign loans and grants, FDI is also an important source of financing development projects. After economic liberalization in the 1990s, FDI has steadily increased in India. In first half of the 2015, India attracted investment of $31 billion compared to $28 billion and $27 billion of China and the US respectively. The Government of India has amended the FDI policy to increase FDI inflow. As of April 2015, FDI inflow in India increased by 48% since the launching of "Make in India" initiative on September 25, 2014. India was ranked 15th in the world in 2013 in terms of FDI inflow, it rose up to 9th position in 2014 and in 2015 India became the top destination for foreign direct investment.
22. Technical assistance is the most productive form of external aid. Transfer of knowledge, skills and productive knowhow from a developed to a developing country can permanently raise the productivity of labor, and make land and capital fruitful. This is evident from India's experience with establishing land grant pattern universities with the technical and financial assistance provided by the USAID, the Rockefeller Foundation and the Ford Foundation.
23. The amount of foreign debt of India has been increasing over time. In 1991 it was estimated to be around ₹959.97 billion, which increased to ₹3,531.30 billion in 2005, and to ₹28,085.68 billion in 2014. This trend indicates that we have yet to go a long way before we reach our proclaimed goal of self-reliance.

Questions for Discussion

1. India's rural sector is starved of capital and, consequently, it has low resources productivity, low incomes, and higher incidence of poverty and unemployment. Outline a strategy for increasing the flow of funds to the rural sector.
2. Discuss how inflation can help the government mop up funds for rural development.

3. Compare and contrast the roles of the Reserve Bank of India (RBI) and the National Bank for Agricultural and Rural Development (NABARD) in increasing the flow of credit to the rural sector.
4. Cooperative credit societies were intended to be an appropriate institutional structure for meeting the credit requirements of rural people. But India's experience with them shows that they have failed to play their intended role. Discuss the reasons why it has been so.
5. Discuss why the RRBs have not been able to be a low-cost alternative to the commercial banks.
6. What are the strengths and weaknesses of Self Help Groups (SHGs) vis-à-vis cooperative credit societies?
7. Identify a few areas/projects in the rural sector where foreign investment could be very useful and why
8. How can the Government of India (GoI) attract more foreign investment to the rural sector?
9. Discuss the pros and cons of foreign aid as a means of financing rural development in India.

Notes

1. http://dacnet.nic.in/eands/agStat06-07.htm (Accessed in March 2008).
2. http://www.indiabudget.nic.in/es2007-08 (Accessed in March 2008).
3. The Committee on Financial Inclusion defined financial inclusion as *"the process of ensuring access to financial services and timely and adequate credit where needed by vulnerable groups such as weaker sections and low income groups at an affordable cost."*
4. https://www.nabard.org/english/FinancialInclusion2.aspx
5. https://en.wikipedia.org/wiki/Foreign_direct_investment_in_India (Accessed on December 27, 2015).
6. http://www.indiabudget.nic.in/es2006-07 (Accessed on March 2008).

Chapter 15

Implementation, Monitoring, and Evaluation

LEARNING OUTCOMES

After having gone through this chapter, students should be able to:

- **Define the terms, "project planning," "project monitoring," and "project evaluation";**
- **Describe the major elements of project planning;**
- **Explain why project control is necessary;**
- **Examine the role of "Integration and Coordination" in rural development planning;**
- **Explain why people's participation in implementation is necessary;**
- **Describe the main functions of project monitoring with reference to a rural development project;**
- **Define and differentiate between "*Ex-ante* Evaluation," "Concurrent Evaluation," and "Ex-post Evaluation"; and**
- **Explain the "with and without" and "before and after" approaches to project evaluation, describe their merits and demerits, and how to use them.**

Introduction

Implementation, monitoring and evaluation of projects are all subsumed in the project management function. Implementation may be regarded as a process by which a set of predetermined activities is carried out in a planned manner, with a view to achieving certain established objectives. As mentioned in Chapter 12, a program is usually implemented through a series of well-defined projects. This means that a program usually consists of a number of projects, the implementation of which is supposed to eventually culminate in its execution. The scope of a plan is still broader, in the sense that it usually comprises a number of programs. Thus, for its implementation, a plan has to be broken down into a number of programs, each of which in turn is broken down into a number of projects. A project treats the questions "what, who, when, and how," more specifically than a program does.

Monitoring is a process of keeping a watch on the progress of a project vis-à-vis its targets and time schedule. The main objective of monitoring is to find out whether there are any deviations of actual physical and financial achievements from the planned/targeted ones, and to help the project authority take necessary corrective measures in time. Evaluation of a project is concerned with the assessment of its impact(s).

The failure of agricultural and rural development programs in India, as also in other developing countries can, in large measure, be traced to the difficulties that hinder their effective implementation. Clearly, a program is no better than its implementation. Emphasizing the importance of implementation, the late Prime Minister Jawaharlal Nehru, who had an unusual grasp of planning problems, once pointedly remarked, "We in the Planning Commission and others concerned have grown more experienced and more expert in planning. But the real question is not planning, but implementing the plans.... I fear we are not quite so expert at implementation as at planning" (quoted in Waterston 1970, 403). This statement is notable because it recognizes that the problems of plan implementation are more difficult than those of plan formulation. But the statement seems to imply that planning and implementation are two different and unrelated functions. As a matter of fact, they are highly interrelated and, therefore, should be considered as an integral whole. Planners cannot limit themselves to saying *what* is to be achieved, without showing *how* and by *whom* it is to be done. Every target must be accompanied by policies and measures that have been devised specifically to fulfill it; otherwise it becomes only a forecast or projection. Monitoring is an important aid to effective and smooth implementation of a project. Concurrent evaluation can help the implementing agency make mid-course corrections in the project, and thereby enhance its positive impacts and minimize its (unintended) negative effects. Therefore, both monitoring and evaluation are necessary for the success of rural development projects.

Massive investments have been made in rural development programs since the beginning of the planning era, and will continue to be made in the near future. Apart from several flaws in planning, there have been numerous operational problems in the implementation, monitoring, and evaluation of the programs. This has adversely affected the efficiency and effectiveness of the programs. The policy makers, the implementing agencies, and the beneficiaries have all to be constantly vigilant and watch closely the progress of implementation of rural development projects. This can be done through an appropriate system of monitoring built into the project design itself. Effective monitoring can cut down the wastage of a lot of resources and help achieve project objectives more effectively and efficiently. The Percentage Progress Technique (PPT) is a commonly used approach adopted to assess the progress of a project. In this approach, the percentage of physical work completed and the percentage of project outlay expended are used to review the progress of the project. The other aids to monitoring include (a) network analysis; (b) objective-oriented project planning (OOPP), also known as ZOPP (*Zielorientierte Projektplanung*); (c) master schedule; and (d) management summary reports (Gopalakrishnan and Ramamoorthy 1993, 332–37).

This chapter is devoted to a discussion of some of the methods and processes of project implementation, monitoring and evaluation and knowledge management (KM).

Project Implementation

We can distinguish between two approaches to implementation, namely, the traditional (blueprint) approach and the open (people-centered) approach. The traditional approach is characterized by a mechanical view of planning and development, in which implementation is simply a tool of the powerful (donors, planners, politicians). Employees are seen variously as cogs in a machine or troublesome but necessary raw materials. Project beneficiaries are seen either as clients (to be "sold" an idea) or employees (to be instructed).

On the other hand, in the open approach, the main focus is on making people important, thinking in terms of "instigators" and "actors," rather than as planners and clients. It recognizes that implementation is about the communication of meaning, and that it is concerned with power and influence. Implementation becomes more important and is seen as the education of both planners and clients to their mutual benefit. It is still a means of getting things done, but it is also concerned with how things are done and their desirable and undesirable consequences. As a result, it becomes much more an integral part of the planning process and influences the technical, financial, and economic aspects of the process.

In the context of rural development, an approach is needed that encourages and fosters decreasing dependence and increasing self-reliance, for which the open approach is suited. The traditional approach, on the other hand, can cause dependence and alienation, rather than reducing it. But it is still the predominant approach to implementation and is used by the majority of rural development agencies. The open approach is pragmatic and flexible and is suited to learning and adapting from experience. It leans heavily on the one great resource that the traditional approach has ignored, which is, the people themselves, their motivation, experience, and common sense. Furthermore, the open view would suggest that implementation cannot be separated from politics. To think of implementation purely in terms of the acquisition of finance, planning of expenditure, acquisition of inputs, budgetary control, and other mechanics of management, is to miss the basic point. Implementation is concerned with action—who plans it, who does it, whom it is done to and why, who has the power, and how the power is organized for action.

Now, we briefly discuss the major components of the implementation process.

Planning for Implementation

Some planning is required for plan implementation as well. A plan for implementation should, at the minimum, specify what is to be done, who is to do it, when it is to be done and how it is to be done. To begin with, the plan should be broken up into a number of projects and then an implementation system should be developed for every project. Clearly, every project will require a unique implementation system tailor-made to suit its peculiar requirements and characteristics. It is not possible to develop universally applicable implementation systems. But a broad frame for implementation systems can be specified as follows (Kohli 1979, 13–17).

Plan for Physical Work

The plan for physical work should include the following:

1. Estimation of requirements of supplies, equipment and implements, labor, power, credit, and managerial and technical staff.
2. Recruitment, orientation and posting of the staff.
3. Surveys, studies, investigations, and reports.
4. Procurement of supplies, equipment and implements, credit, and so on.
5. Arrangements for marketing of the produce of the target beneficiaries.
6. Allocation and distribution of supplies, equipment, credit, and so on.
7. Physical works.
8. Arrangement for decision-making and performing administrative functions at different levels and stages.

All these activities should be clearly defined along with their sequence and interdependence.

Time Plan

First, the estimated time required for each activity, assuming the availability of staff and other resources as planned, should be decided, as well as the dates when each item of work should begin and finish. Techniques such as bar charts, flow charts, Program Evaluation and Review Technique (PERT) and critical path method (CPM) could be used to develop a time plan for the project (Gopalakrishnan and Ramamoorthy 1993, Chapters 5 and 6). Care should be taken to match the requirement with the availability in each time period, both in terms of quantum and pattern.

Input Resource Planning

Input resource planning should include the following:

1. Identification of scarce inputs, which would require detailed planning and matching with availability.
2. Determination of total requirement of each category of inputs.
3. Breaking the total requirement into period-wise components, in line with the time plan formulated.
4. Realistic forecasts of likely availability of inputs for each period of time and specification of assumptions underlying these forecasts.
5. Comparison of requirements with availability for each period.
6. Reworking of the time plan, whenever necessary, so that the revised requirements correspond to the availability.

After the time plan and the input resource plan have been thus integrated, the resultant implementation plan can be termed as realistic or implementable, depending upon how realistically the future conditions have been foreseen.

Equipment Order Planning

Separate lists of equipment and other items to be purchased should be prepared and orders placed accordingly. The purchase plan and the implementation plan should be synchronized.

Project Organization

An appropriate project organization has to be developed, responsibilities for various tasks clearly assigned, and proper use of scientific equipment and tools ensured, both for preparing the implementation plan as well as for executing the project. Filling key positions with adequately skilled and experienced persons on time is also important. It is also better to spell out the monitoring and management information systems to be used during the implementation and to develop the necessary report formats.

Building Inter-linkages

This is necessary to complete the project in time and to derive full benefits from the interrelated projects, such as bridges and roads, irrigation and crop development projects, production, processing and marketing projects, power and industry, and so on. Both backward and forward linkages with other projects should be built and strengthened.

Drawing eclectically on several sources of ideas, Robert Chambers and his colleagues have developed a system for programming and controlling the implementation of rural development programs and projects. It is called the "Programming and Implementation (PIM)" system. The pilot system has been tested in the Special Rural Development Programme (SRDP) in Kenya. The system has the following three main components (Chambers 1974, Chapter 2):

1. A programming exercise, which in the SRDP was done annually and held just before or just after the beginning of the financial year. This meeting is attended by all those directly concerned with implementation, and they jointly and freely draw up a phased work program for the year.
2. A management meeting, which in the SRDP was usually held monthly. It is attended by those concerned directly with implementation. Progress is reviewed against the phased work program, bottlenecks are identified, and remedial action is agreed upon at this meeting.
3. An action report, which in the SRDP was described as a monthly management report, summarizing briefly the progress made and the problems encountered, naming those responsible for action, and sent quickly and simultaneously to those concerned at different levels in the government.

The main principles incorporated in the system are as follows:

1. A procedure requiring joint programming by all those responsible for implementation.
2. Staff taking part in setting their own work targets.
3. Collegial sanctions against poor work.
4. Lean and functional reports.
5. Communication direct from the implementer to the point of bottleneck or delay.
6. Functional meetings used sparingly.
7. Sophistication in simplicity.

These principles might be used in devising other implementation and management systems for other situations, in India and other developing countries. A number of technical, economic, financial, commercial, socio-cultural, and institutional–organizational factors affect the implementation of a rural development program. Knowledge about the nature and magnitude of the effect of each of these factors is necessary for rural development managers to be able to implement and manage the program efficiently and effectively. Similar knowledge is also essential for rural development policy makers and planners in order to formulate realistic policies and plans for rural development. It is the lack or inadequacy of knowledge about some or all of these factors, on the part of both development policy makers and administrators, that explains, to a large extent, the failure of India's development programs.

Project Control

The functions of management and control are linked together because there is no generally agreed definition of them. Indeed, the words are often used interchangeably. However, we prefer to regard them as separate, though linked, functions. Control is concerned with maintaining project operations to meet changing circumstances, particularly those exogenous to the project, such as markets, input and product prices, government policy changes, and so on.

In practice, the control function of rural development projects is frequently so pre-occupied with financial accountability, the prevention of fraud and the policing of project activities that it tends toward a centralized, rigid and non-motivating structure. This preoccupation reflects the attitude of the operating ministries—which are spending—and not that of business institutions. The result is that project control is seen as a major function at the cost of project management, and this accounts for the inflexibility of project operations observed so frequently. Rural development projects rarely operate under static circumstances and, therefore, project management should have the capacity to adjust project operations to change.

The management structures and methods of control should be closely related to the basic physical, technical, social, and economic characteristics of a project. In the early stages of project operation, strong technical and administrative control is likely to be beneficial but, over time, increasing benefits are likely to come from the decentralization of decision-making and greater farmer participation.

Project management performance depends not only on a staffing structure appropriate to the type and size of the project, but also on the quality of staff; this refers to all levels of management. A shortage of high quality, well-motivated manpower is a common characteristic of developing countries, but it is particularly marked in the rural sector where projects are often isolated and sometimes located in unattractive situations, which makes it difficult to attract people to work on them. Perhaps, even more important is the fact that the wages and salaries of project employees as well as access to urban amenities are often unattractive and inadequate when compared with other sectors.

Integration and Coordination

Given the multidisciplinary nature of rural development, and the multitude of governmental and nongovernmental agencies engaged in the implementation of diverse agricultural and rural development programs with different—and often conflicting—objectives, it is absolutely essential that the different development programs under operation in an area be integrated and coordinated for optimum results. In the absence of requisite integration and coordination among various development programs, as is the case at present in India, there is a great deal of unnecessary overlapping, duplication, and wastage of scarce resources. The main reason for the lack of integration and coordination among various development agencies can be traced to India's Constitution, which, until the 73rd Amendment in 1992, did not define the relationship between the State and the district and other lower tiers, with reference to planning.

A review of the experience of PRIs prior to the 73rd Amendment reveals that they had not been successful in achieving the desired integration of the political and administrative systems, and in enlisting people's participation in development plans and programs. The development administration at the district and tehsil/taluka levels still faces the twin problems of horizontal and vertical coordination, and integration of the political and administrative systems. In order to solve these problems and to bring together all the administrative operations under the effective control of a single agency, it would be necessary to evolve a unified administrative structure at the district level, integrating the functions of the Zila Parishad and the DRDA.

The unified organizational structure may have the collector, acting as the overall coordinator, whose authority should be reinforced through local people's institutions brought into the administrative process, with adequate powers and well-defined functions, and which can enforce their policy decisions on the functionaries operating within their jurisdiction. Certain criteria for designing an ideal rural development organization are presented in Chapter 13, Box 13.2.

People's Participation in Implementation

The implementation of any rural development project on a national scale cannot be effective without the active and widespread participation of its clientele. This is why a rural development project authority, to be effective, must know how to make the project's clientele see themselves as partners in the effort, and how to encourage the individual initiative dormant in the people. In other words, the project authority must be capable of maintaining a proper balance between public intervention and private initiative; the former will be greater in the early stage of development and the latter in the advanced stage of development.

It is the task of the project authority to discover the active elements in the local population, to awaken their interest, and to mobilize their initiative. The active elements may be found in the educated middle class, rural leaders, political parties, or in other groups. Their successful activation requires the first-hand knowledge of the population, and their customs and traditions and is often based more on perceptiveness and intuition than on direct rules and principles.

Many different factors may motivate people to participate or refrain from participating in a rural development project. Therefore, it is necessary for those responsible for project implementation to find out the factors that motivate the local people to participate in a project and to formulate, on the basis of this first-hand knowledge, a specific strategy to enlist their participation. A review of India's past efforts in involving people in the processes of plan formulation and implementation would reveal that the decentralization of planning and administrative functions through the PRIs has not brought about the desired results. After the introduction of the 73rd Constitution Amendment Act, 1992, people's participation in planning and implementation of rural development projects was expected to improve. But the experience to date indicates that it has not improved significantly. Most of the rural poor still do not participate in decision-making processes that affect them due to a variety of reasons.

In a few areas, some VAs have been successful in enlisting the support and participation of local people in the implementation of their development projects. But that is more because of the charismatic personality of the project leader, and less because of any institutional innovations that can be replicated on a large scale elsewhere in the country. The Anand-pattern cooperative structure seems to be an appropriate instrument for enlisting people's participation in rural development projects. This has been amply demonstrated under the OF program as described in Chapter 9.

Weitz (1971, Chapter 9) has distilled, from the experience with various development projects, the following simple rules of thumb for enlisting people's participation in development projects:

1. Create a human relationship on the basis of equality between the project clientele and the project employees, and institutionalize it.
2. Know the traditions and social customs of the project's clientele.
3. Introduce programs gradually and adapt them to the ability of the target population, to enable it to absorb the changes involved.
4. Get yourself a partner from amongst the local leaders.
5. Encourage and promote development leadership among both the project employees and the local people.

Project Monitoring

Monitoring is undertaken to fulfill the following purposes:

1. Provide the information required for improving the selection, performance, and cost-effectiveness of projects.
2. Provide the information required by the funding agencies and local level agencies interested in the project.
3. Ensure effective vertical and horizontal information flows between different levels and agencies associated with the projects.

The major components of project monitoring are as follows:

1. Project Progress Reports
   (*i*) Summary,
   (*ii*) Progress of physical implementation compared to targets,
   (*iii*) Financial performance compared to targets, and
   (*iv*) Performance of principal inputs and services.
2. Special Diagnostic Studies
3. Project Completion Reports
4. Project Sustainability

Practically every major agricultural and rural development program provides for monitoring of both the achievement of its physical and financial targets, and the benefits actually accruing to its target group. Usually, a family-based approach is used for monitoring the impact of a program on its clientele. For example, the IRDP provided for the monitoring of incremental income of its beneficiary families and for comparing it with their baseline incomes as assessed at the time of conducting household surveys for selection of beneficiaries. For this purpose, an identity-cum-monitoring card used to be issued to each beneficiary family.

From the management perspective, it is necessary to differentiate between the information needed for control and the information needed for purposes other than control. Therefore, the management needs two types of reports: a control report and an information report. For the purpose of control, what is needed is essentially a comparison of actual performance with planned performance and reasons for the deviations, if any. Therefore, a control report should be very brief and precise. The information report tells the management what is going on in the organization. Such reports may or may not lead to action.

The format and frequency of a monitoring or control report will depend on the nature, size, complexity, and structure of the organization/program that is to be monitored and controlled. But, in general, a monitoring system should be linked with the responsibility centers in the organization concerned. A responsibility center is simply a unit or a subsystem in an organization headed by a responsible manager, who is accountable for the work done by his unit. The manager in charge of a responsibility center should be provided with the information that is relevant for his needs of planning, decision-making, control, and remedial action. The relevant information should, therefore, be identified for each responsibility center and the control report format designed accordingly.

The Ministry of Rural Development places special emphasis on monitoring and evaluating its programs being implemented in rural areas all over the country. Effective monitoring of the programs is considered very important for efficient delivery at the grassroots level, particularly in view of the substantial step up in the allocation of funds for rural development programs.

In order to ensure this, the Ministry has evolved a comprehensive system of monitoring and evaluating the implementation of its programs. Appropriate performance indicators have been developed for the program, for effective monitoring at different levels so that alarm signals are captured well in advance for mid-course corrections.

The important instruments of monitoring and evaluation adopted by the ministry are as follows:

(i) Review by the Union ministers
(ii) Web-based MIS
(iii) Utilization certificates/audit reports
(iv) Performance review committee (PRC) and regional reviews
(v) Concurrent Evaluation/Quick Evaluation
(vi) Web-based monitoring
(vii) Vigilance and monitoring committees (VMCs)
(viii) National-level monitors
(ix) Area officers' scheme

Monitoring of rural development programs at the state level is the responsibility of the State Level Coordination Committee (SLCC) for rural development programs.

A representative of the Union Ministry of Rural Development is also usually invited to participate in the meetings of the SLCC. The chief ministers of the States also review, from time to time, the progress of various programs with members of Parliament (MPs), members of legislative assemblies (MLAs) and senior officers of the state governments concerned.

Apart from the monitoring mechanisms stated previously, the standing committees and the consultative committees and the Public Accounts Committee of the Parliament also take stock of the implementation of various rural development programs at periodical intervals. The shortcomings/lacunae observed by the local MPs in the implementation of the programs are looked into and quick remedial measures are taken to improve the program, wherever required.

Besides the government agencies, other organizations, such as the funding agencies/donors and NGOs also undertake monitoring of the projects supported by them. This is normally done by external agencies/consultants on their behalf.

Project Evaluation

By evaluation we mean assessment. We distinguish between three types of evaluation, namely, *ex-ante* evaluation, concurrent evaluation and *ex-post* evaluation. In *ex-ante* evaluation, a project is assessed before it is executed; in concurrent evaluation, assessment is made while the project is underway; and in *ex-post* evaluation, assessment is made after the project is completed. This section is confined to a discussion of concurrent and *ex-post* evaluation.

Objectives of Evaluation

The main objectives of *ex-post* evaluation are to find out whether, and to what extent, the program has been successful in achieving its objectives and at what cost, to investigate the reasons of both good as well as bad performance, and to bring out the lessons learnt. A secondary objective of evaluation could be to suggest appropriate measures to improve the performance of the program. The main objective of concurrent evaluation is to find out whether the program is progressing as per the plan (and if not, why) and what its impacts are.

Methodological Issues

Evaluation of a rural development program is beset with a number of conceptual and empirical problems. First, there are conceptual problems of devising a composite index of rural development, which can capture its multidimensional nature. Then, there are problems of quantifying all the program interventions and measures that directly and/or indirectly seek to promote rural development, and recording and monitoring their values at the beginning, at the end, and also during the course of the program implementation. These problems are further complicated by the fact that the causal variables or determinants of development keep changing simultaneously, rendering it very difficult to isolate and measure the effect of any one of them. It is difficult—and if at all possible, extravagant in resources—to apply a classical experimental design of studies with random samples, controls, treatments, measurement of effects, and attribution of effects to program measures. Also, a long period may be needed to identify and observe the "after" effects of a rural development program, given the slow diffusion of its effects.

Setting targets is an important management tool, which is commonly used in rural development programs to control and improve the performance, and evaluation is invariably geared toward measuring achievement against the targets. This form of evaluation is liable to biased activity and effort toward achieving outputs that are quantifiable and measurable, to the neglect of those that may be more important, but which are less easy to quantify and measure. For instance, the eradication of poverty was the ultimate goal of IRDP, but its performance was evaluated in terms of achievement of its physical and financial targets. This is mainly because monitoring changes in the magnitude of poverty is more difficult than reporting the progress achieved in fulfilling the physical (number of beneficiaries covered) and financial (amount of subsidy and loans disbursed) targets. It is important, therefore, that program administrators and evaluators take care in choosing evaluation criteria and see the causal links between the program measures, sub-goals, and main goals.

Rural development projects and their outcomes can be seen as long, causal chains of the following type.

Inputs and activities → Production targets → Products (outputs) → Sub-goals → Main goals

An evaluation system has to select points along the chain at which observations and measurements can be carried out. Evaluation could be done at any or all the points along the chain.

Rural development programs usually have multiple effects, only a few of which are usually specified in an evaluation plan. While some of the effects may be anticipated, others may be unanticipated or spillovers. Of the unanticipated effects, some may be harmful and some may be beneficial. For instance, a shortage of good quality milch animals, and the consequent hike in their price, may be an unanticipated harmful effect of provision of milch animals to selected beneficiaries under IRDP, and enhancing of managerial capacity of the beneficiaries may be an unanticipated beneficial effect of the same program. Unless an evaluation design is open to change, and unless perceptive and open-ended research is undertaken concurrently with evaluation, significant unanticipated effects may be missed.

Evaluation is also vulnerable to political insecurity and pressures. External evaluation is usually called upon for three reasons, or for combinations of them: to be quasi-judicial, to be supportive, or to improve performance. Consequently, the evaluator may be regarded as a spy, an investigator, or an enemy; but it is quite likely that he will be co-opted into the system. Co-opted evaluators resemble parasites in their concern not to kill their hosts, and there is a danger that their reports will be muted in criticism and over-lavish in praise, in order to secure their continued employment or the chance of another job.

Besides external evaluation, much informal and unsystematic evaluation takes place within departments/organizations, through the experience gained with implementation, through personal impressions, and through the feedback of internal reporting systems. An external evaluator may contribute a lot by examining the reporting and evaluation systems that already operate within the organization, and trying to improve them and link them up functionally with remedial action and with future resource allocations.

Criteria for Evaluation

The criteria for evaluation of a program should be related to the major goals of the program and should be operational. For example, a simple criterion for evaluating Aajeevika could be the number of people helped to rise above the poverty line on a sustained basis. To operationalize this criterion, we will need to define a poverty line for each state, district, or may be for the block as well, separately at some base year's price, and then keep updating this, year after year, to neutralize the effect of inflation. Once this is done, the next thing required is to develop a system to determine and report the annual per capita income for each beneficiary household every year. This way, we may, at the end of each year, see how many poor families have been helped to rise above the poverty line.

Determining the area-specific poverty line, updating it, and assessing per capita income for each and every beneficiary household are all very difficult tasks, and require the expertise and resources that are not available at present at the block and district levels anywhere in the country. Unless requisite resources and expertise are made available, nothing more or better than the existing system of reporting progress in terms of physical and financial targets can be expected. Universities and research institutes could help in determining poverty lines, updating these, and assessing per capita incomes in a few blocks and districts, but the major brunt of the task will have to be borne by the program itself. The existing official Planning Commission poverty lines for 2011–12 are based on the Tendulkar Expert Group methodology and derived from the MRP private consumption, expenditure size distribution data collected in the 68th round of the NSSO survey (for details, see Chapters 3 and 10).

Approaches to Evaluation

Most evaluation studies have used either the "before and after" or the "with and without" approach to isolate and measure program impacts. Ideally, both these approaches should be used together. The "before and after" approach purges the program impact of the cumulated effect of past programs, and the "with and without" approach eliminates the effects of the natural process of development, as well as of other development programs underway in the area of study. But the "before and after" approach can be used only when the baseline data for the year immediately preceding the year when the program to be evaluated was launched are available.

Under IRDP, baseline household surveys were conducted in all the villages selected for the program and the incomes of the eligible beneficiaries were determined. Assuming that this information is readily available at the block headquarters, one could use both these approaches to evaluate the impact of IRDP. For the "with and without" approach, the households that are otherwise eligible for assistance under the program but were excluded because of the limited target constitute the "control" (without program) group, and the beneficiaries would constitute the "project" (with program) group.

In the "with and without" method, an attempt is made to identify and value the costs and benefits that have arisen from the program, and to compare them with the costs and benefits in the situation that would have prevailed without the program. The difference is the incremental net benefit that can be attributed to the program. The "before and after" method, if used alone, fails to take into account the changes in income, employment, or any other performance indicator that may occur autonomously without the program, and thus may lead to an erroneous estimate of the benefits attributable to the program.

Generally speaking, one may encounter one of three situations in which the program, which is to be evaluated, may be operating (Gittinger 1982, 47–50):

1. A situation in which output, or income, or any other performance indicator has been growing, but at a slow rate, say, 5% per annum, even without the program. With the program, the rate of growth may increase to, say, 10% per annum. So, the incremental effect is 10 – 5 =5% per annum. This situation is represented in Figure 15.1. This kind of situation prevailed in India in the dairy sector before OF-I was launched.
2. A situation in which the output has been declining, say, at a rate of 5% per annum naturally, but with the program, the decrease in output may be checked and output may be stabilized at the normal level. In this case, the benefit from the program is in the form of prevention of loss in output. In agriculture, this kind of situation may arise in areas which are prone to droughts, floods, and wind erosion. This situation is represented in Figure 15.2.
3. A situation in which no change in output is expected without the program, but with the program the output is expected to increase, say, at the rate of 5% per annum. In this case, all the increase (5%) may be attributed to the program. In this situation, the use of "before and after" and "with and without" methods would yield the same

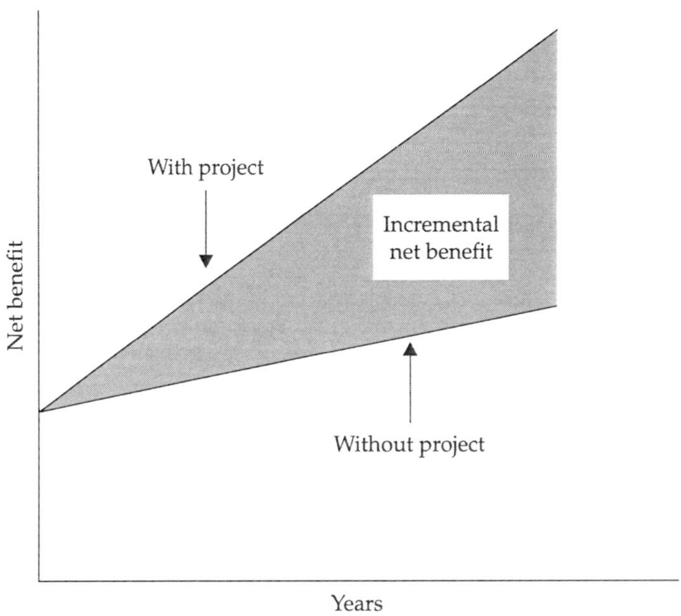

Figure 15.1: *Mechanics of Impact Assessment of a Program Like Operation Flood*

Source: Gittinger (1982).

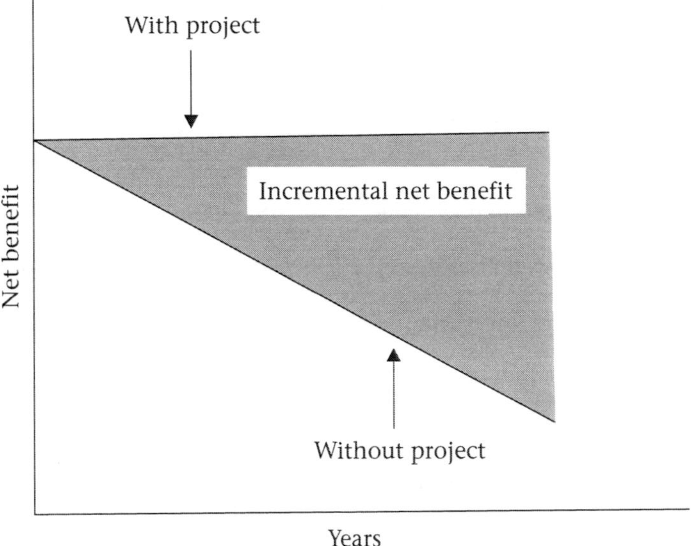

Figure 15.2: *Mechanics of Impact Assessment of a Flood Control Project*

Source: Gittinger (1982).

results. In this kind of situation, one may use either of these methods. This situation (depicted in Figure 15.3) may prevail in the new settlement project areas where, without the project, the productivity of land and other resources is almost stagnant or negligible, but after the project it starts increasing.

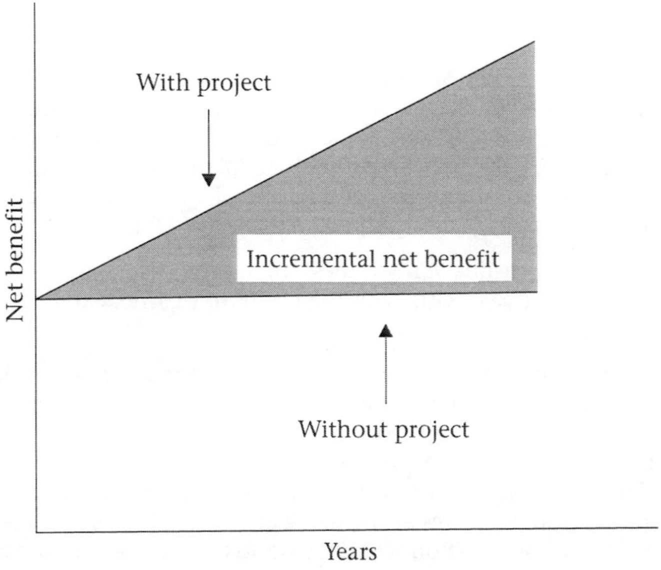

Figure 15.3: *Mechanics of Impact Assessment of a Land Settlement Project*

Source: Gittinger (1982).

Table 15.1: *A Conceptual Design for Impact Measurement*

Type of Group	*Before the Adoption of a Project*	*After the Adoption of a Project*
Beneficiary	I_{PB}	I_{PA}
Non-beneficiary	I_{CB}	I_{CA}

Source: Authors.

Notes: 1. I_{PB} = level of a selected impact indicator for the beneficiary group before the project was launched;

2. I_{PA} = level of a selected indicator for the beneficiary group after the project is over or is still underway;

3. I_{CB} = level of a selected impact indicator for the non-beneficiary group before the project was launched; and

4. I_{CA} = level of a selected impact indicator for the non-beneficiary group after the project is over or is still underway.

A conceptual design that we can use for impact evaluation of a project could be presented as is done in Table 15.1.

The net effect of the project is given as:

$$\text{Net Effect} = (I_{PA} - I_{PB}) - (I_{CA} - I_{CB})$$

Or, alternatively,

$$\text{Net Effect} = (I_{PA} - I_{CA}) - (I_{PB} - I_{CB})$$

$(I_{PA} - I_{PB})$ gives an estimate of the gross effect on the level of an impact indicator over the duration of the project due to the project and non-project activities and $(I_{CA} - I_{CB})$ indicates the change in the level of an impact indicator due to the non-project activities alone.

Uses of Evaluation

The results of evaluation studies should be used as feedback to policy makers, planners, administrators, implementers, bankers, researchers, and to other agencies directly or indirectly associated with the program. Evaluation could make policy makers and implementers aware of the inadequacies of the "blueprint" approach to planning and implementation of rural development programs. To be of any use, the results of evaluation should be presented in a simple and non-technical language, and should be made available to the potential users in time.

The lessons derived from evaluation studies, including the reasons for good and bad performance, should be discussed with both the program planners and administrators, as well as with the beneficiaries.

Any systematic but simple procedure requiring the staff to evaluate the projects on which they are working is likely to be beneficial in heightening their awareness and in communicating their problems to levels at which some of them can be tackled. In the context of Aajeevika, this means that the assistant project officers, extension officers and even VLWs should be encouraged to undertake some simple but systematic evaluation of their activities, and present their findings at annual staff meetings at the block and district levels. Of course, some training in how to conduct scientific evaluation would be necessary before they are asked to do the job.

At the end, we would like to sound caution that it is asking a lot of a social scientist, whether he be in a university or in the government, to make program recommendations that require an assessment of the organizational and management aspects of implementation unless he is also trained in management or has relevant managerial experience. This is perhaps one reason why so many of the proposals that are made by social scientists not trained/experienced in management are never implemented. One way of improving the chances of recommendations being implementable is to give priority to discussion and exchange of ideas between the evaluator who will make the recommendations and the manager who will be faced with implementing them (Chambers 1974, 124).

Knowledge Management (KM) in Rural Development

"Successful organizations are those that consistently create new knowledge, disseminate it widely throughout the organization and quickly embody it in new technologies and products"

—Ikujiro Nonaka, a KM pioneer

As we know by now, India has a long history of governmental and nongovernmental interventions in the form of development schemes to promote rural development.

Since the launch of the First Five Year Plan in 1951–52, the Central and state governments have launched numerous agricultural and rural development programs from time to time. Besides the CSS, a large number of rural development schemes have also been launched by the state governments from time to time. For example, in Gujarat as many as 38 rural and agricultural development schemes are currently underway.[1]

There has been a proliferation of agricultural and rural development schemes since the beginning of the planning era, consequent to the desire of every political party in power to "reinvent the wheel" or "putting the old wine in a new bottle" and the failure to use the experience and knowledge gained from implementation of earlier programs. The number of CSS was 190 at the end of Fifth Plan that had increased to 360 at the end of Ninth Plan. The NDC has duly taken cognizance of the need to reduce the number of CSS. Consequently, the total number of CSS has reduced gradually over time. Further, generally the pattern has been reduction in the number of schemes at the end of each plan after a review. For example, in the Eleventh Plan, the number of schemes declined from 155 in 2005–06 to 99 in 2007–08 at the beginning of Eleventh Plan but subsequently increased to 147 in 2011–12 (Chaturvedi 2011).

Despite the multitude of RD schemes launched in India from time to time over the last 65 years or so and the billions of rupees expended on those schemes, the quality of life of rural people has not improved to the desired extent. This is evidenced from the fact that in 2010–11, India had around 270 million poor people (about 22% of India's total population), which is the highest in the world. Similarly, India has the world's highest number of illiterate and unemployed people.

Although a large number of factors are responsible for such a poor state of affairs and many approaches and strategies have been used to improve the situation, the lack of KM seems to us to be one of the reasons why most of the rural development schemes are not cost-effectively designed nor effectively implemented. For example, Public Distribution Scheme, which is India's oldest program launched after World War II, has been reviewed and evaluated by numerous committees constituted by the Government of India from time to time. It has also been revised and revamped several times but still there are several loopholes in its design and implementation, including large scale leakages of food grains in transit from godowns of the Food Corporation of India to the fair price shops and other form of corrupt practices. These loopholes have not yet been plugged and consequently the scheme still continues to suffer from several drawbacks. Perhaps the lessons learnt from its experience have not been fully incorporated in designing and implementing its latest avatars. Besides, another major lacuna in the implementation of various rural and agricultural development schemes is the overlapping of the objectives and clientele of various schemes, and the consequent confusion among the target groups as to which of those several schemes is intended to benefit them and how. In view of this, KM could be the most cost-effective tool of improving the efficiency and effectiveness of rural development schemes.

KM emerged into the mainstream management arena in the 1990s. It comprises a range of strategies and practices used in an organization to identify, create, represent, distribute, and enable adoption of insights and experiences gained from within the organization. Such insights and experiences comprise knowledge, either embodied in individuals or embedded in organizations as processes or practices.

KM efforts typically focus on organizational objectives such as improved performance, competitive advantage, innovation, the sharing of lessons learned, integration, and continuous improvement of the organization. KM efforts overlap with organizational learning, and may be distinguished from that by a greater focus on the management of knowledge as a strategic asset and a focus on encouraging the sharing of knowledge.

KM efforts typically include on-the-job discussions, formal apprenticeship, discussion forums, corporate libraries, professional training, and mentoring programs. More recently, with the increased use of computers, specific adaptations of technologies such as knowledge bases, expert systems, knowledge repositories, group decision support systems, and intranets have also become important tools of KM.

The following are the main benefits of adopting a systematic approach to managing knowledge in an organization:

1. *Benefits from more efficient processing of information and knowledge, including:*
   - Faster retrieval of information
   - Minimizing duplication, e.g. "one version of the truth"
   - Saving or freeing up the time of busy professionals
   - Knowing who knows what and who is doing what
   - Improved quality of information
   - Access to latest thinking and most current knowledge,

which in turn leads to:

2. *Internal organizational benefits, including efficiencies and effectiveness through:*
   - Sharing of good and best practices
   - Faster time-to-market for new products
   - Reduction of waste and re-work
   - Better management of risk
   - Retention of knowledge before experts leave or retire
   - cost savings, both in people's time and processing of information,

which in turn leads to:

3. *Benefits to external customers and stakeholders including:*
   - Improved customer service and satisfaction
   - Faster solving of intractable and novel problems

- Greater consistency in servicing customers at different locations
- Improved product and service quality, more closely aligned with customer needs
- Better value for money
- Enhanced reputation and market image

Knowledge may be captured at three stages: before, during, or after KM-related activities. Different organizations have tried various knowledge capture incentives, including making content submission mandatory and incorporating rewards into performance measurement plans. Considerable controversy exists over whether incentives work or not in this field and no consensus has emerged.

One strategy to KM involves actively managing knowledge (push strategy). In such an instance, individuals strive to explicitly encode their knowledge into a shared knowledge repository, such as a database, as well as retrieving knowledge they need that other individuals have provided to the repository. This is also commonly known as the codification approach to KM.

Another strategy to KM involves individuals making knowledge requests of experts associated with a particular subject on an ad hoc basis (pull strategy). In such an instance, expert individual(s) can provide their insights to the particular person or people needing this. It is also commonly known as the personalization approach to KM.

Other KM strategies and instruments for organizations include:

- Rewards (as a means of motivating for knowledge sharing)
- Storytelling (as a means of transferring tacit knowledge)
- Cross-project learning
- After action reviews
- Knowledge mapping (a map of knowledge repositories within an organization accessible by all)
- Expert directories (to enable knowledge seeker to reach to the experts)
- Best practice transfer
- knowledge fairs
- Competence management (systematic evaluation and planning of competences of individual organization members)
- Proximity and architecture (the physical situation of employees can be either conducive or obstructive to knowledge sharing)
- Master–apprentice relationship
- Collaborative technologies, for example, groupware
- Knowledge repositories (databases, bookmarking engines, and so on.)
- Measuring and reporting intellectual capital (a way of making explicit knowledge for companies)
- Social software (wikis, social bookmarking, blogs, and so on.)
- Inter-project knowledge transfer

The purpose of setting up a KM system in an organization is to enable its employees to have ready access to the organization's documented base of facts, sources of information, and solutions. For example, a typical claim justifying the creation of a KM system might run something like this: a project manager knows the factors that hinder or facilitate the smooth implementation of the project. Sharing this information organization wide can lead to more efficient design and more effective implementation of similar projects in future.

Here are some guidelines to bear in mind as you embark on institutionalizing a KM program in your organization:

- Start rethinking your organization and your strategy as being knowledge-based: How does knowledge contribute value? Which is your vital knowledge? If you're not sure, conduct a knowledge audit.
- Develop a set of knowledge goals directly from your organizational strategy. Focus on the knowledge areas that directly contribute to achieving your organizational goals.
- As you embark on institutionalizing KM on a pilot basis, start with a few simple well-understood schemes.
- Develop a generic and balanced set of measurement indicators from the chosen schemes. Good indicators are simple and understandable, credible, relevant, measurable, objective, and controllable.
- Engage widely with employees and stakeholders using the full gamut of communications activities. But make sure it is a two-way dialogue.
- Treat the whole process as a learning exercise adapting as necessary from year to year.

Institutionalization of KM in rural development could be effected easily without any drastic change in administrative machinery and without any substantial expenditure. In the Ministry of Rural Development, there is a full-fledged program for monitoring and evaluating on-going schemes. Under this scheme, a KM officer may be appointed or the existing officer of the rank of deputy secretary/director looking after the schemes could be assigned this additional responsibility. The task involved is not highly technical and therefore could be handled easily by an officer in the ministry without any specialized training. Now, there is a growing number of organizations in developed countries that employ knowledge managers and KM has emerged as an important area of specialization in management courses.

In India also, quite a few organizations, mostly in information technology and corporate sectors, are now using KM as a tool for improving their organizational efficiency. Duly recognizing the importance of KM, a National Knowledge Management Commission (NKC) was constituted by the Government of India in June 2005 under the chairmanship of Sam Pitroda to prepare a blueprint for reform of India's knowledge related and other institutions. One of its terms of reference was to promote knowledge applications in agriculture and industry. It had a designated time-frame of three years from October 2, 2005 to October 2, 2008, which was extended to March 31, 2009. In three years NKC had submitted recommendations on 27 focus areas in the form of letters to the Prime Minister. The recommendations have been widely disseminated in three compilations: "Report to the Nation 2006," and "Report to the Nation 2007" as well as "Towards a Knowledge Society," which is a compilation of the education recommendations. The final Report of NKC contains the full text of all the recommendations submitted by the commission in the three years of its tenure. It also includes follow up on the recommendations. NKC recognizes that the challenges facing Indian agriculture can only be addressed through a comprehensive package of measures that includes an emphasis on enhanced knowledge generation and application. NKC has also recommended restructuring of the Agricultural Technology Management Agency (ATMA) to make it more decentralized, participatory and locally responsive, and enhancing the role of private players in agricultural extension delivery. It also has focused on knowledge applications for enhancing the well-being of common people, especially in rural areas. The governments at the Center and states are taking steps for successful implementation of the policy suggestions made by NKC. The government's commitment to NKC's vision is reflected in the Eleventh Five Year Plan where NKC's inputs have been incorporated in formulating the broad contours of the plan.[2]

Key Points

1. Implementation, monitoring, and evaluation of projects are all subsumed in the project management function. Implementation may be regarded as a process by which a set of predetermined activities is carried out in a planned manner, with a view to achieving certain established objectives. Monitoring is a process of keeping a watch on the progress of a project vis-à-vis its targets and time schedule. Evaluation of a project is concerned with the assessment of the impact(s) of the project.
2. Massive investments have been made in rural development programs since the beginning of the planning era in India and will continue to be made in the near future. Apart from several flaws in planning, there have been numerous operational problems in the implementation, monitoring, and evaluation and KM of the programs. This has adversely affected the efficiency and effectiveness of the programs.
3. There are two approaches to implementation, namely, the traditional (blueprint) approach and the open (people-centered) approach. The former is characterized by a mechanical view of planning and development, in which implementation is simply a tool of the powerful (donors, planners, politicians) and the latter places people at the center of the entire process of implementation.
4. Some planning is required for plan implementation as well. A plan for implementation should, at the minimum, specify what is to be done, who is to do it, when it is to be done and how it is to be done. To begin with, the plan should be broken up into a number of projects, and then, for every project, an implementation system should be developed.
5. For discharging various functions of project management including preparation of an implementation plan and executing the project, an appropriate project organization has to be developed, responsibilities for various tasks clearly assigned, and the proper use of scientific equipment and tools ensured. Filling key positions with adequately skilled and experienced persons on time is also important.
6. Building inter-linkages is necessary to complete the project in time and to derive full benefits from the interrelated projects, such as bridges and roads, irrigation and crop development projects, production, processing, and marketing projects, power and industry, and so on. Both backward and forward linkages with other projects should be built and strengthened.
7. Given the multidisciplinary nature of rural development, and the multitude of governmental and nongovernmental agencies engaged in the implementation of diverse agricultural and rural development programs with different—and often conflicting—objectives, it is absolutely essential that the different development programs in operation in an area be integrated and coordinated for optimum results.
8. The Ministry of Rural Development places special emphasis on monitoring and evaluation of its programs being implemented in rural areas all over the country. In order to ensure this, the ministry has evolved a comprehensive system of monitoring and evaluation of the implementation of its programs. Appropriate performance indicators have been developed for program, for effective monitoring at different levels so that alarm signals are captured well in advance for mid-course corrections.
9. The implementation of any rural development project on a national scale cannot be possible without the active and widespread participation of its clientele. This is why a rural development project authority, to be effective, must know how to make the

project's clientele see themselves as partners in the effort and how to encourage the individual initiative dormant in the people.

10. We could distinguish between three types of evaluation, namely, *ex-ante* evaluation, concurrent evaluation and *ex-post* evaluation. In *ex-ante* evaluation, a project is assessed before it is executed; in concurrent evaluation, assessment is made while the project is underway; in *ex-post* evaluation, assessment is made after the project is completed. Both concurrent and *ex-post* evaluations are necessary for efficient and effective implementation of a rural development program.
11. There are two commonly used approaches to evaluation: "with and without" and "before and after." Ideally, both the approaches should be used to assess the impacts of a project on its clientele and other persons. But this is possible only if and when the base line data for the period preceding the launching of the project are available.
12. An external evaluator can contribute a lot by examining the systems of reporting and evaluation that already exist within the organization, and trying to improve them and link them functionally with remedial action.
13. An internal evaluation based on personal impressions and the feedback of internal reporting systems can also be very useful, if it is done objectively and used constructively. Internal evaluation should not be used as an espionage system, and the internal evaluator should not be allowed to become a power-wielding center.
14. The results of evaluation studies should be used as feedback to policy makers, planners, administrators, implementers, bankers, researchers and to other agencies directly or indirectly associated with the program.
15. To be of any use, the results of evaluation should be presented in a simple and non-technical language, and should be made available to the potential users in time.
16. KM emerged into the mainstream management arena in the 1990s. It comprises a range of strategies and practices used in an organization to identify, create, represent, distribute, and enable adoption of insights and experiences gained from within the organization. Such insights and experiences comprise knowledge, either embodied in individuals or embedded in organizations as processes or practices.
17. The lack of KM is one of the reasons why most of the rural development schemes are not cost-effectively designed nor effectively implemented. KM could be the most cost-effective tool of improving the efficiency and effectiveness of rural development schemes.

Questions for Discussion

1. Most of the rural development projects in India fail to achieve their objectives efficiently mainly because of lax implementation. Outline a strategy for improving the implementation of rural development projects.
2. What are the advantages of involving people/stakeholders in the process of implementation of rural development project?
3. Why are the government officers reluctant to involve people in implementation of rural development projects?
4. Illustrate with an example the differences between monitoring and evaluation.
5. Which one of the "With and Without" and "Before and After" approaches to evaluation is suitable in India and why?

6. What are the pros and cons of external evaluation and internal evaluation?
7. Discuss how knowledge management could be an integral part of project management.

Notes

1. Personal communication with Dr H.S. Shylendra, Professor, Institute of Rural Management, Anand.
2. http://knowledgecommissionarchive.nic.in/reports/report09.asp (Accessed on January 5, 2016).

Bibliography

Acharya, S.S. 1997. "Agricultural Price Policy and Development: Some Facts and Emerging Issues." *Indian Journal of Agricultural Economics*, 52 (1): 1–47.

Adelman, Irma and C.T. Morris. 1967. *Society, Politics and Economic Development.* Baltimore, MD: Johns Hopkins University Press.

Agrawal, A.N. and S.P. Singh, eds. 1975. *The Economics of Under Development.* New Delhi: Oxford University Press.

Aiyar, Anklesaria S. Swaminathan. 1995. "Encouraging News About Poverty." *The Economic Times*, 14 December.

Alavi, Hamza and Teodar Shanin, eds. 1982. *Introduction to the Sociology of "Developing Societies."* London: Macmillan.

Alderman, Harold, George Merges and Roger Slade. 1987. "Cooperatives and the Commercialization of Milk Production in India: A Literature Review." IFPRI Working Paper on Commercialization of Agriculture and Nutrition, No. 2, Washington, D.C.

Alex, Alexander V. 1983. *Human Capital Approach to Economic Development.* New Delhi: Metropolitan.

Alvares, Claude. 1985. *Another Revolution Fails.* New Delhi: Ajanta Publications.

Anderson, Terry L. 1982. "The New Resource Economics: Old Ideas and New Applications." *American Journal of Agricultural Economics*, 64: 928–34.

Anonymous. 1968. *Webster's Dictionary,* Third New International Edition, Springfield, MA: G. & C. Merriam Co.

———. 1978. "Mahatma Gandhi on Rural Development." *Indian Farming,* (October–November).

———. 2007. "Poverty in India." *Kurukshetra*, 55 (4): 44.

Ansoff, Igor H., Roger P. Declerck and Robert L. Hayes, eds. 1976. *From Strategic Planning to Strategic Management.* London: John Wiley and Sons.

Atkinson, Anthony B. 1970. "On the Measurement of Equality." *Journal of Economic Theory*, 2 (February): 253–54.

———. 1987. "On the Measurement of Poverty." *Econometrica*, 55: 749–64.

Balooni, Kulbhushan and Katar Singh. 2003. "Institutional Financing of Wastelands Afforestation in India: Some Issues and Options." *Natural Resources Forum*, 27.

Bandyopadhyay, D. 1988. "Direct Intervention Programmes for Poverty Alleviation: An Appraisal." *Economic and Political Weekly*, 25 June: A77–88.

Barbier, Edward B. 1997. "Introduction." *Environment and Development Economics*, Special issue on Environmental Kuznets Curve, 2 (4): 357–67.

Barnett, T. 1988. *Sociology and Development.* London: Hutchinson.

Bartelmus, Peter. 1997. "Whither Economics? From Optimality to Sustainability." *Environment and Development Economics*, 2 (3): 323–45.

Basu, D.N. and G.S. Guha. 1996. *Agro-Climatic Regional Planning in India, Vol. I: Concepts and Application.* New Delhi: Concept Publishing Co.

Basu, D.N. and S.P. Kashyap. 1996. *Agro-Climatic Regional Planning in India, Vol. II: Themes and Cases.* New Delhi: Concept Publishing Co.

Bauer, Peter. 1991. *The Development Frontier.* Cambridge: Harvard University Press.

Berger, Peter L. and Richard John Neuhaus. 1977. *To Empower People: The Role of Mediating Structures in Public Policy.* Washington, D.C.: American Enterprise Institute for Public Policy Research.

Boeke, J.H. 1953. *Economics and Economic Policy of Dual Societies as Exemplified by Indonesia.* New York: Institute of Pacific Relations.

Bromley, D.W. 1991. *Environment and Economy: Property Rights and Public Policy.* Oxford: Basil Blackwell.

Bronfenbrenner, Martin. 1966. "The High Cost of Economic Development." *Land Economics*, August 1953: 209–18 quoted in Benjamin Higgins: *Economic Development: Principles, Problems and Policies.* Allahabad: Central Book Depot.

Brown, Lester R., Alan Durning, Christopher Flavin, Hilary French, Jodi Jacobson, Nicholas Lenssen, Marcia Lowe, Sandra Postel, Michael Renner, Linda Starke, Pater Weber and John Young. 1993. *State of the World 1993.* London and New York: W.W. Norton.

Bryant, Coralee and Louise G. White. 1980. *Managing Rural Development: Peasant Participation in Rural Development.* New Hartford, CT: Kumarian Press.

Buckley, Walter. 1967. *Sociology and Modern Systems Theory.* Englewood Cliffs, NJ: Prentice Hall, Inc.

Chaturvedi, B.K. 2011. *Report of the Committee on Restructuring of Centrally Sponsored Schemes (CSS)* New Delhi: Planning Commission, GOI.

CSO (Central Statistical Organisation). 2004. *National Accounts Statistics.* New Delhi: Central Statistical Organization, Ministry of Statistics and Programme Implementation, Government of India.

———. 2006. *National Accounts Statistics.* New Delhi: Central Statistical Organisation. Ministry of Statistics and Programme Implementation, Government of India.

———. 2008. *National Accounts Statistics.* New Delhi: Central Statistical Organisation. Ministry of Statistics and Programme Implementation, Government of India.

CSE (Centre for Science and Environment). 2001. *Down to Earth: Survival Primer, Society for Environmental Communications*, Centre for Science and Environment, New Delhi.

CMIE (Centre for Monitoring Indian Economy). 1997. *Approach Paper to Ninth Five Year Plan.* Mumbai: Centre for Monitoring Indian Economy, February.

Ciriacy-Wantrup, S.V. 1968. *Resource Conservation: Economics and Policies,* 3rd ed. Berkeley: Division of Agricultural Sciences, University of California.

Chambers, Robert. 1974. *Managing Rural Development, Ideas and Experience From East Africa.* Uppsala: Scandinavian Institute of African Studies.

———. 1983. *Rural Development: Putting the Last First.* London: Longman.

———. 1987. "Sustainable Rural Livelihoods: A Strategy for People, Environment and Development," Commissioned Study No. 7, Institute of Development Studies at the University of Sussex, Brighton, England.

Chand, Ramesh. 1997. "Import Liberalisation and Indian Agriculture: The Challenge and Strategy." Policy Paper No. 6, New Delhi: National Centre for Agricultural Economics and Policy Research.

Cochrane, Willard W. 1969. *The World Food Problem: A Guardedly Optimistic View.* New York: Thomas Y. Crowell Company Inc.

Daly, Herman E. 1990. "Toward Some Operational Principles of Sustainable Development," *Ecological Economics*, 2: 1–6.

Dandekar, V.M. 1972. "Effectiveness in Agricultural Planning," *Teaching Forum: Development Processes and Planning*, 19 July. New York: The Agricultural Development Council.

Dandekar, V.M. and Nilakanth Rath. 1971. *Poverty in India.* Pune: Indian School of Political Economy.

Dantwala, M.L. 1970. "From Stagnation to Growth," *Indian Economic Journal,* 18, (October–December): 165–92.

Dasgupta, A.K. 1978. "Plan Priorities: Some Basic Issue," *Yojana*, 12 (26 January): 16–18.

Desai, D.K. 1983. *Management in Rural Development.* New Delhi: Oxford and IBH.

Deshpande, D.V., M.K. Mudgal and K.K. Gupta. 1996. "Regional Rural Banks at Cross Roads." Working Paper No. 9, Bankers Institute of Rural Development, Lucknow.

Doornbos, Martin and Liana Gertsch. 1994. "Sustainability, Technology and Corporate Interest: Resource Strategies in India's Modern Dairy Sector," *Journal of Development Studies*, 30 (3): 918.

Doornbos, Martin Pietrvan Stuijvenberg and Piet Terhal. 1987. "Operation Flood: Impact and Issues," *Food Policy*, 12 (4): 376–83.

Doornbos, Martin, Frank van Dorsten, Manoshi Mitra and Piet Terhal. 1990. *Dairy Aid and Development: India's Operation Flood*, Indo-Dutch Studies on Development Alternatives, 3. New Delhi/Newbury Park, CA/London: SAGE Publications.

Dorner, Peter. 1973. "Institutions as Aids to Development." Paper presented at the 15th International Conference of Agricultural Economists, Sao Paulo, Brazil, 19–30 August.

Dulfer, E. 1974. "Operational Efficiency of Agricultural Cooperatives in Developing Countries. "Development Paper No. 96, Food and Agriculture Organisation, United Nations Organisation, Rome.

Dunn, Edgar S. 1971. *Economic and Social Development: A Process of Social Learning.* Baltimore: The Johns Hopkins University Press.

ECAFE (Economic Commission for Asia and the Far East). 1950. *Foreign Investment Laws and Regulations in the ECAFE Region.* Bangkok: United Nations Economic Commission for Asia and the Far East, Committee on Industry and Trade.

Ekaus, Richard S. and Kirit S. Parikh. 1968. *Planning for Growth: Multi-sectoral, Intertemporal Models Applied to India.* Cambridge, MA: The MIT Press.

Ekins, Paul. 1991. "A Strategy for Global Environmental Sustainability," *Development*, 2.

Ensminger, Douglas. 1968. *An Evolving Strategy for India's Agricultural Development.* New Delhi: The Ford Foundation.

———. 1972. *Rural India in Transition.* New Delhi: All-India Panchayat Parishad.

Fan, Shenggen, Peter, B.R. Hazell and T. Haque. 1998. "Role of Infrastructure in Production Growth and Poverty Reduction in Indian Rainfed Agriculture." Project report submitted to the Indian Council of Agricultural Research (ICAR), New Delhi; the World Bank, Washington; and the International Food Policy Research Institute, Washington.

FAO (Food and Agriculture Organisation). 1989. *The State of Food and Agriculture 1989*, FAO Agriculture Series No. 22. Rome: Food and Agriculture Organisation.

———. 1996. *Production Year Book, 1995, Vol. 49.* Rome: Food and Agriculture Organisation, United Nations Organisation.

———. 2001. *Global Forest Resources Assessment 2000: Main Report.* FAO Forestry Paper No. 140, Food and Agriculture Organisation, Rome.

———. 2010. *Global Forest Resources Assessment 2010—Main Report.* FAO Forestry Paper No. 163, Food and Agriculture Organization of the United Nations, Rome.

———. 2014. FAO Statistical Yearbook 2014, Asia and the Pacific, Bangkok: Food and Agriculture, Food and Agriculture Organization of the United Nations, Regional Office for Asia and the Pacific, (www.fao.org/3/a-i3590e (Accessed on April 17, 2015).

——— 2015. *AQUASTAT.* Available at: http://www.fao.org/nr/water/aquastat/data/query/results.html (Accessed on August 18, 2015).

FSI (Forest Survey of India). 2001. *State of Forest Report 2001.* Dehradun: Forest Survey of India, Government of India.

———. 2013. *State of Forest Report 2013*, Dehradun: Forest Survey of India. Government of India. Available at: www.fsi.nic.in/forestcover_2013. (Accessed on October 12, 2015).

Foster, John. 1984. "On Economic Poverty: A Survey of Aggregate Measures," *Advances in Econometrics*, 3: 215–51.

Foster, John, Joel Greer and Erick Thorbecke. 1984. "A Class of Decomposable Poverty Measures," *Econometrica*, 52: 761–66.

Fox, Karl A., Jati K. Sengupta and Erik Thorbecke. 1966. *The Theory of Quantitative Economic Policy with Applications to Economic Growth and Stabilization.* Amsterdam: North Holland Publishing Company.

Fei, John C.H. and Gustav Ranis. 1964. *Development of the Labour Surplus Economy: Theory and Policy.* Homewood, IL: Richard D. Irwin for the Economic Growth Centre, Yale University.

Gaikwad, V.R., Gunvant M. Desai, Paul Mampilly and V.S. Vyas. 1977. *Development of Intensive Agriculture: Lessons from IADP.* Ahmedabad: Centre for Management in Agriculture, Indian Institute of Management.

Gangrade, K.D. 1997. "Power to Powerless: A Silent Revolution through Panchayat Raj System," *Journal of Rural Development*, 6 (4): 755–56.

Ghosh, A. 1968. *Planning, Programming, and Input-Output Models: Selected Papers on Indian Planning.* Cambridge: Cambridge University Press.

George, Shanti. 1987. "Stemming Operation Flood: Towards an Alternative Dairy Policy for India," *Economic and Political Weekly*, 26 September.

———. 1988. "Cooperatives and Indian Dairy Policy: More Anand than Pattern." In *Who Shares? Cooperatives and Rural Development*, edited by D.W. Attwood and B.S. Baviskar. New Delhi: Oxford University Press.

Gibbons, David. 1997. "Targetting the Poor and Covering Costs." Paper presented at the Micro-Credit Summit and communicated to the author via e-mail by Robert Gailey, Research Director, Micro-Credit Summit Secretariat, under the auspices of the "Poverty Discussion Group" programme.

Gittinger, J. Price. 1982. *Economic Analysis of Agricultural Projects*, 2nd ed. Baltimore: The Johns Hopkins University Press.

GoI (Government of India). 1961. *Towards a Self Reliant Economy: India's Third Plan, 1961–66.* New Delhi: Planning Commission, Government of India.

———. 1963. *Intensive Agricultural District Programme: Report (1961–63).* New Delhi: Expert Committee on Assessment and Evaluation, Ministry of Food and Agriculture, GoI.

———. 1968. *Modernising Indian Agriculture (1960–68)*, vol. 1. New Delhi: Expert Committee on Assessment and Evaluation, Ministry of Food and Agriculture, C. D. and Cooperation, GoI.

———. 1975. *Report on Evaluation Study of Small Farmers, Marginal Farmers and Agricultural Labourers Project, 1974–75*, Chapter 6. New Delhi: Planning Commission, GoI.

GoI (Government of India). 1976. *Report of the National Commission on Agriculture 1976, Part II: Policy and Strategy*. New Delhi: Ministry of Agriculture and Irrigation, GoI.

———. 1977. *Report of the Review Committee on Pilot Intensive Rural Employment Project (PIREP)*, 11–19. New Delhi: Ministry of Irrigation and Agriculture, GoI.

———. 1978a. *Report of the Finance Commission*. New Delhi: GoI.

———. 1978b. *Report of the Working Group on Block Level Planning (1978)*. New Delhi: Planning Commission, GoI.

———. 1979. *Study of CSRE 1971–74*. New Delhi: Planning Commission, GoI.

———. 1980. *Manual on Integrated Rural Development Programme*. New Delhi: Ministry of Rural Reconstruction, GoI.

———. 1984. *Report of the Evaluation Committee on Operation Flood II*. New Delhi: Department of Agriculture and Cooperation, Ministry of Agriculture, GoI.

———. 1987. *National Water Policy 1987*. New Delhi: Department of Agriculture and Cooperation, Ministry of Agriculture, GoI.

———. 1988. *National Forest Policy 1988*. New Delhi: Ministry of Environment and Forests, GoI.

———. 1997a. *Annual Report 1996–97*. New Delhi: Ministry of Rural Areas and Employment, GoI.

———. 1997b. *Economic Survey 1996–97*. New Delhi: Ministry of Finance, Government of India.

———. 1997c. *Agricultural Statistics at a Glance*. New Delhi: Directorate of Economics and Statistics, Department of Agriculture and Cooperation, Ministry of Agriculture, GoI.

———. 1998a. *India 1998*. New Delhi: Ministry of Information and Broadcasting, Publications Division, GoI.

———. 1998b. *Economic Survey 1997–98*. New Delhi: Ministry of Finance, GoI.

———. 1999. “Integrated Water Resources Development: A Plan for Action.” Report of the National Commission for Integrated Water Resources Development, Vol. I. New Delhi: Ministry of Water Resources, GoI.

———. 2000. *The National Policy on Agriculture*. Department of Agriculture and Cooperation. New Delhi: Ministry of Agriculture, GoI.

———. 2002a. *Annual Report 2001–02*. New Delhi: Department of Rural Development, Ministry of Rural Development, GoI.

———. 2002b. *Tenth Five Year Plan (2002–07), Volume III: State Plans, Trends, Concerns and Strategies*. New Delhi: Planning Commission, GoI.

———. 2002c. *National Water Policy 2002*. New Delhi: Ministry of Water Resources, GoI.

———. 2002d. *National Policy on Cooperatives*. New Delhi: Department of Agriculture and Cooperation, Ministry of Agriculture, GoI.

———. 2004a. *Agricultural Statistics at a Glance 2004*. New Delhi: Department of Agriculture and Cooperation, GoI.

———. 2004b. *Marine Fishing Policy 2004*. New Delhi: Department of Animal Husbandry and Dairying, Ministry of Agriculture, GoI.

———. 2005a. *Seventeenth Livestock Census, 2003*. Department of Animal Husbandry and Dairying, Ministry of Agriculture, GoI, New Delhi. Available at: http://dahd.nic.in/Census.htm. (Accessed on March 2008).

———. 2005b. *National Rural Employment Guarantee Act 2005*. New Delhi: Ministry of Rural Development, GoI.

———. 2006a. *Agricultural Statistics at a Glance 2006*. New Delhi: Ministry of Agriculture, Department of Agriculture and Cooperation, GoI. Available at: http://dacnet.nic.in/eands/agStat06-07htm. (Accessed on March 2008).

———. 2006b. *Report of the XI Plan Working Group on Poverty Elimination Programmes*, New Delhi: Planning Commission (Rural Development Division), GoI.

———. 2006d. *Serving Farmers and Saving Farmers*. Fifth and Final Report, National Commission on Farmers, New Delhi: Ministry of Agriculture, GoI.

———. 2007a. *Agricultural Statistics at a Glance 2006*. New Delhi: Department of Agriculture and Cooperation, GoI.

———. 2007b. *Union Budget and Economic Survey*. New Delhi: Ministry of Finance, GoI.

———. 2012. *National Water Policy 2012*. New Delhi: MoWR, Government of India.

———. 2014. Elucidation of the *Fifth National Report*, submitted to United Nations Convention to Combat Desertification (UNCCD), New Delhi: Secretariat 2012, Ministry of Environment and Forest, GoI.

Gopalakrishnan, P. and V.E. Ramamoorthy. 1993. *Text Book of Project Management.* New Delhi: Macmillan India Ltd.

Gould, Julius and W.L. Kolb. 1967. *A Dictionary of Social Sciences,* 4th Printing. UNRS. Co. Paris: UNESCO.

Gouldner, Alvin. 1959. "Organisational Analysis." In *Sociology Today,* edited by Robert K. Merton, 400–28. New York: Basic Books Inc.

Grafton, R. Quentin, Linwood H. Pendelton and Harry W. Nelson. 2001. *A Dictionary of Environmental Economics, Science, and Policy*. Cheltenham, UK: Edward Elgar.

Gran, Guy. 1983. *Development by People: Citizens Construction of a Just World.* New York: Praeger.

Gulati, Ashok. 1989. "Input Subsidies in Indian Agriculture: A State-wise Analysis," *Economic and Political Weekly*, 24 (25, June): A57–65.

Gulati, Ashok and A.N. Sharma. 1992. "Subsidising Agriculture: A Cross Country View," *Economic and Political Weekly*, 27 (39, September): A106–11.

Gupta, K.R. 1976. *Economics of Development and Planning.* New Delhi: Atma Ram and Sons.

Gupta, S.P. 1995. "Economic Reform and its Impact on Poor," *Economic and Political Weekly*, 3 June: 1295–1313. Mumbai: Halite.

Graham. 1968. *The Economics of Agricultural Policy.* Oxford: Basil.

Haque, M.S. 1997. "Development of India's Wastelands through Institutional Credit: A 15-Year Plan." In *Advances in Wastelands Development,* edited by T.K. Sarkar, R.C. Vaish, V. Verma and S.P. Gawande. New Delhi: Soil Conservation Society of India.

Hardin, G. 1968. "The Tragedy of the Commons," *Science*, 162: 1143–1248.

Harold, Alderman, George Mergos and Roger Slade. 1987. "Cooperatives and the Commercialisation of Milk Production in India: A Literature Review," IFPRI Working Paper on Commercialization of Agriculture and Nutrition No. 2, Washington DC.

Hayami, Yujiro and V.W. Ruttan. 1970. "Agricultural Productivity Differences among Countries," *The American Economic Review*, 60 (5, December): 895–911.

———. 1971. *Agricultural Development: An International Perspective.* Baltimore: The Johns Hopkins University Press.

Heady, Earl O. 1965. *Agricultural Policy Under Economic Development.* Ames (Iowa): Iowa State University Press.

Hickman, Bert G., ed. 1965. *Quantitative Economic Policy.* Washington: The Brookings Institution.

Higgins, Benjamin. 1966. *Economic Development: Principles, Problems and Policies.* Allahabad: Central Book Depot.

Hirway, Indira. 1988. "Reshaping IRDP: Some Issues," *Economic and Political Weekly*, 25 June: A89–95.

Hoda, Anwarul and Prerna Terway. 2015. "Credit Policy for Agriculture in India—An Evaluation," Working Paper No. 302, June 2015. New Delhi: Indian Council for Research on International Economic Relations.

Honadle, George and Rudi Klauss, eds. 1979. *International Development Administration: Implementation Analysis for Development Projects.* New York: Praeger Publishers.

Hunter, Guy. 1970. *The Administration of Agricultural Development: Lessons from India.* London: Oxford University Press.

Ickis, John C. 1983. "Structural Response to New Rural Development Strategies." In *Bureaucracy and the Poor: Closing the Gap,* edited by David C. Korten and Felipe B. Alfonso, 4–33. West Hartford, CT: Kumarian Press.

ICAR and NAAS. 2010. *Degraded and Wastelands of India: Status and Spatial Distribution.* New Delhi: Indian Council of Agricultural Research and National Academy of Agricultural Sciences.

IDC. 1982. *Eleventh Annual Report, 1980–81.* Vadodara: Indian Dairy Corporation.

IDFC. 2013. India Rural Development Report 2012/13. New Delhi: Infrastructure Development Finance Company (IDFC) Rural Development Network, 2013

Jena, A.C. 1998. "PDS: An Overview of Policies and Programme Implementation," In *Fifty Years of Rural Development: Retrospect and Prospect*, Vol. II. edited by R.C. Choudhury and S. Rajakutty. Hyderabad: National Institute of Rural Development.

Jesus, Ed C. De. 1984. "Learning about Bureaucratic Reorientation." Paper presented at the 4th International Conference of Management Institutes Working Group on Social Development Management, Ahmedabad, 23–27 January.

Johnston, Bruce F. and William C. Clark. 1982. *Redesigning Rural Development: A Strategic Perspective.* Baltimore: The Johns Hopkins University Press.

Joshi, P.K. and D. Jha. 1991. "Farm Level Effects of Soil Degradation in Sharda Sahayak Irrigation Project." Working Paper on Future Growth in Indian Agriculture. Washington, D.C.: Central Soil Salinity Research Institute, Indian Council of Agricultural Research, and the International Food Policy Research Institute.

Kakwani, N.C. and N. Poddar. 1976. "Efficiency Estimation of the Lorenz Curve and Associated Inequality Measures From Grouped Observations," *Econometrica*. 44 (1): 137–48.

Kanwar, Rakesh. 2001. "Disaster Management," *The Administrator*, XLIV (December): 96–110.

Katiha, Pradeep K. 2006. "The Status of and Prospects for Inland Aquaculture and Culture-based Fisheries in India." Unpublished paper included in the *Compendium of Abstracts: Water and Equity*, presented at the 5th IWMI-Tata Annual Partners Meet, Institute of Rural Management, Anand, 8–10 March.

Khera, S.S. 1977. *Government in Business*. New Delhi: National Publishing House.

Kirschen, E.S., J. Bernard, H. Besters, F. Blackaby, O. Eckstein, J. Faaland, F. Hartog, L.L. Morissons and E. Tosco. 1964. *Economic Policy in Our Time*. I. Amsterdam: North Holland Publishing Company.

Kohli, Uddesh. 1979. "Implementation Planning," *Yojana*, 23 (11, June): 13–17.

Korten, David C., ed. 1980. "Community Organisation and Rural Development: A Learning, Process Approach," *Public Administration Review*, 40 (5) (September–October): 480–511.

———. 1981. "The Management of Social Transformation," *Public Administration Review*, November–December: 610.

Korten, David C. and Felipe B. Alfonso, eds. 1983. *Bureaucracy and the Poor: Closing the Gap*. West Hartford, CT: Kumarian Press.

Korten, David C. and Rudi Klauss, eds. 1984. *People Centred Development*. West Hartford, CT: Kumarian Press.

Krishnaji, N. 1997. "Human Poverty Index: A Critique," *Economic and Political Weekly*, 30 August: 2202–05.

Kumar, Nalini. 1997. "Operation Flood: Literature Review and Reconciliation," Occasional Publication No. 13. Anand: Institute of Rural Management.

Kumar, Pradeep and S.P. Pal. 1998. "Delivery Makes the Difference," *The Economic Times*, 16 May.

Kundu, Amitabh. 1980. *Measurement of Urban Process: A Study in Regionalisation*. Mumbai: Popular Prakashan.

Kurien, V. 1978. "Food Aid in the Form of Dairy Products." Speech delivered at the 20th International Dairy Congress, Paris, 26–30 June. Anand: National Dairy Development Board.

———. 1992. "Food Aid for Dairy Development," *Dairy India 1992*, 4th Annual ed. New Delhi.

Kuznets, Simon. 1955. "Economic Growth and Income Inequality," *American Economic Review*, 49: 1–28.

Law, Vivek. 2002. "Banking on Fraud," *India Today*, June 10.

Leibenstein, Harvey. 1957. *Economic Backwardness and Economic Growth*. New York: John Wiley.

Lewis, W. Arthur. 1954. "Economic Development with Unlimited Supplies of Labour," *The Manchester School*, 22 May: 139–92.

———. 1955. *The Theory of Economic Growth*. London: George Allen & Unwin Ltd.

Littrell, W. Boyd. 1980. "Bureaucracy in the Eighties: Introduction," *The Journal of Applied Behavioural Science*, 16 (3, July–September): 560–61.

Lorsch, Jay W. and Paul R. Lawrence. 1972. *Organisation Planning: Cases and Concepts*. Homewood, IL: Richard D. Irwin Inc.

Mathur, Ashok. 2005. "Rural Development: Indices and Linkages." In *India: Rural Development Report-Rural Institutions, 2005, by* National Institute of Rural Development (NIRD). Hyderabad: National Institute of Rural Development, Ministry of Rural Development, Government of India.

MIT (Massachusetts Institute of Technology). 1957. *The Objectives of United States Economic Assistance Programmes*. Washington: MIT, Centre for International Studies.

Macy, Joanna. 1983. *Dharma and Development: Religion as Resource in the Sarvodaya Self-Help Movement*. West Hartford, CT: Kumarian Press.

Maheshwari, Shriram. 1987. "Voluntary Action in Rural Development in India," *Indian Journal of Public Administration*,33 (3) (July–September): 560–61.

March, James G. and Herbert A. Simon. 1958. *Organizations*. New York: John Wiley and Sons Inc.

Mascarenhas, R.C. 1988. *A Strategy for Rural Development: Dairy Cooperatives in India*. New Delhi: SAGE Publications.

McKay, John. 1990. "The Development Model," *Development Journal of the Society for International Development*, 33 (3/4): 55.

Meadows, Donella H., Dennis L. Meadows, Jørgen Randers and William W. Behrens III. 1972. *The Limits to Growth*. New York: Universe Books.

Mehta, Shiv R. 1984. *Rural Development Policies and Programmes*. New Delhi: SAGE Publications.
Meier, Gerald M. 1976. *Leading Issues in Economic Development*, 3rd ed. New York: Oxford University Press.
Meier, Gerald M. and R.E. Baldwin. 1957. *Economic Development: Theory, History, and Policy*. New York: Wiley.
Mellor, John W. 1966. *The Economics of Agricultural Development*. Ithaca: Cornell University Press.
Mergos, George and Roger Slade. 1987. "Dairy Development and Milk Cooperatives: The Effect of a Dairy Project in India." Discussion Paper No. 15, Washington DC: World Bank.
Mikesell, Raymond F. 1968. *The Economics of Foreign Aid*. Chicago: Aldine Publishing Company.
Minhas, B.S. 1974. *Planning and the Poor*. New Delhi: S. Chand and Company Limited.
Minhas, B.S., L.R. Jain and S.D. Tendulkar. 1991. "Declining Incidence of Poverty into the 1980s: Evidence vs Artefacts," *Economic and Political Weekly*, July.
Mishra, S.N. and Ramesh Chand. 1995. "Private and Public Capital Formation in Indian Agriculture: Comments on Complementarity Hypothesis and Others," *Economic and Political Weekly*, 30 (24): A64–79.
MoA (Ministry of Agriculture), Government of India. 2010. *National Mission on Sustainable Agriculture.*, New Delhi: Department of Agriculture and Cooperation, MoA, GoI.
———. 2012. *All India Report on Number and Area of Operational Holdings*. New Delhi: Agriculture Census Division, Department of Agriculture and Cooperation, MoA, GoI.
———. 2013. *State of India's Agriculture 2011–12*. New Delhi: Department of Agriculture and Cooperation, MoA, GoI.
———. 2014a. *Agricultural Statistics at a Glance 2014*. New Delhi: Department of Agriculture and Cooperation, MoA, GoI. Available at: (http://agricoop.nic.in/Agristatisticsnew.html (Accessed on April 12, 2015).
———. 2014b. *Basic Animal Husbandry and Fisheries Statistics 2014*. New Delhi: Department of Animal Husbandry, Dairying and Fisheries, MoA, GoI. Available at: http://dahd.nic.in/dahd/default.aspx (Accessed on April 12, 2015).
———. 2014c. *National Mission on Sustainable Agriculture, Operational Guidelines*. New Delhi: Department of Agriculture and Cooperation, MoA, GoI.
———. 2015. *Annual Report 2014-15*. New Delhi: Ministry of Agriculture and Farmer Welfare, GoI.
———. n.d. *Land Degradation and its Management in India*. New Delhi: MoA, GoI, Mimeo. Available at: http://www.moef.nic.in/sites/default/files/Session%20I%20MoA.pdf (Accessed on May 20, 2015).
MoEF (Ministry of Environment, Forests and Climate Change), Government of India. 2015. *Annual Report 2014–15*. New Delhi: MoEF, GoI.
MoF (Ministry of Finance), Government of India. 2008. *Union Budget and Economic Survey*. New Delhi: MoF, GoI.
———. 2015. *Economic Survey 2014–15*. New Delhi: MoF, Department of Economic Affairs, GoI.
MoRD (Ministry of Rural Development). Government of India. 2013a. *Annual Report 2012–13*. New Delhi: GoI.
———. 2013b. *Wastelands Atlas of India 2011*. New Delhi: Department of Land Resources, MoRD, GoI. Available at: www.dolr.nic.in/wasteland2010/dolr/India.pdf (Accessed on April 12, 2015).
Moench, Marcus and Dinesh Kumar. 1997. "Distinction between Efficiency and Sustainability: The Role of Energy Prices in Groundwater Management," in *The Challenge of the Balance: Environmental Economics in India*, Proceedings of a National Environment and Economics Meeting, edited by Anil Agarwal. New Delhi: Centre for Science and Environment.
Morgan, Theodore and George W. Betz, eds. 1970. *Economic Development: Readings in Theory and Practice*. Belmont, CA: Wadsworth Publishing Company Inc.
Moris, Jone. 1981. *Managing Induced Rural Development*. Bloomington, IN: Indiana University, International Development Institute.
Morris, David and Michelle B. McAlpin. 1982. *Measuring the Condition of India's Poor: The Physical Quality of Life Index*. New Delhi: Promilla and Company Publishers.
Mosher, A.T. 1966. *Getting Agriculture Moving*. New York: Frederick A. Praeger Inc.
———. 1976. *Thinking About Rural Development*. New York: Agricultural Development Council.
Murdick, Robert G. and Joel E. Ross. 1971. *Information Systems for Modern Management*, 2nd ed. New Delhi: Prentice-Hall of India Pvt. Ltd.
Muthalagu, K. 2007. "Poverty Eradication in India under Anti-poverty Programmes: Some Observations," *Kurukshetra*, 56 (2): 4.

Myrdal, Gunnar. 1957. *Economic Theory and Under-developed Regions*. Mumbai: Vora and Co. Publishers Pvt. Ltd.

NABARD (National Bank for Agricultural and Rural Development). 1997. *Annual Report 1996–97*. Mumbai: NABARD.

———. 2007. *Annual Report 2006–07*. Mumbai: NABARD.

———. 2015. *Annual Report 2014-15*. Mumbai: NABARD. Available at: https://www.nabard.org/Publication/NABARD_AR_2014_15_ENGLISH.pdf (Accessed on September 10, 2015).

NDDB (National Dairy Development Board). 1997. *Annual Report 1996–97*. Anand: NDDB.

———. 2007. *Annual Report 2006–07*. Anand: NDDB.

———. 2014. Annual Report 2013-14, Anand: NDDB.

NIRD (National Institute of Rural Development). 1996. *Rural Development Statistics 1994–95*. Hyderabad: NIRD.

———. 2005. *India Rural Development Report 2005–06*. Hyderabad: NIRD.

NSSO (National Sample Survey Office), 2005. *Situation Assessment of Farmers Survey: Indebtedness of Farmer Households*, Report No. 498, NSS 9th Round, January-December 2003. New Delhi: NSSO, Ministry of Statistics and Programme Implementation, Government of India.

———. 2006. *61st Round Report, July 2004-June 2005*, Report No. 508 (61/1.0/1), NSSO. New Delhi: NSSO, Ministry of Statistics and Programme Implementation, GoI.

———. 2014. *Drinking Water, Sanitation, Hygiene and Housing Condition in India, (JULY 2012 – DECEMBER 2012)*, NSS Report No. 556 (69/1.2/1), New Delhi: NSSO, Ministry of Statistics and Programme Implementation, Government of India. Available at: http://mospi.nic.in/Mospi_New/upload/nss_rep_556_14aug14.pdf (Accessed on March 14, 2016).

———. 2015. *Employment and Unemployment Situation Among Social Groups in India, NSS 68th Round*, NSS Report No. 563 (68/10/4). New Delhi: NSSO, Ministry of Statistics and Programme Implementation, GoI.

———. 2015. *Energy Statistics 2015*. New Delhi: Central Statistics Office, National Statistical Organisation, Ministry of Statistics and Plan Implementation, GoI. Available at: www.mospi.gov.in (Accessed on March 14, 2016).

NCUI (National Cooperative Union of India). 2012. *Indian Cooperative Movement: A Statistical Profile–2012*. New Delhi: NCUI.

Owens, Edgar and Robert Shaw. 1972. *Development Reconsidered*. New Delhi: Oxford and IBH Publishing Company.

Pal, Suresh and Alka Singh. 1997. "Agricultural Research and Extension in India: Institutional Structure and Investments." Policy Paper No. 7. New Delhi: National Centre for Agricultural Economics and Policy Research.

Panda, Snehlata. 1997. "Political Empowerment of Women: A Case of Orissa," *Journal of Rural Development*, 6 (4): 663.

Patel, Amrita. 1996. "Operation Flood: The Next Step," *Dairy India 1997*. New Delhi.

Paul, Samuel. 1982. *Managing Development Programs: The Lessons of Success*. Boulder, CO: Westview Press.

Pearce, D.W. and R.K. Turner. 1990. *Economics of Natural Resources and the Environment*. Hemel Hempstead and London: Harvester Wheatsheaf.

Pigou, A.C. (1920) 1962. *The Economics of Welfare*. Reprint, London: The English Language Book Society and Macmillan.

Planning Commission, Government of India. 2011. *Report of the Twelfth Plan Working Group on Disadvantaged Farmers including Women*. New Delhi: GoI.

———. 2013. *Twelfth Five Year Plan*, 2012-17, Vol. II, 311–13, New Delhi: SAGE Publications.

———. 2014a. *Data-book compiled for Use of Planning Commission*. New Delhi: GoI. Available at: http://planningcommission.gov.in (Accessed on May 24, 2015).

———. 2014b. *Report of the (Rangarajan) Expert Group to Review the Methodology for Measurement of Poverty*. New Delhi: GoI.

Postel, Sandra. 1990. "Toward a New Economics," *World-Watch*, September–October: 20–28.

Prasad, Brahmanand. 1968. "Foreign Technology and India's Economic Development," *International Development Review*, 10 (June): 18–20. Washington: Society for International Development.

Pursell, G. and Ashok Gulati. 1993. "Liberalizing Indian Agriculture: An Agenda for Reform." Policy Research Working Papers, Working Paper Series No. 1172, International Economic Department. Washington: The World Bank.

Radhakrishna, R., ed. 2008. *India Development Report 2008*. Mumbai: Indira Gandhi Institute of Development Research and New Delhi: Oxford University Press.

Radhakrishna, R. and Shovan Ray, eds. 2005. *Handbook of Poverty: Perspectives, Policies and Programmes.* New Delhi: Oxford University Press.

Ramakrishnaiah, D. 1980. "Area Development Planning for Agriculture in Naurar Watershed, Almora (U.P): A Multi- period Programming Approach." Unpublished Ph.D. Thesis: G. B. Pant University of Agriculture and Technology, Pantnagar, Uttarakhand. 90–131.

Ranis, Gustav and John C.H. Fei. 1970. "A Theory of Economic Development." In *Economic Development: Readings in Theory and Practice,* edited by Theodore Morgan and George W. Betz. Belmont, CA: Wadsworth Publishing Company Inc.

Rath, Nilakanth. 1985. "Garibi Hatao: Can IRDP Do lt?," T.A. Pai Memorial Lecture-2. Manipal, January 17, 1985. Also in *Economic and Political Weekly*, 20 (6) 9 February: 20–21.

———. 1989. "Agricultural Growth and Investment in India," *Journal of Indian School of Political Economy*, 1 (1). 64–83

Raymond, Susan. 1996. "Corporate Voluntarism: Private Support for Social Policy," *Economic Reform Today*, 4. Washington: Centre for International Private Enterprise.

RBI (Reserve Bank of India). 2000. *Report of the High Power Committee on Urban Cooperative Banks*, RBI Bulletin, January. Mumbai: RBI.

———. 2013. *A Profile of Banks 2012–13*. Fort, Mumbai: Reserve Bank of India.

Rosenstein-Rodan, P.N. 1970. "Notes on the Theory of the "Big Plush." In *Economic Development: Readings in Theory and Practice,* edited by Theodore Morgan and George W. Betz. Belmont, CA: Wadsworth Publishing Company Inc.

Rostow. 1960. *The Stages of Economic Growth: A Non-Communist Manifesto*. London: Cambridge University Press.

Salunkhe, Harshal A. and B.B. Deshmush. 2012. "The overview of Government subsidies to agriculture sector in India." *IOSR Journal of Agriculture and Veterinary Science* (IOSR-JAVS), 1 (5, November–December): 43–47.

Satish, P. 2007. "Rural Infrastructure and Growth: An Overview," *Indian Journal of Agricultural Economics*, 62 (1): 32–51

Schickele, Rainer. 1954. *Agricultural Policy: Farm Programmes and National Welfare*. Lincoln: University of Nebraska Press.

Schultz, W. Theodore. 1964. *Transforming Traditional Agriculture*. Ludhiana: Lyall Book Depot.

Schumpeter. 1949. "Economic Theory and Entrepreneurial History',. In *Change and the Entrepreneur–Postulates and Patterns for Entrepreneurial History* edited by Centre for Research in Entrepreneurial History, 63–84, Harvard University, Cambridge, MA: Harvard University Press.

Seers, Dudley. 1969. "The Meaning of Development." Paper presented at the Eleventh World Conference of the Society for International Development, November 14–17, New Delhi.

Sehgal, J. and I.P. Abrol. 1994. *Soil Degradation in India: Status and Impact*. New Delhi: Oxford and IBH.

Sen, A.K. 1976. "Poverty: An Ordinal Approach to Measurement,/" *Econometrica*, 44: 219–31.

Shah, Dilip R. 1992. *Dairy Cooperativization: An Instrument of Social Change*. New Delhi and Jaipur: Rawat Publications.

Sharma, Miriam and Urmila Vanjani. 1993. "When More Means Less: Assessing the Impact of Dairy Development on the Lives and Health of Women in Rural Rajasthan (India)," *Social Science Medicine*, 37: 11.

Shetty, S.L. 1990. "Investment in Agriculture: Brief Review of Recent Trends," *Economic and Political Weekly*, 25 (7 and 8). 389–98

SID (Society for International Development). 1969. *United Nations Panel on Flow of Foreign Capital to Developing Countries*. Washington DC: Society for International Development.

Simon, Julian L. and Herman Kahn. 1984. *The Resourceful Earth: A Response to Global 2000*. New York: Basil Blackwell.

Singh, Hoshiar, ed. 1985. *Rural Development in India: Evaluative Studies in Policies and Programmes*. Jaipur: Printwell Publishers.

Singh, Katar. 1973. "The Impact of New Agricultural Technology on Farm Income Distribution in the Aligarh District of Uttar Pradesh," *Indian Journal of Agricultural Economics*, 28 (2, April–June): 4.

———. 1994. *Managing Common Pool Resources: Principles and Case Studies*. Delhi: Oxford University Press.

———. 1995. "The Watershed Management Approach to Sustainability of Renewable Common Pool Natural Resources: Lessons of India's Experience." Research Paper No. 14, Institute of Rural Management, Anand.

———. 1997. "Property Rights and Tenures in Natural Resources." In *Natural Resource Economics: Theory and Application in India,* edited by John Kerr, Dinesh K. Marothia, Katar Singh, C. Ramasamy and William R. Bentley, 131–59. New Delhi: Oxford and IBH Co.
———. 1998. "Cooperative Property Rights as an Instrument of Managing Groundwater." In *Groundwater Law: The Growing Debate,* edited by Marcus Moench. Ahmedabad: Vikram Sarabhai Centre for Development Interaction-VIKSAT, and Nehru Foundation for Development.
———. 1999. *Rural Development: Principles, Policies and Management,* 2nd ed. New Delhi: SAGE Publications.
———. 2009. *Rural Development: Principles, Policies and Management,* 3rd ed. New Delhi: SAGE Publications.
Singh, Katar and Anil Shishodia. 1992. "Irrigation Management in India: Need for Reforms," *Indian Economic Panorama.* 2 (1): 39–41.
———. 2007. *Environmental Economics: Theory and Applications.* New Delhi: SAGE Publications.
Singh, Katar and J. Acharya. 1986. "The Impact of the Madhya Pradesh Dairy Development Project," Research Report. Anand: Institute of Rural Management.
Singh, Katar and V. Mukunda Das. 1982. "Impact of Operation Flood at the Village Level," IRMA Research Report No. 1. Anand. Institute of Rural Management.
Singh, Katar and Vishwa Ballabh, eds. 1996. *Cooperative Management of Natural Resources.* New Delhi: SAGE Publications.
Singh, Katar, P. Durgaprasad and K. Vengama Raju. 1985. "Impact of Milch Animals Programme of IRDP in Sabarkantha District, Gujarat," Research Report. Anand: Institute of Rural Management.
Singh, Sukhpal, 2012. "New Markets for Smallholders in India: Exclusion, Policy and Mechanisms," *Economic and Political Weekly,* 47 (52): 95–105.
SPWD (Society for Promotion of Wastelands Development). 1984. *Society for Promotion of Wastelands Development.* Monograph. New Delhi: Society for Promotion of Wastelands Development.
Somjee, Geeta and A.H. Somjee. 1989. *Reaching Out to the Poor: The Unfinished Rural Revolution.* London: Macmillan.
Stern, David I. 1998. "Progress on the Environmental Kuznets Curve?," *Environment and Development Economics,* 3 (2): 173–96.
Stoltenberg, Thorvald. 1989. "Devising World Policy Options for Sustainable Development," *Development,* 1.
Swaminathan, M.S. 1996. "Science and Technology for Sustainable Food Security," *Indian Journal of Agricultural Economics,* 51 (1 and 2): 60–75.
Times of India. 1997. "Ground Realities: Soil Degradation." *The Times of India,* 25 August.
———. 1998. "Alarming Rise in Salinity." *The Times of India,* 22 May.
Tinbergen, Jan. 1952. *On the Theory of Economic Policy.* Amsterdam: North Holland Publishing Company.
———. 1966. *Economic Policy: Principles and Design.* Amsterdam: North Holland Publishing Company.
———. 1968. *Central Planning.* New Haven, CT: Yale University Press.
Todaro, Michael P. 1977. *Economic Development in the Third World.* London: Longman.
———. 1995. *Economic Development,* 5th ed. New York and London: Longman.
Toffler, Alvin. 1980. *The Third Wave.* New York: William Morrow and Company Inc.
UN (United Nations). 1992. *Energy Statistics Year Book,* quoted in Katar Singh. 1999. "Sustainable Development: Some Reflections," *Indian Journal of Agricultural Economics,* 54 (1).
———. 1998. *Framework Convention on Climate Change.* New York: United Nations Organisation.
———. 2012. *United Nations Energy Statistics Yearbook: Total Final Consumption,* Table 3, 47–64. New York: United Nations Organization.
UN/FAO (United Nations/Food and Agriculture Organization). 1972. *Interim Evaluation Report of the Inter-Agency (FAO/WFP 1972) Mission on Operation Flood (India-618).* New Delhi: UN/FAO.
———. 1976. Detailed Report of the Second UN/FAO World Food Programme Evaluation Mission on Operation Flood (India-WFP-618). New Delhi: UN/FAO.
UN/FAO World Food Programme. 1981. "Milk Marketing and Dairy Development," (Operation Flood-I), Terminal Evaluation Report on Project India 618, prepared by an inter-agency mission which visited India from 9 February to 8 March 1981. New Delhi: UN/FAO.
UNDP (United Nations Development Programme). 1990. *Human Development Report 1990.* New York: Oxford University Press.
———. 1991. *Human Development Report 1991.* New York: Oxford University Press.
———. 1994. *Human Development Report 1994.* New York. Oxford University Press.
———. 1996a. *Human Development Report 1996.* New York: Oxford University Press.
———. 1996b. *India's External Development Partners; Profiles of Cooperation Programmes.* New Delhi: UNDP.

UNDP (United Nations Development Programme). 1997. *Human Development Report 1997.* New York: Oxford University Press.

———. 2003. *Human Development Report 2003.* New York: Oxford University Press.

———. 2008. *Human Development Reports-2007/2008 Report-Indicators.* New York: Oxford University Press.

———. 2014. *Human Development Report 2014.* Available at: http://hdr.undp.org/sites/default/files/hdr14-report-en-1.pdf (Accessed on 10 March 2016).

Uphoff, Norman T., ed. 1983. *Rural Development and Local Organisations in Asia-3: South East Asia.* New Delhi: Macmillan India Limited.

Uphoff, Norman T. and Milton J. Esman. 1983. *Local Organisation for Rural Development: Analysis of Asian Experience.* Ithaca, NY: Cornell University, and Rural Development Committee, Centre for International Studies.

Vaishnav, P.H. and K.V. Sundaram. 1978. "Integrating Development Administration at the Area Level," a note incorporated in the *Report of the Working Group on Block Level Planning.* New Delhi: Planning Commission, Government of India.

Vyas, V.S. 1998. *Agricultural Trade Policy and Export Strategy,* Presidential Address, XII Annual Conference on Agricultural Marketing, Institute of Development Studies, Jaipur.

Waterston, Albert. 1965. *Development Planning: Lessons of Experience.* Baltimore: The Johns Hopkins University Press.

———. 1970. "A Hard Look at Development Planning." In *Economic Development, Readings in Theory and Practice,* edited by Theodore Morgan and George W. Betz, 400–7. Belmont (California): Wadsworth Publishing Company Inc.

WSSCC (Water Supply and Sanitation Collaborative Council). 1999. "Vision 21: Water for People in the 21st Century." Paper presented at the 25th Water Engineering Development Centre (WEDC) Conference, "Integrated Development for Water Supply and Sanitation," Addis Ababa, Ethiopia, 18–22 May.

WCED (World Commission on Environment and Developments). 1987. *Our Common Future. Report of World Commission on Environment and Development.* New Delhi: Oxford University Press.

Weitz, Raanan. 1971. *From Peasant to Farmer: A Revolutionary Strategy for Development.* New York: Columbia University Press.

WFP (World Food Programme). 1981. *UN/FAO World Food Programme Terminal Evaluation Report on Project India 618–'Milk Marketing and Dairy Development' (Operation Flood I).* Rome: World Food Programme, FAO.

Wharton Jr, Clifton, R. 1970. "Stages in Agricultural Development," In *Economic Development: Readings in Theory and Practice,* edited by Theodore Morgan and George W. Betz, 166–70. Belmont (California): Wadsworth Publishing Company Inc.

World Bank. 1988. *India: Wasteland Development Review.* Washington, DC: World Bank.

———. 1996. *Staff Appraisal Report: India Eco development Project.* Report No. 14914–IN, South Asia Department II, Agriculture and Water Division. Washington, DC: The World Bank.

———. 1997. *World Bank Development Report 1997.* New Delhi: Oxford University Press.

WRI (World Resources Institute). 1992. *World Resources 1992–93: A Report by the World Resources Institute.* Oxford: Oxford University Press.

———. 1998. *World Resources 1998–99: A Guide to Global Environment.* Oxford: The World Resources Institute, Oxford University Press.

Yotopoulos, Pan A. and J.B. Nugent. 1976. *Economics of Development: Empirical Investigation.* New York: Harper and Row Publishers.

Some Important Web Links

Ministry of Agriculture (MoA)
http://www.agricoop.nic.in

Agricultural Marketing Board (Agmarknet)
http://agmarknet.dac.gov.in/

Ministry of Environment, Forest and Climate Change (MoEF)
http://www.envfor.nic.in

Ministry of Finance (MoF)
http://www.finmin.nic.in/

Ministry of Statistics and Plan Implementation (MoSPI)
http://www.mospi.gov.in

Ministry of Rural Development (MoRD)
http://rural.nic.in/netrural/rural/index.aspx
http://www.rural.nic.in/sites/programmes-schemes.asp RD Schemes

National Bank for Agriculture and Rural Development (NABARD)
https://www.nabard.org/

National Dairy Development Board (NDDB)
http://www.nddb.coop

National Cooperative Union of India (NCUI)
http://www.ncui.coop/pdf/National-Cooperative-Union-of-India.pdf

National Horticulture Mission: (http://nhm.nic.in/Archive/midh(English).pdf)

National Institute of Rural Development (NIRD)
http://www.nird.org.in/Rural%20Development%20Statistics%202011-12

Niti Aayog
http://www.niti.gov.in

Planning Commission of India (erstwhile- archived)
http://planningcommissionarchive.nic.in/ Archived http://planningcommission.gov.in/data/datatable/index.php?data=RBI)data

Reserve Bank of India (RBI)
https://www.rbi.org.in/

Index